Third Edition

Classics of
Organization Theory

Brooks/Cole Series in Public Administration

The Foundations of Policy Analysis (1983)
Garry D. Brewer and Peter deLeon

Public Administration:
An Action Orientation (1991)
Robert B. Denhardt

Public Adminsitration in Action:
Readings, Profiles, and Cases (1992)
Robert B. Denhardt and Barry R. Hammond

Thoeories of Public Organization (1984)
Robert B. Denhardt

The Nonprofit Organization:
Essential Readings (1990)
*David L. Gies, J. Steven Ott,
and Jay M. Shafritz*

Organization Theory:
A Public Perspective (1987)
*Harold F. Gortner, Julianne Mahler,
and Jeanne Bell Nicholson*

Governmental Accounting and Control (1984)
*Leo Herbert, Larry N. Killough,
and Alan Walter Steiss*

Governing Public Organizations (1990)
Karen M. Hult and Charles Walcott

Government Budgeting: Theory, Process,
and Politics, 2nd Edition (1992)
Albert C. Hyde

Democratic Politics and Policy Analysis (1990)
Hank C. Jenkins-Smith

Politics and the Bureaucracy: Policymaking
in the Fourth Branch of Government,
Third Edition (1992)
Kenneth J. Meier

Applied Statistics for Public Administration,
Third Edition (1992)
Kenneth J. Meier and Jeffrey L. Brudney

Fiscal Administration: Analysis and
Applications for the Public Sector,
Third Edition (1991)
John L. Mikesell

Managing Urban America,
Third Edition (1989)
David R. Morgan

Classic Readings in Organizational
Behavior (1989)
J. Steven Ott

The Organizational Culture Perspective (1989)
J. Steven Ott

The Job of the Public Manager (1989)
John Rehfuss

Microcomputers and Government
Management: Design and Use of
Applications (1991)
John F. Sacco and John W. Ostrowski

Classics of Organization Theory,
Third Edition (1992)
Jay M. Shafritz and J. Steven Ott

Classics of Public Administration,
Third Edition (1992)
Jay M. Shafritz and Albert C. Hyde

Managing the Public Sector (1986)
Grover Starling

Strategies for Policy Making (1988)
Grover Starling

Financial Management in Public
Organizations (1989)
Alan Walter Steiss

Critical Issues in Public Personnel Policy (1989)
Ronald D. Sylvia

Program Planning and Evaluation for the
Public Manager (1985)
*Ronald D. Sylvia, Kenneth J. Meier,
and Elizabeth M. Gunn*

Classics of Public Personnel Policy, Second
Edition, Revised and Expanded (1991)
Frank J. Thompson

A Casebook of Public Ethics and Issues (1990)
William M. Timmins

Introduction to Budgeting (1978)
John Wanat

Quantitative Methods for Public
Administration, Second Edition (1988)
Susan Welch and John Comer

Third Edition

Classics of
Organization Theory

Jay M. Shafritz
University of Pittsburgh

J. Steven Ott
University of Utah

Brooks/Cole Publishing Company
Pacific Grove, California

About the Authors

Jay M. Shafritz is a professor in the Graduate School of Public and International Affairs at the University of Pittsburgh. Previously he has taught at the University of Colorado in Denver, the University of Houston in Clear Lake City, the State University of New York in Albany, and Rensselaer Polytechnic Institute. He is the author, coauthor, or editor of more than three dozen books on public, private, and nonprofit management as well as various articles. Dr. Shafritz received his master's degree from the Baruch College of the City University of New York and his Ph.D. from Temple University.

J. Steven Ott is an associate professor who teaches organization and management courses at the University of Utah. Previously he was at the University of Maine. Dr. Ott had been executive vice president of a Colorado-based management consulting firm for more than twenty-five years. He is a frequent speaker at management seminars and conferences on intra- and inter-organizational processes and leadership. Dr. Ott has written numerous books and articles, including *The Organizational Culture Perspective*, *Classic Readings in Organizational Behavior*, and *The Nonprofit Organization*. Dr. Ott earned his bachelor's degree from The Pennsylvania State University, his master's degree from the Sloan School of Management at the Massachusetts Institute of Technology, and his Ph.D. from the University of Colorado at Denver.

Brooks/Cole Publishing Company
A Division of Wadsworth, Inc.

Printed in the United States of America

10   9   8   7   6   5   4   3

Library of Congress Cataloging-in-Publication Data
Classics of organization theory / [edited] by Jay M. Shafritz and J. Steven Ott. — 3rd ed.
    p. cm.
    Includes bibliographical references.
    ISBN 0-534-17304-7
    1. Organization. 2. Management. I. Shafritz, Jay M. II. Ott, J. Steven.
    HD31.C56 1991
    658—dc20   91-32705
                                                         CIP

Sponsoring Editor: Cynthia C. Stormer
Editorial Assistant: Cathleen S. Collins
Production Editor: Linda Loba
Manuscript Editor: Barbara Kimmel
Permissions Editor: Marie DuBois
Interior Design: Katherine Minerva
Cover Design: Sharon L. Kinghan
Art Coordinator: Lisa Torri
Typesetting: Execustaff
Cover Printing and Printing and Binding: Malloy Lithographing, Inc.

Preface

About the only thing that is more satisfying to writers than the chance to write the second edition of a book is the opportunity to do a third edition. Warranted or not, publication of a third edition seems to indicate that a book may be earning its place in the literature of a field.

This third edition of *Classics of Organization Theory* has benefited immeasurably from the advice that has come from our friendly critics of the second edition. It also has benefited from our maturing judgment and several years of additional pondering on the subject of organization theory. It has been substantially restructured and rewritten to reflect changes in the field of organization theory and our developing thoughts. Completely new chapters have been added on the organizational behavior perspective or human resource theory, and multiple constituencies theory. The chapter on systems and contingency theory has been expanded to incorporate population ecology theory of organization or natural selection theory. In almost every chapter, some articles have been replaced with others that should prove to be more important and more readable.

On the other hand, we also tried to retain the character of the second edition, to stay close to its formulations. The Introduction still presents an overview of organization theory. And the entire book has a historical flavor intended to highlight the ebbs and flows in the development of organization theory over time. We have updated the "Chronology of Organization Theory" because many readers have told us that it is interesting and helpful for putting works into their contextual perspective.

As with the first and second editions, we sincerely solicit comments, ideas, and suggestions from the scholarly and practitioner communities. Given sufficient encouragement—and long enough lives—we will continue revising this book as new theories and perspectives gain in importance.

Many people contributed to this third edition. Albert Hyde, Edgar Duncan, and Kevin Kearn at the University of Pittsburgh, as well as Ralph Hummel at the University of Oklahoma have been very generous with their time, encouragement, and penetrating questions. Jeffrey Pinto, University of Maine, helped immeasurably, particularly with suggestions on market theory and population ecology. Christine Kreider, currently at the University of Minnesota, guided us through the sociological literature. We owe special thanks to Samuel Overman, our friend and former colleague at the University of Colorado at Denver, who never has (and probably never will) allow us to become complacent. We'd also like to thank the following reviewers for their helpful suggestions and comments: Dr. David V. Day, The Pennsylvania State University; Dr. Gerard Fowler, St. Louis University; Dr. Ira Kaplan, Hofstra University; Dr. Esther Langston,

University of Nevada-Las Vegas; Dr. Dorothy Marcic, Metropolitan State University; Dr. Thomas Marchigiano-Monroy, Rutgers-The State University of New Jersey; Dr. Scott Moore, Colorado State University; and Dr. Maria Papadakis, Syracuse University. Finally, we collectively thank the authors and publishers of these classics for their permission to reproduce their work.

Jay M. Shafritz
J. Steven Ott

Contents

Introduction

This book is about organization theory. By *organization,* we mean a social unit with some particular purposes. By *theory,* we mean a proposition or set of propositions that seeks to explain or predict something. The something in this case is how groups and individuals behave in varying organizational structures and circumstances. This is obviously important information for any manager or leader to have. It is hardly an exaggeration to say that the world is ruled by the underlying premises of organization theory, and that it has been ever since humankind first organized itself for hunting, war, and even family life. Indeed, the newest thing about organization theory is the study of it.

Only in the twentieth century has intellectual substance and tradition been given to a field that was the instinctual domain of adventuresome entrepreneurs and cunning politicos. Organization theory lay largely dormant over the centuries until society found a practical use for it—to help manage the ever-burgeoning national (as opposed to local) industries and institutions that increasingly run the twentieth century. When the problems of managing an organization grew to be more than one head could cope with, the search for guidance on how to manage and arrange large-scale organizations became as noble a quest as the secular world of business could offer. If a commercial society ever had prophets, they were those pioneers of the scientific management movement who claimed that the path to ever-greater prosperity was to be found in the relentless search for the ''one best way.'' They were offering society a theory—abstract guidance for those who knew where they wanted to go but didn't quite know how to get there. They already knew what Kurt Lewin would assert years later: ''There is nothing so practical as a good theory.'' (Marrow, 1969)

Peter Drucker (1954) once observed that the thrust toward scientific management ''may well be the most powerful as well as the most lasting contribution America has made to Western thought since the Federalist Papers.'' Of course, the scientific management movement was just the beginning of a continuous search for the most effective means by which people can be organized into social units in order to achieve the goals of their companies, their governments, or themselves. What was once said of the first atomic bomb is now said of the first U.S. voyage to the moon: It was as much an achievement of organization as it was of engineering and science.

Have our more recent theories of organization kept pace with our industrial and technical achievements? Maybe. But certainly yes when they are compared with the

1

"primitive" notions of the scientific management movement. Yet many of the basics remain the same—remain as givens. The laws of physics and gravity do not change with intellectual fashions or technological advances; nor do the basic social and physical characteristics of people change. Just as those who would build space ships have to start by studying Newton, those who would design and manage organizations must start with Taylor and Fayol. The future will always build upon what is enduring from the past. That is the rationale for this book—to provide those who seek to understand and/or to advance organization theory with a convenient place to find the essentials, indeed the classics, of organization theory's past. However old some of these articles may be, they are not dated. A classic *is* a classic because it continues to be of value to each new generation of students and practitioners who study organizations.

The basic elements of organizations have remained relatively constant through history: Organizations (or their important constituencies) have purposes (which may be explicit or implicit), attract participants, acquire and allocate resources to accomplish goals, use some form of structure to divide and coordinate activities, and rely on certain members to lead or manage others. Although the elements of organizations have remained relatively constant, their purposes, structures, ways of doing things, and methods for coordinating activities have always varied widely. The variations largely (but not exclusively) reflect an organization's adaptation to its environment. Organizations are "open systems" that are influenced by and have an impact on the world around them. The world around organizations includes, for example, their sources of inputs (like raw materials, capital, and labor), markets, technology, politics, and the surrounding society's culture and subcultures. Inherently, organizations are part of the society and the culture in which they exist and function. Human behavior and thus organizational behavior is heavily influenced by culturally rooted beliefs, values, assumptions, and behavioral norms affecting all aspects of organizational life.

Theories about organizations do not develop in a vacuum. They reflect what is going on in the world—including the existing culture. Thus, contributions to organization theory vary over time and across cultures and subcultures. The advent of the factory system, World War II, the "flower child"/anti-establishment/self-development era of the 1960s, the computer/information society of the 1970s, and the pervasive uncertainties of the 1980s all substantially influenced the evolution of organization theory. In order to truly understand organization theory as it exists today, one must appreciate the historical contexts through which it developed and the cultural milieus during and in which important contributions were made to its body of knowledge. In order to help readers place writings in their historical contexts, "A Chronology of Organization Theory," a review of the major events and publications in the field, follows this introduction.

Criteria for Selection

The editors are neither so vain nor so foolish as to assert that these are *the* classics of organization theory. The academic study of organization theory rests on a foundation of primary and secondary sciences: It draws significantly from such diverse disciplines as sociology, psychology, social psychology, cultural anthropology, political science, economics, business administration, and public administration. It draws with less force, but still importantly, from mathematics, statistics, systems theory, industrial engineering, philosophy and ethics, history, and the computer sciences. The field is so diverse that there can be no single definitive list of *the classics*. The editors readily admit that some important contributors and contributions to the field have not found their way into this collection. Omitting some was very painful. However, considerations of space and balance necessarily prevailed.

We used several criteria for making our selections. First, we asked ourselves, "Should the serious student of organization theory be expected to be able to identify these authors and their basic themes?" When the answer was yes, it was so because the contribution has long been, or is increasingly being recognized as, an important theme by a significant writer. Whereas we expect to be criticized for excluding other articles and writers, it will be more difficult to honestly criticize us for our inclusions; the writers and selections chosen are among the most widely quoted and reprinted theorists and theories in the field of organization theory. The possible exceptions are the articles chosen to represent the newer perspectives of organization theory—particularly multiple constituencies/market, power and politics, and organizational culture and symbolic management. Most of the significant writing in these perspectives has been done since 1980, and some of the most impressive works are as recent as 1990. Obviously, new articles have not been quoted as extensively as those written ten, twenty, or thirty years earlier. Thus, we had to be more subjective when making our editorial decisions about inclusions and exclusions in these chapters. In our judgment, these selections will fare well against the test of time.

The second criterion is related to the first: Each article or portion of a book had to make a basic statement that has been echoed or attacked consistently over the years. In other words, the selection had to be important—significant in the sense that it must have been (or will be) an integral part of the foundation for the subsequent building of the field of organization theory.

The third criterion was that articles had to be readable. Those of you who have already had reason to peruse the literature of organization theory will appreciate the importance of this criterion. (We tried very hard to live by this criterion, but we were not completely successful!)

The inclusion of articles from the more recent perspectives raises important questions about our choices of chapters for grouping theories and selections. For example, why did we establish separate chapters for power and politics and organizational culture and symbolic management but not for natural selection? What is the basis for our distinction between the "modern" structuralists and the systemists? The answers to questions such as these reflect our own conceptual and historical construction of organization theory, tempered by the need to limit the size of this volume. As such, it is crucially important to understand where we, the authors/editors, "are coming from." Thus we have written rather lengthy historical and conceptual overviews for each of our eight chapters. Each chapter presents a school or perspective of organization theory, and because there is no universally accepted set of schools or perspectives, a few words of explanation are needed here.

A Framework: The "Perspectives" of Organization Theory

There is no such thing as *the* theory of organizations. Rather, there are many theories that attempt to explain and predict how organizations and the people in them will behave in varying organizational structures, cultures, and circumstances. Some theories of organization are compatible with and build upon others—in what they explain or predict, the aspects of organizations they consider to be important, their assumptions about organizations and the world at large from which they are created, and the methods for studying organizations that work well. They use the same language or jargon. These groupings of compatible theories and theorists usually are called alternately schools, perspectives, traditions, frameworks, models, paradigms or, occasionally, eras of organization theory. We use these terms interchangeably throughout this book.

Organization theorists from one school will quote and cite each other's works regularly. However, they usually ignore theorists and theories from other schools— or acknowledge them only negatively. In 1961, Harold Koontz described management theory as a "semantics jungle." In 1963, Arthur Kuriloff examined the various schools of organization theory and found that "each is at odds with others, each defends its own position, each claims that the others have major deficiencies." But that was 1963, and we have come a long way since then; or have we? Twenty years after Kuriloff's statement, Graham Astley and Andrew Van de Ven (1983) observed: "The problem is that different schools of [organizational] thought tend to focus only on single sides of issues and use such different logics and vocabularies that they do not speak to each other directly." A year later, Lee Bolman and Terrence Deal (1984) remarked: "Within the social sciences, major schools of thought have evolved, each with its own view of organizations, its own well-defined concepts and assumptions, and its own ideas about how managers can best bring social collectives under control."

It is reasonable to conclude that not only is there no consensus on what constitutes knowledge in organization theory, but there is not likely to be any such consensus in the foreseeable future. Anyone who studies this subject is free to join the school of organization theory of his or her choice and is free to accept the philosophic boundaries of one group of serious thinkers over another. But before casting your lot with one school and excluding others, consider the options. Examine each school's strengths and weaknesses. See if its philosophy is in harmony with your already established beliefs, assumptions, and predispositions. You may find that no single perspective deserves your loyalty, that each contains important information and insights that are useful in differing circumstances. Remember these are schools with no tuition, no classes, and no grades. They exist only as intellectual constructs and as mutual support networks of organization theorists. They have one primary purpose: to organize and extend knowledge about organizations and how to study them.

Just as there is disagreement among the various frames about what makes organizations tick, there also are different views about the best way to group organization theories into schools. A few examples of different views on the schools of organization theory are summarized in Figure 1.

Each of the major frames of organization theory is associated with a period in time. For example, the classical school was at its prime in the 1920s and 1930s, and the neoclassical school in the 1940s and 1950s. Each school had its beginnings while another was dominant, gradually gained acceptance, and eventually replaced its predecessor as the dominant perspective. Some years later, another came along to challenge and eventually take its position. Once-dominant frames of organization theory may lose the center stage, but they do not die. Their thinking influences subsequent frames—even those that reject their basic assumptions and tenets. Important works from these earlier perspectives become the timeless classics.

This cycling of schools through struggling ascendancy, dominance, challenge by other schools, and reluctant decline is not unique to organization theory. Thomas Kuhn (1970) postulated that this dialectic process is common in all sciences—including physics, mathematics, and psychiatry. It is quite common for frames that are close to each other chronologically to have widely divergent basic assumptions about the object of their theories.

Despite their differences, most of the better-known approaches to grouping organization theories into schools (including those summarized in Figure 1) have commonalities. First, they group theories by their perspectives on organizations—in other words, by basic assumptions about humans and organizations and by those aspects of organizations that they see as most important for understanding organizational behavior. Second, they usually group the theories by the period of time during which the most important contributions were written. However, there are other organization theorists who use different approaches for labeling them. For example, Harold Koontz in "The Management Theory Jungle Revisited" (1980) expanded his list from six to eleven approaches to the study of management and organizational theory. We find Koontz's more current categorization system, with its Interpersonal Behavior Approach, Cooperative Social System Approach, and Sociotechnical Systems Approach, to be far too detailed to be useful.

Graham Astley and Andrew Van de Ven (1983) use a very different logic to classify schools of organization "thought" into four basic views based on two analytical dimensions: the level of organizational analysis (micro or macro) and the emphasis placed on deterministic versus voluntaristic assumptions about human nature. Thus Astley and Van de Ven conclude that organization theories can be grouped into the cells of a two-by-two matrix. (See Figure 2.) Their voluntaristic-to-deterministic dimension (the horizontal continuum in Figure 2) classifies theories by their assumptions about individual organization members' autonomy and self-direction versus the assumption that behavior in organizations is determined by structural constraints. The macro-to-micro continuum (the vertical continuum in Figure 2) groups organization theories by their focus on communities of organizations or single organizations.

Author	Schools
Scott, W. G. (1961). Organization theory: An overview and an appraisal. *Academy of Management Journal.*	The Classical Doctrine Neoclassical Theory Modern Theory
Koontz, H. (1961). The management theory jungle. *Academy of Management Journal.*	Management Process School Empirical Approach (or Case Approach) Human Behavior School Social System School Decision Theory School Mathematics School

Hutchinson, J. G. (1967). *Organizations: Theory and classical concepts.* New York: Holt, Rinehart & Winston.	Scientific Management
	Environmental and Human Relations School
	Man as a Decision Maker
	Current Theories of Management
	  1. Operational School
	  2. Empirical School
	  3. Human Behavior School
	  4. Social Systems School
	  5. Decision Theory School
	  6. Mathematical School

Scott, W. G., & Mitchell, T. R. (1972). *Organization theory* (rev. ed.). Homewood, IL: Dorsey Press.	The Scientific Management Movement The Human Relations and Industrial Humanism Movements Classical Theory Neoclassical Critique The Systems Concept (Unlabeled, but including) Personality Dynamics and Motivation, Attitudes, and Group Dynamics Organization Processes (Communication Processes, Decision Processes, Balance and Conflict Processes, Status and Role Processes, Influence Processes, Leadership Processes, and Technological Processes) Organization Change
George, C. S. Jr., (1972). *The history of management thought.* Englewood Cliffs, NJ: Prentice-Hall.	Traditional School: Scientific Management Behavioral School Management Process School Quantitative School

(continued)

Author	Schools
Perrow, C. (1973, Summer). The short and glorious history of organizational theory. *Organizational Dynamics.*	Scientific Management Human Relations Bureaucracy ("A Comeback") Power, Conflict, and Decisions The Technological Qualification Goals, Environments, and Systems
Pfeffer, J. (1981). *Power in organizations.* Marshfield, MA: Pitman.	Rational Choice Models Bureaucratic Models of Decision Making Decision Process Models Political Models
Bolman, L., & Deal, T. (1984). *Modern approaches to understanding and managing organizations.* San Francisco: Jossey-Bass.	Structural/Systems Frame Human Resources Frame Power Frame Symbolic Frame

Figure 1

A few examples of how scholars have grouped schools of organization theory

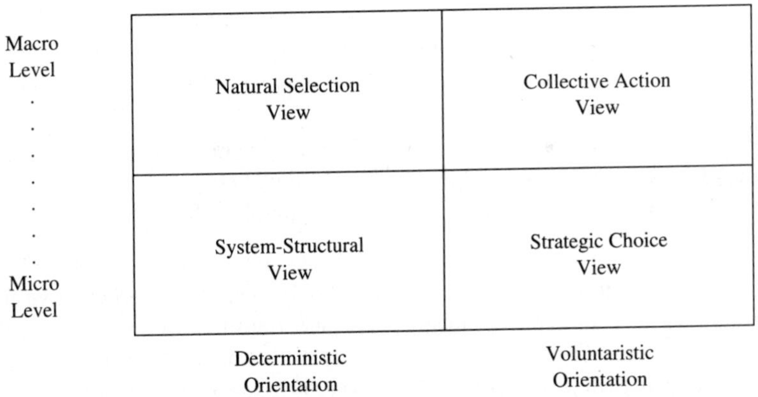

	Deterministic Orientation	Voluntaristic Orientation
Macro Level	Natural Selection View	Collective Action View
Micro Level	System-Structural View	Strategic Choice View

Examples of some representative organization theorists for each of the four views

System-Structural View: Gulick and Urwick (1937), Fayol (1949), Merton (1940), Blau and Scott (1962), Lawrence and Lorsch (1967), James D. Thompson (1967)
Strategic Choice View: Blau (1964), Feldman and March (1981), Strauss et al. (1963), Weick (1979), Bittner (1965)
Natural Selection View: Aldrich (1979), Hannan and Freeman (1977), Porter (1981), Pfeffer and Salancik (1978)
Collective Action View: Emery and Trist (1973), Hawley (1950, 1968), Schön (1971)

Adapted from Astley, W. G., & Van de Ven, A. H. (1983). Central perspectives and debates in organization theory. *Administrative Science Quarterly, 28.*

Figure 2

Astley and Van de Ven's four views of organization

The Organization of This Book

Although different approaches such as Astley and Van de Ven's (1983) and Koontz's (1980) are insightful and thought provoking, they are not well suited to a historical development of organization theory. And, it is our contention that the historical approach offers some clear advantages for the student. Organization theory tends to be somewhat cumulative—theorists and schools of theorists learn from and build upon each other's works. Sometimes the cumulative building of organization theory has been accomplished through the adoption of prior theorists' assumptions, logic, and empirical research methods and findings. In other instances, the building process has advanced by *rejecting* prior assumptions and theories (Kuhn, 1970). Thus, we have used a more traditional, historically oriented approach that allows the reader to follow the ebbs and flows within and between the perspectives. Within chapters, most selections are presented in chronological sequence so the reader can gain a sense of the evolution of thought in the field. Also, the reader can gain a quick overview of the historical development of organization theory by referring to the "Chronology of Organization Theory" that follows this Introduction. Our perspectives, or schools, and their corresponding chapters are:

Chapter I	Classical Organization Theory
Chapter II	Neoclassical Organization Theory
Chapter III	The Organizational Behavior Perspective, or Human Resource Theory
Chapter IV	"Modern" Structural Organization Theory
Chapter V	Systems, Contingency, and Population Ecology Organization Theory
Chapter VI	Multiple Constituencies/Market Organization Theory
Chapter VII	Power and Politics Organization Theory
Chapter VIII	Organizational Culture and Symbolic Management Organization Theory

Each perspective is described and discussed in the first pages of the respective chapters.

Although we have attempted to include only selections that fit into one school, many works span the boundaries, no matter how tightly the boundaries are defined and drawn. For example, Rosabeth Moss Kanter's writings (1977, 1983, and 1989) blend the power politics, human resource, and organizational culture perspectives. Cohen and March's (1974) concept of *organized anarchy* (reprinted here) bridges the power politics and the organizational culture perspectives. Argyris and Schön's (1978) notion of *theories for action* incorporates theory and research from the human resource and the organizational culture perspectives. Thus the reader should remember that the schools—and the chapters—reflect periods in time as well as perspectives of organizations.

In preparing this third edition, we again faced one particularly difficult decision: whether or not to include human resource theory or, as it is often labeled, the organizational behavior perspective. Its omission from the first and second editions has been justifiably questioned by readers and critics alike. Unquestionably, human resource theory is one of the most important perspectives of organization theory. It incorporates a wealth of behavioral science theories that address vital variables, including motivation, leadership, group and intergroup behavior, interactions between people and structure, and the application of applied behavioral sciences to organizational change processes (organization development or OD). Although there are sound arguments for excluding human resource theory, we decided to include it in this third edition. However, organizational behavior is a very large field of study unto itself with an enormous body of literature. We suggest that you should also look at *Essential Readings in Organizational Behavior,* a 1989 Brooks/Cole book edited by Steve Ott, that was designed as a companion to this book. It is impossible to do much more than provide a "flavor" of this body of theory and research in a single chapter.

References

AL-BURAEY, M. A. (1985). *Administrative development: An Islamic perspective.* London: Kegan Paul International.

ALDRICH, H. (1979). *Organizations and environments.* Englewood Cliffs, NJ: Prentice-Hall.

ARGYRIS, C., & SCHÖN, D. A. (1978). *Organizational learning: A theory of action perspective.* Reading, MA: Addison-Wesley.

ASTLEY, W. G., & VAN DE VEN, A. H. (1983, June). Central perspectives and debates in organization theory. *Administrative Science Quarterly, 28,* 245–270.

BITTNER, E. (1965). The concept of organization. *Social Research, 32*(3), 239–255.

BLAU, P. M. (1964). *Exchange and power in social life.* New York: Wiley.

BLAU, P. M., & SCOTT, R. G. (1962). *Formal organizations.* San Francisco: Chandler.

BOLMAN, L. G., & DEAL, T. E. (1984). *Modern approaches to understanding and managing organizations.* San Francisco: Jossey-Bass.

BOLMAN, L. G., & DEAL, T. E. (1991). *Reframing organizations: Artistry, choice, and leadership.* San Francisco: Jossey-Bass.

COHEN, M. D., & MARCH, J. G. (1974). *Leadership and ambiguity: The American college president.* New York: McGraw-Hill.

DRUCKER, P. F. (1954). *The practice of management.* New York: Harper & Row.

EMERY, F. E., and TRIST, E. L. (1973). *Towards a social ecology: Contextual appreciations of the future in the present.* New York: Plenum.

FAYOL, H. (1949). *General and industrial management.* London: Pitman. (Original work published 1916)

FELDMAN, M. S., & MARCH, J. G. (1981). Information in organizations as signal and symbol. *Administrative Science Quarterly, 26,* 171–186.

GEORGE, C. S., Jr. (1972). *The history of management thought.* Englewood Cliffs, NJ: Prentice-Hall.

GULICK, L., & URWICK, L. (Eds.) (1937). *Papers on the science of administration.* New York: Institute of Public Administration.

HANNAN, M., & FREEMAN, J. (1977). The population ecology of organizations. *American Journal of Sociology, 82,* 929–964.

HAWLEY, A. (1950). *Human ecology: A theory of community structure.* New York: Ronald Press.

HAWLEY, A. (1968). Human ecology. In D. L. Sills (Ed.). *The international encyclopedia of the social sciences* (Vol. 4, pp. 328–337). New York: Crowell-Collier & Macmillan.

HUTCHINSON, J. G. (1967). *Organizations: Theory and classical concepts.* New York: Holt, Rinehart & Winston.

IBN KHALDUN. (1969). *The muqaddimah: An introduction to history* (trans. by F. Rosenthal, ed. and abridged by N. J. Dawood). Princeton, NJ: Bollingen Series/Princeton University Press.

KANTER, R. M. (1977). *Men and women of the corporation.* New York: Basic Books.

KANTER, R. M. (1983). *The change masters.* New York: Simon & Schuster.

KANTER, R. M. (1989). *When giants learn to dance.* New York: Simon & Schuster.

KOONTZ, H. (1961). The management theory jungle. *Academy of Management Journal, 4,* 174–188.

KOONTZ, H. (1980). The management theory jungle revisited. *Academy of Management Review, 5,* 175–187.

KUHN, T. S. (1970). *The structure of scientific revolutions* (2nd ed., enlarged.) Chicago: University of Chicago Press.

LAWRENCE, P. R., & LORSCH, J. W. (1967). *Organization and environment.* Cambridge, MA: Harvard University Press.

MARROW, A. J. (1969). *The practical theorist: The life and works of Kurt Lewin.* New York: Basic Books.

MERTON, R. K. (1940). Bureaucratic structure and personality. *Social Forces, 18,* 560–568.

OTT, J. S. (1989). *Classic readings in organizational behavior.* Pacific Grove, CA: Brooks/Cole.

PERROW, C. (1973, Summer). The short and glorious history of organizational theory. *Organizational Dynamics.*

PFEFFER, J. (1981). *Power in organizations.* Marshfield, MA: Pitman.

PFEFFER, J., & SALANCIK, G. R. (1978). *The external control of organizations: A resource dependence perspective.* New York: Harper & Row.

PORTER, M. E. (1981). The contributions of industrial organization to strategic management. *Academy of Management Review, 6,* 609–620.

SCHÖN, D. A. (1971). *Beyond the stable state.* New York: Basic Books.

SCOTT, W. G. (1961, April). Organization theory: An overview and an appraisal. *Academy of Management Journal,* 7–26.

SCOTT, W. G., & MITCHELL, T. R. (1972). *Organization theory* (rev. ed.). Chicago: Dorsey Press.

STRAUSS, A., SCHATZMAN, L., ERLICH, D., BUCHER, R., & SABSHIN, M. (1963). The hospital and its negotiated order. In E. Friedson (Ed.), *The hospital in modern society* (pp. 147–169). New York: Free Press.

THOMPSON, J. D. (1967). *Organizations in action.* New York: McGraw-Hill.

WEICK, K. E. (1979). *The social psychology of organizing* (2nd ed.). Reading, MA: Addison-Wesley.

WREN, D. A. (1972). *The evolution of management thought.* New York: Ronald Press.

A Chronology of Organization Theory

1491 B.C.

- During the exodus from Egypt, Jethro, the father-in-law of Moses, urges Moses to delegate authority over the tribes of Israel along hierarchical lines.

500 B.C.

- Sun Tzu's *The Art of War* recognizes the need for hierarchical organization, inter-organization communications, and staff planning.

400 B.C.

- Socrates argues for the universality of management as an art unto itself.

360 B.C.

- Aristotle in *The Politics* asserts that the specific nature of executive powers and functions cannot be the same for all states (organizations), but must reflect their specific cultural environment.

370 B.C.

- Xenophon records the first known description of the advantages of the division of labor when he describes an ancient Greek shoe factory.

770

- Abu Yusuf, an important pioneering Muslim scholar, explores the administration of essential Islamic government functions, including public financial policy, taxation, and criminal justice, in *Kitab al-Kharaj* (*The Book of Land Taxes*). (Year is approximate.)

1058

- *Al-Ahkam As-Sultaniyyah* (*The Governmental Rules*), by al-Mawardi examines Islamic constitutional law, theoretical and practical aspects of Muslim political thought and behavior, and the behavior of politicians and administrators in Islamic states.

1093

- Al Ghazali emphasizes the role of Islamic creed and teachings for the improvement of administrative and bureaucratic organization in Muslim states, particularly the qualifications and duties of rulers, ministers, and secretaries, in *Ihya 'Ulum ad-Din* (*The Revival of the Religious Sciences*) and *Nasihat al-Muluk* (*Counsel for Kings*). (Year is approximate.)

1300

- In *As-Siyasah ash-Shariyyah* (*The Principles of Religious Government*), ibn Taymiyyah, "the father of Islamic administration," uses the scientific method to outline the principles of administration within the framework of Islam, including: the right man for the right job, patronage, and the spoils system. (Year is approximate.)

1377

- *The Muqaddimah: An Introduction to History,* by Muslim scholar ibn Khaldun, argues that methods for organizational improvement can be developed through the study of the science of culture. Ibn Khaldun specifically introduces conceptions of formal and informal organization, organizations as natural organisms with limits beyond which they cannot grow, and *esprit de corps.*

1513

- Machiavelli in *The Discourses* urges the principle of unity of command: "It is better to confide any expedition to a single man of ordinary ability, rather than to two, even though they are men of the highest merit, and both having equal ability."

1532

- Machiavelli's book of advice to all would-be leaders, *The Prince,* is published five years after its author's death; it will become the progenitor of all "how to succeed" books that advocate practical rather than moral actions.

1776

- Adam Smith's *The Wealth of Nations* discusses the optimal organization of a pin factory; this becomes the most famous and influential statement of the economic rationale of the factory system and the division of labor.

1813

- Robert Owen in his "Address to the Superintendents of Manufactories" puts forth the revolutionary idea that managers should pay as much attention to their "vital machines" (employees) as to their "inanimate machines."

1832

- Charles Babbage's *On the Economy of Machinery and Manufactures* anticipates many of the notions of the scientific management movement, including "basic principles of management" such as the division of labor.

1855

- Daniel C. McCallum in his annual report as superintendent of the New York and Erie Railroad Company states his six basic principles of administration; the first was to use internally generated data for managerial purposes.

1885

- Captain Henry Metcalfe, the manager of an army arsenal, published *The Cost of Manufactures and the Administration of Workshops, Public and Private,* which asserts that there is a "science of administration" that is based upon principles discoverable by diligent observation.

1886

- Henry R. Towne's paper "The Engineer as an Economist," read to the American Society of Mechanical Engineers, encourages the scientific management movement.

1902

- Vilfredo Pareto becomes the "father" of the concept of "social systems"; his societal notions would later be applied by Elton Mayo and the human relationists in an organizational context.

1903

- Frederick W. Taylor publishes *Shop Management.*

1904

- Frank B. and Lillian M. Gilbreth marry; they then proceed to produce many of the pioneering works on time and motion study, scientific management, applied psychology, and twelve children.

1910

- Louis D. Brandeis, an associate of Frederick W. Taylor (and later Supreme Court Justice) coins and popularizes the term *scientific management* in his Eastern Rate Case testimony before the Interstate Commerce Commission by arguing that railroad rate increases should be denied because the railroads could save "a million dollars a day" by applying scientific management methods.

1911

- Frederick W. Taylor publishes *The Principles of Scientific Management.*

1912

- Harrington Emerson publishes *The Twelve Principles of Efficiency,* which put forth an interdependent but coordinated management system.

1913

- Hugo Munsterberg's *Psychology and Industrial Efficiency* calls for the application of psychology to industry.

1914
- Robert Michels in his analysis of the workings of political parties and labor unions, *Political Parties,* formulates his iron law of oligarchy: "Who says organization, says oligarchy."

1916
- In France, Henri Fayol publishes his *General and Industrial Management,* the first complete theory of management.

1922
- Max Weber's structural definition of bureaucracy is published posthumously; it uses an "ideal-type" approach to extrapolate from the real world the central core of features that characterizes the most fully developed form of bureaucratic organization.

1924
- Hawthorne studies begin at the Hawthorne Works of the Western Electric Company in Chicago; they last until 1932 and lead to new thinking about the relationships among work environment, human motivation, and productivity.

1926
- Mary Parker Follett in calling for "power with" as opposed to "power over" anticipates the movement toward more participatory management styles.

1931
- Mooney and Reiley in *Onward Industry* (republished in 1939 as *The Principles of Organization*) show how the newly discovered "principles of organization" have really been known since ancient times.

1933
- Elton Mayo's *The Human Problems of an Industrial Civilization* is the first major report on the Hawthorne studies, the first significant call for a human relations movement.

1937
- Luther Gulick's "Notes on the Theory of Organization" draws attention to the functional elements of the work of an executive with his mnemonic device POSDCORB.

1938
- Chester I. Barnard's *The Functions of the Executive,* his sociological analysis of organizations, encourages and foreshadows the postwar revolution in thinking about organizational behavior.

1939
- Roethlisberger and Dickson publish *Management and the Worker,* the definitive account of the Hawthorne studies.

1940
- Robert K. Merton's article "Bureaucratic Structure and Personality" proclaims that Max Weber's "ideal-type" bureaucracy has inhibiting dysfunctions leading to inefficiency and worse.

1941

- James Burnham in *The Managerial Revolution* asserts that as the control of large organizations passes from the hands of the owners into the hands of professional administrators, the society's new governing class will be the possessors not of wealth but of technical expertise.

1943

- Abraham Maslow's "needs hierarchy" first appears in his *Psychological Review* article, "A Theory of Human Motivation."

1946

- Herbert A. Simon's "The Proverbs of Administration" attacks the principles approach to management for being inconsistent and often inapplicable.

1947

- National Training Laboratories for Group Development (now called the NTL Institute for Applied Behavioral Science) is established to do research on group dynamics and later, sensitivity training.
- Herbert A. Simon's *Administrative Behavior* urges that a true scientific method be used in the study of administrative phenomena, that the perspective of logical positivism should be used in dealing with questions of policy making, and that decision making is the true heart of administration.

1948

- Dwight Waldo publishes *The Administrative State,* which attacks the "gospel of efficiency" that dominated administrative thinking prior to World War II.
- In their *Human Relations* article "Overcoming Resistance to Change," Lester Coch and John R. P. French, Jr., note that employees resist change less when the need for it is effectively communicated to them and when the workers are involved in planning the changes.
- Norbert Wiener coins the term *cybernetics* in his book with the same title, which becomes a critical foundation concept for the systems school of organizational theory.

1949

- Philip Selznick in *TVA and the Grass Roots* discovers "co-optation" when he examines how the Tennessee Valley Authority subsumed new external elements into its policy-making process in order to prevent those elements from becoming a threat to the organization.
- In his *Public Administration Review* article "Power and Administration," Norton E. Long finds that power is the lifeblood of administration, and that managers had to more than just apply the scientific method to problems—they had to attain, maintain, and increase their power or risk failing in their mission.
- Rufus E. Miles, Jr., of the Bureau of the Budget first states Miles' Law: "Where you stand depends on where you sit."
- Air Force Captain Edsel Murphy first states Murphy's Law: "If anything can go wrong, it will."

1950

- George C. Homans publishes *The Human Group*, the first major application of "systems" to organizational analysis.

1951

- Kurt Lewin proposes a general model of change consisting of three phases, "unfreezing, change, refreezing," in his *Field Theory in Social Science*; this model becomes the conceptual frame for organization development.
- Ludwig von Bertalanffy's article "General Systems Theory: A New Approach to the Unity of Science" is published in *Human Biology*; his concepts will become *the* intellectual basis for the systems approach to organizational thinking.

1954

- Peter Drucker's book, *The Practice of Management*, popularizes the concept of management by objectives.
- Alvin Gouldner's *Patterns of Industrial Bureaucracy* describes three possible responses to a formal bureaucratic structure: "mock," where the formal rules are ignored by both management and labor; "punishment-centered," where management seeks to enforce rules that workers resist; and "representative," where rules are both enforced and obeyed.

1956

- William H. Whyte, Jr., first profiles *The Organization Man*, an individual within an organization who accepts its values and finds harmony in conforming to its policies.
- In the premier issue of *Administrative Science Quarterly*, Talcott Parsons' article "Suggestions for a Sociological Approach to the Theory of Organizations" defines an organization as a social system that focuses on the attainment of specific goals and contributes, in turn, to the accomplishment of goals of the larger organization or society itself.
- Kenneth Boulding's *Management Science* article, "General Systems Theory—The Skeleton of Science," integrates Wiener's concept of cybernetics with von Bertalanffy's general systems theory; this will become the most quoted introduction to the systems concept of organization.

1957

- C. Northcote Parkinson discovers his law that "work expands so as to fill the time available for its completion."
- Chris Argyris asserts in his first major book, *Personality and Organization*, that there is an inherent conflict between the personality of a mature adult and the needs of modern organizations.
- Douglas M. McGregor's article "The Human Side of Enterprise," distills the contending traditional (authoritarian) and humanistic managerial philosophies into Theory X and Theory Y; applies the concept of "self-fulfilling prophesies" to organizational behavior.
- Philip Selznick in *Leadership in Administration* anticipates many of the 1980s' notions of "transformational leadership" when he asserts that the function of an institutional

leader is to help shape the environment in which the institution operates and to define new institutional directions through recruitment, training, and bargaining.

- Alvin W. Gouldner in "Cosmopolitans and Locals" identifies two latent social roles that tend to manifest themselves in organizations: "cosmopolitans," who have small loyalty to the employing organization, high commitment to specialized skills, and an outer-reference group orientation; and "locals," who have high loyalty to the employing organization, a low commitment to specialized skills, and an inner-reference group orientation.

1958

- March and Simon in *Organizations* seek to inventory and classify all that is worth knowing about the behavioral revolution in organization theory.
- Leon Festinger, the father of cognitive dissonance theory, writes "The Motivating Effect of Cognitive Dissonance," which becomes the theoretical foundation for the "inequity theories of motivation."
- Robert Tannenbaum and Warren H. Schmidt's *Harvard Business Review* article "How to Choose a Leadership Pattern" describes "democratic management" and devises a leadership continuum ranging from authoritarian to democratic.

1959

- Charles A. Lindblom's "The Science of 'Muddling Through' " rejects the rational model of decision making in favor of incrementalism.
- Herzberg, Mausner, and Snyderman's *The Motivation to Work* puts forth the motivation-hygiene theory of worker motivation.
- Cyert and March postulate that power and politics impact on the formation of organizational goals; their "A Behavioral Theory of Organizational Objectives" is an early precursor of the power and politics school.
- John R. P. French and Bertram Raven identify five bases of power (expert, referent, reward, legitimate, and coercive) in their article "The Bases of Social Power." They argue that managers should not rely on coercive and expert power bases, as they are least effective.

1960

- Richard Neustadt's *Presidential Power* asserts that the president's (or any executive's) essential power is that of persuasion.
- Herbert Kaufman's *The Forest Ranger* shows how organizational and professional socialization can develop the will and capacity to conform in employees.

1961

- Victor A. Thompson's *Modern Organization* finds that there is "an imbalance between ability and authority" causing bureaucratic dysfunctions all over the place.
- Harold Koontz's "The Management Theory Jungle" describes thinking about management as a "semantics jungle."
- Burns and Stalker's *The Management of Innovation* articulates the need for different types of management systems (organic or mechanistic) under differing circumstances.
- Rensis Likert's *New Patterns of Management* offers an empirically based defense of participatory management and organization development techniques.

- Amatai Etzioni in *A Comparative Analysis of Complex Organizations* argues that organizational effectiveness is affected by the match between an organization's goal structure and its compliance structure.

1962

- Robert Presthus' *The Organizational Society* presents his threefold classification of patterns of organizational accommodation: "upward-mobiles," who identify and accept the values of the organization; "indifferents," who reject such values and find personal satisfaction off the job; and "ambivalents," who want the rewards of organizational life but can't cope with the demands.
- Blau and Scott in their *Formal Organizations: A Comparative Approach* assert that all organizations include both a formal and informal element, and that it is impossible to know and understand the true structure of a formal organization without a similar understanding of its parallel informal organization.
- David Mechanic's *Administrative Science Quarterly* article "Sources of Power of Lower Participants in Complex Organizations" anticipates the power and politics perspective of organization theory.

1963

- Strauss, Schatzman, Bucher, Erlich, and Sabshin describe the maintenance of order in a hospital as a dynamic process operating within a framework of negotiated "contracts" among people and groups with different expectations and interests, in "The Hospital and Its Negotiated Order."
- Cyert and March in *A Behavioral Theory of the Firm* demonstrate that corporations tend to "satisfice" rather than engage in economically rational profit-maximizing behavior.

1964

- Blake and Mouton's *The Managerial Grid* uses a graphic gridiron to explain management styles and their potential impacts on an organization development program.
- Michel Crozier in *The Bureaucratic Phenomenon* defines a bureaucracy as "an organization which cannot correct its behavior by learning from its errors."
- Bertram M. Gross publishes his two-volume *The Managing of Organizations*, an historical analysis of thinking about organizations from ancient times to the present.

1965

- Don K. Price publishes *The Scientific Estate*, in which he posits that decisional authority flows inexorably from the executive suite to the technical office.
- Robert L. Kahn's *Organizational Stress* is the first major study of the mental health consequences of organizational role conflict and ambiguity.
- James G. March edits the huge *Handbook of Organizations*, which sought to summarize all existing knowledge on organization theory and behavior.

1966

- Katz and Kahn in *The Social Psychology of Organizations* seek to unify the findings of behavioral science on organizational behavior through open systems theory.
- *Think Magazine* publishes David C. McClelland's article "That Urge to Achieve," in which he identifies two groups of people: the majority of whom aren't concerned

about achieving, and the minority who are challenged by the opportunity to achieve. This notion becomes a premise for future motivation studies.

- Warren Bennis in *Changing Organizations* sounds the death knell for bureaucratic institutions because they are inadequate for a future that will demand rapid organizational change, participatory management, and the growth of a more professionalized work force.

1967

- James D. Thompson's *Organizations in Action* seeks to close the gap between open and closed systems theory by suggesting that organizations deal with the uncertainty of their environments by creating specific elements designed to cope with the outside world while other elements are able to focus on the rational nature of technical operations.
- Anthony Downs' *Inside Bureaucracy* seeks to develop laws and propositions that would aid in predicting the behavior of bureaus and bureaucrats.
- John Kenneth Galbraith's *The New Industrial State* asserts that the control of modern corporations has passed to the technostructure and that this technostructure is more concerned with stability than profits.
- Antony Jay in *Management and Machiavelli* applies Machiavelli's political principles (from *The Prince*) to modern organizational management.

1968

- Harold Wilensky's *Organizational Intelligence* presents the pioneering study of the flow and perception of information in organizations.
- In *Group Dynamics,* Dorwin Cartwright and Alvin Zander propose that the systematic study of group dynamics would advance knowledge of the nature of groups; how they are organized; and relationships among individuals, other groups, and larger institutions.
- John P. Campbell and M. D. Dunnette's "Effectiveness of T-Group Experiences in Managerial Training and Development," appearing in *Psychological Bulletin,* provides a critical review of T-Group literature. They conclude that "an individual's positive feelings about his T-Group experiences" cannot be scientifically measured, nor should they be based entirely on "existential grounds."
- Walker and Lorsch grapple with the perennial structural issue of whether to design organizations by product or function in their *Harvard Business Review* article, "Organizational Choice: Product vs. Function."
- Frederick Herzberg's *Harvard Business Review* article "One More Time, How Do You Motivate Employees?" catapults *motivators* or *satisfiers* and *hygiene factors* into the forefront of organizational motivation theory.

1969

- Laurence J. Peter promulgates his principle that "in a hierarchy every employee tends to rise to his level of incompetence."
- Lawrence and Lorsch in *Organization and Environment* call for a contingency theory that can deal with the appropriateness of different theories under differing circumstances; they state that organizations must solve the problem of simultaneous differentiation and integration.
- Paul Hersey and Kenneth R. Blanchard's "Life Cycle Theory of Leadership," appearing in *Training and Development Journal,* asserts that the appropriate leadership style

for a given situation depends upon the employee's education and experience levels, achievement motivation, and willingness to accept responsibility by the subordinates.

1970

- Burton Clark's *The Distinctive College* identifies ways that three colleges created and maintained their distinctiveness through the management of symbols.
- In "Expectancy Theory," John P. Campbell, Marvin D. Dunnette, Edward E. Lawler III, and Karl E. Weick, Jr., articulate the *expectancy theories of motivation.* People are motivated by calculating how much they want something, how much of it they think they will get, how likely it is their actions will cause them to get it, and how much others in similar circumstances have received.
- Chris Argyris writes *Intervention Theory and Methods,* which becomes one of the most widely cited and enduring works on organizational consulting for change that is written from the organizational behavior/organization development perspective.

1971

- Graham T. Allison's *Essence of Decision* demonstrates the inadequacies of the view that the decisions of a government are made by a "single calculating decisionmaker" who has control over the organizations and officials within his government.
- Irving Janis' "Groupthink," first published in *Psychology Today,* proposes that group cohesion can lead to the deterioration of effective group decision-making efforts.

1972

- Wildcat strike at General Motors Lordstown, Ohio, automobile assembly plant calls national attention to the dysfunctions of dehumanized and monotonous work.
- Harlan Cleveland, in *The Future Executive,* asserts that decision making in the future will call for "continuous improvisation on a general sense of direction."
- Charles Perrow's *Complex Organizations* is a major defense of bureaucratic forms of organization and an attack on those writers who think that bureaucracy can be easily, fairly, or inexpensively replaced.
- Kast and Rosenzweig in their *Academy of Management Journal* article "General Systems Theory: Applications for Organization and Management," assess the level of successful application of general systems theory in organizations and advocate a contingency theory as a less abstract and more applicable theoretical approach.

1973

- Jay Galbraith in *Designing Complex Organizations* articulates the systems/contingency view that the amount of information an organization needs is a function of the levels of its uncertainty, interdependence of units and functions, and adaptation mechanisms.

1974

- In a report for the Carnegie Commission on Higher Education, Michael Cohen and James March introduce the phrase *organized anarchies* to communicate why colleges and universities are distinctive organizational forms with uniquely difficult leadership needs and problems. The report was published as the book, *Leadership and Ambiguity: The American College President.*

- Robert J. House and Terrance R. Mitchell's *Journal of Contemporary Business* article "Path-Goal Theory of Leadership" offers path-goal theory as a useful tool for explaining the effectiveness of certain leadership styles in given situations.
- Victor H. Vroom's *Organizational Dynamics* article "A New Look at Managerial Decision-Making" develops a useful model whereby leaders can perform a diagnosis of a situation to determine which leadership style is most appropriate.
- Steven Kerr's *Academy of Management Journal* article "On the Folly of Rewarding A, While Hoping for B" substantiates that many organizational reward systems are "fouled up"—they pay off for behaviors other than those they are seeking.

1975
- Oliver E. Williamson analyzes organizational decisions to produce products and services internally or to purchase them externally using economic market models, and assesses the implications of such decisions on, for example, organizational authority, in *Markets and Hierarchies: Analysis and Antitrust Implications*.

1976
- Michael Maccoby psychoanalytically interviews 250 corporate managers and discovers "The Gamesman," a manager whose main interest lies in "competitive activity where he can prove himself a winner."
- Jensen and Meckling describe an organization as simply an extension of and a means for satisfying the interests of the multiple individuals and groups that affect and are affected by it, in "Agency Costs and the Theory of the Firm."
- In "A Concept of Organizational Ecology," Eric Trist proposes a concept of organizational population ecology based on the field that is created by a number of organizations whose interrelations comprise a system. The system is the field as a whole, not its component organizations.

1977
- Hannan and Freeman's article "The Population Ecology of Organizations" proposes a new unit of analysis for understanding organizations: the "population of organizations."
- Salancik and Pfeffer's article "Who Gets Power—and How They Hold on to It" explains how power and politics help organizations adapt to their environment by reallocating critical resources to subunits that are performing tasks most vital to organizational survival.
- In *Matrix*, Davis and Lawrence caution against using a matrix form of organization unless there exist specific organizational conditions that are conducive to its success.
- Rosabeth Moss Kanter in *Men and Women of the Corporation* describes the unique problems women encounter with power and politics in organizations.

1978
- Thomas J. Peters' *Organizational Dynamics* article "Symbols, Patterns, and Settings: An Optimistic Case for Getting Things Done" is the first major analysis of symbolic management in organizations to gain significant attention in the "mainstream" literature of organization theory.

1979

- Rosabeth Moss Kanter's *Harvard Business Review* article "Power Failure in Management Circuits" identifies organizational positions that tend to have power problems— then argues that powerlessness is often more of a problem than power for organizations.
- *Structuring Organizations* is published, the first book in Henry Mintzberg's integrative series on "The Theory of Management Policy."

1980

- Connolly, Conlon, and Deutsch argue that evaluations of organizational effectiveness should employ multiple criteria that reflect the diverse interests of the various constituencies that are involved with organizations, in "Organizational Effectiveness: A Multiple-Constituency Approach."

1981

- In "Organization Development: A Political Perspective," Anthony Cobb and Newton Margulies argue that organization development (OD) has developed more political sensitivity and sophistication than most critics realize, but that political activity by OD practitioners is fraught with serious utilitarian and values problems.
- Jeffrey Pfeffer's *Power in Organizations* integrates the tenets and applications of the power and politics school of organization theory.
- Thomas Ouchi's *Theory Z* and Pascale and Athos' *The Art of Japanese Management* popularize the Japanese management "movement."

1982

- Organizational culture becomes "hot" in the general business literature with such books as Peters and Waterman's *In Search of Excellence*, Deal and Kennedy's *Corporate Culture*, and *Business Week's* cover story on "Corporate Culture."

1983

- Henry Mintzberg's *Power in and Around Organizations* molds the power and politics school of organizational theory into an integrative theory of management policy.
- In *The Change Masters*, Rosabeth Moss Kanter defines *change masters* as architects of organizational change; they are the right people in the right places at the right time.
- Meryl R. Louis' article "Organizations as Cultural-Bearing Milieux," becomes the first readable, integrative statement of the organizational cultural school's assumptions and positions.
- "Values in Organizational Theory and Management Education," by Michael Keeley, proposes that organizations exist by virtue of agreement on joint activities to achieve separate purposes of important constituencies, not to achieve organizational goals or purposes.
- Ian Mitroff's *Stakeholders of the Organizational Mind* explains how the perceptions of internal and external organizational stakeholders influence organizational behavior—particularly, decision making about complex problems of organizational policy and design.
- Pondy, Frost, Morgan, and Dandridge edit the first definitive volume on symbolic management, *Organizational Symbolism*.

- Linda Smircich's article "Organizations as Shared Meanings" examines how systems of commonly shared meanings develop and are sustained in organizations through symbolic communications processes, and also how these shared meanings provide members of an organizational culture with a sense of commonality and a distinctive character.

1984

- Sergiovanni and Corbally edit the first notable collection of papers on the organizational culture perspective, *Leadership and Organizational Culture.* Sergiovanni's opening chapter "Cultural and Competing Perspectives in Administrative Theory and Practice" clearly articulates the fundamental underlying assumptions of the organizational culture and symbolic management perspective.
- Siehl and Martin report the findings of the first major quantitative and qualitative empirical study of organizational culture in their "The Role of Symbolic Management: How Can Managers Effectively Transmit Organizational Culture?"

1985

- Edgar Schein writes the most comprehensive and integrative statement of the organizational culture school in his *Organizational Culture and Leadership.*
- In *The Irrational Organization,* Nils Brunsson postulates that rationality may lead to good decisions, but it decreases the probability of organizational action and change.
- *Administrative Development,* by Muhammad A. Al-Buraey, combines Western methodology and technique with Islamic substance, values, and ethics, to demonstrate how the Islamic perspective (as a system and a way of life) is an important moving force in the process and realization of administrative development world-wide.

1986

- *Corporate Culture: Diagnosis and Change,* by Desmond Graves, presents the first serious methodological treatise on "diagnosing" organizational culture.
- Michael Harmon and Richard Mayer write a comprehensive text that applies organization theory in the public sector, *Organization Theory for Public Administration.*
- Gareth Morgan's *Images of Organization* develops the art of reading and understanding organizations starting from the premise that our theories of organization are based on distinctive but partial mental images or metaphors.

1988

- Michael Keeley combines and extends his previous essays on multiple constituencies, organizational purposes, systems of justice, values, and organizational worth into the first comprehensive statement of *A Social-Contract Theory of Organizations.*
- Quinn and Cameron compile *Paradox and Transformation,* an important collection of essays on the necessity for managing with paradoxes in complex organizations, rather than necessarily trying to eliminate them.
- The *American Journal of Sociology* publishes a heated debate between the leading proponents and detractors of population ecology of organization theory.

1989

- Rosabeth Moss Kanter's book *When Giants Learn to Dance* examines how organizations can gain the advantages of smallness (flexibility) and size (staying power) at the same time.

- *Developing Corporate Character,* by Alan Wilkins, explains how it is difficult but possible to change elements of an organizational culture without destroying the positive aspects of the culture that already exist.

1990

- Sally Helgesen creates *diary studies* that explore how women leaders make decisions and gather and disperse information in organizations. Helgesen suggests that "women may be the new Japanese" of management, in *The Female Advantage.*
- "In Praise of Hierarchy," by Elliott Jaques, argues that critics of hierarchy are misguided. Instead of needing new organizational forms, we need to learn how to manage hierarchies better.
- *The Fifth Discipline,* by Peter Senge, explains that few corporations live even half as long as a person because they cannot overcome their organizational learning disabilities.

I

Classical Organization Theory

No single date can be pinpointed as the beginning of serious thinking about how organizations work and how they should be structured and managed. One can trace writings about management and organizations as far back as the known origins of commerce. A lot can be learned from the early organizations of the Muslims, Hebrews, Greeks, and Romans. If we were to take the time, we could make the case that much of what we know about organization theory has its origins in ancient and medieval times. After all, it was Aristotle who first wrote of the importance of culture to management systems, ibn Taymiyyah who used the scientific method to outline the principles of administration within the framework of Islam, and Machiavelli who gave the world the definitive analysis of the use of power.

In order to give the reader a sense of organization theory's deep roots in earlier eras, we offer two examples of ancient wisdom on organization management. The first of our ancient examples is from the Book of Exodus, Chapter 18 (see box 1), in which Jethro, Moses' father-in-law, chastises Moses for failing to establish an organization through which he could delegate his responsibility for the administration of justice. In Verse 25, Moses accepts Jethro's advice; he "chose able men out of all Israel, and made them heads over the people, rulers of thousands, rulers of hundreds, rulers of fifties, and rulers of tens." Moses continued to judge the "hard cases," but his rulers judged "every small matter" themselves. This concept of "management by exception" would later be developed for modern audiences by Frederick Winslow Taylor.

In the second ancient example (see the first selection in this chapter), Socrates anticipates the arguments for "generic management" and "principles of management" as he explains to Nicomachides that a leader who "knows what he needs, and is able to provide it, [can] be a good president, whether he have the direction of a chorus, a family, a city, or an army." (Xenophon, 1869). Socrates lists and discusses the duties of all good presidents—of public and private institutions—and emphasizes the similarities. This is the first known statement that organizations as entities are basically alike; that a manager who could cope well with one would be equally adept at coping with others— even though their purposes and functions might be widely disparate.

Although it is always great fun to delve into the wisdom of the ancients, most analysts of the origins of organization theory view the beginnings of the factory system in Great

---

Box 1

Exodus   Chapter 18

13 And it came to pass on the morrow, that Moses sat to judge the people: and the people stood by Moses from the morning unto the evening.

14 And when Moses' father-in-law saw all that he did to the people, he said, "What *is* this thing that thou doest to the people? why sittest thou thyself alone, and all the people stand by thee from morning unto even?"

15 And Moses said unto his father-in-law, "Because the people come unto me to inquire of God:

16 When they have a matter, they come unto me; and I judge between one and another, and I do make *them* know the statutes of God, and his laws."

17 And Moses' father-in-law said unto him, "The thing that thou doest is not good.

18 Thou wilt surely wear away, both thou, and this people that *is* with thee: for this thing *is* too heavy for thee: thou art not able to perform it thyself alone.

19 Hearken now unto my voice, I will give thee counsel, and God shall be with thee: Be thou for the people to God-ward, that thou mayest bring the causes unto God:

20 And thou shalt teach them ordinances and laws, and shalt shew them the way wherein they must walk, and the work that they must do.

21 Moreover thou shalt provide out of all the people able men, such as fear God, men of truth, hating covetousness; and place *such* over them, *to be* rulers of thousands, *and* rulers of hundreds, rulers of fifties, and rulers of tens:

22 And let them judge the people at all seasons: and it shall be, *that* every great matter they shall bring unto thee, but every small matter they shall judge: so shall it be easier for thyself, and they shall bear *the burden* with thee.

23 If thou shalt do this thing, and God command thee *so,* then thou shalt be able to endure, and all this people shall also go to their place in peace."

24 So Moses hearkened to the voice of his father-in-law, and did all that he had said.

25 And Moses chose able men out of all Israel, and made them heads over the people, rulers of thousands, rulers of hundreds, rulers of fifties, and rulers of tens.

26 And they judged the people at all seasons: the hard cases they brought unto Moses, but every small matter they judged themselves.

27 And Moses let his father-in-law depart; and he went his way into his own land.

Britain in the eighteenth century as the birthpoint of complex economic organizations and, consequently, of the field of organization theory.

Classical organization theory, as its name implies, was the first theory of its kind, is considered traditional, and continues to be the base upon which other schools of organization theory have built. Thus, an understanding of classical organization theory is essential not only because of its historical interest but also, more importantly, because subsequent analyses and theories presume a knowledge of it.

The classical school dominated organization theory into the 1930s and remains highly influential today (Merkle, 1980). Over the years, classical organization theory expanded and matured. Its basic tenets and assumptions, however, which were rooted in the industrial revolution of the 1700s and the professions of mechanical engineering, industrial engineering, and economics, have never changed. They were only expanded upon, refined, and made more sophisticated. These fundamental tenets are that:

1. Organizations exist to accomplish production-related and economic goals.
2. There is one best way to organize for production, and that way can be found through systematic, scientific inquiry.
3. Production is maximized through specialization and division of labor.
4. People and organizations act in accordance with rational economic principles.

The evolution of any theory must be viewed in context. The beliefs of early management theorists about how organizations worked or should work were a direct reflection of the societal values of their times. And the times were harsh. It was well into the twentieth century before the industrial workers of the United States and Europe began to enjoy even limited "rights" as organization citizens. Workers were not viewed as individuals but as the interchangeable parts in an industrial machine whose parts were made of flesh only when it was impractical to make them of steel.

The advent of power-driven machinery and hence the modern factory system spawned our current concepts of economic organizations and organization for production. Power-driven equipment was expensive. Production workers could not purchase and use their own equipment as they had their own tools. Remember the phrase for being fired— "get the sack." It comes from the earliest days of the industrial revolution when a dismissed worker literally was given a sack in which to gather up his tools. Increasingly, workers without their own tools and often without any special skills had to gather for work where the equipment was—in factories. Expensive equipment had to produce enough output to justify their acquisition and maintenance costs.

The advent of the factory system presented managers of organizations with an unprecedented array of new problems. Managers had to arrange for heavy infusions of capital, plan and organize for reliable large-scale production, coordinate and control activities of large numbers of people and functions, contain costs (this was hardly a concern under "cottage industry" production), and maintain a trained and motivated work force.

Under the factory system, organizational success resulted from well-organized production systems that kept machines busy and costs under control. Industrial and mechanical engineers—and their machines—were the keys to production. Organizational structures and production systems were needed to take best advantage of the machines. Organizations, it was thought, should work like machines, using people, capital, and machines as their parts. Just as industrial engineers sought to design "the best" machines to keep factories productive, industrial and mechanical engineering-type thinking dominated theories about "the best way" to organize for production. Thus, the first theories of organizations were concerned primarily with the anatomy—or structure—of formal organizations. This was the milieu, or the environment, the mode of thinking, that shaped and influenced the tenets of classical organization theory.

Centralization of equipment and labor in factories, division of specialized labor, management of specialization, and economic paybacks on factory equipment all were concerns of the Scottish economist Adam Smith's work *An Inquiry into the Nature and Causes of the Wealth of Nations* (1776). The historian Arnold Toynbee (1956) identified Adam Smith (1723–1790) and James Watt (1736–1819) as the two people who were most responsible for pushing the world into industrialization. Watt, of course, invented the steam engine.

Smith, who is considered the "father" of the academic discipline of economics, provided the intellectual foundation for laissez-faire capitalism. *The Wealth of Nations* (1776) devotes its first chapter, "Of the Division of Labour," to a discussion of the optimum organization of a pin factory. Why? Because specialization of labor was one of the pillars of Smith's "invisible hand" market mechanism in which the greatest rewards would go to those who were the most efficient in the competitive marketplace. Traditional pin makers could produce only a few dozen pins a day. When organized in a factory with each worker performing a limited operation, they could produce tens of thousands a day. Smith's "Of the Division of Labour" is reprinted here because, comings as it did at the dawn of the Industrial Revolution, it is the most famous and influential statement on the economic rationale of the factory system. Smith revolutionized thinking about economics and organizations. Thus we have operationally defined 1776, the year in which *Wealth of Nations* was published, as the beginning point of organization theory as an applied science and academic discipline. Besides, 1776 was a good year for other events as well.

Charles Babbage (1792–1871), the British scientist and mathematician who is considered the intellectual "father" of the modern computer, was studying different manufacturing methods to produce one of his many inventions. His studies led him to conclude that there were basic principles of management (including the division of labor), that those principles could be learned through experience, and that they could be applied broadly. He alluded to these conclusions in *On the Economy of Machinery and Manufactures* (1832). His chapter "On the Division of Labour," which is included here, clearly benefited from the earlier writing of Adam Smith, but Babbage carried the concept considerably farther—as is obvious from the conclusions about pervasive principles of management. Sixty years later, Babbage's conclusions would influence the thinking and writing of Frederick Winslow Taylor and his followers and, therefore, of the scientific management movement.

About twenty years after Babbage proposed general principles of management, Daniel C. McCallum (1815–1878), the visionary general superintendent of the New York and Erie Railroad, elucidated general principles of organization that "may be regarded as settled and necessary" (1856). His principles included division of responsibilities, power commensurate with responsibilities, and a reporting system that allowed managers to know promptly if responsibilities were "faithfully executed" and to identify errors and "delinquent" subordinates. McCallum, who is also credited with creating the first modern organization chart, had an enormous influence on the managerial development of the American railroad industry.

In systematizing America's first big business before the Civil War, McCallum provided the model principles and procedures of management for the big businesses that would follow after the war. He became so much *the* authority on running railroads that, as a major general during the Civil War, he was chosen to run the Union's military rail system. Although McCallum was highly influential as a practitioner, he was no scholar, and the only coherent statement of his general principles comes from an annual report he wrote for the New York and Erie Railroad. Excerpts from his "Superintendent's Report" of March 25, 1856, are reprinted here.

During the 1800s, two practicing managers in the United States independently discovered that generally applicable principles of administration could be determined through systematic, scientific investigation—about thirty years before Taylor's *The Principles of Scientific Management* or Fayol's *General and Industrial Management.* The first, Captain Henry Metcalfe (1847–1917) of the United States Army's Frankford Arsenal in Philadelphia, urged managers to record production events and experiences systematically so that they could use the information to improve production processes. He published his propositions in *The Cost of Manufactures and the Administration of Workshops, Public and Private* (1885), which also pioneered in applying "pre-scientific management" methods to the problems of managerial control and asserted that there is a "science of administration" based upon principles discoverable by diligent observation. Although Metcalfe's work is important historically, it is so similar to that of Taylor's and others that it is not included here as a selection.

The second prescientific management advocate of the 1880s was Henry R. Towne (1844–1924), co-founder and president of the Yale & Towne Manufacturing Company. In 1886, Towne proposed that shop management was of equal importance to engineering management and that the American Society of Mechanical Engineers (ASME) should take a leadership role in establishing a multicompany, engineering/management "database" on shop practices or "the management of works." The information could then be shared among established and new enterprises. Several years later, his proposal was adopted by ASME. His paper presented to the society, entitled "The Engineer as an Economist," was published in *Transactions of the American Society of Mechanical Engineers* (1886) and is reprinted here. Historians have often considered Towne's paper the first "call" for scientific management.

Interestingly, Towne had several significant associations with Frederick Winslow Taylor. The two of them were fellow draftsmen at the Midvale Steel works during the 1880s. Towne gave Taylor one of his first true opportunities to succeed at applying scientific management principles at Yale & Towne in 1904. Towne also nominated Taylor for the presidency of ASME in 1906, and thus provided him with an international forum for advocating scientific management. (Upon election, Taylor promptly reorganized the ASME according to scientific management principles.)

While the ideas of Adam Smith, Charles Babbage, Frederick Winslow Taylor, and others are still dominant influences on the design and management of organizations, it was Henri Fayol (1841–1925), a French executive engineer, who developed the first comprehensive theory of management. While Taylor was tinkering with the technology employed by the individual worker, Fayol was theorizing about all of the elements necessary to organize and manage a major corporation. Fayol's major work, *Administration Industrielle et Generale* (published in France in 1916), was almost ignored in the United States until Constance Storr's English translation, *General and Industrial Management,* appeared in 1949. Since that time, Fayol's theoretical contributions have been widely recognized and his work is considered fully as significant as that of Taylor.

Fayol believed that his concept of management was universally applicable to every type of organization. Whereas he had six principles: technical (production of goods), commercial (buying, selling, and exchange activities), financial (raising and using capital), security (protection of property and people), accounting, and managerial (coordination, control, organization, planning, and command of people); Fayol's primary interest and emphasis was on his final principle—managerial. His managerial principle addressed such variables as division of work, authority and responsibility, discipline, unity of command, unity of direction, subordination of individual interest to general interest, remuneration of personnel, centralization, scalar chains, order, equity, stability of personnel tenure, initiative, and esprit de corps. Reprinted here is Fayol's "General Principles of Management," a chapter from his *General and Industrial Management*.

About one hundred years after Adam Smith declared the factory to be the most appropriate means of mass production, Frederick Winslow Taylor and a group of his followers were "spreading the gospel" that factory workers could be much more productive if their work was designed scientifically. Taylor, the acknowledged father of the scientific management movement, pioneered the development of time-and-motion studies, originally under the name "Taylorism" or the "Taylor system." "Taylorism" or its successor scientific management was not a single invention but rather a series of methods and organizational arrangements designed by Taylor and his associates to increase the efficiency and speed of machine-shop production. Premised upon the notion that there was "one best way" of accomplishing any given task, Taylor's scientific management sought to increase output by discovering the fastest, most efficient, and least fatiguing production methods.

The job of the scientific manager, once the "one best way" was found, was to impose this procedure upon his or her organization. Classical organization theory derives from a corollary of this proposition. If there was one best way to accomplish any given production task, then correspondingly, there must also be one best way to accomplish any task of social organization—including organizing firms. Such principles of social organization were assumed to exist and to be waiting to be discovered by diligent scientific observation and analysis.

Scientific management, as espoused by Taylor, also contained a powerful, puritanical, social message. Taylor (1911) offered scientific management as the way for firms to increase profits, get rid of unions, "increase the thrift and virtue of the working classes," and raise productivity so that the broader society could enter a new era of harmony based on higher consumption of mass-produced goods by members of the laboring classes.

Scientific management emerged as a national movement during a series of events in 1910. The railroad companies in the eastern states filed for increased freight rates with the Interstate Commerce Commission. The railroads had been receiving poor press, being blamed for many things including a cost-price squeeze that was bankrupting farmers. Thus the rate hearings received extensive media coverage. Louis D. Brandeis, a self-styled populist lawyer who would later be a Supreme Court justice, took the case against the railroads without pay. Brandeis called in Harrington Emerson, a consultant who had "systematized" the Santa Fe Railroad, to testify that the railroads did not need increased rates: They could "save a million dollars a day" by using what Brandeis initially called "scientific management" methods (Urwick, 1956). At first, Taylor was reluctant to use the phrase because it sounded too academic. But the ICC hearings meant that the national scientific management boom was underway, and Taylor was its leader.

Taylor had a profound—almost revolutionary—effect on the fields of business and public administration. Taylor gained credence for the notion that organizational operations could be planned and controlled systematically by experts using scientific principles. Many of Taylor's concepts and precepts are still in use today. The legacy of scientific management is substantial. Taylor's best known work is his 1911 book *The Principles of Scientific Management,* but he also wrote numerous accounts on the subject. Reprinted here is an article, also entitled "The Principles of Scientific Management," which was the summary of an address given by him on March 3, 1915, two weeks prior to his death.

Several of Taylor's associates subsequently gained wide recognition including, for example, Frank (1868–1924) and Lillian (1878–1972) Gilbreth of *Cheaper by the Dozen* (1948) and "therblig" (Spriegel & Myers, 1953) fame; Henry Laurence Gantt (1861–1919), who invented the Gantt chart for planning work output (Alford, 1932); and Carl G. Barth (1860–1939) who, among his other accomplishments, in 1908 convinced the dean of the new Harvard Business School to adopt "Taylorism" as the "foundation concept" of modern management (Urwick, 1956).

In contrast with the fervent advocates of scientific management, Max Weber (1864–1920) was a brilliant analytical sociologist who happened to study bureaucratic organizations. Bureaucracy has emerged as a dominant feature of the contemporary world. Virtually everywhere one looks in both developed and developing nations, economic, social, and political life are influenced extensively by bureaucratic organizations. Typically *bureaucracy* is used to refer to a specific set of structural arrangements. It is also used to refer to specific patterns of behavior—patterns that are not restricted to formal bureaucracies. It is widely assumed that the structural characteristics of organizations properly defined as "bureaucratic" influence the behavior of individuals—whether clients or bureaucrats—who interact with them. Contemporary thinking along these lines began with the work of Max Weber. His analysis of bureaucracy, first published in 1922, remains the single most influential statement and the point of departure for all further analyses on the subject (including those of the "modern structuralists" in Chapter IV).

Drawing upon studies of ancient bureaucracies in Egypt, Rome, China, and the Byzantine Empire, as well as on the more modern ones emerging in Europe during the nineteenth and early part of the twentieth centuries, Weber used an "ideal-type" approach to extrapolate from the real world the central core of features characteristic of the most fully developed bureaucratic form of organization. Weber's "Characteristics of Bureaucracy," which is included here, is neither a description of reality nor a statement of normative preference. In fact, Weber feared the potential implications of bureaucracies. Rather, his "ideal-type" bureaucracy is merely an identification of the major variables or features that characterize this type of social institution.

Luther Gulick's (b. 1892) "Notes on the Theory of Organization," which clearly was influenced by the work of Henry Fayol, is one of the major statements of the "principles" approach to managing the functions of organizations. It appeared in *Papers on the Science of Administration,* a collection that he and Lyndall Urwick edited in 1937. It was here that Gulick introduced his famous mnemonic, POSDCORB, which stood for the seven major functions of executive management—planning, organizing, staffing, directing, coordinating, reporting, and budgeting. Gulick's principles of administration also included unity of command and span of control. Overall, the *Papers* was a statement of the "state of the art" of organization theory. The study of organizations through analysis of management functions continues within the field of organization theory.

Daniel A. Wren (1972) once observed that "the development of a body of knowledge about how to manage has . . . evolved within a framework of the economic, social, and political facets of various cultures. Management thought is both a process in and a product of its cultural environment." The selections we have chosen to represent the classical school of organization theory vividly demonstrate Wren's thesis. Looking through 1992 "lenses," it is tempting to denigrate the contributions of the classicalists— to view them as narrow and simplistic. In the context of their times, however, they were brilliant pioneers. Their thinking provided invaluable foundations for the field of organization theory, and their influence upon organization theory and theorists continues today.

References

AL-BURAEY, M. A. (1985). *Administrative development: An Islamic perspective.* London: Kegan Paul International.

ALFORD, L. P. (1932). *Henry Laurence Gantt: Leader in industry.* New York: Harper & Row.

BABBAGE, C. (1832). *On the economy of machinery and manufactures.* Phiadelphia, PA: Carey & Lea.

FAYOL, H. (1949). *General and industrial management* (C. Storrs, Trans.) London: Pitman. (Original work published 1916)

GEORGE, C. S., Jr. (1972). *The history of management thought.* (2nd ed.). Englewood Cliffs, NJ: Prentice-Hall.

GILBRETH, F. B., Jr., & CAREY, E. G. (1948). *Cheaper by the dozen.* New York: Grosset & Dunlap.

GULICK, L. (1937). Notes on the theory of organization. In L. Gulick & L. Urwick (Eds.), *Papers on the science of administration* (pp. 3–13). New York: Institute of Public Administration.

MCCALLUM, D. C. (1856). Superintendent's report, March 25, 1856. In *Annual report of the New York and Erie Railroad Company for 1855.* In A. D. Chandler, Jr. (Ed.), *The railroads* (pp. 101–108). New York: Harcourt Brace Jovanovich.

MERKLE, J. A. (1980). *Management and ideology: The legacy of the international scientific management movement.* Berkeley, CA: University of California Press.

METCALFE, H. (1885). *The cost of manufactures and the administration of workshops, public and private.* New York: Wiley.

SMITH, A. (1776). Of the division of labour. In A. Smith, *The wealth of nations* (chap. 1).

SPRIEGEL, W. R., & MYERS, C. E. (Eds.). (1953). *The writings of the Gilbreths.* Homewood, IL: Irwin.

TAYLOR, F. W. (1911). *The principles of scientific management.* New York: Norton.

TAYLOR, F. W. (1916, December). The principles of scientific management. *Bulletin of the Taylor Society.* An abstract of an address given by the late Dr. Taylor before the Cleveland Advertising Club, March 3, 1915.

TOWNE, H. R. (1886, May). The engineer as an economist. *Transactions of the American Society of Mechanical Engineers, 7,* 428–432. Paper presented at a meeting of the Society, Chicago, IL.

TOYNBEE, A. (1956). *The industrial revolution.* Boston: Beacon Press. (Original publication 1884)

URWICK, L. (1956). *The golden book of management.* London: Newman, Neame.

WEBER, M. (1922). Bureaucracy. In H. Gerth & C. W. Mills (Eds.), *Max Weber: Essays in sociology.* Oxford, UK: Oxford University Press.

WREN, D. A. (1972). *The evolution of management thought.* New York: Ronald Press.

XENOPHON. (1869). *The memorabilia of Socrates,* (Rev. J. S. Watson, Trans.) New York: Harper & Row.

1

Socrates Discovers Generic Management

Seeing Nicomachides, one day, coming from the assembly for the election of magistrates, he asked him, "Who have been chosen generals, Nicomachides?"

"Are not the Athenians the same as ever, Socrates?" he replied; "for they have not chosen me, who am worn out with serving on the list, both as captain and centurion, and with having received so many wounds from the enemy (he then drew aside his robe, and showed the scars of the wounds), but have elected Antisthenes, who has never served in the heavy-armed infantry, nor done anything remarkable in the cavalry, and who indeed knows nothing, but how to get money."

"It is not good, however, to know this," said Socrates, "since he will then be able to get necessaries for the troops?"

"But merchants," replied Nicomachides, "are able to collect money; and yet would not on that account, be capable of leading an army."

"Antisthenes, however," continued Socrates, "is given to emulation, a quality necessary in a general. Do you not know that whenever he has been chorus-manager he has gained the superiority in all his choruses?"

"But, but Jupiter," rejoined Nicomachides, "there is nothing similar in managing a chorus and an army."

"Yet Antisthenes," said Socrates, "though neither skilled in music nor in teaching a chorus, was able to find out the best masters in these departments."

SOURCE: Xenophon, *The Anabasis or Expedition of Cyrus and the Memorabilia of Socrates*, trans. J. S. Watson (N.Y.: Harper & Row, 1869), 430–433.

"In the army, accordingly," exclaimed Nicomachides, "he will find others to range his troops for him, and others to fight for him!"

"Well, then," rejoined Socrates, "if he finds out and selects the best men in military affairs, as he has done in the conduct of his choruses, he will probably attain superiority in this respect also; and it is likely that he will be more willing to spend money for a victory in war on behalf of the whole state, than for a victory with a chorus in behalf of his single tribe."

"Do you say, then, Socrates," said he, "that it is in the power of the same man to manage a chorus well, and to manage an army well?"

"I say," said Socrates, "that over whatever a man may preside, he will, if he knows what he needs, and is able to provide it, to be a good president, whether he have the direction of a chorus, a family, a city, or an army."

"By Jupiter, Socrates," cried Nicomachides, "I should never have expected to hear from you that good managers of a family would also be good generals."

"Come, then," proceeded Socrates, "let us consider what are the duties of each of them, that we may understand whether they are the same, or are in any respect different."

"By all means."

"Is it not, then, the duty of both," asked Socrates, "to render those under their command obedient and submissive to them?"

"Unquestionably."

"Is it not also the duty of both to intrust various employments to such as are fitted to execute them?"

"That is also unquestionable."

"To punish the bad, and to honor the good, too, belongs, I think, to each of them."

"Undoubtedly."

"And is it not honorable in both to render those under them well-disposed toward them?"

"That also is certain."

"And do you think it for the interest of both to gain for themselves allies and auxiliaries or not?"

"It assuredly is for their interest."

"Is it not proper for both also to be careful of their resources?"

"Assuredly."

"And is it not proper for both, therefore, to be attentive and industrious in their respective duties?"

"All these particulars," said Nicomachides, "are common alike to both; but it is not common to both to fight."

"Yet both have doubtless enemies," rejoined Socrates.

"That is probably the case," said the other.

"Is it not for the interest of both to gain the superiority over those enemies?"

"Certainly; but to say something on that point, what, I ask, will skill in managing a household avail, if it be necessary to fight?"

"It will doubtless in that case, be of the greatest avail," said Socrates; "for a good manager of a house, knowing that nothing is so advantageous or profitable as to get the better of your enemies when you contend with them, nothing so unprofitable and prejudicial as to be defeated, will zealously seek and provide every thing that may conduce to victory, will carefully watch and guard against whatever tends to defeat, will vigorously engage if he sees that his force is likely to conquer, and, what is not the least important point, will cautiously avoid engaging if he finds himself insufficiently prepared. Do not, therefore, Nicomachides," he added, "despise men skillful in managing a household; for the conduct of private affairs differs from that of public concerns only in magnitude; in other respects they are similar; but what is most to be observed, is, that neither of them are managed without men, and that private matters are not managed by one species of men, and public matters by another; for those who conduct public business make use of men not at all differing in nature from those whom the managers of private affairs employ; and those who know how to employ them conduct either public or private affairs judiciously, while those who do not know will err in the management of both."

2

Of the Division of Labour

Adam Smith

The greatest improvement in the productive powers of labour, and the greater part of the skill, dexterity, and judgment with which it is any where directed, or applied, seem to have been the effects of the division of labour.

The effects of the division of labour, in the general business of society, will be more easily understood, by considering in what manner it operates in some particular manufactures. It is commonly supposed to be carried furthest in some very trifling ones; not perhaps that it really is carried further in them than in others of more importance: but in those trifling manufactures which are destined to supply the small wants of but a small number of people, the whole number of workmen must necessarily be small; and those employed in every different branch of the work can often be collected into the same workhouse, and placed at once under the view of the spectator. In those great manufactures, on the contrary, which are destined to supply the great wants of the great body of the people, every different branch of the work employs so great a number of workmen, that it is impossible to collect them all into the same workhouse. We can seldom see more, at one time, than those employed in one single branch. Though in such manufactures, therefore, the work may really be divided into a much greater number of parts, than in those of a more trifling nature, the division is not near so obvious, and has accordingly been much less observed.

SOURCE: Adam Smith, *The Wealth of Nations* (1776), Chapter 1. Footnotes omitted.

To take an example, therefore, from a very trifling manufacture; but one in which the division of labour has been very often taken notice of, the trade of the pin-maker; a workman not educated to this business (which the division of labour has rendered a distinct trade), nor acquainted with the use of the machinery employed in it (to the invention of which the same division of labour has probably given occasion), could scarce, perhaps, with his utmost industry, make one pin in a day, and certainly could not make twenty. But in the way in which this business is now carried on, not only the whole work is a peculiar trade, but it is divided into a number of branches, of which the greater part are likewise peculiar trades. One man draws out the wire, another straights it, a third cuts it, a fourth points it, a fifth grinds it at the top for receiving the head; to make the head requires two or three distinct operations; to put it on, is a peculiar business, to whiten the pins is another; it is even a trade by itself to put them into the paper; and the important business of making a pin is, in this manner, divided into about eighteen distinct operations, which, in some manufactories, are all performed by distinct hands, though in others the same man will sometimes perform two or three of them. I have seen a small manufactory of this kind where ten men only were employed, and where some of them consequently performed two or three distinct operations. But though they were very poor, and therefore but indifferently accommodated with the necessary machine, they could, when they exerted themselves, make among them about twelve pounds of pins in a day. There are in a pound upwards of four thousand pins of a middling size. Those ten persons, therefore, could make among them upwards of forty-eight thousand pins in a day. Each person, therefore, making a tenth part of forty-eight thousand pins, might be considered as making four thousand eight hundred pins in a day. But if they had all wrought separately and independently, and without any of them having been educated to this peculiar business, they certainly could not each of them have made twenty, perhaps not one pin in a day; that is, certainly, not the two hundred and fortieth, perhaps not the four thousand eight hundredth part of what they are at present capable of performing, in consequence of a proper division and combination of their different operations.

In every other art and manufacture, the effects of the division of labour are similar to what they are in this very trifling one; though, in many of them, the labour can neither be so much subdivided, nor reduced to so great a simplicity of operation. The division of labour, however, so far as it can be introduced, occasions, in every art, a proportionable increase of the productive powers of labour. The separation of different trades and employments from one another, seems to have taken place, in consequence of this advantage. This separation too is generally carried furthest in those countries which enjoy the highest degree of industry and improvement; what is the work of one man in a rude state of society, being generally that of several in an improved one. In every improved society, the farmer is generally nothing but a farmer; the manufacturer, nothing but a manufacturer. The labour too which is necessary to produce any one complete manufacture, is almost always divided among a great number of hands. How many different trades are employed in each branch of the linen and woollen manufactures, from the growers of the flax and the wool, to the bleachers and smoothers of the linen, or to the dyers and dressers of the cloth! The nature of agriculture, indeed, does not admit of so many subdivisions of labour, nor of so complete a separation of one business from another, as manufactures. It is impossible to separate so entirely, the business of the grazier from that of the corn-farmer, as the trade of the carpenter is commonly separated from that of the smith. The spinner is almost always a distinct person from the weaver; but the ploughman, the harrower, the sower of the seed, and the reaper of the corn, are often the same. The occasions for those different sorts of labour returning with the different seasons of the year, it is impossible that one man should be constantly employed in any one of them. This impossibility of making so complete and entire a separation of all the different branches of labour employed in agriculture, is perhaps the reason why the improvement of the productive powers of labour in this art, does not always keep pace with their improvement in manufactures. The most opulent nations, indeed, generally excel all their neighbours in agriculture as well as in manufactures; but they are commonly more distinguished by their superiority in the latter than in the former. Their lands are in general better cultivated, and having more labour and expence bestowed upon them, produce more in proportion to the extent and natural fertility of the ground. But this superiority of produce is seldom much more than in proportion to the superiority of labour and expence. In agriculture, the labour of the rich country is not always much more productive than that of the poor; or, at least, it is never so much more productive, as it commonly is in manufactures. The corn of the rich country, therefore, will not always, in the same degree of goodness, come cheaper to market than that of the poor. The corn of Poland, in the same degree of goodness is as cheap as that of France, notwithstanding the superior opulence and improvement of the latter country. The corn of France is, in the corn provinces, fully as good, and most years nearly about the same price with the corn of England, though, in opulence and improvement, France is perhaps inferior to England. The corn lands of England, however, are better cultivated than those of France, and the corn lands of France are said to be much better cultivated than those of Poland. But though the poor country, notwithstanding the inferiority of its cultivation, can, in some measure, rival the rich in the cheapness and goodness of its corn, it can pretend to no such competition in its manufactures; at least if those manufactures suit the soil, climate, and situation of the rich country. The silks of France are better and cheaper than those of England, because the silk manufacture, at least under the present high duties upon the importation of raw silk, does not so well suit the climate of England as that of France. But the hardware and the coarse woollens of England are beyond all comparison superior to those of France, and much cheaper too in the same degree of goodness. In Poland there are said to be scarce any manufactures of any kind, a few of those coarser household manufactures excepted, without which no country can well subsist.

This great increase of the quantity of work, which, in consequence of the division of labour, the same number of people are capable of performing, is owing to three different circumstances; first, to the increase of dexterity in every particular workman; secondly, to the saving of the time which is commonly lost in passing from one species of work to another; and lastly, to the invention of a great number of machines which facilitate and abridge labour, and enable one man to do the work of many.

First, the improvement of the dexterity of the workman necessarily increases the quantity of the work he can perform; and the division of labour, by reducing every man's business to some one simple operation, and by making this operation the sole employment of his life, necessarily increases very much the dexterity of the workman. A common smith, who, though accustomed to handle the hammer, has never been used to make nails, if upon some particular occasion he is obliged to attempt it, will scarce, I am assured, be able to make above two or three hundred nails in a day, and those too very bad ones. A smith who has been accustomed to make nails, but whose sole or principal business has not been that of a nailer, can seldom with his utmost diligence make more than eight hundred or a thousand nails in a day. I have seen several boys under twenty years of age who had never exercised any other trade but that of making nails, and who, when they exerted themselves, could make, each of them, upwards of two thousand three hundred nails in a day. The making of a nail, however, is by no means one of the simplest operations. The same person blows the bellows, stirs or mends the fire as there is occasion, heats the iron, and forges every part of the nail: In forging the head too he is obliged to change

his tools. The different operations into which the making of a pin, or of a metal button, is subdivided, are all of them much more simple, and the dexterity of the person, of whose life it has been the sole business to perform them, is usually much greater. The rapidity with which some of the operations of those manufactures are performed, exceeds what the human hand could, by those who had never seen them, be supposed capable of acquiring.

Secondly, the advantage which is gained by saving the time commonly lost in passing from one sort of work to another, is much greater than we should at first view be apt to imagine it. It is impossible to pass very quickly from one kind of work to another, that is carried on in a different place, and with quite different tools. A country weaver, who cultivates a small farm, must lose a good deal of time in passing from his loom to his field, and from the field to his loom. When the two trades can be carried on in the same workhouse, the loss of time is no doubt much less. It is even in this case, however, very considerable. A man commonly saunters a little in turning his hand from one sort of employment to another. When he first begins the new work he is seldom very keen and hearty; his mind, as they say, does not go to it, and from some time he rather trifles than applies to good purpose. The habit of sauntering and of indolent careless application, which is naturally, or rather necessarily acquired by every country workman who is obliged to change his work and his tools every half hour, and to apply his hand in twenty different ways almost every day of his life; renders him almost always slothful and lazy, and incapable of any vigorous application even on the most pressing occasions. Independent, therefore, of his deficiency in point of dexterity, this cause alone must always reduce considerably the quantity of work which he is capable of performing.

Thirdly, and lastly, every body must be sensible how much labour is facilitated and abridged by the application of proper machinery. It is unnecessary to give any example. I shall only observe, therefore, that the invention of all those machines by which labour is so much facilitated and abridged, seems to have been originally owing to the division of labour. Men are much more likely to discover easier and readier methods of attaining any object, when the whole attention of their minds is directed towards that single object, than when it is dissipated among a great variety of things. But in consequence of the division of labour, the whole of every man's attention comes naturally to be directed towards some one very simple object. It is naturally to be expected, therefore, that some one or other of those who are employed in each particular branch of labour should soon find out easier and readier methods of performing their own particular work, wherever the nature of it admits of such improvement. A great part of the machines made use of in those manufactures in which labour is most subdivided, were originally the inventions of common workmen, who, being each of them employed in some very simple operation, naturally turned their thoughts towards finding out easier and readier methods of performing it. Whoever has been much accustomed to visit such manufactures, must frequently have been shewn very pretty machines, which were the inventions of such workmen, in order to facilitate and quicken their own particular part of the work. In the first fire-engines, a boy was constantly employed to open and shut alternately the communication between the boiler and the cylinder, according as the piston either ascended or descended. One of those boys, who loved to play with his companions, observed that, by tying a string from the handle of the valve which opened this communication to another part of the machine, the valve would open and shut without his assistance, and leave him at liberty to divert himself with his playfellows. One of the greatest improvements that has been made upon this machine, since it was first invented, was in this manner the discovery of a boy who wanted to save his own labour.

All the improvements in machinery, however, have by no means been the inventions of those who had occasion to use the machines. Many improvements have been made by the ingenuity of the makers of the machines, when to make them become the business of a peculiar trade; and some by that of those who are called philosophers or men of speculation, whose trade it is not to do any thing, but to observe every thing; and who, upon that account, are often capable of combining together the powers of the most distant and dissimilar objects. In the progress of society, philosophy or speculation becomes, like every other employment, the principal or sole trade and occupation of a particular class of citizens. Like every other employment too, it is subdivided into a great number of different branches, each of which affords occupation to a peculiar tribe or class of philosophers; and this subdivision of employment in philosophy, as well as in every other business, improves dexterity, and saves time. Each individual becomes more expert in his own peculiar branch, more work is done upon the whole, and the quantity of science is considerably increased by it.

It is the great multiplication of the productions of all the different arts, in consequence of the division of labour, which occasions, in a well-governed society, that universal opulence which extends itself to the lowest ranks of the people. Every workman has a great quantity of his own work to dispose of beyond what he himself has occasion for; and every other workman being exactly in the same situation, he is enabled to exchange a great quantity of his own goods for a great quantity, or, what comes to the same thing, for the price of a great quantity of theirs. He supplies them abundantly with what they have occasion for, and they accommodate him as amply with what he has occasion for, and a general plenty diffuses itself through all the different ranks of the society.

Observe the accommodation of the most common artificer or day-labourer in a civilized and thriving country, and you will perceive that the number of people of whose industry a part, though but a small part, has been employed in procuring him his accommodation, exceeds all computation. The woollen coat, for example, which covers the day-labourer, as coarse and rough as it may appear, is the produce of the joint labour of a great multitude of workmen.

The shepherd, the sorter of the wool, the wool-comber or carder, the dyer, the scribbler, the spinner, the weaver, the fuller, the dresser, with many others, must all join their different arts in order to complete even this homely production. How many merchants and carriers, besides, must have been employed in transporting the materials from some of those workmen to others who often live in a very distant part of the country! How much commerce and navigation in particular, how many ship-builders, sailors, sail-makers, rope-makers, must have been employed in order to bring together the different drugs made use of by the dyer, which often come from the remotest corners of the world! What a variety of labour too is necessary in order to produce the tools of the meanest of those workmen! To say nothing of such complicated machines as the ship of the sailor, the mill of the fuller, or even the loom of the weaver, let us consider only what a variety of labour is requisite in order to form that very simple machine, the shears with which the shepherd clips the wool. The miner, the builder of the furnace for smelting the ore, the feller of the timber, the burner of the charcoal to be made use of in the smelting-house, the brick-maker, the brick-layer, the work-men who attend the furnace, the millwright, the forger, the smith, must all of them join their different arts in order to produce them. Were we to examine, in the same manner, all the different parts of his dress and household furniture, the coarse linen shirt which he wears next his skin, the shoes which cover his feet, the bed which he lies on, and all the different parts which compose it, the kitchen grate at which he prepares his victuals, the coals which he makes use of for that purpose, dug from the bowels of the earth, and brought to him perhaps by a long sea and a long land carriage, all the other utensils of his kitchen, all the furniture of his table, the knives and forks, the earthen or pewter plates upon which he serves up and divides his victuals, the different hands employed in preparing his bread and his beer, the glass window which lets in the heat and the light, and keeps out the wind and the rain, with all the knowledge and art requisite for preparing that beautiful and happy invention, without which these northern parts of the world could scarce have afforded a very comfortable habitation, together with the tools of all the different workmen employed in producing those different conveniences; if we examine, I say, all these things, and consider what a variety of labour is employed about each of them, we shall be sensible that without the assistance and cooperation of many thousands, the very meanest person in a civilized country could not be provided, even according to, what we very falsely imagine, the easy and simple manner in which he is commonly accommodated. Compared, indeed, with the more extravagant luxury of the great, his accommodation must no doubt appear extremely simple and easy; and yet it may be true, perhaps, that the accommodation of an European prince does not always so much exceed that of an industrious and frugal peasant, as the accommodation of the latter exceeds that of many an African king. . . .

3

On the Division of Labour

Charles Babbage

Perhaps the most important principle on which the economy of a manufacture depends, is the *division of labour* amongst the persons who perform the work. The first application of this principle must have been made in a very early stage of society; for it must soon have been apparent, that more comforts and conveniences could be acquired by one man restricting his occupation to the art of making bows, another to that of building houses, a third boats, and so on. This division of labour into trades was not, however, the result of an opinion that the general riches of the community would be increased by such an arrangement: but it must have arisen from the circumstance, of each individual so employed discovering that he himself could thus make a greater profit of his labour than by pursuing more varied occupations. Society must have made considerable advances before this principle could have been carried into the workshop; for it is only in countries which have attained a high degree of civilization, and in articles in which there is a great competition amongst the producers, that the most perfect system of the division of labour is to be observed. The principles on which the advantages of this system depend, have been much the subject of discussion amongst writers on Political Economy; but the relative importance of their influence does not appear, in all cases, to have been estimated with sufficient

SOURCE: Charles Babbage, *On the Economy of Machinery and Manufactures* (Philadelphia: Carey & Lea, 1832), 121–140.

precision. It is my intention, in the first instance, to state shortly those principles, and then to point out what appears to me to have been omitted by those who have previously treated the subject.

1. *Of the time required for learning.* It will readily be admitted, that the portion of time occupied in the acquisition of any art will depend on the difficulty of its execution; and that the greater the number of distinct processes, the longer will be the time which the apprentice must employ in acquiring it. Five or seven years have been adopted, in a great many trades, as the time considered requisite for a lad to acquire a sufficient knowledge of his art, and to repay by his labour, during the latter portion of his time, the expense incurred by his master at its commencement. If, however, instead of learning all the different processes for making a needle, for instance, his attention be confined to one operation, a very small portion of his time will be consumed unprofitably at the commencement, and the whole of the rest of it will be beneficial to his master: and if there be any competition amongst the masters, the apprentice will be able to make better terms, and diminish the period of his servitude. Again; the facility of acquiring skill in a single process, and the early period of life at which it can be made a source of profit, will induce a greater number of parents to bring up their children to it; and from this circumstance also, the number of workmen being increased, the wages will soon fall.

A certain quantity of material will be consumed unprofitably, or spoiled by every person who learns an art; and, as he applies himself to each new process, he will waste a certain quantity of the raw material, or of the partly manufactured commodity. But whether one man commits this waste in acquiring successively each process, or many persons separately learn the several processes, the quantity of waste will remain the same: in this view of the subject, therefore, the division of labour will neither increase nor diminish the price of production.

2. Another source of the advantage resulting from the division of labour is, that *time is always lost from changing from one occupation to another.* When the human hand, or the human head, has been for some time occupied in any kind of work, it cannot instantly change its employment with full effect. The muscles of the limbs employed have acquired a flexibility during their exertion, and those to be put in action a stiffness during rest, which renders every change slow and unequal in the commencement. A similar result seems to take place in any change of mental exertion; the attention bestowed on the new subject is not so perfect at the first commencement as it becomes after some exercise. Long habit also produces in the muscles exercised a capacity for enduring fatigue to a much greater degree than they could support under other circumstances.

Another cause of the loss of time in changing from one operation to another, arises from the employment of different tools in the two processes. If these tools are simple in their nature, and the change is not frequently repeated, the loss of time is not considerable; but in many processes of the arts the tools are of great delicacy, requiring accurate adjustment whenever they are used. In many cases the time employed in adjusting, bears a large proportion to that employed in using the tool. The sliding-rest, the dividing and the drilling-engine, are of this kind; and hence in manufactories of sufficient extent, it is found to be good economy to keep one machine constantly employed in one kind of work: one lathe, for example, having a screw motion ot its sliding-rest along the whole length of its bed, is kept constantly making cylinders; another, having a motion for rendering uniform the velocity of the work at the point at which it passes the tool, is kept for facing surfaces; whilst a third is constantly employed in cutting wheels.

3. *Skill acquired by frequent repetition of the same processes.* The constant repetition of the same process necessarily produces in the workman a degree of excellence and rapidity in his particular department, which is never possessed by one person who is obliged to execute many different processes. This rapidity is still farther increased from the circumstance that most of the operation in factories, where the division of labour is carried to a considerable extent, are paid for as piece work. It is difficult to estimate in numbers the effect of this cause upon production. In nail-making, Adam Smith has stated, that it is almost three to one; for, he observes, that a smith accustomed to make nails, but whose whole business has not been that of a nailer, can make only from eight hundred to a thousand per day; whilst a lad who had never exercised any other trade, can make upwards of two thousand three hundred a day.

Upon an occasion when a large issue of bank-notes was required, a clerk at the Bank of England signed his name, consisting of seven letters, including the initial of his Christian name, five thousand three hundred times during eleven working hours; and he also arranged the notes he had signed in parcels of fifty each. In different trades the economy of production arising from this cause, will necessarily be different. The case of nail-making is perhaps, rather an extreme one. It must, however, be observed that, in one sense, this is not a permanent source of advantage; for, although it acts at the commencement of an establishment, yet every month adds to the skill of the workmen; and at the end of three or four years they will not be very far behind those who have practised only the particular branch of their art.

4. *The division of labour suggests the contrivance of tools and machinery to execute its processes.* When each process, by which any article is produced, is the sole occupation of one individual, his whole attention being devoted to a very limited and simple operation, any improvement in the form of his tools, or in the mode of using them, is much more likely to occur to his mind than if it were distracted by a greater variety of circumstances. Such an improvement in the tool is generally the first step towards a machine. If a piece of metal is to be cut in a lathe, for example, there is one angle at which the cutting-tool must be held to ensure the cleanest cut; and it is quite natural that the idea of fixing the tool at that angle

should present itself to an intelligent workman. The necessity of moving the tool slowly, and in a direction parallel to itself, would suggest the use of a screw, and thus arises the sliding-rest. It was probably the idea of mounting a chisel in a frame, to prevent its cutting too deeply, which gave rise to the common carpenter's plane. In cases where a blow from a hammer is employed, experience teaches the proper force required. The transition from the hammer held in the hand to one mounted upon an axis, and lifted regularly to a certain height by some mechanical contrivance, requires perhaps a greater degree of invention. Yet it is not difficult to perceive, that, if the hammer alway falls from the same height, its effect must be always the same.

When each process has been reduced to the use of some simple tool, the union of all these tools, actuated by one moving power, constitutes a machine. In contriving tools and simplifying processes, the operative workmen are, perhaps, most successful; but it requires far other habits to combine into one machine these scattered arts. A previous education as a workman in the peculiar trade, is undoubtedly a valuable preliminary; but in order to make such combinations with any reasonable expectation of success, an extensive knowledge of machinery, and the power of making mechanical drawings, are essentially requisite. These accomplishments are now much more common than they were formerly; and their absence was, perhaps, one of the causes of the multitude of failures in the early history of many of our manufactures.

Such are the principles usually assigned as the causes of the advantage resulting from the division of labour. As in the view I have taken of the question, the most important and influential cause has been altogether unnoticed, I shall re-state those principles in the words of Adam Smith: "The great increase in the quantity of work, which, in consequence of the division of labour, the same number of people are capable of performing, is owing to three different circumstances: first, to the increase of dexterity in every particular workman; secondly, to the

saving of time, which is commonly lost in passing from one species of work to another; and, lastly, to the invention of a great number of machines which facilitate and abridge labour, and enable one man to do the work of many.'' Now, although all these are important causes, and each has its influence on the result; yet it appears to me, that any explanation of the cheapness of manufactured articles, as consequent upon the division of labour, would be incomplete if the following principle were omitted to be stated.

That the master manufacturer, by dividing the work to be executed into different processes, each requiring different degrees of skill and force, can purchase exactly that precise quantity of both which is necessary for each process; whereas, if the whole work were executed by one workman, that person must possess sufficient skill to perform the most difficult, and sufficient strength to execute the most laborious, of the operations into which the art is divided. [1]

As the clear apprehension of this principle, upon which so much of the economy arising from the division of labour depends, is of considerable importance, it may be desirable to illustrate it, by pointing out its precise and numerical application in some specific manufacture. The art of making needles is, perhaps, that which I should have selected as comprehending a very large number of processes remarkably different in their nature; but the less difficult art of pin-making, has some claim to attention, from its having been used by Adam Smith, in his illustration of the subject; and I am confirmed in the choice, by the circumstance of our possessing a very accurate and minute description of that art, as practised in France above half a century ago.

Pin-making. In the manufacture of pins in England the following processes are employed:—

1. Wire-drawing. The brass wire used for making pins is purchased by the manufacturer in coils of about twenty-two inches in diameter, each weighing about thirty-six pounds. The coils are wound off into smaller ones of about six inches' diameter, and between one and two pounds' weight. The diameter of this wire is now reduced by drawing it repeatedly through holes in steel plates, until it becomes of the size required for the sort of pins intended to be made. During the process of drawing the wire through these holes it becomes hardened, and it is necessary to anneal it in order to prevent its breaking; and, to enable it to be still farther reduced, it is annealed two or three times, according to the diminution of diameter required. The coils are then soaked in sulphuric acid, largely diluted with water, in order to clean them, and are then beaten on stone for the purpose of removing any oxidated coating which may adhere to them. This process is usually performed by men, who draw and clean from thirty to thirty-six pounds of wire a day. They are paid at the rate of five farthings per pound, and generally earn about 3*s.* 6*d.* per day.

M. Perronet made some experiments on the extension the wire undergoes by this process at each hole: he took a piece of thick Swedish brass wire, and found

	Feet	Inch
Its length to be before drawing	3	8
After passing the first hole	5	5
_____ second hole	7	2
_____ third hole	7	8

It was now, annealed, and the length became

	Feet	Inch
After passing the fourth hole	10	8
_____ fifth hole	13	1
_____ sixth hole	16	8
And finally, after passing through six other holes	144	0

The holes through which the wire was drawn were not, in this experiment, of regularly decreasing diameter; and it is extremely difficult to make such holes, and still more to preserve them in their original dimensions.

2. Straightening the Wire. The coil of wire now passes into the hands of a woman, assisted by a boy or girl. A few nails, or iron pins, not quite in a line, are fixed into one end of a wooden table about twenty feet in length; the end of the wire is passed alternately between these nails, and is then pulled to the other end of the table. The object of this process is to straighten the wire, which had acquired a uniform curvature in the small coils into which it had been wound. The length thus straightened is cut off, and the remainder of the coil is drawn into similar lengths. About seven nails or pins are employed in straightening the wire, and their adjustment is a matter of some nicety. It seems, that by passing the wire between the first three nails or pins, a bend is produced in an opposite direction to that which the wire had in the coil; this bend, by passing the next two nails, is reduced to another of larger curvature in the first direction, and so on till the curvature is at last so large that it may be confounded with a straight line.

3. Pointing. A man next takes about three hundred of these straightened pieces in a parcel, and putting them into a gauge, cuts off from one end, by means of a pair of shears, moved by his foot, a portion equal in length to rather more than six pins. He continues this operation until the entire parcel is reduced into similar pieces. The next step is to sharpen the ends: for this purpose the operator sits before a steel mill, which is kept rapidly revolving; and taking up a parcel between the finger and the thumb of each hand, he passes the ends before the mill, taking care with his fingers and thumbs to make each wire slowly revolve upon its axis. The mill consists of a cylinder about six inches in diameter, and two and a half inches broad, faced with steel, which is cut in the manner of a file. Another cylinder is fixed on the same axis at a few inches distant; the file on the edge of which is of a finer kind, and is used for finishing off the points. Having thus pointed all the pieces at one end, he reverses them, and performs the same process on the other. This process requires considerable skill, but it is not unhealthy whilst the similar process in needle-making is remarkably destructive of health. The pieces, now pointed at both ends, are next placed in gauges, and the pointed ends are cut off, by means of shears, to the proper length of which the pins are to be made. The remaining portions of the wire are now equal to about four pins in length, and are again pointed at each end, and their ends again cut off. This process is repeated a third time, and the small portion of wire left in the middle is thrown amongst the waste, to be melted along with the dust arising from the sharpening. It is usual for a man, his wife, and a child, to join in performing these processes; and they are paid at the rate of five farthings per pound. They can point from thirty-four to thirty-six and a half pounds per day, and gain from 6*s. 6d.* to 7*s.*, which may be apportioned thus: 5*s. 6d.* to the man, 1*s.* to the woman, 6*d.* to the boy or girl.

4. Twisting and Cutting the Heads. The next process is making the heads. For this purpose a boy takes a piece of wire, of the same diameter as the pin to be headed, which he fixes on an axis that can be made to revolve rapidly by means of a wheel and strap connected with it. This wire is called the mould. He then takes a smaller wire, which having passed through an eye in a small tool held in his left hand, he fixes close to the bottom of the mould. The mould is now made to revolve rapidly by means of the right hand, and the smaller wire coils round it until it has covered the whole length of the mould. The boy now cuts the end of the spiral connected with the foot of the mould, and draws it off. When a sufficient quantity of heading is thus made, a man takes from thirteen to twenty of this spirals in his left hand, between his thumb and three outer fingers; these he places in such a manner that two turns of the spiral shall be beyong the upper edge of a pair of shears, and with the forefinger of the same hand he feels these two projecting turns. With his right hand he closes the shears; and the two turns of the spiral being cut off, drop into a basin. The position of the forefinger prevents the heads from flying about when cut off. The

workmen who cut the heads are usually paid at the rate of 2½*d.* to 3*d.* per pound for large, but a higher price is given for the smaller heading. Out of this they pay the boy who spins the spiral; he receives from 4*d.* to 6*d.* per day. A good workman can cut from six to about thirty pounds of heading per day, according to its size.

5. Heading. The process of fixing the head on the body of the pin is usually executed by women and children. Each operator sits before a small steel stake, having a cavity, into which one half of the intended head will fit; immediately above is a steel die, having a corresponding cavity for the other half of the head: this latter die can be raised by a pedal moved by the foot. The cavities in the centre of these dies are connected with the edge by a small groove, to admit of the body of the pin, which is thus prevented from being flattened by the blow of the die. The operator with his left hand dips the pointed end of the body of a pin into a tray of heads; having passed the point through one of them, he carries it along to the other end with the forefinger. He now takes the pin in the right hand, and places the head in the cavity of the stake, and, lifting the die with his foot, allows it to fall on the head. This blow tightens the head on the shank, which is then turned round, and the head receives three or four blows on different parts of its circumference. The women and children who fix the heads are paid at the rate of 1*s. 6d.* for every twenty thousand. A skillful operator can with great exertion do twenty thousand per day; but from ten to fifteen thousand is the usual quantity: children head a much smaller number; varying, of course, with the degree of their skill. The weight of the hammer is from seven to ten pounds, and it falls through a very small space, perhaps from one to two inches. About one percent are spoiled in the process; these are picked out afterwards by women, and are reserved with the waste from other processes for the melting-pot. The form of the dies in which the heads are struck is varied according to the fashion of the time; but the repeated blows to which it is subject renders it necessary that it should be repaired after it has been used for about thirty pounds of pins.

6. Tinning. The pins are now fit to be tinned, a process which is usually executed, by a man, assisted by his wife, or by a lad. The quantity of pins operated upon at this stage is usually fifty-six pounds. They are first placed in a pickle, in order to remove any grease or dirt from their surface, and also to render that surface rough, which facilitates the adherence of the tin with which they are to be covered. They are then placed in a boiler full of a solution of tartar in water, in which they are mixed with a quantity of tin in small grains. They are generally kept boiling for about two hours and a half, and are then removed into a tub of water into which some bran has been thrown; this is for the purpose of washing them. They are then taken out, and, being placed in wooden trays, are well shaken in dry bran: this removes any water adhering to them; and by giving the wooden tray a peculiar kind of motion, the pins are thrown up, and the bran gradually flies off, and leaves them behind in the tray. The man who pickles and tins the pins usually gets one penny per pound for the work, and employs himself, during the boiling of one batch of pins, with drying those previously tinned. He can earn about 9s. per day; but out of this he pays about 3s. for his assistant.

7. Papering. The arranging of pins side by side in paper is generally performed by women. The pins come from the last process in wooden bowls, with the points projecting in all directions. A woman takes up some, and places them on the teeth of a comb, whilst, by a few shakes, some of the pins fall back into the bowl, and the rest, being caught by their heads, are detained between the teeth of the comb. Having thus arranged them in a parallel direction, she fixes the requisite number between two pieces of iron, having twenty-five small grooves, at equal distances; and having previously doubled the paper, she presses it against the points of the pins until they have passed through the two folds which are to retain them. The pins are then relieved from the grasp of the tool, and the process repeated with others. A woman gains about 1s. 6d. per day by papering; but children

are sometimes employed, who earn from 6d. per day, and upwards.

Having thus described the various processes of pin-making, without entering into the minute details, and having stated the usual cost of each, it will be convenient to present a tabular view [Table 1] of the time occupied by each process, and its cost, as well as of the sums which can be earned by the persons who confine themselves solely to each process. As the rate of wages is itself fluctuating, and as the prices paid and quantities executed have been given between certain limits, it is not to be expected that this table can represent with the minutest accuracy the cost of each part of the work, nor even that it shall accord perfectly with the prices above given: but it has been drawn up with some care, and will be quite sufficient for that general view, and for those reasonings, which it is meant to illustrate. A table nearly similar will be subjoined [Table 2], which has been deduced from a statement of M. Perronet, respecting the art of pin-making in France, about seventy years ago.

English Manufacture. Pins, "*Elevens,*" 5,546 weigh one pound; "*one dozen*" = 6,932 pins weigh twenty ounces, and require six ounces of paper.

French Manufacture. Cost of 12,000 pins, N. 6, each being eight-tenths of an English inch in length; with the cost of each operation:— deduced from the observations and statement of M. Perronet:—as they were manufactured in France about 1760.

It appears from the analysis we have given of the art of pin-making, that it occupies rather more than seven hours and a half of time, for ten different individuals working in succession on the same material, to convert it into a pound of pins; and that the total expense of their labour, each being paid in the joint ratio of his skill and of the time he is employed, amounts very nearly to 1s. 1d. But from an examination of the first of these tables, it appears that the wages earned by the persons employed vary from 4½d. per day up to 6s., and consequently the skill which is required for their respective employments may be measured by those sums. Now it is evident, that if one person be required

Table 1

Name of the Process	Workmen	Time of Making 1 lb. of Pins (hours)	Cost of Making 1 lb. of Pins (pence)	Workman Earns per Day (s)	(d)	Price of Making Each Part of a Single Pin, in Millionths of a Penny
1. Drawing Wire	Man	.3636	1.2500	3	3	225
2. Straightening the	Woman	.3000	.2840	1	0	51
Wire	Girl	.3000	.1420	0	6	26
3. Pointing	Man	.3000	1.7750	5	3	319
4. Twisting and	Boy	.0400	.0147	0	4½	3
Cutting the Heads	Man	.0400	.2103	5	4½	38
5. Heading	Woman	4.0000	5.0000	1	3	901
6. Tinning, or	Man	.1071	.6666	6	0	121
Whitening	Woman	.1071	.3333	3	0	60
7. Papering	Woman	2.1314	3.1973	1	6	576
		7.6892	12.8732			2,320

Table 2

Name of the Process	Time of Making Twelve Thousand Pins (hours)	Cost of Making Twelve Thousand Pins (pence)	Workman Usually Earns per Day (pence)	Expense of Tools and Material (pence)
1. Wire	—	—	—	24.75
2. Straightening and Cutting	1.2	.5	4.5	—
Coarse Pointing	1.2	.625	10.0	—
Turning Wheel*	1.2	.875	7.0	—
3. Fine Pointing	.8	.5	9.375	—
Turning Wheel	1.2	.5	4.75	—
Cutting off Pointed Ends	.6	.375	7.5	—
Turning Spiral	.5	.152	3.0	—
4. Cutting off Heads	.8	.375	5.625	—
Fuel to Anneal Ditto	—	—	—	.125
5. Heading	12.0	.333	4.25	—
6. Tartar for Cleaning	—	—	—	.5
Tartar for Whitening	—	—	—	.5
7. Papering	4.8	.5	2.0	—
Paper	—	—	—	1.0
Wear of Tools	—	—	—	2.0
	24.3	4.708		

*The expense of turning the wheel appears to have arisen from the person so occupied being unemployed during half his time, whilst the pointer went to another manufactory.

to make the whole pound of pins, he must have skill enough to earn about 5*s*. 3*d*. per day whilst he is pointing the wires or cutting off the heads from the spiral coil,—and 6*s*. when he is whitening the pins; which three operations together would occupy little more than the seventeenth part of his time. It is also apparent, that during more than one half of his time he must be earning only 1*s*. 3*d*. per day in putting on the heads, although his skill, if properly employed, would, in the same time, produce nearly five times as much. If therefore we were to employ, for each of the processes, the man who whitens the pins, and who earns 6*s*. per day, even supposing that he could make the pounds of pins in an equally short time, yet we must pay him for his time 46.14 pence or about 3*s*. 10*d*. *The pins would therefore cost in making, three times and three quarters as much as they now do by the application of the division of labour.* The higher the skill required of the workman in any one process of a manufacture, and the smaller the time during which it is employed, so much the greater will be the advantage of separating that process from the rest, and devoting one person's attention entirely to it. Had we selected the art of needle-making as our illustration, the economy arising from the division of labour would have been still larger; for the process of tempering the needles requires great skill, attention, and experience; and although from three to four thousand are tempered at once, the workman is paid a very high rate of wages. In another process of the same art, dry-pointing, which is also executed with great rapidity, the wages earned by the workman reach from 7*s*. to 12*s*., 15*s*., and even, in some instances, to 20*s*. per day; whilst other processes in the same art are carried on by children paid at the rate of 6*d*. per day.

Some farther reflections are suggested by the preceding analysis; but it may be convenient, previously, to place before the reader a brief description of a machine for making pins, invented by an American. It is highly ingenious in point of contrivance, and, in respect to its economical principles, will furnish a strong and interesting contrast with the manufacture of pins

by the human hand. In this machine a coil of brass wire is placed on an axis; one end of this wire is drawn by a pair of rollers through a small hole in a plate of steel, and is held there by a forceps. As soon as the machine is put in action—

1. The forceps draws the wire on to a distance equal in length to one pin: a cutting edge of steel then descends close to the hole through which the wire entered, and severs a piece equal in length to one pin.

2. The forceps holding this wire moves on until it brings the wire into the centre of the *chuck* of a small lathe, which opens to receive it. Whilst the forceps returns to fetch another piece of wire, the lathe revolves rapidly, and grinds the projecting end of the wire upon a steel mill, which advances towards it.

3. After this first or coarse pointing, the lathe stops, and another forceps takes hold of the half-pointed pin, (which is instantly released by the opening of the *chuck*,) and conveys it to a similar *chuck* of another lathe, which receives it, and finishes the pointing on a finer steel mill.

4. This mill again stops, and another forceps removes the pointed pin into a pair of strong steel clams, having a small groove in them by which they hold the pin very firmly. A part of this groove, which terminates at that edge of the steel clams which is intended to form the head of the pin, is made conical. A small round steel punch is now driven forcibly against the end of the wire thus clamped, and the head of a pin is partially formed by compressing the wire into the conical cavity.

5. Another pair of forceps now removes the pin to another pair of clams, and the head of the pin is completed by a blow from a second punch, the end of which is slightly concave. Each pair of forceps returns as soon as it has delivered its burden; and thus there are always five pieces of wire at the same moment in different stages of advance towards a finished pin. The pins so formed are received in a tray, and whitened and

papered in the usual manner. About sixty pins can thus be made by this machine in one minute; but each process occupies exactly the same time in performing.

In order to judge of the value of such a machine, compared with hand labour, it would be necessary to inquire:—1. To what defects pins so made are liable? 2. What advantages they possess over those made the usual way? 3. What is the prime cost of a machine for making them? 4. What is the expense of keeping it in repair? 5. What is the expense of moving it and attending to it?

1. Pins made by the machine are more likely to bend, because as the head is punched up out of solid wire, it ought to be in a soft state to admit of this process. 2. Pins made by the machine are better than common ones, because they are not subject to losing their heads. 3. With respect to the prime cost of a machine, it would be very much reduced if numbers should be required. 4. With regard to its wear and tear, experience only can decide the question: but it may be remarked, that the steel clams or dies in which the heads are punched up, will wear quickly unless the wire has been softened by annealing; and that if it has been softened, the bodies of the pins will bend too readily. Such an inconvenience might be remedied, either by making the machine spin the heads and fix them on, or by annealing only that end of the wire which is to become the head of the pin: but this would cause a delay between the operations, since the brass is too brittle while heated to bear a blow without crumbling. 5. On comparing the time occupied by the machine with that stated in the analysis, we find, except in the process of heading, if time alone is considered, that the human hand is more rapid. Three thousand six hundred pins are pointed by the machine in one hour, whilst a man can point fifteen thousand six hundred in the same time. But in the process of heading, the rapidity of the machine is two and a half times that of the human hand. It must, however, be observed, that the process of grinding does not require the application of force to the machine equal to that of one man; for all the processes we have described are executed at once by the machine, and one labourer can easily work it.

Note

1. I have already stated, that this principle presented itself to me after a personal examination of a number of manufactories and workshops devoted to different purposes; but I have since found that it has been distinctly stated, in the work of Gioja, *Nuovo Prospetto delle Scienze Economiche,* 6 tom. 4to. Milano, 1815, tom. i. capo iv.

4

Superintendent's Report

OFFICE GENERAL SUP'T N.Y. &
ERIE R. R.
New York, March 25, 1856

HOMER RAMSDELL, ESQ.
PRESIDENT OF THE NEW YORK AND
ERIE RAILROAD COMPANY:

SIR:

The magnitude of the business of this road, its numerous and important connections, and the large number of employés engaged in operating it, have led many, whose opinions are entitled to respect, to the conclusion, that a proper regard to details, which enter so largely into the elements of success in the management of all railroads, cannot possibly be attained by any plan that contemplates its organization as a whole; and in proof of this position, the experience of shorter roads is referred to, the business operations of which have been conducted much more economically.

Theoretically, other things being equal, a long road should be operated for a less cost per mile than a short one. This position is so clearly evident and so generally admitted, that its truth may be assumed without offering any arguments in support of it; and, notwithstanding the reverse, so far as *practical* results are considered, has generally been the case, we must look to other causes than the mere difference in length of roads for a solution of the difficulty.

SOURCE: Daniel C. McCallum, "Superintendent's Report," March 25, 1856, in *Annual Report of the New York and Erie Railroad Company for 1855* (New York, 1856).

A Superintendent of a road fifty miles in length can give its business his personal attention, and may be almost constantly upon the line engaged in the direction of its details; each employé is familiarly known to him, and all questions in relation to its business are at once presented and acted upon; and any system, however imperfect, may under such circumstances prove comparatively successful.

In the government of a road five hundred miles in length a very different state of things exists. Any system which might be applicable to the business and extent of a short road, would be found entirely inadequate to the wants of a long one; and I am fully convinced, that in the want of a system perfect in its details, properly adapted and vigilantly enforced, lies the true secret of their failure; and that this disparity of cost per mile in operating long and short roads, is not produced by *a difference in length,* but is in proportion to the perfection of the system adopted.

Entertaining these views, I had the honor, more than a year since, to submit for your consideration and approval a plan for the more effective organization of this department. The system then proposed has to some extent been introduced, and experience, so far, affords the strongest assurances that when fully carried out, the most satisfactory results will be obtained.

In my opinion a system of operations, to be efficient and successful, should be such as to give to the principal and responsible head of the running department a complete daily history of details in all their minutiae. Without such supervision, the procurement of a satisfactory annual statement must be regarded as extremely problematical. The fact that dividends are earned without such control does not disprove the position, as in many cases the extraordinarily remunerative nature of an enterprise may ensure satisfactory returns under the most loose and inefficient management.

It may be proper here to remark that in consequence of that want of adaptation before alluded to, we cannot avail ourselves to any great extent of the plan of organization of shorter lines in framing one for this, nor have we any precedent or experience upon which we can fully rely in doing so. Under these circumstances, it will scarcely be expected that we can at once adopt any plan of operations which will not require amendment and a reasonable time to prove its worth. A few general principles, however, may be regarded as settled and necessary in its formation, amongst which are:

1. A proper division of responsibilities.
2. Sufficient power conferred to enable the same to be fully carried out, that such responsibilities may be real in their character.
3. The means of knowing whether such responsibilities are faithfully executed.
4. Great promptness in the report of all derelictions of duty, that evils may be at once corrected.
5. Such information, to be obtained through a system of daily reports and checks that will not embarrass principal officers, nor lessen their influence with their subordinates.
6. The adoption of a system, as a whole, which will not only enable the General Superintendent to detect errors immediately, but will also point out the delinquent.

5

The Engineer as an Economist

Henry R. Towne

The monogram of our national initials, which is the symbol of our monetary unit, the dollar, is almost as frequently conjoined to the figures of an engineer's calculations as are the symbols indicating feet, minutes, pounds, or gallons. The final issue of his work, in probably a majority of cases, resolves itself into a question of dollars and cents, of relative or absolute values. This statement, while true in regard to the work of all engineers, applies particularly to that of the mechanical engineer, for the reason that his functions, more frequently than in the case of others, include the executive duties of organizing and superintending the operations of industrial establishments, and of directing the labor of the artisans whose organized efforts yield the fruition of his work.

To insure the best results, the organization of productive labor must be directed and controlled by persons having not only good executive ability, and possessing the practical familiarity of a mechanic or engineer with the goods produced and the processes employed, but having also, and equally, a practical knowledge of how to observe, record, analyze and compare essential facts in relation to wages, supplies, expense accounts, and all else that enters into or affects the economy of production and the cost of the product. There are many good mechanical engineers;—there are also many good "business men";—but the two are rarely combined in one

SOURCE: *Transactions of The American Society of Mechanical Engineers*, Vol. 7 (Paper presented at May 1886 meeting of the Society, Chicago), 428–432.

person. But this combination of qualities, together with at least some skill as an accountant, either in one person or more, is essential to the successful management of industrial works, and has its highest effectiveness if united in one person, who is thus qualified to supervise, either personally or through assistants, the operations of all departments of a business, and to subordinate each to the harmonious development of the whole.

Engineering has long been conceded a place as one of the modern arts, and has become a well-defined science, with a large and growing literature of its own, and of late years has subdivided itself into numerous and distinct divisions, one of which is that of mechanical engineering. It will probably not be disputed that the matter of shop management is of equal importance with that of engineering, as affecting the successful conduct of most, if not all, of our great industrial establishments, and that the *management of works* has become a matter of such great and far-reaching importance as perhaps to justify its classification also as one of the modern arts. The one is a well-defined science, with a distinct literature, with numerous journals and with many associations for the interchange of experience; the other is unorganized, is almost without literature, has no organ or medium for the interchange of experience, and is without association or organization of any kind. A vast amount of accumulated experience in the art of workshop management already exists, but there is no record of it available to the world in general, and each old enterprise is managed more or less in its own way, receiving little benefit from the parallel experience of other similar enterprises, and imparting as little of its own to them; while each new enterprise, starting *de novo* and with much labor, and usually at much cost for experience, gradually develops a more or less perfect system of its own, according to the ability of its managers, receiving little benefit or aid from all that may have been done previously by others in precisely the same field of work.

Surely this condition of things is wrong and should be remedied. But the remedy must not be looked for from those who are "business men" or clerks and accountants only; it should come from those whose training and experience has given them an understanding of both sides (viz.: the mechanical and the clerical) of the important questions involved. It should originate, therefore, from those who are also engineers, and, for the reasons above indicated, particularly from mechanical engineers. Granting this, why should it not originate from, and be promoted by The American Society of Mechanical Engineers?

To consider this proposition more definitely, let us state the work which requires to be done. The questions to be considered, and which need recording and publication as conducing to discussion and the dissemination of useful knowledge in this specialty, group themselves under two principal heads, namely: Shop Management, and Shop Accounting. A third head may be named which is subordinate to, and partly included in each of these, namely: Shop Forms and Blanks. Under the head of Shop Management fall the questions of organization, responsibility, reports, systems of contract and piece work, and all that relates to the executive management of works, mills and factories. Under the head of Shop Accounting fall the questions of time and wages systems, determination of costs, whether by piece or day-work, the distribution of the various expense accounts, the ascertainment of profits, methods of bookkeeping, and all that enters into the system of accounts which relates to the manufacturing departments of a business, and to the determination and record of its results.

There already exists an enormous fund of information relating to such matters, based upon actual and most extensive experience. What is now needed is a medium for the interchange of this experience among those whom it interests and concerns. Probably no better way for this exists than that obtaining in other instances, namely, by the publication of papers and reports, and by meetings for the discussion of papers and interchange of opinions.

The subject thus outlined, however distinct and apart from the primary functions of this society, is, nevertheless, germane to the interests of most, if not all, of its members. Conceding this, why should not the function of the society be so enlarged as to embrace this new field of usefulness? This work, if undertaken, may be kept separate and distinct from the present work of the society by organizing a new "section" (which might be designated the "Economic Section"), the scope of which would embrace all papers and discussions relating to the topics herein referred to. The meetings of this section could be held either separately from, or immediately following the regular meetings of the society, and its papers could appear as a supplement to the regular transactions. In this way all interference would be avoided with the primary and chief business of the society, and the attendance at the meetings of the new section would naturally resolve itself into such portion of the membership as is interested in the objects for which it would be organized.

As a single illustration of the class of subjects to be covered by the discussions and papers of the proposed new section, and of the benefit to be derived therefrom, there may be cited the case of a manufacturing establishment in which there are now in use, in connection with the manufacturing accounts and exclusive of the ordinary commercial accounts, some twenty various forms of special record and account books, and more than one hundred printed forms and blanks. The primary object to which all of these contribute is the systematic recording of the operations of the different departments of the works, and the computation therefrom of such statistical information as is essential to the efficient management of the business, and especially to increased economy of production. All of these special books and forms have been the outgrowth of experience extending over many years, and represent a large amount of thoughtful planning and intelligent effort at constant development and improvement. The methods thus arrived at would undoubtedly be of great value to others engaged in similar operations, and particularly to persons engaged in organizing and starting new enterprises. It is probable that much, if not all, of the information and experience referred to would be willingly made public through such a channel as is herein suggested, particularly if such action on the part of one firm or corporation would be responded to in like manner by others, so that each member could reasonably expect to receive some equivalent for his contributions by the benefit which he would derive from the experience of others.

In the case of the establishment above referred to, a special system of contract and piece-work has been in operation for some fifteen years, the results from which, in reducing the labor cost on certain products without encroaching upon the earnings of the men engaged, have been quite striking. A few of these results selected at random, are indicated by the accompanying diagram (Figure 1), the diagonal lines on which represent the fluctuations in the labor cost of certain special products during the time covered by the table, the vertical scale representing values.

Undoubtedly a portion of the reductions thus indicated resulted from improved appliances, larger product, and increased experience, but after making due allowance for all of these, there remains a large portion of the reduction which, to the writer's knowledge, is fairly attributable to the operation of the peculiar piece-work system adopted. The details and operations of this system would probably be placed before the society, in due time, through the channel of the proposed new section, should the latter take definite form. Other, and probably much more valuable, information

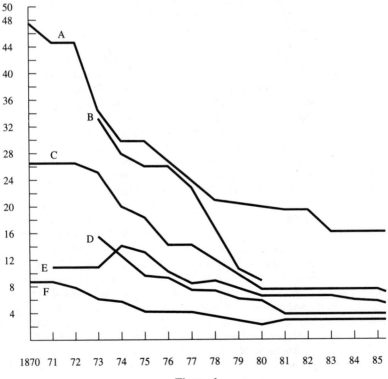

Figure 1

and experience relating to systems of contract and piece-work would doubtless be contributed by other members, and in the aggregate a great amount of information of a most valuable character would thus be made available to the whole membership of the society.

In conclusion, it is suggested that if the plan herein proposed commends itself favorably to the members present at the meeting at which it is presented, the subject had best be referred to a special committee, by whom it can be carefully considered, and by whom, if it seems expedient to proceed further, the whole matter can be matured and formulated in an orderly manner, and thus be so presented at a future meeting as to enable the society then intelligently to act upon the question, and to decide whether or not to adopt the recommendations made by such committee.

6

General Principles of Management

Henri Fayol

The managerial function finds its only outlet through the members of the organization (body corporate). Whilst the other functions bring into play material and machines the managerial function operates only on the personnel. The soundness and good working order of the body corporate depend on a certain number of conditions termed indiscriminately principles, laws, rules. For preference I shall adopt the term principles whilst dissociating it from any suggestion of rigidity, for there is nothing rigid or absolute in management affairs, it is all a question of proportion. Seldom do we have to apply the same principle twice in identical conditions; allowance must be made for different changing circumstances, for men just as different and changing and for many other variable elements.

Therefore principles are flexible and capable of adaptation to every need; it is a matter of knowing how to make use of them, which is a difficult art requiring intelligence, experience, decision and proportion. Compounded of tact and experience, proportion is one of the foremost attributes of the manager. There is no limit to the number of principles of management, every rule or managerial procedure which strengthens the body corporate or facilitates its functioning has a place among the principles so long, at least, as experience confirms its

SOURCE: Henri Fayol, *General and Industrial Management,* trans. Constance Storrs (London: Pitman Publishing, Ltd., 1949), 19–42. (Original work published 1916.) Reprinted by permission.

worthiness. A change in the state of affairs can be responsible for change of rules which had been engendered by that state.

I am going to review some of the principles of management which I have most frequently had to apply; viz.—

1. Division of work.
2. Authority.
3. Discipline.
4. Unity of command.
5. Unity of direction.
6. Subordination of individual interests to the general interest.
7. Remuneration.
8. Centralization.
9. Scalar chain (line of authority).
10. Order.
11. Equity.
12. Stability of tenure of personnel.
13. Initiative.
14. Esprit de corps.

1. Division of Work

Specialization belongs to the natural order; it is observable in the animal world, where the more highly developed the creature the more highly differentiated its organs; it is observable in human societies where the more important the body corporate[1] the closer is the relationship between structure and function. As society grows, so new organs develop destined to replace the single one performing all functions in the primitive state.

The object of division of work is to produce more and better work with the same effort. The worker always on the same part, the manager concerned always with the same matters, acquire an ability, sureness, and accuracy which increase their output. Each change of work brings in its train an adaptation which reduces output. Division of work permits of reduction in the number of objects to which attention and effort must be directed and has been recognized as the best means of making use of individuals and of groups of people. It is not merely applicable to technical work, but without exception to all work involving a more or less considerable number of people and demanding abilities of various types, and it results in specialization of functions and separation of powers. Although its advantages are universally recognized and although possibility of progress is inconceivable without the specialized work of learned men and artists, yet division of work has its limits which experience and a sense of proportion teach us may not be exceeded.

2. Authority and Responsibility

Authority is the right to give orders and the power to exact obedience. Distinction must be made between a manager's official authority deriving from office and personal authority, compounded of intelligence, experience, moral worth, ability to lead, past services, etc. In the make up of a good head personal authority is the indispensable complement of official authority. Authority is not to be conceived of apart from responsibility, that is apart from sanction—reward or penalty—which goes with the exercise of power. Responsibility is a corollary of authority, it is its natural consequence and essential counterpart, and wheresoever authority is exercised responsibility arises.

The need for sanction, which has its origin in a sense of justice, is strengthened and increased by this consideration, that in the general interest useful actions have to be encouraged and their opposite discouraged. Application of sanction to acts of authority forms part of the conditions essential for good management, but it is generally difficult to effect, especially in large concerns. First, the degree of responsibility must be established and then the weight of the sanction. Now, it is relatively easy to establish a workman's responsibility for his acts and a scale of corresponding sanctions; in the case of a foreman it is somewhat difficult, and proportionately as one goes up the scalar chain of businesses, as work grows more complex, as the number of workers involved increases, as the final result is more remote, it is increasingly difficult to isolate the share of the initial act of authority in the ultimate result and to establish the degree of responsibility of the manager. The measurement of this responsibility and its equivalent in material terms elude all calculation.

Sanction, then, is a question of kind, custom, convention, and judging it one must take into account the action itself, the attendant circumstances and potential repercussions. Judgment demands high moral character, impartiality and firmness. If all these conditions are not fulfilled there is a danger that the sense of responsibility may disappear from the concern.

Responsibility valiantly undertaken and borne merits some consideration; it is a kind of courage everywhere much appreciated. Tangible proof of this exists in the salary level of some industrial leaders, which is much higher than that of civil servants of comparable rank but carrying no responsibility. Nevertheless, generally speaking, responsibility is feared as much as authority is sought after, and fear of responsibility paralyses much initiative and destroys many good qualities. A good leader should possess and infuse into those around him courage to accept responsibility.

The best safeguard against abuse of authority and against weakness on the part of a higher manager is personal integrity and particularly high moral character of such a manager, and this integrity, it is well known, is conferred neither by election nor ownership.

3. Discipline

Discipline is in essence obedience, application, energy, behaviour, and outward marks of respect observed in accordance with the standing agreements between the firm and its employees, whether these agreements have been freely debated or accepted without prior discussion, whether they be written or implicit, whether they derive from the wish of the parties to them or from rules and customs, it is these agreements which determine the formalities of discipline.

Discipline, being the outcome of different varying agreements, naturally appears under the most diverse forms; obligations of obedience, application, energy, behavior, vary, in effect, from one firm to another, from one group of employees to another, from one time to another. Nevertheless, general opinion is deeply convinced that discipline is absolutely essential for the smooth running of business and that without discipline no enterprise could prosper.

This sentiment is very forcibly expressed in military hand-books, where it runs that "Discipline constitutes the chief strength of armies." I would approve unreservedly of this aphorism were it followed by this other, "Discipline is what leaders make it." The first one inspires respect for discipline, which is a good thing, but it tends to eclipse from view the responsibility of leaders, which is undesirable, for the state of discipline of any group of people depends essentially on the worthiness of its leaders.

When a defect in discipline is apparent or when relations between superiors and subordinates leave much to be desired, responsibility for this must not be cast heedlessly, and without going further afield, on the poor state of the team, because the ill mostly results from the ineptitude of the leaders. That, at all events, is what I have noted in various parts of France, for I have always found French workmen obedient and loyal provided they are ably led.

In the matter of influence upon discipline, agreements must set side by side with command. It is important that they be clear and, as far as possible, afford satisfaction to both sides. This is not easy. Proof of that exists in the great strikes of miners, railwaymen, and civil servants which, in these latter years, have jeopardized national life at home and elsewhere and which arose out of agreements in dispute or inadequate legislation.

For half a century a considerable change has been effected in the mode of agreements between a concern and its employees. The agreements of former days fixed by the employer alone are being replaced, in ever increasing measure, by understandings arrived at by discussion between an owner or group of owners and workers' associations. Thus each individual owner's responsibility has been reduced and is further diminished by increasingly frequent state intervention in labour problems. Nevertheless, the setting up of agreements binding a firm and its employees from which disciplinary formalities emanate, should remain one of the chief preoccupations of industrial heads.

The well-being of the concern does not permit, in cases of offence against discipline, of the neglect of certain sanctions capable of preventing or minimizing their recurrence. Experience and tact on the part of a manager are put to the proof in the choice and degree of sanctions to be used, such as remonstrances, warning, fines, suspensions, demotion, dismissal. Individual people and attendant circumstances must be taken into account. In fine, discipline is respect for agreements which are directed at achieving obedience, application, energy, and the outward marks of respect. It is incumbent upon managers at high levels as much as upon humble employees, and the best means of establishing and maintaining it are—

1. Good superiors at all levels.
2. Agreements as clear and fair as possible.
3. Sanctions (penalties) judiciously applied.

4. Unity of Command

For any action whatsoever, an employee should receive orders from one superior only. Such is the rule of unity of command, arising from general and ever-present necessity and wielding an influence on the conduct of affairs, which to my way of thinking, is at least equal to any other principle whatsoever. Should it be violated, authority is undermined, discipline is in jeopardy, order disturbed and stability threatened. This rule seems fundamental to me and so I have given it the rank of principle. As soon as two superiors wield their authority over the same person or department, uneasiness makes itself felt and should the cause persist, the disorder increases, the malady takes on the appearance of an animal organism troubled by a foreign body, and the following consequences are to be observed: either the dual command ends in disappearance or elimination of one of the superiors and organic well-being is restored, or else the organism continues to wither away. In no case is there adaptation of the social organism to dual command.

Now dual command is extremely common and wreaks havoc in all concerns, large or small, in home and in state. The evil is all the more to be feared in that it worms its way into the social organism on the most plausible pretexts. For instance—

(a) In the hope of being better understood or gaining time or to put a stop forthwith to an undesirable practice, a superior S^2 may give orders directly to an employee E without going via the superior S^1. If this mistake is repeated there is dual command with its consequences, *viz.*, hesitation on the part of the subordinate, irritation and dissatisfaction on the part of the superior set aside, and disorder in the work. It will be seen later that it is possible to bypass the scalar chain when necessary, whilst avoiding the drawbacks of dual command.

(b) The desire to get away from the immediate necessity of dividing up authority as between two colleagues, two friends, two members of one family, results at times in dual command reigning at the top of a concern right from the outset. Exercising the same powers and having the same authority over the same men, the two colleagues end up inevitably with dual command and its consequences. Despite harsh lessons, instances of this sort are still numerous. New colleagues count on their mutual regard, common interest, and good sense to save them from every conflict, every serious disagreement and, save for rare exceptions, the illusion is short-lived. First an awkwardness makes itself felt, then a certain irritation and, in time, if dual command exists, even hatred. Men cannot bear dual command. A judicious assignment of duties would have reduced the danger without entirely banishing it, for between two superiors on the same footing there must always be some question ill-defined. But it is riding for a fall to set up a business organization with two superiors on equal footing without assigning duties and demarcating authority.

(c) Imperfect demarcation of departments also leads to dual command: two superiors issuing orders in a sphere which each thinks his own, constitutes dual command.

(d) Constant linking up as between different departments, natural intermeshing of functions, duties often badly defined, create an ever-present danger of dual command. If a knowledgeable superior does not put it in order, footholds are established which later upset and compromise the conduct of affairs.

In all human associations, in industry, commerce, army, home, state, dual command is a perpetual source of conflicts, very grave sometimes, which have special claim on the attention of superiors of all ranks.

5. Unity of Direction

This principle is expressed as: one head and one plan for a group of activities having the same objective. It is the condition essential to unity of action, coordination of strength and focusing of effort. A body with two heads is in the social as in the animal sphere a monster, and has difficulty in surviving. Unity of direction (one head one plan) must not be confused with unity of command (one employee to have orders from one superior only). Unit of direction is provided for by sound organization of the body corporate, unity of command turns on the functioning of the personnel. Unity of command cannot exist without unity of direction, but does not flow from it.

6. Subordination of Individual Interest to General Interest

This principle calls to mind the fact that in a business the interest of one employee or group of employees should not prevail over that of the concern, that the interest of the home should come before that of its members and that the interest of the state should have pride of place over that of one citizen or group of citizens.

It seems that such an admonition should not need calling to mind. But ignorance, ambition, selfishness, laziness, weakness, and all human passions tend to cause the general interest to be lost sight of in favour of individual interest and a perpetual struggle has to be waged against them. Two interests of a different order, but claiming equal respect, confront each other and means must be found to reconcile them. That represents one of the great difficulties of management. Means of effecting it are—

1. Firmness and good example on the part of superiors.
2. Agreements as fair as is possible.
3. Constant supervision.

7. Remuneration of Personnel

Remuneration of personnel is the price of services rendered. It should be fair and, as far as is possible, afford satisfaction both to personnel and firm (employee and employer). The rate of remuneration depends, firstly, on circumstances independent of the employer's will and employee's worth, viz. cost of living, abundance or shortage of personnel, general business conditions, the economic position of the business, and after that it depends on the value of the employee and mode of payment adopted. Appreciation of the factors dependent on the employer's will and on the value of employees, demands a fairly good knowledge of business, judgement, and impartiality. Later on in connection with selecting personnel we shall deal with assessing the value of employees; here only the mode of payment is under consideration as a factor operation on remuneration. The method of payment can exercise considerable influence on business progress, so the choice of this method is an important problem. It is also a thorny problem which in practice has been solved in widely different ways, of which so far none has proved satisfactory. What is generally looked for in the method of payment is that—

1. It shall assure fair remuneration.
2. It shall encourage keenness by rewarding well-directed effort.
3. It shall not lead to overpayment going beyond reasonable limits.

I am going to examine briefly the modes of payment in use for workers, junior managers, and higher managers.

Workers

The various modes of payment in use for workers are—

1. Time rates.
2. Job rates.
3. Piece rates.

These three modes of payment may be combined and give rise to important variations by the introduction of bonuses, profit-sharing schemes, payment in kind, and nonfinancial incentives.

1. Time rates. Under this system the workman sells the employer, in return for a predetermined sum, a day's work under definite conditions. This system has the disadvantage of conducing to negligence and of demanding constant supervision. It is inevitable where the work done is not susceptible to measurement and in effect it is very common.

2. Job rates. Here payment made turns upon the execution of a definite job set in advance and may be independent of the length of the job. When payment is due only on condition that the job be completed during the normal work spell, this method merges into time rate. Payment by daily job does not require as close a supervision as payment by the day, but it has the drawback of levelling the output of good workers down to that of mediocre ones. The good ones are not satisfied, because they feel that they could earn more; the mediocre ones find the task set too heavy.

3. Piece rates. Here payment is related to work done and there is no limit. This system is often used in workshops where a large number of similar articles have to be made, and is found where the product can be measured by weight, length, or cubic capacity, and in general is used wherever possible. It is criticized on the grounds of emphasizing quantity at the expense of quality and of provoking disagreements when rates have to be revised in the light of manufacturing improvements. Piece-work becomes contract work when applied to an important unit of work. To reduce the contractor's risk, sometimes there is added to the contract price a payment for each day's work done.

Generally, piece rates give rise to increased earnings which act for some time as a stimulus, then finally a system prevails in which this mode of payment gradually approximates to time rates for a pre-arranged sum.

The above three modes of payment are found in all large concerns; sometimes time rates prevail, sometimes one of the other two. In a workshop the same workman may be seen working now on piece rates, not on time rates. Each one of these methods had its advantages and drawbacks, and their effectiveness depends on circumstances and the ability of superiors. Neither method nor rate of payment absolves management from competence and tact, and keenness of workers and peaceful atmosphere of the workshop depend largely upon it.

Bonuses

To arouse the worker's interest in the smooth running of the business, sometimes an increment in the nature of a bonus is added to the time-, job- or piece-rate: for good time keeping, hard work, freedom from machine breakdown, output, cleanliness, etc. The relative importance, nature and qualifying conditions of these bonuses are very varied. There are to be found the small daily supplement, the monthly sum, the annual award, shares or portions of shares distributed to the most meritorious, and also even profit-sharing schemes such as, for example, certain monetary allocations distributed annually among workers in some large firms. Several French collieries started some years back the granting of a bonus proportional to profits distributed or to extra profits. No contract is required from the workers save that the earning of the bonus is subject to certain conditions, for instance, that there shall have no strike during the year, or that absenteeism shall not have exceeded a given number of days. This type of bonus introduced an element of profit-sharing into miners' wages without any prior discussion as between workers and employer. The workman did not refuse a gift, largely gratuitous, on the part of the employer, that is, the contract was a unilateral one. Thanks to a successful trading period the yearly wages have been appreciably increased by the operation of the bonus. But what is to happen in lean times? This interesting procedure is as yet too new to be judged, but obviously it is no general solution of the problem. . . .

Profit-Sharing

1. Workers. The idea of making workers share in profits is a very attractive one and it would seem that it is from there that harmony as between Capital and Labour should come. But the practical formula for such sharing has not yet been found. Workers' profit-sharing has hitherto come up against insurmountable difficulties of application in the case of large concerns. Firstly, let us note that it cannot exist in enterprises having no monetary objective (State services, religion, philanthropic, scientific societies) and also that it is not possible in the case of businesses running at a loss. Thus profit-sharing is excluded from a great number of concerns. There remain the prosperous business concerns and of these latter the desire to reconcile and harmonize workers' and employers' interests is nowhere so great as in French mining and metallurgical industries. Now, in these industries I know of no clear application of workers' profit-sharing, whence it may be concluded forthwith that the matter is difficult, if not impossible. It is very difficult indeed. Whether a business is making a profit or not the worker must have an immediate wage assured him, and a system which would make workers' payment depend entirely on eventual future profit is unworkable. But perhaps a part of wages might come from business profits. Let us see. Viewing all contingent factors, the workers' greater or lesser share of activity or ability in the final outcome of a large concern is impossible to assess and is, moreover, quite insignificant. The portion accruing to him of distributed dividend would at the most be a few centimes on a wage of five francs for instance, that is to say the smallest extra effort, the stroke of a pick or of a file operating directly on his wage, would prove of greater advantage to him. Hence the worker has no interest in being rewarded by a share in profits proportionate to the effect he has upon profits. It is worthy of note that, in most large concerns, wages increases, operative now for some twenty years, represent a total sum greater than the amount of capital shared out. In effect, unmodified real profit-sharing by workers of large concerns has not yet entered the sphere of practical business politics.

2. Junior managers. Profit-sharing for foremen, superintendents, engineers, is scarcely more advanced than for workers. Nevertheless, the influence of these employees on the results of a business is quite considerable, and if they are not consistently interested in profits the only reason is that the basis for participation is difficult to establish. Doubtless managers have no need of monetary incentive to carry out their duties, but they are not indifferent to material satisfactions and it must be acknowledged that the hope of extra profit is capable of arousing their enthusiasm. So employees at middle levels should, where possible, be induced to have an interest in profits. It is relatively easy in

businesses which are starting out or on trial, where exceptional effort can yield outstanding results. Sharing may then be applied to overall business profits or merely to the running of the particular department of the employee in question. When the business is of long standing and well run the zeal of a junior manager is scarcely apparent in the general outcome, and it is very hard to establish a useful basis on which he may participate. In fact, profit-sharing among junior managers in France is very rare in large concerns. Production or workshop output bonuses —not to be confused with profit-sharing—are much more common.

3. Higher managers. It is necessary to go right up to top management to find a class of employee with frequent interest in the profits of large-scale French concerns. The head of the business, in view of his knowledge, ideas, and actions, exerts considerable influence on general results, so it is quite natural to try and provide him with an interest in them. Sometimes it is possible to establish a close connection between his personal activity and its effects. Nevertheless, generally speaking, there exist other influences quite independent of the personal capability of the manager which can influence results to a greater extent than can his personal activity. If the manager's salary were exclusively dependent upon profits, it might at times be reduced to nothing. There are besides, businesses being built up, wound up, or merely passing through temporary crisis, wherein management depends no less on talent than in the case of prosperous ones, and wherein profit-sharing cannot be a basis for remuneration for the manager. In fine, senior civil servants cannot be paid on a profit-sharing basis. Profit-sharing, then, for either higher managers or workers is not a general rule of remuneration. To sum up, then: profit-sharing is a mode of payment capable of giving excellent results in certain cases, but is not a general rule. It does not seem to me possible, at least for the present, to count on this mode of payment for appeasing conflict between Capital and Labour. Fortunately, there are other means which hitherto have been sufficient to maintain relative social quiet. Such methods have not lost their power and it is up to managers to study them, apply them, and make them work well.

Payment in Kind, Welfare Work, Non-Financial Incentives

Whether wages are made up of money only or whether they include various additions such as heating, light, housing, food, is of little consequence provided that the employee be satisfied.

From another point of view, there is no doubt that a business will be better served in proportion as its employees are more energetic, better educated, more conscientious and more permanent. The employer should have regard, if merely in the interests of the business, for the health, strength, education, morale, and stability of his personnel. These elements of smooth running are not acquired in the workshop alone, they are formed and developed as well, and particularly, outside it, in the home and school, in civil and religious life. Therefore, the employer comes to be concerned with his employees outside the works and here the question of proportion comes up again. Opinion is greatly divided on this point. Certain unfortunate experiments have resulted in some employers stopping short their interest, at the works gate and at the regulation of wages. The majority consider that the employer's activity may be used to good purpose outside the factory confines provided that there be discretion and prudence, that it be sought after rather than imposed, be in keeping with the general level of education and taste of those concerned and that it have absolute respect for their liberty. It must be benevolent collaboration, not tyrannical stewardship, and therein lies an indispensable condition of success. . . .

8. Centralization

Like division of work, centralization belongs to the natural order; this turns on the fact that in every organism, animal or social, sensations converge towards the brain or directive part, and from the brain or directive part orders are sent out which set all parts of the organism in movement. Centralization is not a system of management good or bad of itself, capable of being adopted or discarded at the whim of managers or of circumstances; it is always present to a greater or less extent. The question of centralization or decentralization, is a simple question of proportion, it is a matter of finding the optimum degree for the particular concern. In small firms, where the manager's orders go directly to subordinates there is absolute centralization; in large concerns, where a long scalar chain is interposed between manager and lower grades, orders and counter-information too, have to go through a series of intermediaries. Each employee, intentionally or unintentionally, puts something of himself into the transmission and execution of orders and of information received too. He does not operate merely as a cog in a machine. What appropriate share of initiative may be left to intermediaries depends on the personal character of the manager, on his moral worth, on the reliability of his subordinates, and also on the condition of the business. The degree of centralization must vary according to different cases. The objective to pursue is the optimum utilization of all faculties of the personnel.

If the moral worth of the manager, his strength, intelligence, experience, and swiftness of thought allow him to have a wide span of activities he will be able to carry centralization quite far and reduce his seconds in command to mere executive agents. If, conversely, he prefers to have greater recourse to the experience, opinions, and counsel of his colleagues whilst reserving to himself the privilege of giving general directives, he can effect considerable decentralization.

Seeing that both absolute and relative value of manager and employees are constantly changing, it is understandable that the degree of centralization or decentralization may itself vary constantly. It is a problem to be solved according to circumstances, to the best satisfaction of the interests involved. It arises, not only in the case of higher authority, but for superiors at all levels and not one but can extend or confine, to some extent, his subordinates' initiative.

The finding of the measure which shall give the best overall yield: that is the problem of centralization or decentralization. Everything which goes to increase the importance of the subordinate's rôle is decentralization, everything which goes to reduce it is centralization.

9. Scalar Chain

The scalar chain is the chain of superiors ranging from the ultimate authority to the lowest ranks. The line of authority is the route followed —via every link in the chain—by all communications which start from or go to the ultimate authority. This path is dictated both by the need for some transmission and by the principle of unity of command, but it is not always the swiftest. It is even at times disastrously lengthy in large concerns, notably in governmental ones. Now, there are many activities whose success turns on speedy execution, hence respect for the line of authority must be reconciled with the need for swift action.

Let us imagine that section F has to be put into contact with section P in a business whose scalar chain is represented by the double ladder G–A–Q thus—

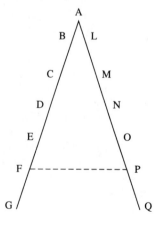

By following the line of authority the ladder must be climbed from F to A and then descended from A to P, stopping at each rung, then ascended again from P to A, and descended once more from A to F, in order to get back to the starting point. Evidently it is much simpler and quicker to go directly from F to P by making use of FP as a "gang plank" and that is what is most often done. The scalar principle will be safeguarded if managers E and O have authorized their respective subordinates F and P to treat directly, and the position will be fully regularized if F and P inform their respective superiors forthwith of what they have agreed upon. So long as F and P remain in agreement, and so long as their actions are approved by their immediate superiors, direct contact may be maintained, but from the instant that agreement ceases or there is no approval from the superiors direct contact comes to an end, and the scalar chain is straightway resumed. Such is the actual procedure to be observed in the great majority of businesses. It provides for the usual exercise of some measure of initiative at all levels of authority. In the small concern, the general interest, viz. that of the concern proper, is easy to grasp, and the employer is present to recall this interest to those tempted to lose sight of it. In government enterprise the general interest is such a complex, vast, remote thing, that it is not easy to get a clear idea of it, and for the majority of civil servants the employer is somewhat mythical and unless the sentiment of general interest be constantly revived by higher authority, it becomes blurred and weakened and each section tends to regard itself as its own aim and end and forgets that it is only a cog in a big machine, all of whose parts must work in concert. It becomes isolated, cloistered, aware only of the line of authority.

The use of the "gang plank" is simple, swift, sure. It allows the two employees F and P to deal at one sitting, and in a few hours, with some question or other which via the scalar chain would pass through twenty transmissions, inconvenience many people, involve masses of paper, lose weeks or months to get to a conclusion less satisfactory generally than the one which could have been obtained via direct contact as between *F* and *P*.

Is it possible that such practices, as ridiculous as they are devastating, could be in current use? Unfortunately there can be little doubt of it in government department affairs. It is usually acknowledged that the chief cause is fear of responsibility. I am rather of the opinion that it is insufficient executive capacity on the part of those in charge. If supreme authority *A* insisted that his assistants *B* and *L* made use of the "gang plank" themselves and made its use incumbent upon their subordinates *C* and *M*, the habit and courage of taking responsibility would be established and at the same time the custom of using the shortest path.

It is an error to depart needlessly from the line of authority, but it is an even greater one to keep to it when detriment to the business ensues. The latter may attain extreme gravity in certain conditions. When an employee is obliged to choose between the two practices, and it is impossible for him to take advice from his superior, he should be courageous enough and feel free enough to adopt the line dictated by the general interest. But for him to be in this frame of mind there must have been previous precedent, and his superiors must have set him the example—for example must always come from above.

10. Order

The formula is known in the case of material things "A place for everything and everything in its place." The formula is the same for human order. "A place for everyone and everyone in his place."

Material Order

In accordance with the preceding definition, so that material order shall prevail, there must be a place appointed for each thing and each thing must be in its appointed place. Is that enough? Is it not also necessary that the place shall have been well chosen? The object of

order must be avoidance of loss of material, and for this object to be completely realized not only must things be in their place suitably arranged but also the place must have been chosen so as to facilitate all activities as much as possible. If this last condition be unfulfilled, there is merely the appearance of order. Appearance of order may cover over real disorder. I have seen a works yard used as a store for steel ingots in which the material was well stacked, evenly arranged and clean and which gave a pleasing impression of orderliness. On close inspection it could be noted that the same heap included five or six types of steel intended for different manufacture all mixed up together. Whence useless handling, lost time, risk of mistakes because each thing was not in its place. It happens, on the other hand, that the appearance of disorder may actually be true order. Such is the case with papers scattered about at a master's whim which a well-meaning but incompetent servant re-arranges and sticks in neat piles. The master can no longer find his way about them. Perfect order presupposes a judiciously chosen place and the appearance of order is merely a false or imperfect image of real order. Cleanliness is a corollary of orderliness, there is no appointed place for dirt. A diagram representing the entire premises divided up into as many sections as there are employees responsible facilitates considerably the establishing and control of order.

Social Order

For social order to prevail in a concern there must, in accordance with the definition, be an appointed place for every employee and every employee be in his appointed place. Perfect order requires, further, that the place be suitable for the employee and the employee for the place—in English idiom, "The right man in the right place."

Thus understood, social order presupposes the successful execution of the two most difficult managerial activities: good organization and good selection. Once the posts essential to the smooth running of the business have been decided upon and those to fill such posts have been selected, each employee occupies that post wherein he can render most service. Such is perfect social order "A place for each one and each one in his place." That appears simple, and naturally we are so anxious for it to be so that when we hear for the twentieth time a government departmental head assert this principle, we conjure up straightway a concept of perfect administration. This is a mirage.

Social order demands precise knowledge of the human requirements and resources of the concern and a constant balance between these requirements and resources. Now this balance is most difficult to establish and maintain and all the more difficult the bigger the business, and when it has been upset and individual interests resulted in neglect or sacrifice of the general interest, when ambition, nepotism, favouritism, or merely ignorance, has multiplied positions without good reason or filled them with incompetent employees, much talent and strength of will and more persistence than current instability of ministerial appointments presupposes, are required in order to sweep away abuses and restore order. . . .

11. Equity

Why equity and not justice? Justice is putting into execution established conventions, but conventions cannot foresee everything, they need to be interpreted or their inadequacy supplemented. For the personnel to be encouraged to carry out its duties with all the devotion and loyalty of which it is capable it must be treated with kindliness, and equity results from the combination of kindliness and justice. Equity excludes neither forcefulness nor sternness and the application of it requires much good sense, experience, and good nature.

Desire for equity and equality of treatment are aspirations to be taken into account in dealing with employees. In order to satisfy these requirements as much as possible without neglecting any principle or losing sight of the general interest, the head of the business must frequently summon up his highest faculties. He should strive to instil a sense of equity throughout all levels of the scalar chain.

12. Stability of Tenure of Personnel

Time is required for an employee to get used to new work and succeed in doing it well, always assuming that he possesses the requisite abilities. If when he has got used to it, or before then, he is removed, he will not have had time to render worthwhile service. If this be repeated indefinitely the work will never be properly done. The undesirable consequences of such insecurity of tenure are especially to be feared in large concerns, where the settling in of managers is generally a lengthy matter. Much time is needed indeed to get to know men and things in a large concern in order to be in a position to decide on a plan of action, to gain confidence in oneself, and inspire it in others. Hence it has often been recorded that a mediocre manager who stays is infinitely preferable to outstanding managers who merely come and go.

Generally the managerial personnel of prosperous concerns is stable, that of unsuccessful ones is unstable. Instability of tenure is at one and the same time cause and effect of bad running. The apprenticeship of a higher manager is generally a costly matter. Nevertheless, changes of personnel are inevitable; age, illness, retirement, death, disturb the human make-up of the firm, certain employees are no longer capable of carrying out their duties, whilst others become fit to assume greater responsibilities. In common with all the other principles, therefore, stability of tenure and personnel is also a question of proportion.

13. Initiative

Thinking out a plan and ensuring its success is one of the keenest satisfactions for an intelligent man to experience. It is also one of the most powerful stimulants of human endeavour. This power of thinking out and executing is what is called initiative, and freedom to propose and to execute belongs too, each in its way, to initiative. At all levels of the organizational ladder zeal and energy on the part of employees are augmented by initiative. The initiative of all, added to that of the manager, and supplementing it if need be, represents a great source of strength for businesses. This is particularly apparent at difficult times; hence it is essential to encourage and develop this capacity to the full.

Much tact and some integrity are required to inspire and maintain everyone's initiative, within the limits imposed, by respect for authority and for discipline. The manager must be able to sacrifice some personal vanity in order to grant this sort of satisfaction to subordinates. Other things being equal, moreover, a manager able to permit the exercise of initiative on the part of subordinates is infinitely superior to one who cannot do so.

14. Esprit de Corps

"Union is strength." Business heads would do well to ponder on this proverb. Harmony, union among the personnel of a concern, is great strength in that concern. Effort, then, should be made to establish it. Among the countless methods in use I will single out specially one principle to be observed and two pitfalls to be avoided. The principle to be observed is unity of command; the dangers to be avoided are (a) a misguided interpretation of the motto "divide and rule," (b) the abuse of written communications.

(a) Personnel must not be split up. Dividing enemy forces to weaken them is clever, but dividing one's own team is a grave sin against the business. Whether this error results from inadequate managerial capacity or imperfect grasp of things, or from egoism which sacrifices general interest to personal interest, it is always reprehensible because harmful to the business.

There is no merit in sowing dissension among subordinates; any beginner can do it. On the contrary, real talent is needed to co-ordinate effort, encourage keenness, use each man's abilities, and reward each one's merit without arousing possible jealousies and disturbing harmonious relations.

(b) Abuse of written communications. In dealing with a business matter or giving an order which requires explanation to complete it, usually it is simpler and quicker to do so verbally than in writing. Besides, it is well known that differences and misunderstandings which a conversation could clear up, grow more bitter in writing. Thence it follows that, wherever possible, contacts should be verbal; there is a gain in speed, clarity and harmony. Nevertheless, it happens in some firms that employees of neighbouring departments with numerous points of contact, or even employees within a department, who could quite easily meet, only communicate with each other in writing. Hence arise increased work and complications and delays harmful to the business. At the same time, there is to be observed a certain animosity prevailing between different departments or different employees within a department. The system of written communications usually brings this result. There is a way of putting an end to this deplorable system and that is to forbid all communications in writing which could easily and advantageously be replaced by verbal ones. There again, we come up against a question of proportion. . . .

There I bring to an end this review of principles, not because the list is exhausted—this list has no precise limits—but because to me it seems at the moment especially useful to endow management theory with a dozen or so well-established principles, on which it is appropriate to concentrate general discussion. The foregoing principles are those to which I have most often had recourse. I have simply expressed my personal opinion in connection with them. Are they to have a place in the management code which is to be built up? General discussion will show.

This code is indispensable. Be it a case of commerce, industry, politics, religion, war, or philanthropy, in every concern there is a management function to be performed, and for its performance there must be principles, that is to say acknowledged truths regarded as proven on which to rely. And it is the code which represents the sum total of these truths at any given moment.

Surprise might be expressed at the outset that the eternal moral principles, the laws of the Decalogue and Commandments of the Church are not sufficient guide for the manager, and that a special code is needed. The explanation is this: the higher laws of religious or moral order envisage the individual only, or else interests which are not of this world, whereas management principles aim at the success of associations of individuals and at the satisfying of economic interests. Given that the aim is different, it is not surprising that the means are not the same. There is no identity, so there is no contradiction. Without principles one is in darkness and chaos; interest, experience, and proportion are still very handicapped, even with the best principles. The principle is the lighthouse fixing the bearings, but it can only serve those who already know the way into port.

Note

1. *"Body corporate."* Fayol's term "corps social," meaning all those engaged in a given corporate activity in any sphere, is best rendered by this somewhat unusual term because (*a*) it retains his implied biological metaphor; (*b*) it represents the structure as distinct from the process of organization. The term will be retained in all contexts where these two requirements have to be met. (Translator's note.)

7

The Principles of Scientific Management

Frederick Winslow Taylor

By far the most important fact which faces the industries of our country, the industries, in fact, of the civilized world, is that not only the average worker, but nineteen out of twenty workmen throughout the civilized world firmly believe that it is for their best interests to go slow instead of to go fast. They firmly believe that it is for their interest to give as little work in return for the money that they get as is practical. The reasons for this belief are twofold, and I do not believe that the workingmen are to blame for holding these fallacious views.

If you will take any set of workmen in your own town and suggest to those men that it would be a good thing for them in their trade if they were to double their output in the coming year, each man turn out twice as much work and become twice as efficient, they would say, "I don't know anything about other people's trades; what you are saying about increasing efficiency being a good thing may be good for other trades, but I know that the only result if you come to our trade would be that half of us would be out of a job before the year was out." That to the average workingman is an axiom; it is not a matter subject to debate at all. And

SOURCE: Bulletin of the Taylor Society (December 1916). An abstract of an address given by the late Dr. Taylor before the Cleveland Advertising Club, March 3, 1915, two weeks prior to his death. It was repeated the following day at Youngstown, Ohio, and this presentation was Dr. Taylor's last public appearance.

even among the average business men of this country that opinion is almost universal. They firmly believe that that would be the result of a great increase in efficiency, and yet directly the opposite is true.

The Effect of Labor-Saving Devices

Whenever any labor-saving device of any kind has been introduced into any trade—go back into the history of any trade and see it—even though that labor-saving device may turn out ten, twenty, thirty times that output that was originally turned out by men in that trade, the result has universally been to make work for more men in that trade, not work for less men.

Let me give you one illustration. Let us take one of the staple businesses, the cotton industry. About 1840 the power loom succeeded the old hand loom in the cotton industry. It was invented many years before, somewhere about 1780 or 1790, but it came in very slowly. About 1840 the weavers of Manchester, England, saw that the power loom was coming, and they knew it would turn out three times the yardage of cloth in a day that the hand loom turned out. And what did they do, these five thousand weavers of Manchester, England, who saw starvation staring them in the face? They broke into the establishments into which those machines were being introduced, they smashed them, they did everything possible to stop the introduction of the power loom. And the same result followed that follows every attempt to interfere with the introduction of any labor-saving device, if it is really a labor-saving device. Instead of stopping the introduction of the power loom, their opposition apparently accelerated it, just as opposition to scientific management all over the country, bitter labor opposition today, is accelerating the introduction of it instead of retarding it. History repeats itself in that repect. The power loom came right straight along.

And let us see the result in Manchester. Just what follows in every industry when any labor-saving device is introduced. Less than a century has gone by since 1840. The population of England in that time has not more than doubled. Each man in the cotton industry in Manchester, England, now turns out, at a restricted estimate ten yards of cloth for every yard of cloth that was turned out in 1840. In 1840 there were 5,000 weavers in Manchester. Now there are 265,000. Has that thrown men out of work? Has the introduction of labor-saving machinery, which has multiplied the output per man by tenfold, thrown men out of work?

What is the real meaning of this? All that you have to do is to bring wealth into this world and the world uses it. That is the real meaning. The meaning is that where in 1840 cotton goods were a luxury to be worn only by rich people when they were hardly ever seen on the street, now every man, woman, and child all over the world wears cotton goods as a daily necessity.

Nineteen-twentieths of the real wealth of this world is used by the poor people, and not the rich, so that the workingman who sets out as a steady principle to restrict output is merely robbing his own kind. That group of manufacturers which adopts as a permanent principle restriction of output, in order to hold up prices, is robbing the world. The one great thing that marks the improvement of this world is measured by the enormous increase in output of the individuals in this world. There is fully twenty times the output per man now that there was three hundred years ago. That marks the increase in the real wealth of the world; that marks the increase of the happiness of the world, that gives us the opportunity for shorter hours, for better education, for amusement, for art, for music, for everything that is worthwhile in this world—goes right straight back to this increase in the output of the individual. The workingmen of today live better than the king did three hundred years ago. From what does the progress the world has made come? Simply from the increase in the output of the individual all over the world.

The Development of Soldiering

The second reason why the workmen of this country and of Europe deliberately restrict output is a very simple one. They, for this reason, are even less to blame than they are for the other. If, for example, you are manufacturing a pen, let us assume for simplicity that a pen can be made by a single man. Let us say that the workman is turning out ten pens per day, and that he is receiving $2.50 a day for his wages. He has a progressive foreman who is up to date, and that foreman goes to the workman and suggests, "Here, John, you are getting $2.50 a day, and you are turning out ten pens. I would suggest that I pay you 25 cents for making that pen." The man takes the job, and through the help of his foreman, through his own ingenuity, through his increased work, through his interest in his business, through the help of his friends, at the end of the year he finds himself turning out twenty pens instead of ten. He is happy, he is making $5, instead of $2.50 a day. His foreman is happy because, with the same room, with the same men he had before, he has doubled the output of his department, and the manufacturer himself is sometimes happy, but not often. Then someone on the board of directors asks to see the payroll, and he finds that we are paying $5 a day where other similar mechanics are only getting $2.50, and in no uncertain terms he announces that we must stop ruining the labor market. We cannot pay $5 a day when the standard rate of wages is $2.50; how can we hope to compete with surrounding towns? What is the result? Mr. Foreman is sent for, and he is told that he has got to stop ruining the labor market of Cleveland. And the foreman goes back to his workman in sadness, in depression, and tells his workman, "I am sorry, John, but I have got to cut the price down for that pen; I cannot let you earn $5 a day; the board of directors has got on to it, and it is ruining the labor market; you ought to be willing to have the price reduced. You cannot earn more than $3 or $2.75 a day, and I will have to cut your wages so that you will only get $3 a day." John, of necessity accepts the cut, but he sees to it that he never makes enough pens to get another cut.

Characteristics of the Union Workman

There seem to be two divergent opinions about the workmen of this country. One is that a lot of the trade unions' workmen, particularly in this country, have become brutal, have become dominating, careless of any interests but their own, and are a pretty poor lot. And the other opinion which those same trade unionists hold of themselves is that they are pretty close to little gods. Whichever view you may hold of the workingmen of this country, and my personal view of them is that they are a pretty fine lot of fellows, they are just about the same as you and I. But whether you hold the bad opinion or the good opinion, it makes no difference. Whatever the workingmen of this country are or whatever they are not, they are not fools. And all that is necessary is for a workingman to have but one object lesson, like that I have told you, and he soldiers for the rest of his life.

There are a few exceptional employers who treat their workmen differently, but I am talking about the rule of the country. Soldiering is the absolute rule with all workmen who know their business. I am not saying it is for their interest to soldier. You cannot blame them for it. You cannot expect them to be large enough minded men to look at the proper view of the matter. Nor is the man who cuts the wages necessarily to blame. It is simply a misfortune in industry.

The Development of Scientific Management

There has been, until comparatively recently, no scheme promulgated by which the evils of rate cutting could be properly avoided, so soldiering has been the rule.

Now the first step that was taken toward the development of those methods, of those principles, which rightly or wrongly have come to be known under the name of scientific management —the first step that was taken in an earnest endeavor to remedy the evils of soldiering; an earnest endeavor to make it unnecessary for workmen to be hypocritical in this way, to deceive themselves, to deceive their employers, to live day in and day out a life of deceit, forced upon them conditions—the very first step that was taken toward the development was to overcome that evil. I want to emphasize that, because I wish to emphasize the one great fact relating to scientific management, the greatest factor: namely, that scientific management is no new set of theories that has been tried on by any one at every step. Scientific management at every step has been an evolution, not a theory. In all cases the practice has preceded the theory, not succeeded it. In every case one measure after another has been tried out, until the proper remedy has been found. That series of proper eliminations, that evolution, is what is called scientific management. Every element of it has had to fight its way against the elements that preceded it, and prove itself better or it would not be there tomorrow.

All the men that I know of who are in any way connected with scientific management are ready to abandon any scheme, and theory in favor of anything else that could be found that is better. There is nothing in scientific management that is fixed. There is no one man, or group of men, who have invented scientific management.

What I want to emphasize is that all of the elements of scientific management are an evolution, not an invention. Scientific management is in use in an immense range and variety of industries. Almost every type of industry in this country has scientific management working successfully. I think I can safely say that on the average in those establishments in which scientific management has been introduced, the average workman is turning out double the output he was before. I think that is a conservative statement.

The Workmen the Chief Beneficiaries

Three or four years ago I could have said there were about fifty thousand men working under scientific management, but now I know there are many more. Company after company is coming under it, many of which I know nothing about. Almost universally they are working successfully. This increasing of the output per individual in the trade, results, of course, in cheapening the product; it results, therefore, in larger profit usually to the owners of the business; it results also, in many cases, in a lowering of the selling price, although that has not come to the extent it will later. In the end the public gets the good. Without any question, the large good which so far has come from scientific management has come to the worker. To the workmen has come, practically right off as soon as scientific management is introduced, an increase in wages amounting from 33 to 100 percent, and yet that is not the greatest good that comes to the workmen from scientific management. The great good comes from the fact that, under scientific management, they look upon their employers as the best friends they have in the world; the suspicious watchfulness which characterizes the old type management, the semi-antagonism, or the complete antagonism between workmen and employers is entirely superseded, and in its place comes genuine friendship between both sides. That is the greatest good that has come under scientific management. As a proof of this in the many businesses in which scientific management has been introduced, I know of not one single strike of workmen working under it after it had been introduced, and only two or three while it was in process of introduction. In this connection I must speak of the fakers, those who have said they can introduce scientific management into a business in six months or a year. That is pure nonsense. There have been many strikes stirred up by that type of man. Not one strike has ever come, and I do not believe ever will come, under scientific management.

What Scientific Management Is

What is scientific management? It is no efficiency device, nor is it any group of efficiency devices. Scientific management is no new scheme for paying men, it is no bonus system, no piecework system, no premium system of payment; it is no new method of figuring costs. It is no one of the various elements by which it is commonly known, by which people refer to it. It is not time study nor man study. It is not the printing of a ton or two of blanks and unloading them on a company and saying, "There is your system, go ahead and use it." Scientific management does not exist and cannot exist until there has been a complete mental revolution on the part of the workmen working under it, as to their duties toward themselves and toward their employers, and a complete mental revolution in the outlook for the employers, toward their duties, toward themselves, and toward their workmen. And until this great mental change takes place, scientific management does not exist. Do you think you can make a great mental revolution in a large group of workmen in a year, or do you think you can make it in a large group of foremen and superintendents in a year? If you do, you are very much mistaken. All of us hold mighty close to our ideas and principles in life, and we change very slowly toward the new, and very properly too.

Let me give you an idea of what I mean by this change in mental outlook. If you are manufacturing a hammer or a mallet, into the cost of that mallet goes a certain amount of raw materials, a certain amount of wood and metal. If you will take the cost of the raw materials and then add to it that cost which is frequently called by various names—overhead expenses, general expense, indirect expense; that is, the proper share of taxes, insurance, light, heat, salaries of officers and advertising—and you have a sum of money. Subtract that sum from the selling price, and what is left over is called the surplus. It is over this surplus that all of the labor disputes in the past have occurred. The workman naturally wants all he can get. His wages come out of that surplus. The manufacturer wants all he can get in the shape of profits, and it is from the division of this surplus that all the labor disputes have come in the past—the equitable division.

The new outlook that comes under scientific management is this: The workmen, after many object lessons, come to see and the management come to see that this surplus can be made so great, providing both sides will stop their pulling apart, will stop their fighting and will push as hard as they can to get as cheap an output as possible, that there is no occasion to quarrel. Each side can get more than ever before. The acknowledgement of this fact represents a complete mental revolution. . . .

What Scientific Management Will Do

I am going to try to prove to you that the old style of management has not a ghost of a chance in competition with the principles of scientific management. Why? In the first place, under scientific management, the initiative of the workmen, their hard work, their goodwill, their best endeavors are obtained with absolute regularity. There are cases all the time where men will soldier, but they become the exception, as a rule, and they give their true initiative under scientific management. That is the least of the two sources of gain. The greatest source of gain under scientific management comes from the new and almost unheard-of duties and burdens which are voluntarily assumed, not by the workmen, but by the men on the management side. These are the things which make scientific management a success. These new

duties, these new burdens undertaken by the management have rightly or wrongly been divided into four groups, and have been called the principles of scientific management.

The first of the great principles of scientific management, the first of the new burdens which are voluntarily undertaken by those on the management side is the deliberate gathering together of the great mass of traditional knowledge which, in the past, has been in the heads of the workmen, recording it, tabulating it, reducing it in most cases to rules, laws, and in many cases to mathematical formulae, which, with these new laws, are applied to the cooperation of the management to the work of the workmen. This results in an immense increase in the output, we may say, of the two. The gathering in of this great mass of traditional knowledge, which is done by the means of motion study, time study, can be truly called the science.

Let me make a prediction. I have before me the first book, so far as I know, that has been published on motion study and on time study. That is, the motion study and time study of the cement and concrete trades. It contains everything relating to concrete work. It is of about seven hundred pages and embodies the motions of men, the time and the best way of doing that sort of work. It is the first case in which a trade has been reduced to the same condition that engineering data of all kinds have been reduced, and it is this sort of data that is bound to sweep the world.

I have before me something which has been gathering for about fourteen years, the time or motion study of the machine shop. It will take probably four or five years more before the first book will be ready to publish on that subject. There is a collection of sixty or seventy thousand elements affecting machine-shop work. After a few years, say three, four or five years more, someone will be ready to publish the first book giving the laws of the movements of men in the machine shop—all the laws, not only a few of them. Let me predict, just as sure as the sun shines, that is going to come in every trade. Why? Because it pays, for no other reason. That results in doubling the output in any shop. Any device which results in an increased output is bound to come in spite of all opposition, whether we want it or not. It comes automatically.

The Selection of the Workman

The next of the four principles of scientific management is the scientific selection of the workman, and then his progressive development. It becomes the duty under scientific management of not one, but of a group of men on the management side, to deliberately study the workmen who are under them; study them in the most careful, thorough and painstaking way; and not just leave it to the poor, over-worked foreman to go out and say, "Come on, what do you want? If you are cheap enough I will give you a trial."

That is the old way. The new way is to take a great deal of trouble in selecting the workmen. The selection proceeds year after year. And it becomes the duty of those engaged in scientific management to know something about the workmen under them. It becomes their duty to set out deliberately to train the workmen in their employ to be able to do a better and still better class of work than ever before, and to then pay them higher wages than ever before. This deliberate selection of the workmen is the second of the great duties that devolve on the management under scientific management.

Bringing Together the Science and the Man

The third principle is the bringing together of this science of which I have spoken and the trained workmen. I say bringing because they don't come together unless someone brings them. Select and train your workmen all you may, but unless there is someone who will make the men and the science come together, they will stay apart. The "make" involves a great many elements. They are not all disagree-able elements. The most important and largest way of "making" is to do something nice for the man whom you wish to make come together with the science. Offer him a plum, something that is worthwhile. There are many plums offered to those who come under scientific management—better treatment, more kindly treatment, more consideration for their wishes, and an opportunity for them to express their wants freely. That is one side of the "make." An equally important side is, whenever a man will not do what he ought, to either make him do it or stop it. If he will not do it, let him get out. I am not talking of any mollycoddle. Let me disabuse your minds of any opinion that scientific management is a mollycoddle scheme. . . .

The Principle of the Divison of Work

The fourth principle is the plainest of all. It involves a complete re-division of the work of the establishment. Under the old scheme of management, almost all of the work was done by the workmen. Under the new, the work of the establishment is divided into two large parts. All of that work which formerly was done by the workmen alone is divided into two large sections, and one of those sections is handed over to the management. They do a whole division of the work formerly done by the workmen. It is this real cooperation, this genuine division of the work between the two sides, more than any other element which accounts for the fact that there never will be strikes under scientific management. When the workman realizes that there is hardly a thing he does that does not have to be preceded by some act of preparation on the part of management, and when that work-man realizes when the management falls down and does not do its part, that he is not only entitled to a kick, but that he can register that kick in the most forcible possible way, he cannot quarrel with the men over him. It is teamwork. There are more complaints made every day on the part of the workmen that the men on the management side fail to do their duties than are made by the management that the men fail. Every one of the complaints of the men have to be heeded, just as much as the complaints from the management that the workmen do not do their share. That is characteristic of scientific management. It represents a democracy, co-operation, a genuine division of work which never existed before in this world.

The Proof of the Theory

I am through now with the theory. I will try to convince you of the value of these four principles by giving you some practical illustrations. I hope that you will look for these four elements in the illustrations. I shall begin by trying to show the power of these four elements when applied to the greatest kind of work I know of that is done by man. The reason I have heretofore chosen pig-iron for an illustration is that it is the lowest form of work that is known.

A pig of iron weighs about ninety-two pounds on an average. A man stoops down and, with no other implement than his hands, picks up a pig of iron, walks a few yards with it, and drops it on a pile. A large part of the community has the impression that scientific management is chiefly handling pig-iron. The reason I first chose pig-iron for an illustration is that, if you can prove to any one the strength, the effect, of those four principles when applied to such rudimentary work as handling pig-iron, the presumption is that it can be applied to something better. The only way to prove it is to start at the bottom and show those four principles all along the line. I am sorry I cannot, because of the lack of time, give you the illustration of handling pig-iron. Many of you doubt whether there is much of any science in it. I am going to try to prove later with a high class mechanic that the workman who is fit to work at any type of work is almost universally incapable of understanding the principles without the help of some one else. I will use shoveling because

it is a shorter illustration, and I will try to show what I mean by the science of shoveling, and the power which comes to the man who knows the science of shoveling. It is a high art compared with pig-iron handling.

The Science of Shoveling

When I went to the Bethlehem Steel Works, the first thing I saw was a gang of men unloading rice coal. They were a splendid set of fellows, and they shoveled fast. There was no loafing at all. They shoveled as hard as you could ask any man to work. I looked with the greatest of interest for a long time, and finally they moved off rapidly down into the yard to another part of the yard and went right at handling iron ore. One of the main facts connected with that shoveling was that the work those men were doing was that, in handling the rice coal, they had on their shovels a load of 3¾ pounds, and when the same men went to handling ore with the same shovel, they had over 38 pounds on their shovels. Is it asking too much of anyone to inquire whether 3¾ pounds is the right load for a shovel, or whether 38 pounds is the right load for a shovel? Surely if one is right the other must be wrong. I think that is a self-evident fact, and yet I am willing to bet that that is what workmen are doing right now in Cleveland.

That is the old way. Suppose we notice that fact. Most of us do not notice it because it is left to the foreman. At the Midvale works, we had to find out these facts. What is the old way of finding them out? The old way was to sit down and write one's friends and ask them the questions. They got answers from contractors about what they thought it ought to be, and then they averaged them up, or took the most reliable man, and said, "That is all right; now we have a shovel load of so much." The more common way is to say, "I want a good shovel foreman." They will send for the foreman of the shovelers and put the job up to him to find what is the proper load to put on a shovel. He will tell you right off the bat. I want to show you the difference under scientific management.

Under scientific management you ask no one. Every little trifle,—there is nothing too small,—becomes the subject of experiment. The experiments develop into a law; they save money; they increase the output of the individual and make the thing worthwhile. How is this done? What we did in shoveling experiments was to deliberately select two first class shovelers, the best we knew how to get. We brought them into the office and said, "Jim and Mike, you two fellows are both good shovelers. I have a proposition to make to you. I am going to pay you double wages if you fellows will go out and do what I want you to do. There will be a young chap go along with you with a pencil and a piece of paper, and he will tell you to do a lot of fool things, and you will do them, and he will write down a lot of fool things, and you will think it is a joke, but it is nothing of the kind. Let me tell you one thing: if you fellows think that you can fool that chap you are very much mistaken, you cannot fool him at all. Don't get it through your heads you can fool him. If you take this double wages, you will be straight and do what you are told." They both promised and did exactly what they were told. What we told them was this: "We want you to start in and do whatever shoveling you are told to do and work at just the pace, all day long, that when it comes night you are going to be good and tired, but not tired out. I do not want you exhausted or anything like that, but properly tired. You know what a good day's work is. In other words, I do not want any loafing business or any overwork business. If you find yourself overworked and getting too tired, slow down." Those men did that and did it in the most splendid kind of way day in and day out. We proved their cooperation because they were in different parts of the yard, and they both got near enough the same results. Our results were duplicated.

I have found that there are a lot of schemes among my working friends, but no more among them than among us. They are good, straight fellows if you only treat them right, and put the matter up squarely to them. We started in at a pile of material, with a very large shovel. We kept innumerable accurate records of all kinds, some of them useless. Thirty or forty different items were carefullly observed about the work of those two men. We counted the number of shovelfuls thrown in a day. We found with a weight of between thirty-eight and thirty-nine pounds on the shovel, the man made a pile of material of a certain height. We then cut off the shovel, and he shoveled again and with a thirty-four pound load his pile went up and he shoveled more in a day. We again cut off the shovel to thirty pounds, and the pile went up again. With twenty-six pounds on the shovel, the pile again went up, and at twenty-one and one-half pounds the men could do their best. At twenty pounds the pile went down, at eighteen it went down, at fourteen it went down, so that they were at the peak of twenty-one and one-half pounds. There is a scientific fact. A first class shoveler ought to take twenty-one and one-half pounds on his shovel in order to work to the best possible advantage. You are not giving that man a chance unless you give him a shovel which will hold twenty-one pounds.

The men in the yard were run by the old fashioned foreman. He simply walked about with them. We at once took their shovels away from them. We built a large labor tool room which held ten to fifteen different kinds of shoveling implements so that for each kind of material that was handled in that yard, all the way from rice coals, ashes, coke, all the way up to ore, we would have a shovel that would just hold twenty-one pounds, or average twenty-one. One time it would hold eighteen, the next twenty-four, but it will average twenty-one.

When you have six hundred men laboring in the yard, as we had there, it becomes a matter of quite considerable difficulty to get, each day, for each one of those six hundred men, engaged in a line one and one-half to two miles long and a half mile wide, just the right shovel for shoveling material. That requires organization to lay out and plan for those men in advance. We had to lay out the work each day. We had to have large maps on which the movements of the men were plotted out a day in advance. When each workman came in the morning, he took out two pieces of paper. One of the blanks gave them a statement of the implements which they had to use, and the part of the yard in which they had to work. That required organization planning in advance.

One of the first principles we adopted was that no man in that labor gang could work on the new way unless he earned sixty percent higher wages than under the old plan. It is only just to the workman that he shall know right off whether he is doing his work right or not. He must not be told a week or month after, that he fell down. He must know it the next morning. So the next slip that came out of the pigeon hole was either a white or yellow slip. We used the two colors because some of the men could not read. The yellow slip meant that he had not earned his sixty per cent higher wages. He knew that he could not stay in that gang and keep on getting yellow slips.

Teaching the Men

I want to show you again the totally different outlook there is under scientific management by illustrating what happened when that man got his yellow slips. Under the old scheme, the foreman could say to him, "You are no good, get out of this; no time for you, you cannot earn sixty percent higher wages; get out of this! Go!" It was not done politely, but the foreman had no time to palaver. Under the new scheme what happened? A teacher of shoveling went down to see that man. A teacher of shoveling is a man who is handy with a shovel, who has made his mark in life with a shovel, and yet who is a kindly fellow and knows how to show the other fellow what he ought to do. When that teacher went there he said, "See here, Jim, you have a lot of those yellow slips, what is the matter with you? What is up? Have you been drunk? Are you tired? Are you sick? Anything wrong with you? Because if you are tired or

sick we will give you a show somewhere else." "Well, no, I am all right." "Then if you are not sick, or there is nothing wrong with you, you have forgotten how to shovel. I showed you how to shovel. You have forgotten something, now go ahead and shovel and I will show you what is the matter with you." Shoveling is a pretty big science, it is not a little thing.

If you are going to use the shovel right you should always shovel off an iron bottom; if not an iron bottom, a wooden bottom; and if not a wooden bottom a hard dirt bottom. Time and again the conditions are such that you have to go right into the pile. When that is the case, with nine out of ten materials it takes more trouble and more time and more effort to get the shovel into the pile than to do all the rest of the shoveling. That is where the effort comes. Those of you again who have taught the art of shoveling will have taught your workmen to do this. There is only one way to do it right. Put your forearm down onto the upper part of your leg, and when you push into the pile, throw your weight against it. That relieves your arm of work. You then have an automatic push, we will say, about eighty pounds, the weight of your body thrown on to it. Time and again we would find men whom we had taught to shovel right were going at it in the same old way, and of course, they could not do a day's work. The teacher would simply stand over that fellow and say, "There is what is the matter with you, Jim, you have forgotten to shovel into the pile."

You are not interested in shoveling, you are not interested in whether one way or the other is right, but I do hope to interest you in the difference of the mental attitude of the men who are teaching under the new system. Under the new system, if a man falls down, the presumption is that it is our fault at first, that we probably have not taught the man right, have not given him a fair show, have not spent time enough in showing him how to do his work.

Let me tell you another thing that is characteristic of scientific management. In my day, we were smart enough to know when the boss was coming, and when he came up we were apparently really working. Under scientific management, there is none of that pretense. I cannot say that in the old days we were delighted to see the boss coming around. We always expected some kind of roast if he came too close. Under the new, the teacher is welcomed; he is not an enemy, but a friend. He comes there to try to help the man get bigger wages, to show him how to do something. It is the great mental change, the change in the outlook that comes, rather than the details of it.

Does Scientific Management Pay?

It took the time of a number of men for about three years to study the art of shoveling in that yard at the Bethlehem Steel Works alone. They were carefully trained college men, and they were busy all the time. That costs money, the tool room costs money, the clerks we had to keep there all night figuring up how much the men did the day before cost money, the office in which the men laid out and planned the work cost money. The very fair and proper question, the only question to ask is "Does it pay?" because if scientific management does not pay in dollars and cents, it is the rankest kind of nonsense. There is nothing philanthropic about it. It has got to pay, because business which cannot be done on a profitable basis, ought not to be done on a philanthropic basis, for it will not last. At the end of three and one-half years we had a very good chance to know whether or not it paid.

Fortunately in the Bethlehem Steel Works they had records of how much it cost to handle the materials under the old system, where the single foreman led a group of men around the works. It costs them between seven and eight cents a ton to handle materials, on an average throughout the year. After paying for all this extra work I have told you about, it cost between three and four cents a ton to handle materials, and there was a profit of between seventy-five and eighty thousand dollars a year in that yard by handling those materials in the new way. What the men got out of it was this: Under the old

system there were between four and six hundred men handling the material in that yard, and when we got through there were about one hundred and forty. Each one was earning a great deal more money. We made careful investigation and found they were almost all saving money, living better, happier; they are the most contented set of laborers to be seen anywhere. It is only by this kind of justification, justification of a profit for both sides, an advantage to both sides, that scientific management can exist.

I would like to give you one more illustration. I want to try to prove to you that even the highest class mechanic cannot possibly understand the philosophy of his work, cannot possibly understand the laws under which he has to operate. There is a man who has had a high school education, an ingenious fellow who courts variety in life, to whom it is pleasant to change from one kind of work to another. He is not a cheap man, he is rather a high grade man among the machinists of this country. The case of which I am going to tell you is one in which my friend Barth went to introduce scientific management in the works of an owner, who, at between 65 and 70 years of age, had built up his business from nothing to almost five thousand men. They had a squabble, and after they got through, Mr. Barth made the proposition, "I will take any machine that you use in your shop, and I will show you that I can double the output of that machine." A very fair machine was selected. It was a lathe on which the workman had been working about twelve years. The product of that shop is a patented machine with a good many parts, 350 men working making those parts year in and year out. Each man had ten or a dozen parts a year.

The first thing that was done was in the presence of the foreman, the superintendent and the owner of the establishment. Mr. Barth laid down the way in which all of the parts were to be machined on that machine by the workman. Then Mr. Barth, with one of his small slide rules, proceeded to analyze the machine. With the aid of this analysis, which embodies the laws of cutting metals, Mr. Barth was able to take his turn at the machine; his gain was from two and one-half times to three times the amount of work turned out by the other man. This is what can be done by science as against the old rule of thumb knowledge. That is not exaggeration; the gain is as great as that in many cases.

Let me tell you something. The machines of this country, almost universally in the machine shops of our country, are speeded two or three hundred percent wrong. I made that assertion before the tool builders in Atlantic City. I said, "Gentlemen, in your own shops, many of your machines are two and three hundred percent wrong in speeds. Why? Because you have guessed at it." I am trying to show you what are the losses under the old opinions, the difference between knowledge on the one hand and guesswork on the other.

In 1882, at the end of a long fight with the machinists of the Midvale Steel Works, I went there as a laborer, and finally became a machinist after serving my apprenticeship outside. I finally got into the shop, and worked up to the place of a clerk who had something wrong with him. I then did a little bit more work than the others were doing, not too much. They came to me and said, "See here, Fred, you are not going to be a piecework hog." I said, "You fellows mean that you think I am not going to try to get any more work off these machines? I certainly am. Now I am on the other side, and I am going to be straight with you, and I will tell you so in advance." They said, "All right then, we will give you fair notice you will be outside the fence inside of six weeks." Let me tell you gentlemen, if any of you have been through a fight like that, trying to get workmen to do what they do not want to do, you will know the meanness of it, and you will never want to go into another one. I never would have gone into it if I had known what was ahead of me. After the meanest kind of a bitter fight, at the end of three years, we fairly won out and got a big increase in output. I had no illusion at the end of that time as to my great ability or anything else. I knew that those workmen knew about ten times as much as I did about doing the work. I set out deliberately to get on our side some of that knowledge that those workmen had.

Mr. William Sellers was the president, and he was a man away beyond his generation in progress. I went to him and said, "I want to spend quite a good deal of money trying to educate ourselves on the management side of our works. I do not know much of anything, and I am just about in the same condition as all the rest of the foremen around here." Very reluctantly, I may say, he allowed us to start to spend money. That started the study of the art of cutting metals. At the end of six months, from the standpoint of how to cut the metal off faster, the study did not amount to anything, but we unearthed a gold mine of information. Mr. Sellers laughed at me, but when I was able to show him the possibilities that lay ahead of us, the number of things we could find out, he said, "Go ahead." So until 1889, that experiment went straight ahead day in and day out. That was done because it paid in dollars and cents.

After I left the Midvale Steel Works, we had no means of figuring those experiments except the information which we had already gotten. Ten different machines were built to develop the art of cutting metals, so that almost continuously from 1882 for twenty-six years, all sorts of experiments went on to determine the twelve great elements that go to make up the art of cutting metals. I am trying to show you just what is going to take place in every industry throughout this world. You must know those facts if you are going to manufacture cheaply, and the only way to know them is to pay for them. . . .

The Effect on the Workman

Almost every one says, "Why, yes, that may be a good thing for the manufacturer, but how about the workmen? You are taking all the initiative away from that workman, you are making a machine out of him; what are you doing for him? He becomes merely a part of the machine." That is the almost universal impression. Again let me try to sweep aside the fallacy of that view by an illustration. The modern surgeon without a doubt is the finest mechanic in the world. He combines the greatest manual dexterity with the greatest knowledge of implements and the greatest knowledge of materials on which he is working. He is a true scientist, and he is a very highly skilled mechanic.

How does the surgeon teach his trade to the young men who come to the medical school? Does he say to them, "Now, young men, we belong to an older generation than you do, but the new generation is going to far outstrip anything that has been done in our generation; therefore, what we want of you is your initiative. We must have your brains, your thought, with your initiative. Of course, you know we old fellows have certain prejudices. For example, if we were going to amputate a leg, when we come down to the bone we are accustomed to take a saw, and we use it in that way and saw the bone off. But, gentlemen, do not let that fact one minute interfere with your originality, with your initiative, if you prefer an axe or a hatchet." Does the surgeon say this? He does not. He says, "You young men are going to outstrip us, but we will show you how. You shall not use a single implement in a single way until you know just which one to use, and we will tell you which one to use, and until you know how to use it, we will tell you how to use that implement, and after you have learned to use that implement our way, if you then see any defects in the implements, any defects in the method, then invent; but, invent so that you can invent upwards. Do not go inventing things which we discarded years ago."

That is just what we say to our young men in the shops. Scientific management makes no pretense that there is any finality in it. We merely say that the collective work of thirty or forty men in this trade through eight or ten years has gathered together a large amount of data. Every man in the establishment must start that way, must start our way, then if he can show us any better way, I do not care what it is, we will make an experiment to see if it is better. It will be named after him, and he will get a prize for having improved on one of our standards. There is the way we make progress under scientific management. There is your justification for all this. It does not dwarf initiative, it makes true initiative. Most of our progress comes through our workmen, but comes in a legitimate way.

8

Bureaucracy

Max Weber

1. Characteristics of Bureaucracy

Modern officialdom functions in the following specific manner:

I. There is the principle of fixed and official jurisdictional areas, which are generally ordered by rules, that is, by laws or administrative regulations.

1. The regular activities required for the purposes of the bureaucratically governed structure are distributed in a fixed way as official duties.

2. The authority to give the commands required for the discharge of these duties is distributed in a stable way and is strictly delimited by rules concerning the coercive means, physical, sacerdotal, or otherwise, which may be placed at the disposal of officials.

3. Methodical provision is made for the regular and continuous fulfillment of these duties and for the execution of the corresponding rights; only persons who have the generally regulated qualifications to serve are employed.

In public and lawful government these three elements constitute "bureaucratic authority." In private economic domination, they constitute bureaucratic "management." Bureaucracy, thus understood, is fully developed in political and ecclesiastical communities only in the

SOURCE: From *From Max Weber: Essays in Sociology* edited and translated by H. H. Gerth and C. Wright Mills. Copyright 1946 by Oxford University Press, Inc.; renewed 1973 by Hans H. Gerth. Reprinted by permission of the publisher. Footnotes omitted.

modern state, and, in the private economy, only in the most advanced institutions of capitalism. Permanent and public office authority, with fixed jurisdiction, is not the historical rule but rather the exception. This is so even in large political structures such as those of the ancient Orient, the Germanic and Mongolian empires of conquest, or of many feudal structures of state. In all these cases, the ruler executes the most important measures through personal trustees, table-companions, or court-servants. Their commissions and authority are not precisely delimited and are temporarily called into being for each case.

II. The principles of office hierarchy and of levels of graded authority mean a firmly ordered system of super- and subordination in which there is a supervision of the lower offices by the higher ones. Such a system offers the governed the possibility of appealing the decision of a lower office to its higher authority, in a definitely regulated manner. With the full development of the bureaucratic type, the office hierarchy is monocratically organized. The principle of hierarchical office authority is found in all bureaucratic structures: in state and ecclesiastical structures as well as in large party organizations and private enterprises. It does not matter for the character of bureaucracy whether its authority is called "private" or "public."

When the principle of jurisdictional "competency" is fully carried through, hierarchical subordination—at least in public office—does not mean that the "higher" authority is simply authorized to take over the business of the "lower." Indeed, the opposite is the rule. Once established and having fulfilled its task, an office tends to continue in existence and be held by another incumbent.

III. The management of the modern office is based upon written documents ("the files"), which are preserved in their original or draught form. There is, therefore, a staff or subaltern officials and scribes of all sorts. The body of officials actively engaged in a "public" office, along with the respective apparatus of material implements and the files, make up a "bureau." In private enterprise, "the bureau" is often called "the office."

In principle, the modern organization of the civil service separates the bureau from the private domicile of the offical, and, in general, bureaucracy segregates official activity as something distinct from the sphere of private life. Public monies and equipment are divorced from the private property of the official. This condition is everywhere the product of a long development. Nowadays, it is found in public as well as in private enterprises; in the latter, the principle extends even to the leading entrepreneur. In principle, the executive office is separated from the household, business from private correspondence, and business assets from private fortunes. The more consistently the modern type of business management has been carried through the more are these separations the case. The beginnings of this process are to be found as early as the Middle Ages.

It is the peculiarity of the modern entrepreneur that he conducts himself as the "first official" of his enterprise, in the very same way in which the ruler of a specifically modern bureaucratic state spoke of himself as "the first servant" of the state. The idea that the bureau activities of the state are intrinsically different in character from the management of private economic offices is a continental European notion and, by way of contrast, is totally foreign to the American way.

IV. Office management, at least all specialized office management—and such management is distinctly modern—usually presupposes thorough and expert training. This increasingly holds for the modern executive and employee of private enterprises, in the same manner as it holds for the state official.

V. When the office is fully developed, official activity demands the full working capacity *of the official, irrespective of the fact that his obligatory time in the bureau may be firmly delimited.* In the normal case, this is only the product of a long development, in the public as well as in the private office. Formerly, in all cases, the normal state of affairs was reversed: official business was discharged as a secondary activity.

VI. The management of the office follows general rules, which are more or less stable, more or less exhaustive, and which can be learned. Knowledge of these rules represents a special technical learning which the officials possess. It involves jurisprudence, or administrative or business management.

The reduction of modern office management to rules is deeply embedded in its very nature. The theory of modern public administration, for instance, assumes that the authority to order certain matters by decree—which has been legally granted to public authorities—does not entitle the bureau to regulate the matter by commands given for each case, but only to regulate the matter abstractly. This stands in extreme contrast to the regulation of all relationships through individual privileges and bestowals of favor, which is absolutely dominant in patrimonialism, at least in so far as such relationships are not fixed by sacred tradition.

2. The Position of the Official

All this results in the following for the internal and external position of the official:

I. Office holding is a "vocation." This is shown, first, in the requirement of a firmly prescribed course of training, which demands the entire capacity for work for a long period of time, and in the generally prescribed and special examinations which are prerequisites of employment. Furthermore, the position of the official is in the nature of a duty. This determines the internal structure of his relations, in the following manner: Legally and actually, office holding is not considered a source to be exploited for rents or emoluments, as was normally the case during the Middle Ages and frequently up to the threshold of recent times. Nor is office holding considered a usual exchange of services for equivalents, as is the case with free labor contracts. Entrance into an office, inclduing one in the private economy, is considered an acceptance of a specific obligation of faithful management in return for a secure existence. It is decisive for the specific nature of modern loyalty to an office that, in the pure type, it does not establish a relationship to a *person,* like the vassal's or disciple's faith in feudal or in patrimonial relations of authority. Modern loyalty is devoted to impersonal and functional purposes. Behind the functional purposes, of course, "ideas of culture-values" usually stand. These are *ersatz* for the earthly or supra-mundane personal master: ideas such as "state," "church," "community," "party," or "enterprise" are thought of as being realized in a community; they provide an ideological halo for the master.

The political official—at least in the fully developed modern state—is not considered the personal servant of a ruler. Today, the bishop, the priest, and the preacher are in fact no longer, as in early Christian times, holders of purely personal charisma. The supra-mundane and sacred values which they offer are given to everybody who seems to be worthy of them and who asks for them. In former times, such leaders acted upon the personal command of their master; in principle, they were responsible only to him. Nowadays, in spite of the partial survival of the old theory, such religious leaders are officials in the service of a functional purpose, which in the present-day "church" has become routinized and, in turn, ideologically hallowed.

II. The personal position of the official is patterned in the following way:

1. Whether he is in a private office or a public bureau, the modern official always strives and usually enjoys a distinct *social esteem* as compared with the governed. His social position is guaranteed by the prescriptive rules of rank order and, for the political official, by special definitions of the criminal code against "insults of officials" and "contempt" of state and church authorities.

The actual social position of the official is normally highest where, as in old civilized countries, the following conditions prevail: a strong demand for administration by trained experts; a strong and stable social differentiation, where the official predominantly derives from socially and economically privileged strata because of the social distribution of power; or where the costliness of the required training and status conventions are binding upon him. The possession of educational certificates—to be discussed elsewhere—are usually linked with qualification for office. Naturally, such certificates or patents enhance the "status element" in the social position of the official. For the rest this status factor in individual cases is explicitly and impassively acknowledged; for example, in the prescription that the acceptance or rejection of an aspirant to an official career depends upon the consent ("election") of the members of the official body. This is the case in the German army with the officer corps. Similar phenomena, which promote this guild-like closure of officialdom, are typically found in patrimonial and, particularly, in prebendal officialdoms of the past. The desire to resurrect such phenomena in changed forms is by no means infrequent among modern bureaucrats. For instance, they have played a role among the demands of the quite proletarian and expert officials (the *tretyj* element) during the Russian revolution.

Usually the social esteem of the officials as such is especially low where the demand for expert administration and the dominance of status conventions are weak. This is especially the case in the United States; it is often the case in new settlements by virtue of their wide fields for profitmaking and the great instability of their social stratification.

2. The pure type of bureaucratic official is *appointed* by a superior authority. An official elected by the governed is not a purely

bureaucratic figure. Of course, the formal existence of an election does not by itself mean that no appointment hides behind the election—in the state, especially, appointment by party chiefs. Whether or not this is the case does not depend upon legal statutes but upon the way in which the party mechanism functions. Once firmly organized, the parties can turn a formally free election into the mere acclamation of a candidate designated by the party chief. As a rule, however, a formally free election is turned into a fight, conducted according to definite rules, for votes in favor of one of two designated candidates.

In all circumstances, the designation of officials by means of an election among the governed modifies the strictness of hierarchical subordination. In principle, an official who is so elected has an autonomous position opposite the superordinate official. The elected official does not derive his position "from above" but "from below," or at least not from a superior authority of the official hierarchy but from powerful party men ("bosses"), who also determine his further career. The career of the elected official is not, or at least not primarily, dependent upon his chief in the administration. The official who is not elected but appointed by a chief normally functions more exactly, from a technical point of view, because, all other circumstances being equal, it is more likely that purely functional points of consideration and qualities will determine his selection and career. As laymen, the governed can become acquainted with the extent to which a candidate is expertly qualified for office only in terms of experience, and hence only after his service. Moreover, in every sort of selection of officials by election, parties quite naturally give decisive weight not to expert considerations but to the services a follower renders to the party boss. This holds for all kinds of procurement of officials by elections, for the designation of formally free, elected officials by party bosses when they determine the slate of candidates, or the free appointment by a chief who has himself been elected. The contrast, however, is relative: substantially similar conditions hold where

legitimate monarchs and their subordinates appoint officials, except that the influence of the followings are then less controllable.

Where the demand for administration by trained experts is considerable, and the party followings have to recognize an intellectually developed, educated, and freely moving "public opinion," the use of unqualified officials falls back upon the party in power at the next election. Naturally, this is more likely to happen when the officials are appointed by the chief. The demand for a trained administration now exists in the United States, but in the large cities, where immigrant votes are "corralled," there is, of course, no educated public opinion. Therefore, popular elections of the administrative chief and also of his subordinate officials usually endanger the expert qualification of the official as well as the precise functioning of the bureaucratic mechanism. It also weakens the dependence of the officials upon the hierarchy. This holds at least for the large administrative bodies that are difficult to supervise. The superior qualification and integrity of federal judges, appointed by the President, as over against elected judges in the United States is well known, although both types of officials have been selected primarily in terms of party considerations. The great changes in American metropolitan administrations demanded by reformers have proceeded essentially from elected mayors working with an apparatus of officials who were appointed by them. These reforms have thus come about in a "Caesarist" fashion. Viewed technically, as an organized form of authority, the efficiency of "Caesarism," which often grows out of democracy, rests in general upon the position of the "Caesar" as a free trustee of the masses (of the army or of the citizenry), who is unfettered by tradition. The "Caesar" is thus the unrestrained master of a body of highly qualified military officers and officials whom he selects freely and personally without regard to tradition or to any other considerations. This "rule of the personal genius," however, stands in contradiction to the formally "democratic" principle of a universally elected officialdom.

3. Normally, the position of the official is held for life, at least in public bureaucracies; and this is increasingly the case for all similar structures. As a factual rule, *tenure for life* is presupposed, even where the giving of notice or periodic reappointment occurs. In contrast to the worker in a private enterprise, the official normally holds tenure. Legal or actual life-tenure, however, is not recognized as the official's right to the possession of office, as was the case with many structures of authority in the past. Where legal guarantees against arbitrary dismissal or transfer are developed, they merely serve to guarantee a strictly objective discharge of specific office duties free from all personal considerations. In Germany, this is the case for all juridical and, increasingly, for all administrative officials.

Within the bureaucracy, therefore, the measure of "independence," legally guaranteed by tenure, is not always a source of increased status for the official whose position is thus secured. Indeed, often the reverse holds, especially in old cultures and communities that are highly differentiated. In such communities, the stricter the subordination under the arbitrary rule of the master, the more it guarantees the maintenance of the conventional seigneurial style of living for the official. Because of the very absence of these legal guarantees of tenure, the conventional esteem for the official may rise in the same way as, during the Middle Ages, the esteem of the nobility of office rose at the expense of esteem for the freemen, and as the king's judge surpassed that of the people's judge. In Germany, the military officer or the administrative official can be removed from office at any time, or at least far more readily than the "independent judge," who never pays with loss of his office for even the grossest offense against the "code of honor" or against social conventions of the salon. For this very reason, if other things are equal, in the eyes of the master stratum the judge is considered less qualified for social intercourse than are officers and administrative officials, whose greater dependence on the master is a greater guarantee of their conformity with status conventions. Of course, the average official strives for a civil-service law, which would materially secure his old age and provide increased guarantees against his arbitrary removal from office. This striving, however, has its limits. A very strong development of the "right to the office" naturally makes it more difficult to staff them with regard to technical efficiency, for such a development decreases the career opportunities of ambitious candidates for office. This makes for the fact that officials, on the whole, do not feel their dependency upon those at the top. This lack of a feeling of dependency, however, rests primarily upon the inclination to depend upon one's equals rather than upon the socially inferior and governed strata. The present conservative movement among the Badenia clergy, occasioned by the anxiety of a presumably threatening separation of church and state, has been expressly determined by the desire not to be turned "from a master into a servant of the parish."

4. The official receives the regular *pecuniary* compensation of a normally fixed *salary* and the old age security provided by a pension. The salary is not measured like a wage in terms of work done, but according to "status," that is, according to the kind of function (the "rank") and, in addition, possibly, according to the length of service. The relatively great security of the official's income, as well as the rewards of social esteem, make the office a sought-after position, especially in countries which no longer provide opportunities for colonial profits. In such countries, this situation permits relatively low salaries for officials.

5. The official is set for a "*career*" within the hierarchical order of the public service. He moves from the lower, less important, and lower paid to the higher positions. The average official naturally desires a mechanical fixing of the conditions of promotion: if not of the offices, at least of the salary levels. He wants these conditions fixed in terms of "seniority," or possibly according to grades achieved in a developed system of expert examinations. Here and there, such examinations actually form a character *indelebilis* of the official and have lifelong effects on his career. To this is joined

the desire to qualify the right to office and the increasing tendency toward status group closure and economic security. All of this makes for a tendency to consider the offices as "prebends" of those who are qualified by educational certificates. The necessity of taking general personal and intellectual qualifications into consideration, irrespective of the often subaltern character of the education certificate, has led to a condition in which the highest political offices, especially the positions of "ministers," are principally filled without reference to such certificates.

9

Notes on the Theory of Organization

Luther Gulick

Every large-scale or complicated enterprise requires many men to carry it forward. Wherever many men are thus working together the best results are secured when there is a division of work among these men. The theory of organization, therefore, has to do with the structure of co-ordination imposed upon the work-division units of an enterprise. Hence it is not possible to determine how an activity is to be organized without, at the same time, considering how the work in question is to be divided. Work division is the foundation of organization; indeed, the reason for organization.

1. The Division of Work

It is appropriate at the outset of this discussion to consider the reasons for and the effect of the division of work. It is sufficient for our purpose to note the following factors.

Why Divide Work?

Because men differ in nature, capacity and skill, and gain greatly in dexterity by specialization; Because the same man cannot be at two places at the same time; Because the range of knowledge and skill is so great that a man cannot within his life-span know more than a

SOURCE: Luther Gulick and Lyndall Urwick, eds., *Papers on the Science of Administration* (New York: Institute of Public Administration, 1937), 3–13. Reprinted with permission.

small fraction of it. In other words, it is a question of human nature, time, and space.

In a shoe factory it would be possible to have 1,000 men each assigned to making complete pairs of shoes. Each man would cut his leather, stamp in the eyelets, sew up the tops, sew on the bottoms, nail on the heels, put in the laces, and pack each pair in a box. It might take two days to do the job. One thousand men would make 500 pairs of shoes a day. It would also be possible to divide the work among these same men, using the identical hand methods, in an entirely different way. One group of men would be assigned to cut the leather, another to putting in the eyelets, another to stitching up the tops, another to sewing on the soles, another to nailing on the heels, another to inserting the laces and packing the pairs of shoes. We know from common sense and experience that there are two great gains in this latter process: first, it makes possible the better utilization of the varying skills and aptitudes of the different workmen, and encourages the development of specialization; and second, it eliminates the time that is lost when a workman turns from a knife, to a punch, to a needle and awl, to a hammer, and moves from table to bench, to anvil, to stool. Without any pressure on the workers, they could probably turn out twice as many shoes in a single day. There would be additional economies, because inserting laces and packing could be assigned to unskilled and low-paid workers. Moreover, in the cutting of the leather there would be less spoilage because the less skillful pattern cutters would be eliminated and assigned to other work. It would also be possible to cut a dozen shoe tops at the same time from the same pattern with little additional effort. All of these advances would follow, without the introduction of new labor saving machinery.

The introduction of machinery accentuates the division of work. Even such a simple thing as a saw, a typewriter, or a transit requires increased specialization, and serves to divide workers into those who can and those who cannot use the particular instrument effectively. Division of work on the basis of the tools and machines used in work rests no doubt in part on aptitude, but primarily upon the development and maintenance of skill through continued manipulation.

Specialized skills are developed not alone in connection with machines and tools. They evolve naturally from the materials handled, like wood, or cattle, or paint, or cement. They arise similarly in activities which center in a complicated series of interrelated concepts, principles, and techniques. These are most clearly recognized in the professions, particularly those based on the application of scientific knowledge, as in engineering, medicine, and chemistry. They are none the less equally present in law, ministry, teaching, accountancy, navigation, aviation, and other fields.

The nature of these subdivisions is essentially pragmatic, in spite of the fact that there is an element of logic underlying them. They are therefore subject to a gradual evolution with the advance of science, the invention of new machines, the progress of technology and the change of the social system. In the last analysis, however, they appear to be based upon differences in individual human beings. But it is not to be concluded that the apparent stability of "human nature," whatever that may be, limits the probable development of specialization. The situation is quite the reverse. As each field of knowledge and work is advanced, constituting a continually larger and more complicated nexus of related principles, practices and skills, any individual will be less and less able to encompass it and maintain intimate knowledge and facility over the entire area, and there will thus arise a more minute specialization because knowledge and skill advance while man stands still. Division of work and integrated organization are the bootstraps by which mankind lifts itself in the process of civilization.

The Limits of Division

There are three clear limitations beyond which the division of work cannot to advantage go. The first is practical and arises from the volume of work involved in man-hours. Nothing is gained by subdividing work if that further subdivision results in setting up a task which requires less than the full time of one man. This is too obvious to need demonstration. The only exception arises where space interferes, and in, such cases the part-time expert must fill in his spare time at other tasks, so that as a matter of fact a new combination is introduced.

The second limitation arises from technology and custom at a given time and place. In some areas nothing would be gained by separating undertaking from the custody and cleaning of churches, because by custom the sexton is the undertaker; in building construction it is extraordinarily difficult to redivide certain aspects of electrical and plumbing work and to combine them in a more effective way, because of the jurisdictional conflicts of craft unions; and it is clearly impracticable to establish a division of cost accounting in a field in which no technique of costing has yet been developed.

This second limitation is obviously elastic. It may be changed by invention and by education. If this were not the fact, we should face a static division of labor. It should be noted, however, that a marked change has two dangers. It greatly restricts the labor market from which workers may be drawn and greatly lessens the opportunities open to those who are trained for the particular specialization.

The third limitation is that the subdivision of work must not pass beyond physical division into organic division. It might seem far more efficient to have the front half of the cow in the pasture grazing and the rear half in the barn being milked all of the time, but this organic division would fail. Similarly there is no gain from splitting a single movement or gesture like licking an envelope, or tearing apart a series of intimately and intricately related activities.

It may be said that there is in this an element of reasoning in a circle; that the test here applied as to whether an activity is organic or not is whether it is divisible or not—which is what we set out to define. This charge is true. It must be a pragmatic test. Does the division work out? Is something vital destroyed and lost? Does it bleed?

The Whole and the Parts

It is axiomatic that the whole is equal to the sum of its parts. But in dividing up any "whole," one must be certain that every part, including unseen elements and relationships, is accounted for. The marble sand to which the Venus de Milo may be reduced by a vandal does not equal the statue, though every last grain be preserved; nor is a thrush just so much feathers, bones, flesh and blood; nor a typewriter merely so much steel, glass, paint, and rubber. Similarly a piece of work to be done cannot be subdivided into the obvious component parts without great danger that the central design, the operating relationships, the imprisoned idea, will be lost. . . .

When one man builds a house alone he plans as he works; he decides what to do first and what next, that is, he "co-ordinates the work." When many men work together to build a house this part of the work, the co-ordinating, must not be lost sight of.

In the "division of the work" among the various skilled specialists, a specialist in planning and coordination must be sought as well. Otherwise, a great deal of time may be lost, workers may get in each other's way, material may not be on hand when needed, things may be done in the wrong order, and there may even be a difference of opinion as to where the various doors and windows are to go. It is self-evident that the more the work is subdivided, the greater is the danger of confusion, and the greter is the need of overall supervision and coordination. Co-ordination is not something that develops by accident. It must be won by intelligent, vigorous, persistent, and organized effort.

2. The Co-ordination of Work

If subdivision of work is inescapable, co-ordination becomes mandatory. There is, however, no one way to co-ordination. Experience shows that it may be achieved in two primary ways. These are:

1. By organization, that is, by interrelating the subdivisions of work by allotting them to men who are placed in a structure of authority, so that the work may be co-ordinated by orders of superiors to subordinates, reaching from the top to the bottom of the entire enterprise.

2. By the dominance of an idea, that is, the development of intelligent singleness of purpose in the minds and wills of those who are working together as a group, so that each worker will of his own accord fit his task into the whole with skill and enthusiasm.

These two principles of co-ordination are not mutually exclusive, in fact, no enterprise is really effective without the extensive utilization of both.

Size and time are the great limiting factors in the development of co-ordination. In a small project, the problem is not difficult; the structure of authority is simple, and the central purpose is real to every worker. In a large complicated enterprise, the organization becomes involved, the lines of authority tangled, and there is danger that the workers will forget that there is any central purpose, and so devote their best energies only to their own individual advancement and advantage.

The interrelated elements of time and habit are extraordinarily important in coordination. Man is a creature of habit. When an enterprise is built up gradually from small beginnings the staff can be "broken in" step by step. And when difficulties develop, they can be ironed out, and the new method followed from that point on as a matter of habit, with the knowledge that that particular difficulty will not develop again. Routines may even be mastered by drill as they are in the army. When, however, a large new interprise must be set up or altered overnight, then the real difficulties of co-ordination make their appearance. The factor of habit, which is thus an important foundation of co-ordination when time is available, becomes a serious handicap when time is not available, that is, when rules change. The question of co-ordination therefore must be approached with different emphasis in small and in large enterprises; in simple and in complex situations; in stable and in new or changing organizations.

Co-ordination through Organization

Organization as a way of co-ordination requires the establishment of a system of authority whereby the central purpose or objective of an enterprise is translated into reality through the combined efforts of many specialists, each working in his own field at a particular time and place.

It is clear from long experience in human affairs that such a structure of authority requires not only many men at work in many places at selected times, but also a single directing executive authority.[1] The problem of organization thus becomes the problem of building up between the executive at the center and the subdivisions of work on the periphery of an effective network of communication and control.

The following outline may serve further to define the problem:

I. First Step: Define the job to be done, such as the furnishing of pure water to all of the people and industries within a given area at the lowest possible cost;
II. Second Step: Provide a director to see that the objective is realized;
III. Third Step: Determine the nature and number of individualized and specialized work units into which the job will have to be divided. As has been seen above, this subdivision depends partly upon the size of the job (no ultimate subdivision can generally be so small as to require less than the full time of one worker) and upon the status of technological and social development at a given time;
IV. Fourth Step: Establish and perfect the structure of authority between the director and the ultimate work subdivisions.

It is this fourth step which is the central concern of the theory of organization. It is the function of this organization (IV) to enable the director (II) to co-ordinate and energize all of the subdivisions of work (III) so that the major objective (I) may be achieved efficiently.

The Span of Control

In this undertaking we are confronted at the start by the inexorable limits of human nature. Just as the hand of man can span only a limited number of notes on the piano, so the mind and will of man can span but a limited number of immediate managerial contacts. The problem has been discussed brilliantly by Graicunas in his paper included in this collection. The limit of control is partly a matter of the limits of knowledge, but even more is it a matter of the limits of time and of energy. As a result the executive of any enterprise can personally direct only a few persons. He must depend upon these to direct others, and upon them in turn to direct still others, until the last man in the organization is reached. . . .

But when we seek to determine how many immediate subordinates the director of an enterprise can effectively supervise, we enter a realm of experience which has not been brought under sufficient scientific study to furnish a final answer. Sir Ian Hamilton says, "The nearer we approach the supreme head of the whole organization, the more we ought to work towards groups of three; the closer we get to the foot of the whole organization (the Infantry of the Line), the more we work towards groups of six."[2]

The British Machinery of Government Committee of 1918 arrived at the conclusions that "The Cabinet should be small in number—preferably ten or, at most, twelve."[3]

Henri Fayol said "[In France] a minister has twenty assistants, where the Administrative Theory says that a manager at the head of a big undertaking should not have more than five or six."[4]

Graham Wallas expressed the opinion that the cabinet should not be increased "beyond the number of ten or twelve at which organized oral discussion is most efficient."[5]

Léon Blum recommended for France a prime minister with a technical cabinet modelled after the British War Cabinet, which was composed of five members.[6]

It is not difficult to understand why there is this divergence of statement among authorities who are agreed on the fundamentals. It arises in part from the differences in the capacities and work habits of individual executives observed, and in part from the noncomparable character of the work covered. It would seem that insufficient attention has been devoted to three factors, first, the element of diversification of function; second, the element of time; and third, the element of space. A chief of public works can deal effectively with more direct subordinates than can the general of the army, because all of his immediate subordinates in the department of public works will be in the general field of engineering, while in the army there will be many different elements, such as communications, chemistry, aviation, ordinance, motorized service, engineering, supply, transportation, etc., each with its own technology. The element of time is also of great significance as has been indicated above. In a stable organization the chief executive can deal with more immediate subordinates than in a new or changing organization. Similarly, space influences the span of control. An organization located in one building can be supervised through more immediate subordinates than can the same organization if scattered in several cities. When scattered there is not only need for more supervision, and therefore more supervisory personnel, but also for a fewer number of contacts with the chief executive because of the increased difficulty faced by the chief executive in learning sufficient details about a far-flung organization to do an intelligent job. The failure to attach sufficient importance to these variables has served to limit the scientific validity of the statements which have been made that one man can supervise but three, or five, or eight, or twelve immediate subordinates.

These considerations do not, however, dispose of the problem. They indicate rather the need for further research. But without further research we may conclude that the chief executive of an organization can deal with only a few immediate subordinates; that this number is determined not only by the nature of the work, but also by the nature of the executive; and that the number of immediate subordinates in a large, diversified and dispersed organization must be even less than in a homogeneous and unified organization to achieve the same measure of coordination.

One Master

From the earliest times it has been recognized that nothing but confusion arises under multiple command. "A man cannot serve two masters" was adduced as a theological argument because it was already accepted as a principle of human relation in everyday life. In administration this is known as the principle of "unity of command."[7] The priniciple may be stated as follows: A workman subject to orders from several superiors will be confused, inefficient, and irresponsible; a workman subject to orders from but one superior may be methodical, efficient, and responsible. Unity of command thus refers to those who are commanded, not to those who issue the commands.[8]

The significance of this principle in the process of co-ordination and organization must not be lost sight of. In building a structure of co-ordination, it is often tempting to set up more than one boss for a man who is doing work which has more than one relationship. Even as great a philosopher of management as Taylor fell into this error in setting up separate foremen to deal with machinery, with materials, with speed, etc., each with the power of giving orders directly to the individual workman.[9] The rigid adherence to the principle of unity of command may have its absurdities; these are, however, unimportant in comparison with the certainty of confusion, inefficiency and irresponsibility which arise from the violation of the principle.

Technical Efficiency

There are many aspects of the problem of securing technical efficiency. Most of these do not concern us here directly. They have been treated extensively by such authorities as Taylor,

Dennison, and Kimball, and their implications for general organization by Fayol, Urwick, Mooney, and Reiley. There is, however, one efficiency concept which concerns us deeply in approaching the theory of organization. It is the principle of homogeneity.

It has been observed by authorities in many fields that the efficiency of a group working together is directly related to the homogeneity of the work they are performing, of the processes they are utilizing, and of the purposes which actuate them. From top to bottom, the group must be unified. It must work together.

It follows from this (1) that any organizational structure which brings together in a single unit work divisions which are non-homogeneous in work, in technology, or in purpose will encounter the danger of friction and inefficiency; and (2) that a unit based on a given specializaton cannot be given technical direction by a layman.

In the realm of government it is not difficult to find many illustrations of the unsatisfactory results of non-homogeneous administrative combinations. It is generally agreed that agricultural development and education cannot be administered by the same men who enforce pest and disease control, because the succcess of the former rests upon friendly co-operation and trust of the farmers, while the latter engenders resentment and suspicion. Similarly, activities like drug control established in protection of the consumer do not find appropriate homes in departments dominated by the interests of the producer. In the larger cities and in states it has been found that hospitals cannot be so well administered by the health department directly as they can be when set up independently in a separate department, or at least in a bureau with an extensive autonomy, and it is generally agreed that public welfare administration and police administration require separation, as do public health administration and welfare administration, though both of these combinations may be found in successful operation under special conditions. No one would think of combining water supply and public education, or tax administration and public recreation. In every one of these cases, it will be seen that there is some element either of work to be done, or of the technology used, or of the end sought which is non-homogeneous.

Another phase of the combination of incompatible functions in the same office may be found in the common American practice of appointing unqualified laymen and politicians to technical positions or to give technical direction to highly specialized services. As Dr. Frank J. Goodnow pointed out a generation ago, we are faced here by two heterogeneous functions, "politics" and "administration," the combination of which cannot be undertaken within the structure of the administration without producing inefficiency.

Caveamus Expertum

At this point a word of caution is necessary. The application of the principle of homogeneity has its pitfalls. Every highly trained technician, particularly in the learned professions, has a profound sense of omniscience and a great desire for complete independence in the service of society. When employed by government he knows exactly what the people need better than they do themselves, and he knows how to render this service. He tends to be utterly oblivious of all other needs, because, after all, is not his particular technology the road to salvation? Any restraint applied to him is "limitation of freedom," and any criticism "springs from ignorance and jealousy." Every budget increase he secures is "in the public interest," while every increase secured elsewhere is "a sheer waste." His efforts and maneuvers to expand are "public education" and "civic organization," while similar efforts by others are "propaganda" and "politics."

Another trait of the expert is his tendency to assume knowledge and authority in fields in which he has no competence. In this particular, educators, lawyers, priests, admirals, doctors, scientists, engineers, accountants, merchants and bankers are all the same—having achieved technical competence or "success" in one field, they come to think this competence is a general quality detachable from the field and inherent in themselves. They step without embarrassment into other areas. They do not remember that the robes of authority of one kingdom confer so sovereignty in another; but that there they are merely a masquerade.

The expert knows his "stuff." Society needs him, and must have him more and more as man's technical knowledge becomes more and more extensive. But history shows us that the common man is a better judge of his own needs in the long run than any cult of experts. Kings and ruling classes, priests and prophets, soldiers and lawyers, when permitted to rule rather than serve mankind, have in the end done more to check the advance of human welfare than they have to advance it. The true place of the expert is, as A. E. said so well, "on tap, not on top." The essential validity of democracy rests upon this philosophy, for democracy is a way of government in which the common man is the final judge of what is good for him.

Efficiency is one of the things that is good for him because it makes life richer and safer. That efficiency is to be secured more and more through the use of technical specialists. These specialists have no right to ask for, and must not be given freedom from supervisory control, but in establishing that control, a government which ignores the conditions of efficiency cannot expect to achieve efficiency.

3. Organizational Patterns

Organization Up or Down?

One of the great sources of confusion in the discussion of the theory of organization is that some authorities work and think primarily from the top down, while others work and think from the bottom up. This is perfectly natural because some authorities are interested primarily in the executive and in the problems of central management, while others are interested primarily in individual services and activities. Those who work from the top down regard the organization as a system of subdividing the enterprise under the chief executive, while those who work from the bottom up, look upon organization as a system of combining the individual units of work into aggregates which are in turn subordinated to the chief executive. It may be argued that either approach leads to a consideration of the entire problem, so that it is of no great significance which way the organization is viewed. Certainly it makes this very important practical difference: those who work from the top down must guard themselves from the danger of sacrificing the effectiveness of the individual services in their zeal to achieve a model structure at the top, while those who start from the bottom, must guard themselves from the danger of thwarting co-ordination in their eagerness to develop effective individual services.

In any practical situation the problem of organization must be approached from both top and bottom. This is particularly true in the reorganization of a going concern. May it not be that this practical necessity is likewise the sound process theoretically? In that case one would develop the plan of an organization or reorganization both from the top downward and from the bottom upward, and would reconcile the two at the center. In planning the first subdivisions under the chief executive, the principle of the limitation of the span of control must apply; in building up the first aggregates of specialized functions, the principle of homogeneity must apply. If any enterprise has such an array of functions that the first subdivisions from the top down do not readily meet the first aggregations from the bottom up, then additional divisions and additional aggregates must be introduced, but at each further step there must be a less and less rigorous adherence to the two conflicting principles until their juncture is effected. . . .

Organizing the Executive

The effect of the suggestion presented above is to organize and institutionalize the executive function as such so that it may be more adequate in a complicated situation. This is in reality not a new idea. We do not, for example, expect the chief executive to write his own letters. We give him a private secretary, who is part of his office and assists him to do this part of his job. This secretary is not a part of any department, he is a subdivision of the executive himself. In just this way, though on a different plane, other phases of the job of the chief executive may be organized.

Before doing this, however, it is necessary to have a clear picture of the job itself. This brings us directly to the question, "What is the work of the chief executive? What does he do?"

The answer is POSDCORB.

POSDCORB is, of course, a made-up word designed to call attention to the various functional elements of the work of a chief executive because "administration" and "management" have lost all specific content.[10] POSDCORB is made up of the initials and stands for the following activities:

Planning, that is working out in broad outline the things that need to be done and the methods for doing them to accomplish the purpose set for the enterprise;

Organizing, that is the establishment of the formal structure of authority through which work subdivisions are arranged, defined and co-ordinated for the defined objective;

Staffing, that is the whole personnel function of bringing in and training the staff and maintaining favorable conditions of work;

Directing, that is the continuous task of making decisions and embodying them in specific and general orders and instructions and serving as the leader of the enterprise;

Co-ordinating, that is the all important duty of interrelating the various parts of the work;

Reporting, that is keeping those to whom the executive is responsible informed as to what is going on, which thus includes keeping himself and his subordinates informed through records, research, and inspection;

Budgeting, with all that goes with budgeting in the form of fiscal planning, accounting, and control.

This statement of the work of a chief executive is adapted from the functional analysis elaborated by Henri Fayol in his "Industrial and General Administration." It is believed that those who know administration intimately will find in this analysis a valid and helpful pattern, into which can be fitted each of the major activities and duties of any chief executive.

If these seven elements may be accepted as the major duties of the chief executive, it follows that they *may* be separately organized as subdivisions of the executive. The need for such subdivision depends entirely on the size and complexity of the enterprise. In the largest enterprises, particularly where the chief executive is as a matter of fact unable to do the work that is thrown upon him, it may be presumed that one or more parts of POSDCORB should be suborganized.

Notes

1. I.e., when *organization is the basis of coordination.* Wherever the central executive authority is composed of several who exercise their functions jointly by majority vote, as on a board, this is from the standpoint of organization still a "single authority"; where the central executive is in reality composed of several men acting freely and independently, then organization cannot be said to be the basis of co-ordination; it is rather the dominance of an idea and falls under the second principle stated above.

2. Sir Ian Hamilton, "The Soul and Body of an Army." Arnold, London, 1921, p. 230.

3. Great Britain. Ministry of Reconstruction. Report of the Machinery of Government Committee. H. M. Stationery Office, London, 1918, p. 5.

4. Henri Fayol, "The Administrative Theory in the State." Address before the Second International Congress of Administrative Science at Brussels, September 13, 1923. Paper IV in this collection.

5. Graham Wallas, "The Great Society." Macmillan, London and New York, 1919, p. 264.

6. Léon Blum, "La Réforme Gouvernementale." Grasset, Paris, 1918. Reprinted in 1936, p. 59.

7. Henri Fayol, "Industrial and General Administration." English translation by J. A. Coubrough. International Management Association, Geneva, 1930.

8. Fayol terms the latter "unity of direction."

9. Frederick Winslow Taylor, "Shop Management." Harper and Brothers, New York and London, 1911, p. 99.

10. See Minutes of the Princeton Conference on Training for the Public Service, 1935, p. 35. See also criticism of this analysis in Lewis Meriam, "Public Service and Special Training," University of Chicago Press, 1936, pp. 1, 2, 10 and 15, where this functional analysis is misinterpreted as a statement of qualifications for appointment.

II

Neoclassical Organization Theory

There is no precise definition of *neoclassical* in the context of organization theory. The general connotation is that of a theoretical perspective that revises and/or is critical of classical organization theory—particularly for minimizing issues related to the humanness of organizational members, coordination needs among administrative units, internal-external organizational relations, and organizational decision processes. The major writers of the classical school did their most significant work before World War II. The Neoclassical writers gained their reputations as organization theorists by attacking the classical writers from the end of the war through the 1950s. Because classical theories were, to a large measure, derived intellectually rather than empirically, their artificial assumptions left them vulnerable to attack. Theorists of the classical period thought that organizations should be based on universally applicable, scientific principles.

In spite of their frequent and vigorous attacks upon the classicalists, the neoclassicalists did not develop a body of theory that could adequately replace the classical school. The neoclassical school modified, added to, and somewhat extended classical theory. It attempted to blend assumptions of classical theory with concepts that subsequently were used by later organization theorists from all subsequent schools. The neoclassical school attempted to save classical theory by introducing modifications based upon research findings in the behavioral sciences. It did not have a bona fide theory of its own. To a great extent, it was an "anti-school."

Despite its limitations, the neoclassical school was very important in the historical development of organization theory. But, like a rebellious teenager, neoclassical theory could not permanently stand on its own. It was a transitional, somewhat reactionary school. Why then was the neoclassical school so important? First, because it initiated the theoretical movement away from the oversimplistic mechanistic views of the classical school. The neoclassicalists challenged some of the basic tenets of the classical school *head on.* And, remember, the classical school was the only school at that time. Organization theory and classical organization theory were virtually synonymous.

Secondly, in the process of challenging the classical school, the neoclassicalists raised issues and initiated theories that became central to the foundations of most of the schools that have followed. The neoclassical school was a critically important forerunner. Most serious post-1960 articles from *any* school of organization theory cite neoclassical theorists.

All of the neoclassical selections that we have chosen to include in this chapter are important precursors of the human relations, "modern" structural, systems, multiple constituency, power and politics, and organizational culture perspectives of organization theory.

Herbert A. Simon certainly was the most influential of the neoclassical organization theorists. He was the first to seriously challenge the tenets of classical organization theory. In his widely quoted 1946 *Public Administration Review* article "The Proverbs of Administration" (the first selection in this chapter), Simon is devastating in his criticism of the classical approach to "general principles of management," such as those proposed by Fayol, Gulick, and others, as being inconsistent, conflicting, and inapplicable to many of the administrative situations facing managers. He suggests that such "principles" as "span of control" and "unity of command" can, with equal logic, be applied in diametrically opposed ways to the same set of circumstances. Simon concludes that the so-called principles of administration are instead proverbs of administration. The basic themes of the article later were incorporated in his landmark book *Administrative Behavior* (1947).

One of the major themes of the neoclassical organization theorists was that organizations did not and could not exist as self-contained islands isolated from their environments. As might be expected, the first significant efforts to "open up" organizations (theoretically speaking) came from analysts whose professional identities required them to take a broad view of things—sociologists.

One such sociologist, Philip Selznick, in his 1948 *American Sociological Review* article, "Foundations of the Theory of Organization," (which is reprinted here) asserts that while it is possible to describe and design organizations in a purely rational manner, such efforts can never hope to cope with the nonrational aspects of organizational behavior. In contrast with the classical theorists, Selznick maintains that organizations consist of individuals whose goals and aspirations might not necessarily coincide with the formal goals of the organization, rather than consist of simply a number of positions for management to control. Selznick is perhaps best known for his concept of "co-optation," which describes the process of an organization bringing and subsuming new elements into its policy-making process in order to prevent such elements from becoming a threat to the organization or its mission. The fullest account of Selznick's "co-optation" is found in *TVA and the Grass Roots,* his 1949 case study of how the Tennessee Valley Authority first gained local support for its programs. Selznick's approach to studying organizations and his intellectual distinction between the concepts of "organization" and "institution" have been lauded as models of organizational theory's insightfulness and usefulness by such writers on organizational culture as Ott (1989), Pedersen and Sorensen (1989), Siehl and Martin (1984), Walker (1986), and Wilkins (1983; 1989).

We have focused on Philip Selznick here, but many other sociologists also made major contributions to the neoclassical school and to the general development of the field of organization theory. For example:

• Melville Dalton (1950; 1959) focused on structural frictions between line and staff units and between the central office of an organization and geographically dispersed facilities. His work drew attention to some of the universal ingredients of conflict within organizations and to problems of educating and socializing managers.

• Talcott Parsons introduced an approach to the analysis of formal organizations using the general theory of social systems. In his 1956 article "Suggestions for a Sociological Approach to the Theory of Organizations," Parsons defined an organization as a social system that focuses on the attainment of specific goals and contributes, in turn, to the accomplishment of goals of a more comprehensive system, such as the larger organization or even society itself.

• William F. Whyte (1948) studied human relations in the restaurant business in order to understand and describe stresses that result from interrelations and status differences in the workplace.

Perhaps the most comprehensive of the neoclassical critiques came in 1957, when James G. March and Herbert A. Simon published *Organizations,* a summary of the knowledge about organization theory/behavior that had been generated primarily by the behavioral science movement. Reprinted here is their well-known section concerning the dysfunctions of bureaucracies, "Theories of Bureaucracy." The piece begins by reviewing the models of bureaucratic behavior developed by three contemporary sociologists—Robert K. Merton (1940), Philip Selznick (1949), and Alvin W. Gouldner (1954). In each case, the sociologists found that efforts to achieve bureaucratic objectives resulted in unforeseen and dysfunctional consequences, because individuals responded in personal ways to organizational stimuli. These studies helped to reveal the dynamic—as opposed to static—nature of organizations and provided a framework for further exploration of the impact of systems on individuals and, more importantly, the impact of individuals on systems.

As we mentioned earlier, Herbert Simon and his associates at the Carnegie Institute of Technology (now, Carnegie-Mellon University) also were major developers of theories of organizational decision making. Simon was a firm believer that decision making should be the focus of a new "administrative science." For example, Simon (1947) asserted that organizational theory is, in fact, the theory of the bounded rationality of human beings who "satisfice" because they do not have the intellectual capacity to maximize. Simon (1960) also drew a distinction between "programmed" and "unprogrammed" organizational decisions and highlighted the importance of the distinction for management information systems. His work on administrative science and decision making went in two major directions: first, he was a pioneer in developing the "science" of improved organizational decision making through quantitive methods, such as operations research and computer technology. Secondly, and perhaps even more important, was his leadership in studying the processes by which administrative organizations make decisions. Herbert Simon's extensive contributions continue to influence the field of organization theory in the 1980s.

Two of Simon's colleagues at Carnegie Tech during the early 1960s, R. M. Cyert and James G. March, analyze the impact of power and politics on the establishment of organizational goals in "A Behavioral Theory of Organizational Objectives" (reprinted here). This was a perspective that did not receive serious attention from organizational theorists until the mid-1970s. Cyert and March discuss the formation and activation of coalitions, as well as negotiations to impose coalitions' demands on the organization.

The article subsequently was merged into their widely cited 1963 book *A Behavioral Theory of the Firm,* which postulated that corporations tended to "satisfice" rather than engage in economically rational profit-maximizing behavior.

The neoclassical school played a very important role in the evolution of organization theory. Its writers provided the intellectual and empirical impetus to break the classicalists' simplistic, mechanically oriented, monopolistic dominance of the field. Neoclassicalists also paved the way—opened the door—for the soon-to-follow explosions of thinking from the human relations, "modern" structural, systems, power and politics, and organizational culture perspectives of organizations.

References

CYERT, R. M., & MARCH, J. G. (1959). Behavioral theory of organizational objectives. In M. Haire (Ed.), *Modern organization theory* (pp. 76–90). New York: Wiley.

CYERT, R. M., & MARCH, J. G., (1963). *A behavioral theory of the firm.* Englewood Cliffs, NJ: Prentice-Hall.

DALTON, M. (1950, June). Conflicts between staff and line managerial officers. *American Sociological Review,* 342–351.

DALTON, M. (1959). *Men who manage.* New York: Wiley.

DURKHEIM, E. (1947). *The division of labor in society.* George Simpson (Trans). New York: Free Press. (Original work published 1893)

ETZIONI, A. (1961). *A comparative analysis of complex organizations.* New York: Free Press.

GORDON, C. W., & BABCHUK, N. (1959). A typology of voluntary associations. *American Sociological Review, 24,* 22–29.

GOULDNER, A. W. (1954). *Patterns of industrial democracy.* Glencoe, IL: Free Press.

MARCH, J. G., & SIMON, H. A. (1958). *Organizations.* New York: Wiley.

MERTON, R. K., (1940). Bureaucratic structure and personality. *Social Forces, 18,* 560–568.

OTT, J. S. (1989). *The organizational culture perspective.* Pacific Grove, CA: Brooks/Cole.

PARSONS, T. (1956, June). Suggestions for a sociological approach to the theory of organizations. *Administrative Science Quarterly, 1,* 63–85.

PEDERSEN, J. S., & SORENSEN, J. S. (1989). *Organisational cultures in theory and practice.* Aldershot, UK: Gower Publishing Company.

SELZNICK, P. (1948). Foundations of the theory of organization. *American Sociological Review, 13,* 25–35.

SELZNICK, P. (1949). *TVA and the grass roots.* Berkeley, CA: University of California Press.

SIEHL, C., & MARTIN, J. (1984). The role of symbolic management: How can managers effectively transmit organizational culture? In J. G. Hunt, D. M. Hosking, C. A. Schriesheim, & R. Stewart (Eds.), *Leaders and managers* (pp. 227–269). New York: Pergamon Press.

SIMON, H. A. (1946, Winter). The proverbs of administration. *Public Administration Review, 6,* 53–67.

SIMON, H. A. (1947). *Administrative behavior.* New York: Macmillan.

SIMON, H. A. (1957). *Administrative behavior* (2nd ed.). New York: Macmillan.

SIMON, H. A. (1960). *The new science of management decisions.* New York: Harper & Row.

WALKER, W. E. (1986). *Changing organizational culture: Strategy, structure, and professionalism in the U. S. General Accounting Office.* Knoxville, TN: The University of Tennessee Press.

WHYTE, W. F. (1948). *Human relations in the restaurant business.* New York: McGraw-Hill.

WILKINS, A. A. (1983). Organizational stories as symbols which control the organization. In L. R. Pondy, P. J. Frost, G. Morgan, & T. C. Dandridge (Eds.), *Organizational symbolism* (pp. 93–107). Greenwich, CT: JAI Press.

WILKINS, A. A. (1989). *Developing corporate character.* San Francisco: Jossey-Bass.

10

The Proverbs of Administration

Herbert A. Simon

A fact about proverbs that greatly enhances their quotability is that they almost always occur in mutually contradictory pairs. "Look before you leap!"—but "He who hesitates is lost."

This is both a great convenience and a serious defect—depending on the use to which one wishes to put the proverbs in question. If it is a matter of rationalizing behavior that has already taken place or justifying action that has already been decided upon, proverbs are ideal. Since one is never at a loss to find one that will prove his point—or the precisely contradictory point, for that matter—they are a great help in persuasion, political debate, and all forms of rhetoric.

But when one seeks to use proverbs as the basis of a scientific theory, the situation is less happy. It is not that the propositions expressed by the proverbs are insufficient; it is rather that they prove too much. A scientific theory should tell what is true but also what is false. If Newton had announced to the world that particles of matter exert either an attraction or a repulsion on each other, he would not have added much to scientific knowledge. His contribution consisted in showing that an attraction was exercised and in announcing the precise law governing its operation.

SOURCE: Reprinted from *Public Administration Review* 6 (Winter 1946): 53–67. © 1946 by the American Society for Public Administration (ASPA), 1120 G Street NW, Suite 500, Washington, DC. All rights reserved. Footnotes renumbered.

Most of the propositions that make up the body of administrative theory today share, unfortunately, this defect of proverbs. For almost every principle one can find an equally plausible and acceptable contradictory principle. Although the two principles of the pair will lead to exactly opposite organizational recommendations, there is nothing in the theory to indicate which is the proper one to apply.[1]

It is the purpose of this paper to substantiate this sweeping criticism of administrative theory, and to present some suggestions—perhaps less concrete than they should be—as to how the existing dilemma can be solved.

Some Accepted Administrative Principles

Among the more common "principles" that occur in the literature of administration are these:

1. Administrative efficiency is increased by a specialization of the task among the group.
2. Administrative efficiency is increased by arranging the members of the group in a determinate hierarchy of authority.
3. Administrative efficiency is increased by limiting the span of control at any point in the hierarchy to a small number.
4. Administrative efficiency is increased by grouping the workers, for purposes of control, according to (*a*) purpose, (*b*) process, (*c*) clientele, or (*d*) place. (This is really an elaboration of the first principle but deserves separate discussion.)

Since these principles appear relatively simple and clear, it would seem that their application to concrete problems of administrative organization would be unambiguous and that their validity would be easily submitted to empirical test. Such, however, seems not to be the case. To show why it is not, each of the four principles just listed will be considered in turn.

Specialization. Administrative efficiency is supposed to increase with an increase in specialization. But is this intended to mean that *any* increase in specialization will increase efficiency? If so, which of the following alternatives is the correct application of the principle in a particular case?

1. A plan of nursing should be put into effect by which nurses will be assigned to districts and do all nursing within that district, including school examinations, visits to homes of school children, and tuberculosis nursing.
2. A functional plan of nursing should be put into effect by which different nurses will be assigned to school examinations, visits to homes of school children, and tuberculosis nursing. The present method of generalized nursing by districts impedes the development of specialized skills in the three very diverse programs.

Both of these administrative arrangements satisfy the requirement of specialization—the first provides specialization by place; the second, specialization by function. The principle of specialization is of no help at all in choosing between the two alternatives.

It appears that the simplicity of the principle of specialization is a deceptive simplicity—a simplicity which conceals fundamental ambiguities. For "specialization" is not a condition of efficient administration; it is an inevitable characteristic of all group effort, however efficient or inefficient that effort may be. Specialization merely means that different persons are doing different things—and since it is physically impossible for two persons to be doing the same thing in the same place at the same time, two persons are always doing different things.

The real problem of administration, then, is not to "specialize," but to specialize in that particular manner and along those particular lines which will lead to administrative efficiency. But, in thus rephrasing this "principle" of administration, there has been brought clearly into the open its fundamental ambiguity: "Administrative efficiency is increased by a specialization of the task among the group in the direction which will lead to greater efficiency."

Further discussion of the choice between competing bases of specialization will be undertaken after two other principles of administration have been examined.

Unity of command. Administrative efficiency is supposed to be enhanced by arranging the members of the organization in a determinate hierarchy of authority in order to preserve "unity of command."

Analysis of this "principle" requires a clear understanding of what is meant by the term "authority." A subordinate may be said to accept authority whenever he permits his behavior to be guided by a decision reached by another, irrespective of his own judgment as to the merits of that decision.

In one sense the principle of unity of command, like the principle of specialization, cannot be violated; for it is physically impossible for a man to obey two contradictory commands—that is what is meant by "contradictory commands." Presumably, if unity of command is a principle of administration, it must assert something more than this physical impossibility. Perhaps it asserts this: that it is undesirable to place a member of an organization in a position where he receives orders from more than one superior. This is evidently the meaning that Gulick attaches to the principle when he says,

> The significance of this principle in the process of co-ordination and organization must not be lost sight of. In building a structure of co-ordination, it is often tempting to set up more than one boss for a man who is doing work which has more than one relationship. Even as great a philosopher of management as Taylor fell into this error in setting up separate foremen to deal with machinery, with materials, with speed, etc., each with the power of giving orders directly to the individual workman. The rigid adherence to the principle of unity of command may have its absurdities; these are, however, unimportant in comparison with the certainty of confusion, inefficiency and irresponsibility which arise from the violation of the principle.[2]

Certainly the principle of unity of command, thus interpreted, cannot be criticized for any lack of clarity or any ambiguity. The definition of authority given above should provide a clear test whether, in any concrete situation, the principle is observed. The real fault that must be found with this principle is that it is incompatible with the principle of specialization. One of the most important uses to which authority is put in organization is to bring about specialization in the work of making decisions, so that each decision is made at a point in the organization where it can be made most expertly. As a result, the use of authority permits a greater degree of expertness to be achieved in decision making than would be possible if each operative employee had himself to make all the decisions upon which his activity is predicated. The individual fireman does not decide whether to use a two-inch hose or a fire extinguisher; that is decided for him by his officers, and the decision is communicated to him in the form of a command.

However, if unity of command, in Gulick's sense, is observed, the decisions of a person at any point in the administrative hierarchy are subject to influence through only one channel of authority; and if his decisions are of a kind that require expertise in more than one field of knowledge, then advisory and informational services must be relied upon to supply those premises which lie in a field not recognized by the mode of specialization in the organization. For example, if an accountant in a school department is subordinate to an educator, and if unity of command is observed, then the finance department cannot issue direct orders to him regarding the technical, accounting aspects of his work. Similarly, the director of motor vehicles in the public works department will be unable to issue direct orders on care of motor equipment to the fire-truck driver.[3]

Gulick, in the statement quoted above, clearly indicates the difficulties to be faced if unity of command is not observed. A certain amount of irresponsibility and confusion are almost certain to ensue. But perhaps this is not too great a price to pay for the increased expertise that can be applied to decisions. What is needed to decide the issue is a principle of administration that would enable one to weigh the relative advantages of the two courses of action. But neither the principle of unity of command nor the principle of specialization is helpful in adjudicating the controversy. They merely contradict each other without indicating any procedure for resolving the contradiction. . . .

The principle of unity of command is perhaps more defensible if narrowed down to the following: In case two authoritative commands conflict, there should be a single determinate person whom the subordinate is expected to obey; and the sanctions of authority should be applied against the subordinate only to enforce his obedience to that one person.

If the principle of unity of command is more defensible when stated in this limited form, it also solves fewer problems. In the first place, it no longer requires, except for settling conflicts of authority, a single hierarchy of authority. Consequently, it leaves unsettled the very important question of how authority should be zoned in a particular organization (i.e., the modes of specialization) and through what channels it should be exercised. Finally, even this narrower concept of unity of command conflicts with the principle of specialization, for whenever disagreement does occur and the organization members revert to the formal lines of authority, then only those types of specialization which are represented in the hierarchy of authority can impress themselves on decisions. If the training officer of a city exercises only functional supervisions over the police training officer, then in case of disagreement with the police chief, specialized knowledge of training problems will be subordinated or ignored. That this actually occurs is shown by the frustration so commonly expressed by functional supervisors at their lack of authority to apply sanctions.

Span of control. Administrative efficiency is supposed to be enhanced by limiting the number of subordinates who report directly to any one administrator to a small number—say six. This notion that the "span of control" should be narrow is confidently asserted as a third incontrovertible principle of administration. The usual common-sense arguments for restricting the span of control are familiar and need not be repeated here. What is not so generally recognized is that a contradictory proverb of administration can be stated which, though it is not so familiar as the principle of span of control, can be supported by arguments of equal plausibility. The proverb in question is the following: Administrative efficiency is enhanced by keeping at a minimum the number of organizational levels through which a matter must pass before it is acted upon.

This latter proverb is one of the fundamental criteria that guide administrative analysis in procedures simplification work. Yet in many situations the results to which this principle leads are in direct contradiction to the requirements of the principle of span of control, the principle of unity of command, and the principle of specialization. The present discussion is concerned with the first of these conflicts. To illustrate the difficulty, two alternative proposals for the organization of a small health department will be presented—one based on the restriction of span of control, the other on the limitation of number of organization levels:

1. The present organization of the department places an administrative overload on the health officer by reason of the fact that all eleven employees of the department report directly to him and the further fact that some of the staff lack adequate technical training. Consequently, venereal disease clinic treatments and other details require an undue amount of the health officer's personal attention.

It has previously been recommended that the proposed medical officer be placed in charge of the venereal disease and chest clinics and all child hygiene work. It is further recommended that one of the inspectors be designated chief inspector and placed in charge of all the department's inspectional activities and that one of the nurses be designated as head nurse. This will relieve the health commissioner of considerable detail and will leave him greater freedom to plan and supervise the health program as a whole, to conduct health education, and to coordinate the work of the department with that of other community agencies. If the department were thus organized, the effectiveness of all employees could be substantially increased.

2. The present organization of the department leads to inefficiency and excessive red tape by reason of the fact that an unnecessary supervisory level intervenes between the health officer and the operative employees, and that those four of the twelve employees who are best trained technically are engaged largely in "overhead" administrative duties. Consequently, unnecessary delays occur in securing the approval of the health officer on matters requiring his attention, and too many matters require review and re-review.

The medical officer should be left in charge of the venereal disease and chest clinics and child hygiene work. It is recommended, however, that the position of chief inspector and head nurse be abolished and that the employees now filling these positions perform regular inspectional and nursing duties. The details of work scheduling now handled by these two employees can be taken care of more economically by the secretary to the health officer, and, since broader matters of policy have, in any event, always required the personal attention of the health officer, the abolition of these two positions will eliminate a wholly unnecessary step in review, will allow an expansion of inspectional and nursing services, and will permit at least a beginning to be made in the recommended program of health education. The number of persons reporting directly to the health officer will be increased to nine, but since there are few matters requiring the coordination of these employees, other than the work schedules and policy questions referred to above, this change will not materially increase his work load.

The dilemma is this: in a large organization with complex interrelations between members, a restricted span of control inevitably produces excessive red tape, for each contact between organization members must be carried upward until a common superior is found. If the organization is at all large, this will involve carrying all such matters upward through several levels of officials for decision and then downward again in the form of orders and instructions—a cumbersome and time-consuming process.

The alternative is to increase the number of persons who are under the command of each officer, so that the pyramid will come more rapidly to a peak, with fewer intervening levels. But this, too, leads to difficulty, for if an officer is required to supervise too many employees, his control over them is weakened.

If it is granted, then, that both the increase and the decrease in span of control has some undesirable consequences, what is the optimum point? Proponents of a restricted span of control have suggested three, five, even eleven, as suitable numbers, but nowhere have they explained the reasoning which led them to the particular number they selected. The principle as stated casts no light on this very crucial question. One is reminded of current arguments about the proper size of the national debt.

Organization by purpose, process, clientele, place. Administrative efficiency is supposed to be increased by grouping workers according to (*a*) purpose, (*b*) process, (*c*) clientele, or (*d*) place. But from the discussion of specialization it is clear that this principle is internally inconsistent; for purpose, process, clientele, and place are competing bases of organization, and at any given point of division the advantages of three must be sacrificed to secure the advantages of the fourth. If the major departments of a city, for example, are organized on the basis of major purpose, then it follows that all the physicians, all the lawyers, all the engineers, all the statisticians will not be located in a single department exclusively composed of members of their profession but will be distributed among the various city departments needing their services. The advantages of organization by process will thereby be partly lost.

Some of these advantages can be regained by organizing on the basis of process *within*

the major departments. Thus there may be an engineering bureau within the public works department, or the board of education may have a school health service as a major division of its work. Similarly, within small units there may be division by area or by clientele: e.g., a fire department will have separate companies located throughout the city, while a welfare department may have intake and case work agencies in various locations. Again, however, these major types of specialization cannot be simultaneously achieved, for at any point in the organization it must be decided whether specialization at the next level will be accomplished by distinction of major purpose, major process, clientele, or area.

The conflict may be illustrated by showing how the principle of specialization according to purpose would lead to a different result from specialization according to clientele in the organization of a health department.

1. Public health administration consists of the following activities for the prevention of disease and the maintenance of healthful conditions: (1) vital statistics; (2) child hygiene—prenatal, maternity, postnatal, infant, preschool, and school health programs; (3) communicable disease control; (4) inspection of milk, foods, and drugs; (5) sanitary inspection; (6) laboratory service; (7) health education.

One of the handicaps under which the health department labors is the fact that the department has no control over school health, that being an activity of the county board of education, and there is little or no coordination between that highly important part of the community health program and the balance of the program which is conducted by the city-county health unit. It is recommended that the city and county open negotiations with the board of education for the transfer of all school health work and the appropriation therefor to the joint health unit. . . .

2. To the modern school department is entrusted the care of children during almost the entire period that they are absent from the parental home. It has three principal responsibilities toward them: (1) to provide for their

education in useful skills and knowledge and in character; (2) to provide them with wholesome play activities outside school hours; (3) to care for their health and to assure the attainment of minimum standards of nutrition.

One of the handicaps under which the school board labors is the fact that, except for school lunches, the board has no control over child health and nutrition, and there is little or no coordination between that highly important part of the child development program and the balance of the program which is conducted by the board of education. It is recommended that the city and county open negotiations for the transfer of all health work for children of school age to the board of education.

Here again is posed the dilemma of choosing between alternative, equally plausible, administrative principles. But this is not the only difficulty in the present case, for a closer study of the situation shows there are fundamental ambiguities in the meanings of the key terms— "purpose," "process," "clientele," and "place."

"Purpose" may be roughly defined as the objective or end for which an activity is carried on; "process" as a means for accomplishing a purpose. Processes, then, are carried on in order to achieve purposes. But purposes themselves may generally be arranged in some sort of hierarchy. A typist moves her fingers in order to type; types in order to reproduce a letter, reproduces a letter in order that an inquiry may be answered. Writing a letter is then the purpose for which the typing is performed; while writing a letter is also the process whereby the purpose of replying to an inquiry is achieved. It follows that the same activity may be described as purpose or as process.

This ambiguity is easily illustrated for the case of an administrative organization. A health department conceived as a unit whose task it is to care for the health of the community is a purpose organization; the same department conceived as a unit which makes use of the medical arts to carry on its work is a process organization. In the same way, an education department may be viewed as a purpose (to

educate) organization, or a clientele (children) organization; the forest service as a purpose (forest conservation), process (forest management), clientele (lumbermen and cattlemen utilizing public forests), or area (publicly owned forest lands) organization. When concrete illustrations of this sort are selected, the lines of demarcation between these categories become very hazy and unclear indeed.

"Organization by major purpose," says Gulick, ". . . serves to bring together in a single large department all of those who are at work endeavoring to render a particular service."[4] But what is a particular service? Is fire protection a single purpose, or is it merely a part of the purpose of public safety?—or is it a combination of purposes including fire prevention and fire fighting? It must be concluded that there is no such thing as a purpose, or a unifunctional (single-purpose) organization. What is to be considered a single function depends entirely on language and techniques.[5] If the English language has a comprehensive term which covers both of two subpurposes it is natural to think of the two together as a single purpose. If such a term is lacking, the two subpurposes become purposes in their own right. On the other hand, a single activity may contribute to several objectives, but since they are technically (procedurally) inseparable, the activity is considered a single function or purpose.

The fact, mentioned previously, that purposes form a hierarchy, each subpurpose contributing to some more final and comprehensive end, helps to make clear the relation between purpose and process. "Organization by major process," says Gulick, ". . . tends to bring together in a single department all of those who are at work making use of a given special skill or technology, or are members of a given profession."[6] Consider a simple skill of this kind—typing. Typing is a skill which brings about a means-end coordination of muscular movements, but a very low level in the means-end hierarchy. The content of the typewritten letter is indifferent to the skill that produces it. The skill consists merely in the ability to hit the letter "*t*" quickly whenever the letter "*t*" is required by the content and to hit the letter "*a*" whenever the letter "*a*" is required by the content.

There is, then, no essential difference between a "purpose" and a "process," but only a distinction of degree. A "process" is an activity whose immediate purpose is at a low level in the hierarchy of means and ends, while a "purpose" is a collection of activities whose orienting value or aim is at a high level in the means-end hierarchy.

Next consider "clientele" and "place" as bases of organization. These categories are really not separate from purpose, but a part of it. A complete statement of the purpose of a fire department would have to include the area served by it: "to reduce fires losses on property in the city of X." Objectives of an administrative organization are phrased in terms of a service to be provided and an area for which it is provided. Usually, the term "purpose" is meant to refer only to the first element, but the second is just as legitimately an aspect of purpose. Area of service, of course, may be a specified clientele quite as well as a geographical area. In the case of an agency which works on "shifts," time will be a third dimension of purpose—to provide a given service in a given area (or to a given clientele) during a given time period.

With this clarification of terminology, the next task is to reconsider the problem of specializing the work of an organization. It is no longer legitimate to speak of a "purpose" organization, a "process" organization, a "clientele" organization, or an "area" organization. The same unit might fall into any one of these four categories, depending on the nature of the larger organizational unit of which it was a part. A unit providing public health and medical services for school-age children in Multnomah County might be considered (1) an "area" organization if it were part of a unit providing the same service for the state of Oregon; (2) a "clientele" organization if it were part of a unit providing similar services for children of all ages; (3) a "purpose" or a "process" organization (it would be impossible to say which) if it were part of an education department.

It is incorrect to say that Bureau A is a process bureau; the correct statement is that Bureau A is a process bureau *within* Department X.[7] This latter statement would mean that Bureau A incorporates all the processes of a certain kind in Department X, without reference to any special subpurposes, subareas, or subclientele of Department X. Now it is conceivable that a particular unit might incorporate all processes of a certain kind but that these processes might relate to only certain particular subpurposes of the department purpose. In this case, which corresponds to the health unit in an education department mentioned above, the unit would be specialized by both purpose and process. The health unit would be the only one in the education department using the medical art (process) and concerned with health (subpurpose).

Even when the problem is solved of proper usage for the terms "purpose," "process," "clientele," and "area," the principles of administration give no guide as to which of these four competing bases of specialization is applicable in any particular situation. The British Machinery of Government Committee had no doubts about the matter. It considered purpose and clientele as the two possible bases of organization and put its faith entirely in the former. Others have had equal assurance in choosing between purpose and process. The reasoning which leads to these unequivocal conclusions leaves something to be desired. The Machinery of Government Committee gives this sole argument for its choice:

Now the inevitable outcome of this method of organization [by clientele] is a tendency to Lilliputian administration. It is impossible that the specialized service which each Department has to render to the community can be of as high a standard when its work is at the same time limited to a particular class of persons and extended to every variety of provision for them, as when the Department concentrates itself on the provision of the particular service only by whomsoever required, and looks beyond the interest of comparatively small classes.[8]

The faults in this analysis are obvious. First, there is no attempt to determine how a service is to be recognized. Second, there is a bald assumption, absolutely without proof, that a child health unit, for example, in a department of child welfare could not offer services of "as high a standard" as the same unit if it were located in a department of health. Just how the shifting of the unit from one department to another would improve or damage the quality of its work is not explained. Third, no basis is set forth for adjudicating the competing claims of purpose and process—the two are merged in the ambiguous term "service." It is not necessary here to decide whether the committee was right or wrong in its recommendation; the important point is that the recommendation represented a choice, without any apparent logical or empirical grounds, between contradictory principles of administration. . . .

These contradictions and competitions have received increasing attention from students of administration during the past few years. For example, Gulick, Wallace, and Benson have stated certain advantages and disadvantages of the several modes of specialization, and have considered the conditions under which one or the other mode might best be adopted.[9] All this analysis has been at a theoretical level—in the sense that data have not been employed to demonstrate the superior effectiveness claimed for the different modes. But though theoretical, the analysis has lacked a theory. Since no comprehensive framework has been constructed within which the discussion could take place, the analysis has tended either to the logical one-sidedness which characterizes the examples quoted above or to inconclusiveness.

The impasse of administrative theory. The four "principles of administration" that were set forth at the beginning of this paper have now been subjected to critical analysis. None of the four survived in very good shape, for in each case there was found, instead of an unequivocal principle, a set of two or more mutually incompatible principles apparently equally applicable to the administrative situation.

Moreover, the reader will see that the very same objections can be urged against the customary discussions of "centralization" versus "decentralization," which usually conclude, in effect, that "on the one hand, centralization of decision-making functions are desirable; on the other hand, there are definite advantages in decentralization."

Can anything be salvaged which will be useful in the construction of an administrative theory? As a matter of fact, almost everything can be salvaged. The difficulty has arisen from treating as "principles of administration" what are really only criteria for describing and diagnosing administrative situations. Closet space is certainly an important item in the design of a successful house; yet a house designed entirely with a view to securing a maximum of closet space—all other considerations being forgotten —would be considered, to say the least, somewhat unbalanced. Similarly, unity of command, specialization by purpose, and decentralization are all items to be considered in the design of an efficient administrative organization. No single one of these items is of sufficient importance to suffice as a guiding principle for the administrative analyst. In the design of administrative organizations, as in their operation, overall efficiency must be the guiding criterion. Mutually incompatible advantages must be balanced against each other, just as an architect weighs the advantages of additional closet space against the advantages of a larger living room.

This position, if it is a valid one, constitutes an indictment of much current writing about administrative matters. As the examples cited in this chapter amply demonstrate, much administrative analysis proceeds by selecting a single criterion and applying it to an administrative situation to reach a recommendation; while the fact that equally valid, but contradictory, criteria exist which could be applied with equal reason, but with a different result, is conveniently ignored. A valid approach to the study of administration requires that *all* the relevant diagnostic criteria be identified; that each administrative situation be analyzed in terms of the entire set of criteria; and that research be instituted to determine how weights can be assigned to the several criteria when they are, as they usually will be, mutually incompatible.

An Approach to Administrative Theory

This program needs to be considered step by step. First, what is included in the description of administrative situations for purposes of such an analysis? Second, how can weights be assigned to the various criteria to give them their proper place in the total picture?

The description of administrative situations. Before a science can develop principles, it must possess concepts. Before a law of gravitation could be formulated, it was necessary to have the notions of "acceleration" and "weight." The first task of administrative theory is to develop a set of concepts that will permit the description in terms relevant to the theory of administrative situations. These concepts, to be scientifically useful, must be operational; that is, their meanings must correspond to empirically observable facts or situations. The definition of *authority* given earlier in this paper is an example of an operational definition.

What is a scientifically relevant description of an organization? It is a description that, so far as possible, designates for each person in the organization what decisions that person makes and the influences to which he is subject in making each of these decisions. Current descriptions of administrative organizations fall far short of this standard. For the most part, they confine themselves to the allocation of *functions* and the formal structure of *authority*. They give little attention to the other types of organizational influence or to the system of communications. . . .[10]

Consider the term "centralization." How is it determined whether the operations of a particular organization are "centralized" or "decentralized"? Does the fact that field offices exist prove anything about decentralization?

Might not the same decentralization take place in the bureaus of a centrally located office? A realistic analysis of centralization must include a study of the allocation of decisions in the organization and the methods of influence that are employed by the higher levels to affect the decisions at the lower levels. Such an analysis would reveal a much more complex picture of the decision-making process than any enumeration of the geographical locations of organizational units at the different levels.

Administrative description suffers currently from superficiality, oversimplification, lack of realism. It had confined itself too closely to the mechanism of authority and has failed to bring within its orbit the other, equally important, modes of influence on organizational behavior. It has refused to undertake the tiresome task of studying the actual allocation of decision-making functions. It has been satisfied to speak of "authority," "centralization," "span of control," "function," without seeking operational definitions of these terms. Until administrative description reaches a higher level of sophistication, there is little reason to hope that rapid progress will be made toward the identification and verification of valid administrative principles.

Does this mean that a purely formal description of an administrative organization is impossible—that a relevant description must include an account of the content of the organization's decisions? This is a question that is almost impossible to answer in the present state of knowledge of administrative theory. One thing seems certain: content plays a greater role in the application of administrative principles than is allowed for in the formal administrative theory of the present time. This is a fact that is beginning to be recognized in the literature of administration. If one examines the chain of publications extending from Mooney and Reilley, through Gulick and the President's Committee controversy, to Schuyler Wallace and Benson, he sees a steady shift of emphasis from the "principles of administration" themselves to a study of the *conditions* under which competing principles are respectively applicable. Recent publications seldom say that "organization should be by purpose," but rather that "under such and such conditions purpose organization is desirable." It is to these conditions which underlie the application of the proverbs of administration that administrative theory and analysis must turn in their search for really valid principles to replace the proverbs.

The diagnosis of administrative situations. Before any positive suggestions can be made, it is necessary to digress a bit and to consider more closely the exact nature of the propositions of administrative theory. The theory of administration is concerned with how an organization should be constructed and operated in order to accomplish its work efficiently. A fundamental principle of administration, which follows almost immediately from the rational character of "good" administration, is that among several alternatives involving the same expenditure that one should always be selected which leads to the greatest accomplishment of administrative objectives; and among several alternatives that lead to the same accomplishment that one should be selected which involves the least expenditure. Since this "principle of efficiency" is characteristic of any activity that attempts rationally to maximize the attainment of certain ends with the use of scarce means, it is as characteristic of economic theory as it is of administrative theory. The "administrative man" takes his place alongside the classical "economic man."[11]

Actually, the "principle" of efficiency should be considered a definition rather than a principle: it is a definition of what is meant by "good" or "correct" administrative behavior. It does not tell *how* accomplishments are to be maximized, but merely states that this maximization is the aim of administrative activity, and that administrative theory must disclose under what conditions the maximization takes place.

Now what are the factors that determine the level of efficiency which is achieved by an administrative organization? It is not possible to make an exhaustive list of these but the principal categories can be enumerated. Perhaps the simplest method of approach is to consider the single member of the administrative organization and ask what the limits are to the quantity and quality of his output. These limits include (a) limits on his ability to perform and (b) limits on his ability to make correct decisions. To the extent that these limits are removed, the administrative organization approaches its goal of high efficiency. Two persons, given the same skills, the same objectives and values, the same knowledge and information, can rationally decide only upon the same course of action. Hence, administrative theory must be interested in the factory that will determine with what skills, values, and knowledge the organization member undertakes his work. These are the "limits" to rationality with which the principles of administration must deal.

On one side, the individual is limited by those skills, habits, and reflexes which are no longer in the realm of the conscious. His performance, for example, may be limited by his manual dexterity or his reaction time or his strength. His decision-making processes may be limited by the speed of his mental processes, his skill in elementary arithmetic, and so forth. In this area, the principles of administration must be concerned with the physiology of the human body and with the laws of skill-training and of habit. This is the field that has been most successfully cultivated by the followers of Taylor and in which has been developed time-and-motion study and the therblig.

On a second side, the individual is limited by his values and those conceptions of purpose which influence him in making decisions. If his loyalty to the organization is high, his decisions may evidence sincere acceptance of the objectives set for the organization; if that loyalty is lacking, personal motives may interfere with his administrative efficiency. If his loyalties are attached to the bureau by which he is employed, he may sometimes make decisions that are inimical to the larger unit of which the bureau is a part. In this area the principles of administration must be concerned with the determinants of loyalty and morale, with leadership and initiative, and with the influences that determine where the individual's organizational loyalties will be attached.

On a third side, the individual is limited by the extent of his knowledge of things relevant to his job. This applies both to the basic knowledge required in decision-making—a bridge designer must know the fundamentals of mechanics—and to the information that is required to make his decisions appropriate to the given situation. In this area, administrative theory is concerned with such fundamental questions as these: What are the limits on the mass of knowledge that human minds can accumulate and apply? How rapidly can knowledge be assimilated? How is specialization in the administrative organization to be related to the specializations of knowledge that are prevalent in the community's occupational structure? How is the system of communication to channel knowledge and information to the appropriate decision-points? What types of knowledge can, and what types cannot, be easily transmitted? How is the need for intercommunication of information affected by the modes of specialization in the organization? This is perhaps the *terra incognita* of administrative theory, and undoubtedly its careful exploration will cast great light on the proper application of the proverbs of administration.

Perhaps this triangle of limits does not completely bound the area of rationality, and other sides need to be added to the figure. In any case, this enumeration will serve to indicate the kinds of considerations that must go into the construction of valid and noncontradictory principles of administration.

An important fact to be kept in mind is that the limits of rationality are variable limits. Most important of all, consciousness of the limits may in itself alter them. Suppose it were discovered in a particular organization, for example, that organizational loyalties attached to small units had frequently led to a harmful degree of intra-organizational competition. Then, a program which trained members of the organization to be conscious of their loyalties, and to subordinate loyalties to the smaller group to those of the large, might lead to a very considerable alteration of the limits in that organization.[12]

A related point is that the term "rational behavior" as employed here, refers to rationality when that behavior is evaluated in terms of the objectives of the larger organization; for, as just pointed out, the difference in direction of the individual's aims from those of the larger organization is just one of those elements of nonrationality with which the theory must deal.

A final observation is that, since administrative theory is concerned with the nonrational limits of the rational, it follows that the larger the area in which rationality has been achieved the less important is the exact form of the administrative organization. For example, the function of plan preparation, or design, if it results in a written plan that can be communicated interpersonally without difficulty, can be located almost anywhere in the organization without affecting results. All that is needed is a procedure whereby the plan can be given authoritative status, and this can be provided in a number of ways. A discussion, then, of the proper location for a planning or designing unit is apt to be highly inconclusive and is apt to hinge on the personalities in the organization and their relative enthusiasm, or lack of it, toward the planning function rather than upon any abstract principles of good administration.[13]

On the other hand, when factors of communication or faiths or loyalty are crucial to the making of a decision, the location of the decision in the organization is of great importance. The method of allocating decisions in the army, for instance, automatically provides (at least in the period prior to the actual battle) that each decision will be made where the knowledge is available for coordinating it with other decisions.

Assigning weights to the criteria. A first step, then, in the overhauling of the proverbs of administration is to develop a vocabulary, along the lines just suggested, for the description of administrative organization. A second step, which has also been outlined, is to study the limits of rationality in order to develop a complete and comprehensive enumeration of the criteria that must be weighed in evaluating an administrative organization. The current proverbs represent only a fragmentary and unsystematized portion of these criteria.

When these two tasks have been carried out, it remains to assign weights to the criteria. Since the criteria, or "proverbs," are often mutually competitive or contradictory, it is not sufficient merely to identify them. Merely to know, for example, that a specified change in organization will reduce the span of control is not enough to justify the change. This gain must be balanced against the possible resulting loss of contact between the higher and lower ranks of the hierarchy.

Hence, administrative theory must also be concerned with the question of the weights that are to be applied to these criteria—to the problems of their relative importance in any concrete situation. This question is not one that can be solved in a vacuum. Arm-chair philosophizing about administration—of which the present paper is an example—has gone about as far as it can profitably go in this particular direction. What is needed now is empirical research and experimentation to determine the relative desirability of alternative administrative arrangements.

The methodological framework for this research is already at hand in the principle of efficiency. If an administrative organization whose activities are susceptible to objective evaluation be subjected to study, then the actual change in accomplishment that results from modifying administrative arrangements in these organizations can be observed and analyzed.

There are two indispensable conditions to successful research along these lines. First, it is necessary that the objectives of the administrative organization under study be defined in concrete terms so that results, expressed in terms of these objectives, can be accurately measured. Second, it is necessary that sufficient experimental control be exercised to make possible the isolation of the particular effect under study from other disturbing factors that might be operating on the organization at the same time.

These two conditions have seldom been even partially fulfilled in so-called "administrative experiments." The mere fact that a legislature passes a law creating an administrative agency, that the agency operates for five years, that the agency is finally abolished, and that a historical study is then made of the agency's operations is not sufficient to make of that agency's history an "administrative experiment." Modern American legislation is full of such "experiments" which furnish orators in neighboring states with abundant ammunition when similar issues arise in their bailiwicks, but which provide the scientific investigator with little or nothing in the way of objective evidence, one way or the other. . . .

Perhaps the program outlined here will appear an ambitious or even a quixotic one. There should certainly be no illusions, in undertaking it, as to the length and deviousness of the path. It is hard to see, however, what alternative remains open. Certainly neither the practitioner of administration nor the theoretician can be satisfied with the poor analytic tools that the proverbs provide him. Nor is there any reason to believe that a less drastic reconversion than that outlined here will rebuild those tools to usefulness.

It may be objected that administration cannot aspire to be a "science"; that by the nature of its subject it cannot be more than an "art." Whether true or false, this objection is irrelevant to the present discussion. The question of how "exact" the principles of administration can be made is one that only experience can answer. But as to whether they should be logical or illogical there can be no debate. Even an "art" cannot be founded on proverbs.

Notes

1. Lest it be thought that this deficiency is peculiar to the science—or "art"—of administration, it should be pointed out that the same trouble is shared by most Freudian psychological theories, as well as by some sociological theories.
2. Luther Gulick, "Notes on the Theory of Organization," in Luther Gulick and L. Urwick (eds.), *Papers on the Science of Administration* (Institute of Public Administration, Columbia University, 1937), p. 9.

3. This point is discussed in Herbert A. Simon, "Decision-Making and Administrative Organization," 4 *Public Administration Review* 20-21 (Winter, 1944).

4. Gulick and Urwick (eds.), *op. cit.,* p. 21.

5. If this is correct, then any attempt to prove that certain activities belong in a single department because they relate to a single purpose is doomed to fail. See, for example, John M. Gaus and Leon Wolcott, *Public Administration and the U.S. Department of Agriculture* (Public Administration Service, 1940).

6. *Op. cit.,* p. 23.

7. This distinction is implicit in most of Gulick's analysis of specialization. However, since he cites as examples single departments within a city, and since he usually speaks of "grouping activities" rather than "dividing work," the relative character of these categories is not always apparent in this discussion (*op. cit.,* pp. 15-30).

8. *Report of the Machinery of Government Committee* (H. M. Stationery Office, 1918).

9. Gulick, "Notes on the Theory of Organization," pp. 21-30; Schuyler Wallace, *Federal Departmentalization* (Columbia University Press, 1941); George C. S. Benson, "International Administrative Organization," 1 *Public Administration Review* 473-486 (Autumn, 1941).

10. The monograph by Macmahon, Millett, and Ogden, *op. cit.,* perhaps approaches nearer than any other published administrative study to the sophistication required in administrative description. See, for example, the discussion on pp. 233-236 of headquarters-field relationships.

11. For an elaboration of the principle of efficiency and its place in administrative theory see Clarence E. Ridley and Herbert A. Simon, *Measuring Municipal Activities* (International City Managers' Association, 2nd ed., 1943), particularly Chapter 1 and the preface to the second edition.

12. For an example of the use of such training, see Herbert A. Simon and William Divine, "Controlling Human Factors in an Administrative Experiment," 1 *Public Administration Review* 487-492 (Autumn, 1941).

13. See, for instance, Robert A. Walker, *The Planning Function in Urban Government* (University of Chicago Press, 1941), pp. 166-175. Walker makes out a strong case for attaching the planning agency to the chief executive. But he rests his entire case on the rather slender reed that "as long as the planning agency is outside the governmental structure . . . planning will tend to encounter resistance from public officials as an invasion of their responsibility and jurisdiction." This "resistance" is precisely the type of nonrational loyalty which has been referred to previously, and which is certainly a variable.

11

Foundations of the Theory of Organization

Philip Selznick

Trades unions, governments, business corporations, political parties, and the like are formal structures in the sense that they represent rationally ordered instruments for the achievement of stated goals. "Organization," we are told, "is the arrangement of personnel for facilitating the accomplishment of some agreed purpose through the allocation of functions and responsibilities."[1] Or, defined more generally, formal organization is "a system of consciously coordinated activities or forces of two or more persons."[2] Viewed in this light, formal organization is the structural expression of rational action. The mobilization of technical and managerial skills requires a pattern of coordination, a systematic ordering of positions and duties which defines a chain of command and makes possible the administrative integration of specialized functions. In this context *delegation* is the primordial organization act, a precarious venture which requires the continuous elaboration of formal mechanisms of coordination and control. The security of all participants, and of the system as a whole, generates a persistent pressure for the institutionalization of relationships, which are thus removed from the uncertainties of individual fealty or sentiment. Moreover, it is necessary for the relations within the structure to be

SOURCE: From *American Sociological Review* 13 (1948): 25–35. Copyright © 1948 American Sociological Association. Reprinted by permission.

determined in such a way that individuals will be interchangeable and the organization will thus be free of dependence upon personal qualities.[3] In this way, the formal structure becomes subject to calculable manipulation, an instrument of rational action.

But as we inspect these formal structures we begin to see that they never succeed in conquering the nonrational dimensions of organizational behavior. The latter remain at once indispensable to the continued existence of the system of coordination and at the same time the source of friction, dilemma, doubt, and ruin. This fundamental paradox arises from the fact that rational action systems are inescapably imbedded in an institutional matrix, in two significant senses: (1) the action system—or the formal structure of delegation and control which is its organizational expression—is itself only an aspect of a concrete social structure made up of individuals who may interact as *wholes,* not simply in terms of their formal roles within the system; (2) the formal system, and the social structure within which it finds concrete existence, are alike subject to the pressure of an institutional environment to which some overall adjustment must be made. The formal administrative design can never adequately or fully reflect the concrete organization to which it refers, for the obvious reason that no abstract plan or pattern can—or may, if it is to be useful—exhaustively describe an empirical totality. At the same time, that which is not included in the abstract design (as reflected, for example, in a staff-and-line organization chart) is vitally relevant to the maintenance and development of the formal system itself.

Organization may be viewed from two standpoints which are analytically distinct but which are empirically united in a context of reciprocal consequences. On the one hand, any concrete organizational system is an economy; at the same time, it is an adaptive social structure. Considered as an economy, organization is a system of relationships which define the availability of scarce resources *and* which may be manipulated in terms of efficiency and effectiveness. It is the economic aspect of organization which commands the attention of management technicians and, for the most part, students of public as well as private administration.[4] Such problems as the span of executive control, the role of staff or auxilary agencies, the relation of headquarters to field offices, and the relative merits of single or multiple executive boards are typical concerns of the science of administration. The coordinative scalar, and functional principles, as elements of the theory of organization, are products of the attempt to explicate the most general features of organization as a "technical problem" or, in our terms, as an economy.

Organization as an economy is, however, necessarily conditioned by the organic states of the concrete structure, outside of the systematics of delegation and control. This becomes especially evident as the attention of leadership is directed toward such problems as the legitimacy of authority and the dynamics of persuasion. It is recognized implicitly in action and explicitly in the work of a number of students that the possibility of manipulating the system of coordination depends on the extent to which that system is operating within an environment of effective inducement to individual participants and of conditions in which the stability of authority is assured. This is in a sense the fundamental thesis of Barnard's remarkable study, *The Functions of the Executive.* It is also the underlying hypothesis which makes it possible for Urwick to suggest that "proper" or formal channels in fact function to "confirm and record" decisions arrived at by more personal means.[5] We meet it again in the concept of administration as a process of education, in which the winning of consent and support is conceived to be a basic function of leadership.[6] In short, it is recognized that control and consent cannot be divorced even within formally authoritarian structures.

The indivisibility of control and consent makes it necessary to view formal organizations as *cooperative* systems, widening the frame of reference of those concerned with the manipulation of organizational resources. At the point of action, of executive decision, the economic aspect of organization provides inadequate tools for control over the concrete structure. This idea may be readily grasped if attention is directed to the role of the individual within the organizational economy. From the standpoint of organization as a formal system, persons are viewed functionally, in respect to their *roles,* as participants in assigned segments of the cooperative system. But in fact individuals have a propensity to resist depersonalization, to spill over the boundaries of their segmentary roles, to participate as *wholes.* The formal systems (at an extreme, the disposition of "rifles" at a military perimeter) cannot take account of the deviations thus introduced, and consequently break down as instruments of control when relied upon alone. The whole individual raises new problems for the organization, partly because of the needs of his own personality, partly because he brings with him a set of established habits as well, perhaps, as commitments to special groups outside of the organization.

Unfortunately for the adequacy of formal systems of coordination, the needs of individuals do not permit a singleminded attention to the stated goals of the system within which they have been assigned. The hazard inherent in the act of delegation derives essentially from this fact. Delegation is an organizational act, having to do with formal assignments to functions and powers. Theoretically, these assignments are made to roles or official positions, not to individuals as such. In fact, however, delegation necessarily involves concrete individuals who have interests and goals which do not always coincide with the goals of the formal system. As a consequence, individual personalities may offer resistance to the demands made upon them by the official conditions of delegation. These resistances are not accounted for within the categories of coordination and delegation, so that when they occur they must be considered as unpredictable and accidental. Observations of this type of situation within formal structures are sufficiently commonplace. A familiar example is that of delegation to a subordinate who is also required to train his own replacement. The subordinate may resist this demand in order to maintain unique access to the "mysteries" of the job, and thus insure his indispensability to the organization.

In large organizations, deviations from the formal system tend to become institutionalized, so that "unwritten laws" and informal associations are established. Institutionalization removes such deviations from the realm of personality differences, transforming them into a persistent structural aspect of formal organizations.[7] These institutionalized rules and modes of informal cooperation are normally attempts by participants in the formal organization to control the group relations which form the environment of organizational decisions. The informal patterns (such as cliques) arise spontaneously, are based on personal relationships, and are usually directed to the control of some specific situation. They may be generated anywhere within a hierarchy, often with deleterious consequences for the formal goals of the organization, but they may also function to widen the available resources of executive control and thus contribute to rather than hinder the achievement of the stated objectives of the organization. The deviations tend to force a shift away from the purely formal system as the effective determinant of behavior to (1) a condition in which informal patterns buttress the formal, as through the manipulation of sentiment within the organization in favor of established authority; or (2) a condition wherein the informal controls effect a consistent modification of formal goals, as in the case of some bureaucratic patterns.[8] This trend will eventually result in the formalization of erstwhile informal activities, with the cycle of deviation and transformation beginning again on a new level.

The relevance of informal structures to organizational analysis underlines the significance of conceiving of formal organizations as cooperative systems. When the totality of interacting groups and individuals becomes the object of inquiry, the latter is not restricted by formal, legal, or procedural dimensions. The *state of the system* emerges as a significant point of analysis, as when an internal situation charged with conflict qualifies and informs actions ostensibly determined by formal relations and objectives. A proper understanding of the organizational process must make it possible to interpret changes in the formal system—new appointments or rules or reorganizations—in their relation to the informal and unavowed ties of friendship, class loyalty, power cliques, or external commitment. This is what it means "to know the score." . . .

To recognize the sociological relevance of formal structures is not, however, to have constructed a theory of organization. It is important to set the framework of analysis, and much is accomplished along this line when, for example, the nature of authority in formal organizations is reinterpreted to emphasize the factors of cohesion and persuasion as against legal or coercive sources.[9] This redefinition is logically the same as that which introduced the conception of the self as social. The latter helps make possible, but does not of itself fulfill, the requirements for a dynamic theory of personality. In the same way, the definition of authority as conditioned by sociological factors of sentiment and cohesion—or more generally the definition of formal organizations as cooperative systems—only sets the stage, as an initial requirement, for the formulation of a theory of organization.

Structural-Functional Analysis

Cooperative systems are constituted of individuals interacting as wholes in relation to a formal system of coordination. The concrete structure is therefore a resultant of the reciprocal influences of the formal and informal aspects of organization. Furthermore, this structure is itself a totality, an adaptive "organism" reacting to influences upon it from an external environment. These considerations help to define the objects of inquiry; but to progress to a system of predicates *about* these objects it is necessary to set forth an analytical method which seems to be fruitful and significant. The method must have a relevance to empirical materials, which is to say, it must be more specific in its reference than discussions of the logic or methodology of social science.

The organon which may be suggested as peculiarly helpful in the analysis of adaptive structures has been referred to as "structural-functional analysis."[10] This method may be characterized in a sentence: *Structural-functional analysis relates contemporary and variable behavior to a presumptively stable system of needs and mechanisms.* This means that a given empirical system is deemed to have basic needs, essentially related to self-maintenance; the system develops repetitive means of self-defense; and day-to-day activity is interpreted in terms of the function served by that activity for the maintenance and defense of the system. Put thus generally, the approach is applicable on any level in which the determinate "states" of empirically isolable systems undergo self-impelled and repetitive transformations when impinged upon by external conditions. This self-impulsion suggests the relevance of the term "dynamic," which is often used in referring to physiological, psychological, or social systems to which this type of analysis has been applied.[11]

It is a postulate of the structural-functional approach that the basic need of all empirical systems is the maintenance of the integrity and continuity of the system itself. Of course, such a postulate is primarily useful in directing attention to a set of "derived imperatives" or needs which are sufficiently concrete to characterize the system at hand.[12] It is perhaps rash to attempt a catalogue of these imperatives for formal organizations, but some suggestive formulation is needed in the interests of setting forth the type of analysis under discussion. In formal organizations, the "maintenance of the system" as a generic need may be specified in terms of the following imperatives:

1. *The security of the organization as a whole in relation to social forces in its environment.* This imperative requires continuous attention to the possibilities of encroachment and to the forestalling of threatened aggressions or deleterious (though perhaps unintended) consequences from the actions of others.

2. *The stability of the lines of authority and communication.* One of the persistent reference-points of administrative decision is the weighing of consequences for the continued capacity of leadership to control and to have access to the personnel or ranks.

3. *The stability of informal relations within the organization.* Ties of sentiment and self-interest are evolved as unacknowledged but effective mechanisms of adjustment of individuals and subgroups to the conditions of life within the organization. These ties represent a cementing of relationships which sustains the formal authority in day-to-day operations and widens opportunities for effective communication.[13] Consequently, attempts to "upset" the informal structure, either frontally or as an indirect consequence of formal reorganization, will normally be met with considerable resistance.

4. *The continuity of policy and of the sources of its determination.* For each level within the organization, and for the organization as a whole, it is necessary that there be a sense that action taken in the light of a given policy will not be placed in continuous jeopardy. Arbitrary or unpredictable changes in policy undermine the significance of (and therefore the attention to) day-to-day action by injecting a note of capriciousness. At the same time, the organization will seek stable roots (or firm statutory authority or popular mandate) so that a sense of the permanency and legitimacy of its acts will be achieved.

5. *A homogeneity of outlook with respect to the meaning and role of the organization.* The minimization of disaffection requires a unity derived from a common understanding of what the character of the organization is meant to be. When this homogeneity breaks down, as in situations of internal conflict over basic issues,

the continued existence of the organization is endangered. On the other hand, one of the signs of "healthy" organization is the ability to effectively orient new members and readily slough off those who cannot be adapted to the established outlook.

This catalogue of needs cannot be thought of as final, but it approximates the stable system generally characteristic of formal organizations. These imperatives are derived, in the sense that they represent the conditions for survival or self-maintenance of cooperative systems of organized action. An inspection of these needs suggests that organizational survival is intimately connected with the struggle for relative prestige, both for the organization and for elements and individuals within it. It may therefore be useful to refer to a *prestige-survival motif* in organizational behavior as a shorthand way of relating behavior needs, especially when the exact nature of the needs remains in doubt. However, it must be emphasized that prestige-survival in organizations does not derive simply from like motives in individuals. Loyalty and self-sacrifice may be individual expressions of organizational or group egotism and self-consciousness.

The concept of organizational need directs analysis to the *internal relevance* of organizational behavior. This is especially pertinent with respect to discretionary action undertaken by agents manifestly in pursuit of formal goals. The question then becomes one of relating the specific act of discretion to some presumptively stable organizational need. In other words, it is not simply action plainly oriented internally (such as in-service training) but also action presumably oriented externally which must be inspected for its relevance to internal conditions. This is of prime importance for the understanding of bureaucratic behavior, for it is of the essence of the latter that action formally undertaken for substantive goals be weighed and transformed in terms of its consequences for the position of the officialdom. . . .

The setting of structural-functional analysis as applied to organizations requires some qualification, however. Let us entertain the suggestion that the interesting problem in social science is not so much why men act the way they do as why men in certain circumstances *must* act the way they do. This emphasis upon constraint, if accepted, releases us from an ubiquitous attention to behavior in general, and especially from any undue fixation upon statistics. On the other hand, it has what would seem to be salutary consequence of focusing inquiry upon certain necessary relationships of the type "if . . . then," for example: If the cultural level of the rank and file members of a formally democratic organization is below that necessary for participation in the formulation of policy, then there will be pressure upon the leaders to use the tools of demagogy.

Is such a statement universal in its applicability? Surely not in the sense that one can predict without remainder the nature of all or even most political groups in a democracy. Concrete behavior is a resultant, a complex vector, shaped by the operation of a number of such general constraints. But there is a test of general applicability: it is that of noting whether the relation made explicit must be *taken into account* in action. This criterion represents an empirical test of the significance of social generalizations. If a theory is significant it will state a relation which will either (1) be taken into account as an element of achieving control; or (2) be ignored only at the risk of losing control and will evidence itself in a ramification of objective or unintended consequences.[14] It is a corollary of this principle of significance that investigation must search out the underlying factors in organizational action, which requires a kind of intensive analysis of the same order as psychoanalytic probing.

A frame of reference which invites attention to the constraints upon behavior will tend to highlight tensions and dilemmas, the characteristic paradoxes generated in the course of action. The dilemma may be said to be the handmaiden of structural-functional analysis, for it introduces the concept of *commitment* or *involvement* as fundamental to organizational analysis. A dilemma in human behavior is represented by an inescapable commitment which cannot be reconciled with the needs of the organism or the social system. There are many spurious dilemmas which have to do with verbal contradictions, but inherent dilemmas to which we refer are of a more profound sort, for they reflect the basic nature of the empirical system in question. An economic order committed to profit as its sustaining incentive may, in Marxist terms, sow the seed of its own destruction. Again, the anguish of man, torn between finitude and pride, is not a matter of arbitrary and replaceable assumptions but is a reflection of the psychological needs of the human organism, and is concretized in his commitment to the institutions which command his life; he is in the world and of it, inescapably involved in its goals and demands; at the same time, the needs of the spirit are compelling, proposing modes of salvation which have continuously disquieting consequences for worldly involvements. In still another context, the need of the human organism for affection and response necessitates a commitment to elements of the culture which can provide them; but the rule of the super-ego is uncertain since it cannot be completely reconciled with the need for libidinal satisfaction. . . .

Organizational analysis, too, must find its selective principle; otherwise the indiscriminate attempts to relate activity functionally to needs will produce little in the way of significant theory. Such a principle might read as follows: *Our frame of reference is to select out those needs which cannot be fulfilled within approved avenues of expression and thus must have recourse to such adaptive mechanisms as ideology and to the manipulation of formal processes and structures in terms of informal goals.* This formulation has many difficulties, and is not presented as conclusive, but it suggests the kind of principle which is likely to separate the quick and the dead, the meaningful and the trite, in the study of cooperative systems in organized action.[15]

The frame of reference outlined here for the theory of organization may now be identified as involving the following major ideas: (1) the concept of organizations as cooperative systems, adaptive social structures, made up of interacting individuals, subgroups, and informal plus formal relationships; (2) structural-functional analysis, which relates variable aspects of organization (such as goals) to stable needs and self-defensive mechanisms; (3) the concept of recalcitrance as a quality of the tools of social action, involving a break in the continuum of adjustment and defining an environment of constraint, commitment, and tension. This frame of reference is suggested as providing a specifiable *area of relations* within which predicates in the theory of organization will be sought, and at the same time setting forth principles of selection and relevance in our approach to the data of organization.

It will be noted that we have set forth this frame of reference within the overall context of social action. The significance of events may be defined by their place and operational role in a means-end scheme. If functional analysis searches out the elements important for the maintenance of a given structure, and that structure is one of the materials to be manipulated in action, then that which is functional in respect to the structure is also functional in respect to the action system. This provides a ground for the significance of functionally derived theories. At the same time, relevance to control in action is the empirical test of their applicability or truth.

Co-optation as a Mechanism of Adjustment

The frame of reference stated above is in fact an amalgam of definition, resolution, and substantive theory. There is an element of *definition* on conceiving of formal organizations as cooperative systems, though of course the interaction of informal and formal patterns is a question of fact; in a sense, we are *resolving* to employ structural-functional analysis on the assumption that it will be fruitful to do so, though here, too, the specification of needs or derived imperatives is a matter for empirical inquiry; and out predication of recalcitrance as a quality of the tools of action is itself a *substantive theory,* perhaps fundamental to a general understanding of the nature of social action.

A theory of organization requires more than a general frame of reference, though the latter is indispensable to inform the approach of inquiry to any given set of materials. What is necessary is the construction of generalizations concerning transformations within and among cooperative systems. These generalizations represent, from the standpoint of particular cases, possible predicates which are relevant to the materials as we know them in general, but which are not necessarily controlling in all circumstances. A theory of transformations in organization would specify those states of the system which resulted typically in predictable, or at least understandable, changes in such aspects of organization as goals, leadership, doctrine, efficiency, effectiveness, and size. These empirical generalizations would be systematized as they were related to the stable needs of the cooperative system.

Changes in the characteristics of organizations may occur as a result of many different conditions, not always or necessarily related to the processes of organization as such. But the theory of organization must be selective, so that explanations of transformations will be sought within its own assumptions or frame of reference. Consider the question of size. Organizations may expand for many reasons—the availability of markets, legislative delegations, the swing of opinion—which may be accidental from the point of view of the organizational process. To explore changes in size (as of, say, a trades union) as related to changes in nonorganizational conditions may be necessitated by the historical events to be described, but it will not of itself advance the frontiers of the theory of organization. However, if "the innate propensity of all organizations to expand" is asserted as a function of "the inherent instability of incentives"[16] then transformations have been stated within the terms of the theory of organization itself. It is likely that in many cases the generalization in question

may represent only a minor aspect of the empirical changes, but these organizational relations must be made explicit if the theory is to receive development.

In a frame of reference which specifies needs and anticipates the formulation of a set of self-defensive responses or mechanisms, the latter appear to constitute one kind of empirical generalization or "possible predicate" within the general theory. The needs of organizations (whatever investigation may determine them to be) are posited as attributes of all organizations, but the responses to disequilibrium will be varied. The mechanisms used by the system in fulfillment of its needs will be repetitive and thus may be described as a specifiable set of assertions within the theory of organization, but any given organization may or may not have recourse to the characteristic modes of response. Certainly no given organization will employ all of the possible mechanisms which are theoretically available. When Barnard speaks of an "innate propensity of organization to expand," he is in fact formulating one of the general mechanisms, namely, expansion, which is a characteristic mode of response available to an organization under pressure from within. These responses necessarily involve a transformation (in this case, size) of some structural aspect of the organization.

Other examples of the self-defensive mechanisms available to organizations may derive primarily from the response of these organizations to the institutional environments in which they live. The tendency to construct ideologies, reflecting the need to come to terms with major social forces, is one such mechanism. Less well understood as a mechanism of organizational adjustment is what we may term *co-optation.* Some statement of the meaning of this concept may aid in clarifying the foregoing analysis.

Co-optation is the process of absorbing new elements into the leadership or policy-determining structure of an organization as a means of averting threats to its stability or existence. This is a defensive mechanism, formulated as one of a number of possible predicates available for the interpretation of organizational behavior. Co-optation tells us something about the process by which an institutional environment impinges itself upon an organization and effects changes in its leadership and policy. Formal authority may resort to co-optation under the following general conditions:

1. When there exists a hiatus between consent and control, so that the legitimacy of the formal authority is called into question. The "indivisibility" of consent and control refers, of course, to an optimum situation. Where control lacks an adequate measure of consent, it may revert to coercive measures or attempt somehow to win the consent of the governed. One means of winning consent is to co-opt elements into the leadership or organization, usually elements which in some way reflect the sentiment, or possess the confidence of the relevant public or mass. As a result, it is expected that the new elements will lend respectability or legitimacy to the organs of control and thus reestablish the stability of formal authority. This process is widely used, and in many different contexts. It is met in colonial countries, where the organs of alien control reaffirm their legitimacy by co-opting native leaders into the colonial administration. We find it in the phenomenon of "crisis-patriotism" wherein formally disfranchised groups are temporarily given representation in the councils of government in order to win their solidarity in a time of national stress. Co-optation is presently being considered by the United States Army in its study of proposals to give enlisted personnel representation in the court-martial machinery—a clearly adaptive response to stresses made explicit during the war, the lack of confidence in the administration of army justice. The "unity" parties of totalitarian states are another form of co-optation; company unions or some employee representation plans in industry are still another. In each of these cases, the response of formal authority (private or public, in a large organization or a small one) is an attempt to correct a state of imbalance by *formal* measures. It will be noted, moreover, that what is shared is the *responsibility* for power rather than power itself. These conditions define what we shall refer to as *formal co-optation.*

2. Co-optation may be a response to the pressure of specific centers of power. This is not necessarily a matter of legitimacy or of a general and diffuse lack of confidence. These may be well established; and yet organized forces which are able to threaten the formal authority may effectively shape its structure and policy. The organization in respect to its institutional environment—or the leadership in respect to its ranks—must take these forces into account. As a consequence, the outside elements may be brought into the leadership or policy-determining structure, may be given a place as a recognition of and consession to the resources they can independently command. The representation of interests through administrative constituencies is a typical example of this process. Or, within an organization, individuals upon whom the group is dependent for funds or other resources may insist upon and receive a share in the determination of policy. This form of cooperation is typically expressed in informal terms, for the problem is not one of responding to a state of imbalance with respect to the "people as a whole" but rather one of meeting the pressure of specific individuals or interest-groups which are in a position to enforce demands. The latter are interested in the substance of power and not its forms. Moreover, an open acknowledgement of capitulation to specific interests may itself undermine the sense of legitimacy of the formal authority within the community. Consequently, there is a positive pressure to refrain from explicit recognition of the relationship established. This form of the co-optative mechanism, having to do with the sharing of power as a response to specific pressures, may be termed *informal co-optation.*

Co-optation reflects a state of tension between formal authority and social power. The former is embodied in a particular structure and leadership, but the latter has to do with subjective and objective factors which control the loyalties and potential manipulability of the community. Where the formal authority is an expression of social power, its stability is assured. On the other hand, when it becomes divorced from the sources of social power its continued existence is threatened. This threat may arise from the sheer alienation of sentiment or from the fact that other leaderships have control over the sources of social power. Where a formal authority has been accustomed to the assumption that its constituents respond to it as individuals, there may be a rude awakening when organization of those constituents on a non-governmental basis creates nuclei of power which are able effectively to demand a sharing of power.[17]

The significance of co-optation for organizational analysis is not simply that there is a change in or a broadening of leadership, and that this is an adaptive response, but also that *this change is consequential for the character and role of the organization.* Co-optation involves commitment, so that the groups to which adaptation has been made constrain the field of choice available to the organization or leadership in question. The character of the co-opted elements will necessarily shape (inhibit or broaden) the modes of action available to the leadership which has won adaptation and security at the price of commitment. The concept of co-optation thus implicitly sets forth the major points of the frame of reference outlined above: it is an adaptive response of a cooperative system to a stable need, generating transformations which reflect constraints enforced by the recalcitrant tools of action.

Notes

1. John M. Gaus, "A Theory of Organization in Public Administration," in *The Frontiers of Public Administration* (Chicago: University of Chicago Press, 1936), p. 66.
2. Chester I. Barnard, *The Functions of the Executive* (Cambridge: Harvard University Press, 1938), p. 73.
3. Cf. Talcott Parsons' generalization (after Max Weber) of the "law of the increasing rationality of action systems," in *The Structure of Social Action* (New York: McGraw-Hill, 1937), p. 752.
4. See Luther Gulick and Lydall Urwick (editors), *Papers on the Science of Administration* (New York: Institute of Public Administration, Columbia University, 1937); Lydall Urwick, *The Elements of Administration* (New York, Harper, 1943); James D. Mooney and Alan C. Reiley, *The Principles of Organization* (New York: Harper, 1939); H. S. Dennison, *Organization Engineering* (New York: McGraw-Hill, 1931).
5. Urwick, *The Elements of Administration, op. cit.,* p. 47.
6. See Gaus, *op. cit.* Studies of the problem of morale are instances of the same orientation, having received considerable impetus in recent years from the work of the Harvard Business School group.
7. The creation of informal structures within various types of organizations has received explicit recognition in recent years. See F. J. Roethlisberger and W. J. Dickson, *Management and the Worker* (Cambridge: Harvard University Press, 1941), p. 524; also Barnard, *op. cit.,* c. ix; and Wilbert E. Moore, *Industrial Relations and the Social Order* (New York: Macmillan, 1946), chap. xv.
8. For an analysis of the latter in these terms, see Philip Selznick, "An Approach to a Theory of Bureaucracy," *American Sociological Review* 8 (February, 1943).
9. Robert Michels, "Authority," *Encyclopedia of the Social Sciences* (New York: Macmillan, 1931), pp. 319ff.; also Barnard, *op cit.,* c. xii.
10. For a presentation of this approach having a more general reference than the study of formal organizations, see Talcott Parsons, "The Present Position and Prospects of Systematic Theory in Sociology," in Georges Gurvitch and Wilbert E. Moore (ed.), *Twentieth Century Sociology* (New York: The Philosophical Library, 1945).
11. "Structure" refers to both the relationships within the system (formal plus informal patterns in organization) and the set of needs and modes of satisfaction which characterize the given type of empirical system. As the utilization of this type of analysis proceeds, the concept of "need" will require further clarification. In particular, the imputation of a "stable set of needs" to organizational systems must not function as a new instinct theory. At the same time,

we cannot avoid using these inductions as to generic needs, for they help us to stake out our area of inquiry. The author is indebted to Robert K. Merton who has, in correspondence, raised some important objections to the use of the term "need" in this context.

12. For "derived imperative" see Bronislaw Malinowski, *The Dynamics of Culture Change* (New Haven: Yale University Press, 1945), pp. 44ff. For the use of "need" in place of "motive" see the same author's *A Scientific Theory of Culture* (Chapel Hill: University of North Carolina Press, 1944), pp. 89–90.

13. They may also *destroy* those relationships, as noted above, but the need remains, generating one of the persistent dilemmas of leadership.

14. See R. M. MacIver's discussion of the "dynamic assessment" which "brings the external world selectively into the subjective realm, conferring on it subjective significance for the ends of action." *Social Causation* (Boston: Ginn, 1942), chaps. 11, 12. The analysis of this assessment within the context of organized action yields the implicit knowledge which guides the choice among alternatives. See also Robert K. Merton, "The Unanticipated Consequences of Purposive Social Action," *American Sociological Review* 1 (December, 1936).

15. This is not meant to deprecate the study of organizations as *economies* or formal systems. The latter represent an independent level, abstracted from organizational structures as cooperative or adaptive systems ("organisms").

16. Barnard, *op. cit.*, pp. 158–159.

17. It is perhaps useful to restrict the concept of co-optation to formal organizations, but in fact it probably reflects a process characteristic of all group leaderships. This has received some recognition in the analysis of class structure, wherein the ruling class is interpreted as protecting its own stability by absorbing new elements. Thus Michels made the point that "an aristocracy cannot maintain an enduring stability by sealing itself off hermetically." See Robert Michels, *Umschichtungen in den herrschenden Klassen nach dem Kriege* (Stuttgart: Kohlhammer, 1934), p. 39; also Gaetano Mosca, *The Ruling Class* (New York: McGraw-Hill, 1939), p. 413ff. The alliance or amalgamation of classes in the face of a common threat may be reflected in formal and informal co-optative responses among formal organizations sensitive to class pressures. In a forthcoming volume, *TVA and the Grass Roots,* the author has made extensive use of the concept of co-optation in analyzing some aspects of the organizational behavior of a government agency.

12

Theories of Bureaucracy

James G. March & Herbert A. Simon

Modern studies of "bureaucracies" date from Weber as to both time and acknowledged intellectual debt.[1] But, . . . his major interests in the study of organizations appear to have been four: (1) to identify the characteristics of an entity he labelled "bureaucracy"; (2) to describe its growth and the reasons for its growth; (3) to isolate the concomitant social changes; (4) to discover the consequences of bureaucratic organization for the achievement of bureaucratic goals (primarily the goals of a political authority). It is in the last-named interest that Weber most clearly differentiates himself from the other writers [discussed in the source]. Weber wishes to show to what extent bureaucratic organization is a rational solution to the complexities of modern problems. More specifically, he wishes to show in what ways bureaucratic organization overcomes the decision-making or "computational" limits of individuals or alternative forms of organization (*i.e.*, through specialization, division of labor, etc.).

Consequently, Weber appears to have more in common with Urwick, Gulick, and others than he does with those who regard themselves as his successors. To be sure, Weber goes beyond the "machine" model in significant ways. In particular, he analyzes in some detail the relation between an official and his office. But, in general, Weber perceives bureaucracy as

an adaptive device for using specialized skills, and he is not exceptionally attentive to the character of the human organism.

When we turn from Weber to the more recent students of bureaucracy, however, we find them paying increasing attention to the "unanticipated" responses of the organization members.[2] Without denying Weber's essential proposition that bureaucracies are more efficient (with respect to the goals of the formal hierarchy) than are alternative forms of organization, the research and analyses of Merton,[3] Selznick,[4] and Gouldner[5] have suggested important dysfunctional consequences of bureaucratic organization. In addition —explicitly in the case of Gouldner and implicitly in the other two authors—they have hypothesized that the unintended consequences of treating individuals as machines actually encourage a continued use of the "machine" model.

The general structure of the theoretical systems of all three writers is remarkably similar. They use as the basic independent variable some form of organization or organizational procedure designed to control the activities of the organization members. These procedures are based primarily on what we have called the machine model of human behavior. They are shown to have the consequences anticipated by the organizational leaders, but also to have other, unanticipated, consequences. In turn, these consequences reinforce the tendency to use the control device. Thus, the systems may be depicted as in Figure 1.

The several systems examined here posit different sets of variables and theoretical relations. However, their structures are sufficiently similar to suggest that these studies in "bureaucracy" belong to a single class of theories.

The Merton Model

Merton[6] is concerned with dysfunctional organizational learning: organization members generalize a response from situations where the

SOURCE: From James G. March and Herbert A. Simon, *Organizations*, 36–47. Copyright © 1958 John Wiley & Sons, Inc. Reprinted by permission of John Wiley & Sons, Inc. Footnotes renumbered.

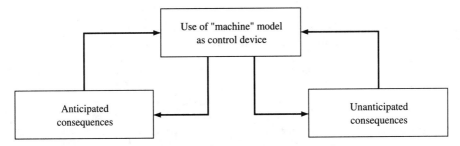

Figure 1
The General Bureaucracy Model

response is appropriate to similar situations where it results in consequences unanticipated and undesired by the organization. Merton asserts that changes in the personality of individual members of the organization stem from factors in the organizational structure. Here personality refers to any fairly reliable connection between certain stimuli and the characteristic responses to them. The label "personality" is attached to such a response pattern when the pattern does not change easily or rapidly.

Merton's system of propositions begins with a *demand for control* (3.1) made on the organization by the top hierarchy. This demand takes the form of an increased *emphasis on the reliability of behavior* (3.2) within the organization [3.2:3.1].[7] From the point of view of the top hierarchy, this represents a need for accountability and predictability of behavior. The techniques used to secure reliability draw upon what has been called here the "machine" model of human behavior. Standard operating procedures are instituted, and control consists largely in checking to ensure that these procedures are, in fact, followed.

Three consequences follow from this emphasis on reliability in behavior and the techniques used to install it:

1. There is a reduction in the *amount of personalized relationships* (3.3) [3.3:3.2]. The bureaucracy is a set of relationships between offices, or roles. The official reacts to other members of the organization not as more or less unique individuals but as representatives of positions that have specified rights and duties. Competition within the organization occurs within closely defined limits; evaluation and promotion are relatively independent of individual achievement (*e.g.,* promotion by seniority).

2. *Internalization of the rules of the organization* (3.4) by the participants is increased [3.4:3.2]. Rules originally devised to achieve organizational goals assume a positive value that is independent of the organizational goals. However, it is important to distinguish two phenomena, both of which have been called the "displacement of goals." In one case, a given stimulus evokes an activity perceived as leading to a preferred state of affairs. In a series of such situations, the repeated choice of the acceptable alternative causes a gradual transfer of the preference from the final state of affairs to the instrumental activity. In the other case, the choice of a desired alternative reveals additional desirable consequences not originally anticipated. The instrumental activity has, therefore, positively valued consequences even when it does not have the originally anticipated outcomes. It is this latter phenomenon (secondary reinforcement) that is operating in the present situation: the organizational setting brings about new personal or subunit consequences through participation in organizationally motivated actions.

3. There is increased *use of categorization as a decision-making technique* (3.5) [3.5:3.2]. To be sure, categorizing is a basic part of thinking in any situation. The special feature involved here is a tendency to restrict the categories used to a relatively small number and to enforce the

first formally applicable category rather than search for the possible categories that might be applied and choose among them. An increase in the use of categorization for decision making decreases the *amount of search for alternatives* (3.6) [3.6:3.5].

The reduction in personalized relationships, the increased internalization of rules, and the decreased search for alternatives combine to make the behavior of members of the organization highly predictable; *i.e.,* they result in an increase in the *rigidity of behavior* (3.7) of participants [3.7:3.3, 3.4, 3.6]. At the same time, the reduction in personalized relationships (particularly with respect to internal competition) facilitates the development of an *esprit de corps,* i.e., increases the *extent to which goals are perceived as shared among members of the group* (3.8) [3.8:3.3]. Such a sense of commonness of purpose, interests, and character increases the *propensity of organization members to defend each other against outside pressures* (3.9) [3.9:3.8]. This, in turn, solidifies the tendency toward rigid behavior [3.7:3.9].

The rigidity of behavior has three major consequences. First, it substantially satisfies the original demands for reliability [3.2:3.7]. Thus, it meets an important maintenance need of the system. Further needs of this sort are met by strengthening in-group identification, as previously mentioned [3.2:3.8]. Second, it increases the *defensibility of individual action* (3.10) [3.10:3.7]. Simple categories rigorously applied to individual cases without regard for personal features can only be challenged at a higher level of the hierarchy. Third, the rigidity of behavior increases the *amount of difficulty with clients* (3.11) of the organization [3.11:3.7] and complicates the achievement of client satisfaction—a near-universal organizational goal. Difficulty with clients is further increased by an increase in the *extent of use of trappings of authority* (3.12) by subordinates in the organization [3.11:3.12], a procedure that is encouraged by the in-group's defensiveness [3.12:3.9].

The maintenance of part of the system by the techniques previously outlined produces

a continuing pressure to maintain these techniques, as would be anticipated. It is somewhat more difficult to explain why the organization would continue to apply the same techniques in the face of client dissatisfaction. Why do organizational members fail to behave in each case in a manner appropriate to the situation? For the answer one must extend Merton's explicit statements by providing at least one, and perhaps two, additional feedback loops in the system. (It is not enough to say that such behavior becomes a part of the "personality." One must offer some explanation of why this apparently maladaptive learning takes place.)

The second major consequence of rigidity in behavior mentioned above (increased defensibility of individual action) is a deterrent to discrimination that reinforces the emphasis on reliability of behavior [3.2:3.10]. In addition, client dissatisfaction may in itself reinforce rigidity. On the one hand, client pressure at lower levels in the hierarchy tends to increase the *felt need for the defensibility of individual action* (3.13) [3.13:3.11]. On the other hand, remedial action demanded by clients from higher officials in the hierarchy may be misdirected. To the extent to which clients perceive themselves as being victims of discrimination (a perception that is facilitated in American culture by the importance attached to "equal treatment"), the proposals of clients or of the officials to whom they complain will probably strengthen the emphasis on reliability of behavior. This conflict between "service" and "impartiality" as goals for public organizations seems to lie behind a good deal of the literature on public bureaucracies.

We see that Merton's model is a rather complex set of relations among a relatively large number of variables. A simplified version of the model designed to illustrate its major features, is provided in Figure 2.

The Selznick Model

Where Merton emphasizes rules as a response to the demand for control, Selznick

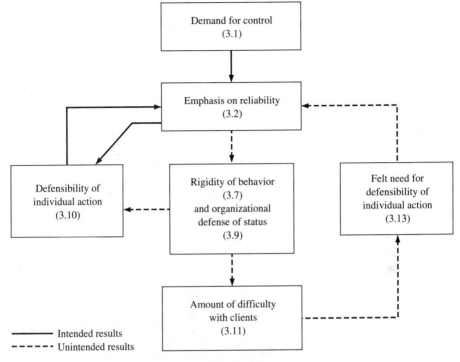

Figure 2
The Simplified Merton Model

emphasizes the delegation of authority.[8] Like Merton, however, Selznick wishes to show how the use of a control technique (*i.e.*, delegation) brings about a series of unanticipated consequences. Also, like Merton, Selznick shows how these consequences stem from the problems of maintaining highly interrelated systems of interpersonal relations.

Selznick's model starts with the demand for control made by the top hierarchy. As a result of this demand, an increased *delegation of authority* (3.14) is instituted [3.14:3.1].

Delegation, however, has several immediate consequences. As intended, it increases the *amount of training in specialized competences* (3.15) [3.15:3.14]. Restriction of attention to a relatively small number of problems increases experience within these limited areas and improves the employee's ability to deal with

these problems. Operating through this mechanism, delegation tends to decrease the *difference between organizational goals and achievement* (3.16) [3.16:3.15], and thus to stimulate more delegation [3.14:3.16]. At the same time, however, delegation results in departmentalization and an increase in the *bifurcation of interests* (3.17) among the subunits in the organization [3.17:3.14]. The maintenance needs of the subunits dictate a commitment to the subunit goals over and above their contribution to the total organizational program. Many individual needs depend on the continued success and even expansion of the subunit. As in the previous example, the activities originally evaluated in terms of the organization goals are seen to have additional important ramifications for the subunits.

Bifurcation of interests is also stimulated by the specialized training that delegation (intendedly) produces. Training results in increased competence and, therefore, in increased *costs of changing personnel* (3.18) [3.18:3.15] and this results, in turn, in further differentiation of subunit goals [3.17:3.18].

The bifurcation within the organization leads to increased *conflict among organizational subunits* (3.19) [3.19:3.17]. As a consequence, the *content of decisions* (3.20) made within the organization depends increasingly upon considerations of internal strategy, particularly if there is little *internalization of organizational goals by participants* (3.21) [3.20:3.19, 3.21]. As a result there is an increase in the difference between organizational goals and achievement [3.16:3.20] and this results in an increase in delegation [3.14:3.16]. . . .

This effect on daily decisions is accentuated by two other mechanisms in Selznick's system. The struggle for internal control not only affects directly the content of decisions, but also causes greater *elaboration of subunit ideologies* (3.22) [3.22:3.19]. Each subunit seeks success by fitting its policy into the official doctrine of the large organization to legitimize its demands. Such a tactic increases the *internalization of subgoals by participants* (3.23) within subunits [3.23:3.22].

At the same time, the internalization of subgoals is reinforced by a feedback from the daily decisions it influences. The necessity for making daily decisions creates a system of precedents. Decisions depend primarily on the operational criteria provided by the organization, and, among these criteria, subunit goals are of considerable importance [3.20:3.23]. Precedents tend to become habitual responses to the situations for which they are defined as relevant and thus to reinforce the internalization of subunit goals [3.23:3.20]. Obviously, internalization of subgoals is partially dependent on the *operationality of organizational goals* (3.24). By operationality of goals, we mean the extent to which it is possible to observe and test how well goals are being achieved. Variations in the operationality of organizational goals affect the content of daily decisions [3.20:3.24] and thus the extent of subunit goal internalization.

From this it is clear that delegation has both functional and dysfunctional consequences for the achievement of organizational goals. It contributes both to their realization and to their deflection. Surprisingly, the theory postulates that both increases and decreases in goal achievement cause an increase in delegation. Why does not normal learning occur here? The answer seems to be that when goals are not achieved, delegation is—within the framework of the "machine" model—the correct response, and the model does not consider alternatives to simple delegation. On the other hand, the model offers explicitly at least two "dampers" that limit the operation of the dysfunctional mechanisms. As is indicated in Figure 3 where the skeleton of the Selznick model is outlined, there are two (not entirely independent) variables treated as independent but potentially amenable to organizational control, each of which restrains the runaway features of daily decision-making. By suitable changes in the extent to which organizational goals are operational or in the internalization of organizational goals by participants, some of the dysfunctional effects of delegation can be reduced. (To be sure, this ignores the possible effect of such procedures on the maintenance problems of the subunits and the consequent results for the larger organizations, but these are problems we are not prepared to attack at the moment.)

The Gouldner Model

In terms of number of variables and relations, Gouldner's model[9] is the simplest of the three presented here; but it exhibits the major features of the two previous systems. Like Merton, Gouldner is concerned with the consequences of bureaucratic rules for the maintenance of organization structure. Like both Merton and Selznick, he attempts to show how a control technique designed to maintain the equilibrium of a subsystem disturbs the

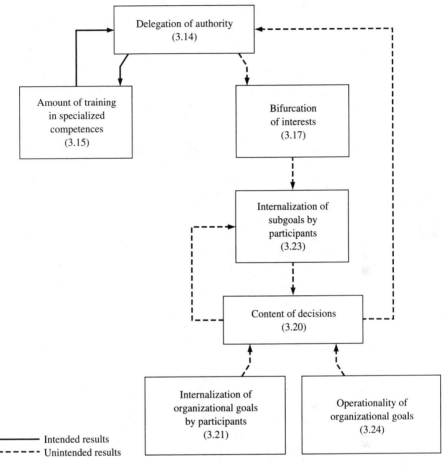

Figure 3
The Simplified Selznick Model

equilibrium of a larger system, with a subsequent feedback on the subsystem.

In Gouldner's system, the *use of general and impersonal rules* (3.25) regulating the work procedures is part of the response to the demand for control from the top hierarchy [3.25:3.1]. One consequence of such rules is to decrease the *visibility of power relations* (3.26) within the group [3.26:3.25]. The visibility of authority differences within the work group interacts with the *extent to which equality norms are held* (3.27) to affect the *legitimacy of the supervisory role* (3.28) [3.28:3.26, 3.27]. This, in turn, affects the *level of interpersonal tension* (3.29) in the work group [3.29:3.28]. In the American culture of egalitarian norms, decreases in power visibility increase the legitimacy of the supervisory position and therefore decrease tension within the group.

Gouldner argues that these anticipated consequences of rule-making do occur, that the survival of the work group as an operating unit is substantially furthered by the creation of general rules, and that consequently the use of such rules is reinforced [3.25:3.29].

At the same time, however, work rules provide cues for organizational members beyond those intended by the authority figures in the organization. Specifically, by defining unacceptable behavior, they increase *knowledge about minimum acceptable behavior* (3.30) [3.30:3.25]. In conjunction with a low level of internalization of organizational goals, specifying a minimum level of permissible behavior increases the disparity between organization goals and achievement by depressing behavior to the minimum level [3.16:3.21, 3.30].

Performance at the minimum level is perceived by hierarchical superiors as a failure. In short, the internal stabilizing effects of the rules are matched by the unbalance they produce in the larger organization. The response to the unbalance is an increase in the *closeness of supervision* (3.31) over the work group [3.31:3.16]. This response is based on the "machine" model of human behavior: low performance indicates a need for more detailed inspection and control over the operation of the "machine."

In turn, however, close supervision increases the visibility of power relations within the organization [3.26:3.31], raises the tension level in the work group, and thereby upsets the equilibrium originally based on the institution of rules. The broad outline of the model is shown in Figure 4.

Gouldner's model leaves some puzzles unexplained. In particular, why is increased supervision the supervisory response to low performance? It seems reasonable that the tendency

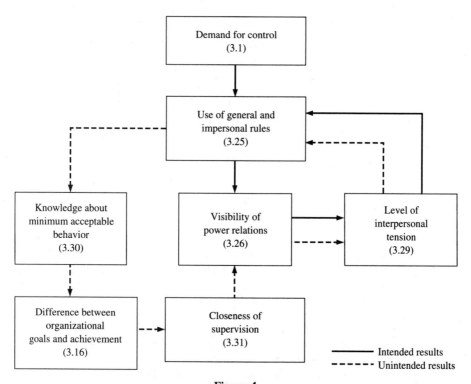

Figure 4
The Simplified Gouldner Model

to make such a response is affected both by role perceptions and by a third equilibrating process in the system—the individual needs of the supervisors. Thus, the intensity of supervision is a function of the *authoritarianism of supervisors* (3.32) and a function of the *punitivity of supervisory role perception* (3.33) [3.31:3.32, 3.33].

As in the Selznick model, the existence of "dampers" on the system poses the question of their treatment as external variables. Appropriate manipulation of equality norms, perceived commonality of interest, and the needs of supervisors will restrict the operation of the dysfunctional features of the system. The failure of top management to use such techniques of control suggests that the system may be incompletely defined.

Problems of Verification

We have sketched three major "models" of bureaucratic behavior. To what extent are the hypotheses empirically verified? Both Selznick and Gouldner base their propositions on extended observations of single organizations in the field. The data on which Merton relies are somewhat less specific but appear to be distilled from a set of generally accepted characterizations of organizational behavior.

Such evidence raises two major problems. First, what is the role of field research in verifying hypotheses about organizational behavior? The field situation fails to meet many of the major assumptions underlying standard techniques of statistical inference. The second problem is distinctly related to the first. What is the standing of the single case as evidence? For example, one of the knottier complications in this area is deciding what the sample size really is.

At least some of the propositions advanced by these three writers will be reexamined below in different contexts. . . . As we will suggest, . . . there is evidence for some of the propositions over and above the single field studies discussed here. The evidence is scarcely conclusive and far from complete, but on the whole tends to be consistent with the general models used by Merton, Selznick, and Gouldner. What little we can say beyond that is indicated below.

Implications of the Bureaucracy Models

Other quite comparable models can be added to those examined here. Bendix has discussed limits on technical rationality within an organization and pointed out the intriguing complications involved in the use of spy systems as systems of control.[10] Dubin has presented a model quite similar to that of Merton.[11] Blau has examined the changes in operating procedures that occur at a relatively low level in the hierarchy under the pressure of work group needs.[12]

In the sample of three cases from the "bureaucracy" literature we have presented (as well as in the others mentioned), complications arise in each of the three ways predicted from the influence model outlined previously. The elaboration of evoking connections, the presence of unintended cues, and organizationally dysfunctional learning appear to account for most of the unanticipated consequences with which these theories deal.

Many of the central problems for the analysis of human behavior in large-scale organizations stem from the operation of subsystems within the total organizational structure. The sociological studies of the work group analyzed here have focussed on the ways in which the needs of individuals, the primary work group, and the large organization interact to affect each other. . . .

Notes

1. M. Weber, *From Max Weber: Essays in Sociology,* trans. Gerth and Mills (Oxford, 1946).

M. Weber, *The Theory of Social and Economic Organization,* trans. Henderson and Parsons (Oxford, 1947).

2. R. K. Merton, "The Unanticipated Consequences of Purposive Social Action," *American Sociological Review* 1 (1936): 894–904. A. W. Gouldner, "Theoretical Requirements of the Applied Social Sciences," *American Sociological Review* 22 (1957): 91–102.

3. R. K. Merton, "Bureaucratic Structure and Personality," *Social Forces* 18 (1940): 560–568.

4. P. Selznick, *TVA and the Grass Roots* (Berkeley, Calif., 1949).

5. A. W. Gouldner, *Patterns of Industrial Bureaucracy* (Glencoe, Ill., 1954).

6. Merton, *Bureaucratic Structure, op. cit.*

7. See pp. 8–9 of [the source] for an explanation of the numbering system used for the propositions.

8. Selznick, *op. cit.*

9. Gouldner, *Patterns, op. cit.*

10. R. Bendix, "Bureaucracy: The Problem and Its Setting," *American Sociological Review* 12 (1947): 493–507.

11. R. Dubin, "Decision-Making by Management Relations," *Administrative Science Quarterly* 2 (1957): 60–81.

12. P. M. Blau, *The Dynamics of Bureaucracy* (Chicago, 1955).

13

A Behavioral Theory of Organizational Objectives

Richard M. Cyert & James G. March

Organizations make decisions. They make decisions in the same sense in which individuals make decisions: The organization as a whole behaves as though there existed a central coordination and control system capable of directing the behavior of the members of the organization sufficiently to allow the meaningful imputation of purpose to the total system. Because the central nervous system of most organizations appears to be somewhat different from that of the individual system, we are understandably cautious about viewing organization decision-making in quite the same terms as those applied to individual choice. Nevertheless, organizational choice is a legitimate and important focus of research attention.

As in theories of individual choice, theories of organizational decision-making fall into two broad classes. Normative theorists—particularly economic theorists of the firm—have been dedicated to the improvement of the rationality of organizational choice. Recent developments in the application of mathematics to the solution of economic decision-problems are fully and effectively in such a tradition (Cooper, Hitch, Baumol, Shubik, Schelling, Valavanis, and Ellsberg, 1958). The empirical theory of organizational decision-making has a much more checkered tradition and is considerably less well-developed (March and Simon, 1958).

SOURCE: Mason Haire, ed. *Modern Organization Theory* (New York: Wiley, 1959), 76–90. Copyright © Vivian Haire. Reprinted by permission.

The present efforts to develop a behavioral theory of organizational decision-making represent attempts to overcome the disparity between the importance of decision-making in organizations and our understanding of how, in fact, such decisions are made. The research as a whole, as well as that part of it discussed below, is based on three initial commitments. The first of these is to develop an explicitly empirical theory rather than a normative one. Our interest is in understanding how complex organizations make decisions, not how they ought to do so. Without denying the importance of normative theory, we are convinced that the major current needs are for empirical knowledge.

The second commitment is to focus on the classic problems long explored in economic theory—pricing, resource allocation, and capital investment. This commitment is intended to overcome some difficulties with existing organization theory. By introducing organizational propositions into models of rather complex systems, we are driven to increase the precision of the propositions considerably. At present, anyone taking existing organization theory as a base for predicting behavior within organizations finds that he can make a number of rather important predictions of the general form: If x varies, y will vary. Only rarely will he find either the parameters of the functions or more elaborate predictions for situations in which the *ceteris paribus* assumptions are not met.

The third commitment is to approximate in the theory the process by which decisions are made by organizations. This commitment to a process-oriented theory is not new. It has typified many organization theorists in the past (Marshall, 1919; Weber, 1947). The sentiment that one should substitute observation for assumption whenever possible seems, a priori, reasonable. Traditionally, the major dilemma in organization theory has been between putting into the theory all the features of organizations we think are relevant and thereby making the theory unmanageable, or pruning the model down to a simple system, thereby making it unrealistic. So long as we had to deal primarily with classical mathematics, there was, in fact, little we could do. With the advent of the computer and use of simulation, we have a methodology that will permit us to expand considerably the emphasis on actual process without losing the predictive precision essential to testing (Cyert and March, in press, 1959).

In models currently being developed there are four major subsystems. Since they operate more or less independently, it is possible to conceive them as the four basic subtheories required for a behavioral theory of organizational decision-making; first, the theory of organizational objectives; second, the theory of organizational expectations; third, the theory of organizational choice; fourth, the theory of organizational implementation. In this paper we discuss the first of these only, the theory of organizational objectives.

The Organization as a Coalition

Let us conceive the organization as a coalition. It is a coalition of individuals, some of them organized into subcoalitions. In the business organization, one immediately thinks of such coalition members as managers, workers, stockholders, suppliers, customers, lawyers, tax collectors, etc. In the governmental organization, one thinks of such members as administrators, workers, appointive officials, elective officials, legislators, judges, clientele, etc. In the voluntary charitable organization, one thinks of paid functionaries, volunteers, donors, donees, etc.

This view of an organization as a coalition suggests, of course, several different recent treatments of organization theory in which a similar basic position is adopted. In particular, inducements-contributions theory (Barnard, 1938; Simon, 1947), theory of games (von Neumann and Morgenstern, 1947), and theory of teams (Marschak, in this volume). Each of these theories is substantially equivalent on this score. Each specifies:

1. That organizations include individual participants with (at least potentially) widely varying preference orderings.
2. That through bargaining and side payments the participants in the organization enter into a coalition agreement for purposes of the game. This agreement specifies a joint preference-ordering (or organizational objective) for the coalition.
3. That thereafter the coalition can be treated as a single strategist, entrepreneur, or what have you.

Such a formulation permits us to move immediately to modern decision theory, which has been an important part of recent developments in normative organization theory. In our view, however, a joint preference ordering is not a particularly good description of actual organization goals. Studies of organizational objectives suggest that to the extent to which there is agreement on objectives, it is agreement on highly ambiguous goals (Truman, 1951; Kaplan, Dirlam, and Lanzillotti, 1958). Such agreement is undoubtedly important to choice within the organization, but it is a far cry from a clear preference ordering. The studies suggest further that behind this agreement on rather vague objectives there is considerable disagreement and uncertainty about subgoals; that organizations appear to be pursuing one goal at one time and another (partially inconsistent) goal at another; and that different parts of the organization appear to be pursuing different goals at the same time (Kaplan, Dirlam, and Lanzillotti, 1958; Selznick, 1949). Finally, the studies suggest that most organization objectives take the form of an aspiration level rather than an imperative to "maximize" or "minimize," and that the aspiration level changes in reponse to experience (Blau, 1955; Alt, 1949).

In the theory to be outlined here, we consider three major ways in which the objectives of a coalition are determined. The first of these is the bargaining process by which the composition and general terms of the coalition are fixed. The second is the internal organizational process of control by which objectives are stabilized and elaborated. The third is the process of adjustment to experience, by which coalition agreements are altered in response to environmental changes. Each of these processes is considered, in turn, in the next three sections of the paper.

Formation of Coalition Objectives through Bargaining

A basic problem in developing a theory of coalition formation is the problem of handling side payments. No matter how we try we simply cannot imagine that the side payments by which organizational coalitions are formed even remotely satisfy the requirements of unrestricted transferability of utility. Side payments are made in many forms: money, personal treatment, authority, organization policy, etc. A winning coalition does not have a fixed booty which it then divides among its members. Quite to the contrary, the total value of side payments available for division among coalition members is a function of the composition of the coalition; and the total utility of the actual side payments depends on the distribution made within the coalition. There is no conservation of utility.

For example, if we can imagine a situation in which any dyad is a viable coalition (e.g., a partnership to exploit the proposition that two can live more cheaply in coalition than separately), we would predict a greater total utility for those dyads in which needs were complementary than for those in which they were competitive. Generally speaking, therefore, the partitioning of the adult population into male-female dyads is probably more efficient from the point of view of total utility accruing to the coalition than is a partition into sexually homogeneous pairs.

Such a situation makes game theory as it currently exists virtually irrelevant for a treatment of organizational side payments (Luce and Raiffa, 1957). But the problem is in part even deeper than that. The second requirement of such theories as game theory, theory of teams, and inducements-contributions theory, is that after the side payments are made, a joint preference ordering is defined. All conflict is settled by the side-payment bargaining. The employment-contract form of these theories, for example, assumes that the entrepreneur has an objective. He then purchases whatever services he needs to achieve the objective. In return for such payments, employees contract to perform whatever is required of them—at least within the range of permissible requirements. For a price, the employee adopts the "organization" goal.

One strange feature of such a conception is that it describes a coalition asymmetrically. To what extent is it arbitrary that we call wage payments "costs" and dividend payments "profits"—rather than the other way around? Why is it that in our quasi-genetic moments we are inclined to say that in the beginning there was a manager and he recruited workers and capital? For the development of our own theory we make two major arguments. First, the emphasis on the asymmetry has seriously confused our understanding of organizational goals. The confusion arises because ultimately it makes only slightly more sense to say that the goals of a business organization is to maximize profit than it does to say that its goal is to maximize the salary of Sam Smith, Assistant to the Janitor.

Second, despite this there are important reasons for viewing some coalition members as quite different from others. For example, it is clear that employees and management make somewhat different demands on the organization. In their bargaining, side payments appear traditionally to have performed the classical function of specifying a joint preference ordering. In addition, some coalition members (e.g., many stockholders) devote substantially less time to the particular coalition under consideration than do others. It is this characteristic that has usually been used to draw organizational boundaries between "external" and "internal" members of the coalition. Thus, there are important classes of coalition members who are passive most of the time. A condition of such passivity must be that the payment demands they make are of such a character that most of the time they can be met rather easily.

Although we thereby reduce substantially the size and complexity of the coalition relevant for most goal-setting, we are still left with something more complicated than an individual entrepreneur. It is primarily through bargaining within this active group that what we call organizational objectives arise. Side payments, far from being incidental distribution of a fixed, transferable booty, represent the central process of goal specification. That is, a significant number of these payments are in the form of policy commitments.

The distinction between demands for monetary side payments and demands for policy commitments seems to underlie management-oriented treatments of organizations. It is clear that in many organizations this distinction has important ideological and therefore affective connotations. Indeed, the breakdown of the distinction in our generation has been quite consistently violent. Political party-machines in this country have changed drastically the ratio of direct monetary side payments (e.g., patronage, charity) to policy commitments (e.g., economic legislation). Labor unions are conspicuously entering into what has been viewed traditionally as the management prerogatives of policy-making, and demanding payments in that area. Military forces have long since given up the substance—if not entirely the pretense—of being simply hired agents of the regime. The phenomenon is especially obvious in public (Dahl and Lindblom, 1953; Simon, Smithburg, and Thompson, 1950) and voluntary (Sills, 1957; Messinger, 1955) organizations; but all organizations use policy side payments. The marginal cost to other coalition members is typically quite small.

This trend toward policy side payments is particularly observable in contemporary organizations, but the important point is that we have never come close to maintenance of a sharp distinction in the kinds of payments made and demanded. Policy commitments have (one is tempted to say always) been an important part of the method by which coalitions are formed. In fact, an organization that does not use such devices can exist in only a rather special environment.

To illustrate coalition formation under conditions where the problem is not scarce resources for side payments, but varying complementarities of policy demands, imagine a nine-man committee appointed to commission a pointing for the village hall. The nine members make individually the following demands:

Committeeman A: The painting must be an abstract monotone.

Committeeman B: The painting must be an impressionistic oil.

Committeeman C: The painting must be small and oval in shape.

Committeeman D: The painting must be small and in oil.

Committeeman E: The painting must be square in shape and multicolored.

Committeeman F: The painting must be an impressionistic square.

Committeeman G: The painting must be a monotone and in oil.

Committeeman H: The painting must be multicolored and impressionistic.

Committeeman I: The painting must be small and oval.

In this case, each potential coalition member makes two simple demands. Assuming that five members are all that are required to make the decision, there are three feasible coalitions. A, C, D, G, and I can form a coalition and commission a small, oval, monotone, oil abstract. B, C, D, H, and I can form a coalition and commission a small, oval, multicolored, impressionistic oil. B, D, E, F, and H can form a coalition and commission a small, square, multicolored, impressionistic oil.

Committeeman D, it will be noted, is in the admirable position of being included in every possible coalition. The reason is clear; his demands are completely consistent with the demands of everyone else.

Obviously at some level of generality the distinction between money and policy payments disappears because any side payment can be viewed as a policy constraint. When we agree to pay someone $35,000 a year, we are constrained to that set of policy decisions that will allow such a payment. Any allocation of scarce resources (such as money) limits the alternatives for the organization. But the scarcity of resources is not the only kind of problem. Some policy demands are strictly inconsistent with other demands. Others are completely complementary. If I demand of the organization that John Jones be shot and you demand that he be sainted, it will be difficult for us both to stay in the organization. This is not because either bullets or haloes are in short supply or because we don't have enough money for both.

To be sure, the problems of policy consistency are in *principle* amenable to explicit optimizing behavior. But they add to the computational difficulties facing the coalition members and make it even more obvious why the bargaining leading to side payment and policy agreements is only slightly related to the bargaining anticipated in a theory of omniscient rationality. The tests of short-run feasibility that they represent lead to the familiar complications of conflict, disagreement, and rebargaining.

In the process of bargaining over side payments many of the organizational objectives are defined. Because of the form the bargaining takes, the objectives tend to have several important attributes. First, they are imperfectly rationalized. Depending on the skill of the leaders involved, the sequence of demands leading to the new bargaining, the aggressiveness of various parts of the organization, and the scarcity of resources, the new demands will be tested for consistency with existing policy. But this testing is normally far from complete. Second, some objectives are stated in the form

of aspiration-level constraints. Objectives arise in this form when demands which are consistent with the coalition are stated in this form. For example, the demand, "We must allocate ten percent of our total budget to research." Third, some objectives are stated in a nonoperational form. In our formulation such objectives arise when potential coalition members have demands which are nonoperational or demands which can be made nonoperational. The prevalence of objectives in this form can be explained by the fact that nonoperational objectives are consistent with virtually any set of objectives.

Stabilization and Elaboration of Objectives

The bargaining process goes on more or less continuously, turning out a long series of commitments. But a description of goal formation simply in such terms is not adequate. Organizational objectives are, first of all, much more stable than would be suggested by such a model, and secondly, such a model does not handle very well the elaboration and clarification of goals through day-to-day bargaining.

Central to an understanding of these phenomena is again an appreciation for the limitations of human capacities and time to devote to any particular aspect of the organizational system. Let us return to our conception of a coalition having monetary and policy side payments. These side-payment agreements are incomplete. They do not anticipate effectively all possible future situations, and they do not identify all considerations that might be viewed as important by the coalition members at some future time. Nevertheless, the coalition members are motivated to operate under the agreements and to develop some mutual control-systems for enforcing them.

One such mutual control-system in many organizations is the budget. A budget is a highly explicit elaboration of previous commitments. Although it is usually viewed as an asymmetric control-device (i.e., a means for superiors to control subordinates), it is clear that it represents a form of mutual control. Just as there are usually severe costs to the department in exceeding the budget, so also are there severe costs to other members of the coalition if the budget is not paid in full. As a result, budgets in every organization tend to be self-confirming.

A second major, mutual control-system is the allocation of functions. Division of labor and specialization are commonly treated in management textbooks simply as techniques of rational organization. If, however, we consider the allocation of functions in much the way we would normally view the allocation of resources during budgeting, a somewhat different picture emerges. When we define the limits of discretion, we constrain the individual or subgroup from acting outside those limits. But at the same time, we constrain any other members of the coalition from prohibiting action within those limits. Like the allocation of resources in a budget, the allocation of discretion in an organization chart is largely self-confirming.

The secondary bargaining involved in such mutual control-systems serves to elaborate and revise the coalition agreements made on entry (Thompson and McEwen, 1958). In the early life of an organization, or after some exceptionally drastic organizational upheaval, this elaboration occurs in a context where very little is taken as given. Relatively deliberate action must be taken on everything from pricing policy to paperclip policy. Reports from individuals who have lived through such early stages emphasize the lack of structure that typifies settings for day-to-day decisions (Simon, 1953).

In most organizations most of the time, however, the elaboration of objectives occurs within much tighter constraints. Much of the situation is taken as given. This is true primarily because organizations have memories in the form of precedents, and individuals in the coalition are strongly motivated to accept the precedents as binding. Whether precedents are formalized in the shape of an official standard-operating-procedure or are less formally stored,

they remove from conscious consideration many agreements, decisions, and commitments that might well be subject to renegotiation in an organization without a memory (Cyert and March, to be published, 1960). Past bargains become precedents for present situations. A budget becomes a precedent for future budgets. An allocation of functions becomes a precedent for future allocations. Through all the well-known mechanisms, the coalition agreements of today are institutionalized into semipermanent arrangements. A number of administrative aphorisms come to mind: an unfilled position disappears; see an empty office and fill it up; there is nothing temporary under the sun. As a result of organizational precedents, objectives exhibit much greater stability than would typify a pure bargaining situation. The "accidents" of organizational genealogy tend to be perpetuated.

Changes in Objectives through Experience

Although considerably stabilized by memory and institutionalization-phenomena, the demands made on the coalition by individual members do change with experience. Both the nature of the demands and their quantitative level vary over time.

Since many of the requirements specified by individual participants are in the form of attainable goals rather than general maximizing constraints, objectives are subject to the usual phenomena associated with aspiration levels. As an approximation to the aspiration-level model, we can take the following set of propositions:

1. In the steady state, aspiration level exceeds achievement by a small amount.
2. Where achievement increases at an increasing rate, aspiration level will exhibit short-run lags behind achievement.
3. Where achievement decreases, aspiration level will be substantially above achievement.

These propositions derive from simpler assumptions requiring that current aspiration be an optimistic extrapolation of past achievement and past aspiration. Although such assumptions are sometimes inappropriate, the model seems to be consistent with a wide range of human goal-setting behavior (Lewin, Dembo, Festinger, and Sears, 1944). Two kinds of achievement are, of course, important. The first is the achievement of the participant himself. The second is the achievement of others in his reference group (Festinger, 1954).

Because of these phenomena, our theory of organizational objectives must allow for drift in the demands of members of the organization. No one doubts that aspirations with respect to monetary compensation vary substantially as a function of payments received. So also do aspirations regarding advertising budget, quality of product, volume of sales, product mix, and capital investment. Obviously, until we know a great deal more than we do about the parameters of the relation between achievement and aspiration we can make only relatively weak predictions. But some of these predictions are quite useful, particularly in conjunction with search theory (Cyert, Dill, and March, 1958).

For example, two situations are particularly intriguing. What happens when the rate of improvement in the environment is great enough so that it outruns the upward adjustment of aspiration? Second, what happens when the environment becomes less favorable? The general answer to both of these questions involves the concept of organizational slack (Cyert and March, 1956). When the environment outruns aspiration-level adjustment, the organization secures, or at least has the potentiality of securing, resources in excess of its demands. Some of these resources are simply not obtained—although they are available. Others are used to meet the revised demands of those members of the coalition whose demands adjust most rapidly—usually those most deeply involved in the organization. The excess resources would not be subject to very general bargaining because they do not involve allocation in the face of scarcity. Coincidentally

perhaps, the absorption of excess resources also serves to delay aspiration-level adjustment by passive members of the coalition.

When the environment becomes less favorable, organizational slack represents a cushion. Resource scarcity brings on renewed bargaining and tends to cut heavily into the excess payments introduced during plusher times. It does not necessarily mean that precisely those demands that grew abnormally during better days are pruned abnormally during poorer ones; but in general we would expect this to be approximately the case.

Some attempts have been made to use these very simple propositions to generate some meaningful empirical predictions. Thus, we predict that, discounting for the economies of scale, relatively successful firms will have higher unit-costs than relatively unsuccessful ones. We predict that advertising expenditures will be a function of sales in the previous time period at least as much as the reverse will be true.

The nature of the demands also changes with experience in another way. We do not conceive that individual members of the coalition will have a simple listing of demands, with only the quantitative values changing over time. Instead we imagine each member as having a rather disorganized file case full of demands. At any point in time, the member attends to only a rather small subset of his demands, the number and variety depending again on the extent of his involvement in the organization and on the demands of his other commitments on his attention.

Since not all demands are attended to at the same time, one important part of the theory of organizational objectives is to predict when particular units in the organization will attend to particular goals. Consider the safety goal in a large corporation. For the safety engineers, this is a very important goal most of the time. Other parts of the organization rarely even consider it. If, however, the organization has some drastic experience (e.g., a multiple fatality), attention to a safety goal is much more widespread and safety action quite probable.

Whatever the experience, it shifts the attention-focus. In some (as in the safety example), adverse experience suggests a problem area to be attacked. In others, solutions to problems stimulate attention to a particular goal. An organization with an active personnel-research department will devote substantial attention to personnel goals not because it is necessarily a particularly pressing problem but because the subunit keeps generating solutions that remind other members of the organization of a particular set of objectives they profess.

The notion of attention-focus suggests one reason why organizations are successful in surviving with a large set of unrationalized goals. They rarely see the conflicting objectives simultaneously. For example, let us reconsider the case of the pair of demands that John Jones be either (a) shot or (b) sainted. Quite naturally, these were described as inconsistent demands. Jones cannot be simultaneously shot and sainted. But the emphasis should be on *simultaneously*. It is quite feasible for him to be first shot and then sainted, or vice versa. It is logically feasible because a halo can be attached as firmly to a dead man as to a live one and a saint is as susceptible to bullets as a sinner. It is organizationally feasible because the probability is low that both of these demands will be attended to simultaneously.

The sequential attention to goals is a simple mechanism. A consequence of the mechanism is that organizations ignore many conditions that outside observers see as direct contradictions. They are contradictions only if we imagine a well-established, joint preference ordering or omniscient bargaining. Neither condition exists in an organization. If we assume that attention to goals is limited, we can explain the absence of any strong pressure to resolve apparent internal inconsistencies. This is not to argue that all conflicts involving objectives can be resolved in this way, but it is one important mechanism that deserves much more intensive study.

Constructing a Predictive Theory

Before the general considerations outlined above can be transformed into a useful predictive theory, a considerable amount of precision must be added. The introduction of precision depends, in turn, on the future success of research into the process of coalition formation. Nevertheless, some steps can be taken now to develop the theory. In particular, we can specify a general framework for a theory and indicate its needs for further development.

We assume a set of coalition members, actual or potential. Whether these members are individuals or groups of individuals is unimportant. Some of the possible subsets drawn from this set are viable coalitions. That is, we will identify a class of combinations of members such that any of these combinations meet the minimal standards imposed by the external environment on the organization. Patently, therefore, the composition of the viable set of coalitions will depend on environmental conditions.

For each of the potential coalition members we require a set of demands. Each such individual set is partitioned into an active part currently attended to and an inactive part currently ignored. Each demand can be characterized by two factors; first, its marginal resource requirements, given the demands of all possible other combinations of demands from potential coalition members; second, its marginal consistency with all possible combinations of demands from potential coalition members.

For each potential coalition member we also require a set of problems, partitioned similarly into an active and an inactive part.

This provides us with the framework of the theory. In addition, we need five basic mechanisms. First, we need a mechanism that changes the quantitative value of the demands over time. In our formulation, this becomes a version of the basic aspiration-level and mutual control theory outlined earlier.

Second, we need an attention-focus mechanism that transfers demands among the three possible states; active set, inactive set, not-considered set. We have said that some organizational participants will attend to more demands than other participants and that for all participants some demands will be considered at one time and others at other times. But we know rather little about the actual mechanisms that control this attention factor.

Third, we need a similar attention-focus mechanism for problems. As we have noted, there is a major interaction between what problems are attended to and what demands are attended to, but research is also badly needed in this area.

Fourth, we need a demand-evaluation procedure that is consistent with the limited capacities of human beings. Such a procedure must specify how demands are checked for consistency and for their resource demands. Presumably, such a mechanism will depend heavily on a rule that much of the problem is taken as given and only incremental changes are considered.

Fifth, we need a mechanism for choosing among the potentially viable coalitions. In our judgment, this mechanism will probably look much like the recent suggestions of game theorists that only small changes are evaluated at a time (Luce and Raiffa, 1957).

Given these five mechanisms and some way of expressing environmental resources, we can describe a process for the determination of objectives in an organization that will exhibit the important attributes of organizational goal-determination. At the moment, we can approximate some of the required functions. For example, it has been possible to introduce into a complete model a substantial part of the first mechanism, and some elements of the second, third, and fourth (Cyert, Feigenbaum, and March, 1959). Before the theory can develop further, however, and particularly before it can focus intensively on the formation of objectives through bargaining and coalition formation (rather than on the revision of such objectives and the selective attention to them), we require greater empirical clarification of the phenomena involved.

References

ALT, R. M. (1949). The internal organization of the firm and price formation: An illustrative case. *Quarterly J. of Econ., 63,* 92–110.

BARNARD, C. I. (1938). *The functions of the executive.* Cambridge: Harvard University Press.

BLAU, P. M. (1955). *The dynamics of bureaucracy.* Chicago: University of Chicago Press.

COOPER, W. W., HITCH, C., BAUMOL, W. J., SHUBIK, M., SCHELLING, T. C., VALAVANIS, S., & ELLSBERG, D. (1958). Economics and operations research: A symposium. *The Rev. of Econ. and Stat., 40,* 195–229.

CYERT, R. M., & MARCH, J. G. (1956). Organizational factors in the theory of oligopoly. *Quarterly J. of Econ., 70,* 44–64.

CYERT, R. M., DILL, W. R., & MARCH, J. G. (1958). The role of expectations in business decision making. *Adm. Sci. Quarterly, 3,* 307–340.

CYERT, R. M., & MARCH, J. G. (1959). Research on a behavioral theory of the firm. *Management Rev.*

CYERT, R. M., FEIGENBAUM, E. A., & MARCH, J. G. (1959). Models in a behavioral theory of the firm. *Behavioral Sci., 4,* 81–95.

CYERT, R. M., & MARCH, J. G. (1960). Business operating procedure. In B. von H. Gilmer (Ed.), *Industrial psychology.* New York: McGraw-Hill.

DAHL, R. A., & LINDBLOM, C. E. (1953). *Politics, economics, and welfare.* New York: Harper.

FESTINGER, L. (1954). A theory of social comparison processes. *Human Relations, 7,* 117–140.

KAPLAN, A. D. H., DIRLAM, J. B., & LANZILLOTTI, R. F. (1958). *Pricing in big business.* Washington: Brookings Institution.

LEWIN, L., DEMBO, T., FESTINGER, L., & SEARS, P. (1944). Level of aspiration. In J. M. Hunt (Ed.), *Personality and the behavior disorders.* (Vol I). New York: Ronald Press.

LUCE, R. D., & RAIFFA, H. (1957). *Games and decisions.* New York: Wiley.

MARCH, J. G., & SIMON, H. A. (1958). *Organizations.* New York: Wiley.

MARSCHAK, J. Efficient and viable organization forms. In this volume.

MARSHALL, A. (1919). *Industry and trade.* London: Macmillan.

MESSINGER, S. L. (1955). Organizational transformation: A case study of a declining social movement. *Amer. sociol. Rev., 20,* 3–10.

SELZNICK, P. (1949). *TVA and the grass roots.* Berkeley: University of California Press.

SILLS, D. L. (1957). *The volunteers.* Glencoe, IL: Free Press.

SIMON, H. A. (1947). *Administrative behavior.* New York: Macmillan.

SIMON, H. A., SMITHBURG, D. W., & THOMPSON, V. A. (1950). *Public administration.* New York: Knopf.

SIMON, H. A. (1953). Birth of an organization: The economic cooperation administration. *Public Adm. Rev., 13,* 227–236.

THOMPSON, J. D., & MCEWEN, W. J. (1958). Organizational goals and environment: Goal setting as an interaction process. *Amer. sociol. rev., 23,* 23–31.

TRUMAN, D. B. (1951). *The governmental process.* New York: Knopf.

VON NEUMANN, J., & MORGENSTERN, O. (1947). *Theory of games and economic behavior.* (2nd ed.) Princeton, NJ: Princeton University Press.

WEBER, M. (1947). *The theory of social and economic organization* (A. M. Henderson & T. Parsons, Trans.). New York: Oxford University Press.

III

The Organizational Behavior Perspective, or Human Resource Theory

Students and practitioners of management have always been interested in and concerned with the behavior of people in organizations. But fundamental assumptions about the behavior of people at work did not change dramatically from the beginnings of humankind's attempts to organize until only a few decades ago. Using the traditional "the boss knows best" mind-set (set of assumptions), Hugo Münsterberg (1863–1916), the German-born psychologist whose later work at Harvard would earn him the title of "father" of industrial or applied psychology, pioneered the application of psychological findings from laboratory experiments to practical matters. He sought to match the abilities of new hires with a company's work demands, to positively influence employee attitudes toward their work and their company, and to understand the impact of psychological conditions on employee productivity (H. Münsterberg, 1913; M. Münsterberg, 1922). Münsterberg's approach characterized how the behavioral sciences tended to be applied in organizations well into the 1950s. During and following World War II, the armed services were particularly active in conducting and sponsoring research into how the military could best *find and shape people to fit its needs.*

In contrast to the Hugo Münsterberg-type perspective on organizational behavior, the 1960s, 1970s, and 1980s "modern breed" of applied behavioral scientists have focused their attention on seeking to answer questions such as how organizations could and should allow and encourage their people to grow and develop. From this perspective, it is *assumed* that organizational creativity, flexibility, and prosperity flow naturally from employee growth and development. The essence of the relationship between organization and people is redefined from dependence to codependence. People are considered to be as or more important than the organization itself. The organizational behavior methods and techniques of the 1960s, 1970s, and 1980s could not have been used in Münsterberg's days *because we didn't believe (assume) that codependence was the "right" relationship between an organization and its employees.*

Although practitioners and researchers have been interested in the behavior of people inside organizations for a very long time, it has only been since about 1957—when our basic assumptions about the relationship between organizations and people truly began to change—that the organizational behavior perspective, or human resource theory, came into being. Those who see organizations through the "lenses" of the organizational behavior perspective focus on people, groups, and the relationships among them and the organizational environment. Because the organizational behavior perspective places a very high value on humans as individuals, things typically are done very openly and honestly, providing employees with maximum amounts of accurate information so they can make informed decisions with free will about their future (Argyris, 1970).

Human resource theory draws on a body of research and theory built around the following assumptions:

1. Organizations exist to serve human needs (rather than the reverse).
2. Organizations and people need each other. (Organizations need ideas, energy, and talent; people need careers, salaries, and work opportunities.)
3. When the fit between the individual and the organization is poor, one or both will suffer: individuals will be exploited, or will seek to exploit the organizations, or both.
4. A good fit between individual and organization benefits both: human beings find meaningful and satisfying work, and organizations get the human talent and energy that they need. (Bolman & Deal, 1991, p. 121)

No other perspective of organizations has ever had such a wealth of research findings and methods at its disposal.

The one most significant set of events that preceded and presaged a conscious theory (and field) of organizational behavior was the multiyear work done by the Elton Mayo team at the Hawthorne plant of the Western Electric Company beginning in 1927 (Mayo, 1933; Roethlisberger & Dixon, 1939). It is important to note that the Mayo team began its work trying to fit into the mold of classical organization theory thinking. The team phrased its questions in the language and concepts industry was accustomed to using to see and explain problems such as: productivity in relationship to such factors as the amount of light, the rate of flow of materials, and alternative wage payment plans. The Mayo team succeeded in making significant breakthroughs in understanding only after it redefined the Hawthorne problems as social psychological problems—problems conceptualized in such terms as interpersonal relations in groups, group norms, control over one's own environment, and personal recognition. It was only after the Mayo team achieved this breakthrough that it became the "grandfather"—the direct precursor—of the field of organizational behavior and human resource theory. The Hawthorne studies laid the foundation for a set of assumptions that would be fully articulated and would displace the assumptions of classical organization theory twenty years later. The Hawthorne experiments were the emotional and intellectual wellspring of the organizational behavior perspective and modern theories of motivation. The Hawthorne experiments showed that complex, interactional variables make the difference in motivating people—things like attention paid to workers as individuals, workers' control over their own work, differences between individuals' needs, management's willingness to listen, group norms, and direct feedback.

According to human resource theory, the organization is not the independent variable to be manipulated in order to change behavior (as a dependent variable)—even though organizations pay employees to help them achieve organizational goals. Instead, the organization must be seen as the context in which behavior occurs. It is both an independent and dependent variable. The organization influences human behavior just as behavior shapes the organization. The interactions shape conceptualizations of jobs, human communication and interaction in work groups, the impact of participation in decisions about one's own work, roles (in general), and the roles of leaders.

It should be evident that human resource organization theory is an enormous field of study supported by a large body of literature both because it addresses numerous subfields and because it has so much research available for use. In this chapter, we can only introduce a few of its most important ideas and best-known authors. For a more thorough presentation, we suggest J. Steven Ott's (1989) anthology *Classic Readings in Organizational Behavior.* Ott groups the literature of human resource theory by its most pervasive themes:

- Motivation
- Group and intergroup relations
- Leadership
- The person–organization interface (the context of organizational behavior)
- Power and dependence
- Processes for creating organizational change [including the subfield of organization development (OD)]

In this chapter, we have limited the selections to a few classic readings on leadership, motivation, group dynamics, and organizational change. The first article reprinted here is a truly pioneering treatise on the situational or contingency approach to leadership, "The Giving of Orders," by Mary Parker Follett. Follett discusses how orders should be given in any organization: They should be depersonalized "to unite all concerned in a study of the situation, to discover the law of the situation and obey that." Follett thus argues for a participatory leadership style, whereby employees and employers cooperate to assess the situation and decide what should be done at that moment—in that situation. Once the "law" of the situation is discovered, "the employee can issue it to the employer as well as employer to employee." This manner of giving orders facilitates better attitudes within an organization because nobody is necessarily under another person; rather, all take their cues from the situation.

All discussions of motivation start with Abraham Maslow. His hierarchy of needs stands alongside the Hawthorne experiments and Douglas McGregor's Theory X and Theory Y as *the* departure points for studying motivation in organizations. An overview of Maslow's basic theory of needs is presented here from his 1943 *Psychological Review* article "A Theory of Human Motivation." Maslow's theoretical premises can be summarized in a few phrases:

- All humans have needs that underlie their motivational structure
- As lower levels of needs are satisfied, they no longer "drive" behavior
- Satisfied needs are not motivators
- As lower level needs of workers become satisfied, higher order needs take over as the motivating forces

Maslow's theory has been attacked frequently. Few empirical studies have supported it, and it oversimplifies the complex structure of human needs and motivations. Several modified needs hierarchies have been proposed over the years that reportedly are better able to withstand empirical testing (for example, Alderfer, 1969). But, despite the criticisms and the continuing advances across the spectrum of applied behavioral sciences, Abraham Maslow's theory continues to occupy a most honored and prominent place in organizational behavior and management textbooks.

Between 1957 and 1960, the organizational behavior perspective literally exploded onto the organization scene. On April 9, 1957, Douglas M. McGregor delivered the Fifth Anniversary Convocation address to the School of Industrial Management at the Massachusetts Institute of Technology. He titled his address "The Human Side of Enterprise." McGregor expanded his talk into some of the most influential articles and books on organizational behavior and organization theory. In "The Human Side of Enterprise," McGregor articulated how managerial assumptions about employees become self-fulfilling prophesies. He labeled his two sets of contrasting assumptions Theory X and Theory Y, but they are more than just theories. McGregor had articulated the basic assumptions of the organizational behavior perspective.

"The Human Side of Enterprise" is a cogent articulation of the basic assumptions of the organizational behavior perspective. Theory X and Theory Y are contrasting basic managerial assumptions about employees that, in McGregor's words, become self-fulfilling prophesies. Managerial assumptions *cause* employee behavior. Theory X and Theory Y are ways of seeing and thinking about people that, in turn, affect their behavior. Thus, "The Human Side of Enterprise" (1957b), which is reprinted in this chapter, is a landmark theory of motivation.

Theory X assumptions represent a restatement of the tenets of the scientific management movement. For example, Theory X holds that human beings inherently dislike work and will avoid it if possible. Most people must be coerced, controlled, directed, or threatened with punishment to get them to work toward the achievement of organizational objectives; and humans prefer to be directed, to avoid responsibility, and will seek security above all else. These assumptions serve as polar opposites to McGregor's Theory Y.

Theory Y assumptions postulate, for example, that people do not inherently dislike work; work can be a source of satisfaction. People will exercise self-direction and self-control if they are committed to organization objectives. People are willing to seek and to accept responsibility; avoidance of responsibility is not natural, it is a consequence of experiences. The intellectual potential of most humans is only partially utilized at work.

David McClelland is one of the most widely cited of the many students and theorists who studied and wrote about motivation in organizations during the 1960s. David McClelland began the construction of his motivation theory with Abraham Maslow's need theory and was also influenced substantially by the Theory X and Theory Y assumptions of Douglas McGregor. McClelland postulates that people have three basic needs (or drives), which vary in intensity under different circumstances: achievement, power, and affiliation. In his 1966 article "That Urge to Achieve," which is included in this chapter, McClelland focuses on people with a high need to achieve, which he calls *achievement motivation.* Even though all people have some need to achieve, McClelland asserts that "most people in this world . . . can be divided into two broad groups. There is that minority which is challenged by opportunity and willing to work hard to achieve something, and the majority which really does not care all that much"—people with high and low achievement motivation. Business executives, particularly if they are in positions of real responsibility, and salesmen tend to score high in achievement need. McClelland's article presents the techniques that he and his associates have used to develop achievement needs in people, and it describes their failures in trying to develop high achievement attitudes among low-income groups. It isn't enough to change people's motivation if the environment in which they live doesn't support their new efforts. In balance, however, McClelland contends that achievement motivation can be raised through training.

Chris Argyris's 1970 book *Intervention Theory and Methods* is one of the most comprehensive, widely cited, and enduring works on organizational consulting for change written from an organizational behavior/organization development perspective. A portion of the first chapter from *Intervention Theory and Methods* is reprinted here. The book has remained central to the field because Argyris unambiguously lays out the fundamental tenets that undergird the organizational behavior perspective of change. These tenets define such fundamentals as the nature of the change-agent/client relationship, the necessity for valid and usable information, and necessary preconditions for organization members to internalize change.

The final reading in this chapter is Irving Janis' widely cited 1971 article "Groupthink," a study of pressures for conformance—the reasons that social conformity is encountered so frequently in groups. Janis examines high-level decision makers and decision making during times of major fiascoes: the 1962 Bay of Pigs, the Johnson administration's decision to escalate the Vietnam War, and the 1941 failure to prepare for the attack on Pearl Harbor. Groupthink is "the mode of thinking that persons engage in when *concurrence seeking* becomes so dominant in a cohesive in-group that it tends to override realistic appraisal of alternative courses of action . . . the desperate drive for consensus at any cost that suppresses dissent among the mighty in the corridors of power." Janis identifies eight symptoms of groupthink that are relatively easy to observe:

- An illusion of invulnerability
- Collective construction of rationalizations that permit group members to ignore warnings or other forms of negative feedback
- Unquestioning belief in the morality of the in-group
- Strong, negative, stereotyped views about the leaders of enemy groups
- Rapid application of pressure against group members who express even momentary doubts about virtually any illusions the group shares
- Careful, conscious, personal avoidance of deviation from what appears to be a group consensus

- Shared illusions of unanimity of opinion
- Establishment of *mindguards*—people who "protect the leader and fellow members from adverse information that might break the complacency they shared about the effectiveness and morality of past decisions."

Janis concludes with an assessment of the negative influence of groupthink on executive decision making (including overestimation of the group's capability and self-imposed isolation from new or opposing information and points of view), as well as preventive and remedial steps for dealing with groupthink.

The organizational behavior perspective is the most optimistic of all perspectives or theories of organization. Building from Douglas McGregor's Theory X and Theory Y assumptions, organizational behavior has assumed that under the right circumstances, people and organizations will grow and prosper together. The ultimate worth of people is an overarching value of the human relations movement—a worthy end in and of itself—not simply a means or process for achieving a higher-order organizational end. Individuals and organizations are not necessarily antagonists. Managers can learn to unleash previously stifled energies and creativities. The beliefs, values, and tenets of organizational behavior are noble, uplifting, and exciting. They hold a promise for humankind, especially those who will spend their lifetime working in organizations.

As one would expect of a very optimistic and humanistic set of assumptions and values, they (and the strategies of organizational behavior) became strongly normative (prescriptive). For many organizational behavior practitioners of the 1960s, 1970s, and 1980s the perspective's assumptions and methods became a cause. Hopefully, through the choice of articles and the introductions to each chapter, this volume communicates these optimistic tenets and values, and articulates the logical and emotional reasons why the organizational behavior perspective developed into a virtual movement. This is the true essence of *organizational behavior.*

References

ALDERFER, J. S. (1969). An empirical test of a new theory of human needs. *Organizational Behavior and Human Performance, 4,* 142–175.

ARGYRIS, C. (1962). *Interpersonal competence and organizational effectiveness.* Homewood, IL: The Dorsey Press and Richard D. Irwin.

ARGYRIS, C. (1970). Intervention theory and method. Reading, MA: Addison-Wesley.

ARGYRIS, C. (1990). *Overcoming organizational defenses: Facilitating organizational learning.* Boston: Allyn & Bacon.

BENNIS, W. G. (1976). *The unconscious conspiracy: Why leaders can't lead.* New York: AMACOM.

BOLMAN, L. G., & DEAL, T. E. (1991). *Reframing Organizations.* San Francisco: Jossey-Bass.

COHEN, A. R., FINK, S. L., GADON, H., & WILLITS, R. D. (1988). *Effective behavior in organizations* (4th ed.). Homewood, IL: Irwin.

FOLLETT, M. P. (1926). The giving of orders. In H. C. Metcalf (Ed.), *Scientific foundations of business administration.* Baltimore, MD: Williams & Wilkins.

HAIRE, M. (1954). Industrial social psychology. In G. Lindzey (Ed.), *Handbook of social psychology, Volume II: Special fields and applications* (pp. 1104–1123). Reading, MA: Addison-Wesley.

HAMPTON, D. R., SUMMER, C. E., & WEBBER, R. A. (1987). *Organizational behavior and the practice of management* (5th ed.). Glenview, IL: Scott, Foresman.

HERSEY, P., & BLANCHARD, K. H. (1982). *Management of organizational behavior: Utilizing human resources* (4th ed.). Englewood cliffs, NJ: Prentice-Hall.

JANIS, I. L. (November 1971). Groupthink. *Psychology Today,* 44–76.

LEWIN, K. (1947). Frontiers in group dynamics: Concept, method and reality in social science: Social equilibrium and social change. *Human Relations, 1,* 5–41.

LEWIN, K. (1948). *Resolving social conflicts.* New York: Harper.

MASLOW, A. H. (1943). A theory of human motivation. *Psychological Review, 50.*

MAYO, G. E. (1933). *The human problems of an industrial civilization.* Boston, MA: Harvard Business School, Division of Research.

McGREGOR, D. M. (1957a, April). The human side of enterprise. Address to the Fifth Anniversary Convocation of the School of Industrial Management, Massachusetts Institute of Technology. In *Adventure in thought and action.* Cambridge, MA: M.I.T. School of Industrial Management, 1957. Reprinted in W. G. Bennis, E. H. Schein, & C. McGregor (Eds.), (1966). *Leadership and motivation: Essays of Douglas McGregor* (pp. 3–20). Cambridge, MA: The M.I.T. Press.

McGREGOR, D. M. (November 1957b). The human side of enterprise. *Management Review,* 22–28, 88–92.

McGREGOR, D. M. (1960). *The human side of enterprise.* New York: McGraw-Hill.

MÜNSTERBERG, H. (1913). *Psychology and industrial efficiency.* Boston: Houghton Mifflin Company.

MÜNSTERBERG, M. (1922). *Hugo Münsterberg, His life and work.* New York: Appleton.

OTT, J. S. (Ed.). (1989). *Classic readings in organizational behavior.* Pacific Grove, CA: Brooks/Cole.

REITZ, H. J. (1987). *Behavior in organizations* (3rd ed.). Homewood, IL: Irwin.

ROETHLISBERGER, F. J., & DIXON, W. J. (1939). *Management and the worker.* Cambridge, MA: Harvard University Press.

WREN, D. A. (1972). *The evolution of management thought.* New York: Ronald Press.

14

The Giving of Orders

Mary Parker Follett

To some men the matter of giving orders seems a very simple affair; they expect to issue their own orders and have them obeyed without question. Yet, on the other hand, the shrewd common sense of many a business executive has shown him that the issuing of orders is surrounded by many difficulties; that to demand an unquestioning obedience to orders not approved, not perhaps even understood, is bad business policy. Moreover, psychology, as well as our own observation, shows us not only that you cannot get people to do things most satisfactorily by ordering them or exhorting them; but also that even reasoning with them, even convincing them intellectually, may not be enough. Even the "consent of the governed" will not do all the work it is supposed to do, an important consideration for those who are advocating employee representation. For all our past life, our early training, our later experience, all our emotions, beliefs, prejudices, every desire that we have, have formed certain habits of mind that the psychologists call habit-patterns, action-patterns, motor-sets.

Therefore it will do little good merely to get intellectual agreement; unless you change the habit-patterns of people, you have not really changed your people. Business administration, industrial organization, should build up certain habit-patterns, that is, certain mental attitudes.

SOURCE: Henry C. Metcalf, ed., *Scientific Foundations of Business Administration* (Baltimore: Williams & Wilkins Co., 1926). Copyright © 1926 The Williams & Wilkins Co. Footnotes omitted.

For instance, the farmer has a general disposition to "go it alone," and this is being changed by the activities of the co-operatives, that is, note, *by the farmer's own activities.* So the workman has often a general disposition of antagonism to his employers which cannot be changed by argument or exhortation, but only through certain activities which will create a different disposition. One of my trade union friends told me that he remembered when he was a quite small boy hearing his father, who worked in a shoe-shop, railing daily against his boss. So he grew up believing that it was inherent in the nature of things that the workman would be against his employer. I know many working men who have a prejudice against getting college men into factories. You could all give me examples of attitudes among your employees which you would like to change. We want, for instance, to create an attitude of respect for expert opinion.

If we analyse this matter a little further we shall see that we have to do three things. I am now going to use psychological language: (1) build up certain attitudes; (2) provide for the release of these attitudes; (3) augment the released response as it is being carried out. What does this mean in the language of business? A psychologist has given us the example of the salesman. The salesman first creates in you the attitude that you want his article; then, at just the "psychological" moment, he produces his contract blank which you may sign and thus release that attitude; then if, as you're preparing to sign, some one comes in and tells you how pleased he has been with his purchase of this article, that augments the response which is being released.

If we apply this to the subject of orders and obedience, we see that people can obey an order only if previous habit patterns are appealed to or new ones created. When the employer is considering an order, he should also be thinking of the way to form the habits which will ensure its being carried out. We should first lead the salesmen selling shoes or the bank clerk cashing cheques to see the desirability of a different method. Then the rules of the store or bank should be so changed as to make it possible for salesman or cashier to adopt the new method. In the third place they could be made more ready to follow the new method by convincing in advance some one individual who will set an example to the others. You can usually convince one or two or three ahead of the rank and file. This last step you all know from your experience to be good tactics; it is what the psychologists call intensifying the attitude to be released. But we find that the released attitude is not by one release fixed as a habit; it takes a good many responses to do that.

This is an important consideration for us, for from one point of view business success depends largely on this—namely, whether our business is so organized and administered that it tends to form certain habits, certain mental attitudes. It has been hard for many old-fashioned employers to understand that *orders will not take the place of training.* I want to italicize that. Many a time an employer has been angry because, as he expressed it, a workman "wouldn't" do so and so, when the truth of the matter was that the workman couldn't, actually couldn't, do as ordered because he could not go contrary to life-long habits. This whole subject might be taken up under the heading of education, for there we could give many instances of the attempt to make arbitrary authority take the place of training. In history, the aftermath of all revolutions shows us the results of the lack of training.

In this matter of prepared-in-advance behaviour patterns—that is, in preparing the way for the reception of orders, psychology makes a contribution when it points out that the same words often rouse in us a quite different response when heard in certain places and on certain occasions. A boy may respond differently to the same suggestion when made by his teacher and when made by his schoolmate. Moreover, he may respond differently to the same suggestion made by the teacher in the schoolroom and made by the teacher when they are taking a walk together. Applying this to the giving of orders, we see that the place in which orders are given, the circumstances under which they are given, may make all the difference in the world as to the response which we get. Hand them down a long way from President or Works Manager and the effect is weakened. One might say that the strength of favourable response to an order is in inverse ratio to the distance the order travels. Production efficiency is always in danger of being affected whenever the long-distance order is substituted for the face-to-face suggestion. There is, however, another reason for that which I shall consider in a moment.

All that we said in the foregoing paper of integration and circular behaviour applies directly to the anticipation of response in giving orders. We spoke then of what the psychologists call linear and circular behaviour. Linear behaviour would be, to quote from Dr. Cabot's review of my book, *Creative Experience,* when an order is accepted as passively as the woodshed accepts the wood. In circular behaviour you get a "come-back." But we all know that we get the come-back every day of our life, and we must certainly allow for it, or for what is more elegantly called circular behaviour, in the giving of orders. Following out the thought of the previous paper, I should say that the giving of orders and the receiving of orders ought to be a matter of integration through circular behaviour, and that we should seek methods to bring this about.

Psychology has another important contribution to make on this subject of issuing orders or giving directions: before the integration can be made between order-giver and order-receiver, there is often an integration to be made within one or both of the individuals concerned. There are often two dissociated paths in the individual; if you are clever enough to recognize these, you can sometimes forestall a Freudian conflict, make the integration appear before there is an acute stage.

To explain what I mean, let me run over briefly a social worker's case. The girl's parents had been divorced and the girl placed with a jolly, easy-going, slack and untidy family, consisting of the father and mother and eleven children, sons and daughters. Gracie was very happy here, but when the social worker in charge of the case found that the living conditions involved a good deal of promiscuity, she thought the girl should be placed elsewhere. She therefore took her to call on an aunt who had a home with some refinement of living, where they had "high tastes," as one of the family said. This aunt wished to have Gracie live with her, and Gracie decided that she would like to do so. The social worker, however, in order to test her, said "But I thought you were so happy where you are." "Can't I be happy and high, too?" the girl replied. There were two wishes here, you see. The social worker by removing the girl to the aunt may have forestalled a Freudian conflict, the dissociated paths may have been united. I do not know the outcome of this story, but it indicates a method of dealing with our co-directors—make them "happy and high, too."

Business administration has often to consider how to deal with the dissociated paths in individuals or groups, but the methods of doing this successfully have been developed much further in some departments than in others. We have as yet hardly recognized this as part of the technique of dealing with employees, yet the clever salesman knows that it is the chief part of his job. The prospective buyer wants the article and does not want it. The able salesman does not suppress the arguments in the mind of the purchaser against buying, for then the purchaser might be sorry afterwards for his purchase, and that would not be good salesmanship. Unless he can unite, integrate, in the purchaser's mind, the reasons for buying and the reasons for not buying, his future sales will be imperilled, he will not be the highest grade salesman.

Please note that this goes beyond what the psychologist whom I quoted at the beginning of this section told us. He said, "The salesman must create in you the attitude that you want his article." Yes, but only if he creates this attitude by integration, not by suppression.

Apply all this to orders. An order often leaves the individual to whom it is given with two dissociated paths; an order should seek to unite, to integrate, dissociated paths. Court decisions often settle arbitrarily which of two ways is to be followed without showing a possible integration of the two, that is, the individual is often left with an internal conflict on his hands. This is what both courts and business administration should try to prevent, the internal conflicts of individuals or groups.

In discussing the preparation for giving orders, I have not spoken at all of the appeal to certain instincts made so important by many writers. Some writers, for instance, emphasize the instinct of self-assertion; this would be violated by too rigid orders or too clumsily-exercised authority. Other writers, of equal standing, tell us that there is an instinct of submission to authority. I cannot discuss this for we should first have to define instincts, too long an undertaking for us now. Moreover, the exaggerated interest in instincts of recent years, an interest which in many cases has received rather crude expression, is now subsiding. Or, rather, it is being replaced by the more fruitful interest in habits.

There is much more that we could learn from psychology about the forming of habits and the preparation for giving orders than I can even hint at now. But there is one point, already spoken of by implication, that I wish to consider more explicitly—namely, the manner of giving orders. Probably more industrial trouble has been caused by the manner in which orders are given than in any other way. In the *Report on Strikes and Lockout,* a British Government publication, the cause of a number of strikes is given as "alleged harassing conduct of the foreman," "alleged tyrannical conduct of an under-foreman," "alleged overbearing conduct of officials." The explicit statement, however, of the tyranny of superior officers as the direct cause of strikes is I should say, unusual, yet resentment smoulders and breaks out in other issues. And the demand for better treatment is often explicit enough. We find it made by the metal and wood-working trades in an aircraft factory, who declared that any treatment of men without regard to their feelings of self-respect would be answered by a stoppage of work. We find it put in certain agreements with employers the ''the men must be treated with proper respect, and threats and abusive language must not be used.''

What happens to man, *in* a man, when an order is given in a disagreeable manner by foreman, head of department, his immediate superior in store, bank or factory? The man addressed feels that his self-respect is attacked, that one of his most inner sanctuaries is invaded. He loses his temper or becomes sullen or is on the defensive; he begins thinking of his ''rights''—a fatal attitude for any of us. In the language we have been using, the wrong behaviour pattern is aroused, the wrong motor-set; that is, he is now ''set'' to act in a way which is not going to benefit the enterprise in which he is engaged.

There is a more subtle psychological point here, too; the more you are ''bossed'' the more your activity of thought will take place within the bossing-pattern, and your part in that pattern seems usually to be opposition to the bossing.

This complaint of the abusive language and the tyrannical treatment of the one just above the worker is an old story to us all, but there is an opposite extreme which is far too little considered. The immediate superior officer is often so close to the worker that he does not exercise the proper duties of his position. Far from taking on himself an aggressive authority, he has often evaded one of the chief problems of his job: how to do what is implied in the fact that he has been put in a position over others. The head of the woman's cloak department in a store will call out, ''Say, Sadie, you're 36, aren't you? There's a woman down in the Back Bay kicking about something she says you promised yesterday.'' ''Well, I like that,'' says Sadie, ''Some of those Back Bay women would kick in Heaven.'' And that perhaps is about all that happens. Of course, the Back Bay lady

has to be appeased, but there is often no study of what has taken place for the benefit of the store. I do not mean that a lack of connection between such incidents and the improvement of store technique is universal, but it certainly exists far too often and is one of the problems of those officials who are just above the heads of departments. Naturally, a woman does not want to get on bad terms with her fellow employees with whom she talks and works all day long. Consider the chief operator of the telephone exchanges, remembering that the chief operator is a member of the union, and that the manager is not.

Now what is our problem here? How can we avoid the two extremes: too great bossism in giving orders, and practically no orders given? I am going to ask how *you* are avoiding these extremes. My solution is to depersonalize the giving of orders, to unite all concerned in a study of the situation, to discover the law of the situation and obey that. Until we do this I do not think we shall have the most successful business administration. This is what does take place, what has to take place, when there is a question between two men in positions of equal authority. The head of the sales departments does not give orders to the head of the production department, or vice versa. Each studies the market and the final decision is made as the market demands. This is, ideally, what should take place between foremen and the rank and file, between any head and his subordinates. One *person* should not give orders to another *person,* but both should agree to take their orders from the situation. If orders are simply part of the situation, the question of someone giving and someone receiving does not come up. Both accept the orders given by the situation. Employers accept the orders given by the situation; employees accept the orders given by the situation. This gives, does it not, a slightly different aspect to the whole of business administration through the entire plant?

We have here, I think, one of the largest contributions of scientific management: it tends to depersonalize orders. From one point of view, one might call the essence of scientific management the attempt to find the law of the situation. With scientific management the managers are as much under orders as the workers, for both obey the law of the situation. Our job is not how to get people to obey orders, but how to devise methods by which we can best *discover* the order integral to a particular situation. When that is found, the employee can issue it to the employer, as well as employer to employee. This often happens easily and naturally. My cook or my stenographer point out the law of the situation, and I, if I recognize it as such, accept it, even although it may reverse some "order" I have given.

If those in supervisory positions should depersonalize orders, then there would be no overbearing authority on the one hand, nor on the other that dangerous *laissez-aller* which comes from the fear of exercising authority. Of course we should exercise authority, but always the authority of the situation. I do not say that we have found the way to a frictionless existence, far from it, but we now understand the place which we mean to give to friction. We intend to set it to work for us as the engineer does when he puts the belt over the pulley. There will be just as much, probably more, room for disagreement in the method I am advocating. The situation will often be seen differently, often be interpreted differently. But we shall know what to do with it, we shall have found a method of dealing with it.

I call it depersonalizing because there is not time to go any further into the matter. I think it really is a matter of *repersonalizing*. We, persons, have relations with each other, but we should find them in and through the whole situation. We cannot have any sound relations with each other as long as we take them out of that setting which gives them their meaning and value. This divorcing of persons and the situation does a great deal of harm. I have just said that scientific management depersonalizes; the deeper philosophy of scientific management shows us personal relations within the whole setting of that thing of which they are a part.

There is much psychology, modern psychology particularly, which tends to divorce person and situation. What I am referring to is the present zest for "personality studies." When some difficulty arises, we often hear the psychologist whose specialty is personality studies say, "Study the psychology of that man." And this is very good advice, but only if at the same time we study the entire situation. To leave out the whole situation, however, is so common a blunder in the studies of these psychologists that it constitutes a serious weakness in their work. And as those of you who are personnel directors have more to do, I suppose, with those psychologists who have taken personality for their specialty than with any others, I wish you would watch and see how often you find that this limitation detracts from the value of their conclusions.

I said above that we should substitute for the long-distance order the face-to-face suggestion. I think we can now see a more cogent reason for this than the one then given. It is not the face-to-face suggestion that we want so much as the joint study of the problem, and such joint study can be made best by the employee and his immediate superior or employee and special expert on that question.

I began this talk by emphasizing the advisability of preparing in advance the attitude necessary for the carrying out of orders, and in the previous paper we considered preparing the attitude for integration; but we have now, in our consideration of the joint study of situations, in our emphasis on obeying the law of the situation, perhaps got a little beyond that, or rather we have now to consider in what sense we wish to take the psychologist's doctrine of prepared-in-advance attitudes. By itself this would not take us far, for everyone is studying psychology nowadays, and our employees are going to be just as active in preparing us as we in preparing them! Indeed, a girl working in a factory said to me, "We had a course in psychology last winter, and I see now that you have to be pretty careful how you put things to the managers if you want them to consider favourably what you're asking for." If this prepared-in-advance idea were all that the psychologists think it, it would have to be printed privately as secret doctrine. But the truth is that the best preparation for integration in the matter of orders or in anything else, is a joint study of the situation. We should not try to create the attitude we *want,* although that is the usual phrase, but the attitude required for cooperative study and decision. This holds good even for the salesman. We said above that when the salesman is told that he should create in the prospective buyer the attitude that he wants the article, he ought also to be told that he should do this by integration rather than by suppression. We have now a hint of *how* he is to attain this integration.

I have spoken of the importance of changing some of the language of business personnel relations. We considered whether the words "grievances," complaints," or Ford's "trouble specialists" did not arouse the wrong behaviour-patterns. I think "order" certainly does. If that word is not to mean any longer external authority, arbitrary authority, but the law of the situation, then we need a new word for it. It is often the order that people resent as much as the thing ordered. People do not like to be ordered even to take a holiday. I have often seen instances of this. The wish to govern one's own life is, of course, one of the most fundamental feelings in every human being. To call this "the instinct of self-assertion," "the instinct of initiative," does not express it wholly. I think it is told in the life of some famous American that when he was a boy and his mother said, "Go get a pail of water," he always replied, "I won't," before taking up the pail and fetching the water. This is significant; he resented the command, the command of a person; but he went and got the water, not, I believe, because he had to, but because he recognized the demand of the situation. *That,* he knew he had to obey; *that,* he was willing to obey. And this kind of obedience is not opposed to the wish to govern one's self, but each is involved in the other; both are part of the same fundamental urge at the root of one's being. We have here something far more

profound than "the egoistic impulse" or "the instinct of self-assertion." We have the very essence of the human being.

This subject of orders has led us into the heart of the whole question of authority and consent. When we conceive of authority and consent as parts of an inclusive situation, does that not throw a flood of light on this question? The point of view here presented gets rid of several dilemmas which have seemed to puzzle people in dealing with consent. The feeling of being "under" someone, of "subordination," of "servility," of being "at the will of another," comes out again and again in the shop stewards movement and in the testimony before the Coal Commission. One man said before the Coal Commission, "It is all right to work with anyone; what is disagreeable is to feel too distinctly that you are working *under* anyone." *With* is a pretty good preposition, not because it connotes democracy, but because it connotes functional unity, a much more profound conception than that of democracy as usually held. The study of the situation involves the *with* preposition. Then Sadie is not left alone by the head of the cloak department, nor does she have to obey her. The head of the department says, "Let's see how such cases had better be handled, then we'll abide by that." Sadie is not under the head of the department, but both are *under* the situation.

Twice I have had a servant applying for a place ask me if she would be treated as a menial. When the first woman asked me that, I had no idea what she meant, I thought perhaps she did not want to do the roughest work, but later I came to the conclusion that to be treated as a menial meant to be obliged to be under someone, to follow orders without using one's own judgment. If we believe that what heightens self-respect increases efficiency, we shall be on our guard here.

Very closely connected with this is the matter of pride in one's work. If an order goes against what the craftsman or the clerk thinks is the way of doing his work which will bring the best results, he is justified in not wishing to obey that order. Could not that difficulty be met by a joint study of the situation? It is said that it is characteristic of the British workman to feel, "I know my job and won't be told how." The peculiarities of the British workman might be met by a joint study of the situation, it being understood that he probably has more to contribute to that study than anyone else. . . .

There is another dilemma which has to be met by everyone who is in what is called a position of authority: how can you expect people merely to obey orders and at the same time to take that degree of responsibility which they should take? Indeed, in my experience, the people who enjoy following orders blindly, without any thought on their own part, are those who like thus to get rid of responsibility. But the taking of responsibility, each according to his capacity, each according to his function in the whole . . . , this taking of responsibility is usually the most vital matter in the life of every human being, just as the allotting of responsibility is the most important part of business administration.

A young trade unionist said to me, "how much dignity can I have as a mere employee?" He can have all the dignity in the world if he is allowed to make his fullest contribution to the plant *and to assume definitely the responsibility therefor.*

I think one of the gravest problems before us is how to make the reconciliation between receiving orders and taking responsibility. And I think the reconciliation can be made through our conception of the law of the situation. . . .

We have considered the subject of symbols. It is often very apparent that an order is a symbol. The referee in the game stands watch in hand and says, "Go." It is an order, but order only as symbol. I may say to an employee, "Do so and so," but I should say it only because we have both agreed, openly or tacitly, that that which I am ordering done is the best thing to be done. The order is then a symbol. And if it is a philosophical and psychological truth that we owe obedience only to a functional unity to which we are contributing, we should remember that a more accurate way of stating that would be to say that our obligation is to a unifying, to a process.

This brings us now to one of our most serious problems in this matter of orders. It is important, but we can touch on it only briefly; it is what we spoke of . . . as the evolving situation. I am trying to show here that the order must be integral to the situation and must be recognized as such. But we saw that the situation was always developing. If the situation is never stationary, then the order should never be stationary, so to speak; how to prevent it from being so is our problem. The situation is changing while orders are being carried out. How is the order to keep up with the situation? External orders never can, only those drawn fresh from the situation.

Moreover, if taking a *responsible* attitude toward experience involves recognizing the evolving situation, a *conscious* attitude toward experience means that we note the change which the developing situation makes in ourselves; the situation does not change without changing us.

To summarize, . . . integration being the basic law of life, orders should be the composite conclusion of those who give and those who receive them; more than this, that they should be the integration of the people concerned and the situation; even more than this, that they should be the integration involved in the evolving situation. If you accept my three fundamental statements on this subject: (1) that the order should be the law of the situation; (2) that the situation is always evolving; (3) that orders should involve circular not linear behaviour—then we see that our old conception of orders has somewhat changed, and that there should therefore follow definite changes in business practice.

There is a problem so closely connected with the giving of orders that I want to put it before you for future discussion. After we have decided on our orders, we have to consider how much and what kind of supervision is necessary or advisable in order that they shall be carried out. We all know that many workers object to being watched. What does that mean, how far is it justifiable? How can the objectionable element be avoided and at the same time necessary supervision given? I do not think that this matter has been studied sufficiently. When I asked a very intelligent girl what she thought would be the result of profit sharing and employee representation in the factory where she worked, she replied joyfully, "We shan't need foremen any more." While her entire ignoring of the fact that the foreman has other duties than keeping workers on their jobs was amusing, one wants to go beyond one's amusement and find out what this objection to being watched really means.

In a case in Scotland arising under the Minimum Wage Act, the overman was called in to testify whether or not a certain workman did his work properly. The examination was as follows:

Magistrate: "But isn't it your duty under the Mines Act to visit each working place twice a day?"
Overman: "Yes."
Magistrate: "Don't you do it?"
Overman: "Yes."
Magistrate: "Then why didn't you ever see him work?"
Overman: "They always stop work when they see an overman coming and sit down and wait till he's gone—even take out their pipes, if it's a mine free from gas. They won't let anyone watch them."

An equally extreme standard was enforced for a part of the war period at a Clyde engineering works. The chairman of shop stewards was told one morning that there was a grievance at the smithy. He found one of the blacksmiths in a rage because the managing director in his ordinary morning's walk through the works had stopped for five minutes or so and watched this man's fire. After a shop meeting the chairman took up a deputation to the director and secured the promise that this should not happen again. At the next works meeting the chairman reported the incident to the body of workers, with the result that a similar demand was made throughout the works and practically acceded to, so that the director hardly dared to stop at all in his morning's walk.

I have seen similar instances cited. Many workmen feel that being watched is unbearable. What can we do about it? How can we get proper supervision without this watching which a worker resents? Supervision is necessary; supervision is resented—how are we going to make the integration there? Some say, "Let the workers elect the supervisors." I do not believe in that.

There are three other points closely connected with the subject of this paper which I should like merely to point out. First, when and how do you point out mistakes, misconduct? One principle can surely guide us here: don't blame for the sake of blaming, make what you have to say accomplish something; say it in that form, at that time, under those circumstances, which will make it a real education to your subordinate. Secondly, since it is recognized that the one who gives the orders is not as a rule a very popular person, the management sometimes tries to offset this by allowing the person who has this onus upon him to give any pleasant news to the workers, to have the credit of any innovation which the workers very much desire. One manager told me that he always tried to do this. I suppose that this is good behaviouristic psychology, and yet I am not sure that it is a method I wholly like. It is quite different, however, in the case of a mistaken order having been given; then I think the one who made the mistake should certainly be the one to rectify it, not as a matter of strategy, but because it is better for him too. It is better for all of us not only to acknowledge our mistakes, but to do something about them. If a foreman discharges someone and it is decided to reinstate the man, it is obviously not only good tactics but a square deal to the foreman to allow him to do the reinstating.

There is, of course, a great deal more to this matter of giving orders than we have been able to touch on; far from exhausting the subject, I feel that I have only given hints. I have been told that the artillery men suffered more mentally in the war than others, and the reason assigned for this was that their work was directed from a distance. The combination of numbers by which they focused their fire was telephoned to them. The result was also at a distance. Their activity was not closely enough connected with the actual situation at either end.

15

A Theory of Human Motivation

A. H. Maslow

I. Introduction

In a previous paper [13] various propositions were presented which would have to be included in any theory of human motivation that could lay claim to being definitive. These conclusions may be briefly summarized as follows:

1. The integrated wholeness of the organism must be one of the foundation stones of motivation theory.

2. The hunger drive (or any other physiological drive) was rejected as a centering point or model for a definitive theory of motivation. Any drive that is somatically based and localizable was shown to be atypical rather than typical in human motivation.

3. Such a theory should stress and center itself upon ultimate or basic goals rather than partial or superficial ones, upon ends rather than means to these ends. Such a stress would imply a more central place for unconscious than for conscious motivations.

4. There are usually available various cultural paths to the same goal. Therefore conscious, specific, local-cultural desires are not as fundamental in motivation theory as the more basic, unconscious goals.

5. Any motivated behavior, either preparatory or consummatory, must be understood to be a channel through which many basic needs may be simultaneously expressed

SOURCE: From *Psychological Review* 50 (1943): 370–396.

or satisfied. Typically an act has *more* than one motivation.

6. Practically all organismic states are to be understood as motivated and as motivating.

7. Human needs arrange themselves in hierarchies of prepotency. That is to say, the appearance of one need usually rests on the prior satisfaction of another, more pre-potent need. Man is a perpetually wanting animal. Also no need or drive can be treated as if it were isolated or discrete; every drive is related to the state of satisfaction or dissatisfaction of other drives.

8. *Lists* of drives will get us nowhere for various theoretical and practical reasons. Furthermore any classification of motivations must deal with the problem of levels of specificity or generalization of the motives to be classified.

9. Classifications of motivations must be based upon goals rather than upon instigating drives or motivated behavior.

10. Motivation theory should be human-centered rather than animal-centered.

11. The situation or the field in which the organism reacts must be taken into account but the field alone can rarely serve as an exclusive explanation for behavior. Furthermore the field itself must be interpreted in terms of the organism. Field theory cannot be a substitute for motivation theory.

12. Not only the integration of the organism must be taken into account, but also the possibility of isolated, specific, partial or segmental reactions.

It has since become necessary to add to these another affirmation.

13. Motivation theory is not synonymous with behavior theory. The motivations are only one class of determinants of behavior. While behavior is almost always motivated, it is also almost always biologically, culturally and situationally determined as well.

The present paper is an attempt to formulate a positive theory of motivation which will satisfy these theoretical demands and at the same time conform to the known facts, clinical and observational as well as experimental. It derives most directly, however, from clinical experience. This theory is, I think, in the functionalist tradition of James and Dewey, and is fused with the holism of Wertheimer [19], Goldstein [6], and Gestalt Psychology, and with the dynamicism of Freud [4] and Adler [1]. This fusion or synthesis may arbitrarily be called a 'general-dynamic' theory.

It is far easier to perceive and to criticize the aspects in motivation theory than to remedy them. Mostly this is because of the very serious lack of sound data in this area. I conceive this lack of sound facts to be due primarily to the absence of a valid theory of motivation. The present theory then must be considered to be a suggested program or framework for future research and must stand or fall, not so much on facts available or evidence presented, as upon researches yet to be done, researches suggested perhaps, by the questions raised in this paper.

II. The Basic Needs

The 'physiological' needs.   The needs that are usually taken as the starting point for motivation theory are the so-called physiological drives. Two recent lines of research make it necessary to revise our customary notions about these needs, first, the development of the concept of homeostasis, and second, the finding that appetites (preferential choices among foods) are a fairly efficient indication of actual needs or lacks in the body.

Homeostasis refers to the body's automatic efforts to maintain a constant, normal state of the blood stream. Cannon [2] has described this process for (1) the water content of the blood, (2) salt content, (3) sugar content, (4) protein content, (5) fat content, (6) calcium content, (7) oxygen content, (8) constant hydrogen-ion level (acid-base balance) and (9) constant temperature of the blood. Obviously this list

can be extended to include other minerals, the hormones, vitamins, etc.

Young in a recent article [21] has summarized the work on appetite in its relation to body needs. If the body lacks some chemical, the individual will tend to develop a specific appetite or partial hunger for that food element.

Thus it seems impossible as well as useless to make any list of fundamental physiological needs for they can come to almost any number one might wish, depending on the degree of specificity of description. We can not identify all physiological needs as homeostatic. That sexual desire, sleepiness, sheer activity and maternal behavior in animals, are homeostatic, has not yet been demonstrated. Furthermore, this list would not include the various sensory pleasures (tastes, smells, tickling, stroking) which are probably physiological and which may become the goals of motivated behavior.

In a previous paper [13] it has been pointed out that these physiological drives or needs are to be considered unusual rather than typical because they are isolable, and because they are localizable somatically. That is to say, they are relatively independent of each other, of other motivations and of the organism as a whole, and secondly, in many cases, it is possible to demonstrate a localized, underlying somatic base for the drive. This is true less generally than has been thought (exceptions are fatigue, sleepiness, maternal responses) but it is still true in the classic instances of hunger, sex, and thirst.

It should be pointed out again that any of the physiological needs and the consummatory behavior involved with them serve as channels for all sorts of other needs as well. That is to say, the person who thinks he is hungry may actually be seeking more for comfort, or dependence, than for vitamins or proteins. Conversely, it is possible to satisfy the hunger need in part by other activities such as drinking water or smoking cigarettes. In other words, relatively isolable as these physiological needs are, they are not completely so.

Undoubtedly these physiological needs are the most prepotent of all needs. What this means specifically is, that in the human being who is missing everything in life in an extreme fashion, it is most likely that the major motivation would be the physiological needs rather than any others. A person who is lacking food, safety, love, and esteem would most probably hunger for food more strongly than for anything else.

If all the needs are unsatisfied, and the organism is then dominated by the physiological needs, all other needs may become simply non-existent or be pushed into the background. It is then fair to characterize the whole organism by saying simply that it is hungry, for consciousness is almost completely preempted by hunger. All capacities are put into the service of hunger-satisfaction, and the organization of these capacities is almost entirely determined by the one purpose of satisfying hunger. The receptors and effectors, the intelligence, memory, habits, all may not be defined simply as hunger-gratifying tools. Capacities that are not useful for this purpose lie dormant, or are pushed into the background. The urge to write poetry, the desire to acquire an automobile, the interest in American history, the desire for a new pair of shoes are, in the extreme case, forgotten or become of secondary importance. For the man who is extremely and dangerously hungry, no other interests exist but food. He dreams food, he remembers food, he thinks about food, he emotes only about food, he perceives only food and he wants only food. The more subtle determinants that ordinarily fuse with the physiological drives in organizing even feeding, drinking or sexual behavior, may not be so completely overwhelmed as to allow us to speak at this time (but *only* at this time) of pure hunger drive and behavior, with the one unqualified aim of relief.

Another peculiar characteristic of the human organism when it is dominated by a certain need is that the whole philosophy of the future tends also to change. For our chronically and extremely hungry man, Utopia can be defined very simply as a place where there is plenty of food. He tends to think that, if only he is guaranteed food for the rest of his life, he will be perfectly happy and will never want anything more. Life itself tends to be defined in terms of eating. Anything else will be defined as unimportant. Freedom, love, community feeling, respect, philosophy, may all be waved aside as fripperies which are useless since they fail to fill the stomach. Such a man may fairly be said to live by bread alone.

It cannot possibly be denied that such things are true but their *generality* can be denied. Emergency conditions are, almost by definition, rare in the normally functioning peaceful society. That this truism can be forgotten is due mainly to two reasons. First, rats have few motivations other than physiological ones, and since so much of the research upon motivation has been made with these animals, it is easy to carry the rat-picture over to the human being. Secondly, it is too often not realized that culture itself is an adaptive tool, one of whose main functions is to make the physiological emergencies come less and less often. In most of the known societies, chronic extreme hunger of the emergency type is rare, rather than common. In any case, this is still true in the United States. The average American citizen is experiencing appetite rather than hunger when he says "I am hungry." He is apt to experience sheer life-and-death hunger only by accident and then only a few times through his entire life.

Obviously a good way to obscure the 'higher' motivations, and to get a lopsided view of human capacities and human nature, is to make the organism extremely and chronically hungry or thirsty. Anyone who attempts to make an emergency picture into a typical one, and who will measure all of man's goals and desires by his behavior during extreme physiological deprivation is certainly being blind to many things. It is quite true that man lives by bread alone—when there is no bread. But what happens to man's desires when there *is* plenty of bread and when his belly is chronically filled?

At once other (and 'higher') needs emerge and these, rather than physiological hungers, dominate the organism. And when these in turn are satisfied, again new (and still 'higher') needs emerge and so on. This is what we mean by saying that the basic human needs are organized into a hierarchy of relative prepotency.

One main implication of this phrasing is that gratification becomes as important a concept as deprivation in motivation theory, for it releases the organism from the domination of a relatively more physiological need, permitting thereby the emergence of other more social goals. The physiological needs, along with their partial goals, when chronically gratified cease to exist as active determinants or organizers of behavior. They now exist only in a potential fashion in the sense that they may emerge again to dominate the organism if they are thwarted. But a want that is satisfied is no longer a want. The organism is dominated and its behavior organized only by unsatisfied needs. If hunger is satisfied, it becomes unimportant in the current dynamics of the individual.

This statement is somewhat qualified by a hypothesis to be discussed more fully later, namely that it is precisely those individuals in whom a certain need has always been satisfied who are best equipped to tolerate deprivation of that need in the future, and that furthermore, those who have been deprived in the past will react differently to current satisfactions than the one who has never been deprived.

The safety needs.   If the physiological needs are relatively well gratified, there then emerges a new set of needs, which we may categorize roughly as the safety needs. All that has been said of the physiological needs is equally true, although in lesser degree, of these desires. The organism may equally well be wholly dominated by them. They may serve as the almost exclusive organizers of behavior, recruiting all the capacities of the organism in their service, and we may then fairly describe the whole organism as a safety-seeking mechanism. Again we may say of the receptors, the effectors, of the intellect and the other capacities that they are primarily safety-seeking tools. Again, as in the hungry man, we find that the dominating goal is a strong determinant not only of his current world-outlook and philosophy but also of his philosophy of the future. Practically

everything looks less important than safety, (even sometimes the physiological needs which being satisfied, are now underestimated). A man, in this state, if it is extreme enough and chronic enough, may be characterized as living almost for safety alone.

Although in this paper we are interested primarily in the needs of the adult, we can approach an understanding of his safety needs perhaps more efficiently by observation of infants and children, in whom these needs are much more simple and obvious. One reason for the clearer appearance of the threat or danger reaction in infants, is that they do not inhibit this reaction at all, whereas adults in our society have been taught to inhibit it at all costs. Thus even when adults do feel their safety threatened we may not be able to see this on the surface. Infants will react in a total fashion and as if they were endangered, if they are disturbed or dropped suddenly, startled by loud noises, flashing light, or other unusual sensory stimulation, by rough handling, by general loss of support in the mother's arms, or by inadequate support.[1]

In infants we can also see a much more direct reaction to bodily illnesses of various kinds. Sometimes these illnesses seem to be immediately and *per se* threatening and seem to make the child feel unsafe. For instance, vomiting, colic or other sharp pains seem to make the child look at the whole world in a different way. At such a moment of pain, it may be postulated that, for the child, the appearance of the whole world suddenly changes from sunniness to darkness, so to speak, and becomes a place in which anything at all might happen, in which previously stable things have suddenly become unstable. Thus a child who because of some bad food is taken ill may, for a day or two, develop fear, nightmares, and a need for protection and reassurance never seen in him before his illness.

Another indication of the child's need for safety is his preference for some kind of undisrupted routine or rhythm. He seems to want a predictable, orderly world. For instance, injustice, unfairness, or inconsistency in the parents seems to make a child feel anxious and unsafe. This attitude may be not so much because of the injustice *per se* or any particular pains involved, but rather because this treatment threatens to make the world look unreliable, or unsafe, or unpredictable. Young children seem to thrive better under a system which has at least a skeletal outline of rigidity, in which there is a schedule of a kind, some sort of routine, something that can be counted upon, not only for the present but also far into the future. Perhaps one could express this more accurately by saying that the child needs an organized world rather than an unorganized or unstructured one.

The central role of the parents and the normal family setup are indisputable. Quarreling, physical assault, separation, divorce or death within the family may be particularly terrifying. Also parental outbursts of rage or threats of punishment directed to the child, calling him names, speaking to him harshly, shaking him, handling him roughly, or actual physical punishment sometimes elicit such total panic and terror in the child that we must assume more is involved than the physical pain alone. While it is true that in some children this terror may represent also a fear of loss of parental love, it can also occur in completely rejected children, who seem to cling to the hating parents more for sheer safety and protection than because of hope and love.

Confronting the average child with new, unfamiliar, strange, unmanageable stimuli or situations will too frequently elicit the danger or terror reaction, as for example, getting lost or even being separated from the parents for a short time, being confronted with new faces, new situations or new tasks, the sight of strange, unfamiliar or uncontrollable objects, illness or death. Particularly at such times, the child's frantic clinging to his parents is eloquent testimony to their role as protectors (quite apart from their roles as food-givers and love-givers).

From these and similar observations, we may generalize and say that the average child in our society generally prefers a safe, orderly, predictable, organized world, which he can count on, and in which unexpected, unmanageable or other dangerous things do not happen, and in which, in any case, he has all-powerful parents who protect and shield him from harm.

That these reactions may so easily be observed in children is in a way a proof of the fact that children in our society, feel too unsafe (or, in a word, are badly brought up). Children who are reared in an unthreatening, loving family do *not* ordinarily react as we have described above [17]. In such children the danger reactions are apt to come mostly to objects or situations that adults too would consider dangerous.[2]

The healthy, normal, fortunate adult in our culture is largely satisfied in his safety needs. The peaceful, smoothly running, 'good' society ordinarily makes its members feel safe enough from wild animals, extremes of temperature, criminals, assault and murder, tyranny, etc. Therefore, in a very real sense, he no longer has any safety needs as active motivators. Just as a sated man no longer feels hungry, a safe man no longer feels endangered. If we wish to see these needs directly and clearly we must turn to neurotic or near-neurotic individuals, and to the economic and social underdogs. In between these extremes, we can perceive the expressions of safety needs only in such phenomena as, for instance, the common preference for a job with tenure and protection, the desire for a savings account, and for insurance of various kinds (medical, dental, unemployment, disability, old age).

Other broader aspects of the attempt to seek safety and stability in the world are seen in the very common preference for familiar rather than unfamiliar things, or for the known rather than the unknown. The tendency to have some religion or world-philosophy that organizes the universe and the men in it into some sort of satisfactorily coherent, meaningful whole is also in part motivated by safety-seeking. Here too we may list science and philosophy in general as partially motivated by the safety needs (we shall see later that there are also other motivations to scientific, philosophical or religious endeavor).

Otherwise the need for safety is seen as an active and dominant mobilizer of the organism's resources only in emergencies, *e.g.,* war, disease, natural catastrophes, crime waves, societal disorganization, neurosis, brain injury, chronically bad situation.

Some neurotic adults in our society are, in many ways, like the unsafe child in their desire for safety, although in the former it takes on a somewhat special appearance. Their reaction is often to unknown, psychological dangers in a world that is perceived to be hostile, overwhelming and threatening. Such a person behaves as if a great catastrophe were almost always impending, *i.e.,* he is usually responding as if to an emergency. His safety needs often find specific expression in a search for a protector, or a stronger person on whom he may depend, or perhaps, a Fuehrer.

The neurotic individual may be described in a slightly different way with some usefulness as a grown-up person who retains his childish attitudes toward the world. That is to say, a neurotic adult may be said to behave 'as if' he were actually afraid of a spanking, or of his mother's disapproval, or of being abandoned by his parents, or having his food taken away from him. It is as if his childish attitudes of fear and threat reaction to a dangerous world had gone underground, and untouched by the growing up and learning processes, were now ready to be called out by any stimulus that would make a child feel endangered and threatened.[3]

The neurosis in which the search for safety takes its clearest form is in the compulsive-obsessive neurosis. Compulsive-obsessives try frantically to order and stabilize the world so that no unmanageable, unexpected or unfamiliar dangers will ever appear [14]. They hedge themselves about with all sorts of ceremonials, rules and formulas so that every possible contingency may be provided for and so that no new contingencies may appear. They are much like the brain injured cases, described by Goldstein [6], who manage to maintain their equilibrium by avoiding everything unfamiliar and strange and by ordering their restricted world in such a neat, disciplined, orderly fashion that everything in the world can be

counted upon. They try to arrange the world so that anything unexpected (dangers) cannot possibly occur. If, through no fault of their own, something unexpected does occur, they go into a panic reaction as if this unexpected occurrence constituted a grave danger. What we can see only as a none-too-strong preference in the healthy person, *e.g.,* preference for the familiar, becomes a life-and-death necessity in abnormal cases.

The love needs. If both the physiological and the safety needs are fairly well gratified, then there will emerge the love and affection and belongingness needs, and the whole cycle already described will repeat itself with this new center. Now the person will feel keenly, as never before, the absence of friends, or a sweetheart, or a wife, or children. He will hunger for affectionate relations with people in general, namely, for a place in his group, and he will strive with great intensity to achieve this goal. He will want to attain such a place more than anything else in the world and may even forget that once, when he was hungry, he sneered at love.

In our society the thwarting of these needs is the most commonly found core in cases of maladjustment and more severe psychopathology. Love and affection, as well as their possible expression in sexuality, are generally looked upon with ambivalence and are customarily hedged about with many restrictions and inhibitions. Practically all theorists of psychopathology have stressed thwarting of the love needs as basic in the picture of maladjustment. Many clinical studies have therefore been made of this need and we know more about it perhaps than any of the other needs except the physiological ones [14].

One thing that must be stressed at this point is that love is not synonymous with sex. Sex may be studied as a purely physiological need. Ordinarily sexual behavior is multi-determined, that is to say, determined not only by sexual but also by other needs chief among which are the love and affection needs. Also not to be overlooked is the fact that the love needs involve both giving *and* receiving love.[4]

The esteem needs.   All people in our society (with a few pathological exceptions) have a need or desire for a stable, firmly based, (usually) high evaluation of themselves, for self-respect, or self-esteem, and for the esteem of others. By firmly based self-esteem, we mean that which is soundly based upon real capacity, achievement and respect from others. These needs may be classified into two subsidiary sets. These are, first, the desire for strength, for achievement, for adequacy, for confidence in the face of the world, and for independence and freedom.[5] Secondly, we have what we may call the desire for reputation or prestige (defining it as respect or esteem from other people), recognition, attention, importance or appreciation.[6] These needs have been relatively stressed by Alfred Adler and his followers, and have been relatively neglected by Freud and the psychoanalysts. More and more today however there is appearing widespread appreciation of their central importance.

Satisfaction of the self-esteem need leads to feelings of self-confidence, worth, strength, capability and adequacy of being useful and necessary in the world. But thwarting of these needs produces feelings of inferiority, of weakness and of helplessness. These feelings in turn give rise to either basic discouragement or else compensatory or neurotic trends. An appreciation of the necessity of basic self-confidence and an understanding of how helpless people are without it, can be easily gained from a study of severe traumatic neurosis [8].[7]

The need for self-actualization.   Even if all these needs are satisfied, we may still often (if not always) expect that a new discontent and restlessness will soon develop, unless the individual is doing what he is fitted for. A musician must make music, an artist must paint, a poet must write, if he is to be ultimately happy. What a man can be, he must be. This need we may call self-actualization.

This term, first coined by Kurt Goldstein, is being used in this paper in a much more specific and limited fashion. It refers to the desire for self-fulfillment, namely, to the tendency for him to become actualized in what he is potentially. This tendency might be phrased as the desire to become more and more what one is, to become everything that one is capable of becoming.

The specific form that these needs will take will of course vary greatly from person to person. In one individual it may take the form of the desire to be an ideal mother, in another it may be expressed athletically, and in still another it may be expressed in painting pictures or in inventions. It is not necessarily a creative urge although in people who have any capacities for creation it will take this form.

The clear emergence of these needs rests upon prior satisfaction of the physiological, safety, love and esteem needs. We shall call people who are satisfied in these needs, basically satisfied people, and it is from these that we may expect the fullest (and healthiest) creativeness.[8] Since, in our society, basically satisfied people are the exception, we do not know much about self-actualization, either experimentally or clinically. It remains a challenging problem for research.

The preconditions for the basic need satisfactions.   There are certain conditions which are immediate prerequisites for the basic need satisfactions. Danger to these is reacted to almost as if it were a direct danger to the basic needs themselves. Such conditions as freedom to speak, freedom to do what one wishes so long as no harm is done to others, freedom to express one's self, freedom to investigate and seek for information, freedom to defend one's self, justice, fairness, honesty, orderliness in the group are examples of such preconditions for basic need satisfactions. Thwarting in these freedoms will be reacted to with a threat or emergency response. These conditions are not ends in themselves but they are *almost* so since they are so closely related to the basic needs, which are apparently the only ends in themselves. These conditions are defended because without them the basic satisfactions are quite impossible, or at least, very severely endangered.

If we remember that the cognitive capacities (perceptual, intellectual, learning) are a set of adjustive tools, which have, among other functions, that of satisfaction of our basic needs, then it is clear that any danger to them, any deprivation or blocking of their free use, must also be indirectly threatening to the basic needs themselves. Such a statement is a partial solution of the general problems of curiosity, the search for knowledge, truth and wisdom, and the ever-persistent urge to solve the cosmic mysteries.

We must therefore introduce another hypothesis and speak of degrees of closeness to the basic needs, for we have already pointed out that *any* conscious desires (partial goals) are more or less important as they are more or less close to the basic needs. The same statement may be made for various behavior acts. An act is psychologically important if it contributes directly to satisfaction of basic needs. The less directly it so contributes, or the weaker this contribution is, the less important this act must be conceived to be from the point of view of dynamic psychology. A similar statement may be made for the various defense or coping mechanisms. Some are very directly related to the protection or attainment of the basic needs, other are only weakly and distantly related. Indeed if we wished, we could speak of more basic and less basic defense mechanisms, and then affirm that danger to the more basic defenses is more threatening than danger to less basic defenses (always remembering that this is so only because of their relationship to the basic needs).

The desires to know and to understand. So far, we have mentioned the cognitive needs only in passing. Acquiring knowledge and systematizing the universe have been considered as, in part, techniques for the achievement of basic safety in the world, or, for the intelligent man, expressions of self-actualization. Also freedom of inquiry and expression have been discussed as preconditions of satisfactions of the basic needs. True though these formulations may be, they do not constitute definitive answers to the question as to the motivation role of curiosity, learning, philosophizing, experimenting, etc. They are, at best, no more than partial answers.

This question is especially difficult because we know so little about the facts. Curiosity, exploration, desire for the facts, desire to know may certainly be observed easily enough. The fact that they often are pursued even at great cost to the individual's safety is an earnest of the partial character of our previous discussion. In addition, the writer must admit that, though he has sufficient clinical evidence to postulate the desire to know as a very strong drive in intelligent people, no data are available for unintelligent people. It may then be largely a function of relatively high intelligence. Rather tentatively, then, and largely in the hope of stimulating discussion and research, we shall postulate a basic desire to know, to be aware of reality, to get the facts, to satisfy curiosity, or as Wertheimer phrases it, to see rather than to be blind.

This postulation, however, is not enough. Even after we know, we are impelled to know more and more minutely and microscopically on the one hand, and on the other, more and more extensively in the direction of a world philosophy, religion, etc. The facts that we acquire, if they are isolated or atomistic, inevitably get theorized about, and either analyzed or organized or both. This process has been phrased by some as the search for 'meaning.' We shall then postulate a desire to understand, to systematize, to organize, to analyze, to look for relations and meanings.

Once these desires are accepted for discussion, we see that they too form themselves into a small hierarchy in which the desire to know is prepotent over the desire to understand. All the characteristics of a hierarchy of prepotency that we have described above, seem to hold for this one as well.

We must guard ourselves against the too easy tendency to separate these desires from the basic needs we have discussed above, *i.e.*, to make a sharp dichotomy between 'cognitive' and 'conative' needs. The desire to know and to understand are themselves conative, *i.e.*, have a striving character, and are as much personality needs as the 'basic needs' we have already discussed [19].

III. Further Characteristics of the Basic Needs

The degree of fixity of the hierarchy of basic needs. We have spoken so far as if this hierarchy were a fixed order but actually it is not nearly as rigid as we may have implied. It is true that most of the people with whom we have worked have seemed to have these basic needs in about the order that has been indicated. However, there have been a number of exceptions.

(1) There are some people in whom, for instance, self-esteem seems to be more important than love. This most common reversal in the hierarchy is usually due to the development of the notion that the person who is most likely to be loved is a strong or powerful person, one who inspires respect or fear, and who is self confident or aggressive. Therefore such people who lack love and seek it, may try hard to put on a front of aggressive, confident behavior. But essentially they seek high self-esteem and its behavior expressions more as a means-to-an-end than for its own sake; they seek self-assertion for the sake of love rather than for self-esteem itself.

(2) There are other, apparently innately creative people in whom the drive to creativeness seems to be more important than any other counter-determinant. Their creativeness might appear not as self-actualization released by basic satisfaction, but in spite of lack of basic satisfaction.

(3) In certain people the level of aspiration may be permanently deadened or lowered. That is to say, the less prepotent goals may simply be lost, and may disappear forever, so that the person who has experienced life at a very low level, i.e., chronic unemployment, may continue to be satisfied for the rest of his life if only he can get enough food.

(4) The so-called 'psychopathic personality' is another example of permanent loss of the love needs. These are people who, according to the best data available [9], have been starved for love in the earliest months of their lives and have simply lost forever the desire and the ability to give and to receive affection (as animals lose sucking or pecking reflexes that are not exercised soon enough after birth).

(5) Another cause of reversal of the hierarchy is that when a need has been satisfied for a long time, this need may be underevaluated. People who have never experienced chronic hunger are apt to underestimate its effects and to look upon food as a rather unimportant thing. If they are dominated by a higher need, this higher need will seem to be the most important of all. It then becomes possible, and indeed does actually happen, that they may, for the sake of this higher need, put themselves into the position of being deprived in a more basic need. We may expect that after a long-time deprivation of the more basic needs there will be a tendency to reevaluate both needs so that the more prepotent need will actually become consciously prepotent for the individual who may have given it up very lightly. Thus, a man who has given up his job rather than lose his self respect, and who then starves for six months or so, may be willing to take his job back even at the price of losing his self-respect.

(6) Another partial explanation of *apparent* reversals is seen in the fact that we have been talking about the hierarchy of prepotency in terms of consciously felt wants or desires rather than behavior. Looking at behavior itself may give us the wrong impression. What we have claimed is that the person will *want* the more basic of two needs when deprived in both. There is no necessary implication here that he will act upon his desires. Let us say again that there are many determinants of behavior other than the needs and desires.

(7) Perhaps more important than all these exceptions are the ones that involve ideals, high social standards, high values and the like. With such values people become martyrs; they will give up everything for the sake of a particular ideal, or value. These people may be understood, at least in part, by reference to one basic concept (or hypothesis) which may be called 'increased frustration-tolerance through early gratification.' People who have been satisfied in their basic needs throughout their lives, particularly in their earlier years, seem to develop exceptional power to withstand present or future thwarting of these needs simply because they have strong, healthy character structure as a result of basic satisfaction. They are the 'strong' people who can easily weather disagreement or opposition, who can swim against the stream of public opinion and who can stand up for the truth at great personal cost. It is just the ones who have loved and been well loved, and who have had many deep friendships who can hold out against hatred, rejection or persecution.

I say all this in spite of the fact that there is a certain amount of sheer habituation which is also involved in any full discussion of frustration tolerance. For instance, it is likely that those persons who have been accustomed to relative starvation for a long time, are partially enabled thereby to withstand food deprivation. What sort of balance must be made between these two tendencies, of habituation on the one hand, and of past satisfaction breeding present frustration tolerance on the other hand, remains to be worked out by further research. Meanwhile we may assume that they are both operative, side by side, since they do not contradict each other. In respect to this phenomenon of increased frustration tolerance, it seems probable that the most important gratifications come in the first two years of life. That is to say, people who have been made secure and strong in the earliest years, tend to remain secure and strong thereafter in the face of whatever threatens.

Degrees of relative satisfaction. So far, our theoretical discussion may have given the impression that these five sets of needs are somehow in a step-wise, all-or-none relationships to each other. We have spoken in such terms as the following: "If one need is satisfied, then another emerges." This statement might give the false impression that a need must be satisfied 100 per cent before the next need emerges. In actual fact, most members of our society who are normal, are partially satisfied in all their basic needs and partially unsatisfied in all their basic needs at the same time. A more realistic description of the hierarchy would be in terms of decreasing percentages of satisfaction as we go upon the hierarchy of prepotency. For instance, if I may assign arbitrary figures for the sake of illustration, it is as if the average citizen is satisfied perhaps 85 per cent in his physiological needs, 70 per cent in his safety needs, 50 per cent in his love needs, 40 per cent in his self-esteem needs, and 10 per cent in his self-actualization needs.

As for the concept of emergence of a new need after satisfaction of the prepotent need, this emergence is not a sudden, saltatory phenomenon but rather a gradual emergence by slow degrees from nothingness. For instance, if prepotent need A is satisfied only 10 per cent then need B may not be visible at all. However, as this need A becomes satisfied 25 per cent, need B may emerge 5 per cent, as need A becomes satisfied 75 per cent need B may emerge 90 per cent, and so on.

Unconscious character of needs. These needs are neither necessarily conscious nor unconscious. On the whole, however, in the average person, they are more often unconscious rather than conscious. It is not necessary at this point to overhaul the tremendous mass of evidence which indicates the crucial importance of unconscious motivation. It would by now be expected, on a priori grounds alone, that unconscious motivations would on the whole be rather more important than the conscious motivations. What we have called the basic needs are very often largely unconscious although they may, with suitable techniques, and with sophisticated people become conscious.

Cultural specificity and generality of needs. This classification of basic needs makes some attempt to take account of the relative unity behind the superficial differences in specific desires from one culture to another. Certainly in any particular culture an individual's conscious motivational content will usually be extremely different from the conscious motivational content of an individual in another society. However, it is the common experience of anthropologists that people, even in different societies, are much more alike than we would think from our first contact with them, and that as we know them better we seem to find more and more of this commonness. We than recognize the most startling differences to be superficial rather than basic, *e.g.*, differences in style of hairdress, clothes, tastes in food, etc. Our classification of basic needs is in part an attempt to account for this unity behind the apparent diversity from culture to culture. No claim is made that it is ultimate or universal for all cultures. The claim is made only that it is relatively more ultimate, more universal, more basic, than the superficial conscious desires from culture to culture, and makes a somewhat closer approach to common-human characteristics. Basic needs are *more* common-human than superficial desires or behaviors.

Multiple motivations of behavior. These needs must be understood *not* to be *exclusive* or single determiners of certain kinds of behavior. An example may be found in any behavior that seems to be physiologically motivated, such as eating, or sexual play or the like. The clinical psychologists have long since found that any behavior may be a channel through which flow various determinants. Or to say it in another way, most behavior is multi-motivated. Within the sphere of motivational determinants any behavior tends to be determined by several or *all* of the basic needs simultaneously rather than by only one of them. The latter would be more an exception than the former. Eating may be partially for the sake of filling the stomach, and partially for the sake of comfort and amelioration of other needs. One may make love not only for

pure sexual release, but also to convince one's self of one's masculinity, or to make a conquest, to feel powerful, or to win more basic affection. As an illustration, I may point out that it would be possible (theoretically if not practically) to analyze a single act of an individual and see in it the expression of his physiological needs, his safety needs, his love needs, his esteem needs and self-actualization. This contrasts sharply with the more naive brand of trait psychology in which one trait or one motive accounts for a certain kind of act, *i.e.*, an aggressive act is traced solely to a trait of aggressiveness.

Multiple determinants of behavior. Not all behavior is determined by the basic needs. We might even say that not all behavior is motivated. There are many determinants of behavior other than motives.[9] For instance, one other important class of determinants is the so-called 'field' determinants. Theoretically, at least, behavior may be determined completely by the field, or even by specific isolated external stimuli, as in association of ideas, or certain conditioned reflexes. If in response to the stimulus word 'table,' I immediately perceive a memory image of a table, this response certainly has nothing to do with my basic needs.

Secondly, we may call attention again to the concept of 'degree of closeness to the basic needs' or 'degree of motivation.' Some behavior is highly motivated, other behavior is only weakly motivated. Some is not motivated at all (but all behavior is determined).

Another important point[10] is that there is a basic difference between expressive behavior and coping behavior (functional striving, purposive goal seeking). An expressive behavior does not try to do anything; it is simply a reflection of the personality. A stupid man behaves stupidly, not because he wants to, or tries to, or is motivated to, but simply because he *is* what he is. The same is true when I speak in a bass voice rather than tenor or soprano. The random movements of a healthy child, the smile on the face of a happy man even when he is alone, the springiness of the healthy man's walk, and the erectness of his carriage are other examples of expressive, non-functional behavior. Also the *style* in which a man carries out almost all his behavior, motivated as well as unmotivated, is often expressive.

We may then ask, is *all* behavior expressive or reflective of the character structure? The answer is 'No.' Rote, habitual, automatized, or conventional behavior may or may not be expressive. The same is true for most 'stimulus-bound' behaviors.

It is finally necessary to stress that expressiveness of behavior, and goal-directedness of behavior are not mutually exclusive categories. Average behavior is usually both.

Goals as centering principle in motivation theory.   It will be observed that the basic principle in our classification has been neither the instigation nor the motivated behavior but rather the functions, effects, purposes, or goals of the behavior. It has been proven sufficiently by various people that this is the most suitable point for centering any motivation theory.[11]

Animal- and human-centering.   This theory starts with the human being rather than any lower and presumably 'simpler' animal. Too many of the findings that have been made in animals have been proven to be true for animals but not for the human being. There is no reason whatsoever why we should start with animals in order to study human motivation. The logic or rather illogic behind this general fallacy of 'pseudo-simplicity' has been exposed often enough by philosophers and logicians as well as by scientists in each of the various fields. It is no more necessary to study animals before one can study man than it is to study mathematics before one can study geology or psychology or biology.

We may also reject the old, naive, behaviorism which assumed that it was somehow necessary, or at least more 'scientific' to judge human beings by animal standards. One consequence of this belief was that the whole notion of purpose and goal was excluded from motivational psychology simply because one could not ask a white rat about his purposes. Tolman [18] has long since proven in animal studies themselves that this exclusion was not necessary.

Motivation and the theory of psychopathogenesis.   The conscious motivational content of everyday life has, according to the foregoing, been conceived to be relatively important or unimportant accordingly as it is more or less closely related to the basic goals. A desire for an ice cream cone might actually be an indirect expression of a desire for love. If it is, then this desire for the ice cream cone becomes extremely important motivation. If however the ice cream is simply something to cool the mouth with, or a casual appetitive reaction, then the desire is relatively unimportant. Everyday conscious desires are to be regarded as symptoms, as *surface indicators of more basic needs*. If we were to take these superficial desires at their face value we would find ourselves in a state of complete confusion which could never be resolved, since we would be dealing seriously with symptoms rather than with what lay behind the symptoms.

Thwarting of unimportant desires produces no psychopathological results; thwarting of a basically important need does produce such results. Any theory of psychopathogenesis must then be based on a sound theory of motivation. A conflict or a frustration is not necessarily pathogenic. It becomes so only when it threatens or thwarts the basic needs, or partial needs that are closely related to the basic needs [10].

The role of gratified needs.   It has been pointed out above several times that our needs usually emerge only when more prepotent needs have been gratified. Thus gratification has an important role in motivation theory. Apart from this, however, needs cease to play an active determining or organizing role as soon as they are gratified.

What this means is that, *e.g.,* a basically satisfied person no longer has the needs for esteem, love, safety, etc. The only sense in which he might be said to have them is in the almost metaphysical sense that a sated man has hunger, or a filled bottle has emptiness. If we are interested in what *actually* motivates us, and not in what has, will, or might motivate us, then a satisfied need is not a motivator. It must be considered for all practical purposes simply not to exist, to have disappeared. This point should be emphasized because it has been either overlooked or contradicted in every theory of motivation I know.[12] The perfectly healthy, normal, fortunate man has no sex needs or hunger needs, or needs for safety, or for love, or for prestige, or self-esteem, except in stray moments of quickly passing threat. If we were to say otherwise, we should also have to aver that every man had all the pathological reflexes, *e.g.*, Babinski, etc., because if his nervous system were damaged, these would appear.

It is such considerations as these that suggest the bold postulation that a men who is thwarted in any of his basic needs may fairly by envisaged simply as a sick man. This is a fair parallel to our designation as 'sick' of the man who lacks vitamins or minerals. Who is to say that a lack of love is less important than a lack of vitamins? Since we know the pathogenic effects of love starvation, who is to say that we are invoking value-questions in an unscientific or illegitimate way, any more than the physician does who diagnoses and treats pellagra or scurvy? If I were permitted this usage, I should then say simply that a healthy man is primarily motivated by his needs to develop and actualize his fullest potentialities and capacities. If a man has any other basic needs in any active, chronic sense, then he is simply an unhealthy man. He is as surely sick as if he had suddenly developed a strong salt-hunger or calcium hunger.[13]

If this statement seems unusual or paradoxical the reader may be assured that this is only one among many such paradoxes that will appear as we revise our ways of looking at man's deeper motivations. When we ask what man wants of life, we deal with his very essence.

IV. Summary

(1) There are at least five sets of goals, which we may call basic needs. These are briefly physiological, safety, love, esteem, and self-actualization. In addition, we are motivated by the desire to achieve or maintain the various conditions upon which these basic satisfactions rest and by certain more intellectual desires.

(2) These basic goals are related to each other, being arranged in a hierarchy of prepotency. This means that the most prepotent goal will monopolize consciousness and will tend of itself to organize the recruitment of the various capacities of the organism. The less prepotent needs are minimized, even forgotten or denied. But when a need is fairly well satisfied, the next prepotent ('higher') need emerges, in turn to dominate the conscious life and to serve as the center of organization of behavior, since gratified needs are not active motivators.

Thus man is a perpetually wanting animal. Ordinarily the satisfaction of these wants is not altogether mutually exclusive, but only tends to be. The average member of our society is most often partially satisfied and partially unsatisfied in all of his wants. The hierarchy principle is usually empirically observed in terms of increasing percentages of non-satisfaction as we go up the hierarchy. Reversals of the average order of the hierarchy are sometimes observed. Also it has been observed that an individual may permanently lose the higher wants in the hierarchy under special conditions. There are not only ordinarily multiple motivations for usual behavior, but in addition many determinants other than motives.

(3) Any thwarting or possibility of thwarting of these basic human goals, or danger to the defenses which protect them, or to the conditions upon which they rest, is considered to be a psychological threat. With a few exceptions, all psychopathology may be partially traced to such threats. A basically thwarted man may actually be defined as a 'sick' man, if we wish.

(4) It is such basic threats which bring about the general emergency reactions.

(5) Certain other basic problems have not been dealt with because of limitations of space. Among these are (*a*) the problem of values in any definitive motivation theory, (*b*) the relation between appetites, desires, needs and what

is 'good' for the organism, (c) the etiology of the basic needs and their possible derivation in early childhool, (d) redefinition of motivational concepts, *i.e.*, drive, desire, wish, need, goal, (e) implication of our theory for hedonistic theory, (f) the nature of the uncompleted act, of success and failure, and of aspiration-level, (g) the role of association, habit and conditioning, (h) relation to the theory of inter-personal relations, (i) implications for psychotherapy, (j) implication for theory of society, (k) the theory of selfishness, (l) the relation between needs and cultural patterns, (m) the relation between this theory and Allport's theory of functional autonomy. These as well as certain other less important questions must be considered as motivation theory attempts to become definitive.

Notes

1. As the child grows up, sheer knowledge and familiarity as well as better motor development make these 'dangers' less and less dangerous and more and more manageable. Throughout life it may be said that one of the main conative functions of education is this neutralizing of apparent dangers through knowledge, e.g., I am not afraid of thunder because I know something about it.
2. A 'test battery' for safety might be confronting the child with a small exploding firecracker, or with a bewhiskered face, having the mother leave the room, putting him upon a high ladder, a hypodermic injection, having a mouse crawl up to him, etc. Of course I cannot seriously recommend the deliberate use of such 'tests' for they might very well harm the child being tested. But these and similar situations come up by the score in the child's ordinary day-to-day living and may be observed. There is no reason why these stimuli should not be used with, for example, young chimpanzees.
3. Not all neurotic individuals feel unsafe. Neurosis may have at its core a thwarting of the affection and esteem needs in a person who is generally safe.
4. For further details see [12] and [16, Chap. 5].

5. Whether or not this particular desire is universal we do not know. The crucial question, especially important today, is "Will men who are enslaved and dominated, inevitably feel dissatisfied and rebellious?" We may assume on the basis of commonly known clinical data that a man who has known true freedom (not paid for by giving up safety and security but rather built on the basis of adequate safety and security) will not willingly or easily allow his freedom to be taken away from him. But we do not know that this is true for the person born into slavery. The events of the next decade should give us our answer. See discussion of this problem in [5].
6. Perhaps the desire for prestige and respect from others is subsidiary to the desire for self-esteem or confidence in oneself. Observation of children seems to indicate that this is so, but clinical data give no clear support for such a conclusion.
7. For more extensive discussion of normal self-esteem, as well as for reports of various researchers, see [11].
8. Clearly creative behavior, like painting, is like any other behavior in having multiple determinants. It may be seen in 'innately creative' people whether they are satisfied or not, happy or unhappy, hungry or sated. Also it is clear that creative activity may be compensatory, ameliorative or purely economic. It is my impression (as yet unconfirmed) that it is possible to distinguish that artistic and intellectual products of basically satisfied people from those of basically unsatisfied people by inspection alone. In any case, here to we must distinguish, in a dynamic fashion, the overt behavior itself from its various motivations or purposes.
9. I am aware that many psychologists and psychoanalysts use the term 'motivated' and 'determined' synonymously, *e.g.*, Freud. But I consider this an obfuscating usage. Sharp distinctions are necessary for clarity of thought, and precision in experimentation.
10. To be discussed fully in a subsequent publication.
11. The interested reader is referred to the very excellent discussion of this point in Murray's *Explorations in Personality* [15].
12. Note that acceptance of this theory necessitates basic revision of the Freudian theory.
13. If we were to use the word 'sick' in this way, we should then also have to face squarely the relations of man to his society. One clear implication of our definition would be that (1) since a

man is to be called sick who is basically thwarted, and (2) since such basic thwarting is made possible ultimately only by forces outside the individual, then (3) sickness in the individual must come ultimately from a sickness in the society. The 'good' or healthy society would then be defined as one that permitted man's highest purposes to emerge by satisfying all his prepotent basic needs.

References

ADLER, A. *Social interest,* London: Faber & Faber, 1938.

CANNON, W. B. *Wisdom of the body.* New York: Norton, 1932.

FREUD, A. *The ego and the mechanisms of defense.* London: Hogarth, 1937.

FREUD, S. *New introductory lectures on psychoanalysis,* New York: Norton, 1933.

FROMM, E. *Escape from freedom.* New York: Farrar and Rinehart, 1941.

GOLDSTEIN, K. *The organism.* New York: American Book Co., 1939.

HORNEY, K. *The neurotic personality of our time.* New York: Norton, 1937.

KARDINER, A. *The traumatic neuroses of war.* New York: Hoeber, 1941.

LEVY, D. M. Primary effect of hunger. *Amer. J. Psychiat.,* 1937, 94, 643–652.

MASLOW, A. H. Conflict, frustration, and the theory of threat. *J. abnorm. (soc.) Psychol.,* 1943, 38, 81–86.

———. Dominance, personality and social behavior in women. *J. soc. Psychol.,* 1939, 10, 3–39.

———. The dynamics of psychological security-insecurity. *Character & Pers.,* 1942, 10, 331–344.

———. A preface to motivation theory. *Psychosomatic Med.,* 1943, 5, 85–92.

———, & MITTLEMANN, B. *Principles of abnormal psychology.* New York: Harper & Bros., 1941.

MURRAY, H. A., *et al. Explorations in personality.* New York: Oxford University Press, 1938.

PLANT, J. *Personality and the cultural pattern.* New York: Commonwealth Fund, 1937.

SHIRLEY, M. Children's adjustments to a strange situation. *J. abnorm. (soc.) Psychol.,* 1942, 37, 201–217.

TOLMAN, E. C. *Purposive behavior in animals and men.* New York: Century, 1932.

WERTHEIMER, M. Unpublished lectures at the New School for Social Research.

YOUNG, P. T. *Motivation of behavior.* New York: Wiley, 1936.

———. The experimental analysis of appetite. *Psychol. Bull.,* 1941, 38, 129–164.

16

The Human Side of Enterprise

Douglas Murray McGregor

It has become trite to say that industry has the fundamental know-how to utilize physical science and technology for the material benefit of mankind, and that we must now learn how to utilize the social sciences to make our human organizations truly effective.

To a degree, the social sciences today are in a position like that of the physical sciences with respect to atomic energy in the thirties. We know that past conceptions of the nature of man are inadequate and, in many ways, incorrect. We are becoming quite certain that, under proper conditions, unimagined resources of creative human energy could become available within the organizational setting.

We cannot tell industrial management how to apply this new knowledge in simple economic ways. We know it will require years of exploration, much costly development research, and a substantial amount of creative imagination on the part of management to discover how to apply this growing knowledge to the organization of human effort in industry.

SOURCE: Reprinted by permission of the publisher, from "The Human Side of Enterprise" by Douglas Murray McGregor, *Management Review*, November, 1957. Copyright © 1957 by the American Management Association, New York. All rights reserved.
NOTE: This article is based on an address by Dr. McGregor before the Fifth Anniversary Convocation of the M.I.T. School of Industrial Management.

Management's Task: The Conventional View

The conventional conception of management's task in harnessing human energy to organizational requirements can be stated broadly in terms of three propositions. In order to avoid the complications introduced by a label, let us call this set of propositions "Theory X":

1. Management is responsible for organizing the elements of productive enterprise—money, materials, equipment, people—in the interest of economic ends.
2. With respect to people, this is a process of directing their efforts, motivating them, controlling their actions, modifying their behavior to fit the needs of the organization.
3. Without this active intervention by management, people would be passive—even resistant—to organizational needs. They must therefore be persuaded, rewarded, punished, controlled—their activities must be directed. This is management's task. We often sum it up by saying that management consists of getting things done through other people.

Behind this conventional theory there are several additional beliefs—less explicit, but widespread:

4. The average man is by nature indolent—he works as little as possible.
5. He lacks ambition, dislikes responsibility, prefers to be led.
6. He is inherently self-centered, indifferent to organizational needs.
7. He is by nature resistant to change.
8. He is gullible, not very bright, the ready dupe of the charlatan and the demagogue.

The human side of economic enterprise today is fashioned from propositions and beliefs such as these. Conventional organization structures and managerial policies, practices, and programs reflect these assumptions.

In accomplishing its task—with these assumptions as guides—management has conceived of a range of possibilities.

At one extreme, management can be "hard" or "strong." The methods for directing behavior involve coercion and threat (usually disguised), close supervision, tight controls over behavior. At the other extreme, management can be "soft" or "weak." The methods for directing behavior involve being permissive, satisfying people's demands, achieving harmony. Then they will be tractable, accept direction.

This range has been fairly completely explored during the past half century, and management has learned some things from the exploration. There are difficulties in the "hard" approach. Force breeds counter-forces: restriction of output, antagonism, militant unionism, subtle but effective sabotage of management objectives. This "hard" approach is especially difficult during times of full employment.

There are also difficulties in the "soft" approach. It leads frequently to the abdication of management—to harmony, perhaps, but to indifferent performance. People take advantage of the soft approach. They continually expect more but they give less and less.

Currently, the popular theme is "firm but fair." This is an attempt to gain the advantages of both the hard and the soft approaches. It is reminiscent of Teddy Roosevelt's "speak softly and carry a big stick."

Is the Conventional View Correct?

The findings which are beginning to emerge from the social sciences challenge this whole set of beliefs about man and human nature and about the task of management. The evidence is far from conclusive, certainly, but it is suggestive. It comes from the laboratory, the clinic, the schoolroom, the home, and even to a limited extent from industry itself.

The social scientist does not deny that human behavior in industrial organization today is approximately what management perceives it to be. He has, in fact, observed it and studied it fairly extensively. But he is pretty sure that this behavior is *not* a consequence of man's inherent nature. It is a consequence rather of the nature of industrial organizations, of management philosophy, policy, and practice. The conventional approach of Theory X is based on mistaken notions of what is cause and what is effect.

Perhaps the best way to indicate why the conventional approach of management is inadequate is to consider the subject of motivation.

Physiological Needs

Man is a wanting animal—as soon as one of his needs is satisfied, another appears in its place. This process is unending. It continues from birth to death.

Man's needs are organized in a series of levels—a hierarchy of importance. At the lowest level, but pre-eminent in importance when they are thwarted, are his *physiological needs*. Man lives for bread alone, when there is no bread. Unless the circumstances are unusual, his needs for love, for status, for recognition are inoperative when his stomach has been empty for a while. But when he eats regularly and adequately, hunger ceases to be an important motivation. The same is true of the other physiological needs of man—for rest, exercise, shelter, protection from the elements.

A satisfied need is not a motivator of behavior! This is a fact of profound significance that is regularly ignored in the conventional approach to the management of people. Consider your own need for air: Except as you are deprived of it, it has no appreciable motivating effect upon your behavior.

Safety Needs

When the physiological needs are reasonably satisfied, needs at the next higher level begin to dominate man's behavior—to motivate him. These are called *safety needs*. They are needs for protection against danger, threat, deprivation. Some people mistakenly refer to these as needs for security. However, unless man is in a dependent relationship where he fears arbitrary deprivation, he does not demand security. The need is for the "fairest possible break." When he is confident of this, he is more than willing to take risks. But when he feels threatened or dependent, his greatest need is for guarantees, for protection, for security.

The fact needs little emphasis that, since every industrial employee is in a dependent relationship, safety needs may assume considerable importance. Arbitrary management actions, behavior which arouses uncertainty with respect to continued employment or which reflects favoritism or discrimination, unpredictable administration of policy—these can be powerful motivators of the safety needs in the employment relationship *at every level,* from worker to vice president.

Social Needs

When man's physiological needs are satisfied and he is no longer fearful about his physical welfare, his *social needs* become important motivators of his behavior—needs for belonging, for association, for acceptance by his fellows, for giving and receiving friendship and love.

Management knows today of the existence of these needs, but it often assumes quite wrongly that they represent a threat to the organization. Many studies have demonstrated that the tightly knit, cohesive work group may, under proper conditions, be far more effective than an equal number of separate individuals in achieving organization goals.

Yet management, fearing group hostility to its own objectives, often goes to considerable lengths to control and direct human efforts in ways that are inimical to the natural "groupiness" of human beings. When man's social needs—and perhaps his safety needs, too—are thus thwarted, he behaves in ways which tend to defeat organizational objectives. He becomes resistant, antagonistic, uncooperative. But this behavior is a consequence, not a cause.

Ego Needs

Above the social needs—in the sense that they do not become motivators until lower needs are reasonably satisfied—are the needs of greatest significance to management and to man himself. They are the *egoistic needs,* and they are of two kinds:

1. Those needs that relate to one's self-esteem—needs for self-confidence, for independence, for achievement, for competence, for knowledge.
2. Those needs that relate to one's reputation—needs for status, for recognition, for appreciation, for the deserved respect of one's fellows.

Unlike the lower needs, these are rarely satisfied: man seeks indefinitely for more satisfaction of these needs once they have become important to him. But they do not appear in any significant way until physiological, safety, and social needs are all reasonably satisfied.

The typical industrial organization offers few opportunities for the satisfaction of these egoistic needs to people at lower levels in the hierarchy. The conventional methods of organizing work, particularly in mass-production industries, give little heed to these aspects of human motivation. If the practices of scientific management were deliberately calculated to thwart these needs, they could hardly accomplish this purpose better than they do.

Self-Fulfillment Needs

Finally—a capstone, as it were, on the hierarchy of man's needs—there are what we may call the *needs for self-fulfillment.* These are the needs for realizing one's own potentialities, for continued self-development, for being creative in the broadest sense of that term.

It is clear that the conditions of modern life give only limited opportunity for these relatively weak needs to obtain expression. The deprivation most people experience with respect to other lower-level needs diverts their energies into the struggle to satisfy *those* needs, and the needs for self-fulfillment remain dormant.

Management and Motivation

We recognize readily enough that a man suffering from a severe-dietary deficiency is sick. The deprivation of physiological needs has behavioral consequences. The same is true—although less well recognized—of deprivations of higher-level needs. The man whose needs for safety, association, independence, or status are thwarted is sick just as surely as the man who has rickets. And his sickness will have behavioral consequences. We will be mistaken if we attribute his resultant passivity, his hostility, his refusal to accept responsibility to his inherent "human nature." These forms of behavior are *symptoms* of illness—of deprivation of his social and egoistic needs.

The man whose lower-level needs are satisfied is not motivated to satisfy those needs any longer. For practical purposes they exist no longer. Management often asks, "Why aren't people more productive. We pay good wages, provide good working conditions, have excellent fringe benefits and steady employment. Yet people do not seem to be willing to put forth more than minimum effort."

The fact that management has provided for these physiological and safety needs has shifted the motivational emphasis to the social

and perhaps to the egoistic needs. Unless there are opportunities *at work* to satisfy these higher-level needs, people will be deprived; and their behavior will reflect this deprivation. Under such conditions, if management continues to focus its attention on physiological needs, its efforts are bound to be ineffective.

People *will* make insistent demands for more money under these conditions. It becomes more important than ever to buy the material goods and services which can provide limited satisfaction of the thwarted needs. Although money has only limited value in satisfying many higher-level needs, it can become the focus of interest if it is the *only* means available.

The Carrot-and-Stick Approach

The carrot-and-stick theory of motivation (like Newtonian physical theory) works reasonably well under certain circumstances. The *means* for satisfying man's physiological and (within limits) his safety needs can be provided or withheld by management. Employment itself is such a means, and so are wages, working conditions, and benefits. By these means the individual can be controlled so long as he is struggling for subsistence.

But the carrot-and-stick theory does not work at all once man has reached an adequate subsistence level and is motivated primarily by higher needs. Management cannot provide a man with self-respect, or with the respect of his fellows, or with the satisfaction of needs for self-fulfillment. It can create such conditions that he is encouraged and enabled to seek such satisfactions for *himself,* or it can thwart him by failing to create those conditions.

But this creation of conditions is not "control." It is not a good device for directing behavior. And so management finds itself in an odd position. The high standard of living created by our modern technological know-how provides quite adequately for the satisfaction of physiological and safety needs. The only significant exception is where management practices have not created confidence in a "fair break"—and thus where safety needs are thwarted. But by making possible the satisfaction of low-level needs, management has deprived itself of the ability to use as motivators the devices on which conventional theory has taught it to rely—rewards, promises, incentives, or threats and other coercive devices.

The philosophy of management by direction and control—*regardless of whether it is hard or soft*—is inadequate to motivate because the human needs on which this approach relies are today unimportant motivators of behavior. Direction and control are essentially useless in motivating people whose important needs are social and egoistic. Both the hard and the soft approach fail today because they are simply irrelevant to the situation.

People, deprived of opportunities to satisfy at work the needs which are now important to them, behave exactly as we might predict—with indolence, passivity, resistance to change, lack of responsibility, willingness to follow the demagogue, unreasonable demands for economic benefits. It would seem that we are caught in a web of our own weaving.

A New Theory of Management

For these and many other reasons, we require a different theory of the task of managing people based on more adequate assumptions about human nature and human motivation. I am going to be so bold as to suggest the broad dimensions of such a theory. Call it "Theory Y," if you will.

1. Management is responsible for organizing the elements of productive enterprise—money, materials, equipment, people—in the interest of economic ends.

2. People are *not* by nature passive or resistant to organizational needs. They have become so as a result of experience in organizations.

3. The motivation, the potential for development, the capacity for assuming responsibility, the readiness to direct behavior toward organizational goals are all present in people. Management does not put them there. It is a responsibility of management to make it possible for people to recognize and develop these human characteristics for themselves.

4. The essential task of management is to arrange organizational conditions and methods of operation so that people can achieve their own goals *best* by directing *their own* efforts toward organizational objectives.

This is a process primarily of creating opportunities, releasing potential, removing obstacles, encouraging growth, providing guidance. It is what Peter Drucker has called "management by objectives" in contrast to "management by control." It does *not* involve the abdication of management, the absence of leadership, the lowering of standards, or the other characteristics usually associated with the "soft" approach under Theory X.

Some Difficulties

It is no more possible to create an organization today which will be a full, effective application of this theory than it was to build an atomic power plant in 1945. There are many formidable obstacles to overcome.

The conditions imposed by conventional organization theory and by the approach of scientific management for the past half century have tied men to limited jobs which do not utilize their capabilities, have discouraged the acceptance of responsibility, have in an industrial organization—have been conditioned by his experience under these circumstances.

People today are accustomed to being directed, manipulated, controlled in industrial organizations and to finding satisfaction for their social, egoistic, and self-fulfillment needs away from the job. This is true of much of management as well as of workers. Genuine "industrial citizenship"—to borrow again a term from Drucker—is a remote and unrealistic idea, the meaning of which has not even been considered by most members of industrial organizations.

Another way of saying this is that Theory X places exclusive reliance upon external control of human behavior, while Theory Y relies heavily on self-control and self-direction. It is worth noting that this difference is the difference between treating people as children and treating them as mature adults. After generations of the former, we cannot expect to shift to the latter overnight.

Steps in the Right Direction

Before we are overwhelmed by the obstacles, let us remember that the application of theory is always slow. Progress is usually achieved in small steps. Some innovative ideas which are entirely consistent with Theory Y are today being applied with some success.

Decentralization and Delegation

These are ways of freeing people from the too-close control of conventional organization, giving them a degree of freedom to direct their own activities, to assume responsibility, and, importantly, to satisfy their egoistic needs. In this connection, the flat organization of Sears, Roebuck and Company provides an interesting example. It forces "management by objectives," since it enlarges the number of people reporting to a manager until he cannot direct and control them in the conventional manner.

Job Enlargement

This concept, pioneered by I.B.M. and Detroit Edison, is quite consistent with Theory Y. It encourages the acceptance of responsibility at the bottom of the organization; it provides opportunities for satisfying social and egoistic needs. In fact, the reorganization of work at the factory level offers one of the more challenging opportunities for innovation consistent with Theory Y.

Participation and Consultative Management

Under proper conditions, participation and consultative management provide encouragement to people to direct their creative energies toward organizational objectives, give them some voice in decisions that affect them, provide significant opportunities for the satisfaction of social and egoistic needs. The Scanlon Plan is the outstanding embodiment of these ideas in practice.

Performance Appraisal

Even a cursory examination of conventional programs of performance appraisal within the ranks of management will reveal how completely consistent they are with Theory X. In fact, most such programs tend to treat the individual as though he were a product under inspection on the assembly line.

A few companies—among them General Mills, Ansul Chemical, and General Electric—have been experimenting with approaches which involve the individual in setting "targets" or objectives *for himself* and in a *self*-evaluation of performance semiannually or annually. Of course, the superior plays an important leadership role in this process—one, in fact, which demands substantially more competence than the conventional approach. The role is, however, considerably more congenial to many managers than the role of "judge" or "inspector" which is usually forced upon them. Above all, the individual is encouraged to take a greater responsibility for planning and appraising his own contribution to organizational objectives; and the accompanying effects on egoistic and self-fulfillment needs are substantial.

Applying the Ideas

The not infrequent failure of such ideas as these to work as well as expected is often attributable to the fact that a management has "bought the idea" but applied it within the framework of Theory X and its assumptions.

Delegation is not an effective way of exercising management by control. Participation becomes a farce when it is applied as a sales gimmick or a device for kidding people into thinking they are important. Only the management that has confidence in human capacities and is itself directed toward organizational objectives rather than toward the preservation of personal power can grasp the implications of this emerging theory. Such management will find and apply successfully other innovative ideas as we move slowly toward the full implementation of a theory like Y.

The Human Side of Enterprise

It is quite possible for us to realize substantial improvements in the effectiveness of industrial organizations during the next decade or two. The social sciences can contribute much to such developments; we are only beginning to grasp the implications of the growing body of knowledge in these fields. But if this conviction is to become a reality instead of a pious hope, we will need to view the process much as we view the process of releasing the energy of the atom for constructive human ends— as a slow, costly, sometimes discouraging approach toward a goal which would seem to many to be quite unrealistic.

The ingenuity and the perseverance of industrial management in the pursuit of economic ends have changed many scientific and technological dreams into commonplace realities. It is now becoming clear that the application of these same talents to the human side of enterprise will not only enhance substantially these materialistic achievements, but will bring us one step closer to "the good society."

17

That Urge to Achieve

David C. McClelland

Most people in this world, psychologically, can be divided into two broad groups. There is that minority which is challenged by opportunity and willing to work hard to achieve something, and the majority which really does not care all that much.

For nearly twenty years now, psychologists have tried to penetrate the mystery of this curious dichotomy. Is the need to achieve (or the absence of it) an accident, is it hereditary, or is it the result of environment? Is it a single, isolatable human motive, or a combination of motives—the desire to accumulate wealth, power, fame? Most important of all, is there some technique that could give this will to achieve to people, even whole societies, who do not now have it?

While we do not yet have complete answers for any of these questions, years of work have given us partial answers to most of them and insights into all of them. There is a distinct human motive, distinguishable from others. It can be found, in fact tested for, in any group.

Let me give you one example. Several years ago, a careful study was made of 450 workers who had been thrown out of work by a plant shutdown in Erie, Pennsylvania. Most of the unemployed workers stayed home for a while and then checked back with the United States Employment Service to see if their old jobs

SOURCE: Reprinted by permission from *Think* magazine, pp. 82–89, published by IBM. Copyright © 1966 by International Business Machines Corporation.

or similar ones were available. But a small minority among them behaved differently: the day they were laid off, they started job-hunting.

They checked both the United States and the Pennsylvania Employment Office; they studied the "Help Wanted" sections of the papers; they checked through their union, their church, and various fraternal organizations; they looked into training courses to learn a new skill; they even left town to look for work, while the majority when questioned said they would not under any circumstances move away from Erie to obtain a job. Obviously the members of that active minority were differently motivated. All the men were more or less in the same situation objectively: they needed work, money, food, shelter, job security. Yet only a minority showed initiative and enterprise in finding what they needed. Why? Psychologists, after years of research, now believe they can answer that question. They have demonstrated that these men possessed in greater degree a specific type of human motivation. For the moment let us refer to this personality characteristic as "Motive A" and review some of the other characteristics of the men who have more of the motive than other men.

Suppose they are confronted by a work situation in which they can set their own goals as to how difficult a task they will undertake. In the psychological laboratory, such a situation is very simply created by asking them to throw rings over a peg from any distance they may choose. Most men throw more or less randomly, standing now close, now far away, but those with Motive A seem to calculate carefully where they are most likely to get a sense of mastery. They stand nearly always at moderate distances, not so close as to make the task ridiculously easy, not so far away as to make it impossible. They set moderately difficult, but potentially achievable goals for themselves, where they objectively have only about a one-in-three chance of succeeding. In other words, they are always setting challenges for themselves, tasks to make them stretch themselves a little.

But they behave like this only if *they* can influence the outcome by performing the work themselves. They prefer not to gamble at all. Say they are given a choice between rolling dice with one in three chances of winning and working on a problem with a one-in-three chance of solving in the time allotted, they choose to work on the problem even though rolling the dice is obviously less work and the odds of winning are the same. They prefer to work at a problem rather than leave the outcome to chance or to others.

Obviously they are concerned with personal achievement rather than with the rewards of success *per se,* since they stand just as much chance of getting those rewards by throwing the dice. This leads to another characteristic the Motive A men show—namely, a strong preference for work situations in which they get concrete feedback on how well they are doing, as one does, say in playing golf, or in being a salesman, but as one does not in teaching, or in personnel counseling. A golfer always knows his score and can compare how well he is doing with par or with his own performance yesterday or last week. A teacher has no such concrete feedback on how well he is doing in "getting across" to his students.

The *n* Ach Men

But why do certain men behave like this? At one level the reply is simple: because they habitually spend their time thinking about doing things better. In fact, psychologists typically measure the strength of Motive A by taking samples of a man's spontaneous thoughts (such as making up a story about a picture they have been shown) and counting the frequency with which he mentions doing things better. The count is objective and can even be made these days with the help of a computer program for content analysis. It yields what is referred to technically as an individual's *n* Ach score

(for "need for Achievement"). It is not difficult to understand why people who think constantly about "doing better" are more apt to do better at job-hunting, to set moderate, achievable goals for themselves, to dislike gambling (because they get no achievement satisfaction from succcess), and to prefer work situations where they can tell easily whether they are improving or not. But why some people and not others come to think this way is another question. The evidence suggests it is not because of special training they get in the home from parents who set moderately high achievement goals but who are warm, encouraging, and nonauthoritarian in helping their children reach these goals.

Such detailed knowledge about one motive helps correct a lot of common sense ideas about human motivation. For example, much public policy (and much business policy) is based on the simple-minded notion that people will work harder "if they have to." As a first appproximation, the idea isn't totally wrong, but it is only a half-truth. The majority of unemployed workers in Erie "had to" find work as much as those with higher *n* Ach but they certainly didn't work as hard at it. Or again, it is frequently assumed that *any* strong motive will lead to doing things better. Wouldn't it be fair to say that most of the Erie workers were just "unmotivated"? But our detailed knowledge of various human motives shows that each one leads a person to behave in *different* ways. The contrast is not between being "motivated" or "unmotivated" but between being motivated toward A or toward B or C, etc.

A simple experiment makes the point nicely: subjects were told that they could choose as a working partner either a close friend or a stranger who was known to be an expert on the problem to be solved. Those with higher *n* Ach (more "need to achieve") chose the experts over their friends, whereas those with more *n* Aff (the "need to affiliate with others") chose friends over experts. The latter were not "unmotivated;" their desire to be with someone they liked was simply a stronger motive than their desire to excel at the task. Other such needs have been studied by psychologists. For instance, the need for Power is often confused with the need for Achievement because both may lead to "outstanding" activities. There is a distinct difference. People with a strong need for Power want to command attention, get recognition, and control others. They are more active in political life and tend to busy themselves primarily with controlling the channels of communication both up to the top and down to the people so that they are more "in charge." Those with high n Power are not as concerned with improving their work performance daily as those with high n Ach.

It follows, from what we have been able to learn, that not all "great achievers" score high in n Ach. Many generals, outstanding politicians, great research scientists do not, for instance, because their work requires other personality characteristics, other motives. A general or a politician must be more concerned with power relationships, a research scientist must be able to go for long periods without the immediate feedback the person with high n Ach requires, etc. On the other hand, business executives, particularly if they are in positions of real responsibility or if they are salesmen, tend to score high in n Ach. This is true even in a Communist country like Poland: apparently there, as well as in a private economy, a manager succeeds if he is concerned about improving all the time, setting moderate goals, keeping track of his or the company's performance, etc.

Motivation and Half-Truths

Since careful study has shown that common sense notions about motivation are at best half-truths, it also follows that you cannot trust what people tell you about their motives. After all, they often get their ideas about their own motives from common sense. Thus a general may say he is interested in achievement (because he has obviously achieved), or a businessman that he is interested only in making money (because he has made money), or one of the majority of unemployed in Erie that he desperately wants

a job (because he knows he needs one); but a careful check of what each one thinks about and how he spends his time may show that each is concerned about quite different things. It requires special measurement techniques to identify the presence of n Ach and other such motives. Thus what people say and believe is not very closely related to these "hidden" motives which seem to affect a person's "style of life" more than his political, religious or social attitudes. Thus n Ach produces enterprising men among labor leaders or managers, Republicans or Democrats, Catholics or Protestants, capitalists or Communists.

Wherever people begin to think often in n Ach terms, things begin to move. Men with high n Ach get more raises and are promoted more rapidly, because they keep actively seeking ways to do a better job. Companies with many such men grow faster. In one comparison of two firms in Mexico, it was discovered that all but one of the top executives of a fast growing firm had higher n Ach scores than the highest scoring executive in an equally large but slow-growing firm. Countries with many such rapidly growing firms tend to show above average rates of national economic growth. This appears to be the reason why correlations have regularly been found between the n Ach content in popular literature (such as popular songs or stories in children's textbooks) and subsequent rates of national economic growth. A nation which is thinking about doing better all the time (as shown in its popular literature) actually does do better economically speaking. Careful quantitative studies have shown this to be true in Ancient Greece, in Spain in the Middle Ages, in England from 1400–1800, as well as among contemporary nations, whether capitalist or Communist, developed or underdeveloped.

Contrast these two stories for example. Which one contains more n Ach? Which one reflects a state of mind which ought to lead to harder striving to improve the way things are?

• Excerpt from story A (4th grade reader): "Don't Ever Owe a Man—The world is an illusion. Wife, children, horses, and cows are all just ties of fate. They are ephemeral. Each after fulfilling his part in life disappears. So we should not clamour after riches which are not permanent. As long as we live it is wise not to have any attachments and just think of God. We have to spend our lives without trouble, for is it not time that there is an end to grievances? So it is better to live knowing the real state of affairs. Don't get entangled in the meshes of family life.''

• Excerpt from story B (4th grade reader): "How I do Like to Learn—I was sent to an accelerated technical high school. I was so happy I cried. Learning is not very easy. In the beginning I couldn't understand what the teacher taught us. I always got a red cross mark on my papers. The boy sitting next to me was very enthusiastic and also an outstanding student. When he found I couldn't do the problems he offered to show me how he had done them. I could not copy his work. I must learn through my own reasoning. I gave his paper back and explained I had to do it myself. Sometimes I worked on a problem until midnight. If I couldn't finish, I started early in the morning. The red cross marks on my work were getting less common. I conquered my difficulties. My marks rose. I graduated and went on to college.''

Most readers would agree, without any special knowledge of the *n* Ach coding system, that the second story shows more concern with improvement than the first, which comes from a contemporary reader used in Indian public schools. In fact the latter has a certain Horatio Alger quality that is reminiscent of our own McGuffey readers of several generations ago. It appears today in the textbooks of Communist China. It should not, therefore, come as a surprise if a nation like Communist China, obsessed as it is with improvement, tended in the long run to outproduce a nation like India, which appears to be more fatalistic.

The *n* Ach level is obviously important for statesmen to watch and in many instances to try to do something about, particularly if a nation's economy is lagging. Take Britain, for example. A generation ago (around 1925) it ranked fifth among 25 countries where children's readers were scored for *n* Ach—and its economy was doing well. By 1950 the *n* Ach level had dropped to 27th out of 39 countries—well below the word average—and today, its leaders are feeling the severe economic effects of this loss in the spirit of enterprise.

Economics and *n* Ach

If psychologists can detect *n* Ach levels in individuals or nations, particularly before their effects are widespread, can't the knowledge somehow be put to use to foster economic development? Obviously detection or diagnosis is not enough. What good is it to tell Britain (or India for that matter) that it needs more *n* Ach, a greater spirit of enterprise? In most such cases, informed observers of the local scene know very well that such a need exists, though they may be slower to discover it than the psychologist hovering over *n* Ach scores. What is needed is some method of developing *n* Ach in individuals or nations.

Since about 1960, psychologists in my research group at Harvard have been experimenting with techniques designed to accomplish this goal, chiefly among business executives whose work requires the action characteristics of people with high *n* Ach. Initially, we had real doubts as to whether we could succeed, partly because like most American psychologists we had been strongly influenced by the psychoanalytic view that basic motives are laid down in childhood and cannot really be changed later, and partly because many studies of intensive psychotherapy and counseling have shown minor if any long-term personality effects. On the other hand we were encouraged by the nonprofessionals: those enthusiasts like Dale Carnegie, the Communist idealogue or the Church missionary, who felt they could change adults and in fact seemed to be doing so. At any rate we ran some brief (7 to 10 days) "total push" training courses for businessmen designed to increase their *n* Ach.

Four Main Goals

In broad outline the courses had four main goals: (1) They were designed to teach the participants how to think, talk, and act like a person with high *n* Ach, based on our knowledge of such people gained through 17 years of research. For instance, men learned how to make up stories that would code high in *n* Ach (i.e., how to think in *n* Ach terms), how to set moderate goals for themselves in the ring toss game (and in life). (2) The courses stimulated the participants to set higher but carefully planned and realistic work goals for themselves over the next two years. Then we checked back with them every six months to see how well they were doing in terms of their own objectives. (3) The courses also utilized techniques for giving the participants knowledge about themselves. For instance, in playing the ring toss game, they could observe that they behaved differently from others—perhaps in refusing to adjust a goal downward after failure. This would then become a matter for group discussion and the man would have to explain what he had in mind in setting such unrealistic goals. Discussion could then lead on to what a man's ultimate goals in life were, how much he cared about actually improving performance v. making a good impression or having many friends. In this way the participants would be freer to realize their achievement goals without being blocked by old habits and attitudes. (4) The courses also usually created a group *esprit de corps* from learning about each other's hopes and fears, successes and failures, and from going through an emotional experience together, away from everyday life, in a retreat setting. This membership in a new group helps a man achieve his goals, partly because he knows he has their sympathy and support and partly because he knows they will be watching to see how well he does. The same effect has been noted in other therapy groups like Alcoholics Anonymous. We are not sure which of these course "inputs" is really absolutely essential—that remains a research question—but we were taking no chances at the outset in view of the general pessimism about such efforts, and we wanted to include any and all techniques that were thought to change people.

The courses have been given: to executives in a large American firm, and in several Mexican firms, to underachieving high school boys; and to businessmen in India from Bombay and from a small city—Kakinada in the state of Andhra Pradesh. In every instance save one (the Mexican case), it was possible to demonstrate statistically, some two years later, that the men who took the course had done better (made more money, got promoted faster, expanded their businesses faster) than comparable men who did not take the course or who took some other management course.

Consider the Kakinada results, for example. In the two years preceding the course 9 men, 18 percent of the 52 participants, had shown "unusual" enterprise in their businesses. In the 18 months following the course 25 of the men, in other words nearly 50 percent, were unusually active. And this was not due to a general upturn of business in India. Data from a control city, some forty-five miles away, show the same base rate of "unusually active" men as in Kakinada before the course—namely, about 20 percent. Something clearly happened in Kakinada: the owner of a small radio shop started a chemical plant; a banker was so successful in making commercial loans in an enterprising way that he was promoted to a much larger branch of his bank in Calcutta; the local political leader accomplished his goal (it was set in the course) to get the federal government to deepen the harbor and make it into an all-weather port; plans are far along for establishing a steel rolling mill, etc. All this took place without any substantial capital from the outside. In fact, the only costs were for our 10-day courses plus some brief follow-up visits every six months. The men are raising their own capital and using their own resources for getting business and industry moving in a city that had been considered stagnant and unenterprising.

The promise of such a method of developing achievement motivation seems very great. It has obvious applications in helping underdeveloped countries, or "pockets of poverty" in the United States, to move faster economically. It has great potential for businesses that need to "turn around" and take a more enterprising approach toward their growth and development. It may even be helpful in developing more *n* Ach among low-income groups. For instance, data show that lower-class Negro Americans have a very low level of *n* Ach. This is not surprising. Society has systematically discouraged and blocked their achievement striving. But as the barriers to upward mobility are broken down, it will be necessary to help stimulate the motivation that will lead them to take advantage of new opportunities opening up.

Extreme Reactions

But a word of caution: Whenever I speak of this research and its great potential, audience reaction tends to go to opposite extremes. Either people remain skeptical and argue that motives can't really be changed, that all we are doing is dressing Dale Carnegie up in fancy "psychologese," or they become converts and want instant course descriptions by a return mail to solve their local motivation problems. Either response is unjustified. What I have described here in a few pages has taken 20 years of patient research effort, and hundreds of thousands of dollars in basic research costs. What remains to be done will involve even larger sums and more time for development to turn a promising idea into something of wide practical utility.

Encouragement Needed

To take only one example, we have not yet learned how to develop *n* Ach really well among low-income groups. In our first effort—a summer course for bright underachieving 14-year olds—we found that boys from the middle class improved steadily in grades in school over a two-year period, but boys from the lower class showed an improvement after the first year followed by a drop back to their beginning low grade average. (*See Figure 1.*) Why? We speculated that it was because they moved back into an environment in which neither parents nor friends encouraged achievement or upward mobility. In other words, it isn't enough to change a man's motivation if the environment in which he lives doesn't support at least to some degree his new efforts. Negroes striving to rise out of the ghetto frequently confront this problem: they are often faced by skepticism at home and suspicion on the job, so that even if their *n* Ach is raised, it can be lowered again by the heavy odds against their success. We must learn not only to raise *n* Ach but also to find methods of instructing people in how to manage it, to create a favorable environment in which it can flourish.

Many of these training techniques are now only in the pilot testing stage. It will take time and money to perfect them, but society should be willing to invest heavily in view of their tremendous potential for contributing to human betterment.

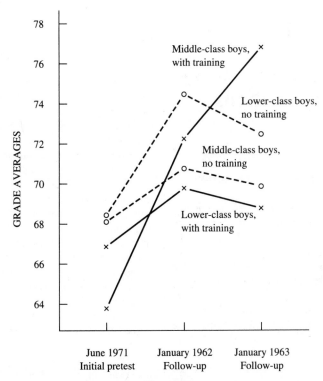

Figure 1

In a Harvard study, a group of underachieving 14-year-olds was given a six-week's course designed to help them do better in school. Some of the boys were also given training in achievement motivation, or *n* Ach (solid lines). As graph reveals, the only boys who continued to improve after a two-year period were the middle-class boys with the special *n* Ach training. Psychologists suspect the lower-class boys dropped back, even with *n* Ach training, because they returned to an environment in which neither parents nor friends encouraged achievement.

18

Intervention Theory and Methods

Chris Argyris

A Definition of Intervention

To intervene is to enter into an ongoing system of relationship, to come between or among persons, groups, or objects for the purpose of helping them. There is an important implicit assumption in the definition that should be made explicit: the system exists independently of the intervenor. There are many reasons one might wish to intervene. These reasons may range from helping the clients make their own decisions about the kind of help they need to coercing the clients to do what the intervenor wishes them to do. Examples of the latter are modern black militants who intervene to demand that the city be changed in accordance with their wishes and choices (or white racists who prefer the same); executives who invite interventionists into their system to manipulate subordinates for them; trade union leaders who for years have resisted systematic research in their own bureaucratic functioning at the highest levels because they fear that valid information might lead to entrenched interests—especially at the top—being unfrozen.

The more one conceives of the intervenor in this sense, the more one implies that the client system should have little autonomy from the intervenor; that its boundaries are

SOURCE: Chris Argyris, *Intervention Theory and Methods*, pp. 15–20. Copyright 1970 by Addison-Wesley Publishing Company, Inc. Reprinted with permission of the publisher.

indistinguishable from those of the intervenor; that its health or effectiveness are best controlled by the intervenor.

In contrast, our view acknowledges interdependencies between the intervenor and the client system but focuses on how to maintain, or increase, the client system's autonomy; how to differentiate even more clearly the boundaries between the client system and the intervenor; and how to conceptualize and define the client system's health independently of the intervenor's. This view values the client system as an ongoing, self-responsible unity that has the obligation to be in control over its own destiny. An intervenor, in this view, assists a system to become more effective in problem solving, decision making, and decision implementation in such a way that the system can continue to be increasingly effective in these activities and have a decreasing need for the intervenor.

Another critical question the intervenor must ask is, who is he helping—management or employees, black militants or Negro moderates, white racists or white moderates? Several chapters of the book are concerned with this question. At this point, it is suggested that the intevenor must be concerned with the system as a whole even though his initial contact may be made with only a few people. He therefore focuses on those intervention activities that eventually (not necessarily immediately) will provide *all* the members opportunities to enhance their competence and effectiveness. If any individual or subsystem wishes help to prevent other individuals or subsystems from having these opportunities, then the intervenor may well have to question seriously his involvement in the project.[1]

Basic Requirements for Intervention Activity

Are there any basic or necessary processes that must be fulfilled regardless of the substantive issues involved, if intervention activity is to be helpful with any level of client (individual, group, or organizational)? One condition that seems so basic as to be defined axiomatic is the generation of *valid information*. Without valid information, it would be difficult for the client to learn and for the interventionist to help.

A second condition almost as basic flows from our assumption that intervention activity, no matter what its substantive interests and objectives, should be so designed and executed that the client system maintains its discreteness and autonomy. Thus *free, informed choice* is also a necessary process in effective intervention activity.

Finally, if the client system is assumed to be ongoing (that is, existing over time), the clients require strengthening to maintain their autonomy not only vis-à-vis the interventionist but also vis-à-vis other systems. This means that their commitment to learning and change has to be more than temporary. It has to be so strong that it can be transferred to relationships other than those with the interventionist and can do so (eventually) without the help of the interventionist. The third basic process for any intervention activity is therefore the client's *internal commitment* to the choices made.

In summary, valid information, free choice, and internal commitment are considered integral parts of any intervention activity, no matter what the substantive objectives are (for example, developing a management performance evaluation scheme, reducing intergroup rivalries, increasing the degree of trust among individuals, redesigning budgetary systems, or redesigning work). These three processes are called the primary intervention tasks.

Primary Tasks of an Interventionist

Why is it necessary to hypothesize that in order for an interventionist to behave effectively and in order that the integrity of the client system be maintained, the interventionist has to focus on three primary tasks, regardless of the substantive problems that the client system may be experiencing?

Valid and Useful Information

First, it has been accepted as axiomatic that valid and useful information is the foundation for effective intervention. Valid information is that which describes the factors, plus their interrelationships, that create the problem for the client system. There are several tests for checking the validity of the information. In increasing degrees of power they are public verifiability, valid prediction, and control over the phenomena. The first is having several independent diagnoses suggest the same picture. Second is generating predictions from the diagnosis that are subsequently confirmed (they occurred under the conditions that were specified). Third is altering the factors systematically and predicting the effects upon the system as a whole. All these tests, if they are to be valid, must be carried out in such a way that the participants cannot, at will, make them come true. This would be a self-fulfilling prophecy and not a confirmation of a prediction. The difficulty with a self-fulfilling prophecy is its indication of more about the degree of power an individual (or subset of individuals) can muster to alter the system than about the nature of the system when the participants are behaving without knowledge of the diagnosis. For example, if an executive learns that the interventionist predicts his subordinates will behave (a) if he behaves (b), he might alter (b) in order not to lead to (a). Such an alteration indicates the executive's power but does not test the validity of the diagnosis that if (a), then (b).

The tests for valid information have important implications for effective intervention activity. First, the interventionist's diagnoses must strive to represent the total client system and not the point of view of any subgroup or individual. Otherwise, the interventionist could not be seen only as being under the control of a particular individual or subgroup, but also his predictions would be based upon inaccurate information and thus might not be confirmed.

This does not mean that an interventionist may not begin with, or may not limit his relationship to, a subpart of the total system. It is totally possible, for example, for the interventionist to help management, blacks, trade union leaders, etc. With whatever subgroup he works he simply should not agree to limit his diagnosis to its wishes.

It is conceivable that a client system may be helped even though valid information is not generated. Sometimes changes occur in a positive direction without the interventionist having played any important role. These changes, although helpful in that specific instance, lack the attribute of helping the organization to learn and to gain control over its problem-solving capability.

The importance of information that the clients can use to control their destiny points up the requirement that the information must not only be valid, it must be useful. Valid information that cannot be used by the clients to alter their system is equivalent to valid information about cancer that cannot be used to cure cancer eventually. An interventionist's diagnosis should include variables that are manipulable by the clients and are complete enough so that if they are manipulated effective change will follow.

Free Choice

In order to have free choice, the client has to have a cognitive map of what he wishes to do. The objectives of his action are known at the moment of decision. Free choice implies voluntary as opposed to automatic; proactive rather than reactive. The act of selection is rarely accomplished by maximizing or optimizing. Free and informed choice entails what Simon has called "satisficing," that is, selecting the alternative with the highest probability of succeeding, given some specified cost constraints. Free choice places the locus of decision making in the client system. Free choice makes it possible for the clients to remain responsible for their destiny. Through free choice the clients can maintain the autonomy of their system.

It may be possible that clients prefer to give up their responsibility and their autonomy, especially if they are feeling a sense of failure. They may prefer, as we shall see in several examples, to turn over their free choice to the interventionist. They may insist that he make recommendations and tell them what to do. The interventionist resists these pressures because if he does not, the clients will lose their free choice and he will lose his own free choice also. He will be controlled by the anxieties of the clients.

The requirement of free choice is especially important for those helping activities where the processes of help are as important as the actual help. For example, a medical doctor does not require that a patient with a bullet wound participate in the process by defining the kind of help he needs. However, the same doctor may have to pay much more attention to the processes he uses to help patients when he is attempting to diagnose blood pressure or cure a high cholesterol. If the doctor behaves in ways that upset the patient, the latter's blood pressure may be distorted. Or, the patient can develop a dependent relationship if the doctor cuts down his cholesterol—increasing habit only under constant pressure from the doctor—and the moment the relationship is broken off, the count goes up.

Effective intervention in the human and social spheres requires that the processes of help be congruent with the outcome desired. Free choice is important because there are so many unknowns, and the interventionist wants the client to have as much willingness and motivation as possible to work on the problem. With high client motivation and commitment, several different methods for change can succeed.

A choice is free to the extent the members can make their selection for a course of action with minimal internal defensiveness; can define the path (or paths) by which the intended consequence is to be achieved; can relate the choice to their control needs; and can build into their choices a realistic and challenging level of aspiration. Free choice therefore implies that the members are able to explore as many alternatives as they consider significant and select those that are central to their needs.

Why must the choice be related to the central needs and why must the level of aspiration be realistic and challenging? May people not choose freely unrealistic or unchallenging objectives? Yes, they may do so in the short run, but not for long if they still want to have free and informed choice. A freely chosen course of action means that the action must be based on an accurate analysis of the situation and not on the biases or defenses of the decision makers. We know, from the level of aspiration studies, that choices which are too high or too low, which are too difficult or not difficult enough will tend to lead to psychological failure. Psychological failure will lead to increased defensiveness, increased failure, and decreased self-acceptance on the part of the members experiencing the failure. These conditions, in turn, will tend to lead to distorted perceptions by the members making the choices. Moreover, the defensive members may unintentionally create a climate where the members of surrounding and interrelated systems will tend to provide carefully censored information. Choices made under these conditions are neither informed nor free.

Turning to the question of centrality of needs, a similar logic applies. The degree of commitment to the processes of generating valid information, scanning, and choosing may significantly vary according to the centrality of the choice to the needs of the clients. The more central the choice, the more the system will strive to do its best in developing valid information and making free and informed choices. If the research from perceptual psychology is valid, the very perception of the clients is altered by the needs involved. Individuals tend to scan more, ask for more information, and be more careful in their choices when they are making decisions that are central to them. High involvement may produce perceptual distortions, as does low involvement. The interventionist, however, may have a greater probability of helping the clients explore possible distortion when the choice they are making is a critical one.

Internal Commitment

Internal commitment means the course of action or choice that has ben internalized by each member so that he experiences a high degree of ownership and has a feeling of responsibility about the choice and its implications. Internal commitment means that the individual has reached the point where he is acting on the choice because it fulfills his own needs and sense of responsibility, as well as those of the system.

The individual who is internally committed is acting primarily under the influence of his own forces and not induced forces. The individual (or any unity) feels a minimal degree of dependence upon others for the action. It implies that he has obtained and processed valid information and that he has made an informed and free choice. Under these conditions there is a high probability that the individual's commitment will remain strong over time (even with reduction of external rewards) or under stress, or when the course of action is challenged by others. It also implies that the individual is continually open to reexamination of his position because he believes in taking action based upon valid information.

Note

1. There is an important function within the scope of responsibility of the interventionist that will not be discussed systematically in this volume. It is the public health function. There are many individuals who do not ask for help because they do not know they need help or that help could be

available to them. The societal strategy for developing effective intervention activity must therefore include a function by which potential clients are educated about organizational health and illness as well as the present state of the art in effecting change. The writer hopes that this volume plays a role in facilitating this function.

19

Groupthink: The Desperate Drive for Consensus at Any Cost

Irving L. Janis

"How could we have been so stupid?" President John F. Kennedy asked after he and a close group of advisers had blundered into the Bay of Pigs invasion. For the last two years I have been studying that question, as it applies not only to the Bay of Pigs decision-makers but also to those who led the United States into such other major fiascoes as the failure to be prepared for the attack on Pearl Harbor, the Korean War stalemate and the escalation of the Vietnam War.

Stupidity certainly is not the explanation. The men who participated in making the Bay of Pigs decision, for instance, comprised one of the greatest arrays of intellectual talent in the history of American Government—Dean Rusk, Robert McNamara, Douglas Dillon, Robert Kennedy, McGeorge Bundy, Arthur Schlesinger Jr., Allen Dulles and others.

It also seemed to me that explanations were incomplete if they concentrated only on disturbances in the behavior of each individual within a decision-making body: temporary emotional states of elation, fear, or anger that reduce a man's mental efficiency, for example, or chronic blind spots arising from a man's social prejudices or idiosyncratic biases.

I preferred to broaden the picture by looking at the fiascoes from the standpoint of group dynamics as it has been explored over the past

SOURCE: From "Groupthink" by Irving L. Janis. Reprinted with permission from *Psychology Today Magazine*. Copyright © 1971 (Sussex Publishers, Inc.).

three decades, first by the great social psychologist Kurt Lewin and later in many experimental situations by myself and other behavioral scientists. My conclusion after poring over hundreds of relevant documents—historical reports about formal group meetings and informal conversations among the members—is that the groups that committed the fiascoes were victims of what I call "groupthink."

"Groupy." In each case study, I was surprised to discover the extent to which each group displayed the typical phenomena of social conformity that are regularly encountered in studies of group dynamics among ordinary citizens. For example, some of the phenomena appear to be completely in line with findings from social-psychological experiments showing that powerful social pressures are brought to bear by the members of a cohesive group whenever a dissident begins to voice his objections to a group consensus. Other phenomena are reminiscent of the shared illusions observed in encounter groups and friendship cliques when the members simultaneously reach a peak of "groupy" feelings.

Above all, there are numerous indications pointing to the development of group norms that bolster morale at the expense of critical thinking. One of the most common norms appears to be that of remaining loyal to the group by sticking with the policies to which the group has already committed itself, even when those policies are obviously working out badly and have unintended consequences that disturb the conscience of each member. This is one of the key characteristics of groupthink.

1984. I use the term groupthink as a quick and easy way to refer to the mode of thinking that persons engage in when *concurrence-seeking* becomes so dominant in a cohesive ingroup that it tends to override realistic appraisal of alternative courses of action. Groupthink is a term of the same order as the words in the newspeak vocabulary George Orwell used in his dismaying world of *1984.* In that context, groupthink takes on an invidious connotation. Exactly such a connotation is intended, since the term refers to a deterioration in mental efficiency, reality testing and moral judgments as a result of group pressures.

The symptoms of groupthink arise when the members of decision-making groups become motivated to avoid being too harsh in their judgments of their leaders' or their colleagues' ideas. They adopt a soft line of criticism, even in their own thinking. At their meetings, all the members are amiable and seek complete concurrence on every important issue, with no bickering or conflict to spoil the cozy, "we-feeling" atmosphere.

Kill. Paradoxically, soft-headed groups are often hard-hearted when it comes to dealing with outgroups or enemies. They find it relatively easy to resort to dehumanizing solutions—they will readily authorize bombing attacks that kill large numbers of civilians in the name of the noble cause of persuading an unfriendly government to negotiate at the peace table. They are unlikely to pursue the more difficult and controversial issues that arise when alternatives to a harsh military solution come up for discussion. Nor are they inclined to raise ethical issues that carry the implication that *this fine group of ours, with its humanitarianism and its high-minded principles, might be capable of adopting a course of action that is inhumane and immoral.*

Norms. There is evidence from a number of social-psychological studies that as the members of a group feel more accepted by the others, which is a central feature of increased group cohesiveness, they display less overt conformity to group norms. Thus we would expect that the more cohesive a group becomes, the less the members will feel constrained to censor what they say out of fear of being socially

punished for antagonizing the leader or any of their fellow members.

In contrast, the groupthink type of conformity tends to increase as group cohesiveness increases. Groupthink involves nondeliberate suppression of critical thoughts as a result of internalization of the group's norms, which is quite different from deliberate suppression on the basis of external threats of social punishment. The more cohesive the group, the greater the inner compulsion on the part of each member to avoid creating disunity, which inclines him to believe in the soundness of whatever proposals are promoted by the leader or by a majority of the group's members.

In a cohesive group, the danger is not so much that each individual will fail to reveal his objections to what the others propose but that he will think the proposal is a good one, without attempting to carry out a careful, critical scrutiny of the pros and cons of the alternatives. When groupthink becomes dominant, there also is considerable suppression of deviant thoughts, but it takes the form of each person's deciding that his misgivings are not relevant and should be set aside, that the benefit of the doubt regarding any lingering uncertainties should be given to the group consensus.

Stress. I do not mean to imply that all cohesive groups necessarily suffer from groupthink. All ingroups may have a mild tendency toward groupthink, displaying one or another of the symptoms from time to time, but it need not be so dominant as to influence the quality of the group's final decision. Neither do I mean to imply that there is anything necessarily inefficient or harmful about group decisions in general. On the contrary, a group whose members have properly defined roles, with traditions concerning the procedures to follow in pursuing a critical inquiry, probably is capable of making better decisions than any individual group member working alone.

The problem is that the advantages of having decisions made by groups are often lost because of powerful psychological pressures that arise when the members work closely together, share the same set of values and, above all, face a crisis situation that puts everyone under intense stress.

The main principle of groupthink, which I offer in the spirit of Parkinson's Law, is this: *The more amiability and esprit de corps there is among the members of a policy-making ingroup, the greater the danger that independent critical thinking will be replaced by groupthink, which is likely to result in irrational and dehumanizing actions directed against outgroups.*

Symptoms. In my studies of high-level governmental decision-makers, both civilian and military, I have found eight main symptoms of groupthink.

1. *Invulnerability.* Most or all of the members of the ingroup share an illusion of invulnerability that provides for them some degree of reassurance about obvious dangers and leads them to become over-optimistic and willing to take extraordinary risks. It also causes them to fail to respond to clear warnings of danger.

The Kennedy ingroup, which uncritically accepted the Central Intelligence Agency's disastrous Bay of Pigs plan, operated on the false assumption that they could keep secret the fact that the United States was responsible for the invasion of Cuba. Even after news of the plan began to leak out, their belief remained unshaken. They failed even to consider the danger that awaited them: a worldwide revulsion against the U.S.

A similar attitude appeared among the members of President Lyndon B. Johnson's ingroup, the "Tuesday Cabinet," which kept escalating the Vietnam War despite repeated setbacks and failures. "There was a belief," Bill Moyers commented after he resigned, "that if we indicated a willingness to use our power, they [the North Vietnamese] would get the message and back away from an all-out confrontation. . . . There was a confidence—it

was never bragged about, it was just there—that when the chips were really down, the other people would fold."

A most poignant example of an illusion of invulnerability involves the ingroup around Admiral H. E. Kimmel, which failed to prepare for the possibility of a Japanese attack on Pearl Harbor despite repeated warnings. Informed by his intelligence chief that radio contact with Japanese aircraft carriers had been lost, Kimmel joked about it: "What, you don't know where the carriers are? Do you mean to say that they could be rounding Diamond Head (at Honolulu) and you wouldn't know it?" The carriers were in fact moving full-steam toward Kimmel's command post at the time. Laughing together about a danger signal, which labels it as a purely laughing matter, is a characteristic manifestation of groupthink.

2. *Rationale.* As we see, victims of groupthink ignore warnings; they also collectively construct rationalizations in order to discount warnings and other forms of negative feedback that, taken seriously, might lead the group members to reconsider their assumptions each time they recommit themselves to past decisions. Why did the Johnson ingroup avoid reconsidering its escalation policy when time and again the expectations on which they based their decisions turned out to be wrong? James C. Thomson, Jr., a Harvard historian who spent five years as an observing participant in both the State Department and the White House, tells us that the policymakers avoided critical discussion of their prior decisions and continually invented new rationalizations so that they could sincerely recommit themselves to defeating the North Vietnamese.

In the fall of 1964, before the bombing of North Vietnam began, some of the policymakers predicted that six weeks of air strikes would induce the North Vietnamese to seek peace talks. When someone asked, "What if they don't?" the answer was that another four weeks certainly would do the trick.

Later, after each setback, the ingroup agreed that by investing just a bit more effort (by stepping up the bomb tonnage a bit, for instance), their course of action would prove to be right. *The Pentagon Papers* bear out those observations.

In *The Limits of Intervention,* Townsend Hoopes, who was acting Secretary of the Air Force under Johnson, says that Walt W. Rostow in particular showed a remarkable capacity for what has been called "instant rationalization." According to Hoopes, Rostow buttressed the group's optimism about being on the road to victory by culling selected scraps of evidence from news reports or, if necessary, by inventing "plausible" forecasts that had no basis in evidence at all.

Admiral Kimmel's group rationalized away their warnings, too. Right up to December 7, 1941, they convinced themselves that the Japanese would never dare attempt a full-scale surprise assault against Hawaii because Japan's leaders would realize that it would precipitate an all-out war which the United States would surely win. They made no attempt to look at the situation through the eyes of the Japanese leaders—another manifestation of groupthink.

3. *Morality.* Victims of groupthink believe unquestioningly in the inherent morality of their ingroup; this belief inclines the members to ignore the ethical or moral consequences of their decisions.

Evidence that this symptom is at work usually is of a negative kind—the things that are left unsaid in group meetings. At least two influential persons had doubts about the morality of the Bay of Pigs adventure. One of them, Arthur Schlesinger Jr., presented his strong objections in a memorandum to President Kennedy and Secretary of State Rusk but suppressed them when he attended meetings of the Kennedy team. The other, Senator J. William Fulbright, was not a member of the group, but the President invited him to express his misgivings in a speech to the policymakers. However, when Fulbright finished speaking the President moved on to other agenda items without asking for reactions of the group.

David Kraslow and Stuart H. Loory, in *The Secret Search for Peace in Vietnam,* report that

during 1966 President Johnson's ingroup was concerned primarily with selecting bomb targets in North Vietnam. They based their selections on four factors—the military advantage, the risk to American aircraft and pilots, the danger of forcing other countries into the fighting, and the danger of heavy civilian casualties. At their regular Tuesday luncheons, they weighed these factors the way school teachers grade examination papers, averaging them out. Though evidence on this point is scant, I suspect that the group's ritualistic adherence to a standardized procedure induced the members to feel morally justified in their destructive way of dealing with the Vietnamese people—after all, the danger of heavy civilian casualties from U.S. air strikes was taken into account on their checklists.

4. *Stereotypes.* Victims of groupthink hold stereotyped views of the leaders of enemy groups: they are so evil that genuine attempts at negotiating differences with them are unwarranted, or they are too weak or too stupid to deal effectively with whatever attempts the ingroup makes to defeat their purposes, no matter how risky the attempts are.

Kennedy's groupthinkers believed that Premier Fidel Castro's air force was so ineffectual that obsolete B-26's could knock it out completely in a surprise attack before the invasion began. They also believed that Castro's army was so weak that a small Cuban-exile brigade could establish a well-protected beachhead at the Bay of Pigs. In addition, they believed that Castro was not smart enough to put down any possible internal uprisings in support of the exiles. They were wrong on all three assumptions. Though much of the blame was attributable to faulty intelligence, the point is that none of Kennedy's advisers even questioned the CIA planners about these assumptions.

The Johnson advisers' sloganistic thinking about "the Communist apparatus" that was "working all around the world" (as Dean Rusk put it) led them to overlook the powerful nationalistic strivings of the North Vietnamese government and its efforts to ward off Chinese domination. The crudest of all stereotypes used by Johnson's inner circle to justify their policies was the domino theory ("If we don't stop the Reds in South Vietnam, tomorrow they will be in Hawaii and next week they will be in San Francisco," Johnson once said). The group so firmly accepted this stereotype that it became almost impossible for any adviser to introduce a more sophisticated viewpoint.

In the documents on Pearl Harbor, it is clear to see that the Navy commanders stationed in Hawaii had a naive image of Japan as a midget that would not dare to strike a blow against a powerful giant.

5. *Pressure.* Victims of groupthink apply direct pressure to any individual who momentarily expresses doubts about any of the group's shared illusions or who questions the validity of the arguments supporting a policy alternative favored by the majority. This gambit reinforces the concurrence-seeking norm that loyal members are expected to maintain.

President Kennedy probably was more active than anyone else in raising skeptical questions during the Bay of Pigs meetings, and yet he seems to have encouraged the group's docile, uncritical acceptance of defective arguments in favor of the CIA's plan. At every meeting, he allowed the CIA representatives to dominate the discussion. He permitted them to give their immediate refutations in response to each tentative doubt that one of the others expressed, instead of asking whether anyone shared the doubt or wanted to pursue the implications of the new worrisome issue that had just been raised. And at the most crucial meeting, when he was calling on each member to give his vote for or against the plan, he did not call on Arthur Schlesinger, the one man there who was known by the President to have serious misgivings.

Historian Thomson informs us that whenever a member of Johnson's ingroup began to express doubts, the group used subtle social pressures to "domesticate" him. To start with, the dissenter was made to feel at home provided that he lived up to two restrictions: 1) that he did not voice his doubts to outsiders, which would play into the hands of the opposition; and 2) that he kept his criticisms within the bounds of acceptable deviation, which meant not challenging any of the fundamental assumptions that went into the group's prior commitments. One such "domesticated dissenter" was Bill Moyers. When Moyers arrived at a meeting, Thomson tells us, the President greeted him with, "Well, here comes Mr. Stop-the-Bombing."

6. *Self-Censorship.* Victims of groupthink avoid deviating from what appears to be group consensus; they keep silent about their misgivings and even minimize to themselves the importance of their doubts.

As we have seen, Schlesinger was not at all hesitant about presenting his strong objections to the Bay of Pigs plan in a memorandum to the President and the Secretary of State. But he became keenly aware of his tendency to suppress objections at the White House meetings. "In the months after the Bay of Pigs, I bitterly reproached myself for having kept so silent during those crucial discussions in the cabinet room," Schlesinger writes in *A Thousand Days,* "I can only explain my failure to do more than raise a few timid questions by reporting that one's impulse to blow the whistle on this nonsense was simply undone by the circumstances of the discussion."

7. *Unanimity.* Victims of groupthink share an illusion of unanimity within the group concerning almost all judgments expressed by members who speak in favor of the majority view. This symptom results partly from the preceding one, whose effects are augmented by the false assumption that any individual who remains silent during any part of the discussion is in full accord with what the others are saying.

When a group of persons who respect each other's opinions arrives at a unanimous view, each member is likely to feel that the belief must be true. This reliance on consensual validation within the group tends to replace individual critical thinking and reality testing, unless there are clear-cut disagreements among the members. In contemplating a course of action such as the invasion of Cuba, it is painful for the members to confront disagreements within their group, particularly if it becomes apparent that there are widely divergent views about whether the preferred course of action is too risky to undertake at all. Such disagreements are likely to arouse anxieties about making a serious error. Once the sense of unanimity is shattered, the members no longer can feel complacently confident about the decision they are inclined to make. Each man must then face the annoying realization that there are troublesome uncertainties and he must diligently seek out the best information he can get in order to decide for himself exactly how serious the risks might be. This is one of the unpleasant consequences of being in a group of hard-headed, critical thinkers.

To avoid such an unpleasant state, the members often become inclined, without quite realizing it, to prevent latent disagreements from surfacing when they are about to initiate a risky course of action. The group leader and the members support each other in playing up the areas of convergence in their thinking, at the expense of fully exploring divergencies that might reveal unsettled issues.

"Our meetings took place in a curious atmosphere of assumed consensus," Schlesinger writes. His additional comments clearly show that, curiously, the consensus was an illusion— an illusion that could be maintained only because the major participants did not reveal their own reasoning or discuss their idiosyncratic assumptions and vague reservations. Evidence from several sources makes it clear that even the three principals—President Kennedy, Rusk and McNamara—had widely differing assumptions about the invasion plan.

8. *Mindguards.* Victims of groupthink sometimes appoint themselves as mindguards to protect the leader and fellow members from adverse information that might break the complacency they shared about the effectiveness and morality of past decisions. At a large birthday party for his wife, Attorney General Robert F. Kennedy, who had been constantly informed about the Cuban invasion plan, took Schlesinger aside and asked him why he was opposed. Kennedy listened coldly and said, "You may be right or you may be wrong, but the President has made his mind up. Don't push it any further. Now is the time for everyone to help him all they can."

Rusk also functioned as a highly effective mindguard by failing to transmit to the group the strong objections of three "outsiders" who had learned of the invasion plan—Undersecretary of State Chester Bowles, USIA Director Edward R. Murrow, and Rusk's intelligence chief, Roger Hilsman. Had Rusk done so, their warnings might have reinforced Schlesinger's memorandum and jolted some of Kennedy's ingroup, if not the President himself, into reconsidering the decision.

Products. When a group of executives frequently displays most or all of these interrelated symptoms, a detailed study of their deliberations is likely to reveal a number of immediate consequences. These consequences are, in effect, products of poor decision-making practices because they lead to inadequate solutions to the problems under discussion.

First, the group limits its discussions to a few alternative courses of action (often only two) without an initial survey of all the alternatives that might be worthy of consideration.

Second, the group fails to reexamine the course of action initially preferred by the majority after they learn of risks and drawbacks they had not considered originally.

Third, the members spend little or no time discussing whether there are nonobvious gains they may have overlooked or ways of reducing the seemingly prohibitive costs that made rejected alternatives appear undesirable to them.

Fourth, members make little or no attempt to obtain information from experts within their own organizations who might be able to supply more precise estimates of potential losses and gains.

Fifth, members show positive interest in facts and opinions that support their preferred policy, and they tend to ignore facts and opinions that do not.

Sixth, members spend little time deliberating about how the chosen policy might be hindered by bureaucratic inertia, sabotaged by political opponents, or temporarily derailed by common accidents. Consequently, they fail to work out contingency plans to cope with foreseeable setbacks that could endanger the overall success of their chosen course.

Support. The search for an explanation of why groupthink occurs has led me through a quagmire of complicated theoretical issues in the murky area of human motivation. My belief, based on recent social psychological research, is that we can best understand the various symptoms of groupthink as a mutual effort among the group members to maintain self-esteem and emotional equanimity by providing social support to each other, especially at times when they share responsibility for making vital decisions.

Even when no important decision is pending, the typical administrator will begin to doubt the wisdom and morality of his past decisions each time he receives information about setbacks, particularly if the information is accompanied by negative feedback from prominent men who originally had been his supporters. It should not be surprising, therefore, to find that individual members strive to develop unanimity and esprit de corps that will help bolster each other's morale, to create an optimistic outlook about the success of pending decisions, and to reaffirm the positive value of past policies to which all of them are committed.

Pride. Shared illusions of invulnerability, for example, can reduce anxiety about taking risks. Rationalizations help members believe that the risks are really not so bad after all. The assumption of inherent morality helps the members to avoid feelings of shame or guilt. Negative stereotypes function as stress-reducing devices to enhance a sense of moral righteousness as well as pride in a lofty mission.

The mutual enhancement of self-esteem and morale may have functional value in enabling the members to maintain their capacity to take action, but it has maladaptive consequences insofar as concurrence-seeking tendencies interfere with critical, rational capacities and lead to serious errors of judgment.

While I have limited my study to decision-making bodies in government, groupthink symptoms appear in business, industry and any other field where small, cohesive groups make the decisions. It is vital, then, for all sorts of people—and especially group leaders—to know what steps they can take to prevent groupthink.

Remedies. To counterpoint my case studies of the major fiascoes, I have also investigated two highly successful group enterprises, the formulation of the Marshall Plan in the Truman Administration and the handling of the Cuban missile crisis by President Kennedy and his advisers. I have found it instructive to examine the steps Kennedy took to change his group's decision-making processes. These changes ensured that the mistakes made by his Bay of Pigs ingroup were not repeated by the missile-crisis ingroup, even though the membership of both groups was essentially the same.

The following recommendations for preventing groupthink incorporate many of the good practices I discovered to be characteristic of the Marshall Plan and missile crisis groups:

1. The leader of a policy-forming group should assign the role of critical evaluator to each member, encouraging the group to give high priority to open airing of objections and doubts. This practice needs to be reinforced by the leader's acceptance of criticism of his own judgments in order to discourage members from soft-pedaling their disagreements and from allowing their striving for concurrence to inhibit critical thinking.

2. When the key members of a hierarchy assign a policy-planning mission to any group within their organization, they should adopt an impartial stance instead of stating preferences and expectations at the beginning. This will encourage open inquiry and impartial probing of a wide range of policy alternatives.

3. The organization routinely should set up several outside policy-planning and evaluation groups to work on the same policy question, each deliberating under a different leader. This can prevent the insulation of an ingroup.

4. At intervals before the group reaches a final consensus, the leader should require each member to discuss the group's deliberations with associates in his own unit of the organization—assuming that those associates can be trusted to adhere to the same security regulations that govern the policy-makers—and then to report back their reactions to the group.

5. The group should invite one or more outside experts to each meeting on a staggered basis and encourage the experts to challenge the views of the core members.

6. At every general meeting of the group, whenever the agenda calls for an evaluation of policy alternatives, at least one member should play devil's advocate, functioning as a good lawyer in challenging the testimony of those who advocate the majority position.

7. Whenever the policy issue involves relations with a rival nation or organization, the group should devote a sizable block of time, perhaps an entire session, to a survey of all warning signals from the rivals and should write alternative scenarios on the rivals' intentions.

8. When the group is surveying policy alternatives for feasibility and effectiveness, it should from time to time divide into two or more subgroups to meet separately, under different chairmen, and then come back together to hammer out differences.

9. After reaching a preliminary consensus about what seems to be the best policy, the group should hold a "second-chance" meeting at which every member expresses as vividly as he can all his residual doubts, and rethinks the entire issue before making a definitive choice.

How.   These recommendations have their disadvantages. To encourage the open airing of objections, for instance, might lead to prolonged and costly debates when a rapidly growing crisis requires immediate solution. It also could cause rejection, depression and anger. A leader's failure to set a norm might create cleavage between leader and members that could develop into a disruptive power struggle if the leader looks on the emerging consensus as anathema. Setting up outside evaluation groups might increase the risk of security leakage. Still, inventive executives who know their way around the organizational maze probably can figure out how to apply one or another of the prescriptions successfully, without harmful side effects.

They also could benefit from the advice of outside experts in the administrative and behavioral sciences. Though these experts have much to offer, they have had few chances to work on policy-making machinery within large organizations. As matters now stand, executives innovate only when they need new procedures to avoid repeating serious errors that have deflated their self-images.

In this era of atomic warheads, urban disorganization and ecocatastrophes, it seems to me that policymakers should collaborate with behavioral scientists and give top priority to preventing groupthink and its attendant fiascoes.

IV

"Modern" Structural Organization Theory

Usually when someone refers to the structure of an organization, that person is talking about the relatively stable relationships among the positions, groups of positions (units), and work processes that make up the organization. Structural organization theory is concerned with vertical differentiations—hierarchical levels of organizational authority and coordination, and horizontal differentiations between organizational units—for example, between product or service lines, geographical areas, or skills. The organization chart is the ever-present "tool" of a structural organization theorist.

Why do we use the label "modern" to modify structural organization theory? Most organizational theorists from the classical school were structuralists. They focused their attention on the structure—or design—of organizations and their production processes. Some examples that are reprinted in Chapter I include those by Adam Smith, Henri Fayol, Charles Babbage, Daniel McCallum, Frederick Winslow Taylor, and Max Weber. Thus we use the word "modern" (always in quotation marks) merely to differentiate between the structural organization theorists of the 1960s and 1970s and the pre-World War II classical school structuralists.

The "modern" structuralists are concerned with many of the same issues that the classical structuralists were, but their theories have been influenced by and have benefited greatly from advancements in organization theory since World War II. Modern structuralists' roots are in the thinking of Fayol, Taylor, Gulick, and Weber, and their underlying tenets are quite similar: Organizational efficiency is the essence of organizational rationality; the goal of rationality is to increase the production of wealth in terms of real goods and services. However, "modern" structural theories also have been influenced substantially by the neoclassical, human relations-oriented, and systems theorists of organization.

Bolman and Deal (1984) identify the basic assumptions of the "modern" structural school:

1. Organizations are rational institutions whose primary purpose is to accomplish established objectives; rational organizational behavior is achieved best through systems of defined rules and formal authority. Organizational control and coordination are key for maintaining organizational rationality.

2. There is a "best" structure for any organization—or at least a most appropriate structure—in light of its given objectives, the environmental conditions surrounding it (for example, its markets, the competition, and the extent of government regulation), the nature of its products and/or services (the "best" structure for a management consulting firm probably is substantially different from that for a certified public accounting firm), and the technology of the production processes (a coal mining company has a different "best structure" than the "high tech" manufacturer of computer microcomponents).

3. Specialization and the division of labor increase the quality and quantity of production—particularly in highly skilled operations and professions.

4. Most problems in an organization result from structural flaws and can be solved by changing the structure.

What sorts of practical issues are best addressed by "modern" structural organization theory? Is it useful? The most immediate issue in the design of any organization is the question of structure. What should it look like? How should it work? How will it deal with the most common structural questions of specialization, departmentalization, span of control, and the coordination and control of specialized units?

Tom Burns and G. M. Stalker of the Tavistock Institute in London—which is widely acknowledged as the birthplace of the "socio-technical approach" to organizations—developed their widely cited theory of "mechanistic and organic systems" of organization while examining rapid technological change in the British and Scottish electronics industry in the post–World War II years. Their account of "Mechanistic and Organic Systems" from their 1961 book, *The Management of Innovation,* is reprinted here.

Burns and Stalker found that stable conditions may suggest the use of a mechanistic form of organization where a traditional pattern of hierarchy, reliance on formal rules and regulations, vertical communications, and structured decision making is possible. However, more dynamic conditions—situations in which the environment changes rapidly—require the use of an organic form of organization where there is less rigidity, more participation, and more reliance on workers to define and redefine their positions and relationships. For example, technological creativity, an essential ingredient in an organic system, requires an organizational climate and management systems that are supportive of innovation. The impacts of these two organizational forms on individuals are substantially different. Supervisors and managers find that the mechanistic form provides them with a greater sense of security in dealing with their environment than the organic form, which introduces much greater uncertainty. Burns and Stalker conclude that either form of organization may be appropriate in particular situations.

In "The Concept of Formal Organization," a chapter from their 1962 book *Formal Organizations: A Comparative Approach,* Peter M. Blau and W. Richard Scott assert that all organizations include both a formal and informal element. The informal organization by its nature is rooted in the formal structure and supports its formal organization by establishing norms for the operation of the organization—which cannot always be spelled out by rules and policies. For these reasons, Blau and Scott maintain that it is impossible to know and understand the true structure of a formal organization without a similar understanding of its parallel informal organization. Clearly, Blau and Scott were influenced by the "classical philosopher" Chester Barnard's 1938 book *The Functions of the Executive,* in which he held that:

> informal organization, although comprising the processes of society which are unconscious as contrasted with those of formal organizations which are conscious, has two important classes of effects: (*a*) it establishes certain attitudes, understandings, customs, habits, institutions, and (*b*) it creates the condition under which formal organization may arise.

Arthur H. Walker and Jay W. Lorsch, in their 1968 *Harvard Business Review* article "Organizational Choice: Product vs. Function," grapple with one of the perennial questions facing those who would design organizations: Should an organization be structured according to product or function? "Should all specialists in a given function be grouped under a common boss, regardless of differences in products they are involved in, or should the various functional specialists working on a single product be grouped together under the same superior?" Walker and Lorsch tackle this problem by examining two firms in the same industry—one organized by product and the other by function. They conclude that either structural arrangement can be appropriate, depending upon the organization's environment and the nature of the organization itself.

In 1776, Adam Smith advocated the division of labor to increase the effectiveness of the factory system of production. In 1922, Max Weber described two strong and opposing forces that have an impact on all organizations: the need for division of labor and specialization, and the need for centralizing authority. Division of labor is an inevitable consequence of specialization by skills, products, or processes. Most "modern" structuralists now use the word *differentiation*—which means essentially the same thing as specialization but also reflects increased appreciation of the myriad and rapidly changing external environmental forces with which organizations interact (for example, different markets, sociopolitical cultures, regulatory environments, technologies, competition, and the economy). Thus, complex differentiation is essential for organizational effectiveness as well as efficiency. However, differentiation *means* diverse forces that "pull organizations apart." Differentiation increases the need for organizational coordination and control that, in the language of "modern" structuralists, is labeled "integration."

Paul R. Lawrence and Jay W. Lorsch have received wide acclaim for their chapter "The Organization-Environment Interface," from their 1969 book *Developing Organizations: Diagnosis and Action,* which asserts that the single most important problem all organizations must solve is achieving a balance between the conflicting needs for and demands of differentiation and integration. Lawrence and Lorsch advocate a contingency approach to organization theory—an approach that utilizes different organization theories that may be appropriate under different circumstances and conditions. (See Chapter V for a discussion of contingency theories.)

Matrix organization structures originated with the U.S. aerospace program of the 1960s and the aerospace companies' extraordinary and conflicting needs for freedom (for innovation) and order (for regulation and control). Thus, matrix organization theory addresses the same inherent, organizational design need that was described by Max Weber (division of labor versus centralized authority) and Paul Lawrence and Jay Lorsch (differentiation versus integration). However, the enormity, complexity, importance, and temporary nature of the aerospace projects rendered traditional structural solutions to organizational problems inadequate for the task. Thus, great interest developed in matrix structures.

In their book *Matrix* (1977), Stanley Davis and Paul Lawrence define a "matrix as any organization that employs a *multiple command system* that includes not only a multiple command structure but also related support mechanisms and an associated organizational culture and behavior pattern." In their Chaper 2, "The Matrix Organization—Who Needs It?," Davis and Lawrence warn against unquestioning implementation of a matrix. Is a matrix a useful form of organizational structure? According to Davis and Lawrence, only if all necessary conditions exist. A matrix structure is only one element of a matrix organization: matrix systems, culture, and behavior also are needed. Additionally, a matrix organization is not desirable unless: (1) the organization must cope regularly with two or more "critical sectors" (critical sectors include functions, products, services, markets, and/or areas), (2) organizational tasks are uncertain, complex, and highly inter-dependent, and (3) there are economies of scale.

Henry Mintzberg has emerged as one of the most widely respected management and organizational theorists of the 1970s and 1980s. Since the 1960s, Mintzberg has been compiling a theory of management policy—a field of management and organization theory that has lacked attention. An adaptation of his early conceptual model of manage-ment policy is in Figure 1. The model demonstrates why Mintzberg is so influential: He is synthesizing many schools of organization and management theory—and doing so with coherence. His 1979 book *The Structuring of Organizations* addresses the first component of the model. (His 1983 book *Power in and Around Organizations* addresses the second component of the model. A chapter from it is reprinted in our Chapter VII.) In his chapter "Five Basic Parts of the Organization," which is reprinted here, Mintzberg uses James D. Thompson's (1967) concepts of "pooled, sequential, and reciprocal organizational coupling" to create a model of organizations with five interdependent parts: the strategic apex, the middle line, the operating core, the technostructure, and the support staff. His model is a creative and useful departure from traditional views of formal organization structure.

From the mid-1960s until well into the late 1980s, the historical attacks against the bureaucratic form of organization were renewed and expanded. For example, in *Changing Organizations* (1966), Warren Bennis predicted that bureaucratic organiza-tions as we know them will disappear within this century because they are unable to adapt to rapidly changing environments. Alvin Toffler's chapter in *Future Shock* (1970), "Organization: The Coming Ad-hocracy," reflects Bennis' thinking, and Bennis and Philip Slater's *The Temporary Society* (1968) extended Bennis' (1966) theme to predict a rise in democracy within organizations as well as in general society. Frederick Thayer (1981) identifies hierarchy as *the* root cause of alienation in organizations. Yet, all theories of organizational democracy are based on the assumption that hierarchy is desirable, necessary, and inevitable. More recently, Peter Drucker (1988) has predicted

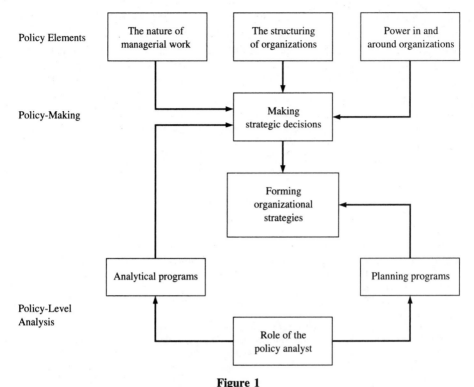

Figure 1

Mintzberg's basic model of management policy Adapted from Mintzberg, H. (1979). *The structuring of organizations* (p. iv). Englewood Cliffs, NJ: Prentice-Hall.

flatter, information-based, task- and mission-focused organizations. Edgar Schein (1989) foresees that information technology will eliminate the need for most functions currently performed by supervisors and thus eliminate the need for hierarchical arrangements. However, as much as we may need new non-hierarchical models, "we may have difficulty inventing them because of the automatic tendency to think hierarchically" (p. 63).

Is the bureaucratic form of organization on an inevitable road to extinction? Is it being replaced by systems of temporary democratic networks or structures without hierarchical layers of authority, responsibility, and accountability? If so, the trend isn't apparent yet. In fact, bureaucracy appears to be holding its own quite well in practice—even if not in the mainstream literature of organization theory. A small body of literature has even developed within the discipline of public administration that justifies the bureaucratic form of organization because of its efficiency and its promotion of equity and representativeness (Kaufman, 1977; Krislov & Rosenbloom, 1981; Goodsell, 1983).

Elliott Jaques, whose studies of organizations and structure have spanned more than forty years—from the Tavistock Institute's socio-technical systems "Glacier Project" (1950) to the present, has asserted himself as a foremost defender of the hierarchical-bureaucratic form of organization in the early 1990s. Jaques contends that those who argue against hierarchy are "simply wrong, and all their proposals are based on an inadequate understanding of not only hierarchy but also human nature." Hierarchical layers enable organizations to cope with discontinuities in mental and physical complexities, thereby separating tasks into manageable series of steps: "What we need is not some new kind of organization. What we need is managerial hierarchy that understands its own nature and purpose." According to Jaques, hierarchy is *the* best alternative for large organizations: "We need to stop casting about fruitlessly for organizational Holy Grails and settle down to the hard work of putting our managerial hierarchies in order."

References

BARNARD, C. I. (1938). *The functions of the executive.* Cambridge, MA: Harvard University Press.

BENNIS, W. G. (1966). *Changing organizations.* New York: McGraw-Hill.

BENNIS, W. G., & SLATER, P. E. (1968). *The temporary society.* New York: Harper & Row.

BLAU, P. M., & SCOTT, W. R. (1962). *Formal organizations: A comparative approach.* San Francisco: Chandler Publishing.

BOLMAN, L. G., & DEAL, T. E. (1984). *Modern approaches to understanding and managing organizations.* San Francisco: Jossey-Bass.

BURNS, T., & STALKER, G. M. (1961). *The management of innovation.* London: Tavistock Publications.

CROZIER, M. (1964). *The bureaucratic phenomenon.* Chicago: University of Chicago Press.

DAVIS, S. M., & LAWRENCE, P. R. (1977). *Matrix.* Reading, MA: Addison-Wesley.

DRUCKER, P. F. (1988, January-February). The coming of the new organization. *Harvard Business Review,* 45–53.

ETZIONI, A. (1961). *A comparative analysis of complex organizations.* Englewood Cliffs, NJ: Prentice-Hall.

GOODSELL, C. T. (1983). *The case for bureaucracy: A public administration polemic.* Chatham, NJ: Chatham House.

JAQUES, E. (1950). Collaborative group methods in a wage negotiation situation (The Glacier Project—I). *Human Relations, 3*(3).

JAQUES, E. (1990, January-February). In praise of hierarchy. *Harvard Business Review,* 127–133.

KAUFMAN, H. (1977). *Red tape.* Washington, DC: Brookings Institution.

KRISLOV, S., & ROSENBLOOM, D. H. (1981). *Representative bureaucracy and the American political system.* New York: Praeger.

LAWRENCE, P. R., & LORSCH, J. W. (1969). *Developing organizations.* Reading, MA: Addison-Wesley.

MINTZBERG, H. (1979). *The structuring of organizations.* Englewood Cliffs, NJ: Prentice-Hall.

MINTZBERG, H. (1983). *Power in and around organizations.* Englewood Cliffs, NJ: Prentice-Hall.

SCHEIN, E. H. (1989, Winter). Reassessing the "divine rights" of managers. *Sloan Management Review, 30*(2), 63–68.

THAYER, F. C. (1981). *An end to hierarchy and competition: Administration in the post-affluent world* (2d ed.). New York: New Viewpoints.

THOMPSON, J. D. (1967). *Organizations in action.* New York: McGraw-Hill.

THOMPSON, V. A. (1961). *Modern organization.* New York: Knopf.

TOFFLER, A. (1970). *Future Shock.* New York: Random House.

WALKER, A. H., & LORSCH, J. W. (1968, November-December). Organizational choice: Product vs. function. *Harvard Business Review, 46,* 129–138.

20

Mechanistic and Organic Systems

Tom Burns and G. M. Stalker

We are now at the point at which we may set down the outline of the two management systems which represent for us . . . the two polar extremities of the forms which such systems can take when they are adapted to a specific rate of technical and commercial change. The cases we have tried to establish from the literature, as from our research experience exhibited in the last chapter, is that the different forms assumed by a working organization do exist objectively and are not merely interpretations offered by observers of different schools.

Both types represent a "rational" form of organization, in that they may both, in our experience, be explicitly and deliberately created and maintained to exploit the human resources of a concern in the most efficient manner feasible in the circumstances of the concern. Not surprisingly, however, each exhibits characteristics which have been hitherto associated with different kinds of interpretation. For it is our contention that empirical findings have usually been classified according to sociological ideology rather than according to the functional specificity of the working organization to its task and the conditions confronting it.

We have tried to argue that these are two formally contrasted forms of management system. These we shall call the mechanistic and organic forms.

SOURCE: From Tom Burns and G. M. Stalker, *The Management of Innovation* (London: Tavistock Publications, 1961), 119–125. Reprinted by permission. References omitted; footnotes retained.

A *mechanistic* management system is appropriate to stable conditions. It is characterized by:

(a) the specialized differentiation of functional tasks into which the problems and tasks facing the concern as a whole are broken down;

(b) the abstract nature of each individual task, which is pursued with techniques and purposes more or less distinct from those of the concern as a whole; *i.e.*, the functionaries tend to pursue the technical improvement of means, rather than the accomplishment of the ends of the concern;

(c) the reconciliation, for each level in the hierarchy, of these distinct performances by the immediate superiors, who are also, in turn, responsible for seeing that each is relevant in his own special part of the main task.

(d) the precise definition of rights and obligations and technical methods attached to each functional role;

(e) the translation of rights and obligations and methods into the responsibilities of a functional position;

(f) hierarchic structure of control, authority, and communication;

(g) a reinforcement of the hierarchic structure by the location of knowledge of actualities exclusively at the top of the hierarchy, where the final reconciliation of distinct tasks and assessment of relevance is made.[1]

(h) a tendency for interaction between members of the concern to be vertical, *i.e.*, between superior and subordinate;

(i) a tendency for operations and working behavior to be governed by the instructions and decisions issued by superiors;

(j) insistence on loyalty to the concern and obedience to superiors as a condition of membership;

(k) a greater importance and prestige attaching to internal (local) than to general (cosmopolitan) knowledge, experience, and skill.

The *organic* form is appropriate to changing conditions, which give rise constantly to fresh problems and unforeseen requirements for action which cannot be broken down or distributed automatically arising from the functional roles defined within a hierarchic structure. It is characterized by:

(a) the contributive nature of special knowledge and experience to the common task of the concern;

(b) the "realistic" nature of the individual task, which is seen as set by the total situation of the concern;

(c) the adjustment and continual redefinition of individual tasks through interaction with others;

(d) the shedding of "responsibility" as a limited field of rights, obligations and methods. (Problems may not be posted upwards, downwards or sideways as being someone else's responsibility);

(e) the spread of commitment to the concern beyond any technical definition;

(f) a network structure of control, authority, and communication. The sanctions which apply to the individual's conduct in his working role derive more from presumed community of interest with the rest of the working organization in the survival and growth of the firm, and less from a contractual relationship between himself and a nonpersonal corporation, represented for him by an immediate superior;

(g) omniscience no longer imputed to the head of the concern; knowledge about the technical or commercial nature of the here and now task may be located anywhere in the network; this location becoming the ad hoc centre of control authority and communication;

(h) a lateral rather than a vertical direction of communication through the organization, communication between people of different rank, also, resembling consultation rather than command;

(i) a content of communication which consists of information and advice rather than instructions and decisions;

(j) commitment to the concern's task and to the "technological ethos" of material progress and expansion is more highly valued than loyalty and obedience;

(k) importance and prestige attach to affiliations and expertise valid in the industrial and technical and commercial milieux external to the firm.

One important corollary to be attached to this account is that while organic systems are not hierarchic in the same sense as are mechanistic, they remain stratified. Positions are differentiated according to seniority—i.e., greater expertise. The lead in joint decisions is frequently taken by seniors, but it is an essential presumption of the organic system that the lead, i.e., "authority," is taken by whoever shows himself most informed and capable, i.e., the "best authority." The location of authority is settled by consensus.

A second observation is that the area of commitment to the concern—the extent to which the individual yields himself as a resource to be used by the working organization—is far more extensive in organic than in mechanistic systems. Commitment, in fact, is expected to approach that of the professional scientist to his work, and frequently does. One further consequence of this is that it becomes far less feasible to distinguish "informal" from "formal" organization.

Thirdly, the emptying out of significance from the hierarchic command system, by which co-operation is ensured and which serves to monitor the working organization under a mechanistic system, is countered by the development of shared beliefs about the values and goals of the concern. The growth and accretion of institutionalized values, beliefs, and conduct, in the form of commitments, ideology, and manners, around an image of the concern in its industrial and commercial setting make good the loss of formal structure.

Finally, the two forms of systems represent a polarity, not a dichotomy; there are, as we have tried to show, intermediate stages between the extremities empirically known to us. Also, the relation of one form to the other is elastic, so that a concern oscillating between relative stability and relative change may also oscillate between the two forms. A concern may (and frequently does) operate with a management system which includes both types.

The organic form, by departing from the familiar clarity and fixity of the hierarchic structure, is often experienced by the individual manager as an uneasy, embarrassed, or chronically anxious quest for knowledge about what he should be doing, or what is expected of him, and similar apprehensiveness about what others are doing. Indeed, as we shall see later, this kind of response is necessary if the organic form of organization is to work effectively. Understandably, such anxiety finds expression in resentment when the apparent confusion besetting him is not explained. In these situations, all managers some of the time, and many managers all of the time, yearn for more definition and structure.

On the other hand, some managers recognize a rationale of nondefinition, a reasoned basis for the practice of those successful firms in which designation of status, function, and line of responsibility and authority has been vague or even avoided.

The desire for more definition is often in effect a wish to have the limits of one's task more neatly defined—to know what and when one doesn't have to bother about as much as to know what one does have to. It follows that the more definition is given, the more omniscient the management must be, so that no functions are left whole or partly undischarged, no person is overburdened with undelegated responsibility, or left without the authority to do his job properly. To do this, to have all the separate functions attached to individual roles fitting together and comprehensively, to have communication between persons constantly maintained on a level adequate to the needs of each functional role, requires rules or traditions of behavior proved over a long time and an equally fixed, stable task. The omniscience which may then be credited to the head of the concern is expressed throughout its body through the lines of command, extending in a clear, explicitly titled hierarchy of officers and subordinates.

The whole mechanistic form is instinct with this twofold principle of definition and dependence which acts as the frame within which action is conceived and carried out. It works, unconsciously, almost in the smallest minutiae of daily activity. "How late is late?" The answer to this question is not to be found in the rule book, but in the superior. Late is when the boss thinks it is late. Is he the kind of man who thinks 8:00 is the time, and 8:01 is late? Does he think that 8:15 is all right occasionally if it is not a regular thing? Does he think that everyone should be allowed a 5-minute grace after 8:00 but after that they are late?

Settling questions about how a person's job is to be done in this way is nevertheless simple, direct, and economical of effort. We shall, in a later chapter, examine more fully the nature of the protection and freedom (in other respects than his job) which this affords the individual.

One other feature of mechanistic organization needs emphasis. It is a necessary condition of its operation that the individual "works on his own," functionally isolated; he "knows his job," he is "responsible for seeing it's done." He works at a job which is in a sense artificially abstracted from the realities of the situation the concern is dealing with, the accountant "dealing with the costs side," the works manager "pushing production," and so on. As this works out in practice, the rest of the organization becomes part of the problem situation the individual has to deal with in order to perform successfully; *i.e.*, difficulties and problems arising from work or information which has been handed over the "responsibility barrier" between two jobs or departments are regarded as "really" the responsibility of the person from whom they were received. As a design engineer put in,

When you get designers handing over designs completely to production, it's "their responsibility" now. And you get tennis games played with the responsibility for anything that goes wrong. What happens is that you're constantly getting unsuspected faults arising from characteristics which you didn't think important in the design. If you get to hear of these through a sales person, or a production person, or somebody to whom the design was handed over to in the dim past, then, instead of being a design problem, it's an annoyance caused by that particular person, who can't do his own job— because you'd thought you were finished with that one, and you're on to something else now.

When the assumptions of the form of organization make for preoccupation with specialized tasks, the chances of career success, or of greater influence, depend rather on the relative importance which may be attached to each special function by the superior whose task it is to reconcile and control a number of them. And, indeed, to press the claims of one's job or department for a bigger share of the firm's resources is in many cases regarded as a mark of initiative, of effectiveness, and even of "loyalty to the firm's interests." The state of affairs thus engendered squares with the role of the superior, the man who can see the wood instead of just the trees, and gives it the reinforcement of the aloof detachment belonging to a court of appeal. The ordinary relationship prevailing between individual managers "in charge of" different functions is one of rivalry, a rivalry which may be rendered innocuous to the persons involved by personal friendship or the norms of sociability, but which turns discussion about the situations which constitute the real problems of the concern—how to make the products more cheaply, how to sell more, how to allocate resources, whether to curtail activity in one sector, whether to risk expansion in another and so on—into an arena of conflicting interests.

The distinctive feature of the second, organic system is the pervasiveness of the working organization as an institution. In concrete terms, this makes itself felt in a preparedness to combine with others in serving the general aims of the concern. Proportionately to the rate and extent of change, the less can the omniscience appropriate to command organizations be ascribed to the head of the organization; for executives, and even operatives, in a changing firm it is always theirs to reason why. Furthermore, the less definition can be given to status roles, and modes of communication, the more do the activities of each member of the organization become determined by the real tasks of the firm as he sees them than by instruction and routine. The individual's job ceases to be self-contained; the only way in which "his" job can be done is by his participating continually with others in the solution of problems which are real to the firm, and put in a language of requirements and activities meaningful to them all. Such methods of working put much heavier demands on the individual. . . .

We have endeavored to stress the appropriateness of each system to its own specific set of conditions. Equally, we desire to avoid the suggestion that either system is superior under all circumstances to the other. In particular, nothing in our experience justifies the assumption that mechanistic systems should be superseded by organic in conditions of stability.[2] The beginning of administrative wisdom is the awareness that there is no one optimum type of management system.

Notes

1. This functional attribute to the head of a concern often takes on a clearly expressive aspect. It is common enough for concerns to instruct all people with whom they deal to address correspondence to the firm (*i.e.*, to its formal head) and for all outgoing letters and orders to be signed by the head of the concern. Similarly, the printed letter heading used by Government departments carries instructions for the replies to be addressed to the Secretary, etc. These instructions are not always taken seriously, either by members of the organization or their correspondents, but in one company this practice was insisted upon and was taken to somewhat unusual lengths; *all* correspondence was delivered to the managing director,

who would thereafter distribute excerpts to members of the staff, synthesizing their replies into the letter of reply which he eventually sent. Telephone communication was also controlled by limiting the number of extensions, and by monitoring incoming and outgoing calls.

2. A recent instance of this assumption is contained in H. A. Shepard's paper addressed to the Symposium on the Direction of Research Establishments, 1956. "There is much evidence to suggest that the optimal use of human resources in industrial organizations requires a different set of conditions, assumptions, and skills from those traditionally present in industry. Over the past twenty-five years, some new orientations have emerged from organizational experiments, observations, and inventions. The new orientations depart radically from doctrines associated with 'Scientific Management' and traditional bureaucratic patterns.

The central emphases in this development are as follows:

1. Wide participation in decision-making, rather than centralized decision-making.
2. The face-to-face group, rather than the individual, as the basic unit of organization.
3. Mutual confidence, rather than authority, the integrative force in organization.
4. The supervisor as the agent for maintaining intragroup and intergroup communication, rather than as the agent of higher authority.
5. Growth of members of the organization to greater responsibility, rather than external control of the member's performance or their tasks."

21

The Concept of Formal Organization

Peter M. Blau and W. Richard Scott

Social Organization and Formal Organizations

Although a wide variety of organizations exists, when we speak of an organization it is generally quite clear what we mean and what we do not mean by this term. We may refer to the American Medical Association as an organization, or to a college fraternity; to the Bureau of Internal Revenue, or to a union; to General Motors, or to a church; to the Daughters of the American Revolution, or to an army. But we would not call a family an organization, nor would we so designate a friendship clique, or a community, or an economic market, or the political institutions of a society. What is the specific and differentiating criterion implicit in our intuitive distinction of organizations from other kinds of social groupings or institutions? It has something to do with how human conduct becomes socially organized, but it is not, as one might first suspect, whether or not social controls order and organize the conduct of individuals, since such social controls operate in both types of circumstances.

Before specifying what is meant by formal organization, let us clarify the general concept of social organization. "Social organization" refers to the ways in which human conduct

SOURCE: From Peter M. Blau and W. Richard Scott, *Formal Organizations: A Comparative Approach,* (Chandler Publishing, 1962), 2–8. Copyright © 1962 by Peter M. Blau and W. Richard Scott. Reprinted by permission of the authors.

becomes socially organized, that is, to the observed regularities in the behavior of people that are due to the social conditions in which they find themselves rather than to their physiological or psychological characteristics as individuals. The many social conditions that influence the conduct of people can be divided into two main types, which constitute the two basic aspects of social organizations: (1) the structure of social relations in a group or larger collectivity of people, and (2) the shared beliefs and orientations that unite the members of the collectivity and guide their conduct.

The conception of structure or system implies that the component units stand in some relation to one another and, as the popular expression "The whole is greater than the sum of its parts" suggests, that the relations between units add new elements to the situation.[1] This aphorism, like so many others, is a half-truth. The sum of fifteen apples, for example, is no more than fifteen times one apple. But a block of ice is more than the sum of the atoms of hydrogen and oxygen that compose it. In the case of the apples, there exist no linkages or relations between the units comprising the whole. In the case of the ice, however, specific connections have been formed between H and O atoms and among H_2O molecules that distinguish ice from hydrogen and oxygen, on the one hand, and from water, on the other. Similarly, a busload of passengers does not constitute a group, since no social relations unify individuals into a common structure.[2] But a busload of club members on a Sunday outing is a group, because a network of social relations links the members into a social structure, a structure which is an emergent characteristic of the collectivity that cannot be reduced to the attributes of its individual members. In short, a network of social relations transforms an aggregate of individuals into a group (or an aggregate of groups into a larger social structure), and the group is more than the sum of the individuals composing it since the structure of social relations is an emergent element that influences the conduct of individuals.

To indicate the nature of social relations, we can briefly dissect this concept. Social relations involve, first, patterns of social interaction: the frequency and duration of the contacts between people, the tendency to initiate these contacts, the direction of influence between persons, the degree of cooperation, and so forth. Second, social relations entail people's sentiments to one another, such feelings of attraction, respect, and hostility. The differential distribution of social relations in a group, finally, defines its status structure. Each member's status in the group depends on his relations with the others—their sentiments toward and interaction with him. As a result, integrated members become differentiated from isolates, those who are widely respected from those who are not highly regarded, and leaders from followers. In addition to these relations between individuals within groups, relations also develop between groups, relations that are a source of still another aspect of social status, since the standing of the group in the larger social system becomes part of the status of any of its members. An obvious example is the significance that membership in an ethnic minority, say, Puerto Rican, has for an individual's social status.

The networks of social relations between individuals and groups, and the status structure defined by them, constitute the core of the social organization to a collectivity, but not the whole of it. The other main dimension of social organization is a system of shared beliefs and orientations, which serve as standards for human conduct. In the course of social interaction common notions arise as to how people should act and interact and what objectives are worthy of attainment. First, common values crystallize, values that govern the goals for which men strive—their ideals and their ideas of what is desirable—such as our belief in democracy or the importance financial success assumes in our thinking. Second, social norms develop—that is, common expectations concerning how people ought to behave—and social sanctions are used

to discourage violations of these norms. These socially sanctioned rules of conduct vary in significance from moral principles or mores, as Sumner calls them, to mere customs or folkways. If values define the ends of human conduct, norms distinguish behavior that is a legitimate means for achieving these ends from behavior that is illegitimate. Finally, aside from the norms to which everybody is expected to conform, differential role expectations also emerge, expectations that become associated with various social positions. Only women in our society are expected to wear skirts, for example. Or, the respected leader of a group is expected to make suggestions, and the other members will turn to him in times of difficulties, whereas group members who have not earned the respect of others are expected to refrain from making suggestions and generally to participate little in group discussions.

These two dimensions of social organization —the networks of social relations and the shared orientations—are often referred to as the social structure and the culture, respectively.[3] Every society has a complex social structure and a complex culture, and every community within a society can be characterized by these two dimensions of social organization, and so can every group within a community (except that the specific term "culture" is reserved for the largest social systems). The prevailing cultural standards and the structure of social relations serve to organize human conduct in the collectivity. As people conform more or less closely to the expectations of their fellows, and as the degree of their conformity in turn influences their relations with others and their social status, and as their status in further turn affects their inclinations to adhere to social norms and their chances to achieve valued objectives, their patterns of behavior become socially organized.

In contrast to the social organization that emerges whenever men are living together, there are organizations that have been deliberately established for a certain purpose.[4] If the accomplishment of an objective requires collective effort, men set up an organization designed to coordinate the activities of many persons and to furnish incentives for others to join them for this purpose. For example, business concerns are established in order to produce goods that can be sold for a profit, and workers organize unions in order to increase their bargaining power with employers. In these cases, the goals to be achieved, the rules the members of the organization are expected to follow, and the status structure that defines the relations between them (the organizational chart) have not spontaneously emerged in the course of social interaction but have been had consciously designed a priori to anticipate and guide interaction and activities. Since the distinctive characteristic of these organizations is that they have been formally established for the explicit purpose of achieving certain goals, the term "formal organization" is used to designate them. And this formal establishment for explicit purpose is the criterion that distinguishes our subject matter from the study of social organization in general.

Formal Organization and Informal Organization

The fact that an organization has been formally established, however, does not mean that all activities and interactions of its members conform strictly to the official blueprint. Regardless of the time and effort devoted by management to designing a rational organization chart and elaborate procedure manuals, this official plan can never completely determine the conduct and social relations of the organization's members. Stephen Vincent Benét illustrates this limitation when he contrasts the military blueprint with military action:

If you take a flat map
And move wooden blocks upon it strategically,
The thing looks well, the blocks behave as they should.
The science of war is moving live men like blocks.

And getting the blocks into place at a fixed moment.
But it takes time to mold your men into blocks
And flat maps turn into country where creeks and gullies
Hamper you wooden squares. They stick in the brush,
They are tired and rest, they straggle after ripe blackberries.
And you cannot lift them up in your hand and move them.[5]

In every formal organization there arise informal organizations. The constituent groups of the organization, like all groups, develop their own practices, values, norms, and social relations as their members live and work together. The roots of these informal systems are embedded in the formal organization itself and nurtured by the very formality of its arrangements. Official rules must be general to have sufficient scope to cover the multitude of situations that may arise. But the application of these general rules to particular cases often poses problems of judgment, and informal practices tend to emerge that provide solutions for these problems. Decisions not anticipated by official regulations must frequently be made, particularly in times of change, and here again unofficial practices are likely to furnish guides for decisions long before the formal rules have been adapted to the changing circumstances. Moreover, unofficial norms are apt to develop that regulate performance and productivity. Finally, complex networks of social relations and informal status structures emerge, within groups and between them, which are influenced by many factors besides the organizational chart, for example by the background characteristics of various persons, their abilities, their willingness to help others, and their conformity to group norms. But to say that these informal structures are not completely determined by the formal institutions is not to say that they are entirely independent of it. For informal organizations develop in response to the opportunities created and the problems posed by their environment, and the formal organization constitutes the immediate environment of the groups within it.

When we speak of formal organizations in this book, we do not mean to imply that attention is confined to formally instituted patterns; quite the contrary. It is impossible to understand the nature of a formal organization without investigating the networks of informal relations and the unofficial norms as well as the formal hierarchy of authority and the official body of rules, since the formally instituted and the informally emerging patterns are inextricably intertwined. The distinction between the formal and the informal aspects of organizational life is only an analytical one and should not be reified; there is only one actual organization. Note also that one does not speak of the informal organization of a family or of a community. The term "informal organization" does not refer to all types of emergent patterns of social life but only to those that evolve within the framework of a formally established organization. Excluded from our purview are social institutions that have evolved without explicit design; included are the informally emerging as well as the formally instituted patterns within formally established organizations.

The decision of the members of a group to formalize their endeavors and relations by setting up a specific organization, say, a social and athletic club, is not fortuitous. If a group is small enough for all members to be in direct social contact, and if it has no objectives that require coordination of activities, there is little need for explicit procedures or a formal division of labor. But the larger the group and the more complex the task it seeks to accomplish, the greater are the pressures to become explicitly organized.[6] Once a group of boys who merely used to hang around a drugstore decide to participate in the local baseball league, they must organize a team. And the complex coordination of millions of soldiers with thousands of specialized duties in a modern army requires extensive formalized procedures and a clearcut authority structure.

Since formal organizations are often very large and complex, some authors refer to them as "large-scale" or as "complex" organizations. But we have eschewed these terms as misleading in two respects. First, organizations vary in size and complexity, and using these variables as defining criteria would result in such odd expressions as "a small large-scale organization" or "a very complex complex organization." Second, although formal organizations often become very large and complex, their size and complexity do not rival those of the social organization of a modern society, which includes such organizations and their relations with one another in addition to other nonorganizational patterns. (Perhaps the complexity of formal organizations is so much emphasized because it is man-made whereas the complexity of societal organization has slowly emerged, just as the complexity of modern computers is more impressive than that of the human brain. Complexity by design may be more conspicuous than complexity by growth or evolution.)

The term "bureaucratic organization" which also is often used, calls attention to the fact that organizations generally possess some sort of administrative machinery. In an organization that has been formally established, a specialized administrative staff usually exists that is responsible for maintaining the organization as a going concern and for coordinating the activities of its members. Large and complex organizations require an especially elaborate administrative apparatus. In a large factory, for example, there is not only an industrial work force directly engaged in production but also an administration composed of executive, supervisory, clerical, and other staff personnel. The case of a government agency is more complicated, because such an agency is part of the administrative arm of the nation. The entire personnel of, say, a law-enforcement agency is engaged in administration, but administration of different kinds; whereas operating officials administer the law and thereby help maintain social order in the society, their superiors and the auxiliary staff administer agency procedures and help maintain the organization itself.

One aspect of bureaucratization that has received much attention is the elaboration of detailed rules and regulations that the members of the organization are expected to faithfully follow. Rigid enforcement of the minutiae of extensive official procedures often impedes effective operations. Colloquially, the term "bureaucracy" connotes such rule-encumbered inefficiency. In sociology, however, the term is used neutrally to refer to the administrative aspects of organizations. If bureaucratization is defined as the amount of effort devoted to maintaining the organization rather than to directly achieving its objectives, all formal organizations have at least a minimum of bureaucracy—even if this bureaucracy involves no more than a secretary-treasurer who collects dues. But wide variations have been found in the degree of bureaucratization in organizations, as indicated by the amount of effort devoted to administrative problems, the proportion of administrative personnel, the hierarchical character of the organization, or the strict enforcement of administrative procedures and rigid compliance with them.

Notes

1. For a discussion of some of the issues raised by this assertion, see Ernest Nagel, "On the statement 'The Whole Is More Than the Sum of Its Parts'," Paul F. Lazarsfeld and Morris Rosenberg (eds.), *The Language of Social Research* (Glencoe, Ill.: Free Press, 1955), pp. 519–527.

2. A purist may, concededly, point out that all individuals share the role of passenger and so are subject to certain generalized norms, courtesy for example.

3. See the recent discussion of these concepts by Kroeber and Parsons, who conclude by defining culture as "transmitted and created content and patterns of values, ideas, and other symbolic meaningful systems" and social structure or system as "the specifically relational system of interaction among individuals and collectivities." A. L. Kroeber and Talcott Parsons, "The Concepts of Culture and of Social System," *American Sociological Review, 23* (1958), p. 583.

4. Sumner makes this distinction between, in his terms, *crescive* and *enacted* social institutions. William Graham Sumner, *Folkways* (Boston: Ginn, 1907), p. 54.

5. From *John Brown's Body*. Holt, Rinehart & Winston, Inc. Copyright, 1927, 1928, by Stephen Vincent Benét. Copyright renewed, 1955, 1956, by Rosemary Carr Benét.

6. For a discussion of size and its varied effects on the characteristics of social organization, see Theodore Caplow, "Organizational Size," *Administrative Science Quarterly,* 1 (1957), pp. 484–505.

22

Organizational Choice: Product versus Function

Arthur H. Walker and Jay W. Lorsch

Of all the issues facing a manager as he thinks about the form of his organization, one of the thorniest is the question of whether to group activities primarily by product or by function. Should all specialists in a given function be grouped under a common boss, regardless of differences in products they are involved in, or should the various functional specialists working on a single product be grouped together under the same superior?

In talks with managers we have repeatedly heard them anguishing over this choice. For example, recently a divisional vice president of a major U.S. corporation was contemplating a major organizational change. After long study, he made this revealing observation to his subordinate managers:

> We still don't know which choice will be the best one. Should the research, engineering, marketing, and production people be grouped separately in departments for each function? Or would it be better to have them grouped together in product departments, each department dealing with a particular product group?
>
> We were organized by product up until a few years ago. Then we consolidated our

organization into specialized functional departments, each dealing with all of our products. Now I'm wondering if we wouldn't be better off to divide our operations again into product units. Either way I can see advantages and disadvantages, trade-offs. What criteria should I use? How can we predict what the outcomes will be if we change?

Companies that have made a choice often feel confident that they have resolved this dilemma. Consider the case of a large advertising agency that consolidated its copy, art, and television personnel into a "total creative department." Previously they had reported to group heads in their areas of specialization. In a memo to employees the company explained the move:

> Formation of the "total creative" department completely tears down the walls between art, copy, and television people. Behind this move is the realization that for best results all creative people, regardless of their particular specialty, must work together under the most intimate relationship as total advertising people, trying to solve creative problems together from start to finish.
>
> The new department will be broken into five groups reporting to the senior vice president and creative director, each under the direction of an associate creative director. Each group will be responsible for art, television, and copy in their accounts.

But our experience is that such reorganizations often are only temporary. The issues involved are so complex that many managements oscillate between these two choices or try to effect some compromise between them.

In this article we shall explore—from the viewpoint of the behavioral scientist—some of the criteria that have been used in the past to make these choices, and present ideas from recent studies that suggest more relevant criteria for making the decision. We hope to provide a way of thinking about these problems that will lead to the most sensible decisions for the accomplishment of organizational goals.

The dilemma of products versus function is by no means new; managers have been facing the same basic question for decades. As large corporations like Du Pont and General Motors grew, they found it necessary to divide their activities among product divisions.[1] Following World War II, as companies expanded their sales of existing products and added new products and businesses, many of them implemented a transition from functional organizations handling a number of different products to independently managed product divisions. These changes raised problems concerning divisionalization, decentralization, corporate staff activities, and the like.

As the product divisions grew and prospered, many companies extended the idea of product organization further down in their organizations under such labels as "the unit management concept." Today most of the attention is still being directed to these changes and innovations *within* product or market areas below the divisional level.

We are focusing therefore on these organizational issues at the middle and lower echelons of management, particularly on the crucial questions being faced by managers today within product divisions. The reader should note, however, that a discussion of these issues is immensely complicated by the fact that a choice at one level of the corporate structure affects the choices and criteria for choice at other levels. Nonetheless, the ideas we suggest in this article are directly relevant to organizational choice at any level.

Elements to Consider

To understand more fully the factors that make these issues so difficult, it is useful to review the criteria often relied on in making this decision. Typically, managers have used technical and economic criteria. They ask themselves, for instance, "Which choice will minimize payroll costs?" Or, "Which will best utilize equipment and specialists?" This approach not only makes real sense in the traditional logic of management, but it has strong support from the classical school of organization theorists. Luther Gulick, for example, used it in arguing for organization by function:

> It guarantees the maximum utilization of up-to-date technical skill and . . . makes it possible in each case to make use of the most effective divisions of work and specialization. . . . [It] makes possible also the economies of the maximum use of labor-saving machinery and mass production. . . . [It] encourages coordination in all of the technical and skilled work of the enterprise. . . . [It] furnishes an excellent approach to the development of central coordination and control.[2]

In pointing to the advantages of the product basis of organization, two other classical theorists used the same approach:

> Product or product line is an important basis for departmentalizing, because it permits the maximum use of personal skills and specialized knowledge, facilitates the employment of specialized capital and makes easier a certain type of coordination.[3]

In sum, these writers on organization suggested that the manager should make the choice based on three criteria:

1. Which approach permits maximum use of special technical knowledge?
2. Which provides the most efficient utilization of machinery and equipment?
3. Which provides the best hope of obtaining the required control and coordination?

There is nothing fundamentally wrong with these criteria as far as they go, and, of course, managers have been using them. But they fail to recognize the complex set of trade-offs involved in these decisions. As a consequence, managers make changes that produce unanticipated results and may even reduce the effectiveness of their organization. For example:

A major manufacturer of corrugated containers a few years ago shifted from a product basis to a functional basis. The rationale for the decision was that it would lead to improved control of production costs and efficiencies in production and marketing. While the organization did accomplish these aims, it found itself less able to obtain coordination among its local sales and production units. The functional specialists now reported to the top officers in charge of production and sales, and there was no mechanism for one person to coordinate their work below the level of division management. As a result, the company encountered numerous problems and unresolved conflicts among functions and later returned to the product form.

This example pinpoints the major trade-off that the traditional criteria omit. Developing highly specialized functional units makes it difficult to achieve coordination or integration among these units. On the other hand, having product units as the basis for organization promotes collaboration between specialists, but the functional specialists feel less identification with functional goals.

Behaviorists' Findings

We now turn to some new behavioral science approaches to designing organization structure. Recent studies[4] have highlighted three other important factors about specialization and coordination:

• As we have suggested, the classical theorists saw specialization in terms of grouping similar activities, skills, or even equipment. They did not look at its psychological and social consequences. Recently, behavioral scientists (including the authors) have found that there is an important relationship between a unit's or individual's assigned activities and the unit members' patterns of thought and behavior. Functional specialists tend to develop patterns of behavior and thought that are in tune with the demands of their jobs and their prior training, and as a result these specialists (*e.g.*, industrial engineers and production supervisors) have different ideas and orientation about what is important in getting the job done. This is called *differentiation,* which simply means the differences in behavior and thought patterns that develop among different specialists in relation to their respective tasks. Differentiation is necessary for functional specialists to perform their jobs effectively.

• Differentiation is closely related to achievement of coordination, or what behavioral scientists call *integration*. This means collaboration between specialized units or individuals. Recent studies have demonstrated that there is an inverse relationship between differentiation and integration: the more two functional specialists (or their units) differ in their patterns of behavior and thought, the more difficult it is to bring about integration between them. Nevertheless, this research has indicated, achievement of both differentiation and integration is essential if organizations are to perform effectively.

• While achievement of both differentiation and integration is possible, it can occur only when well-developed means of communication among specialists exist in the organization and when the specialists are effective in resolving the inevitable cross-functional conflicts.

These recent studies, then, point to certain related questions that managers must consider when they choose between a product or functional basis of organization.

1. How will the choice affect differentiation among specialists? Will it allow the necessary differences in viewpoint to develop so that specialized tasks can be performed effectively?

2. How does the decision affect the prospects of accomplishing integration? Will it lead, for instance, to greater differentiation, which will increase the problems of achieving integration?

3. How will the decision affect the ability of organization members to communicate with each other, resolve conflicts, and reach the necessary joint decisions?

There appears to be a connection between the appropriate extent of differentiation and integration and the organization's effectiveness in accomplishing its economic goals. What the appropriate pattern is depends on the nature of external factors—markets, technology, and so on—facing the organization, as well as the goals themselves. The question of how the organizational pattern will affect individual members is equally complex. Management must consider how much stress will be associated with a certain pattern and whether such stress should be a serious concern.

To explore in more detail the significance of modern approaches to organizational structuring, we shall describe one recent study conducted in two manufacturing plants—one organized by *product*, the other on a *functional* basis.[5]

Plant F and Plant P

The two plants where this study was conducted were selected because they were closely matched in several ways. They were making the same product; their markets, technology, and even raw materials were identical. The parent companies were also similar: both were large, national corporations that developed, manufactured, and marketed many consumer products. In each case divisional and corporate headquarters were located more than 100 miles from the facilities studied. The plants were separated from other structures at the same site, where other company products were made.

Both plants had very similar management styles. They stressed their desire to foster employees' initiative and autonomy and placed great reliance on selection of well-qualified department heads. They also identified explicitly the same two objectives. The first was to formulate, package, and ship the products in minimum time at specified levels of quality and at minimum costs—that is, within existing capabilities. The second was to improve the capabilities of the plant.

In each plant there were identical functional specialists involved with the manufacturing units and packing unit, as well as quality control, planning and scheduling, warehousing, industrial engineering, and plant engineering. In Plant F (with the *functional* basis of organization), only the manufacturing departments and the planning and scheduling function reported to the plant manager responsible for the product (see Figure 1). All other functional specialists reported to the staff of the divisional manufacturing manager, who was also responsible for plants manufacturing other products. At Plant P (with the *product* basis of organization), all functional specialists with the exception of plant engineering reported to the plant manager (see Figure 2).

State of Differentiation

In studying differentiation, it is useful to focus on the functional specialists' differences in outlook in terms of: orientation toward goals, orientation toward time, and perception of the formality of organization.

Goal orientation. The bases of organization in the two plants had a marked effect on the specialists' differentiated goal orientations. In Plant F they focused sharply on their specialized goals and objectives. For example, quality control specialists were concerned almost exclusively with meeting quality standards, industrial engineers with methods improvements and cost reduction, and scheduling specialists with how to meet requirements. An industrial engineer in Plant F indicated this intensive interest in his own activity:

> We have 150 projects worth close to a million dollars in annual savings. I guess I've completed some that save as much as $90,000 a year. Right now I'm working on cutting departmental costs. You need a hard shell in this work. No one likes to have his costs cut, but that is my job.

That these intense concerns with specialized objectives were expected is illustrated by the

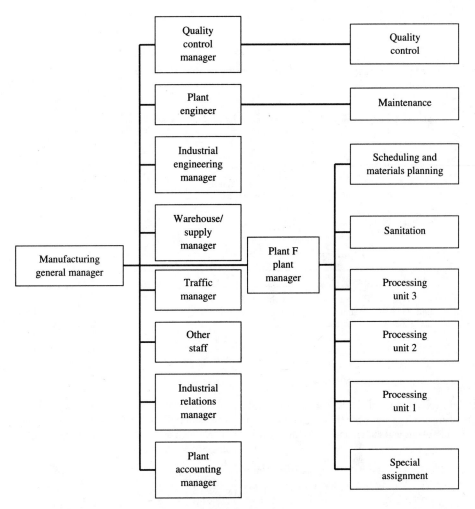

Figure 1
Organizational chart at Plant F

apologetic tone of a comment on production goals by an engineering supervisor at Plant F:

At times we become too much involved in production. It causes a change in heart. We are interested in production, but not at the expense of our own standards of performance. If we get too much involved, then we may become compromised.

A final illustration is when production employees stood watching while members of the maintenance department worked to start a new production line, and a production supervisor remarked:

I hope that they get that line going soon. Right now, however, my hands are tied. Maintenance has the job. I can only wait. My people have to wait, too.

This intense concern with one set of goals is analogous to a rifle shot; in a manner of speaking, each specialist took aim at one set of

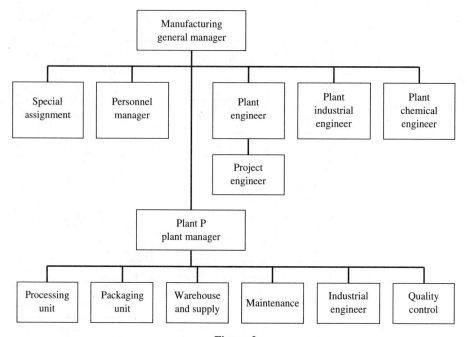

Figure 2
Organizational chart at Plant P

goals and fired at it. Moreover, the specialists identified closely with their counterparts in other plants and at divisional headquarters. As one engineer put it:

> We carry the ball for them (the central office). We carry a project through and get it working right.

At Plant P the functional specialists' goals were more diffuse—like buckshot. Each specialist was concerned not only with his own goals, but also with the operation of the entire plant. For example, in contrast to the Plant F production supervisor's attitude about maintenance, a Plant P maintenance manager said, under similar circumstances:

> We're all interested in the same thing. If I can help, I'm willing. If I have a mechanical problem, there is no member of the operating department who wouldn't go out of his way to solve it.

Additional evidence of this more diffuse orientation toward goals is provided by comments such as these which came from Plant P engineers and managers:

> We are here for a reason—to run this place the best way we know how. There is no reluctance to be open and frank despite various backgrounds and ages.
>
> The changeovers tell the story. Everyone shows willingness to dig in. The whole plant turns out to do cleaning up.

Because the functional specialists at Plant F focused on their individual goals, they had relatively wide differences in goals and objectives. Plant P's structure, on the other hand, seemed to make functional specialists more aware of common product goals and reduced differences in goal orientation. Yet, as we shall see, this lesser differentiation did not hamper their performance.

Time orientation. The two organizational bases had the opposite effect, however, on the time orientation of functional managers. At Plant F, the specialists shared a concern with short-term issues (mostly daily problems). The time orientation of specialists at Plant P was more differentiated. For example, its production managers concentrated on routine matters, while planning and industrial engineering focused on issues that needed solution within a week, and quality control specialists worried about even longer-term problems.

The reason is not difficult to find. Since Plant P's organization led its managers to identify with product goals, those who could contribute to the solution of longer-term problems became involved in these activities. In Plant F, where each unit focused on its own goals, there was more of a tendency to worry about getting daily progress. On the average, employees of Plant P reported devoting 30 percent of their time to daily problems, while at Plant F this figure was 49 percent. We shall have more to say shortly about how these factors influenced the results achieved in the two plants.

Organizational formality. In the study, the formality of organizational structure in each functional activity was measured by three criteria: clarity of definition of job responsibilities, clarity of dividing lines between jobs, and importance of rules and procedures.

It was found that at Plant F there were fewer differences among functional activities in the formality of organization structure than at Plant P. Plant F employees reported that a uniform degree of structure existed across functional specialities; job responsibilities were well defined, and the distinctions between jobs were clear. Similarly, rules and procedures were extensively relied on. At Plant P, on the other hand, substantial differences in the formality of organization existed. Plant engineers and industrial engineers, for example, were rather vague about their responsibilities and about the dividing line between their jobs and other jobs. Similarly, they reported relatively low reliance on rules and procedures. Production managers, on the other hand, noted that their jobs were well defined and that rules and procedures were more important to them.

The effects of these two bases of organization on differentiation along these three dimensions are summarized in Figure 3. Overall, differentiation was greater between functional specialists at Plant P than at Plant F.

Integration Achieved

While the study found that both plants experienced some problems in accomplishing integration, these difficulties were more noticeable at Plant F. Collaboration between maintenance and production personnel and between production and scheduling was a problem there. In Plant P the only relationship where integration was unsatisfactory was that between production and quality control specialists. Thus Plant P seemed to be getting slightly better integration in spite of the greater differentiation among specialists in that organization. Since differentiation

Figure 3
Differentiation in Plants F and P

Dimensions of Differentiation	Plant F	Plant P
Goal orientation	More differentiated and focused	Less differentiated and more diffuse
Time orientation	Less differentiated and shorter term	More differentiated and longer term
Formality of structure	Less differentiated, with more formality	More differentiated, with less formality

and integration are basically antagonistic, the only way managers at Plant P could get both was by being effective at communication and conflict resolution. They were better at this than were managers at Plant F.

Communication patterns.   In Plant P, communication among employees was more frequent, less formal, and more often of a face-to-face nature than was the case with Plant F personnel. One Plant P employee volunteered:

> Communications are no problem around here. You can say it. You can get an answer.

Members of Plant F did not reflect such positive feelings. They were heard to say:

> Why didn't they tell me this was going to happen? Now they've shut down the line.
> When we get the information, it is usually too late to do any real planning. We just do our best.

The formal boundaries outlining positions that were more prevalent at Plant F appeared to act as a damper on communication. The encounters observed were often a succession of two-man conversations, even though more than two may have been involved in a problem. The telephone and written memoranda were more often employed than at Plant P, where spontaneous meetings involving several persons were frequent, usually in the cafeteria.

Dealing with conflict.   In both plants, *confrontation* of conflict was reported to be more typical than either the use of power to *force* one's own position or an attempt to *smooth* conflict by "agreeing to disagree." There was strong evidence, nevertheless, that in Plant P managers were coming to grips with conflicts more directly than in Plant F. Managers at Plant F reported that more conflicts were being smoothed over. They worried that issues were often not getting settled. As they put it:

> We have too many nice guys here.
> If you can't resolve an issue, you go to the plant manager. But we don't like to bother him often with small matters. We

should be able to settle them ourselves. The trouble is we don't. So it dies.

Thus, by ignoring conflict in the hope it would go away, or by passing it to a higher level, managers at Plant F often tried to smooth over their differences. While use of the management hierarchy is one acceptable way to resolve conflict, so many disagreements at Plant F were pushed upstairs that the hierarchy became overloaded and could not handle all the problems facing it. So it responded by dealing with only the more immediate and pressing ones.

At Plant P the managers uniformly reported that they resolved conflicts themselves. There was no evidence that conflicts were being avoided or smoothed over. As one manager said:

> We don't let problems wait very long. There's no sense to it. And besides, we get together frequently and have plenty of chances to discuss differences over a cup of coffee.

As this remark suggests, the quicker resolution of conflict was closely related to the open and informal communication pattern prevailing at Plant P. In spite of greater differentiation in time and orientation and structure, then, Plant P managers were able to achieve more satisfactory integration because they could communicate and resolve conflict effectively.

Performance and Attitudes

Before drawing some conclusions from the study of these two plants, it is important to make two more relevant comparisons between them—their effectiveness in terms of the goals set for them and the attitudes of employees.

Plant performance.   As we noted before, the managements of the two plants were aiming at the same two objectives: maximizing current output within existing capabilities and improving the capabilities of the plant. Of the two facilities, Plant F met the first objective more effectively; it was achieving a higher production rate with greater efficiency and at less cost than was Plant P. In terms of the second objective, however, Plant P was clearly superior to

Plant F; the former's productivity had increased by 23 percent from 1963 to 1966 compared with the latter's increment of only 3 percent. One key manager at Plant F commented:

> There has been a three- or four-year effort to improve our capability. Our expectations have simply not been achieved. The improvement in performance is just not there. We are still where we were three years ago. But our targets for improvements are realistic.

By contrast, a key manager at Plant P observed:

> Our crews have held steady, yet our volume is up. Our quality is consistently better too.

Another said:

> We are continuing to look for and find ways to improve and consolidate jobs.

Employee attitudes. Here, too, the two organizations offer a contrast, but the contrast presents a paradoxical situation. Key personnel at Plant P appeared to be more deeply involved in their work than did managers at Plant F, and they admitted more often to feeling stress and pressure than did their opposite numbers at Plant F. But Plant F managers expressed more satisfaction with their work than did those at Plant P; they liked the company and their jobs more than did managers at Plant P.

Why Plant P managers felt more involved and had a higher level of stress, but were less satisfied than Plant F managers, can be best explained by linking these findings with the others we have reported.

Study Summary

The characteristics of these two organizations are summarized in Figure 4. The nature of the organization at Plant F seemed to suit its stable but high rate of efficiency. Its specialists concentrated on their own goals and performed well, on the whole. The jobs were well defined and managers worked within procedures and rules. The managers were concerned primarily with short-term matters. They were not particularly effective in communicating with each other and in resolving conflict. But this was not very important to achieve steady, good performance, since the coordination necessary to meet this objective could be achieved through plans and procedures and through the manufacturing technology itself.

As long as top management did not exert much pressure to improve performance dramatically, the plant's managerial hierarchy was

Figure 4
Observed characteristics of the two organizations

Characteristics	Plant F	Plant P
Differentiation	Less differentiation except in goal orientation	Greater differentiation in structure and time orientation
Integration	Somewhat less effective	More effective
Conflict management	Confrontation, but also "smoothing over" and avoidance; rather restricted communication pattern	Confrontation of conflict; open, face-to-face communication
Effectiveness	Efficient, stable production; but less successful in improving plant capabilities	Successful in improving plant capabilities, but less effective in stable production
Employee attitudes	Prevalent feeling of satisfaction, but less feeling of stress and involvement	Prevalent feeling of stress and involvement, but less satisfaction

able to resolve the few conflicts arising from daily operations. And as long as the organization avoided extensive problem solving, a great deal of personal contact was not very important. It is not surprising therefore that the managers were satisfied and felt relatively little pressure. They attended strictly to their own duties, remained uninvolved, and got the job done. For them, this combination was satisfying. And higher management was pleased with the facility's production efficiency.

The atmosphere at Plant P, in contrast, was well suited to the goal of improving plant capabilities, which it did very well. There was less differentiation between goals, since the functional specialists to a degree shared the product goals. Obviously, one danger in this form of organization is the potential attraction of specialist managers to total goals to the extent that they lose sight of their particular goals and become less effective in their jobs. But this was not a serious problem at Plant P.

Moreover, there was considerable differentiation in time orientation and structure; some specialists worked at the routine and programmed tasks in operating the plant, while others concentrated on longer-term problems to improve manufacturing capability. The latter group was less constrained by formal procedures and job definitions, and this atmosphere was conducive to problem solving. The longer time orientation of some specialists, however, appeared to divert their attention from maintaining schedules and productivity. This was a contributing factor to Plant P's less effective current performance.

In spite of the higher degree of differentiation in these dimensions, Plant P managers were able to achieve the integration necessary to solve problems that hindered plant capability. Their shared goals and a common boss encouraged them to deal directly with each other and confront their conflicts. Given this pattern, it is not surprising that they felt very involved in their jobs. Also they were under stress because of their great involvement in their jobs. This stress could lead to dissatisfaction with their situation. Satisfaction for its own sake, however, may not

be very important; there was no evidence of higher turnover of managers at Plant P.

Obviously, in comparing the performance of these two plants operating with similar technologies and in the same market, we might predict that, because of its greater ability to improve plant capabilities, Plant P eventually will reach a performance level at least as high as Plant F's. While this might occur in time, it should not obscure one important point: the functional organization seems to lead to better results in a situation where stable performance of a routine task is desired, while the product organization leads to better results in situations where the task is less predictable and requires innovative problem solving.

Clues for Managers

How can the manager concerned with the function versus product decision use these ideas to guide him in making the appropriate choice? The essential step is identifying the demands of the task confronting the organization.

Is it a routine, repetitive task? Is it one where integration can be achieved by plan and conflict managed through the hierarchy? This was the way the task was implicitly defined at Plant F. If this is the nature of the task, or, to put it another way, if management is satisfied with this definition of the task, then the functional organization is quite appropriate. While it allows less differentiation in time orientation and structure, it does encourage differentiation in goal orientation. This combination is important for specialists to work effectively in their jobs.

Perhaps even more important, the functional structure also seems to permit a degree of integration sufficient to get the organization's work done. Much of this can be accomplished through paper systems and through the hardware of the production line itself. Conflict that comes up can more safely be dealt with through the management hierarchy, since the difficulties of resolving conflict are less acute. This is so because the tasks provide less opportunity for conflict and because the specialists have less differentiated viewpoints to overcome. This form of organization is less phychologically demanding for the individuals involved.

On the other hand, if the task is of a problem-solving nature, or if management defines it this way, the product organization seems to be more appropriate. This is especially true where there is a need for tight integration among specialists. As illustrated at Plant P, the product organization form allows the greater differentiation in time orientation and structure that specialists need to attack problems. While encouraging identification with superordinate goals, this organizational form does allow enough differentiation in goals for specialists to make their contributions.

Even more important, to identify with product ends and have a common boss encourages employees to deal constructively with conflict, communicate directly and openly with each other, and confront their differences, so they can collaborate effectively. Greater stress and less satisfaction for the individual may be unavoidable, but it is a small price to pay for the involvement that accompanies it.

The manager's problem in choosing between product and functional forms is complicated by the fact that in each organization there are routine tasks and tasks requiring problem solving, jobs requiring little interdependence among specialists and jobs requiring a great deal. Faced with these mixtures, many companies have adopted various compromises between product and functional bases. They include (in ascending order of structural complexity):

1. *The use of cross-functional teams to facilitate integration.* These teams provide some opportunity for communication and conflict resolution and also a degree of the common identification with product goals that characterizes the product organization. At the same time, they retain the differentiation provided by the functional organization.

2. *The appointment of full-time integrators or coordinators around a product.* These product managers or project managers encourage the functional specialists to become committed to product goals and help resolve conflicts between them. The specialists stell retain their primary identification with their functions.[6]

3. *The "matrix" or grid organization, which combines the product and functional forms by overlaying them.* Some managers wear functional hats and are involved in the day-to-day, more routine activities. Naturally, they identify with functional goals. Others, wearing product or project hats, identify with total product goals and are more involved in the problem-solving activity required to cope with long-range issues and to achieve cross-functional coordination.

These compromises are becoming popular because they enable companies to deal with multiple tasks simultaneously. But we do not propose them as a panacea, because they make sense only for those situations where the differentiation and integration required by the sum of all the tasks make a middle approach necessary. Further, the complexity of interpersonal plus organizational relationships in these forms and the ambiguity associated with them make them difficult to administer effectively and psychologically demanding on the persons involved.

In our view, the only solution to the product versus function dilemma lies in analysis of the multiple tasks that must be performed, the differences between specialists, the integration that must be achieved, and the mechanisms and behavior required to resolve conflict and arrive at these states of differentiation and integration. This analysis provides the best hope of making a correct product or function choice or of arriving at some appropriate compromise solution.

Notes

1. For a historical study of the organizational structure of U.S. corporations, see Alfred D. Chandler, Jr., *Strategy and Structure* (Cambridge: The M.I.T. Press, 1962).

2. Luther Gulick, "Notes on the Theory of Organization," in *Papers on the Science of Administration,*

edited by Luther Gulick and Lyndall F. Urwick (New York Institute of Public Administration, 1917), pp. 23–24.

3. Harold D. Koontz, and C. J. O'Donnell, *Principles of Management* (New York, McGraw-Hill, 2nd ed. 1959), p. 111.

4. See Paul R. Lawrence and Jay W. Lorsch, *Organization and Environment* (Boston, Division of Research, Harvard Business School, 1967); and

Eric J. Miller and A. K. Rice, *Systems of Organization* (London, Tavistock Publications, 1967).

5. Arthur H. Walker, *Behavioral Consequences of Contrasting Patterns of Organization* (Boston, Harvard Business School, unpublished doctoral dissertation, 1967).

6. See Paul R. Lawrence and Jay W. Lorsch, "New Management Job: The Integrator," HBR November-December 1967, p. 142.

23

Organization-Environment Interface

Paul R. Lawrence and Jay W. Lorsch

It is no mystery that organizations must carry on transactions with their environment simply to survive, and, even more importantly, to grow. In the first chapter, we identified the quality of these transactions as posing one of the fundamental developmental problems of any organization. Other analysts of organizational affairs have consistently mentioned transactions with the environment as a crucial if not the most crucial issues. It is an issue that has been dealt with extensively by economists and by specialists in business policy and strategy. They have dealt primarily with the content of these relationships—the actual kind and amount of goods, services, and funds that are part of these transactions. But the issue has not been extensively studied by specialists in the application of behavioral sciences, and attention has not been focused on such human aspects affecting the quality of these transactions as: What is the quality of the information exchanged across the organizational boundaries? What are the major determinants of the quality? What are its consequences? Such questions have been asked many times of the relations between individuals and groups within the organization, but the boundary-spanning relations have simply not been subjected to comparable scrutiny. It is not surprising therefore, that systematic efforts

SOURCE: From Paul R. Lawrence and Jay W. Lorsch, *Developing Organizations: Diagnosis and Action,* © 1969, by Addison-Wesley Publishing Company, Inc., Reading, Massachusetts. Chapter 3, pages 23–30. Reprinted with permission of the publisher. Footnotes omitted.

to diagnose and improve the quality of these organization-environment relations have also lagged behind the effort applied to improving internal relations. It is worth speculating about the reasons for this lack of attention.

Perhaps the focus has been placed on internal transactions because both parties to a faulty relation, being within the institution, tend to bring their troubles to a single source—their shared superior up the chain of command. This focuses attention on the costs of unsatisfactory work relations and triggers corrective action. There is less likelihood that this will happen in connection with boundary transactions. It is, moreover, not so easy to collect information about the status of the boundary-spanning relation since the outside participants may feel no obligation to cooperate. The relative neglect may also be due to the traditional division of labor between academic disciplines. It may be automatically assumed that economists are the experts on boundary transactions while the psychologist and the sociologist are expected to confine their efforts to internal relations. Even within business schools, it is traditional for the functional specialities, such as marketing and finance, to have exclusive concern with the quality of salesman-customer and treasurer-banker relationships. Only recently have such specialists drawn on behavioral disciplines to aid them in the study of these matters.

The authors themselves became involved in the study and improvement of relations at this interface by approaching the topic through the back door. We had been concerned for some years with the quality of intergroup relations in organizations. This interest led us to the observation that major groups in industry displayed some distinctive characteristics that persisted in spite of efforts from top management toward consistency. We came to the conclusion that this persistence could be accounted for if these groups needed these characteristics to conduct favorable transactions with the segment of the firm's environment with which they were especially involved. So, in order to account for some important sources of intergroup conflict, we began to study each group's relations with its special segment of the environment. Our research findings tended strongly to confirm our theory. This, in turn, led us into a new interest not only in understanding these transactions from a behavioral standpoint, but also in helping organizations and their managers diagnose the quality of these relations and improve them.

The Certainty-
Uncertainty Continuum

Our research findings with specific relevance to this interface can be quickly summarized since they were generally reviewed in Chapter 2. We started our inquiry with the simple notion that the characteristics of an organizational unit would in some way need to match up with those of its segment of the environment if healthy transactional relations were to prevail. We were particularly interested in information flows across these boundaries. It seemed to us that if the sector of the environment involved was in a fairly steady, unchanging state, the amount and complexity of the information needed would be much less than if the opposite were true—namely, if there existed a high degree of uncertainty and change in the relevant part of the environment. As the environment varies along this certainty-uncertainty continuum, we expected to find matching differences in the organizational unit concerned if the transactions were to be sound. We identified four measurable features of groups that we thought might vary with the certainty-uncertainty of their parts of the environment. These were:

1. the degree of reliance on formalized rules and formal communication channels within the unit;
2. the time horizon of managers and professionals in the groups;
3. their orientation toward goals, either diffuse or concentrated; and

4. their interpersonal style, either relationship- or task-oriented.

Using measures of these four characteristics, we made a study of high- and low-performance companies in three different industries, and arrived at the specific conclusion that there was a closer fit in the high-performing organizations than in the low performers between the attributes of each unit and the demands of its relevant part of the environment.

One way to visualize the meaning of these findings is to think again in terms of information flows. In order to relate effectively to its environment, any organization must have reasonably accurate and timely information about the environment and especially about environmental changes. This is clearly an easier job if the environment is relatively stable. The job can be specified in a predetermined set of operating rules. The necessary messages can be handled through the traditional superior-subordinate channels, which may be few and constricted but are probably less subject to error and relatively inexpensive. Fairly short time horizons are usually adequate to take account of the reactions of such an environment to the firm's actions. This makes it sensible to use a straight-forward, task-oriented approach in managerial style.

On the other hand, life in an organizational unit must become more complex in order to deal adequately with an uncertain and rapidly changing sector of the environment. To have more points of contact with the environment, a flatter organization is employed. Formal rules cannot be formulated that will be suitable for any appreciable time period, so it seems better not to rely heavily on them. More of an all-to-all communications pattern is indicated, which can keep environmental clues moving throughout the unit for interpretation at all points instead of just through superior-subordinate channels. A longer time orientation is usually needed. The growth of this necessarily more complex and sophisticated (as well as more costly) communication network is fostered by an interpersonal style that emphasizes building strong relationships rather than just accomplishing the task, per se.

Stability versus Change in the Environment

Securing and processing relevant information from the environment, while highly critical, is not the only requirement for high-quality transactions at the organization-environment interface. In addition to exchanging information, people at these interfaces must frequently negotiate the terms of exchange of tangible goods and less tangible services of many kinds. These bargaining and/or problem-solving kinds of relationships can also be analyzed in terms of the findings of research. Fouraker has used his findings from experimental research to develop the idea that organizational units with different internal features are more or less effective depending upon whether their environment is characterized by harsh competition for scarce resources or by more beneficent circumstances. In a relatively unchanging environment, it is likely that time has brought more competitors into the struggle and that therefore resources are scarce. In this circumstance, he argues that the organizations which can conduct more favorable transactions will operate with tighter internal controls, more rules, and simpler channels of communication. In short, they will have closed ranks and geared up for a competitive fight. Again, it is a matching process.

At the other extreme is an organization unit dealing with a rapidly changing environment. The resources are plentiful and diverse, but the organization must be capable of creative and flexible problem-solving to discover potential opportunities for conducting more favorable transactions. Here again that unit will thrive which relies not on rules but on a more complex and flatter communication network which serves to stimulate new ideas. Such a unit would be oriented to a longer time perspective. It would thus be matched with the features of its environment as it works at solving the problem of defining and continually redefining the terms of its environmental transactions.

These, then, are the highlights of current research on the matching of organizational units with their respective sectors of the environment. Good matching seems to foster sound transactions at this organization-environment interface. In our research we studied this interface only for the important functions of sales, research, and production; but [Figure 1] indicates how many additional interfaces of this type are relevant to most business organizations. Similar lists could be drawn for other types of organizations.

One of the ways of evolving an overall strategy for any organization is to develop within the organization the capacity to carry on fully adequate transactions at each of these important interfaces, with some special advantages in regard to one or two of them where a favorable exchange is possible. These are areas of "distinctive competence," to use Selznick's term. An organization in which each

Figure 1

Organizational Unit	Relevant Environmental Sector
Sales	Customers and competitors
Research	Science and technology
Production and engineering	Technology and equipment suppliers
Purchasing	Suppliers
Finance	Financial institutions
Personnel	Labor and professional markets
Public relations	The press and legislative bodies
Legal	Governmental regulatory agencies

of its boundary-spanning units is well matched with its corresponding environmental sector is in a desirable position to detect opportunities for new kinds of favorable transactions with the environment and to anticipate newly developing hazards in the environment. This matching process is a highly flexible way to maintain the kind of continuous search that is recommended by a pioneering study recently conducted by Aguilar on how business firms scan their relevant environments.

As the relevant environment changes, however, organizations not only need suitable matched units, but on occasion also need to establish new units to address emerging environmental facts and to regroup old units. For instance, the emergence of the computer as a new environmental fact has led many firms to create a new unit such as management-information services; and the development of newly relevant mathematical techniques has led to the emergence of operations-research groups and long-range planning groups. Such new groups not only draw together people with different technical skills, but also they often need different orientations, structures, and styles to transact their business successfully.

In addition, as firms grow in terms of product variety and geographical coverage, a need frequently arises to switch the first big structural division of work in the company from the traditional functional basis, implicit in our discussion so far, to some other basis. Valid arguments can be mustered for various choices of first-level structural division, but the soundest arguments will be based on environmental facts. For instance, if different geographical areas require quite different ways of marketing, while the products of a firm are quite similar technically, a first-level split *by geography* is usually indicated, and vice versa. If, on the other hand, the products and the geographical conditions are relatively homogeneous, an initial division *by function* is probably the soundest basis.

This analysis of differences and similarities needs to be complemented by an analysis of the intensity of the interdependencies between various units to find the best possible trade-off.

Once the primary basis for structurally dividing work is selected, secondary means can be provided not only at lower levels but also by staff groups. In some instances where two factors, such as functions and products, are both highly different and critical, some firms, as in the aerospace industry, are turning to a matrix organization. In such an organization two bases are used simultaneously as a first-level division of labor.

We have seen that whether we view the environmental transaction primarily as a problem of information exchange or as one of bargaining and problem-solving, we are pointed toward a matching of organizational traits and orientations with environmental features. We are now in a position to explain how we use this method of analysis as a practical tool in helping specific organizations improve the quality of their environmental transactions. We will do this by examining several specific cases.

The first set of cases involves situations where mismatches could be directly addressed by making adjustments in the internal arrangements of the unit concerned. A second set of cases will also be examined where other types of adjustments were needed to improve the matching process:

1. by releasing counterpressures in the organization for consistency among all units;
2. by adjusting units to accommodate shifts in the environment;
3. by creating new units to meet newly important environmental conditions; and
4. by realigning units to cope with the increased scope of the business.

In reviewing these cases emphasis will be given to the variety of variables in the organizational systems that were selected as the initial means of implementing planned change.

Before turning to the cases, however, we need to get a feel for the way problems at this interface are likely to first present themselves to managers and in turn to behaviorally-oriented consultants. Problems at the environment-organization interface are likely to manifest themselves eventually through economic results.

For example, at the sales-customer interface, it is in a loss of sales volume; in research and development, it is in a drop in the flow of new products, etc. However, these indicators of interface trouble are fairly slow to show up, and managers learn to be sensitive to earlier clues of difficulty. These often take the form of complaints from the outside—letters from customers, a private word dropped at lunch by a banker, an important move by a competitor that caught everyone flatfooted. The customer may be saying that your organization is unresponsive, that you cannot seem to tailor your products to his needs, that he is getting tired of fighting his way through your red tape. In other cases, the concern will develop because a competitor seems too frequently to be first with a new-product introduction, or a new marketing technique. Perhaps in the production area it is a failure to realize economies through process innovation or falling behind in the race with rising wages and salaries. Another clue might be that the best specialists are not staying in the company—there is a worrisome amount of turnover among the more promising professionals in the physical or managerial sciences. These are the clues that might well be traced back to human problems at the environment-organization interface.

24

The Matrix Organization— Who Needs It?

Stanley M. Davis and
Paul R. Lawrence

At this point we need to remind ourselves that every organization, based on matrix or not, is set up as a way of inducing the desired work behavior on the part of its members. This chapter will address the question of what actual organizational behavior one is trying to induce by using the matrix model as against the more conventional types. Even more importantly we will address the "why" question—under what environmental conditions would one want to induce these "matrix" behaviors? When is the matrix a sensible and practical way to bridge between the specific requirements for healthy survival that are thrust upon an organization and the actual work activities of organizational members? When does such a model serve to channel people's energies into needed tasks.

Our study of these questions has led us to the conclusion that the matrix is the preferred structural choice when three basic conditions exist simultaneously. This chapter examines these three conditions and their connection to matrix structures, systems, and behavior.

SOURCE: Stanley M. Davis and Paul R. Lawrence, *Matrix,* © 1977, Addison Wesley Publishing Company, Inc., Reading, Massachusetts. Chapter 2, pp. 11–24. Reprinted with permission of the publisher.

Condition 1: Outside Pressure for Dual Focus

One of the principal reasons people form organizations is to focus attention and energy on a selected goal. Organizations serve as a lens that catches the sun's rays and bends them into a spot of focused energy. This is the source of the power of organizations and their leaders. It is why organizations can undertake tasks that are "too big" for a single individual or a simple small group. The initial way organizations focus human energy is to group people physically into different organizational units each with a defined boundary and a common boss. These groups are formed around a theme or symbol that identifies their purpose to the rest of the organization. Group members develop their own distinctive way of thinking, working, and relating to each other. They share a common task to be performed as their contribution to the work of the entire organization.

At a simple level, tasks can be "too big" for an individual for two basic reasons. The first is simply because an individual cannot be in two places at the same time. The second is because our mental capacity is finite—one individual cannot be expert and skilled in everything. (If this book had been written a century ago we would have had to add a third basic reason— that human physical strength is finite. But the spread of powered machinery has for all practical purposes removed this constraint.) When organizations initially form to get around the first constraint, they very naturally tend to set up their organizational units in terms of different physical locations. This tendency is especially apparent in transport and communication companies such as railroads, postal services, telegraph, and telephone. The same principle is at work when we assign a group to look after a defined set of customers. We expect to have the resulting organizational units bear names that identify both the location or set of customers and the service or product provided. We are familiar with the Milwaukee Airport, the New England Telephone Company, Saks Fifth Avenue, etc. This type of organizational grouping tends to focus attention and energy on performing the entire task or service for a given area or set of customers.

When organizations form to get around the second constraint (mental limits) they tend to group people initially around technical specialties so that the group members can enrich and reinforce one another's technical proficiencies. In conventional language this is known as a functional organization that identifies its primary groups with words such as manufacturing, sales, engineering, purchasing, finance, personnel, etc. These labels serve to orient each group to one technical specialty and focus energy accordingly.

Each of these ways of establishing a division of labor is widely used and each division has performed successfully over many years. But which is best, organizing around functions, areas, products, or services? It quite clearly depends on which constraint is more critical. If the geographical coverage is absolutely essential to the existence of an organization such as the telephone service, then it is wise to organize first of all into geographic units that focus on providing a complete service responsive to the special needs of customers in its area, even at the expense of the potential depth of expertise that could be achieved by grouping by technologies. Likewise, when technical expertise is critical to an organization's existence, then initially using functional (technology) groupings is sensible and perhaps essential. In such an arrangement, organizational power will center in these functional groups and the state of technical proficiency can be expected to advance, even at the expense of providing services and products tailored to the special needs of a particular locality or set of customers.

So each mode of organizing has its special strength and its corresponding weakness. But what if both types of constraints are truly critical and equally compelling? What if focusing attention on both is essential to survival? This is, we suggest, the first of the three basic conditions that call out for some form of a matrix design.

It is no accident that matrix first came into widespread use in the aerospace industry. To survive and prosper in the aerospace industry, any firm needs to focus intensive attention *both* on complex technical issues and on the unique project requirements of the customer. These companies cannot afford to give a second-level status to either the functional groupings around technical specialties or to the project groupings around unique customer needs. They need to create a balance of power between project-oriented managers and the managers of the engineering and scientific specialists. Neither can be allowed to, arbitrarily, overrule the other. Both orientations need to be brought to bear in a simultaneous fashion on a host of tradeoff decisions involving schedules, costs, and product quality. The needed behavior is epitomized by a picture of two middle managers with equal power, but very different orientations and goals, sitting down to debate and argue over each and every point in their search for the answers that would optimize decisions for both technical excellence and unique customer requirements. The dual command structure of a matrix serves to induce this kind of simultaneous decisionmaking behavior. It was to induce this kind of behavior that matrix was developed. . . .

Condition 2: Pressures for High Information-Processing Capacity

The second condition that generates pressure to·adopt a matrix is the requirement for high information-processing capacity among organizational members. Once any organization is formed to do work "too big" for individuals, it must pay the basic price of organizing—it must establish and maintain a network of communciation channels among members. When only one person is doing a job, a single nervous system is used to keep the right and left hands coordinated. When many people are involved in a task, the extra "overhead" cost of coordinating the messages sent back and forth between people must be borne. Since communication uses resources, organization planners try to arrange clusters of people and channels between them to minimize the cost of required communications. The hierarchical pyramid of a conventional organization, depicted with its boxes and lines, represents an attempt to conserve resources by channeling communications through selected managers. Such a communication hierarchy can be supplemented by rules, job descriptions, standard procedures, schedules and budgets which, in addition to personal instructions from the boss, indicate to members what behavior they are expected to engage in that will fit in a coordinated way with the work of others. These coordination arrangements work fine, if they do not get overloaded with information. But under certain conditions they do get very overloaded.

The symptoms of such overloading are familiar to managers. The issues urgently awaiting managerial action pile up. The queue to see the boss gets long. Schedules and budgets start slipping but nothing gets done about it. Bureaucracy sets in. There are too many rules, it is felt, but more probably it is that the channels are not organized properly. The communication process bogs down. In effect, the right hand loses track of what the left hand is doing.

Why do smart, hardworking, well-intentioned managers sometimes get themselves into this situation? Sometimes, better schedules, better budgets, bigger computers, better rules, and clearer job descriptions can cure the problem. As often as not, however, they are an inadequate cure. There are still too many real issues

that have to get resolved and not enough hours in the day to resolve them. Under such conditions only a fundamental redesign of the organization can relieve the information overload. What conditions tend to generate an overwhelming need for information processing and complex problem solving? Only a special combination of circumstances can lead to a very high information-processing requirement.

First, the kinds of demands placed on the organization have to be changing and relatively unpredictable. If the demands are stable, and therefore reasonably predictable, there is not much important new information for the organization to cope with. Plans can be made in advance and the assumptions about future events that the plans were made for will prove valid. There will seldom be a need for quick replanning. Things can go according to schedule. But the future frequently holds major surprises such as sudden changes in market demand, competitive moves, technological advances, ecological restrictions and other governmental regulations, currency and stock-market fluctuations, and the appearance of protest groups. When these surprises occur, plans do not hold up, and large amounts of new information must be assimilated and responded to in a coherent way. *Uncertainty* in the external environment calls for an enriched information-processing capacity within the organization.

Second, even these uncertainties would not be unmanageable if one's organization was doing a simple job such as making and marketing a single product in s single area, or providing a single service to a single customer. It should be remembered that, before the matrix, the last major change in organization design occurred in the 1920s and 1930s when businesses diversified their activities in both product and market terms, leading to the shift from centralized functionally departmentalized organizations to decentralized ones based on a product division design. While the increased complexity of tasks led to a major adaptation in terms of management and organization, both the centralized and the decentralized models maintained the traditional singular chain of command. Information and communication were organized either along functional lines, or by product category or market unit. Simultaneous diversification of both products/services and markets, however, increased the *complexity* of an organization's tasks severalfold. When this complexity is "added" to environmental uncertainty, the result is a major multiplication of information processing requirements.

Finally, the question arises concerning how many individuals and groups must be involved in order to make a reasoned response to new events. The more *interdependence* there is among people on any one issue, the greater the information-processing load. If people can accomplish their tasks, no matter how complex and uncertain, by themselves, then they will not have to share information with others and the information-processing load will not be great. If, on the other hand, their tasks are highly interrelated, the opposite is bound to be the case.

So all three generators of the information load—uncertainty, complexity, and interdependence—have to be examined. If all three are high, conventional ways of handling the load tend to break down. If such a compound piling up of information-processing requirements were a rare, once-in-a-hundred occurrence, we could afford to ignore it. But it appears that this set of circumstances is to be the fate of more and more organizations, even in industries that we could label as stable and mature in the recent past. When organizations have to come to terms with heavy information-processing loads, they have to open up and legitimate a more complex communication and decision network.

If the problem were only one of keeping more people informed of events, the response could be handled through increasing the flow of reports, briefings, and informal communications. But, of course, the tough part is weighing the significance of the new information and making decisions that commit the organization to a response that will prove to be wise over time.

To accomplish this, more people simply must be in a position to think and act as general managers—more people who seek out and pull together the relevant information and opinion, who weigh alternatives, who make commitments in the best interest of the wole and who stand ready to be judged by the eventual results. This is the kind of behavior that is called for when managers handle large amounts of complex information for the organization. This behavior on the part of more people is the ultimate cure for information overload.

The matrix design, properly applied, tends to develop more people who think and act in a general management mode. By inducing this kind of action, the matrix increases an organization's information-processing capacity.

Condition 3: Pressures for Shared Resources

The third and final condition we see as an indication to adopt a matrix is so obvious that its importance is easy to ignore. It is the condition of the organization's being under considerable pressure to achieve economies of scale in human terms and high performance in terms of both costs and benefits by fully utilizing scarce human resources and by meeting high-quality standards.

While all organizations probably feel some degree of pressure for high performance, the amount of such pressure varies a good deal. If an organization has a truly dominant position in a given market, it may not feel much pressure to avoid redundancies in the use of human resources or to attain high-quality outputs. It may feel comfortable increasing its costs by hiring extra specialists to fill out the needs of multiple product divisions, even though these specialists wind up spending much of their time unproductively. On the other hand, it could hire one jack-of-all-trades to perform the jobs of several specialists with a corresponding loss of quality. But when performance pressures are real and strong, the need arises to fully utilize expensive and highly specialized talents. The size of an organization may enable it to acquire skilled human resources in large numbers, but nevertheless there is bound to be an upper limit. Whatever that limit is, when it is reached, pressures will develop to share existing human resources. These internal pressures will be greater when there are external forces pressing to achieve economies of scale. These resources will need to be redeployed in a flexible manner so that people can work on more than one task at a time or at least be readily available for assignment from one task to the next.

A similar agrument holds for the sharing of expensive capital resources and physical facilities. For example, several product divisions may need access to a fleet of different test aircraft (helicopters, propeller-driven and jet aircraft) to evaluate their products, but no divisions can afford to maintain them full time. High performance will result from high utilization of such facilities through effective sharing and redeployment of them among specialist groups.

Organizations with conventional designs tend to develop resistances to the rapid redeployment of specialists across organizational lines. Structures are traditionally thought of as stolid and static. They do not change very often, and when they do it is in a discrete quantum jump to another static state. Since environmental and strategic changes tend to evolve in a continual process, the organization is often catching up with already changed circumstances. And each change is experienced by its members as a wrenching of established patterns of behavior and the need to learn new ones. Also, the more rapidly the environment and the firm's strategy change, the shorter will be the duration for which a given structure is appropriate. In such circumstances, it is helpful to think of optimal structural change as being frequent and in small doses, rather than infrequent major shake-ups. Structure, then, becomes flexible, if not fluid; and people can become accustomed to a structure that is always changing but that rarely erupts and causes severe dislocations. The matrix design helps induce the kind of behavior that views rapid redeployment and the shared use of scarce human resources as basic.

Review: The Three Necessary and Sufficient Conditions

Based on our observations of why managers adopt a matrix, we initially stated that all three conditions discussed above need to be present simultaneously before a matrix is indicated. Why is not the presence of one or two of these conditions an adequate reason? Our analysis runs as follows: learning how to use a matrix is not easy. A matrix organization is not simply a matter of understanding and creating a formal design. For us:

$$\text{Matrix Organization} = \text{Matrix Structure} + \text{Matrix Systems} + \text{Matrix Culture} + \text{Matrix Behavior}.$$

The structure involves the dual chains of command that we have spoken about. The system must also operate along two dimensions simultaneously: planning, controlling, appraising and rewarding, etc., along both functional and product lines at the same time. Moreover, every organization has a culture of its own and . . . for the matrix to succeed the ethos or spirit of the organization must be consonant with the new form. Finally, people's behavior, especially those with two bosses and those who share subordinates, must reflect an understanding, and an ability to work within such overlapping boundaries.

The change to a matrix cannot be accomplished by issuing a new organization chart. People are brought up, by and large, to think in terms of "one person, one boss" and such habits of mind are not easily changed. People must learn to work comfortably and effectively in a different way of managing and organizing. Our experience suggests that successful passage through the early evolution of a matrix, until it is firmly established in its mature form, is a process that will likely take two or three years. That is not a long time in the evolution and life span of an organization, but to those involved in the change, the period of transition can be quite difficult. Furthermore, the limited evidence suggests that going to a matrix will initially add to managerial overhead. So one is ill-advised to view the matrix as one of many exciting new managerial tools and techniques; something that can be tried and discarded if it doesn't seem to be succeeding. The move to a matrix should be a serious decision, made by the top level of management, signalling a major commitment, and thoroughly implemented through many layers of the organization. It is too difficult to undertake superficially, too costly in human terms to attempt haphazardly, and too encompassing to experiment with unnecessarily.

The presence of only two of the three necessary conditions is not sufficient for us to recommend a matrix approach. There are simpler, partial methods for coping with the additional needs. Taking each partial set of conditions separately:

• It is clear that without performance pressures, the problems generated by conditions 1 and/or 2, the pressure for dual focus and for high information-processing requirements, could be handled without a matrix simply by accepting a lower performance level. One could either take whatever time was needed in a conventional organization design to process all the information up to the top level where a dual focus would be brought into play—at the cost of very slow performance—or one could split the organization into decentralized autonomous parts thereby increasing the information-processing capacity, but at the expense of high costs or low quality.

• The presence of only conditions 1 and/or 3, pressures from two critical sectors and pressures to achieve human economies of scale and performance, could reasonably be handled by creating a small top-management team that represented the dual focus and that given the limited informational requirements could then generate high quality and timely decisions.

• Finally, if only conditions 2 and/or 3 were present—to perform uncertain, complex, and interdependent tasks with scarce human resources—the problem could be solved by placing the most critical focus on the chain of command or line roles while using subordinate or staff positions to represent the less critical focus.

As summarized in Figure 1 there are three environmental conditions, each of which calls for organizational response, and all of which must be present simultaneously for an organization to appropriately adopt and adapt the matrix.

In summarizing the three conditions which call for a matrix, we must point out a very real hazard. It is easy for managers from all kinds of organizations to read over the three conditions and readily nod their heads in a quick agreement that all three conditions are present in their situation. Such an initial reaction is understandable. After all, most managers feel pressured from multiple sides and swamped with information. If they felt otherwise, they would

Figure 1
Necessary and sufficient conditions

	Environmental Pressure	*Behavioral Linkage*
Condition 1	Two or more critical sectors; functions, products, services, markets, areas	Balance of power, dual command, simultaneous decision making
Condition 2	Performance of uncertain, complex and interdependent tasks	Enriched information-processing capacity
Condition 3	Economies of scale	Shared and flexible use of scarce human resources

have trouble justifying their salaries. But a facile reaction is dangerous. Organizations do, in fact, vary in the extent to which they experience these pressures. Until these three conditions are overwhelmingly present, in a literal sense, the matrix will almost certainly be an unnecessary complexity. Caution should be exercised in judging the presence or absence of these conditions and one is well advised to err on the conservative side. Clearly, only a limited, even if growing, number of organizations really need a fully evolved matrix.

While the logic of the three conditions is clear, it may not be clear just exactly how the matrix tends to induce the complex behavior that can simultaneously meet all three pressures. Much of the remainder of the book addresses this question, but at least a partial answer is called for now.

The threefold behavior we are trying to induce with the matrix is (1) the focusing of undivided human effort on two (or more) essential organizational tasks simultaneously, (2) the human processing of a great deal of information and the commitment of the organization to a balanced reasoned response (a general management response), and (3) the rapid redeployment of human resources to various projects, products, services, clients, or markets. Figure 2 can help in clarifying how the matrix induces these behaviors.

We see here a diamond-shaped organization rather than the conventional pyramid. The top of the diamond represents the same top management symbolized by the top of the pyramid. The two arms of the diamond symbolize the dual chain of command. In the typical case the left arm would array the functional specialist groups or what could be thought of as the resource or input side of the organization. The right arm arrays the various products, projects, markets, clients, services, or areas the organization is set up to provide. This is the output or transaction side of the matrix. Depending on how many people holding a specialist orientation, either resource or output, the organization needs, these groupings can develop several echelons in response to the practical limits of the span

of control of any line manager. At the foot of the matrix is the 2-boss manager. This manager is responsible for the performance of a defined package of work. The manager is given agreed-upon financial resources and performance targets by superiors on the output side, and negotiated human and equipment resources from the resource manager. The two streams, taken together, constitute the work package. The manager is responsible for managing these resources to meet performance targets. To perform, the manager must handle high volumes of information, weigh alternatives, make commitments on behalf of the organization as a whole, and be prepared to be judged by the results. This form of organization induces the manager to think and behave like a general manager.

This 2-boss manager is subject to dual demands of both the resource hierarchy and the transaction hierarchy, but can also draw upon their specialized help. The manager who cannot reconcile the dual demands is expected to convene a meeting with the two bosses and present the problem for the two of them to solve. In the resulting debate neither boss can, according to the authority structure, overrule the other. They must search for mutually agreeable and timely solutions. While they can, if needed, have recourse to their respective two bosses, they cannot refer too many such disputes upward without reflecting on their own managerial capacity. The matrix induces many peer debates on key trade-off decisions. It tends to ensure that each of these decisions are made on their respective merits and not on the basis of any arbitrary form.

When the mix of tasks undertaken by the output or transaction side of the matrix shifts over time, the resources of the other side need to be redeployed. While it is never completely simple to move people from one task to another, the matrix can help this process along. The resource specialists can be engaged in a time-limited way to help any matrix product manager who needs their type of talent. This can be done over and over again without shifting the individual specialist from his or her "home base" resource group. People who are subject to redeployment

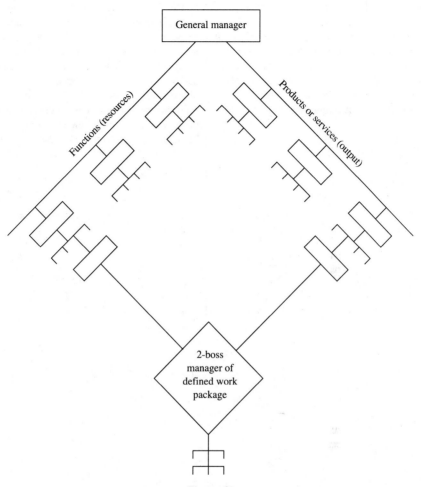

Figure 2
Example of a matrix design

in conventional organizations almost always develop a very understandable resistance to being uprooted and forced to join up with a set of strangers time after time. They cannot build a reputation for performance that carries them past the occasional mistake. They must work to create relations of trust and mutual respect again and again. While these problems are not totally avoided in a matrix, they can be greatly mitigated. Human resources can be redeployed with a minimum amount of the kind of associated human costs that also usually wind up as economic costs.

Finally, we must point out that even in a fully developed matrix organization, only a relatively small proportion of the total number of people in the organization will be directly in the matrix. Whereas a middle-level manager may have two bosses, those people reporting beneath that manager are likely to have only one boss. In an organization with 50,000 employees only 500–1,500 may be in the matrix; and in one with 500 people, only 50 may be in the matrix. To keep in perspective the proportion of people that will be affected directly, it may be helpful to envision the diamond of the matrix perched on top of the traditional design of the pyramid. Drawn to scale, proportionate to the numbers of people involved in the matrix, the total organization chart might look like this:

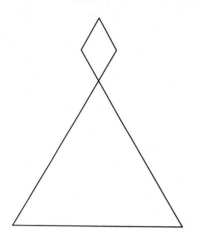

The Printer case study which follows [not included here] provides a concrete example of an organization that is experiencing the need for a matrix. The case study indicates how the matrix can make a major contribution to inducing the kinds of behavior described above. The matrix that is evolving at Printer can serve as the organizational link between the pressures of the environment and the three kinds of complex behaviors needed to respond to these pressures.

25

The Five Basic Parts of the Organization

Henry Mintzberg

In Chapter 1 organizations were described in terms of their use of the coordinating mechanisms. We noted that, in theory, the simplest organization can rely on mutual adjustment to coordinate its basic work of producing a product or service. Its *operators*—those who do this basic work—are largely self-sufficient.

As the organization grows, however, and adopts a more complex division of labor among its operators, the need is increasingly felt for direct supervision. Another brain—that of a *manager*—is needed to help coordinate the work of the operators. So, whereas the division of labor up to this point has been between the operators themselves, the introduction of a manager introduces a first *administrative* division of labor in the structure—between those who do the work and those who supervise it. And as the organization further elaborates itself, more managers are added—not only managers of operators but also managers of managers. An administrative *hierarchy* of authority is built.

As the process of elaboration continues, the organization turns increasingly to standardization as a means of coordinating the work of its operators. The responsibility for much of this standardization falls on a third group, composed of *analysts*. Some, such as work study analysts and industrial engineers, concern themselves with the standardization of work processes;

SOURCE: Henry Mintzberg, *The Structure of Organizations,* © 1979, pp. 18–34. Reprinted by permission of Prentice-Hall, Englewood Cliffs, New Jersey.

others, such as quality control engineers, accountants, planners, and production schedulers, focus on the standardization of outputs; while a few, such as personnel trainers, are charged with the standardization of skills (although most of this standardization takes place outside the organization, before the operators are hired). The introduction of these analysts brings a second kind of administrative division of labor to the organization, between those who do and who supervise the work, and those who standardize it. Whereas in the first case managers assume responsibility from the operators for some of the coordination of their work by substituting direct supervision for mutual adjustment, the analysts assumed responsibility from the managers (and the operators) by substituting standardization for direct supervision (and mutual adjustment). Earlier, some of the control over the work was removed from the operator; now it begins to be removed from the manager as well, as the systems designed by the analysts take increasing responsibility for coordination. The analyst "institutionalizes" the manager's job.

We end up with an organization that consists of a core of operators, who do the basic work of producing the products and services, and an *administrative* component of managers and analysts, who take some of the responsibility for coordinating their work. This leads us to the conceptual description of the organization shown in Figure 1. This figure will be used repeatedly throughout the book, sometimes overlaid to show flows, sometimes distorted to illustrate special structures. It emerges, in effect, as the "logo," or symbol, of the book.

At the base of the logo is the *operating core*, wherein the operators carry out the basic work of the organization—the input, processing, output, and direct support tasks associated with producing the products or services. Above them sits the administrative component, which is shown in three parts. First, are the managers, divided into two groups. Those at the very top

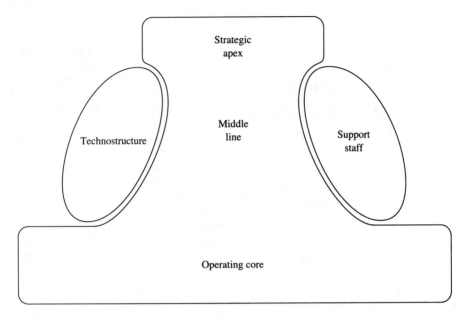

Figure 1
The five basic parts of organizations

of the hierarchy, together with their own personal staff, form the *strategic apex*. And those below, who join the strategic apex to the operating core through the chain of command (such as it exists), make up the *middle line*. To their left stands the *technostructure,* wherein the analysts carry out their work of standardizing the work of others, in addition to applying their analytical techniques to help the organization adapt to its environment. Finally, we add a fifth group, the *support staff,* shown to the right of the middle line. This staff support the functioning of the operating core indirectly, that is, outside the basic flow of operating work. The support staff goes largely unrecognized in the literature of organizational structuring, yet a quick glance at the chart of virtually any large organization indicates that it is a major segment, one that should not be confused with the other four. Examples of support groups in a typical manufacturing firm are research and development, cafeteria, legal council, payroll, public relations, and mailroom.

Figure 1 shows a small strategic apex connected by a flaring middle line to a large, flat operating core. These three parts of the organization are shown in one uninterrupted sequence to indicate that they are typically connected through a single line of formal authority. The technostructure and the support staff are shown off to either side to indicate that they are separate from this main line of authority, and influence the operating core only indirectly.

It might be useful at this point to relate this scheme to some terms commonly used in organizations. The term "middle management," although seldom carefully defined, generally seems to include all members of the organization not at the strategic apex or in the operating core. In our scheme, therefore, "middle management" would comprise three distinct groups—the middle-line managers, the analysts, and the support staff. To avoid confusion, however, the term *middle level* will be used here to describe these three groups together, the term "management" being reserved for the managers of the strategic apex and the middle line.

The word "staff" should also be put into this context. In the early literature, the term was used in contrast to "line": in theory, line positions had formal authority to make decisions, while staff positions did not; they merely advised those who did. (This has sometimes been referred to as "functional" authority, in contrast to the line's formal or "hierarchical" authority.) Allen (1955), for example, delineates the staff's major activities as (1) providing advice, counsel, suggestions, and guidance on planning objectives, policies, and procedures to govern the operations of the line departments on how best to put decisions into practice; and (2) performing specific service activities for the line, for example, installing budgeting systems and recruiting line personnel, "which may include making decisions that the line has asked it to make" (p. 348). As we shall see later, this distinction between line and staff holds up in some kinds of structures and breaks down in others. Nevertheless, the distinction between line and staff is of some use to us, and we shall retain the terms here though in somewhat modified form. *Staff* will be used to refer to the technostructure *and* the support staff, those groups shown on either side in Figure 1. *Line* will refer to the central part of Figure 1, those managers in the flow of formal authority from the strategic to the operating core. Note that this definition does not mention the power to decide or advise. As we shall see, the support staff does not primarily advise; it has distinct functions to perform and decisions to make, although these relate only indirectly to the functions of the operating core. The chef in the plant cafeteria may be engaged in a production process, but it has nothing to do with the basic manufacturing process. Similarly, the technostructure's power to advise sometimes amounts to the power to decide, but that is outside the flow of formal authority that oversees the operating core.[1]

Some conceptual ideas of James D. Thompson. Before proceeding with a more detailed description of each of the five basic parts of the organization, it will be helpful to introduce at this point some of the important conceptual ideas of James D. Thompson (1967). To Thompson, "Uncertainty appears as the fundamental problem for complex organizations, and coping with uncertainty, as the essence of the administrative process" (p. 159). Thompson describes the organization in terms of a "technical core," equivalent to our operating core, and a group of "boundary spanning units." In his terms, the organization reduces uncertainty by sealing off this core from the environment so that the operating activities can be protected. The boundary spanning units face the environment directly and deal with its uncertainties. For example, the research department interprets the confusing scientific environment for the organization, while the public relations department placates a hostile social environment. . . .

Thompson also introduces a conceptual scheme to explain the *interdependencies* among organizational members. He distinguishes three ways in which the work can be coupled, shown in Figure 2. First is *pooled coupling,* where members share common resources but are otherwise independent. Figure 2(a) could represent teachers in a school who share common facilities and budgets but work alone with their pupils. In *sequential coupling,* members work in series, as in a relay race where the baton passes from runner to runner. Figure 2(b) could represent a mass production factory, where raw materials enter at one end, are sequentially fabricated and machined, then fed into an assembly line at various points, and finally emerge at the other end as finished products. In *reciprocal coupling,* the members feed their work back and forth among themselves; in effect each receives inputs from and provides outputs to the others. "This is illustrated by the airline which contains both operations and maintenance units. The production of the maintenance unit is an input for operations, in the form of a serviceable aircraft; and the product (or by-product) of operations is an input for

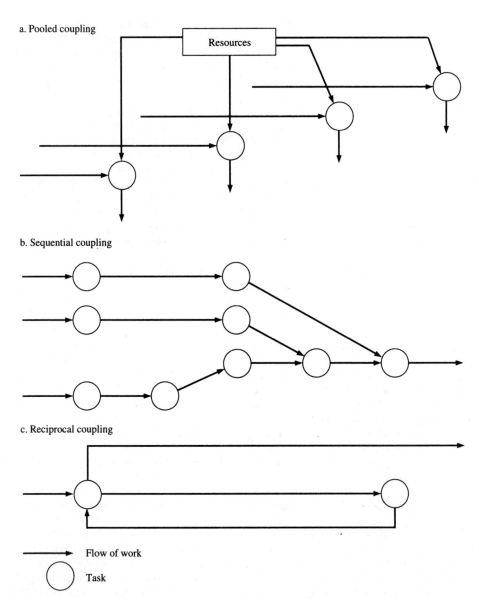

Figure 2
Pooled, sequential, and reciprocal coupling of work

maintenance, in the form of an aircraft needing maintenance" (Thompson, 1967, p. 55). Figure 2(c) could be taken to represent this example, or one in a hospital in which the nurse "preps" the patient, the surgeon operates, and the nurse then takes care of the postoperative care.

Clearly, pooled coupling involves the least amount of interdependence among members. Anyone can be plucked out; and, as long as there is no great change in the resources available, the others can continue to work uninterrupted. Pulling out a member of a sequentially coupled organization, however, is like breaking a link in a chain—the whole activity must cease to function. Reciprocal coupling is, of course, more interdependent still, since a change in one task affects not only those farther along but also those behind.

Now let us take a look at each of the five parts of the organization.

The Operating Core

The operating core of the organization encompasses those members—the operators—who perform the basic work related directly to the production of products and services. The operators perform four prime functions: (1) They *secure the inputs* for production. For example, in a manufacturing firm, the purchasing department buys the raw materials and the receiving department takes it in the door. (2) They *transform the inputs into outputs.* Some organizations transform raw materials, for example, by chopping down trees and converting them to pulp and then paper. Others transform individual parts into complete units, for example, by assembling typewriters, while still others transform information or people, by writing consulting reports, educating students, cutting hair, or curing illness. (3) They *distribute the outputs,* for example, by selling and physically distributing what comes out of the transformation process. (4) They *provide direct support* to the input, transformation, and output functions, for example, by performing maintenance on the operating machines and inventorying the raw materials.

Since it is the operating core that the other parts of the organization seek to protect, standardization is generally carried furthest here. How far, of course, depends on the work being done: assemblers in automobile factories and professors in universities are both operators, although the work of the former is far more standardized than that of the latter.

The operating core is the heart of every organization, the part that produces the essential outputs that keep it alive. But except for the very smallest one, organizations need to build *administrative* components. The administrative component comprises the strategic apex, middle line, and technostructure.

The Strategic Apex

At the other end of the organization lies the strategic apex. Here are found those people charged with overall responsibility for the organization—the chief executive officer (whether called president, superintendent, Pope, or whatever), and any other top-level managers whose concerns are global. Included here as well are those who provide direct support to the top managers—their secretaries, assistants, and so on.[2] In some organizations, the strategic apex includes the executive committee (because its mandate is global even if its members represent specific interests); in others, it includes what is known as the chief executive office—two or three individuals who share the job of chief executive.

The strategic apex is charged with ensuring that the organization serve its mission in an effective way, and also that it serve the needs of those people who control or otherwise have power over the organization (such as owners, government agencies, unions of the employees, pressure groups). This entails three sets of duties. One already discussed is that of direct supervision. To the extent that the organization relies on this mechanism of coordination, it is the managers of the strategic apex and middle line who effect it. Among the managerial roles (Mintzberg, 1973) associated with direct supervision are resource allocator, including the design of the structure itself, the assignment of people and resources to tasks, the issuing of work orders, and the authorization of major decisions made by the employees; disturbance handler, involving the resolution of conflicts, exceptions, and disturbances sent up the hierarchy for resolution; monitor, involving the review of employees' activities; disseminator, involving the transmission of information to employees; and leader, involving the staffing of the organization and the motivating and rewarding of them. In its essence, direct supervision at the strategic apex means ensuring that the whole organization function smoothly as a single integrated unit.

But there is more to managing an organization than direct supervision. That is why even organizations with a minimal need for direct supervision, for example the very smallest that can rely on mutual adjustment, or professional ones that rely on formal training, still need managers. The second set of duties of the strategic apex involves the management of the organization's boundary conditions—its relationships with its environment. The managers of the strategic apex must spend a good deal of their time acting in the roles of spokesman, in informing influential people in the environment about the organization's activities; liaison, to develop high-level contact for the organization, and monitor, to tap these for information and to serve as the contact point for those who wish to influence the organization's goals; negotiator, when major agreements must be reached with outside parties; and sometimes even figurehead, in carrying out ceremonial duties, such as greeting important customers. (Someone once defined the manager, only half in jest, as that person who sees the visitors so that everyone else can get their work done.)

The third set of duties relates to the development of the organization's strategy. Strategy may be viewed as a mediating force between the organization and its environment. Strategy formulation therefore involves the interpretation of the environment and the development of consistent patterns in streams of organizational decisions ("strategies") to deal with it. Thus, in managing the boundary conditions of the organization, the managers of the strategic apex develop an understanding of its environment; and in carrying out the duties of direct supervision, they seek to tailor a strategy to its strengths and its needs, trying to maintain a pace of change that is responsive to the environment without being disruptive to the organization. Specifically, in the entrepreneur role, the top managers search for effective ways to carry out the organization's "mission" (i.e., its production of basic products and services), and sometimes even seek to change that mission. . . .

In general, the strategic apex takes the widest, and as a result the most abstract, perspective of the organization. Work at this level is generally characterized by a minimum of repetition and standardization, considerable discretion, and relatively long decision-making cycles. Mutual adjustment is the favored mechanism for coordination among the managers of the strategic apex itself.

The Middle Line

The strategic apex is joined to the operating core by the chain of middle-line managers with formal authority. This chain runs from the senior managers just below the strategic apex to the *first-line supervisors* (e.g., the shop foremen), who have direct authority over the operators, and embodies the coordinating mechanism that we have called direct supervision. Figure 3 shows one famous chain of authority, that of the U.S. Army, from four-star general at the strategic apex to sergeant as first-line supervisor. This particular chain of authority is *scalar,* that is, it runs in a single line from top to bottom. But as we shall see later, not all need be: some divide and rejoin; a "subordinate" can have more than one "superior."

What do all these levels of managers do? If the strategic apex provides overall direction and the operating core produces the products or services, why does the organization need this whole chain of middle-line managers? One answer seems evident. To the extent that the organization is large and reliant on direct supervision for coordination, it requires middle-line managers. In theory, one manager—the chief

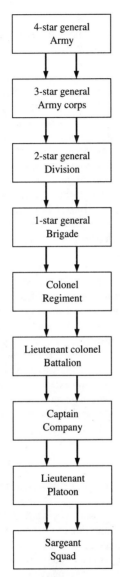

Figure 3
The scalar chain of
command in the
U.S. Army

executive at the strategic apex—can supervise all the operators. In practice, however, direct supervision requires close personal contact between manager and operator, with the result that there is some limit to the number of operators any one manager can supervise—his so-called span of control. Small organizations can get along with one manager (at the strategic apex); bigger ones require more (in the middle-line). As Moses was told in the desert:

> Thou shalt provide out of all the people able men, such as fear God, men of truth, hating covetousness; and place such over them, to be rulers of thousands, and rulers of hundreds, rulers of fifties, and rulers of tens: and let them judge the people at all seasons: and it shall be, that every great matter they shall bring unto thee, but every small matter they shall judge: so shall it be easier for thyself, and they shall bear the burden with thee. If thou shalt do this thing, and God command thee so, then thou shalt be able to endure, and all this people shall also go to their place in peace (Exodus 18:21–24).

Thus, an organizational *hierarchy* is built as a first-line supervisor is put in charge of a number of operators to form a basic organizational unit, another manager is put in charge of a number of these units to form a higher level unit, and so on until all the remaining units can come under a single manager at the strategic apex—designated the "chief executive officer" —to form the whole organization.

In this hierarchy, the middle-line manager performs a number of tasks in the flow of direct supervision above and below him. He collects "feedback" information on the performance of his own unit and passes some of this up to the managers above him, often aggregating it in the process. The sales manager of the machinery firm may receive information on every sale, but he reports to the district sales manager only a monthly total. He also intervenes in the flow of decisions. Flowing up are disturbances in the unit, proposals for change, decisions requiring authorization. Some the middle-line manager handles himself, while others he passes on up for action at a higher level in the hierarchy. Flowing down are resources that he must allocate in his unit, rules and plans that he must elaborate and projects that he must implement there. For example, the strategic apex in the Postal Service may decide to implement a project to sell "domestograms." Each regional manager and, in turn, each district manager must elaborate the plan as it applies to his geographical area.

But like the top manager, the middle manager is required to do more than simply engage in direct supervision. He, too, has boundary conditions to manage, horizontal ones related to the environment of his own unit. That environment may include other units within the larger organization as well as groups outside the organization. The sales manager must coordinate by mutual adjustment with the managers of production and of research, and he must visit some of the organization's customers. The foreman must spend a good deal of time with the industrial engineers who standardize the work processes of the operators and with the supplier installing a new machine in his shop, while the plant manager may spend his time with the production scheduler and the architect designing a new factory. In effect, each middle-line manager maintains liaison contacts with the other managers, analysts, support staffers, and outsiders whose work is interdependent with that of his own unit. Furthermore, the middle-line manager, like the top manager, is concerned with formulating the strategy for his unit, although this strategy is, of course, significantly affected by the strategy of the overall organization.

In general, the middle-line manager performs all the managerial roles of the chief executive, but in the context of managing his own unit (Mintzberg, 1973). He must serve as a figurehead for his unit and lead its members; develop a network of liaison contacts; monitor the environment and his unit's activities and transmit some of the information he receives into his own unit, up the hierarchy, and outside the chain of command; allocate resources within his unit; negotiate with outsiders; initiate strategic change; and handle exceptions and conflicts.

Managerial jobs do, however, shift in orientation as they descend in the chain of authority. There is clear evidence that the job becomes more detailed and elaborated, less abstract and aggregated, more focused on the work flow itself. Thus, the "real-time" roles of the manager—in particular, negotiation and the handling of disturbances—become especially important at lower levels in the hierarchy (Mintzberg, 1973, pp. 110–113). Martin (1956) studied the decisions made by four levels of production managers in the chain of authority and concluded that at each successively lower level, the decisions were more frequent, of shorter duration, and less elastic, ambiguous, and abstract; solutions tended to be more pat or predetermined; the significance of events and interrelationships was more clear; in general, lower-level decision making was more structured.

Figure 4 shows the line manager in the middle of a field of forces. Sometimes these forces become so great—especially those of the analysts to institutionalize his job by the imposition of rules on the unit—that the individual in the job can hardly be called a "manager" at all, in the sense of really being "in charge" of an organizational unit. This is common at the level of first-line supervisor—for example, the foreman in some mass production manufacturing firms and branch managers in some large banking systems.

The Technostructure

In the technostructure we find the analysts (and their supporting clerical staff) who serve the organization by affecting the work of others. These analysts are removed from the operating work flow—they may design it, plan it, change it, or train the people who do it, but they do not do it themselves. Thus, the technostructure is effective only when it can use its analytical techniques to make the work of others more effective.[3]

Who makes up the technostructure? There are the analysts concerned with adaptation, with changing the organization to meet environmental change, and those concerned with control, with

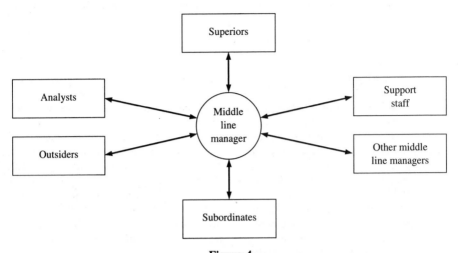

Figure 4
The line manager in the middle

stabilizing and standardizing patterns of activity in the organization (Katz and Kahn, 1966). In this book we are concerned largely with the control analysts, those who focus their attention directly on the design and functioning of structure. The control analysts of the technostructure serve to effect standardization in the organization. This is not to say that operators cannot standardize their own work, just as everyone establishes his or her own procedure for getting dressed in the morning, or that managers cannot do it for them. But in general, the more standardization an organization uses, the more it relies on its technostructure. Such standardization reduces the need for direct supervision, in effect enabling clerks to do what managers once did.

We can distinguish three types of control analysts who correspond to the three forms of standardization: work study analysts (such as industrial engineers), who standardize work processes; planning and control analysts (such as long-range planners, budget analysts, and accountants), who standardize outputs; and personnel analysts (including trainers and recruiters), who standardize skills.

In a fully developed organization, the technostructure may perform at all levels of the hierarchy. At the lowest levels of the manufacturing firm, analysts standardize the operating work flow by scheduling production, carrying out time-and-method studies of the operator's work, an instituting systems of quality control. At middle levels, they seek to standardize the intellectual work of the organization (e.g., by training middle managers) and carry out operations research studies of informational tasks. On behalf of the strategic apex, they design strategic planning systems and develop financial systems to control the goals of major units.

While the analysts exist to standardize the work of others, their own work would appear to be coordinated with others largely through mutual adjustment. (Standardization of skills does play a part in this coordination, however, because analysts are typically highly trained specialists.) Thus, analysts spend a good deal of their time in informal communication. Guetzkow (1965, p. 537), for example, notes that staff people typically have wider communication contacts than line people, and my review of the literature on managerial work (Mintzberg, 1973, pp. 116–118) showed some evidence that staff managers pay more attention to the information processing roles—

monitor, disseminator, spokesman—than do line managers.

Support Staff

A glance at the chart of almost any large contemporary organization reveals a great number of units, all specialized, that exist to provide support to the organization outside the operating work flow. Those comprise the *support staff.* For example, in a university, we find the alma mater fund, building and grounds department, museum, university press, bookstore, printing service, payroll department, janitorial service, endowment office, mailroom, real estate office, security department, switchboard, athletics department, student placement office, student residence, faculty club, guidance service, and chaplainery. None is a part of the operating core, that is, none engages in teaching or research, or even supports it directly (as does, say, the computing center or the library), yet each exists to provide indirect support to these basic missions. In the manufacturing firm, these units run the gamut from legal counsel to plant cafeteria. . . .

The support units can be found at various levels of the hierarchy, depending on the receivers of their service. In most manufacturing firms, public relations and legal counsel are located near the top, since they tend to serve the strategic apex directly. At middle levels are found the units that support the decisions made there, such as industrial relations, pricing, and research and development. And at the lower levels are found the units with more standardized work, that akin to the work of the operating core—cafeteria, mailroom, reception, payroll. Figure 5 shows all these support groups overlaid on our logo, together with typical groups from the other four parts of the organization, again using the manufacturing firm as our example.

Because of the wide variations in the types of support units, we cannot draw a single definitive conclusion about the favored coordinating mechanism for all of them. Each unit relies on whatever mechanism is most appropriate for itself—standardization of skills in the office of legal counsel, mutual adjustment in the research laboratory, standardization of work processes in the cafeteria. However, because many of the support units are highly specialized and rely on professional staff, standardization of skills may be the single most important coordinating mechanism. . . .

The most dramatic growth in organizations in recent decades has been in these staff groups, both the technostructure and the support staff. For example, Litterer (1973, pp. 584–585), in a study of thirty companies, noted the creation of 292 new staff units between 1920 and 1960, nearly ten units per company. More than half these units were in fact created between 1950 and 1960.

Organizations have always had operators and top managers, people to do the basic work and people to hold the whole system together. As they grew, typically they first elaborated their middle-line component, on the assumption in the early literature that coordination had to be effected by direct supervision. But as standardization became an accepted coordinating mechanism, the technostructure began to emerge. The work of Frederick Taylor gave rise to the "scientific management" movement of the 1920s, which saw the hiring of many work study analysts. Just after World War II, the establishing of operations research and the advent of the computer pushed the influence of the technostructure well into the middle levels of the organization, and with the more recent popularity of techniques such as strategic planning and sophisticated financial controls, the technostructure has entrenched itself firmly at the highest levels of the organization as well. And the growth of the support staff has perhaps been even more dramatic, as all kinds of specializations developed during this century —scientific research in a wide number of fields, industrial relations, public relations and many more. Organizations have sought increasingly to bring these as well as the more traditional support functions such as maintenance and cafeteria within their boundaries. Thus, the

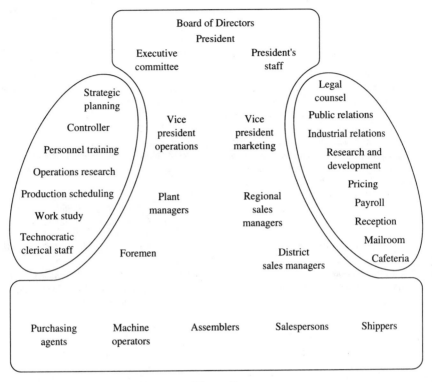

Figure 5
Some members and units of the parts of the manufacturing firm

ellipses to the left and right in the logo have become great bulges in many organizations. Joan Woodward (1965, p. 60) found in her research that firms in the modern process industries (such as oil refining) averaged one staff member for less than three operators, and in some cases the staff people actually outnumbered the operators by wide margins.[4]

Notes

1. There are other, completely different, uses of the term "staff" that we are avoiding here. The military "chiefs of staff" are really managers of the strategic apex; the hospital "staff" physicians are really operators. Also, the introduction of the line/staff distinction here is not meant to sweep all of its problems under the rug, only to distinguish those involved directly from those involved peripherally with the operating work of organizations. By our definition, the production and sales functions in the typical manufacturing firm are clearly line activities, marketing research and public relations clearly staff. To debate whether engineering is line or staff—does it serve the operating core indirectly or is it an integral part of it?—depends on the importance one imputes to engineering in a particular firm. There is a gray area between line and staff: where it is narrow, for many organization, we retain the distinction; where it is wide, we shall explicitly discard it.

2. Our subsequent discussion will focus only on the managers of the strategic apex, the work of the latter group being considered an integral part of their own.

3. This raises an interesting point: that the techno-structure has a built-in commitment to change, to perpetual improvement. The modern organization's obsession with change probably derives in part at least from large and ambitious techno-structures seeking to ensure their own survival. The perfectly stable organization has no need for a technostructure.

4. Woodward's tables and text here are very confusing, owing in part at least to some line errors in the page makeup. The data cited above are based on Figure 18, page 60, which seems to have the title that belongs to Figure 17 and which seems to relate back to Figure 7 on page 28, not to Figure 8 as Woodward claims.

References

ALLEN, L. A. (1955, September). The line-staff relationship. *Management Record*, 346–349, 374–376.

GUETZKOW, H. (1965). Communications in organizations. In J. G. March (Ed.), *Handbook of organizations* (Chap. 12). Chicago: Rand McNally.

KATZ, D., & KAHN, R. L. (1966). *The social psychology of organizations*. New York: Wiley.

KAUFMAN, H., & SEIDMAN, D. (1970). The morphology of organization. *Administrative Science Quarterly*, 439–445.

LITTERER, J. A. (1973). *The analysis of organizations* (2nd ed.). New York: Wiley. Used with permission.

MARTIN, N. H. (1956). Differential decisions in the management of an industrial plant. *The Journal of Business*, 249–260.

MINTZBERG, H. (1973). The nature of managerial work. New York: Harper & Row.

———. (1978). Patterns in strategy formation. *Management Science*, 934–948.

THOMPSON, J. D. (1967). *Organizations in action*. New York: McGraw-Hill.

WOODWARD, J. (1965). *Industrial organization: Theory and practice*. New York: Oxford University Press. Used with permission.

26

In Praise
of Hierarchy

Elliott Jaques

At first glance, hierarchy may seem difficult to praise. Bureaucracy is a dirty word even among bureaucrats, and in business there is a widespread view that managerial hierarchy kills initiative, crushes creativity, and has therefore seen its day. Yet 35 years of research have convinced me that managerial hierarchy is the most efficient, the hardiest, and in fact the most natural structure ever devised for large organizations. Properly structured, hierarchy can release energy and creativity, rationalize productivity, and actually improve morale. Moreover, I think most managers know this intuitively and have only lacked a workable structure and a decent intellectual justification for what they have always known could work and work well.

As presently practiced, hierarchy undeniably has its drawbacks. One of business's great contemporary problems is how to release and sustain among the people who work in corporate hierarchies the thrust, initiative, and adaptability of the entrepreneur. This problem is so great that it has become fashionable to call for a new kind of organization to put in place of managerial hierarchy, an organization that will better meet the requirements of what is variously called the Information Age, the Services Age, or the Post-Industrial Age.

As vague as the description of the age is the definiton of the kind of new organization

SOURCE: Reprinted by permission of *Harvard Business Review*. Elliott Jaques, "In Praise of Hierarchy," *Harvard Business Review* (January–February 1990). Copyright © 1990 by the President and Fellows of Harvard College. All rights reserved.

required to suit it. Theorists tell us it ought to look more like a symphony orchestra or a hospital or perhaps the British raj. It ought to function by means of primus groups or semiautonomous work teams or matrix overlap groups. It should be organic or entrepreneurial or tight-loose. It should hinge on skunk works or on management by walking around or perhaps on our old friend, management by objective.

All these approaches are efforts to overcome the perceived faults of hierarchy and find better ways to improve morale and harness human creativity. But the theorists' belief that our changing world requires an alternative to hierarchical organization is simply wrong, and all their proposals are based on an inadequate understanding of not only hierarchy but also human nature.

Hierarchy is not to blame for our problems. Encouraged by gimmicks and fads masquerading as insights, we have burdened our managerial systems with a makeshift scaffolding of inept structures and attitudes. What we need is not simply a new, flatter organization but an understanding of how managerial hierarchy functions —how it relates to the complexity of work and how we can use it to achieve a more effective deployment of talent and energy.

The reason we have a hierarchical organization of work is not only that tasks occur in lower and higher degrees of complexity—which is obvious—but also that there are sharp discontinuities in complexity that separate tasks into a series of steps or categories—which is not so obvious. The same discontinuities occur with respect to mental work and to the breadth and duration of accountability. The hierarchical kind of organization we call bureaucracy did not emerge accidentally. It is the only form of organization that can enable a company to employ large numbers of people and yet preserve unambiguous accountability for the work they do. And that is why, despite its problems, it has so doggedly persisted.

Hierarchy has not had its day. Hierarchy never did have its day. As an organizational system, managerial hierarchy has never been adequately described and has just as certainly never been adequately used. The problem is not to find an alternative to a system that once worked well but no longer does; the problem is to make it work efficiently for the first time in its 3,000-year history.

What Went Wrong . . .

There is no denying that hierarchical structure has been the source of a great deal of trouble and inefficiency. Its misuse has hampered effective management and stifled leadership, while it's track record as a support for entrepreneurial energy has not been exemplary. We might almost say that successful businesses have had to succeed despite hierarchical organization rather than because of it.

One common complaint is excessive layering —too many rungs on the ladder. Information passes through too many people, decisions through too many levels, and managers and subordinates are too close together in experience and ability, which smothers effective leadership, cramps accountability, and promotes buck passing. Relationships grow stressful when managers and subordinates bump elbows, so to speak, within the same frame of reference.

Another frequent complaint is that few managers seem to add real value to the work of their subordinates. The fact that the breakup value of many large corporations is greater than their share value shows pretty clearly how much value corporate managers can *subtract* from their subsidiary businesses, but in fact few of us know exactly what managerial added value would look like as it was occurring.

Many people also complain that our present hierarchies bring out the nastier aspects of human behavior, like greed, insensitivity, careerism, and self-importance. These are the qualities that have sent many behavioral scientists in search of cooperative, group-oriented, nonhierarchical organizational forms. But are they the inevitable companions of hierarchy, or perhaps a product of the misuse of hierarchy that would disappear if hierarchy were properly understood and structured?

. . . And What Continues to Go Wrong

The fact that so many of hierarchy's problems show up in the form of individual misbehavior has led to one of the most widespread illusions in business, namely, that a company's managerial leadership can be significantly improved solely by doing psychotherapeutic work on the personalities and attitudes of its managers. Such methods can help individuals gain greater personal insight, but I doubt that individual insight, personality matching, or even exercises in group dynamics can produce much in the way of organizational change or an overall improvement in leadership effectiveness. The problem is that our managerial hierarchies are so badly designed as to defeat the best effort even of psychologically insightful individuals.

Solutions that concentrate on groups, on the other hand, fail to take into account the real nature of employment systems. People are not employed in groups. They are employed individually, and their employment contracts—real or implied—are individual. Group members may insist in moments of great esprit de corps that the group as such is the author of some particular accomplishment, but once the work is completed, the members of the group look for individual recognition and individual progression in their careers. And it is not groups but individuals whom the company will hold accountable. The only true group is the board of directors, with its corporate liability.

None of the group-oriented panaceas face this issue of accountability. All the theorists refer to group authority, group decisions, and group concensus, none of them to group accountability. Indeed, they avoid the issue of accountability altogether, for to hold a group accountable, the employment contract would have to be with the group, not with the individuals, and companies simply do not employ groups as such.

To understand hierarchy, you must first understand employment. To be employed is to have an ongoing contract that holds you accountable for doing work of a given type for a specified number of hours per week in exchange for payment. Your specific tasks within that given work are assigned to you by a person called your manager (or boss or supervisor), who *ought to be held accountable* for the work you do.

If we are to make our hierarchies function properly, it is essential to place the emphasis on *accountability for getting work done*. This is what hierarchical systems ought to be about. Authority is a secondary issue and flows from accountability in the sense that there should be just that amount of authority needed to discharge the accountability. So if a group is to be given authority, its members must be held accountable as a group, and unless this is done, it is very hard to take so-called group decisions seriously. If the CEO or the manager of the group is held accountable for outcomes, then in the final analysis, he or she will have to agree with group decisions or have the authority to block them, which means that the group never really had decision-making power to begin with. Alternatively, if groups are allowed to make decisions without their manager's seal of approval, then accountability as such will suffer, for if a group does badly, the group is never fired. (And it would be shocking if it were.)

In the long run, therefore, group authority *without* group accountability is dysfunctional, and group authority *with* group accountability is unacceptable. So images of organizations that are more like symphony orchestras or hospitals or the British raj are surely nothing more than metaphors to express a desired feeling of togetherness—the togetherness produced by a conductor's baton, the shared concern of doctors and nurses for their patients, or the apparent unity of the British civil service in India.

In employment systems, after all, people are not mustered to play together as their manager beats time. As for hospitals, they are the essence of everything bad about burearcratic organization. They function in spite of the system, only because of the enormous professional devotion of their staffs. The Indian civil service was in many ways like a hospital, its people bound together by the struggle to survive in a hostile environment. Managers do need authority, but authority based appropriately on the accountabilities they must discharge.

Why Hierarchy?

The bodies that govern companies, unions, clubs, and nations all employ people to do work, and they all organize these employees in managerial hierarchies, systems that allow organizations to hold people accountable for getting assigned work done. Unfortunately, we often lose sight of this goal and set up the organizational layers in our managerial hierarchies to accomodate pay brackets and facilitate career development instead. If work happens to get done as well, we consider that a useful bonus.

But if our managerial hierarchical organizations tend to choke so readily on debilitating bureaucratic practices, how do we explain the persistence and continued spread of this form of organization for more than 3,000 years? And why has the determined search for alternatives proved so fruitless?

The answer is that managerial hierarchy is and will remain the *only* way to structure unified working systems with hundreds, thousands, or tens of thousands of employees, for the very good reason that managerial hierarchy is the expression of two fundamental characteristics of real work. First, the tasks we carry out are not only more or less complex but they also become more complex as they separate out into discrete categories or types of complexity. Second, the same is true of the mental work that people do on the job, for as this work grows more complex, it too separates out into distinct categories or types of mental activity. In turn, these two characteristics permit hierarchy to meet four of any organization's fundamental needs: to add real value to work as it moves through the organization, to identify and nail down accountability at each stage of the value-adding process, to place people with the necessary competence at each organizational layer, and to build a general consensus and acceptance of the managerial structure that achieves these ends.

Hierarchical Layers

The complexity of the problems encountered in a particular task, project, or strategy is a function on the variables involved—their number, their clarity or ambiguity, the rate at which they change, and, overall, the extent to which they are distinct or tangled. Obviously, as you move higher in a managerial hierarchy the most difficult problems you have to contend with become increasingly complex. The biggest problems faced by the CEO of a large corporation are vastly more complex than those encountered on the shop floor. The CEO must cope not only with a huge array of often amorphous and constantly changing data but also with variables so tightly interwoven that they must be disentangled before they will yield useful information. Such variables might include the cost of capital, the interplay of corporate cash flow, the structure of the international competitive market, the uncertainties of Europe after 1992, the future of Pacific Rim development, social developments with respect to labor, political developments in Eastern Europe, the Middle East, and the Third World, and technological research and change.

That the CEO's and the lathe operator's problems are different in quality as well as quantity will come as no surprise to anyone. The question is—and always has been—where does the change in quality occur? On a continuum of complexity from the bottom of the structure to the top, where are the discontinuities that will allow us to identify layers of hierarchy

that are distinct and separable, as different as ice is from water and water from steam? I spent years looking for the answer, and what I found was somewhat unexpected.

My first step was to recognize the obvious, that the layers have to do with manager-subordinate relationships. The manager's position is in one layer and the subordinate's is in the next layer below. What then sets the necessary distance between? This question cannot be answered without knowing just what it is that a manager does.

The managerial role has three critical features. First, and *most* critical, every manager must be held accountable not only for the work of subordinates but also for adding value to their work. Second, every manager must be held accountable for sustaining a team of subordinates capable of doing this work. Third, every manager must be held accountable for setting direction and getting subordinates to follow willingly, indeed enthusiastically. In brief, every manager is accountable for work and leadership.

In order to make accountability possible, managers must have enough authority to ensure that their subordinates can do the work assigned to them. This authority must include at least these four elements: (1) the right to veto any applicant who, in the manager's opinion, falls below the minimum standards of ability; (2) the power to make work assignments; (3) the power to carry out performance appraisals and, within the limits of company policy, to make decisions—not recommendations—about raises and merit rewards; and (4) the authority to initiate removal —at least from the manager's own team—of anyone who seems incapable of doing the work.

But defining the basic nature of the managerial role reveals only part of what a managerial layer means. It cannot tell us how wide a managerial layer should be, what the difference in responsibility should be between a manager and a subordinate, or, most important, where the break should come between one managerial layer and another. Fortunately, the next step in the research process supplied the missing piece of the puzzle.

Responsibility and Time

This second step was the unexpected and startling discovery that the level of responsibility in any organizational role—whether a manager's or an individual contributor's—can be objectively measured in terms of the target completion time of the *longest* task, project, or program assigned to that role. The more distant the target completion date of the longest task or program, the heavier the weight of responsibility is felt to be. I call this measure the responsibility time span of the role. For example, a supervisor whose principal job is to plan tomorrow's production assignments and next week's work schedule but who also has ongoing responsibility for uninterrupted production supplies for the month ahead has a responsibility time span of one month. A foreman who spends most of his time riding herd on this week's production quotas but who must also develop a program to deal with the labor requirements of next year's retooling has a responsibility time span of a year or a little more. The advertising vice president who stays late every night working on next week's layouts but who also has to begin making contingency plans for the expected launch of two new local advertising media campaigns three years hence has a responsibility time span of three years.

To my great surprise, I found that in all types of managerial organizations in many different countries over 35 years, people in roles at the same time span experience the same weight of responsibility and declare the same level of pay to be fair, regardless of their occupation or actual pay. The time-span range runs from a day at the bottom of a large corporation to more than 20 years at the top, while the felt-fair pay ranges from $15,000 to $1 million and more.

Armed with my definition of a manager and my time-span measuring instrument, I then bumped into the second surprising finding—repeatedly confirmed—about layering in managerial hierarchies: the boundaries between successive managerial layers occur at certain specific time-span increments, just as ice changes to water and water to steam at certain specific temperatures. And the fact that everyone in the hierarchy, regardless of status, seems to see these boundaries in the same places suggests that the boundaries reflect some universal truth about human nature.

The illustration "Managerial Hierarchy in Fiction and in Fact" shows the hierarchical structure of part of a department at one company I studied, along with the approximate responsibility time span for each position. The longest task for manager A was more than five years, while for B, C, and D, the longest task fell between two and five years. Note also that according to the organization chart, A is the designated manager of B, B of C, and C of D.

In reality, the situation was quite different. Despite the managerial roles specified by the company, B, C, and D all described A as their "real" boss. C complained that B was "far too close" and "breathing down my neck." D had the same complaint about C. B and C also admitted to finding it very difficult to manage their immediate subordinates, C and D respectively, who seemed to do better if treated as colleagues and left alone.

In short, there appeared to be a cutoff at five years, such that those with responsibility time spans of less than five years felt they needed a manager with a responsibility time span of more than five years. Manager D, with a time span of two to three years, did not feel that C, with a time span of three to four, was distant

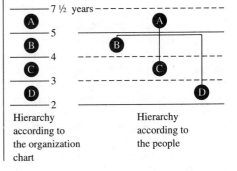

Hierarchy according to the organization chart

Hierarchy according to the people

enough hierarchically to take order from. D felt the same way about B. Only A filled the bill for *any* of the other three.

As the responsibility time span increased in the example from two years to three to four and approached five, no one seemed to perceive a qualitative difference in the nature of the responsibility that a manager discharged. Then, suddenly, when a manager had responsibility for tasks and projects that exceeded five years in scope, everyone seemed to perceive a difference not only in the scope of responsibility but also in its quality and in the kind of work and worker required to discharge it.

I found several such discontinuities that appeared consistently in more than 100 studies. Real managerial and hierarchical boundaries occur at time spans of three months, one year, two years, five years, ten years, and twenty years.

These natural discontinuities in our perception of the responsibility time span create hierarchical strata that people in different companies, countries, and circumstances all seem to regard as genuine and acceptable. The existence of such boundaries has important implications in nearly every sphere of organizational management. One of these is performance appraisal. Another is the capacity of managers to add value to the work of their subordinates.

The only person with the perspective and authority to judge and communicate personal effectiveness is an employee's accountable manager, who, in most cases, is also the only person from whom an employee will accept evaluation and coaching. This accountable manager must be the supervisor one real layer higher in the hierarchy, not merely the next higher employee on the pay scale.

As I suggested earlier, part of the secret to making hierarchy work is to distinguish carefully between hierarchical layers and pay grades. The trouble is that companies need two to three times as many pay grades as they do working layers, and once they've established the pay grades, which are easy to describe and set up, they fail to take the next step and set up a different managerial hierarchy based on

responsibility rather than salary. The result is too many layers.

My experience with organizations of all kinds in many different countries has convinced me that effective value-adding managerial leadership of subordinates can come only from an individual one category higher in cognitive capacity, working one category higher in problem complexity. By contrast, wherever managers and subordinates are in the same layer—separated only by pay grade—subordinates see the boss as too close, breathing down their necks, and they identify their "real" boss as the next manager at a genuinely higher level of cognitive and task complexity. This kind of overlayering is what produces the typical symptoms of bureaucracy in its worst form—too much passing problems up and down the system, bypassing, poor task setting, frustrated subordinates, anxious managers, wholly inadequate performance appraisals, "personality problems" everywhere, and so forth.

Layering at Company X

Companies need more than seven pay grades —as a rule, many more. But seven hierarchical layers is enough or more than enough for all but the largest corporations.

Let me illustrate this pattern of hierarchical layering with the case of two divisions of Company X, a corporation with 32,000 employees and annual sales of $7 billion. As shown in "Two Divisions of Corporation X," the CEO sets strategic goals that look ahead as far as 25 years and manages executive vice presidents with responsibility for 12- to 15-year development programs. One vice president is accountable for several strategic business units, each with a president who works with critical tasks of up to 7 years duration.

One of these units (Y Products) employs 2,800 people, has annual sales of $250 million, and is engaged in the manufacture and sale of engineering products, with traditional semiskilled shop-floor production at Layer I. The other unit

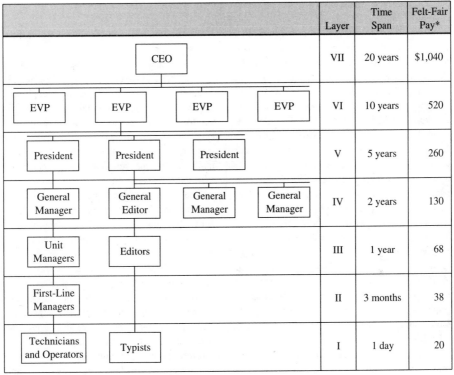

	Layer	Time Span	Felt-Fair Pay*
CEO	VII	20 years	$1,040
EVP EVP EVP EVP	VI	10 years	520
President President President	V	5 years	260
General Manager General Editor General Manager General Manager	IV	2 years	130
Unit Managers Editors	III	1 year	68
First-Line Managers	II	3 months	38
Technicians and Operators Typists	I	1 day	20

* (In thousands of dollars)

Two divisions of Corporation X

(Z Press) publishes books and employs only 88 people. Its funding and negotiations with authors are in the hands of a general editor at Layer IV, assisted by a small group of editors at Layer III, each working on projects that may take up to 18 months to complete.

So the president of Y Products manages more people, governs a greater share of corporate resources, and earns a lot more money for the parent company than does the president of Z Press. Yet the two presidents occupy the same hierarchical layer, have similar authority, and take home comparable salaries. This is neither coincidental nor unfair. It is natural, correct, and efficient.

It is the level of responsibility, *measured in terms of time span,* that tells you how many layers you need in an enterprise—not the number of subordinates or the magnitude of

sales or profits. These factors may have a marginal influence on salary; they have no bearing at all on hierarchical layers.

Changes in the Quality of Work

The widespread and striking consistency of this underlying pattern of true managerial layers leads naturally to the question of why it occurs. Why do people perceive a sudden leap in status from, say, four-and-a-half years to five and from nine to ten?

The answer goes back to the earlier discussion of complexity. As we go higher in a managerial hierarchy, the most difficult problems that arise grow increasingly complex, and, as the complexity of a task increases, so does the complexity of the mental work required to handle it. What I found when I looked at this problem over the course of ten years was that this complexity, like responsibility time span, also occurs in leaps or jumps. In other words, the most difficult tasks found within any given layer are all characterized by the same type or category of complexity, just as water remains in the same liquid state from $0°$ to $100°$ Celsius, even though it ranges from very cold to very hot. (A few degrees cooler or hotter and water changes in state, to ice or steam.)

It is this suddenly increased level of necessary mental capacity, experience, knowledge, and mental stamina that allows managers to add value to the work of their subordinates. What they add is a new perspective, one that is broader, more experienced, and, most important, one that extends further in time. If, at Z Press, the editors at Layer III find and develop manuscripts into books with market potential, it is their general editor at Layer IV who fits those books into the press's overall list, who thinks ahead to their position on next year's list and later allocates resources to their production and marketing, and who makes projections about the publishing and book-buying trends of the next two to five years.

It is also this sudden change in the quality, not just the quantity, of managerial work that subordinates accept as a natural and appropriate break in the continuum of hierarchy. It is why they accept the boss's authority and not just the boss's power.

So the whole picture comes together. Managerial hierarchy or layering is the only effective organizational form for deploying people and tasks at complementary levels, where people can do the tasks assigned to them, where the people in any given layer can add value to the work of those in the layer below them, and, finally, where this stratification of management strikes everyone as necessary and welcome.

What we need is not some new kind of organization. What we need is managerial hierarchy that understands its own nature and purpose. Hierarchy is the best structure for getting work done in big organizations. Trying to raise efficiency and morale without first setting this structure to rights is like trying to lay bricks without mortar. No amount of exhortation, attitudinal engineering, incentive planning, or even leadership will have any permanent effect unless we understand what hierarchy is and why and how it works. We need to stop casting about fruitlessly for organizational Holy Grails and settle down to the hard work of putting our managerial hierarchies in order.

V
Systems, Contingency, and Population Ecology Organization Theory

Since World War II, the social sciences increasingly have used systems analysis to examine their assertions about human behavior. The field of management, which to the extent that it deals with human resources can be said to be a social science, has been no exception. In fact, the systems perspective has dominated organization theory since 1966–1967, when two of the most infulential modern works in organization theory appeared: Robert Katz and Daniel Kahn's *The Social Psychology of Organizations* (1966), which articulated the concept of organizations as *open systems;* and James D. Thompson's coherent statement of the rational systems/contingency perspective of organizations, in *Organizations in Action* (1967).

Perhaps the field of organization theory was simply ripe for advancement in the late 1960s. The human relations orientation had lost much of its vigor, and the cultural milieu was moving away from the introspective, self-developmental, optimism of the "flower-child generation" and the "T-groups" of the early 1960s. Society was becoming enamored with computers, statistics, heuristic models, information systems, and measurement. Whatever the reasons may have been, Katz and Kahn and James D. Thompson provided the intellectual basis for the systems perspective to emerge as *the* mainstream of organization theory.

Systems theories of organization have two major conceptual themes or components: (1) applications to organizations of Ludwig von Bertalanffy's (1951) general systems theory, and (2) the use of quantitative tools and techniques to understand complex relationships among organizational and environmental variables and, thereby, to optimize decisions. Each theme is considered in the paragraphs that follow.

A *system* is any organized collection of parts united by prescribed interactions and designed for the accomplishment of specific goals or general purposes (Boulding, 1956). Thus, it is easy to see why general systems theory provides an important perspective for understanding modern organizations. Systems theory views an organization as a complex set of dynamically intertwined and interconnected elements, including its inputs, processes, outputs, feedback loops, and the environment in which it operates and with which it continuously interacts. A change in any element of the system causes changes in other elements. The interconnections tend to be complex, dynamic, and often unknown; thus when management makes decisions involving one organizational element, unanticipated impacts usually occur throughout the organizational system. Systems theorists study these interconnections, frequently using organizational decision processes and information and control systems as their focal points of analysis.

Whereas classical organization theory tends to be one-dimensional and somewhat simplistic, systems theories tend to be multidimensional and complex in their assumptions about organizational cause-and-effect relationships. The classicalists viewed organizations as static structures; systems theorists see organizations as always-changing processes of interactions among organizational and environmental elements. Organizations are not static, but rather are in constantly shifting states of dynamic equilibrium. They are adaptive systems that are integral parts of their environments. Organizations must adjust to changes in their environment if they are to survive; in turn, virtually all of their decisions and actions affect their environment.

Norbert Wiener's classic model of an organization as an adaptive system, from his 1948 book *Cybernetics,* epitomizes these basic theoretical perspectives of the systems perspective (see Figure 1). *Cybernetics,* a Greek word meaning *steersman,* was used by Wiener to mean the multidisciplinary study of the structures and functions of control and information processing systems in animals and machines. The basic concept behind cybernetics is self-regulation—through biological, social, or technological systems that can identify problems, do something about them, and then receive feedback to adjust themselves automatically. Wiener, a mathematician, developed the concept of cybernetics while working on anti-aircraft systems during World War II. Variations on this simple model of a system have been used extensively by systems theorists for many years, particularly around the development and use of management information systems, but we have not been able to locate anyone who used it before Wiener did in 1948.

The search for order among complex variables has led to an extensive reliance on quantitative analytical methods and models. The systems approach is strongly cause-and-effect oriented (logical-positivist) in its philsophy and methods (Ott, 1989, Chapter 5). In these respects, systems theories have close ties to the scientific management approach of Frederick Winslow Taylor. Whereas Taylor used quantitative scientific methods to find "the one best way," the systems theorist uses quantitative scientific methods to identify cause–effect relationships and to find *optimal solutions.* In this sense, the conceptual approaches and purposes between the two perspectives are strikingly

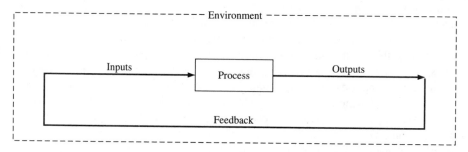

Figure 1
Norbert Wiener's model of an organization as an adaptive system

similar. Thus, systems theories are often called *management sciences* or *administrative sciences*. (But be careful not to make the unpardonable error of calling them *scientific management.*)

Computers, models, and interdisciplinary teams of analysts are the basic "tools" of the systems perspective. Studies of organizations done by its members typically use the scientific method and quasi-experimental research techniques, or computer models. This quantitative orientation reflects the systems school's origins, the years immediately following World War II when the first serious attempts were made to apply mathematical and statistical probability models to organizational processes and decision making. Many of the early efforts started under the label of operations analysis, or operations research, in defense industry-related "think tanks" such as the RAND Corporation of Santa Monica, California. *Operations research* or *operations analysis* refers to the use of mathematical and scientific techniques to develop a quantitative basis for organizational decision making (Raiffa, 1968). During the subsequent decades, defense and aerospace programs provided the development and testing settings for many of the tools and techniques of operations research, including PERT, CPM, statistical inference, linear programming, gaming, Monte Carlo methods, and simulation.

Pioneering neoclassical theories provided important conceptual foundations for the systems approach. Herbert Simon and his associates contributed some of the most important of these (see Chapter II). Simon's visionary theories addressed *bounded rationality* and *satisficing* in organizational decision making (1957), and programmed and unprogrammed decisions (1960). With James March and others, Simon also made major contributions in the areas of cognitive limits on rationality and organizational innovation (1958). Indeed, it was Simon's further work in the areas of management decision making that led to his 1978 Nobel Prize for economics.

As the systems perspective ascended to the center stage of the field of organization theory during the later half of the 1960s, its focus on computers, information technology, and control systems spawned many heated debates between systems theorists and human relations-oriented organization theorists over philosophical issues such as computer domination of social structures, negative effects of centralized organizational decision making, and irresolvable conflicts between the individual freedom of organizational members and technology-based organizational confinement. Thus, for example, Norbert Wiener (1964), the "father" of cybernetics and a visionary systems-oriented scientist, wrote:

> Render unto man the things which are man's and unto the computer the things which are the computer's. This would seem the intelligent policy to adopt when we employ men and computers together in common undertakings. It is a policy as far removed from that of the gadget worshipper as it is from the man who sees only blasphemy and the degradation of man in the use of any mechanical adjuvants whatever to thoughts. [An adjuvant is defined as something that serves to help or assist.]

It is important to remember—and easy to forget—that there are *social* systems as well as *management* systems within the systems approach. The social systems theories have roots in the traditions and philosophies of social psychology, cultural anthropology, and sociology, as well as in the pioneering humanistically oriented philosophers of organization: including Elton Mayo (1933), Chester Barnard (1938), Roethlisberger and Dickson (1939), and Mary Parker Follett (1940).

Daniel Katz and Robert L. Kahn produced the first major statement on the applicability of social systems to organizations in their 1966 book *The Social Psychology of Organizations.* Katz and Kahn provided the intellectual basis for merging classical, neoclassical, human relations/behavioral, "modern" structural, and systems perspectives of organizations. Katz and Kahn balance these perspectives through their concept of organizations as open systems—systems that include organizations and their environments. Because organizations are open systems, they must continuously adapt to changing environmental factors, and managers must recognize that all organizational decisions and actions in turn influence their environments. Reprinted here is "Organizations and the System Concept," a chapter from *The Social Psychology of Organizations,* wherein Katz and Kahn conclude that the traditional closed system view of organizations has led to a failure to fully appreciate the interdependences and interactions between organizations and their environments.

Katz and Kahn's concept of open systems has influenced the thinking of many organization theorists. Several articles that are reprinted here and in Chapter IV provide excellent examples. They include James D. Thompson's writing on technology and tasks, Paul Lawrence and Jay Lorsch's chapter on the need to balance between organizational differentiation and integration, and Jay Galbraith's work on information processing models of organizations.

Classical organization theorists saw organizations as rational but closed systems that pursued the goal of economic efficiency. Because the systems were viewed as "closed" and not subject to influence from the external environment, major attention could be focused on such functions as planning and/or controlling. James D. Thompson, in his influential 1967 book *Organizations in Action,* classifies most organizations as open systems. Reprinted here are the first two chapters from his book in which he suggests that the closed system approach may be realistic at the technical level of organizational operations. Thompson seeks to bridge the gap between open and closed systems by postulating that organizations "abhor uncertainty" and deal with uncertainty in the environment by creating specific elements designed to cope with the outside world, while other elements are able to focus on the rational nature of technical operations. The dominant technology used by an organization strongly influences its structure, activities, and evaluation/control processes.

In a 1972 *Academy of Management Journal* article, "General Systems Theory: Applications for Organization and Management," Fremont E. Kast and James E. Rosenzweig examine the "state of the art" of practical applications of systems theory. They attempt to assess the degree of success we have had in utilizing the "key concepts of general systems theory" in the development of "modern organization theory." After discussing some practical problems of applying systems theory to organizations, Kast and Rosenzweig observe that "many managers have used and will continue to use a systems approach and contingency views intuitively and implicitly,"; thus, systems and contingency views are not new to most managers. The authors conclude with a call for ways to make systems views more usable by practicing managers.

Kast and Rosenzweig use the phrase "contingency views." Contingency theory is a "close cousin" of systems theories in which the effectiveness of an organizational action (for example, a decision) is viewed as dependent upon the relationship between the element in question and all other aspects of the system—at the particular moment. Everything is situational: there are no absolutes or universals. Thus, contingency views of organizations place high importance on rapid, accurate information systems. This linkage between systems theories and the contingency views caused us to place a selection from Jay Galbraith's 1973 book *Designing Complex Organizations* here—rather than in Chapter IV on "modern" structural organization theory. Galbraith is in fact a "modern" structuralist who is concerned primarily with organizational design strategies; however, his chapter "Information Processing Model" captures the essence of the systems/contingency perspective on organizations. He constructs theories about the amount of information an organization must process under different levels of (*a*) uncertainty, (*b*) interdependence among organizational elements, *and* (*c*) organizational adaptation mechanisms.

According to Galbraith and other contingency theorists, uncertainty is the gap between the amount of information an organization needs and the amount of information it possesses. Thus, uncertainty limits an organization's ability to plan and to make decisions. The greater the level of uncertainty, the more an organization must use contingency approaches to planning and decision making.

The theories that are known as population ecology of organizations, organizational ecology, ecological-evolutionary, and natural selection might warrant a separate chapter. However, their place in the field of organization theory is still the subject of heated controversy (Young, 1988; Hannan & Freeman, 1989a). Further, these theories represent logical extensions of systems and contingency theories (Grandori, 1987), and we find it most useful to consider them in conjunction with systems theory.

Theories of organizational ecology focus on the reasons for organizational diversity, formation, survival, and death. They seek to discover why there are so many kinds and sizes of organizations: "An ecology of organizations seeks to understand how social conditions affect the rates at which new organizations and new organizational forms arise, the rates at which organizations change forms, and the rates at which organizations and forms die out" (Hannan & Freeman, 1989b, p. 7). Population ecology theories are concerned with competition, selection, and survival of the fittest in populations (groupings) of organizations. They closely resemble Darwinian theories of evolution in that survival of an organization depends on its ability to acquire adequate supplies of critical resources. These theories are also interested in the distribution of organizational forms across environmental conditions and limitations on various organizational forms in different environments.

Population ecology theory of organizations assumes that natural selection processes operate among organizations. Organizations do not adapt to their changing environments by making decisions; instead, the environment selects among organizational forms based on:

- The magnitude of economies of specialization and scale in using a specialist *versus* a generalist organizational form
- The trade-off costs of generalist organizations adapting to (coping with) environmental states *versus* the costs of errors resulting from maladaptation in specialist organizations

Thus, according to organizational ecology theories, organizational forms are selected naturally based on economies in production, organizational specialization, and change costs.

Organizational ecology theory is most applicable and useful

- When there is competition among the organizations in a population
- When there are many organizations in a population (so that natural selection can occur)
- Among newer rather than older organizations

In "A Concept of Organizational Ecology" (reprinted here), Eric Trist (1976) proposes a concept of organizational ecology based on the organizational field that is created by a number of organizations whose interrelations comprise a system—at the level of the field as a whole. The overall field is the unit of analysis, rather than single organizations in relation to their organizational field. Trist contends that changes in organizational environments have made the world much more complex and interdependent. In order to understand organizations, we must examine the relationships among dissimilar organizations that share boundaries.

The best known and most frequently cited work on natural selection or population ecology is Michael Hannan and John Freeman's 1977 *American Journal of Sociology* article "The Population Ecology of Organizations." Hannan and Freeman propose a model (or set of theories) for use in the study of organizational-environment relations. They assess the applicability and limitations of bioecological models to the study of organizational-environment relations. Populations of organizations—rather than individual organizations—are the appropriate units of analysis. The model incorporates an evolutionary explanation of the principle of isomorphism. They also suggest an organizational selection process based on competition theory and address dynamic considerations of excess capacity using fitness-set theory.

References

BARNARD, C. I. (1938). *The functions of the executive.* Cambridge, MA: Harvard University Press.

BERTALANFFY, L. VON. (1951, December). General systems theory: A new approach to unity of science. *Human Biology, 23,* 303–361.

BERTALANFFY, L. VON. (1968). *General systems theory: Foundations, development, applications.* New York: George Braziller.

BLUMENTHAL, S. C. (1969). *Management information systems.* Englewood Cliffs, NJ: Prentice-Hall.

BOULDING, K. E. (1956, April). General systems theory—The skeleton of science. *Management Science, 2, 3,* 197–208.

CARROLL, G. R. (1987). *Publish and perish: The organizational ecology of newspaper industries.* Greenwich, CT: JAI Press.

CARROLL, G. R. (Ed.). (1988). *Ecological models of organizations.* Cambridge, MA: Ballinger.

CARZO, R., Jr., & YANOUZAS, J. N. (1967). *Formal organizations: A systems approach.* Homewood, IL: Richard D. Irwin.

DEARDEN, J. F., & McFARLAN, F. W. (1966). *Management information systems.* Homewood, IL: Richard D. Irwin.

FOLLETT, M. P. (1940). *Dynamic administration: The collected papers of Mary Parker Follett.* E. M. Fox & L. Urwick (Eds.). New York: Hippocrene Books.

GALBRAITH, J. (1973). *Designing complex organizations.* Reading, MA: Addison-Wesley.

GRANDORI, A. (1987). *Perspectives on organization theory.* Cambridge, MA: Ballinger.

HANNAN, M. T., & FREEMAN, J. (1977). The population ecology of organizations. *American Journal of Sociology, 82,* 929–964.

HANNAN, M. T., & FREEMAN, J. (1984). Where do organizational forms come from? *Sociological Forum, 1,* 50–72.

HANNAN, M. T., & FREEMAN, J. (1989a). Setting the record straight on organizational ecology: Rebuttal to Young. *American Journal of Sociology, 95*(2), 425–438.

HANNAN, M. T., & FREEMAN, J. (1989b). *Organizational ecology.* Cambridge, MA: Harvard University Press.

KAST, F. E. & ROSENZWEIG, J. E. (1970). *Organization and management: A systems approach.* New York: McGraw-Hill.

KAST, F. E., & ROSENZWEIG, J. E. (1972, December). General systems theory: Applications for organization and management. *Academy of Management Journal,* 447–465.

KATZ, D., & KAHN, R. L. (1966). *The social psychology of organizations.* New York: Wiley.

MARCH, J. G., & SIMON, H. A. (1958). *Organizations.* New York: Wiley.

MAYO, E. (1933). *The human problems of an industrial civilization.* New York: Viking Press.

OTT, J. S. (1989). *The organizational culture perspective.* Pacific Grove, CA: Brooks/Cole.

RAIFFA, H. (1968). *Decision analysis.* Reading, MA: Addison-Wesley.

ROETHLISBERGER, F. J., & DICKSON, W. J. (1939). *Management and the worker.* Cambridge, MA: Harvard University Press.

SIMON, H. A. (1957). *Administrative behavior* (2nd ed.). New York: Macmillan.

SIMON, H. A. (1960). *The new science of management decisions.* New York: Harper & Row.

SINGH, J., HOUSE, R. J., & TUCKER, D. J. (1986). Organizational change and organizational mortality. *Administrative Science Quarterly, 31,* 587–611.

THOMPSON, J. D. (1967). *Organizations in action.* New York: McGraw-Hill.

TRIST, E. (1977). A concept of organizational ecology. *Australian Journal of Management, 2,* 162–175.

TRIST, E. (1983). Referent organizations and the development of inter-organizational domains. *Human Relations, 36*(3), 269–284.

WIENER, N. (1948). *Cybernetics.* Cambridge, MA: MIT Press.

WIENER, N. (1950). *The human use of human beings.* Boston: Houghton Mifflin.

WIENER, N. (1964). *God and golem, inc.* Cambridge, MA: MIT Press.

YOUNG, R. C. (1988). Is population ecology a useful paradigm for the study of organizations? *American Journal of Sociology, 94*(1), 1–24.

27

Organizations and the System Concept

Daniel Katz and Robert L. Kahn

The aims of social science with respect to human organizations are like those of any other science with respect to the events and phenomena of its domain. The social scientist wishes to understand human organizations, to describe what is essential in their form, aspects, and functions. He wishes to explain their cycles of growth and decline, to predict their effects and effectiveness. Perhaps he wishes as well to test and apply such knowledge by introducing purposeful changes into organizations—by making them, for example, more benign, more responsive to human needs.

Such efforts are not solely the prerogative of social science, however; common sense approaches to understanding and altering organizations are ancient and perpetual. They tend, on the whole, to rely heavily on two assumptions: that the location and nature of an organization are given by its name; and that an organization is possessed of built-in goals—because such goals were implanted by its founders, decreed by its present leaders, or because they emerged mysteriously as the purposes of the organizational system itself. These assumptions scarcely provide an adequate basis for the study of organizations and at times can be misleading and even fallacious. We propose, however, to make use of the information to which they point.

SOURCE: Daniel Katz and Robert L. Kahn, *The Social Psychology of Organizations,* 14–29. Copyright © 1966 John Wiley & Sons, Inc. Reprinted by permission of John Wiley & Sons, Inc. Footnotes renumbered.

The first problem in understanding an organization or a social system is its location and identification. How do we know that we are dealing with an organization? What are its boundaries? What behavior belongs to the organization and what behavior lies outside it? Who are the individuals whose actions are to be studied and what segments of their behavior are to be included?

The fact that popular names exist to label social organizations is both a help and a hindrance. These popular labels represent the socially accepted stereotypes about organizations and do not specify their role structure, their psychological nature, or their boundaries. On the other hand, these names help in locating the area of behavior in which we are interested. Moreover, the fact that people both within and without an organization accept stereotypes about its nature and functioning is one determinant of its character.

The second key characteristic of the common sense approach to understanding an organization is to regard it simply as the epitome of the purposes of its designer, its leaders, or its key members. The teleology of this approach is again both a help and a hindrance. Since human purpose is deliberately built into organizations and is specifically recorded in the social compact, the bylaws, or other formal protocol of the undertaking, it would be inefficient not to utilize these sources of information. In the early development of a group, many processes are generated which have little to do with its rational purpose, but over time there is a cumulative recognition of the devices for ordering group life and a deliberate use of these devices.

Apart from formal protocol, the primary mission of an organization as perceived by its leaders furnishes a highly informative set of clues for the researcher seeking to study organizational functioning. Nevertheless, the stated purposes of an organization as given by its bylaws or in the reports of its leaders can be misleading. Such statements of objectives may idealize, rationalize, distort, omit, or even conceal some essential aspects of the functioning of the organization. Nor is there always agreement about the mission of the organization among its leaders and members. The university president may describe the purpose of his institution as one of turning out national leaders; the academic dean sees it as imparting the cultural heritage of the past, the academic vice-president as enabling students to move toward self-actualization and development, the graduate dean as creating new knowledge, the dean of men as training youngsters in technical and professional skills which will enable them to earn their living, and the editor of the student newspaper as inculcating the conservative values which will preserve the status quo of an outmoded capitalistic society.

The fallacy here is one of equating the purposes or goals of organizations with the purposes and goals of individual members. The organization as a system has an output, a product or an outcome, but this is not necessarily identical with the individual purposes of group members. Though the founders of the organization and its key members do think in teleological terms about organization objectives, we should not accept such practical thinking, useful as it may be, in place of a theoretical set of constructs for purposes of scientific analysis. Social science, too frequently in the past, has been misled by such short-cuts and has equated popular phenomenology with scientific explanation.

In fact, the classic body of theory and thinking about organizations has assumed a teleology of this sort as the easiest way of identifying organizational structures and their functions. From this point of view an organization is a social device for efficiently accomplishing through group means some stated purpose; it is the equivalent of the blueprint for the design of the machine which is to be created for some practical objective. The essential difficulty with this purposive or design approach is that an organization characteristically includes more and less than is indicated by the design of its founder or the purpose of its leader. Some of the factors assumed in the design may be lacking or so distorted in operational practice as to be meaningless, while unforeseen embellishments dominate the organizational structure. Moreover, it is not always possible to ferret out the designer of the organization or to discover the intricacies of the design which he carried in his head. The attempt by Merton to deal with the latent function of the organization in contrast with its manifest function is one way of dealing with this problem.[1] The study of unanticipated consequences as well as anticipated consequences of organizational functioning is a similar way of handling the matter. Again, however, we are back to the purposes of the creator or leader, dealing with unanticipated consequences on the assumption that we can discover the consequences anticipated by him and can lump all other outcomes together as a kind of error variance.

It would be much better theoretically, however, to start with concepts which do not call for identifying the purposes of the designers and then correcting for them when they do not seem to be fulfilled. The theoretical concepts should begin with the input, output, and functioning of the organization as a system and not with the rational purposes of its leaders. We may want to utilize such purposive notions to lead us to sources of data or as subjects of special study, but not as our basic theoretical constructs for understanding organizations.

Our theoretical model for the understanding of organizations is that of an energic input-output system in which the energic return from the output reactivates the system. Social organizations are flagrantly open systems in that the input of energies and the conversion of output into further energic input consist of transactions between the organization and its environment.

All social systems, including organizations, consist of the patterned activities of a number of individuals. Moreover, these patterned activities are complementary or interdependent with respect to some common output or outcome; they are repeated, relatively enduring, and bounded in space and time. If the activity pattern occurs only once or at unpredictable intervals, we could not speak of an organization. The stability or recurrence of activities can be examined in relation to the *energic input* into the system, the *transformation of energies within the system,* and the *resulting product or energic output.* In a factory the raw materials and the human labor are the energic input, the patterned activities of production the transformation of energy, and the finished product the output. To maintain this patterned activity requires a continued renewal of the inflow of energy. This is guaranteed in social systems by the energic return from the product or outcome. Thus the outcome of the cycle of activities furnishes new energy for the initiation of a renewed cycle. The company which produces automobiles sells them and by doing so obtains the means of securing new raw materials, compensating its labor force, and continuing the activity pattern.

In many organizations outcomes are converted into money and new energy is furnished through this mechanism. Money is a convenient way of handling energy units both on the output and input sides, and buying and selling represent one set of social rules for regulating the exchange of money. Indeed, these rules are so effective and so widespread that there is some danger of mistaking the business of buying and selling for the defining cycles of organization. It is a commonplace executive observation that businesses exist to make money, and the observation is usually allowed to go unchallenged. It is, however, a very limited statement about the purposes of business.

Some human organizations do not depend on the cycle of selling and buying to maintain themselves. Universities and public agencies depend rather on bequests and legislative appropriations, and in so-called voluntary organizations the output reenergizes the activity of organization members in a more direct fashion. Member activities and accomplishments are rewarding in themselves and tend therefore to be continued, without the mediation of the outside environment. A society of bird watchers can wander into the hills and engage in the rewarding activities of identifying birds for their mutual edification and enjoyment. Organizations thus differ on this important dimension of the source of energy renewal, with the great majority utilizing both intrinsic and extrinsic sources in varying degree. Most large-scale organizations are not as self-contained as small voluntary groups and are very dependent upon the social effects of their output for energy renewal.

Our two basic criteria for identifying social systems and determining their functions are (1) tracing the pattern of energy exchange or activity of people as it results in some output and (2) ascertaining how the output is translated into energy which reactivates the pattern. We shall refer to organizational functions or objectives not as the conscious purposes of group leaders or group members but as the outcomes which are the energic source for a maintenance of the same type of output.

This model of an energic input-output system is taken from the open system theory as promulgated by von Bertalanffy.[2] Theorists have pointed out the applicability of the system concepts of the natural sciences to the problems of social science. It is important, therefore, to examine in more detail the constructs of system theory and the characteristics of open systems.

System theory is basically concerned with problems of relationships, of structure, and of interdependence rather than with the constant attributes of objects. In general approach it resembles field theory except that its dynamics deal with temporal as well as spatial patterns. Older formulations of system constructs dealt with the closed systems of the physical sciences, in which relatively self-contained structures could be treated successfully as if they were independent of external forces. But living systems, whether biological organisms or social organizations, are acutely dependent upon their external environment and so must be conceived of as open systems.

Before the advent of open-system thinking, social scientists tended to take one of two approaches in dealing with social structures; they tended either (1) to regard them as closed systems to which the laws of physics applied or (2) to endow them with some vitalistic concept like entelechy. In the former case they ignored the environmental forces affecting the organization and in the latter case they fell back upon some magical purposiveness to account for organizational functioning. Biological theorists, however, have rescued us from this trap by pointing out that the concept of the open system means that we neither have to follow the laws of traditional physics, nor in deserting them do we have to abandon science. The laws of Newtonian physics are correct generalizations but they are limited to closed systems. They do not apply in the same fashion to open systems which maintain themselves through constant commerce with their environment, i.e., a continuous inflow and outflow of energy through permeable boundaries.

One example of the operation of closed versus open systems can be seen in the concept of entropy and the second law of thermodynamics. According to the second law of thermodynamics a system moves toward equilibrium; it tends to run down, that is, its differentiated structures tend to move toward dissolution as the elements composing them become arranged in random disorder. For example, suppose that a bar of iron has been heated by the application of a blowtorch on one side. The arrangement of all the fast (heated) molecules on one side and all the slow molecules on the other is an unstable state, and over time the distribution of molecules becomes in effect random, with the resultant cooling of one side and heating of the other, so that all surfaces of the iron approach the same temperature. A similar process of heat exchange will also be going on between the iron bar and its environment, so that the bar will gradually approach the temperature of the room in which it is located, and in so doing will elevate somewhat the previous temperature of the room. More technically, entropy increases toward a maximum and equilibrium occurs as the physical system attains the state of the most probable distribution of its elements. In social systems, however, structures tend to become more elaborated rather than less differentiated. The rich may grow richer and the poor may grow poorer. The open system does not run down, because

it can import energy from the world around it. Thus the operation of entropy is counteracted by the importation of energy and the living system is characterized by negative rather than positive entropy.

Common Characteristics of Open Systems

Though the various types of open systems have common characteristics by virtue of being open systems, they differ in other characteristics. If this were not the case, we would be able to obtain all our basic knowledge about social organizations through the study of a single cell.

The following nine characteristics seem to define all open systems.

1. Importation of Energy

Open systems import some form of energy from the external environment. The cell receives oxygen from the blood stream; the body similarly takes in oxygen from the air and food from the external world. The personality is dependent upon the external world for stimulation. Studies of sensory deprivation show that when a person is placed in a darkened soundproof room, where he has a minimal amount of visual and auditory stimulation, he develops hallucinations and other signs of mental stress.[3] Deprivation of social stimulation also can lead to mental disorganization.[4] Köhler's studies of the figural after-effects of continued stimulation show the dependence of perception upon its energic support from the external world.[5] Animals deprived of visual experience from birth for a prolonged period never fully recover their visual capacities.[6] In other words, the functioning personality is heavily dependent upon the continuous inflow of stimulation from the external environment. Similarly, social organizations must also draw renewed supplies of energy from other institutions, or people, or the material environment. No social structure is self-sufficient or self-contained.

2. The Through-Put

Open systems transform the energy available to them. The body converts starch and sugar into heat and action. The personality converts chemical and electrical forms of stimulation into sensory qualities, and information into thought patterns. The organization creates a new product, or processes materials, or trains people, or provides a service. These activities entail some reorganization of input. Some work gets done in the system.

3. The Output

Open systems export some products into the environment, whether it be the invention of an inquiring mind or a bridge constructed by an engineering firm. Even the biological organism exports physiological products such as carbon dioxide from the lungs which helps to maintain plants in the immediate environment.

4. Systems as Cycles of Events

The pattern of activities of the energy exchange has a cyclic character. The product exported into the environment furnishes the sources of energy for the repetition of the cycle of activities. The energy reinforcing the cycle of activities can derive from some exchange of the product in the external world or from the activity itself. In the former instance, the industrial concern utilizes raw materials and human labor to turn out a product which is marketed, and the monetary return is used to obtain more raw materials and labor to perpetuate the cycle of activities. In the latter instance, the voluntary organization can provide expressive satisfactions to its members so that the energy renewal comes directly from the organizational activity itself.

The problem of structure, or the relatedness of parts, can be observed directly in some physical arrangement of things where the larger unit is physically bounded and its subparts are also bounded within the larger structure. But how do we deal with social structures, where physical boundaries in this sense do not exist? It was the genius of F. H. Allport which contributed the answer, namely that the structure is to be found in an interrelated set of events which return upon themselves to complete and renew a cycle of activities.[7] It is events rather than things which are structured, so that social structure is a dynamic rather than a static concept. Activities are structured so that they comprise a unity in their completion or closure. A simple linear stimulus-response exchange between two people would not constitute social structure. To create structure, the responses of A would have to elicit B's reactions in such a manner that the responses of the latter would stimulate A to further responses. Of course the chain of events may involve many people, but their behavior can be characterized as showing structure only when there is some closure to the chain by a return to its point of origin with the probability that the chain of events will then be repeated. The repetition of the cycle does not have to involve the same set of phenotypical happenings. It may expand to include more subevents of exactly the same kind or it may involve similar activities directed toward the same outcomes. In the individual organism the eye may move in such a way as to have the point of light fall upon the center of the retina. As the point of light moves, the movements of the eye may also change but to complete the same cycle of activity, i.e., to focus upon the point of light.

A single cycle of events of a self-closing character gives us a simple form of structure. But such single cycles can also combine to give a larger structure of events or an event system. An event system may consist of a circle of smaller cycles or hoops, each one of which makes contact with several others. Cycles may also be tangential to one another from other types of subsystems. The basic method for the identification of social structures is to follow the energic chain of events from the input of energy through its transformation to the point of closure of the cycle.

5. Negative Entropy

To survive, open systems must move to arrest the entropic process; they must acquire negative entropy. The entropic process is a universal law of nature in which all forms of organization move toward disorganization or death. Complex physical systems move toward simple random distribution of their elements and biological organisms also run down and perish. The open system, however, by importing more energy from its environment than it expends, can store energy and can acquire negative entropy. There is then a general trend in an open system to maximize its ratio of imported to expended energy, to survive and even during periods of crisis to live on borrowed time. Prisoners in concentration camps on a starvation diet will carefully conserve any form of energy expenditure to make the limited food intake go as far as possible.[8] Social organizations will seek to improve their survival position and to acquire in their reserves a comfortable margin of operation.

The entropic process asserts itself in all biological systems as well as in closed physical systems. The energy replenishment of the biological organism is not of a qualitative character which can maintain indefinitely the complex organizational structure of living tissue. Social systems, however, are not anchored in the same physical constancies as biological organisms and so are capable of almost indefinite arresting of the entropic process. Nevertheless the number of organizations which go out of existence every year is large.

6. Information Input, Negative Feedback, and the Coding Process

The inputs into living systems consist not only of energic materials which become transformed or altered in the work that gets done. Inputs are also informative in character and furnish signals to the structure about the environment and about its own functioning in relation to the environment. Just as we recognize the distinction between cues and drives in individual psychology, so must we take account of information and energic inputs for all living systems.

The simplest type of information input found in all systems is negative feedback. Information feedback of a negative kind enables the system to correct its deviations from course. The working parts of the machine feed back information about the effects of their operation to some central mechanism or subsystem which acts on such information to keep the system on target. The thermostat which controls the temperature of the room is a simple example of a regulatory device which operates on the basis of negative feedback. The automated power plant would furnish more complex examples. Miller emphasizes the critical nature of negative feedback in his proposition: *"When a system's negative feedback discontinues, its steady state vanishes, and at the same time its boundary disappears and the system terminates."*[9] If there is no corrective device to get the system back on its course, it will expend too much energy or it will ingest too much energic input and no longer continue as a system.

The reception of inputs into a system is selective. Not all energic inputs are capable of being absorbed into every system. The digestive system of living creatures assimilates only those inputs to which it is adapted. Similarly, systems can react only to those information signals to which they are attuned. The general term for the selective mechanisms of a system by which incoming materials are rejected or accepted and translated for the structure is coding. Through the coding process, the "blooming, buzzing confusion" of the world is simplified into a few meaningful and simplified categories for a given system. The nature of the functions performed by the system determines its coding mechanisms, which in turn perpetuate this type of functioning.

7. The Steady State and Dynamic Homeostasis

The importation of energy to arrest entropy operates to maintain some constancy in energy exchange, so that open systems which survive are characterized by a steady state. A steady state is not motionless or a true equilibrium. There is a continuous inflow of energy from the external environment and a continuous export of the products of the system, but the character of the system, the ratio of the energy exchanges and the relations between parts, remains the same. The catabolic and anabolic processes of tissue breakdown and restoration within the body preserve a steady state so that the organism from time to time is not the identical organism it was but a highly similar organism. The steady state is seen in clear form in the homeostatic processes for the regulation of body temperature; external conditions of humidity and temperature may vary, but the temperature of the body remains the same. The endocrine glands are a regulatory mechanism for preserving an evenness of physiological functioning. The general principle here is that of Le Châtelier who maintains that any internal or external factor making for disruption of the system is countered by forces which restore the system as closely as possible to its previous state.[10] Krech and Crutchfield similarly hold, with respect to psychological organization, that cognitive structures will react to influences in such a way as to absorb them with minimal change to existing cognitive integration.[11]

The homeostatic principle does not apply literally to the functioning of all complex living systems, in that in counteracting entropy they move toward growth and expansion. This apparent contradiction can be resolved, however, if we recognize the complexity of the subsystems and their interaction in anticipating changes necessary for the maintenance of an overall steady state. Stagner has pointed out that the initial disturbance of a given tissue constancy within the biological organism will result in mobilization of energy to restore the balance, but that recurrent upsets will lead to actions to anticipate the disturbance:

We eat before we experience intense hunger pangs. . . . energy mobilization for fore-stalling tactics must be explained in terms of a *cortical tension* which reflects the visceral-proprioceptive pattern of the original biological disequilibration. . . . *Dynamic homeostasis* involves the maintenance of tissue constancies by establishing a constant physical environment—by reducing the variability and disturbing effects of external stimulation. Thus the organism does not simply restore the prior equilibrium. A new,

more complex and more comprehensive equilibrium is established.[12]

Though the tendency toward a steady state in its simplest form is homeostatic, as in the preservation of a constant body temperature, the basic principle is *the preservation of the character of the system.* The equilibrium which complex systems approach is often that of a quasi-stationary equilibrium, to use Lewin's concept.[13] An adjustment in one direction is countered by a movement in the opposite direction and both movements are approximate rather than precise in their compensatory nature. Thus a temporal chart of activity will show a series of ups and downs rather than a smooth curve.

In preserving the character of the system, moreover, the structure will tend to import more energy than is required for its output, as we have already noted in discussing negative entropy. To insure survival, systems will operate to acquire some margin of safety beyond the immediate level of existence. The body will store fat, the social organization will build up reserves, the society will increase its technological and cultural base. Miller has formulated the proposition that the rate of growth of a system—within certain ranges—is exponential if it exists in a medium which makes available unrestricted amounts of energy for input.[14]

In adapting to their environment, systems will attempt to cope with external forces by ingesting them or acquiring control over them. The physical boundedness of the single organism means that such attempts at control over the environment affect the behavioral system rather than the biological system of the individual. Social systems will move, however, towards incorporating within their boundaries the external resources essential to survival. Again the result is an expansion of the original system.

Thus, the steady state which at the simple level is one of homeostasis over time, at more complex levels becomes one of preserving the character of the system through growth and expansion. The basic type of system does not change directly as a consequence of expansion. The most common type of growth is a multiplication of the same type of cycles or subsystems—a change in quantity rather than in quality. Animal and plant species grow by multiplication. A social system adds more units of the same essential type as it already has. Haire has studied the ratio between the sizes of different subsystems in growing business organizations.[15] He found that though the number of people increased in both the production subsystem and the subsystem concerned with the external world, the ratio of the two groups remained constant. Qualitative change does occur, however, in two ways. In the first place, quantitative growth calls for supportive subsystems of a specialized character not necessary when the system was smaller. In the second place, there is a point where quantitative changes produce a qualitative difference in the functioning of a system. A small college which triples its size is no longer the same institution in terms of the relation between its administration and faculty, relations among the various academic departments, or the nature of its instruction.

In time, living systems exhibit a growth or expansion dynamic in which they maximize their basic character. They react to change or they anticipate change through growth which assimilates the new energic inputs to the nature of their structure. In terms of Lewin's quasi-stationary equilibrium the ups and downs of the adjustive process do not always result in a return to the old level. Under certain circumstances a solidification or freezing occurs during one of the adjustive cycles. A new base line level is thus established and successive movements fluctuate around this plateau which may be either above or below the previous plateau of operation.

8. Differentiation

Open systems move in the direction of differentiation and elaboration. Diffuse global patterns are replaced by more specialized functions. The sense organs and the nervous system evolved as highly differentiated structures from the primitive nervous tissues. The growth of the personality proceeds from primitive, crude organizations of mental functions to hierarchically structured and well-differentiated systems of beliefs and feelings. Social organizations move toward the multiplication and elaboration of roles with greater specialization of function. In the United States today medical specialists now outnumber the general practitioners.

One type of differentiated growth in systems is what von Bertalanffy terms progressive mechanization. It finds expression in the way in which a system achieves a steady state. The early method is a process which involves an interaction of various dynamic forces, whereas the later development entails the use of a regulatory feedback mechanism. He writes:

It can be shown that the *primary* regulations in organic systems, that is, those which are most fundamental and primitive in embryonic development as well as in evolution, are of such nature of dynamic interaction. . . . Superimposed are those regulations which we may call *secondary,* and which are controlled by fixed arrangements, especially of the feedback type. This state of affairs is a consequence of a general principle of organization which may be called progressive mechanization. At first, systems—biological, neurological, psychological or social—are governed by dynamic interaction of their components; later on, fixed arrangements and conditions of constraint are established which render the system and its parts more efficient, but also gradually diminish and eventually abolish its equipotentiality.[16]

9. Equifinality

Open systems are further characterized by the principle of equifinality, a principle suggested by von Bertalanffy in 1940.[17] According to this principle, a system can reach the same final state from differing initial conditions and by a variety of paths. The well-known biological experiments on the sea urchin show that a normal creature of that species can develop from a complete ovum, from each half of a divided ovum, or from the fusion product of two whole ova. As open systems move toward regulatory mechanisms to control their operations, the amount of equifinality may be reduced.

Some Consequences of Viewing Organizations as Open Systems

In the following chapter we shall inquire into the specific implications of considering organizations as open systems and into the ways in which social organizations differ from other types of living systems. At this point, however, we should call attention to some of the misconceptions which arise both in theory and practice when social organizations are regarded as closed rather than open systems.

The major misconception is the failure to recognize fully that the organization is continually dependent upon inputs from the environment and that the inflow of materials and human energy is not a constant. The fact that organizations have built-in protective devices to maintain stability and that they are notoriously difficult to change in the direction of some reformer's desires should not obscure the realities of the dynamic interrelationships of any social structure with its social and natural environment. The very efforts of the organization to maintain a constant external environment produce changes in organizational structure. The reaction to changed inputs to mute their possible revolutionary implications also results in changes.

The typical models in organizational theorizing concentrate upon principles of internal functioning as if these problems were independent of changes in the environment and as if they did not affect the maintenance inputs of motivation and morale. Moves toward tighter integration and coordination are made to insure stability, when flexibility may be the more important requirement. Moreover, coordination and control become ends in themselves rather than means to an end. They are not seen in full perspective as adjusting the system to its environment but as desirable goals within a closed system. In fact, however, every attempt at coordination which is not functionally required may produce a host of new organizational problems.

One error which stems from this kind of misconception is the failure to recognize the equifinality of the open system, namely that there are more ways than one of producing a given outcome. In a closed physical system the same initial conditions must lead to the same final result. In open systems this is not true even at the biological level. It is much less true at the social level. Yet in practice we insist that there is one best way of assembling a gun for all recruits, one best way for the baseball player to hurl the ball in from the outfield and that we standardize and teach these best methods. Now it is true under certain conditions that there is one best way, but these conditions must first be established. The general principle, which characterizes all open systems, is that there does not have to be a single method for achieving an objective.

A second error lies in the notion that irregularities in the functioning of a system due to environmental influences are error variances and should be treated accordingly. According to this conception, they should be controlled out of studies of organizations. From the organization's own operations they should be excluded as irrelevant and should be guarded against. The decisions of officers to omit a consideration of external factors or to guard against such influences in a defensive fashion, as if they would go away if ignored, is an instance of this type of thinking. So is the now outmoded "public be damned" attitude of businessmen toward the clientele upon whose support they depend. Open system theory, on the other hand, would maintain that environmental influences are not sources of error variance but are integrally related to the functioning of a social system, and that we cannot understand a system without a constant study of the forces that impinge upon it.

Thinking of the organization as a closed system, moreover, results in a failure to develop the intelligence or feedback function of obtaining adequate information about the changes in environmental forces. It is remarkable how weak many industrial companies are in their market research departments when they are so dependent upon the market. The prediction can be hazarded that organizations in our society will increasingly move toward the improvements of the facilities for research in assessing environmental forces. The reason is that we are in the process of correcting our misconception of the organization as a closed system.

Emery and Trist have pointed out how current theorizing on organizations still reflects the older closed system conceptions. They write:

> In the realm of social theory, however, there has been something of a tendency to continue thinking in terms of a "closed" system, that is, to regard the enterprise as sufficiently independent to allow most of its problems to be analyzed with reference to its internal structure and without reference to its external environment. . . . In practice the system theorists in social science . . . did "tend to focus on the statics of social structure and to neglect the study of structural change." In an attempt to overcome this bias, Merton suggested that "the concept of strain, stress and tension on the structural level, provides an analytical approach to the study of dynamics and change." This concept has been widely accepted by system theorists but while it draws attention to sources of imbalance within an organization it does not conceptually reflect the mutual permeation of an organization and its environment that is the cause of such imbalance. It still retains the limiting perspectives of "closed system" theorizing. In the administrative field the same limitations may be seen in the otherwise invaluable contributions of Barnard and related writers.[18]

Summary

The open-system approach to organizations is contrasted with common-sense approaches, which tend to accept popular names and stereotypes as basic organizational properties and to identify the purpose of an organization in terms of the goals of its founders and leaders.

The open-system approach, on the other hand, begins by identifying and mapping the repeated cycles of input, transformation, output, and renewed input which comprise the organizational pattern. This approach to organizations represents the adaptation of work in biology and in the physical sciences by von Bertalanffy and others.

Organizations as a special class of open systems have properties of their own, but they share other properties in common with all open systems. These include the importation of energy from the environment, the through-put or transformation of the imported energy into some product form which is characteristic of the system, the exporting of that product into the environment, and the reenergizing of the system from sources in the environment.

Open systems also share the characteristics of negative entropy, feedback, homeostasis, differentiation, and equifinality. The law of negative entropy states that systems survive and maintain their characteristic internal order only so long as they import from the environment more energy than they expend in the process of transformation and exportation. The feedback principle has to do with information input, which is a special kind of energic importation, a kind of signal to the system about environmental conditions and about the functioning of the system in relation to its environment. The feedback of such information enables the system to correct for its own malfunctioning or for changes in the environment, and thus to maintain a steady state or homeostasis. This is a dynamic rather than a static balance, however. Open systems are not at rest but tend toward differentiation and elaboration, both because of subsystem dynamics and because of the relationship between growth and survival. Finally, open systems are characterized by the principle of equifinality, which asserts that systems can reach the same final state from different initial conditions and by different paths of development.

Traditional organizational theories have tended to view the human organization as a closed system. This tendency has led to a disregard of differing organizational environments and the nature of organizational dependency on environment. It has led also to an overconcentration on principles of internal organizational functioning, with consequent failure to develop and understand the processes of feedback which are essential to survival.

Notes

1. Merton, R. K. 1957. *Social theory and social structure*, rev. ed. New York: Free Press.
2. von Bertalanffy, L. 1956. General system theory. *General Systems*. Yearbook of the Society for the Advancement of General System Theory, *1*, 1–10.
3. Solomon, P., *et al.* (Eds.) 1961. *Sensory deprivation*. Cambridge, Mass: Harvard University Press.
4. Spitz, R. A. 1945. Hospitalism: an inquiry into the genesis of psychiatric conditions in early childhood. *Psychoanalytic Study of the Child*, *1*, 53–74.
5. Kohler, W., & H. Wallach. 1944. Figural aftereffects: an investigation of visual processes. *Proceedings of the American Philosophical Society,* *88*, 269–357. Also, Kohler, W., & D. Emery. 1947. Figural after-effects in the third dimension of visual space. *American Journal of Psychology*, *60*, 159–201.
6. Melzack, R., & W. Thompson. 1956. Effects of early experience on social behavior. *Canadian Journal of Psychology*, *10*, 82–90.
7. Allport, F. H. 1962. A structuronomic conception of behavior: individual and collective. I. Structural theory and the master problem of social psychology. *Journal of Abnormal and Social Psychology*, *64*, 3–30.
8. Cohen, E. 1954. *Human behavior in the concentration camp*. London: Jonathan Cape.
9. Miller, J. G. 1955. Toward a general theory for the behavioral sciences. *American Psychologist*, *10*, 513–531; quote from p. 529.
10. See Bradley, D. F., & M. Calvin. 1956. Behavior: imbalance in a network of chemical transformations. *General Systems*. Yearbook of the Society for the Advancement of General System Theory, *1*, 56–65.
11. Krech, D., & R. Crutchfield. 1948. *Theory and problems of social psychology*. New York: McGraw-Hill.
12. Stagner, R. 1951. Homeostasis as a unifying concept in personality theory. *Psychological Review*, *58*, 5–17; quote from p. 5.
13. Lewin, K. 1947. Frontiers in group dynamics. *Human Relations*, *1*, 5–41.
14. Miller, *op cit*.
15. Haire, M. 1959. Biological models and empirical histories of the growth of organizations. In M. Haire (Ed.), *Modern organization theory*, New York: Wiley, 272–306.
16. von Bertalanffy. 1956, *op cit*, p. 6.
17. von Bertalanffy, L. 1940. Der organismus als physikalisches system betrachtet. *Naturwissenschaften*, *28*, 521 ff.
18. Emery, F. E., & E. L. Trist. 1960. Sociotechnical systems. In *Management sciences models and techniques*. Vol. 2, London: Pergamon Press; quote from p. 84.

28

Organizations in Action

James D. Thompson

Strategies for Studying Organizations

Complex organizations—manufacturing firms, hospitals, schools, armies, community agencies—are ubiquitous in modern societies, but our understanding of them is limited and segmented.

The fact that impressive and sometimes frightening consequences flow from organizations suggests that some individuals have had considerable insight into these social instruments. But insight and private experiences may generate private understandings without producing a public body of knowledge adequate for the preparation of a next generation of administrators, for designing new styles of organizations for new purposes, for controlling organizations, or for appreciation of distinctive aspects of modern societies.

What we know or think we know about complex organizations is housed in a variety of fields or disciplines, and communication among them more nearly resembles a trickle than a torrent.[1] Although each of the several schools has its unique terminology and special heroes, Gouldner was able to discern two fundamental models underlying most of the literature.[2] He labeled these the "rational" and "natural-

SOURCE: James D. Thompson, *Organizations in Action*, 3–24. Copyright © 1967 by McGraw-Hill, Inc. Used with permission of McGraw-Hill Book Company. References converted to footnotes.

system" models of organizations, and these labels are indeed descriptive of the results.

To Gouldner's important distinction we wish to add the notion that the rational model results from a *closed-system strategy* for studying organizations, and that the natural-system model flows from an *open-system strategy*.

Closed-System Strategy

The search for certainty. If we wish to predict accurately the state a system will be in presently, it helps immensely to be dealing with a *determinate system*. As Ashby observes, fixing the present circumstances of a determinate system will determine the state it moves to next, and since such a system cannot go to two states at once, the transformation will be unique.[3]

Fixing the present circumstances requires, of course, that the variables and relationships involved by few enough for us to comprehend and that we have control over or can reliably predict all of the variables and relations. In other words, it requires that the system be closed or, if closure is not complete, that the outside forces acting on it be predictable.

Now if we have responsibility for the future states or performances of some system, we are likely to opt for a closed system. Bartlett's research on mental processes, comparing "adventurous thinking" with "thinking in closed systems," suggests that there are strong human tendencies to reduce various forms of knowledge to the closed-system variety, to rid them of all ultimate uncertainty.[4] If such tendencies appear in puzzle-solving as well as in everyday situations, we would especially expect them to be emphasized when responsibility and high stakes are added. Since much of the literature about organizations has been generated as a by-product of the search for improved efficiency or performance, it is not surprising that it employs closed-system assumptions—employs a rational model—about organizations. Whether we consider *scientific management,*[5] *administrative management,*[6] or *bureaucracy,*[7] the ingredients of the organization are deliberately chosen for their necessary contribution to a goal, and the structures established are those deliberately intended to attain highest efficiency.

Three schools in caricature. Scientific management, focused primarily on manufacturing or similar production activities, clearly employs economic efficiency as its ultimate criterion, and seeks to maximize efficiency by planning procedures according to a technical logic, setting standards, and exercising controls to ensure conformity with standards and thereby with the technical logic. Scientific management achieves conceptual closure of the organization by assuming that goals are known, tasks are repetitive, output of the production process somehow disappears, and resources in uniform qualities are available.

Administrative-management literature focuses on structural relationships among production, personnel, supply, and other service units of the organization; and again employs as the ultimate criterion economic efficiency. Here efficiency is maximized by specializing tasks and grouping them into departments, fixing responsibility according to such principles as span of control or delegation, and controlling action to plans. Administrative management achieves closure by assuming that ultimately a master plan is known, against which specialization, departmentalization, and controls are determined. (That this master plan is elusive is shown by Simon.[8]) Administrative management also assumes that production tasks are known, that output disappears, and that resources are automatically available to the organization.

Bureaucracy also follows the pattern noted above, focusing on staffing and structure as means of handling clients and disposing of cases. Again the ultimate criterion is efficiency, and this time it is maximized by defining offices according to jurisdiction and place in a hierarchy,

appointing experts to offices, establishing rules for categories of activity, categorizing cases or clients, and then motivating proper performance of expert officials by providing salaries and patterns for career advancement. [The extended implications of the assumptions made by bureaucratic theory are brought out by Merton's discussion of "bureaucratic personality."[9]] Bureaucratic theory also employs the closed system of logic. Weber saw three holes through which empirical reality might penetrate the logic, but in outlining his "pure type" he quickly plugged these holes. Policymakers, somewhere above the bureaucracy, could alter the goals, but the implications of this are set aside. Human components—the expert officeholders—might be more complicated than the model describes, but bureaucratic theory handles this by divorcing the individual's private life from his life as an office-holder through the use of rules, salary, and career. Finally, bureaucratic theory takes note of outsiders—clientele—but nullifies their effects by depersonalizing and categorizing clients.

It seems clear that the rational-model approach uses a closed-system strategy. It also seems clear that the developers of the several schools using the rational model have been primarily students of performance or efficiency, and only incidentally students of organizations. Having focused on control of the organization as a target, each employs a closed system of logic and conceptually closes the organization to coincide with that type of logic, for this elimination of uncertainty is the way to achieve determinateness. The rational model of an organization results in everything being functional—making a positive, indeed an optimum, contribution to the overall result. All resources are appropriate resources, and their allocation fits a master plan. All action is appropriate action, and its outcomes are predictable.

It is no accident that much of the literature on the management or administration of complex organization centers on the concepts of *planning* or *controlling.* Nor is it any accident that such views are dismissed by those using the open-system strategy.

Open-System Strategy

The expectation of uncertainty. If, instead of assuming closure, we assume that a system contains more variables than we can comprehend at one time, or that some of the variables are subject to influences we cannot control or predict, we must resort to a different sort of logic. We can, if we wish, assume that the system is determinate by nature, but that it is our incomplete understanding which forces us to expect surprise or the intrusion of certainty. In this case we can employ a natural-system model.

Approached as a natural system, the complex organization is a set of interdependent parts which together make up a whole because each contributes something and receives something from the whole, which in turn is interdependent with some larger environment. Survival of the system is taken to be the goal, and the parts and their relationships presumably are determined through evolutionary processes. Dysfunctions are conceivable, but it is assumed that an offending part will adjust to produce a net positive contribution or be disengaged, or else the system will degenerate.

Central to the natural-system approach is the concept of homeostasis, or self-stabilization, which spontaneously, or naturally, governs the necessary relationships among parts and activities and thereby keeps the system viable in the face of disturbances stemming from the environment.

Two examples in caricature. Study of the *informal organization* constitutes one example of research in complex organizations using the natural-system approach. Here attention is focused on variables which are not included in any of the rational models—sentiments, cliques, social controls via informal norms, status and status striving, and so on. It is clear that students of informal organization regard these variables not as random deviations or error, but as patterned, adaptive responses of human beings in problematic situations.[10] In this view the formal organization is a spontaneous and functional development, indeed a necessity, in complex organizations, permitting the system to adapt and survive.

A second version of the natural-system approach is more global but less crystallized under a label. This school views the organization as a unit in interaction with its environment, and its view was perhaps most forcefully expressed by Chester Barnard[11] and by the empirical studies of Selznick[12] and Clark.[13] This stream of work leads to the conclusion that organizations are not autonomous entities; instead, the best laid plans of managers have unintended consequences and are conditioned or upset by other social units—other complex organizations or publics—on whom the organization is dependent.

Again it is clear that in contrast to the rational-model approach, this research area focuses on variables not subject to complete control by the organization and hence not contained within a closed system of logic. It is also clear that students regard interdependence of organization and environment as inevitable or natural, and as adaptive or functional.

Choice or Compromise?

The literature about organizations, or at least much of it, seems to fall into one of the two categories, each of which at best tends to ignore the other and at worse denies the relevance of the other. The logics associated with each appear to be incompatible, for one avoids uncertainty to achieve determinateness, while the other assumes uncertainty and indeterminateness. Yet the phenomena treated by each approach, as distinct from the explanations of each, cannot be denied.

Viewed in the large, complex organizations are often effective instruments for achievement, and that achievement flows from planned, controlled action. In every sphere—educational, medical, industrial, commercial, or governmental—the quality or costs of goods or services may be challenged and questions may be raised about the equity of distribution within the society of the fruits of complex organizations. Still millions live each day on the assumption that a reasonable degree of purposeful, effective action will be forthcoming from the many complex organizations on which they depend. Planned action, not random behavior, supports our daily lives. Specialized, controlled, patterned action surround us.

There can be no question but that the rational model of organizations directs our attention to important phenomena—to important "truth" in the sense that complex organizations viewed in the large exhibit some of the patterns and results to which the rational model attends, but which the natural-system model tends to ignore. But it is equally evident that phenomena associated with the natural-system approach also exist in complex organizations. There is little room to doubt the universal emergence of the informal organization. The daily news about labor-management negotiations, interagency jurisdictional squabbles, collusive agreements, favoritism, breeches of contract, and so on, are impressive evidence that complex organizations are influenced in significant ways by elements of their environments, a phenomenon addressed by the natural-system approach but avoided by the rational. Yet most versions of the natural-system approach treat organizational purposes and achievements as peripheral matters.

It appears that each approach leads to some truth, but neither alone affords an adequate understanding of complex organizations. Gouldner calls for a synthesis of the two models, but does not provide the synthetic model.

Meanwhile, a serious and sustained elaboration of Barnard's work[14] has produced a newer tradition which evades the closed- versus open-system dilemma.

A Newer Tradition

What emerges from the Simon-March-Cyert stream of study is the organization as a problem-facing and problem-solving phenomenon. The focus is on organizational processes related to choice of courses of action in an environment which does not fully disclose the alternatives available or the consequences of those alternatives. In this view, the organization has limited capacity to gather and process information or to predict consequences of alternatives. To deal with situations of such great complexity, the organization must develop processes for *searching* and *learning*, as well as for *deciding*. The complexity, if fully faced, would overwhelm the organization, hence it must set limits to its definitions of situations; it must make decisions in *bounded rationality*.[15] This requirement involved replacing the maximum-efficiency criterion with one of satisfactory accomplishment, decision-making now involving *satisficing* rather than *maximizing*.[16]

These are highly significant notions, and it will become apparent that this book seeks to extend this "newer tradition." The assumptions it makes are consistent with the open-system strategy, for it holds that the processes going on within the organization are significantly affected by the complexity of the organization's environment. But this tradition also touches on matters important in the closed-system strategy; performance and deliberate decisions.

But despite what seem to be obvious advantages, the Simon-March-Cyert stream of work has not entirely replaced the more extreme strategies, and we need to ask why so many intelligent men and women in a position to make the same observations we have been making should continue to espouse patently incomplete views of complex organizations.

The cutting edge of uncertainty.   Part of the answer to that question undoubtedly lies in the fact that supporters of each strategy have had different purposes in mind, with open-system strategists attempting to understand organizations per se, and closed-system strategists interested in organizations mainly as vehicles for rational achievements. Yet this answer does not seem completely satisfactory, for these students could not have been entirely unaware of the challenges to their assumptions and beliefs.

We can suggest now that rather than reflecting weakness in those who use them, the two strategies reflect something fundamental about the cultures surrounding complex organizations— the fact that our culture does not contain concepts for simultaneously thinking about rationality and indeterminateness. These appear to be incompatible concepts, and we have no ready way of thinking about something as half-closed, half-rational. One alternative, then, is the closed-system approach of ignoring uncertainty to see rationality; another is to ignore rational action in order to see spontaneous processes. The newer tradition with its focus on organizational coping with uncertainty is indeed a major advance. It is notable that a recent treatment by Crozier starts from the bureaucratic position but focuses on coping with uncertainty as its major topic.[17]

Yet in directing our attention to processes for meeting uncertainty, Simon, March, and Cyert may lead us to overlook the useful knowledge amassed by the older approaches. If the phenomena of rational models are indeed observable, we may want to incorporate some elements of those models; and if natural-system phenomena occur, we should also benefit from the relevant theories. For purposes of this volume, then, *we will conceive of complex organizations as open systems, hence indeterminate and faced with uncertainty, but at the same time as subject to criteria of rationality and hence needing determinateness and certainty.*

The Location of Problems

As a starting point, we will suggest that the phenomena associated with open- and closed-system strategies are not randomly distributed through complex organizations, but instead tend to be specialized by location. To introduce this notion we will start with Parsons' suggestion that organizations exhibit three distinct levels of responsibility and control—*technical, managerial,* and *institutional.*[18]

In this view, every formal organization contains a suborganization whose "problems" are focused around effective performance of the technical function—the conduct of classes by teachers, the processing of income tax returns and the handling of recalcitrants by the bureau, the processing of material and supervision of these operations in the case of physical production. The primary exigencies to which the technical suborganization is oriented are those imposed by the nature of the technical task, such as the materials, which must be processed and the kinds of cooperation of different people required to get the job done effectively.

The second level, the managerial, *services* the technical suborganization by (1) mediating between the technical suborganization and those who use its products—the customers, pupils, and so on—and (2) procuring the resources necessary for carrying out the technical functions. The managerial level *controls,* or administers, the technical suborganization (although Parsons notes that its control is not unilateral) by deciding such matters as the broad technical task which is to be performed, the scale of operations, employment and purchasing policy, and so on.

Finally, in the Parsons formulation, the organization which consists of both technical and managerial suborganizations is also part of a wider social system which is the source of the "meaning," or higher-level support which makes the implementation of the organization's goals possible. In terms of "formal" controls, an organization may be relatively independent; but in terms of the meaning of the functions performed by the organization and hence of its "rights" to command resources and to subject its customers to discipline, it is never wholly independent. This overall articulation of the organization and the institutional structure and agencies of the community is the function of the third, or institutional, level of the organization.

Parsons' distinction of the three levels becomes more significant when he points out that at each of the two points of articulation between them there is a *qualitative* break in the simple continuity of "line" authority because the functions at each level are qualitatively different. Those at the second level are not simply lower-order spellings-out of the top-level functions. Moreover, the articulation of levels and functions rests on a two-way interaction, with each side, by withholding its important contribution, in a position to interfere with the functioning of the other and of the larger organization.

If we now reintroduce the conception of the complex organization as an open system subject to criteria of rationality, we are in a position to speculate about some dynamic properties of organizations. As we suggested, the logical model for achieving complete technical rationality uses a closed system of logic—closed by the elimination of uncertainty. In practice, it would seem, the more variables involved, the greater the likelihood of uncertainty, and it would therefore be advantageous for an organization subject to criteria of rationality to remove as much uncertainty as possible from its *technical core* by reducing the number of variables operating on it. Hence if both resource-acquisition and output-disposal problems—which are in part controlled by environmental elements and hence to a degree uncertain or problematic—can be removed from the technical core, the logic can be brought closer to closure, and the rationality, increased.

Uncertainty would appear to be greatest, at least potentially, at the other extreme, the institutional level. Here the organization deals largely with elements of the environment over which it has no formal authority or control. Instead, it is subjected to generalized norms, ranging from formally codified law to informal standards of good practice, to public authority, or to elements expressing the public interest.

At this extreme the closed system of logic is clearly inappropriate. The organization is open to influence by the environment (and vice versa) which can change independently of the actions of the organization. Here an open system of logic, permitting the intrusion of variables penetrating the organization from outside, and facing up to uncertainty, seems indispensable.

If the closed-system aspects of organizations are seen most clearly at the technical level, and the open-system qualities appear most vividly at the institutional level, it would suggest that a significant function of the managerial level is to mediate between the two extremes and the emphases they exhibit. If the organization must approach certainty at the technical level to satisfy its rationality criteria, but must remain flexible and adaptive to satisfy environmental requirements, we might expect the managerial level to mediate between them, ironing out some irregularities stemming from external

sources, but also pressing the technical core for modifications as conditions alter. One exploration of this notion was offered in Thompson.[19]

Possible sources of variation. Following Parsons' reasoning leads to the expectation that differences in technical functions, or *technologies,* cause significant differences among organization, and since the three levels are interdependent, differences in technical functions should also make for differences at managerial and institutional levels of the organization. Similarly, differences of the institutional structures in which organizations are imbedded should make for significant variations among organizations at all three levels.

Relating this back to the Simon-March-Cyert focus on organizational processes of searching, learning, and deciding, we can also suggest that while these adaptive processes may be generic, the ways in which they proceed may well vary with differences in technologies or in environments.

Recapitulation

Most of our beliefs about complex organizations follow from one or the other of two distinct strategies. The closed-system strategy seeks certainty by incorporating only those variables positively associated with goal achievement and subjecting them to a monolithic control network. The open-system strategy shifts attention from goal achievement to survival, and incorporates uncertainty by recognizing organizational interdependence with environment. A newer tradition enables us to conceive of the organization as an open system, indeterminate and faced with uncertainty, but subject to criteria of rationality and hence needing certainty.

With this conception the central problem for complex organizations is one of coping with uncertainty. As a point of departure, we suggest that organizations cope with uncertainty by creating certain parts specifically to deal with it, specializing other parts in operating under conditions of certainty or near certainty. In this case, articulation of these specialized parts becomes significant.

We also suggest that technologies and environments are major sources of uncertainty for organizations, and that differences in those dimensions will result in differences in organizations. To proceed, we now turn to a closer examination of the meaning of "rationality," in the context of complex organizations.

Rationality in Organizations

Instrumental action is rooted on the one hand in *desired outcomes* and on the other hand in *beliefs about cause/effect relationships*. Given a desire, the state of man's knowledge at any point in time dictates the kinds of variables required and the manner of their manipulation to bring that desire to fruition. To the extent that the activities thus dictated by man's beliefs are judged to produce the desired outcomes, we can speak of technology, or *technical rationality*.

Technical rationality can be evaluated by two criteria: instrumental and economic. The essence of the instrumental question is whether the specified actions do in fact produce the desired outcome, and the instrumentally perfect technology is one which inevitably achieves such results. The economic question in essence is whether the results are obtained with the least necessary expenditure of resources, and for this there is no absolute standard. Two different routes to the same desired outcome may be compared in terms of cost, or both may be compared with some abstract ideal, but in practical terms the evaluation of economy is relative to the state of man's knowledge at the time of evaluation.

We will give further consideration to the assessment of organizational action in a later chapter, but it is necessary to distinguish at this point between the instrumental and economic questions because present literature and organization gives considerable attention to the economic dimension of technology but hides the importance of the instrumental question, which in fact takes priority. The cost of doing something can be considered only after we know that the something can be done.

Complex organizations are built to operate technologies which are found to be impossible or impractical for individuals to operate. This does not mean, however, that technologies operated by complex organizations are instrumentally perfect. The instrumentally perfect technology would produce the desired outcome inevitably, and this perfection is approached in the case of continous processing of chemicals or in mass manufacturing—for example, of automobiles. A less perfect technology will produce the desired outcome only part of the time; nevertheless, it may be incorporated into complex organizations, such as the mental hospital, because the desire for the possible outcome is intense enough to settle for possible rather than highly probable success. Sometimes the intensity of desire for certain kinds of outcomes, such as world peace, leads to the creation of complex organizations, such as the United Nations to operate patently imperfect technologies.

Variations in Technologies

Clearly, technology is an important variable in understanding the actions of complex organizations. In modern societies the variety of desired outcomes for which specific technologies are available seems infinite. A complete but simple typology of technologies which has found order in this variety would be quite helpful. Typologies are available for industrial production[20] and for mental therapy[21] but are not general enough to deal with the range of technologies found in complex organizations. Lacking such a typology, we will simply identify three varieties which are (1) widespread in modern society and (2) sufficiently different to illustrate the propositions we wish to develop.

The long-linked technology.[22] A long-linked technology involves serial interdependence in the sense that act Z can be performed only after successful completion of act Y, which in turn rests on act X, and so on. The original symbol of technical rationality, the mass production assembly line, is of this long-linked nature. It approaches instrumental perfection when it produces a single kind of standard product, repetitively and at a constant rate. Production of only one kind of product means that a single technology is required, and this in turn permits the use of clear-cut criteria for the selection of machines and tools, construction of work-flow arrangements, acquisition of raw materials, and selection of human operators. Repetition of the productive process provides experience as a means of eliminating imperfections in the technology; experience can lead to the modification of machines and provide the basis for scheduled preventive maintenance. Repetition means that human motions can also be examined, and through training and practice, energy losses and errors minimized. It is in this setting that the scientific-management movement has perhaps made its greatest contribution.

The constant rate of production means that, once adjusted, the proportion of resources involved can be standardized to the point where each contributes to its capacity; none need to be underemployed. This of course makes important contributions to the economic aspect of the technology.

The mediating technology. Various organizations have, as a primary function, the linking of clients or customers who are or wish to be interdependent. The commerical bank links depositors and borrowers. The insurance firm links those who would pool common risks. The telephone utility links those who would call and those who would be called. The post office provides a possible linkage of virtually every member of the modern society. The employment agency mediates the supply of labor and the demand for it.

Complexity in the mediating technology comes not from the necessity of having each activity geared to the requirements of the next but rather from the fact that the mediating technology requires operating in *standardized ways,* and *extensively; e.g.,* with multiple clients or customers distributed in time and space.

The commercial bank must find and aggregate deposits from diverse depositors; but however diverse the depositors, the transaction must conform to standard terms and to uniform bookkeeping and accounting procedures. It must also find borrowers; but no matter how varied their needs or desires, loans must be made according to standardized criteria and on terms uniformly applied to the category appropriate to the particular borrower. Poor risks who receive favored treatment jeopardize bank solvency. Standardization permits the insurance organization to define categories of risk and hence to sort its customers or potential customers into appropriate aggregate categories; the insured who is not a qualified risk but is so defined upsets the probabilities on which insurance rests. The telephone company became viable only when the telephone became regarded as a necessity, and this did not occur until equipment was standardized to the point where it could be incorporated into one network. Standardization enables the employment agency to aggregate job applicants into categories which can be matched against standardized requests for employees.

Standardization makes possible the operation of the mediating technology over time and through space by assuring each segment of the organization that other segments are operating in compatible ways. It is in such situations that the bureaucratic techniques of categorization and impersonal application of rules have been most beneficial.[23]

The intensive technology. This third variety we label *intensive* to signify that a variety of techniques is drawn upon in order to achieve a change in some specific object; but the selection, combination, and order of application are determined by feedback from the object itself. When the object is human, this intensive technology is regarded as "therapeutic," but the same technical logic is found also in the construction industry[24] and in research where the objects of concern are nonhuman. . . .

The intensive technology is a custom technology. Its successful employment rests in part on the availability of all the capacities potentially needed, but equally on the appropriate custom combination of selected capacities as required by the individual case or project.

Boundaries of technical rationality. Technical rationality, as a system of cause/effect relationships which lead to a desired result, is an abstraction. It is instrumentally perfect when it becomes a closed system of logic. The closed system of logic contains all relevant variables, and only relevant variables. All other influences, or *exogenous variables,* are excluded; and the variables contained in the system vary only to the extent that the experimenter, the manager, or the computer determines they should.

When a technology is put to use, however, there must be not only desired outcomes and knowledge of relevant cause/effect relationships, but also power to control the empirical resources which correspond to the variables in the logical system. A closed system of action corresponding to a closed system of logic would result in instrumental perfection in reality.

The mass production assembly operation and the continuous processing of chemicals are more nearly perfect, in application, than the other two varieties discussed above because they achieve a high degree of control over relevant variables and are relatively free from disturbing influences. Once started, most of the action involved in the long-linked technology is dictated by the internal logic of the technology itself. With the mediating technology, customers or clients intrude to make difficult the standardized activities required by the technology. And with the intensive technology, the specific case defines the component activities and their combination from the larger array of components contained in the abstract technology.

Since technical perfection seems more nearly approachable when the organization has control over all the elements involved,

Proposition 2.1: Under norms of rationality, organizations seek to seal off their core technologies from environmental influences.

Organizational Rationality

When organizations seek to translate the abstractions called technologies into action, they immediately face problems for which the core technologies do not provide solutions.

Mass production manufacturing technologies are quite specific, *assuming* that certain inputs are provided and finished products are somehow removed from the premises before the productive process is clogged; but mass production technologies do not include variables which provide solutions to either the input- or output-disposal problems. The present technology of medicine may be rather specific if certain tests indicate an appendectomy is in order, if the condition of the patient meets certain criteria, and if certain medical staff, equipment, and medications are present. But medical technology contains no cause/effect statements about bringing sufferers to the attention of medical practitioners, or about the provision of the specified equipment, skills, and medications. The technology of education rests on abstract systems of belief about relationships among teachers, teaching materials, and pupils; but learning theories assume the presence of these variables and proceed from that point.

One or more technologies constitute the core of all purposive organizations. But this technical core is always an incomplete representation of what the organization must do to accomplish desired results. Technical rationality is a necessary component but never alone sufficient to provide *organizational rationality,* which involves acquiring the inputs which are taken for granted by the technology, and dispensing outputs which again are outside the scope of the core technology.

At a minimum, then, organizational rationality involves three major component activities. (1) input activities, (2) technological activities, and (3) output activities. Since these are interdependent, organizational rationality requires that they be appropriately geared to one another. The inputs acquired must be within the scope of the technology, and it must be within the capacity of the organization to dispose of the technological production.

Not only are these component activities interdependent, but both input and output activities are interdependent with environmental elements. Organizational rationality, therefore, never conforms to closed-system logic but demands the logic of an open system. Moreover, since the technological activities are embedded in and interdependent with activities which are open to the environment, the closed system can never be completely attained for the technological component. Yet we have offered the proposition that organizations subject to rationality norms seek to seal off their core technologies from environmental influences. How do we reconcile these two contentions?

Proposition 2.2: Under norms of rationality, organizations seek to buffer environmental influences by surrounding their technical cores with input and output components.

To maximize productivity of a manufacturing technology, the technical core must be able to operate as if the market will absorb the single kind of product at a continuous rate, and as if inputs flowed continuously, at a steady rate and with specified quality. Conceivably both sets of conditions could occur; realistically they do not. But organizations reveal a variety of devices for approximating these "as if" assumptions, with input and output components meeting fluctuating environments and converting them into steady conditions for the technological core.

Buffering on the input side is illustrated by the stockpiling of materials and supplies acquired in an irregular market, and their steady insertion into the production process. Preventive maintenance, whereby machines or equipment are repaired on a scheduled basis, thus minimizing surprise, is another example of buffering by the input component. The recruitment of dissimilar personnel and their conversion into reliable performers through training or indoctrination is another; it is most dramatically illustrated by basic training or boot camp in military organizations.[25]

Buffering on the output side of long-linked technologies usually takes the form of maintaining warehouse inventories and items in transit or in distributor inventories, which permits the technical core to produce at a constant rate, but distribution to fluctuate with market conditions.

Buffering on the input side is an appropriate and important device available to all types of organizations. Buffering on the output side is especially important for mass-manufacturing organizations, but is less feasible when the product is perishable or when the object is inextricably involved in the technological process, as in the therapeutic case.

Buffering of an unsteady environment obviously brings considerable advantages to the technical core, but it does so with costs to the organization. A classic problem in connection with buffering is how to maintain inventories, input or output, sufficient to meet all needs without recurring obsolescence as needs change. Operations research recently has made important contributions toward this problem of "run out versus obsolescence," both of which are costly.

Thus while a fully buffered technological core would enjoy the conditions for maximum technical rationality, organizational rationality may call for compromises between conditions for maximum technical efficiency and the energy required for buffering operations. In an unsteady environment, then, the organization under rationality norms must seek other devices for protecting its technical core.

Proposition 2.3: Under norms of rationality, organizations seek to smooth out input and output transactions.

Whereas buffering absorbs environmental fluctuations, smoothing or leveling involves attempts to reduce fluctuations in the environment. Utility firms—electric, gas, water, or telephone—may offer inducements to those who use their services during "trough" periods, or charge premiums to those who contribute to "peaking." Retailing organizations faced with seasonal or other fluctuations in demand, may offer inducements in the form of special promotions or sales during slow periods. Transportation organizations such as airlines may offer special reduced fare rates on light days or during slow seasons.

Organizations pointed toward emergencies, such as fire departments, attempt to level the need for their services by activities designed to prevent emergencies, and by emphasis on the early detection so that demand is not allowed to grow to the point that would overtax the capacity of the organization. Hospitals accomplish some smoothing through the scheduling of nonemergency admissions.

Although action by the organization may thus reduce fluctuations in demand, complete smoothing of demand is seldom possible. But a core technology interrupted by constant fluctuation and change must settle for a low degree of technical rationality. What other services do organizations employ to protect core technologies?

Proposition 2.4: Under norms of rationality, organizations seek to anticipate and adapt to environmental changes which cannot be buffered or leveled.

If environmental fluctuations penetrate the organization and require the technical core to alter its activities, then environmental fluctuations are exogenous variables within the logic of technical rationality. To the extent that environmental fluctuations can be anticipated, however, they can be treated as *constraints* on the technical core within which a closed system of logic can be employed.

The manufacturing firm which can correctly forecast demand for a particular time period can thereby plan or schedule operations of its technical core at a steady rate during that period. Any changes in technical operations due to changes in the environment can be made at the end of the period on the basis of forecasts for the next period.

Organizations often learn that some environmental fluctuations are patterned, and in these cases forecasting and adjustment appear almost automatic. The post office knows, for example, that in large commercial centers large volumes of business mail are posted at the end of the business day, when secretaries leave offices. Recently the post office has attempted to buffer that load by promising rapid treatment of mail posted in special locations during morning hours. Its success in buffering is not known at this writing, but meanwhile the post office schedules its technical activities to meet known daily fluctuations. It can also anticipate heavy demand during November and December, thus allowing its input components lead time in acquiring additional resources.

Banks likewise learn that local conditions and customs result in peak loads at predictable times during the day and week, and can schedule their operations to meet these shifts.[26]

In cases such as these, organizations have amassed sufficient experience to know that fluctuations are patterned with a high degree of regularity or probability; but when environmental fluctuations are the result of combinations of more dynamic factors, anticipation may require something more than the simple projection of previous experience. It is in these situations that forecasting emerges as a specialized and elaborate activity, for which some of the emerging management-science or statistical-decision theories seem especially appropriate.

To the extent that environmental fluctuations are unanticipated they interfere with the orderly operation of the core technology and thereby reduce its performance. When such influences are anticipated and considered as constraints for a particular period of time, the technical core can operate as if it enjoyed a closed system.

Buffering, leveling, and adaptation to anticipated fluctuations are widely used devices for reducing the influence of the environment on the technological cores of organizations. Often they are effective, but there are occasions when these devices are not sufficient to ward off environmental penetration.

Proposition 2.5: When buffering, leveling, and forecasting do not protect their technical cores from environmental fluctuations, organizations under norms of rationality resort to rationing.

Rationing is most easily seen in organizations pointed toward emergencies, such as hospitals. Even in nonemergency situations hospitals may ration beds to physicians by establishing priority systems for nonemergency admissions. In emergencies, such as community disasters, hospitals may ration pharmaceutical dosages or nursing services by dilution—by assigning a fixed number of nurses to a larger patient population. Mental hospitals, especially state mental hospitals, may ration technical services by employing primarily organic-treatment procedures—electroshock, drugs, insulin—which can be employed more economically than psychoanalytic or *milieu* therapies.[27] Teachers and caseworkers in social welfare organizations may ration effort by accepting only a portion of those seeking service, or if not empowered to exercise such discretion, may concentrate their energies on the more challenging cases or on those which appear most likely to yield satisfactory outcomes.[28]

But rationing is not a device reserved for therapeutic organizations. The post office may assign priority to first-class mail, attending to lesser classes only when the priority task is completed. Manufacturers of suddenly popular items may ration allotments to wholesalers or dealers, and if inputs are scarce, may assign priorities to alternative uses of those resources. Libraries may ration book loans, acquisitions, and search efforts.[29]

Rationing is an unhappy solution, for its use signifies that the technology is not operating at its maximum. Yet some system of priorities for the allocation of capacity under adverse conditions is essential if a technology is to be instrumentally effective—if action is to be other than random.

The logic of organizational rationality. Core technologies rest on closed systems of logic, but are invariably embedded in a larger organizational rationality which pins the technology to a time and place, and links it with the larger environment through input and output activities. Organizational rationality thus calls for an open-system logic, for when the organization is opened to environmental influences, some of the factors involved in organizational action become *constraints;* for some meaningful period of time they are not variables but fixed conditions to which the organization must adapt. Some of the factors become *contingencies,* which may or may not vary, but are not subject to arbitrary control by the organization.

Organizational rationality therefore is some result of (1) constraints which the organization must face, (2) contingencies which the organization must meet, and (3) variables which the organization can control.

Recapitulation

Perfection in technical rationality requires complete knowledge of cause/effect relations plus control over all of the relevant variables, or closure. Therefore, under norms of rationality (Prop. 2.1), organizations seek to seal off their core technologies from environmental influences. Since complete closure is impossible (Prop. 2.2), they seek to buffer environmental influences by surrounding their technical cores with input and output components.

Because buffering does not handle all variations in an unsteady environment, organizations seek to smooth input and output transactions (Prop. 2.3), and to anticipate and adapt to environmental changes which cannot be buffered or smoothed (Prop. 2.4), and finally, when buffering, leveling, and forecasting do not protect their technical cores from environmental fluctuations (Prop. 2.5), organizations resort to rationing.

These are maneuvering devices which provide the organization with some self-control despite interdependence with the environment. But if we are to gain understanding of such maneuvering, we must consider both the direction toward which maneuvering is designed and the nature of the environment in which maneuvering takes place.

Notes

1. William R. Dill, "Desegregation or Integration? Comments about Contemporary Research in Organizations," in *New Perspectives in Organization Research*, eds. W. W. Cooper, Harold J. Leavitt, & Maynard W. Shelly II (New York:

John Wiley & Sons, Inc., 1964). James G. March, "Introduction," in *Handbook of Organizations,* ed. James G. March (Chicago: Rand McNally, 1965).

2. Alvin W. Gouldner, "Organizational Analysis," in *Sociology Today,* eds. Robert K. Merton, Leonard Broom, and Leonard S. Cottrell, Jr. (New York: Basic Books, 1959).

3. W. Ross Ashby, *An Introduction to Cybernetics* (London: Chapman and Hall, Ltd., 1956).

4. Sir Frederic Bartlett, *Thinking: An Experimental and Social Study* (New York: Basic Books, 1958).

5. Frederick W. Taylor, *Scientific Management* (New York: Harper & Row, 1911).

6. Luther Gulick, & L. Urwick, eds., *Papers on the Science of Administration* (New York: Institute of Public Administration, 1937).

7. Max Weber, *The Theory of Social and Economic Organization,* ed. Talcott Parsons, trans. A. M. Henderson and Talcott Parsons (New York: Free Press, 1947).

8. Herbert A. Simon, *Administrative Behavior,* 2nd ed. (New York: Macmillan, 1957).

9. Robert K. Merton, "Bureaucratic Structure and Personality," in *Social Theory and Social Structure,* rev. ed., ed. Robert K. Merton (New York: Free Press, 1957).

10. Fritz L. Roethlisberger, & W. J. Dickson, *Management and the Worker* (Cambridge, Mass.: Harvard University Press, 1939).

11. Chester I. Barnard, *The Functions of the Executive* (Cambridge, Mass.: Harvard University Press, 1938).

12. Philip Selznick, *TVA and the Grass Roots* (Berkeley, Calif.: University of California Press, 1949).

13. Burton R. Clark, *Adult Education in Transition* (Berkeley, Calif.: University of California Press, 1956).

14. Simon, *Administrative Behavior.* James G. March, & Herbert A. Simon, *Organizations* (New York: Wiley, 1958). Richard M. Cyert, & James G. March, *A Behavioral Theory of the Firm* (Englewood Cliffs, N.J.: Prentice-Hall, 1963).

15. Herbert A. Simon, *Models of Man, Social and Rational* (New York: Wiley, 1957).

16. *Ibid.*

17. Michel Crozier, *The Bureaucratic Phenomenon* (Chicago: The University of Chicago Press, 1964).

18. Talcott Parsons, *Structure and Process in Modern Societies* (New York: Free Press, 1960).

19. James D. Thompson, "Decision-making, the Firm, and the Market, in *New Perspectives in Organization Research,* eds., W. W. Cooper et al. (New York: Wiley, 1964).

20. Joan Woodward, *Industrial Organization: Theory and Practice* (London: Oxford University Press, 1965).

21. Robert W. Hawkes, "Physical Psychiatric Rehabilitation Models Compared," (Paper presented at the Ohio Valley Sociological Society, 1962).

22. The notions in this section rest especially on conversations some years ago with Frederick L. Bates. For a different but somewhat parallel analysis of work flows, see Robert Dubin, "Stability of Human Organizations," in *Modern Organization Theory,* ed. Mason Haire (New York: Wiley, 1959).

23. Weber, *Theory of Organization.* Merton, *Social Theory and Structure.*

24. Arthur L. Stinchcombe, "Bureaucratic and Craft Administration of Production: A Comparative Study," *Administrative Science Quarterly* 4 (September 1959): 168–187.

25. Sanford M. Dornbusch, "The Military Academy as an Assimilating Institution," *Social Forces* 33 (May 1955): 316–321.

26. Chris Argyris, *Organization of a Bank* (New Haven, Conn.: Labor and Management Center, Yale University, 1954).

27. Ivan Belknap, *The Human Problems of a State Mental Hospital* (New York: McGraw-Hill, 1956).

28. Peter M. Blau, *The Dynamics of Bureaucracy* (Chicago: The University of Chicago Press, 1955).

29. Richard L. Meier, "Communications Overload," *Administrative Science Quarterly* 7 (March 1963): 521–544.

29

General Systems Theory: Applications for Organization and Management

Fremont E. Kast and
James E. Rosenzweig

Biological and social scientists generally have embraced systems concepts. Many organization and management theorists seem anxious to identify with this movement and to contribute to the development of an approach which purports to offer the ultimate—the unification of all science into one grand conceptual model. Who possibly could resist? General systems theory seems to provide a relief from the limitations of more mechanistic approaches and a rationale for rejecting "principles" based on relatively "closed-system" thinking. This theory provides the paradigm for organization and management theorists to "crank into their systems model" all of the diverse knowledge from relevant underlying disciplines. It has become almost mandatory to have the word "system" in the title of recent articles and books (many of us have compromised and placed it only in the subtitle).[1]

But where did it all start? This question takes us back into history and brings to mind the longstanding philosophical arguments between mechanistic and organismic models of the 19th and early 20th centuries. As Deutsch says:

SOURCE: Fremont E. Kast and James E. Rosenzweig, "General Systems Theory: Applications for Organization and Management," *Academy of Management Journal* (December 1972): 447–465.

Both mechanistic and organismic models were based substantially on experiences and operations known before 1850. Since then, the experience of almost a century of scientific and technological progress has so far not been utilized for any significant new model for the study of organization and in particular of human thought [12, p. 389].

General systems theory even revives the specter of the "vitalists" and their views on "life force" and most certainly brings forth renewed questions of teleological or purposeful behavior of both living and nonliving systems. Phillips and others have suggested that the philosophical roots of general systems theory go back even further, at least to the German philosopher Hegel (1770–1831) [29, p. 56]. Thus, we should recognize that in the adoption of the systems approach for the study of organizations we are not dealing with newly discovered ideas—they have a rich genealogy.

Even in the field of organization and management theory, systems views are not new. Chester Barnard used a basic systems framework.

A cooperative system is a complex of physical, biological, personal, and social components which are in a specific systematic relationship by reason of the cooperation of two or more persons for at least one definite end. Such a system is evidently a subordinate unit of larger systems from one point of view; and itself embraces subsidiary systems—physical, biological, etc.—from another point of view. One of the systems comprised within a cooperative system, the one which is implicit in the phrase "cooperation of two or more persons," is called an "organization" [3, p. 65].

And Barnard was influenced by the "systems views" of Vilfredo Pareto and Talcott Parsons. Certainly this quote (dressed up a bit to give the term "system" more emphasis) could be the introduction to a 1972 book on organizations.

Miller points out that Alexander Bogdanov, the Russian philosopher, developed a theory of tektology or universal organization science in 1912 which foreshadowed general systems theory and used many of the same concepts as modern systems theorists [26, p. 249–250].

However, in spite of a long history of organismic and holistic thinking, the utilization of the systems approach did not become the accepted model for organization and management writers until relatively recently. It is difficult to specify the turning point exactly. The momentum of systems thinking was identified by Scott in 1961 when he described the relationship between general systems theory and organization theory.

The distinctive qualities of modern organization theory are its conceptual-analytical base, its reliance on empirical research data, and above all, its integrating nature. These qualities are framed in a philosophy which accepts the premise that the only meaningful way to study organization is to study it as a system. . . . Modern organization theory and general system theory are similar in that they look at organization as an integrated whole [33, pp. 15–21].

Scott said explicitly what many in our field had been thinking and/or implying—he helped us put into perspective the important writings of Herbert Simon, James March, Talcott Parsons, George Homans, E. Wight Bakke, Kenneth Boulding, and many others.

But how far have we really advanced over the past decade in applying general systems theory to organizations and their management? Is it still a "skeleton," or have we been able to "put some meat on the bones?" The systems approach has been touted because of its potential usefulness in understanding the complexities of "live" organizations. Has this approach really helped us in this endeavor or has it compounded confusion with chaos? Herbert Simon describes the challenge for the systems approach:

In both science and engineering, the study of "systems" is an increasingly popular activity. Its popularity is more a response to a pressing need for synthesizing and analyzing complexity than it is to any large development of a body of knowledge and technique for dealing with complexity. If this popularity is to be more than a fad, necessity will have to mother invention and provide substance to go with the name [35, p. 114].

In this article we will explore the issue of whether we are providing substance for the term *systems approach* as it relates to the study of organizations and their management. There are many interesting historical and philosophical questions concerning the relationship between the mechanistic and organistic approaches and their applicability to the various fields of science, as well as other interesting digressions into the evolution of systems approaches. However, we will resist those temptations and plunge directly into a discussion of the key concepts of general systems theory, the way in which these ideas have been used by organization theorists, the limitations in their application, and some suggestions for the future.

Key Concepts of General Systems Theory

The key concepts of general systems theory have been set forth by many writers [6, 7, 13, 17, 25, 28, 39] and have been used by many organization and management theorists [10, 14, 18, 19, 22, 23, 24, 32]. It is not our purpose here to elaborate on them in great detail because we anticipate that most readers will have been exposed to them in some depth. Figure 1 provides a very brief review of those characteristics of systems which seem to have wide acceptance. The review is far from complete. It is difficult to identify a "complete" list of characteristics derived from general systems theory; moreover, it is merely a first-order classification. There are many derived second- and third-order characteristics which could be considered. For example, James G. Miller sets forth *165*

Subsystems or Components: A system by definition is composed of interrelated parts or elements. This is true for all systems—mechanical, biological, and social. Every system has at least two elements, and these elements are interconnected.

Holism, Synergism, Organicism, and Gestalt: The whole is not just the sum of the parts; the system itself can be explained only as a totality. Holism is the opposite of elementarism, which views the total as the sum of its individual parts.

Open Systems View: Systems can be considered in two ways: (1) closed or (2) open. Open systems exchange information, energy, or material with their environments. Biological and social systems are inherently open systems; mechanical systems may be open or closed. The concepts of open and closed systems are difficult to defend in the absolute. We prefer to think of open-closed as a dimension; that is, systems are relatively open or relatively closed.

Input-Transformation-Output Model: The open system can be viewed as a transformation model. In a dynamic relationship with its environment, it receives various inputs, transforms these inputs in some way, and exports outputs.

System Boundaries: It follows that systems have boundaries which separate them from their environments. The concept of boundaries helps us understand the distinction between open and closed systems. The relatively closed system has rigid, impenetrable boundaries; whereas the open system has permeable boundaries between itself and a broader suprasystem. Boundaries are relatively easily defined in physical and biological systems, but are very difficult to delineate in social systems, such as organizations.

Negative Entropy: Closed, physical systems are subject to the force of entropy which increases until eventually the entire system fails. The tendency toward maximum entropy is a movement to disorder, complete lack of resource transformation, and death. In a closed system, the change in entropy must always be positive; however, in open biological or social systems, entropy can be arrested and may even be transformed into negative entropy—a process of more complete organization and ability to transform resources—because the system imports resources from its environment.

Steady State, Dynamic Equilibrium, and Homeostasis: The concept of steady state is closely related to that of negative entropy. A closed system eventually must attain an equilibrium state with maximum entropy—death or disorganization. However, an open system may attain a state where the system remains in dynamic equilibrium through the continuous inflow of materials, energy, and information.

Feedback: The concept of feedback is important in understanding how a system maintains a steady state. Information concerning the outputs or the process of the system is fed back as an input into the system, perhaps leading to changes in the transformation process and/or future outputs. Feedback can be both positive and negative, although the field of cybernetics is based on negative feedback. Negative feedback is informational input which indicates that the system is deviating from a prescribed course and should readjust to a new steady state.

Hierarchy: A basic concept in systems thinking is that of hierarchical relationships between systems. A system is composed of subsystems of a lower order and is also part of a suprasystem. Thus, there is a hierarchy of the components of the system.

Internal Elaboration: Closed systems move toward entropy and disorganization. In contrast, open systems appear to move in the direction of greater differentiation, elaboration, and a higher level of organization.

Multiple Goal-Seeking: Biological and social systems appear to have multiple goals or purposes. Social organizations seek multiple goals, if for no other reason than that they are composed of individuals and subunits with different values and objectives.

(continued)

Equifinality of Open Systems: In mechanistic systems there is a direct cause and effect relationship between the initial conditions and the final state. Biological and social systems operate differently. Equifinality suggests that certain results may be achieved with different intial conditions and in different ways. This view suggests that social organizations can accomplish their objectives with diverse inputs and with varying internal activities (conversion processes).

Figure 1
Key concepts of general systems theory

hypotheses, stemming from open systems theory, which might be applicable to two or more levels of systems [25]. He suggests that they are *general* systems theoretical hypotheses and qualifies them by suggesting that they are propositions applicable to general systems *behavior* theory and would thus exclude non-living systems. He does not limit these propositions to individual organisms, but considers them appropriate for social systems as well. His hypotheses are related to such issues as structure, process, subsystems, information, growth, and integration. It is obviously impossible to discuss all of these hypotheses; we want only to indicate the extent to which many interesting propositions are being posed which might have relevance to many different types of systems. It will be a very long time (if ever) before most of these hypotheses are validated; however, we are surprised at how many of them can be agreed with intuitively, and we can see their possible verification in studies of social organizations.

We turn now to a closer look at how successful or unsuccessful we have been in utilizing these concepts in the development of "modern organization theory."

A Beginning: Enthusiastic but Incomplete

We have embraced general systems theory but, really, how completely? We could review a vast literature in modern organization theory which has explicitly or implicitly adopted systems theory as a frame of reference, and we have investigated in detail a few representative examples of the literature in assessing the "state of the art" [18, 19, 22, 23, 31, 38]. It was found that most of these books professed to utilize general systems theory. Indeed, in the first few chapters, many of them did an excellent job of presenting basic systems concepts and showing their relationship to organizations; however, when they moved further into the discussion of more specific subject matter, they departed substantially from systems theory. The studies appear to use a "partial systems approach" and leave for the reader the problem of integrating the various ideas into a systemic whole. It also appears that many of the authors are unable, because of limitations of knowledge about subsystem relationships, to carry out the task of using general systems theory as a conceptual basis for organization theory.

Furthermore, it is evident that each author had many "good ideas" stemming from the existing body of knowledge or current research on organizations which did not fit neatly into a "systems model." For example, they might discuss leadership from a relatively closed-system point of view and not consider it in relation to organizational technology, structure, or other variables. Out review of the literature suggests that much remains to be done in applying general systems theory to organization theory and management practice.

Some Dilemmas in Applying GST to Organizations

Why have writers embracing general systems theory as a basis for studying organizations had so much difficulty in following through? Part of this difficulty may stem from the newness of the paradigm and our inability to operationalize "all we think we know" about this approach. Or it may be because we know too little about the systems under investigation. Both of these possibilities will be covered later, but first we need to look at some of the more specific conceptual problems.

Organizations as Organisms

One of the basic contributions of general systems theory was the rejection of the traditional closed-system or mechanistic view of social organizations. But, did general systems theory free us from this constraint only to impose another, less obvious one? General systems theory grew out of the organismic views of von Bertalanffy and other biologists; thus, many of the characteristics are relevant to the living organism. It is conceptually easy to draw the analogy between living organisms and social organizations. "There is, after all, an intuitive similarity between the organization of the human body and the kinds of organizations men create. And so, undaunted by the failures of the human-social analogy through time, new theorists try afresh in each epoch" [2, p. 660]. General systems theory would have us accept this analogy between organism and social organization. Yet, we have a hard time swallowing it whole. Katz and Kahn warn us of the danger:

There has been no more pervasive, persistent, and futile fallacy handicapping the social sciences than the use of the physical model for the understanding of social structures. The biological metaphor, with its crude comparisons of the physical parts of the body to the parts of the social system, has been replaced by more subtle but equally misleading analogies between biological and social functioning. This figurative type of thinking ignores the essential difference between the socially contrived nature of social systems and the physical structure of the machine or the human organism. So long as writers are committed to a theoretical

framework based upon the physical model, they will miss the essential social-psychological facts of the highly variable, loosely articulated character of social systems [19, p. 31].

In spite of this warning, Katz and Kahn do embrace much of the general systems theory concepts which are based on the biological metaphor. We must be very cautious about trying to make this analogy too literal. We agree with Silverman who says, "It may, therefore, be necessary to drop the analogy between an organization and an organism: organizations may be systems but not necessarily *natural* systems" [34, p. 31].

Distinction between Organization and an Organization

General systems theory emphasizes that systems are organized—they are composed of interdependent components in some relationship. The social organization would then follow logically as just another system. But, we are perhaps being caught in circular thinking. It is true that all systems (physical, biological, and social) are by definition organized, but are all systems organizations? Rapoport and Horvath distinguish "organization theory" and "the theory of organizations" as follows:

We see organization theory as dealing with general and abstract organizational principles; it applies to any system exhibiting organized complexity. As such, organization theory is seen as an extension of mathematical physics or, even more generally, of mathematics designed to deal with organized systems. The theory of organizations, on the other hand, purports to be a social science. It puts real human organizations at the center of interest. It may study the social structure of organizations and so can be viewed as a branch of sociology; it can study the behavior of individuals or groups as members of organizations and can be viewed as a part of social psychology; it can study power relations and principles of control in organizations and so fits into political science [30, pp. 74–75].

Why make an issue of this distinction? It seems to use that there is a vital matter involved. All systems may be considered to be organized, and more advanced systems may display differentiation in the activities of component parts—such as the specialization of human organs. However, all systems *do not* have purposeful entities. Can the heart or lungs be considered as purposeful entities in themselves or are they only components of the larger purposeful system, the human body? By contrast, the social organization is composed of two or more purposeful elements. "An organization consists of elements that have and can exercise their own wills" [1, p. 669]. Organisms, the foundation stone of general systems theory, do not contain purposeful elements which exercise their own will. This distinction between the organism and the social organization is of importance. In much of general systems theory, the concern is primarily with the way in which the *organism* responds to environmentally generated inputs. Feedback concepts and the maintenance of a steady state are based on internal adaptations to environmental forces. (This is particularly true of cybernetic models.) But, what about those changes and adaptations which occur from *within* social organizations? Purposeful elements within the social organization may initiate activities and adaptations which are difficult to subsume under feedback and steady state concepts.

Open and Closed Systems

Another dilemma stemming from general systems theory is the tendency to dichotomize all systems as opened or closed. We have been led to think of physical systems as closed, subject to the laws of entropy, and to think of biological systems as open to their environment and, possibly, becoming negentropic. But applying this strict polarization to social organizations creates many difficulties. In fact, most social organizations and their subsystems are "partially open" and "partially closed." Open and closed are a matter of degree. Unfortunately, there seems to be a widely held view (often more implicit than explicit) that *open-system thinking is good and closed-system thinking is bad.* We have not become sufficiently sophisticated to recognize that both are appropriate under cerain conditions. For example, one of the most useful conceptualizations set forth by Thompson is that the social organization *must seek* to use closed-system concepts (particularly at the technical core) to reduce uncertainty and to create more effective performance at this level.

Still Subsystems Thinking

Even though we preach a general systems approach, we often practice subsystems thinking. Each of the academic disciplines and each of us personally have limited perspective of the system we are studying. While proclaiming a broad systems viewpoint, we often dismiss variables outside our interest or competence as being irrelevant, and we only open our system to those inputs which we can handle with our disciplinary bag of tools. We are hampered because each of the academic disciplines has taken a narrow "partial systems view" and find comfort in the relative certainty which this creates. Of course, this is not a problem unique to modern organization theory. Under the more traditional process approach to the study of management, we were able to do an admirable job of delineating and discussing planning, organizing, and controlling as separate activities. We were much less successful in discussing them as integrated and interrelated activities.

How Does Our Knowledge Fit?

One of the major problems in utilizing general systems theory is that we know (or think we know) more about certain relationships than we can fit into a general systems model. For example, we are beginning to understand the two-variable relationship between technology and structure. But, when we introduce another variable, say psychosocial relationships, our models become too complex. Consequently, in order to discuss all the things we know about organizations, we depart from a systems approach. Perhaps it is because we know a great deal more about the elements or subsystems of an organization than we do about the interrelationships and interactions between these subsystems. And, general systems theory forces us to consider those relationships about which we know the least—a true dilemma. So we continue to elaborate on those aspects of the organization which we know best—a partial systems view.

Failure to Delineate a Specific System

When the social sciences embraced general systems theory, the total system became the focus of attention and terminology tended toward vagueness. In the utilization of systems theory, we should be more precise in delineating the specific system under consideration. Failure to do this leads to much confusion. As Murray suggests:

> I am wary of the word "system" because social scientists use it very frequently without specifying which of several possible different denotations they have in mind; but more particularly because, today, "system" is a highly cathected term, loaded with prestige; hence, we are all strongly tempted to employ it even when we have nothing definite in mind and its only service is to indicate that we subscribe to the general premise respecting the interdependence of things—basic to organismic theory, holism, field theory, interactionism, transactionism, etc. . . .
> When definitions of the units of a system are lacking, the term stands for no more than an article of faith, and is misleading to boot, insofar as it suggests a condition of affairs that may not actually exist [27, pp. 50–51].

We need to be much more precise in delineating both the boundaries of the system under consideration and the level of our analysis. There is a tendency for current writers in organization theory to accept general systems theory and then to move indiscriminately across systems boundaries and between levels of systems without being very precise (and letting their readers in on what is occurring). James Miller suggests the need for clear delineation of levels in applying systems theory, "It is important to follow one procedural rule in systems

theory in order to avoid confusion. Every discussion should begin with an identification of the level of reference, and the discourse should not change to another level without a specific statement that this is occurring" [25, p. 216]. Our field is replete with these confusions about systems levels. For example, when we use the term *organizational behavior* are we talking about the way the organization behaves as a system or are we talking about the behavior of the individual participants? By goals, do we mean the goals of the organization or the goals of the individuals within the organization? In using systems theory we must become more precise in our delineation of systems boundaries and systems levels if we are to prevent confusing conceptual ambiguity.

Recognition That Organizations Are "Contrived Systems"

We have a vague uneasiness that general systems theory truly does not recognize the "contrived" nature of social organizations. With its predominate emphasis on natural organisms, it may understate some characteristics which are vital for the social organization. Social organizations do not occur naturally in nature; they are contrived by man. They have structure; but it is the structure of events rather than of physical components, and it cannot be separated from the processes of the system. The fact that social organizations are contrived by human beings suggests that they can be established for an infinite variety of purposes and do not follow the same life-cycle patterns of birth, growth, maturity, and death as biological systems. As Katz and Kahn say:

> Social structures are essentially contrived systems. They are made of men and are imperfect systems. They can come apart at the seams overnight, but they can also outlast by centuries the biological organisms which originally created them. The cement which holds them together is essentially psychological rather than biological. Social systems are anchored in the attitudes, perceptions, beliefs, motivations, habits, and expectations of human beings [19, p. 33].

Recognizing that the social organization is contrived again cautions us against making an exact analogy between it and physical or biological systems.

Questions of Systems Effectiveness

General systems theory with its biological orientation would appear to have an evolutionary view of system effectiveness. That living system which best adapts to its environment prospers and survives. The primary measure of effectiveness is perpetuation of the organism's species. Teleological behavior is therefore directed toward survival. But, is survival the only criterion of effectiveness of the social system? It is probably an essential but not all-inclusive measure of effectiveness.

General systems theory emphasizes the organism's survival goal and does not fully relate to the question of the effectiveness of the system in its suprasystem—the environment. Parsonian functional-structural views provide a contrast. "The *raison d'etre* of complex organizations, according to this analysis, is mainly to benefit the society in which they belong, and that society is, therefore, the appropriate frame of reference for the evaluation of organizational effectiveness" [41, p. 896].

But, this view seems to go to the opposite extreme from the survival view of general systems theory—the organization exists to serve the society. It seems to us that the truth lies somewhere between these two viewpoints. And it is likely that a systems viewpoint (modified from the species survival view of general systems theory) will be most appropriate. Yuchtman and Seashore suggest:

> The organization's success over a period of time in this competition for resources—i.e., its bargaining position in a given environment—is regarded as an expression of its overall effectiveness. Since the resources are of various kinds, and the competitive relationships are multiple, and since there is interchangeability among classes of resources, the assessment of organizational effectiveness must be in terms not of any single criterion but of an open-ended multidimensional set of criteria [41, p. 891].

This viewpoint suggests that questions of organizational effectiveness must be concerned with at least three levels of analysis. The level of the environment, the level of the social organization as a system, and the level of the subsystems (human participants) within the organization. Perhaps much of our confusion and ambiguity concerning organizational effectiveness stems from our failure to clearly delineate the level of our analysis and, even more important, our failure really to understand the relationships among these levels.

Our discussion of some of the problems associated with the application of general systems theory to the study of social organizations might suggest that we completely reject the appropriateness of this model. On the contrary, we see the systems approach as the new paradigm for the study of organizations; but, like all new concepts in the sciences, one which has to be applied, modified, and elaborated to make it as useful as possible.

Systems Theory Provides the New Paradigm

We hope the discussion of GST and organizations provides a realistic appraisal. We do not want to promote the value of the systems approach as a matter of faith; however, we do see systems theory as vital to the study of social organizations and as providing the major new paradigm for our field of study.

Thomas Kuhn provides an interesting interpretation of the nature of scientific revolution [20]. He suggests that major changes in all fields of science occur with the development of new conceptual schemes of "paradigms." These new paradigms do not just represent a step-by-step advancement in "normal" science (the science generally accepted and practiced) but, rather, a revolutionary change in the way the scientific field is perceived by the practitioners. Kuhn says:

The historian of science may be tempted to exclaim that when paradigms change, the world itself changes with them. Led by a new paradigm, scientists adopt new instruments and look in new places. Even more important, during revolutions scientists see new and different things when looking with familiar instruments in places they have looked before. It is rather as if the professional community has been suddenly transported to another planet where familiar objects are seen in a different light and are joined by unfamiliar ones as well. . . . Paradigm changes do cause scientists to see the world of their research-engagement differently. Insofar as their only recourse to that world is through what they see and do, we may want to say that after a revolution scientists are responding to a different world [20, p. 110].

New paradigms frequently are rejected by the scientific community. (At first they may seem crude and limited—offering very little more than older paradigms.) They frequently lack the apparent sophistication of the older paradigms which they ultimately replace. They do not display the clarity and certainty of older paradigms which have been refined through years of research and writing. But, a new paradigm does provide for a "new start" and opens up new directions which were not possible under the old. "We must recognize how very limited in both scope and precision a paradigm can be at the time of its first appearance. Paradigms gain their status because they are more successful than their competitors in solving a few problems that the group of practitioners has come to recognize as acute. To be more successful is not, however, to be either completely successful with a single problem or notably successful with any large number" [20, p.23].

Systems theory does provide a new paradigm for the study of social organizations and their management. At this stage it is obviously crude and lacking in precision. In some ways it may not be much better than older paradigms which have been accepted and used for a long time (such as the management process approach). As in other fields of scientific endeavor, the new paradigm must be applied, clarified, elaborated, and made more precise. But, it does provide a fundamentally different view of the reality of social organizations and can serve as the basis for major advancements in our field.

We see many exciting examples of the utilization of the new systems paradigm in the field of organization and management. Several of these have been referred to earlier [7, 13, 19, 22, 23, 24, 31, 38], and there have been many others. Burns and Stalker made substantial use of systems views in setting forth their concepts of mechanistic and organic managerial systems [8]. Their studies of the characteristics of these two organization types lack precise definition to the variables and relationships, but their colleagues have used the systems approach to look at the relationship of organizations to their environment and also among the technical, structural, and behavioral characteristics within the organization [24]. Chamberlain used a system view in studying enterprises and their environment, which is substantially different from traditional microeconomics [9]. The emerging field of "environmental sciences" and "environmental administration" has found the systems paradigm vital.

Thus, the systems theory paradigm is being used extensively in the investigation of relationships between subsystems within organizations and in studying the environmental interfaces. But, it still has not advanced sufficiently to meet the needs. One of the major problems is that the practical need to deal with comprehensive systems of relationships is over-running our ability to fully understand and predict these relationships. *We vitally need the systems paradigm but we are not sufficiently sophisticated to use it appropriately.* This is the dilemma. Do our current failures to fully utilize the systems paradigm suggest that we reject it and return to the older, more traditional, and time-tested paradigms? Or do we work with systems theory to make it more precise, to understand the relationships among subsystems, and to gather the informational inputs which are necessary to make the systems approach really work? We think the latter course offers the best opportunity.

Thus, we prefer to accept current limitations of systems theory, while working to reduce them and to develop more complete and sophisticated approaches for its application. We agree with Rapoport who says:

> The system approach to the study of man can be appreciated as an effort to restore meaning (in terms of intuitively grasped understanding of wholes) while adhering to the principles of *disciplined* generalizations and rigorous deduction. It is, in short, an attempt to make the study of man both scientific and meaningful [7, p. xxii].

We are sympathetic with the second part of Rapoport's comment, the need to apply the systems approach but to make disciplined generalizations and rigorous deductions. This is a vital necessity and yet a major current limitation. We do have some indication that progress (although very slow) is being made.

What Do We Need Now?

Everything is related to everything else—but how? General systems theory provides us with the macro paradigm for the study of social organizations. As Scott and others have pointed out, most sciences go through a macro-micro-macro cycle or sequence of emphasis [33]. Traditional bureaucratic theory provided the first major macro view of organizations. Administrative management theorists concentrated on the development of macro "principles of management" which were applicable to all organizations. When these macro views seemed incomplete (unable to explain important phenomena), attention turned to the micro level—more detailed analysis of components or parts of the organization, thus the interest in human relations, technology, or structural dimensions.

The systems approach returns us to the macro level with a new paradigm. General systems theory emphasizes a very high level of abstraction. Phillips classifies it as a third-order study [29] that attempts to develop macro concepts appropriate for all types of biological, physical, and social systems.

In our view, we are now ready to move down a level of abstraction to consider second-order systems studies or mid-range concepts. These will be based on general systems theory but will be more concrete and will emphasize more specific characteristics and relationships in social organizations. They will operate within the broad paradigm of systems theory but at a less abstract level.

What should we call this new mid-range level of analysis? Various authors have referred to it as a "contingency view," a study of "patterns of relationships," or a search for "configurations among subsystems." Lorsch and Lawrence reflect this view:

> During the past few years there has been evident a new trend in the study of organizational phenomena. Underlying this new approach is the idea that the internal functioning of organizations must be consistent with the demands of the organization task, technology, or external evninment, and the needs of its members if organization is to be effective. Rather than searching for the panacea of the one best way to organize under all conditions, investigators have more and more tended to examine the functioning of organizations in relation to the needs of their particular members and the external pressures facing them. Basically, this approach seems to be leading to the development of a "contingency" theory of organization with the appropriate internal states and processes of the organization contingent upon external requirements and member needs [21, p. 1].

Numerous others have stressed a similar viewpoint. Thompson suggests that the essence of administration lies in understanding basic configurations which exist between the various subsystems and with the environment. "The basic function of administration appears to be co-alignment, not merely of people (in coalitions) but of institutionalized action—of technology and task environment into a viable domain, and of organizational design and structure appropriate to it [38, p. 157].

Bringing these ideas together we can provide a more precise definition of the contingency view:

> The contingency view of organizations and their management suggests that an organization is a system composed of subsystems and delineated by identifiable boundaries from its environmental suprasystem. The contingency view seeks to understand the interrelationships within and among subsystems as well as between the organization and its environment and to define patterns of relationships or configurations of variables. It emphasizes the multivariate nature of organizations and attempts to understand how organizations operate under varying conditions and in specific circumstances. Contingency views are ultimately directed toward suggesting organizational designs and managerial systems most appropriate for specific situations.

But, it is not enough to suggest that a "contingency view" based on systems concepts of organizations and their management is more appropriate than the simplistic "principles approach." If organization theory is to advance and make contributions to managerial practice, it must define more explicitly certain patterns of relationships between organizational variables. This is the major challenge facing our field.

Just how do we go about using systems theory to develop these midrange or contingency views. We see no alternative but to engage in intensive comparative investigation of many organizations following the advice of Blau:

> A theory of organization, whatever its specific nature, and regardless of how subtle the organizational processes it takes into account, has as its central aim to establish the constellations of characteristics that develop in organizations of various kinds. Comparative studies of many organizations are necessary, not alone to test the hypotheses implied by

such a theory, but also to provide a basis for initial exploration and refinement of the theory by indicating the conditions on which relationships, originally assumed to hold universally are contingent. . . . Systematic research on many organizations that provides the data needed to determine the interrelationships between several organizational features is, however, extremely rare [5, p. 332].

Various conceptual designs for the comparative study of organizations and their subsystems are emerging to help in the development of a contingency view. We do not want to impose our model as to what should be considered in looking for these patterns of relationships. However, the tentative matrix shown in Figure 2 suggests this approach. We have used as a starting point the two polar organization types which have been emphasized in the literature—closed/stable-mechanistic and open/adaptive/organic.

We will consider the environmental suprasystem and organizational subsystems (goals and values, technical, structural, psychosocial, and managerial) plus various dimensions or characteristics of each of these systems. By way of illustration we have indicated several specific subcategories under the Environmental Suprasystem as well as the Goals and Values subsystem. This process would have to be completed and extended to all of the subsystems. The next step would be the development of appropriate descriptive language (based on research and conceptualization) for each relevant characteristic across the continuum of organization types. For example, on the "stability" dimension for Goals and Values we would have High, Medium, and Low at appropriate places on the continuum. If the entire matrix were filled in, it is likely that we would begin to see discernible patterns of relationships among subsystems.

We do not expect this matrix to provide *the* midrange model for every one. It is highly doubtful that we will be able to follow through with the field work investigations necessary to fill in all the squares. Nevertheless, it does illustrate a possible approach for the translation

Figure 2

Matrix of patterns of relationships between organization types and systems variables

Organizational Supra- and Subsystems	Continuum of Organization Types	
	Closed/Stable/Mechanistic	*Open/Adaptive/Organic*
Environmental relationships		
General nature	Placid	Turbulent
Predictability	Certain, determinate	Uncertain, Indeterminate
Boundary relationships	Relatively closed; limited to few participants (sales, purchasing, etc.); fixed and well-defined	Relatively open; many participants have external relationships; varied and not clearly defined
Goals and values		
Organizational goals in general	Efficient performance, stability, maintenance	Effective problem-solving, innovation, growth
Goal set	Single, clear-cut	Multiple, determined by necessity to satisfy a set of constraints
Stability	Stable	Unstable
Technical		
Structural		
Psychosocial		
Managerial		

of more abstract general systems theory into an appropriate midrange model which is relevant for organization theory and management practice. Frankly, we see this as a major long-term effort on the part of many researchers, investigating a wide variety of organizations. In spite of the difficulties involved in such research, the endeavor has practical significance. Sophistication in the study of organizations will come when we have a more complete understanding of organizations as total systems (configurations of subsystems) so that we can prescribe more appropriate organizational designs and managerial systems. Ultimately, organization theory should serve as the foundation for more effective management practice.

Application of Systems Concepts to Management Practice

The study of organizations is an applied science because the resulting knowledge is relevant to problem-solving in on-going institutions. Contributions to organization theory come from many sources. Deductive and inductive research in a variety of disciplines provide a theoretical base of propositions which are useful for understanding organizations and for managing them. Experience gained in management practice is also an important input to organization theory. In short, management is based on the body of knowledge generated by practical experience *and* eclectic scientific research concerning organizations. The body of knowledge developed through theory and research should be translatable into more effective organizational design and managerial practices.

Do systems concepts and contingency views provide a panacea for solving problems in organizations? The answer is an emphatic *no;* this approach does not provide "ten easy steps" to success in management. Such cookbook approaches, while seemingly applicable and easy to grasp, are usually shortsighted, narrow in perspective, and superficial—in short, unrealistic. Fundamental ideas, such as systems concepts and contingency views, are more difficult to comprehend. However, they facilitate more thorough understanding of complex situations and increase the likelihood of appropriate action.

It is important to recognize that many managers have used and will continue to use a systems approach and contingency views intuitively and implicitly. Without much knowledge of the underlying body of organization theory, they have an intuitive "sense of the situation," are flexible diagnosticians, and adjust their actions and decisions accordingly. Thus, systems concepts and contingency views are not new. However, if this approach to organization theory and management practice can be made more explicit, we can facilitate better management and more effective organizations.

Practicing managers in business firms, hospitals, and government agencies continue to function on a day-to-day basis. Therefore, they must use whatever theory is available, they cannot wait for the *ultimate* body of knowledge (there is none!). Practitioners should be included in the search for new knowledge because they control access to an essential ingredient—organizational data—and they are the ones who ultimately put the theory to the test. Mutual understanding among managers, teachers, and researchers will facilitate the development of a relevant body of knowledge.

Simultaneously with the refinement of the body of knowledge, a concerted effort should be directed toward applying what we do know. We need ways of making systems and contingency views more usable. Without oversimplification, we need some relevant guidelines for practicing managers.

The general tenor of the contingency view is somewhere between simplistic, specific principles and complex, vague notions. It is a midrange concept which recognizes the complexity involved in managing modern organizations but uses patterns of relationships and/or configurations of subsystems in order to facilitate improved practice. The art of management depends on a reasonable success rate for actions in a probabilistic environment. Our hope is that systems concepts and contingency views, while continually being refined by scientists/researchers/theorists, will also be made more applicable.

Note

1. An entire article could be devoted to a discussion of ingenious ways in which the term "systems approach" has been used in the literature pertinent to organization theory and management practice.

References

1. ACKOFF, RUSELL L., "Towards a System of Systems Concepts," *Management Science* (July 1971).
2. BACK, KURT W., "Biological Models of Social Change," *American Sociological Review* (August 1971).
3. BARNARD, CHESTER I., *The Functions of the Executive* (Cambridge, Mass.: Harvard University Press, 1938).
4. BERRIEN, F. KENNETH, *General and Social Systems* (New Brunswick, NJ: Rutgers University Press, 1968).
5. BLAU, PETER M., "The Comparative Study of Organizations," *Industrial and Labor Relations Review* (April 1965).
6. BOULDING, KENNETH E., "General Systems Theory: The Skeleton of Science," *Management Science* (April 1956).
7. BUCKLEY, WALTER, ed., *Modern Systems Research for the Behavioral Scientist* (Chicago: Aldine, 1968).
8. BURNS, TOM, & G. M. STALKER, *The Management of Innovation* (London: Tavistock Publications, 1961).
9. CHAMBERLAIN, NEIL W., *Enterprise and Environment: The Firm in Time and Place* (New York: McGraw-Hill, 1968).
10. CHURCHMAN, C. WEST, *The Systems Approach* (New York: Dell, 1968).
11. DeGREENE, KENYON, ed., *Systems Psychology* (New York: McGraw-Hill, 1970).
12. DEUTSCH, KARL W., "Toward a Cybernetic Model of Man and Society," in Walter Buckley,

ed., *Modern Systems Research for the Behavioral Scientist* (Chicago: Aldine, 1968).

13. EASTON, DAVID, *A Systems Analysis of Political Life* (New York: Wiley, 1965).

14. EMERY, F. E., & E. L. TRIST, "Sociotechnical Systems," in C. West Churchman and Michele Verhulst, eds., *Management Sciences: Models and Techniques* (New York: Pergamon Press, 1960).

15. EMSHOFF, JAMES R., *Analysis of Behavioral Systems* (New York: Macmillan, 1971).

16. GROSS, BERTRAM M., "The Coming General Systems Models of Social Systems," *Human Relations* (November 1967).

17. HALL, A. D., & R. E. EAGEN, "Definition of System," *General Systems, Yearbook for the Society for the Advancement of General Systems Theory*, Vol. 1 (1956).

18. KAST, FREMONT E., & JAMES E. ROSENZWEIG, *Organization and Management Theory: A Systems Approach* (New York: McGraw-Hill, 1970).

19. KATZ, DANIEL, & ROBERT L. KAHN, *The Social Psychology of Organizations* (New York: Wiley, 1966).

20. KUHN, THOMAS S., *The Structure of Scientific Revolutions* (Chicago: University of Chicago Press, 1962).

21. LORSCH, JAY W., & PAUL R. LAWRENCE, *Studies in Organizational Design* (Homewood, IL: Irwin-Dorsey, 1970).

22. LITTERER, JOSEPH A., *Organizations: Structure and Behavior*, Vol. 1 (New York: Wiley, 1969).

23. ———, *Organizations: Systems, Control and Adaptation*, Vol. 2 (New York: Wiley, 1969).

24. MILLER, E. J., & A. K. RICE, *Systems of Organizations* (London: Tavistock Publications, 1967).

25. MILLER, JAMES G., "Living Systems: Basic Concepts," *Behavioral Science* (July 1965).

26. MILLER, ROBERT F., "The New Science of Administration in the USSR," *Administrative Science Quarterly* (September 1971).

27. MURRAY, HENRY A., "Preparation for the Scaffold of a Comprehensive System," in Sigmund Koch, ed., *Psychology: A Study of a Science*, Vol. 3 (New York: McGraw-Hill, 1959).

28. PARSONS, TALCOTT, *The Social System* (New York: Free Press, 1951).

29. PHILLIPS, D. C., "Systems Theory—A Discredited Philosophy," in Peter P. Schoderbek, *Management Systems* (New York: Wiley, 1971).

30. RAPOPORT, ANATOL, & WILLIAM J. HORVATH, "Thoughts on Organization Theory," in Walter Buckley, ed., *Modern Systems Research for the Behavioral Scientist* (Chicago: Aldine, 1968).

31. RICE, A. K., *The Modern University* (London: Tavistock Publications, 1970).

32. SCHEIN, EDGAR, *Organizational Psychology*, rev. ed. (Englewood Cliffs, NJ: Prentice-Hall, 1970).

33. SCOTT, WILLIAM G., "Organization Theory: An Overview and an Appraisal," *Academy of Management Journal* (April 1961).

34. SILVERMAN, DAVID, *The Theory of Organizations* (New York: Basic Books, 1971).

35. SIMON, HERBERT A., "The Architecture of Complexity," in Joseph A. Litterer, *Organizations: Systems, Control and Adaptation*, Vol. 2 (New York: Wiley, 1969).

36. SPRINGER, MICHAEL, "Social Indicators, Reports, and Accounts: Toward the Management of Society," *The Annals of the American Academy of Political and Social Science* (March 1970).

37. TERREBERRY, SHIRLEY, "The Evolution of Organizational Environments," *Administrative Science Quarterly* (March 1968).

38. THOMPSON, JAMES D., *Organizations in Action* (New York: McGraw-Hill, 1967).

39. VON BERTALANFFY, LUDWIG, *General System Theory* (New York: George Braziller, 1968).

40. ———, The Theory of Open Systems in Physics and Biology," *Science* (January 13, 1950).

41. YUCHTMAN, EPHRAIM, & STANLEY E. SEASHORE, "A System Resource Approach to Organizational Effectiveness," *American Sociological Review* (December 1967).

30

Information Processing Model

Jay Galbraith

In this chapter the basic model is created and the overall structure of the framework is outlined. . . . The purpose is to conceive of organizations as information-processing networks and to explain why and through what mechanisms uncertainty and information relate to structure. In order to accomplish this explanation, the basic bureaucratic mechanical model is created. The value of the model is not that it describes reality but that it creates a basis from which various strategies are formed to adapt the bureaucratic structure for handling greater complexity.

Mechanistic Model

In order to develop the model and the design strategies, assume that we have a task which requires several thousand employees divided among many subtasks. For example, the task of designing and manufacturing an aircraft or space capsule requires a group to design the capsule, a group to design the manufacturing methods, a group to fabricate parts and components, a group to assemble the parts, and a group to test the completed unit. The result is a division of labor which involves considerable

SOURCE: Jay Galbraith, *Designing Complex Organizations,* © 1973, Addison-Wesley Publishing Company, Reading, Mass. Chapter 2, pp. 8–21. Reprinted with permission of the publisher.

interdependence and therefore coordination among the groups. The workflow is shown schematically in Figure 1.

In order to complete the task at a high level of performance, the activities that take place in the various groups must be coordinated. The behavior of the product design engineer must be consistent with the behavior of the process design engineers, etc. Although the behavior of several thousand people must be coordinated, it is impossible for all of them to communicate with each other. The organization is simply too large to permit face-to-face communication to be the mechanism for coordination. The organization design problem is to create mechanisms by which an integrated pattern of behavior can be obtained across all the interdependent groups. In order to see what these mechanisms are and the conditions under which they are appropriate, let us start with a very predictable task and slowly increase the degree of task uncertainty.

First we have a task, like the one represented in Figure 1 in which there is a high degree of division of labor, a high level of performance, and relatively large size. A good deal of information must be processed to coordinate the interdependent subtasks. As the degree of uncertainty increases, the amount of information processing during task execution increases. Organizations must evolve strategies to process the greater amount of information necessary to maintain the level of performance. Let us follow the history of a fictitious organization performing the task represented in Figure 1 and observe the mechanisms that are created to deal with increasing information loads caused by increasing task uncertainty.

Rules, Programs, Procedures

The simplest method of coordinating interdependent subtasks is to specify the necessary behaviors in advance of their execution in the form of rules or programs.[1] In order to make effective use of programs, the organization's

Concept

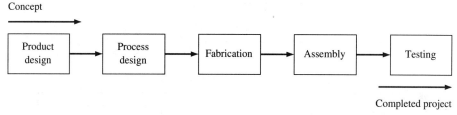

Completed project

Figure 1
Horizontal workflow across a functional division of labor

employees are taught the job-related situations with which they will be faced and the behaviors appropriate to those situations. Then as situations arise daily, the employees act out the behaviors appropriate to the situations. If everyone adopts the appropriate behavior, the resultant aggregate response is an integrated or coordinated pattern of behavior.

The primary virtue of rules is that they eliminate the need for further communication among the subunits. If an organization has hundreds of employees, they cannot all communicate with each other in order to guarantee coordinated action. To the extent that the job-related situations can be anticipated in advance and rules derived for them, integrated activity is guaranteed without communication. These rules and programs perform the same functions for organizations that habits perform for individuals. They eliminate the need for treating each situation as new. The amount of communication and decision making is reduced each time a situation is repeatedly encountered. In addition, rules provide a stability to the organization's operations. As people come and go through an organization, the rules provide a memory for handling routine situations.

The best example of a programmed task is the automobile assembly operation. Each employee learns a specific set of behaviors for each possible situation he will face, e.g., station wagon, convertible, deluxe sedan, standard sedan, etc. For assembly operations the programs and procedures are created by engineers. In other situations individuals simply program themselves.

That is, after confronting the same situation many times, individuals coordinate their behavior by following the same approach as in the past. Many standard operating procedures arise in this manner.

The use of rules and programs as coordination devices is limited, however. It is limited to those job-related situations which can be anticipated in advance and to which an appropriate response can be identified. As the organization faces new and different situations, the use of rules must be supplemented by other integrating devices.

Hierarchy

As the organization that depends on rules encounters situations it has not faced before, it has no ready-made response. When a response is developed for the new situation it must take into account all the subtasks that are affected. The information collection and problem solving activities may be substantial. To handle this task new roles are created, called managerial roles, and arranged in a hierarchy as shown in Figure 2.[2] The occupants of these roles handle the information collection and decision-making tasks necessitated by uncertainty.

Then as unanticipated events arise, the problem is referred to the manager who has the information to make a new decision. In addition, the hierarchy is also a hierarchy of authority and reward power, so that the decisions of the role occupants are effective determinants of the behavior of the task performers. In this manner the hierarchy of authority is employed on an

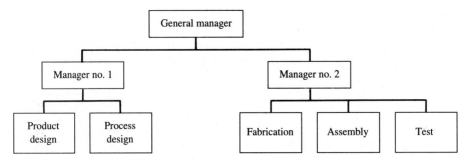

Figure 2
Hierarchical organization structure

exception basis. That is, the new situation, for which there is no preplanned response, is referred upward in the hierarchy to permit the creation of a new response. Since the process we are describing remains rather mechanical, the new situation is referred upward in the hierarchy to that point where a shared superior exists for all subunits affected by the new situation. For example, in Figure 2, if a problem arises during testing which requires product design work, it is referred to the general manager. If a situation arises affecting assembly and fabrication, it is referred to manager No. 2.

It is important to point out that the hierarchy is employed *in addition to, not instead of,* the use of rules. That is, the rules achieve coordination for the uniform and repetitive situations, whereas the new and unique situations are referred upward. This combination guarantees an integrated coordinated organizational response to the situations which the organization faces.

The weakness of hierarchical communication systems is that each link has a finite capacity for handling information. As the organization's subtasks increase in uncertainty, more exceptions arise which must be referred upward in the hierarchy. As more exceptions are referred upward, the hierarchy becomes overloaded. Serious delays develop between the upward transmission of information about new situations and a response to that information downward. In this situation, the organization must develop new processes to supplement rules and hierarchy.

Targeting or Goal Setting

As task uncertainty increases, the volume of information from the points of action to points of decision making overload the hierarchy. In this situation it becomes more efficient to bring the points of decision down to the points of action where the information originates. This can be accomplished by increasing the amount of discretion exercised by employees at lower levels of the organization. However, as the amount of discretion exercised at lower levels of the organization is increased, the organization faces a potential behavior control problem. That is, how can the organization be sure that the employees will consistently choose the appropriate response to the job-related situations which they will face?

In order to increase the probability that employees will select the appropriate behavior, organizations make two responses to deal with the behavior control problem.[3] The first change involves the substitution of craft or professional training of the work force for the detailed centralized programming of the work processes.[4] This is illustrated by a comparison between manufacturing industries and construction industries. In mass production, the work processes that are planned in advance are:

1. the location at which a particular task will be performed
2. the movement of tools, of materials and of workers to this work place and the

most efficient arrangement of these work-place characteristics

3. sometimes the particular movements to be performed in getting the task done
4. the schedules and time allotments for particular operations
5. inspection criteria for particular operations.

In construction all these characteristics of the work process are governed by the worker in accordance with the empirical lore that makes up craft principles.[5]

These two descriptions represent a shift from control based on supervision and surveillance to control based on selection of responsible workers. Workers who have the appropriate skills and attitudes are selected.

Professionalization by itself may not be sufficient to shift decision making to lower levels of the organization. The reason is that in the presence of interdependence, an alternative which is based on professional or craft standards may not be best for the whole organization. Thus alternatives which are preferred from a local or departmental perspective may not be preferred from a global perspective. The product design that is technically preferred may not be preferred by the customer, may be costly to produce, or may require a schedule which takes too long to complete. In order to deal with the problem, organizations undertake processes to set goals or targets to cover the primary interdependencies.

An example of the way goals are used can be demonstrated by considering the design group responsible for an aircraft wing structure. The group's interdependence with other design groups is handled by technical specifications elaborating the points of attachment of the wing to the body, forces transmitted at these points, centers of gravity, etc. The group also has a set of targets (not to be exceeded) for weight, design man-hours to be used, and a completion date. They are given minimum stress specifications below which they cannot design. The group then designs the structures and assemblies which combine to form the wing. They need not communicate with any other design group

on work related matters if they and the interdependent groups are able to operate within the planned targets.

Thus goal setting helps coordinate interdependent subtasks and still allows discretion at the local subtask level. Instead of specifying specific behaviors through rules and programs, the organization specifies targets to be achieved and allows the employees to select behaviors appropriate to the target.[6]

The ability of the design groups to operate within the planned targets, however, depends partly on the degree of task uncertainty. If the task is one that has been performed before, the estimates of man-hours, weight, due date, etc., will probably be realized. If it is a new design involving new materials, the estimates will probably be wrong. The targets will have to be set and reset throughout the design effort.

The violation of planned targets usually requires additional decision making and hence additional information processing. The additional information processing takes place through the hierarchy in the same way that rule exceptions were handled. Problems are handled on an exception basis. They are raised to higher levels of the hierarchy for resolution. The problem rises to the first level at which a shared superior exists for all affected subunits. A decision is made, and the new targets are communicated to the subunits. In this manner the behavior of the interdependent subunits remains integrated.

However, as the organization performs more uncertain tasks, such as designing and building a 747 jumbo jet, the hierarchical channels become overloaded once again. The organization does not have the information to estimate how many man-hours are needed to design the new titanium wings. How much weight will the wings require? Will it take 9 months, a year, or 18 months to complete the design? The information necessary to make these decisions can only be discovered during the actual design. The decisions must be made and remade each time new information is discovered. The volume of information processing can overwhelm an organization behaving in the mechanical fashion outlined in this chapter. The organization must adopt a strategy to either reduce the information necessary to coordinate its activities or increase its capacity to process more information. In the next section these strategies are identified and integrated into the framework. Subsequent chapters explain the strategies in detail.

Design Strategies

The ability of an organization to successfully coordinate its activities by goal setting, hierarchy, and rules depends on the combination of the frequency of exceptions and the capacity of the hierarchy to handle them. As task uncertainty increases, the number of exceptions increases until the hierarchy is overloaded. Then the organization must employ new design strategies. Either it can act in two ways to reduce the amount of information that is processed, or it can act in two ways to increase its capacity to handle more information. An organization may choose to develop in both of these ways. The two methods for reducing the need for information and the two methods for increasing processing capacity are shown schematically in Figure 3. The effect of all these actions is to reduce the number of exceptional cases referred upward into the organization through hierarchical channels.

Creation of Slack Resources

An organization can reduce the number of exceptions that occur by simply reducing the required level of performance. In the example of the wing design, the scheduled time, weight allowance, or man-hours could be increased. In each case more resources could be consumed. These additional resources are called slack resources.[7]

Slack resources are an additional cost to the organization or the customer. However, the longer the scheduled time available, the lower the likelihood of a target being missed. The fewer the exceptions, the less the overload on the hierarchy. Thus the creation of slack resources, through reduced performance levels, reduces the amount of information that must be processed during task execution and prevents the overloading of hierarchical channels. Whether the organization chooses this strategy depends on the relative costs of the other three strategies for handling the overload.

Creation of Self-Contained Tasks

The second method for reducing the amount of information processed is to change from the

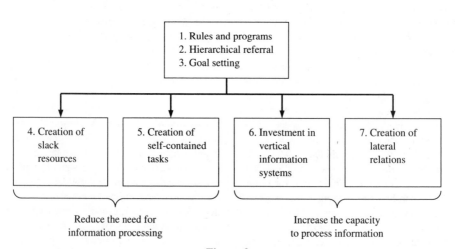

1. Rules and programs
2. Hierarchical referral
3. Goal setting

4. Creation of slack resources

5. Creation of self-contained tasks

6. Investment in vertical information systems

7. Creation of lateral relations

Reduce the need for information processing

Increase the capacity to process information

Figure 3
Organization design strategies

functional task design to one in which each group has all the resources it needs to perform its task. In the example of the 747, self-contained units could be created around major sections of the aircraft—wing, cabin, tail, body, etc. Each group would have its own product engineers, process engineers, fabricating and assembly operations, and test facilities. In other situations, groups can be created around product lines, geographical areas, projects, client groups, markets, etc., each of which would contain the input resources necessary for the task.

The strategy of self-containment shifts the basis of the authority structure from one based on input, resource, skill, or occupational categories, to one based on output or geographical categories. The shift reduces the amount of information processing through several mechanisms—two are described here.

First, it reduces the amount of output diversity faced by a single collection of resources. For example, a professional organization with multiple skill specialties that provides service to three different client groups must schedule the use of these specialties across three demands for their services and determine priorities when conflicts occur. But if the organization changes to three groups, one for each client category, each with its own full complement of specialties, the schedule conflicts across client groups disappears, and there is no need to process information to determine priorities.

The second source of information reduction occurs through a reduced division of labor. The functional or resource specialized structure pools the demand for skills across all output categories. In the example above, each client generates approximately one-third of the demand for each skill. Since the division of labor is determined by the extent of the market, the division of labor must decrease as the demand decreases. In the professional organization, each client group may have generated a need for one-third of a computer programmer. The functional organization would have hired one programmer and shared him across the groups. In the self-contained structure, there is insufficient demand in each group for a programmer,

and so the professionals must do their own programming. Specialization is reduced but there is no problem of scheduling the programmer's time across the three possible uses for it.

Thus the first two strategies reduce overloads on the hierarchy by reducing the number of exceptions that occur. The reduction occurs by reducing the level of performance, diversity of output, or division of labor. According to the theory put forth earlier, reducing the level of performance, etc., reduces the amount of information required to coordinate resources in creating the organization's services or products. In this way, the amount of information to be acquired and processed during task execution, and as a consequence the amount of task uncertainty, is reduced.

In contrast, the other two strategies take the required level of information as given, and create processes and mechanisms to acquire and process information during task execution.

Investment in Vertical Information Systems

The organization can invest in mechanisms which allow it to process information acquired during task performance without overloading the hierarchical communication channels. The investment occurs according to the following logic. After the organization has created its plan or set of targets for weight, stress, budget, and schedule, unanticipated events occur which generate exceptions requiring adjustments to the original plan. At some point when the number of exceptions becomes substantial, it is preferable to generate a new plan rather than make incremental changes in the old one with each exception. The issue is then how frequently plans should be revised—yearly, quarterly, or monthly? The greater the uncertainty, the greater the frequency of replanning. The greater the frequency of replanning, the greater the resources, such as clerks, computer time, input-output devices, etc., required to process information about relevant factors.

Providing more information more often may simply overload the decision maker. Investment may be required to increase the capacity of the decision maker by employing computers, various man-machine combinations, assistants-to, etc. The cost of this strategy is the cost of information processing resources.

The investment strategy is to collect information at the points of origin and direct it, at appropriate times, to the appropriate places in the hierarchy. The strategy increases the information processing at planning time while reducing the number of exceptions which have overloaded the hierarchy.

Creation of Lateral Relations

The last strategy is to selectively employ lateral decision processes which cut across lines of authority. The strategy moves the level of decision making down to where the information exists rather than bringing it up to the points of decision. It decentralizes decisions but without creating self-contained groups. Several mechanisms are employed. The number and types depend upon the level of uncertainty.

The simplest form of lateral relation is direct contact between two people who share a problem. If a problem arises in testing (see Figure 3), the manager of tests may contact the manager of assembly and secure the necessary change. Direct contact avoids the upward referral to another manager and removes overloads from the hierarchy.

In some cases there is a large volume of contact between two subtasks such as process design and assembly. Under these circumstances a new role, a liaison role, may be created to handle the interdepartmental contacts.

As tasks of higher uncertainty are encountered, problems are detected in testing which require the joint efforts of product and process design, assembly, and testing. Rather than refer the problem upwards, managers of these areas form a task force or team to jointly resolve the issue. In this manner interdepartmental group problem solving becomes a mechanism to decentralize decisions and reduce hierarchical overloads.

As more decisions and more decisions of consequence are made at lower levels of the organization through interdepartmental groups, problems of leadership arise. The response is the creation of a new role, an integrating role.[8] The function of the role is to represent the general manager in the interdepartmental decisions for a particular brand, product line, project, country, or geographical unit. These roles are called product managers in commercial firms, project managers in aerospace, and unit managers in hospitals.

After the role is created the issue is, how much and what kind of influence does the role occupant need in order to achieve integration for the project, unit, or product. Mechanisms from supporting information and budget control all the way to dual reporting relations and the matrix design are employed under various circumstances. . . .

In summary, lateral relations permit the moving of decisions to lower levels of the organization and yet guarantee that all information is included in the process. The cost of the strategy is the greater amounts of managerial time that must be spent in group processes and the overhead expense of liaison and integating roles.

Choice of Strategy

Four strategies have been briefly presented. The organization can choose to follow one or some combination of several if it chooses. It will choose that strategy which is least expensive in its environmental context.

It is important to note that the four strategies are hypothesized to be an exhaustive set of alternatives. That is, if the organization is faced with greater uncertainty, due to technological change, higher performance standards, increased competition, or diversified product line to reduce dependence, the amount of information processing is increased. *The organization must adopt at least one of the four strategies when faced with greater uncertainty.* If it does not consciously choose one of the four, then the first, reduced performance standards, will happen automatically. The task information requirements and the capacity of the organization to process information are always matched. If the organization does not consciously match them, reduced performance through budget overruns or schedule overruns will occur in order to bring about equality. Thus the organization should be planned and designed simultaneously with the planning of the strategy and resource allocations. But if the strategy involves introducing new products, entering new markets etc., then some provision for increased information must be made. Not to decide is to decide, and it is to decide upon slack resources as the only strategy for removing hierarchical overload.

Summary

. . . Starting from the observation that uncertainty appears to make a difference in type of organization structure, it was postulated that uncertainty increased the amount of information that must be processed during task execution. Therefore perceived variation in organization form was hypothesized to be variation in the capability of the organization to process information about events that could not be anticipated in advance.

Uncertainty was conceived as the relative difference in the amount of information required and the amount possessed by the organization. The amount required was a function of the output diversity, division of labor, and level of performance. In combination the task uncertainty, division of labor, diversity of output, and level of performance determine the amount of information that must be processed.

Next the basic, mechanistic bureaucratic model was introduced along with explanations of its information processing capabilities. It was shown that hierarchical communication channels can coordinate large numbers of interdependent subtasks but have a limited capacity to remake decisions. In response four strategies were articulated which either reduced the amount of information or increased the capacity of the organization to process more information. The way to decrease information was to reduce the determinants of the amount of information: performance levels, diversity, and division of labor.

The strategies to increase capacity were to invest in the formal, hierarchical information process and to introduce lateral decision processes. Each of these strategies has its effects and costs. Subsequent chapters will discuss each strategy in more detail. In addition, case studies will be presented which highlight the various choices.

Notes

1. James G. March & Herbert A. Simon, *Organizations* (New York: John Wiley, 1958), 142–150.
2. For a more detailed discussion of hierarchical arrangements, see James C. Emery, *Organizational Planning and Control Systems* (New York: Macmillan, 1969), 11–12.
3. There are two aspects to this problem. First, individuals may choose behaviors which are ineffective because they do not have the information or knowledge to make a rational choice. This is the cognitive problem addressed here. The other aspect is that individuals may have goals which are different from organizational goals. Processes for dealing with this problem have been discussed already in this series. See Richard Beckhard, *Organization Development: Strategies and Models* (Reading, Mass.: Addison-Wesley, 1969), 35–40.
4. Arthur Stinchcombe, "Bureaucratic and Craft Administration of Production: A Comparative Study," *Administrative Science Quarterly* (September 1959): 168–187.
5. Ibid., p. 170.
6. Here again there are motivation questions. How difficult should the goals be? Should incentives be attached to them? Should the manager participate in setting them? See John Campbell, Marvin Dunette, Edward Lawler, III, and Karl Weick, Jr., *Managerial Behavior, Performance and Effectiveness* (New York: McGraw-Hill, 1970), Chapter 15.
7. James G. March & Herbert A. Simon, *Organizations* (New York: John Wiley, 1958); and Richard Cyert and James G. March, *A Behavioral Theory of the Firm* (Englewood Cliffs, NJ: Prentice-Hall, 1963).
8. Paul Lawrence & Jay Lorsch, *Organization and Environment* (Boston: Division of Research, Harvard Business School, 1967), Chapter 3.

31

A Concept of Organizational Ecology

Eric Trist

The purpose of this paper is to introduce a concept of organizational ecology.

Obviously, organizational ecology has something to do with interorganizational relations. Let me distinguish what this something is by contrasting it with the main thrust of much of the work which has recently been done in the field. This work has been concerned with a focal organization as related to the other organizations in the environment with which it has direct relations, both on the input and output sides of its activities. My Wharton colleague William Evan (1966) has called this system of relations the organization-set.

By the term organizational ecology, I refer not to a focal organization and its organization-set, but to the organizational field created by a number of organizations whose interrelations compose a system at the level of the whole field. The character of this overall field, as a system, now becomes the object of inquiry, not the single organization as related to its organization-set. The re-centering intended is similar to that suggested by Warren (1967).

If I look back on the way organization theory has developed since World War II, it seems to me that in the first decade we were predominantly concerned with structures and processes

SOURCE: Eric Trist, "A Concept of Organizational Ecology," *Australian Journal of Management,* Volume 2, 1977, pp. 162-175. Reprinted with permission.

internal to the single organization. The excitement was in the discovery of group dynamics, at the unconscious as well as the conscious level, and in the complex infra-structure of interpersonal relations that existed behind the screen of formal role systems. But as we strove to relate these micro-systems to the larger organizational whole, we realized that we could no longer treat this whole as a relatively closed system. The boundary was permeable, penetrating and being penetrated by its environment. Closed system thinking had to be replaced by open system thinking.

In the second decade of post World War II organizational theory, a new emphasis on the environment became apparent. Dill (1958) introduced the term "task environment" and Lawrence and Lorsch (1967) followed with their now classic book, *Organization and Environment.* They showed that key parts of organizations tend to have different environments so that different organizational forms and climates become appropriate for these parts. Recognition of internal differentiation led to the problem of integration being explored in a new way: namely, as negotiation within a pluralistic internal organizational society rather than simply as bureaucratic control of an essentially homogeneous structure.

Most of the studies involved did not take the matter quite as far as my rather sharp statement would suggest. This line of work, however, contains the implication that it would be relevant to consider the single organization, as it becomes more complex, to be governed to some extent (but an important extent) by principles of ecological as well as bureaucratic regulation.

I contrast the two principles and will attempt to show that the socioecological perspective becomes more relevant the more organization-environment relations (as distinct from intra-organizational relations) are subjected to examination.

But so far we have been considering only the focal organization and its organization-set: that is to say, the relation of the organization to its task or transactional environment. There is, however, a wider environment, beyond the task environment, which needs to be distinguished from it. For the various organizations which compose the organization-set of a focal organization have relations with other organizations, which overlap in their relations with still others and others still again. These have only indirect relations with the focal organization. The field of these interwoven indirect relations constitutes the contextual, as distinct from transactional, environment. What goes on in the contextual environment influences to a considerable extent, as a set of boundary conditions, what goes on in the transactional environment, and thence in the organization itself. The character of the contextual environment and the nature of its influences have to be investigated for their own sake.

In the third decade of post World War II organizational theory, problems arising from the contextual environment have begun to claim serious attention from organizational scientists for the first time, albeit that others might have long been concerned with them. I do not think that this new concern is accidental for, as the present age began to disclose its character as an age of discontinuity (to use Peter Drucker's [1968] term), it has become ever clearer that a persistent and pervasive quality, which my Australian colleague Fred Emery and I have called turbulence (and which I will explain later), is increasingly present in the contextual environment of organizations.

This quality of turbulence is causing traditional bureaucratic organizations, with their long familiar policies and strategies designed to solve separate problems and reach single objectives, to work considerably less well than they have hitherto been experienced to do, even at the satisficing level (to use Herb Simon's (1958) term). We seem to have to deal increasingly with problems of the management of large scale systems [macro-systems, as Metcalfe (1974, 1976)], calls them, whose multiple aspects are for better or worse indissolubly interconnected. Such systems my colleague

Russell Ackoff (1975) has called messes. Messes would seem to be piling up in all sectors of modern societies and are scarcely absent in the developing countries. They are the result of the manifold unanticipated consequences of innumerable separate and largely independent lines of action, which Karl Mannheim (1936) once referred to as collective phenomena. Such collective phenomena are creating social slag heaps which none of our policy-planning efforts seem to be having much success in removing, as John Friedmann has shown (1973). Indeed at the macro level we seem to be beset with an increasing number of persistent maladies, called "crises" (a word which permeates current rhetoric), stock examples being energy, the urban condition, inflation, pollution, drugs and crime, the creakings of big government, not to speak of poverty and overpopulation in the third world.

At a more micro level, organizations of many kinds are becoming less able to meet the demands which rapid change places upon them. Last semester, groups of students from one of my courses in the Wharton School undertook field projects in twelve widely different organizations in the Philadelphia area, public and private, statutory and voluntary. In all of them, mini (if not maxi) crises of transition and transformation were present. In degree, the crisis balance, if I may use such a term, tended to be tipped toward the maxi rather than the mini end of the scale. This tends to become so the more that long term rather than immediate survival is taken as the criterion.

As the 1950s gave way to the 1960s, several of us, then working at the Tavistock Institute in London, found that the action research projects in which we were now more frequently becoming engaged changed, in response to client needs, from those primarily concerned with single organizations to endeavors concerned with large-scale social systems involving many and often diverse organizations. That is to say, we had entered the field of organizational ecology. This change in the need for our assistance seemed to reflect the change that was occurring in the texture of the contextual environment towards increased turbulence. The new condition of society required the identification of a new unit of analysis on the part of the social sciences, namely, the organizational ecology system.

The new projects might involve a whole industry, as when we became engaged in the agricultural sector as a whole, through the National Union of Farmers of England and Wales [Higgin, Emery and Trist (1966)]. The presenting problem was stated as a breakdown in communication between Head Office and County Branches, but the reason for this breakdown turned out to be not so much the unwillingness of either side to talk to the other, as a change in the environment in which the N.F.U. was operating. This was the change which was not being "communicated."

Changes taking place towards capital intensive large scale industry in the contextual environment of the wider society had caught up with farming and affected its transactional environment. To meet these changes successfully entailed a switch in emphasis from competition to collaboration. This switch is critical for survival in turbulent environments and for strategies of organizational ecology. In the farmer's case, cooperation involved developing agreed marketing and distributing and even growing and breeding systems which represented collaborative strategies. The arrangements had to be negotiated by the many parties concerned. Only through their participation could interdependent schemes be fashioned and constraints on the individual be accepted which created opportunities for the group. Coercion by an authoritarian power is not available as (shall we say) "a methodology" in this type of situation. Herein lies another clue to a critical feature of systems of organizational ecology as contrasted with bureaucracies. They involve the evolution of a negotiated order, founded on collaboration rather than competition.

Further insights into the properties of systems of organizational ecology were obtained at about this same time from another Tavistock project in the aerospace industry, in which the government of the day had caused the merger of two large engine makers into a vast new complex

[Emery (1976b)]. No sooner had this event taken place than technological developments in the worldwide context, especially in the U.S., undermined the logic of the fusion. In the ensuing situation the joint management seemed unable to develop new strategies because, it was alleged, yesterday's protagonists were unable to collaborate. The problem was brought to us as one of interpersonal conflict within a top management group. However, when Emery and I went away with the eleven people principally concerned to a residential lab, under social island conditions, we found that what they needed most was time in a supporting environment to share their common anxieties, and through doing this intensively to become able to make a collective re-appreciation of their entire situation. There were no deep incompatibilities; nor was there stubborn adherence to previous loyalties. T group procedures intended to facilitate the disclosure of hidden agendas and eyeball to eyeball levelling became rather marginal. The anxieties were existential rather than interpersonal. For the issue was survival. In a turbulent environment the issue is survival. The need is to stop the flight into personal paralysis and interpersonal discord and to replace these by participation in a process of group innovation. In systems of organizational ecology the locus of innovation is in the set of the partners involved.

The sharing of the existential anxiety released the creative resources of the group. By the end of the week decisions had been taken to diversify not only into a new and an unthought-of product line but, unheard of, to seek a partner for a joint venture. Joint ventures and the clustering they produce are organizational ecological phenomena.

The behavioral scientists involved in these projects felt not only a need to understand such processes but to obtain better cognitive maps of large scale socio-ecological systems: models which we lacked. We knew that certain people in O.R. had made advances in modelling such systems. Accordingly, we negotiated with the British O.R. society for the setting up of an Institute for Operational Research linked to the Tavistock.

There was a need to complement the studies made of large scale organizational ecology systems in the industrial field by similar studies in the community field. The first such project, under the leadership of the new O.R. Institute but including behavioral scientists, was undertaken in collaboration with the Lord Mayor and Council of a medium sized British city of 300,000: Coventry. The object was to gain a better understanding of policy-planning processes and to develop new methodologies and strategies and strategies for decision-making under conditions of complexity and uncertainty. We needed to forge a link between the field of organizational behavior and the planning field, a link of critical importance for organizational ecology.

As Jay Forrester (1971) has said, complexity is counter-intuitive. Though I do not believe this to be true of all its aspects, models are nevertheless necessary, otherwise one gets lost in tracing out the implications of one component system for others. A model was developed called A.I.D.A. for the Analysis of Interconnected Decision Areas. As regards uncertainty, further work came up with a new conceptualization of the sources of uncertainty. Means were found of reducing a manifold of solutions to a manageable set of leading solutions and thence of keeping open as many options as possible when decisions had to be taken, under time constraints, to commit resources for a future whose emergent properties could be predicted. This work by John Friend and the late Neil Jessop (1969), published under the title "Local Government and Strategic Choice," has been continued by Friend (1974) with several colleagues, at the regional level.

On the behavioral side, access was gained not only to members of the City Council but to the caucuses of both political parties, the set of administrative departments, the unions concerned, and groups of voluntary workers out in the wards. Attempts were made to educate such people in the use of the conceptual tools which had been developed and to provide them with cognitive maps more pertinent to their affairs than those to which they were accustomed.

Since then, regular seminars and working conferences have been held with an increasing number of mayors and administrative officers of British cities, and chairmen and executives of some of the new regional authorities, so that a learning network is being brought into existence which provides diffusion channels for innovation. Let me say at this point that the concept of social network is as basic to the understanding of systems of organizational ecology as that of the primary work group is to the understanding of the single organization.

John Stringer (1967), who participated in the work just described, and who has now joined the new Australian Graduate School of Management, has called the systems of organizational ecology involved in these studies multi-organizations. I will reserve this conceptualization for one class of such system: namely, that in which member organizations are linked to a key organization among them which acts as a central referent organization. It does this even though many of them are only partially under its control or linked to it only through interface relations. Let me add that interface relations are as basic to systems of organizational ecology as superior-subordinate relations are to bureaucratic organizations. Interface relations require negotiation as distinct from compliance. This, as I stated earlier, is a basic distinction between the two types of system.

As well as multi-organizations, there is a second class in which the referent organization is of a different kind. It is a new organization brought into being and controlled by the member organizations rather than being one of the key constituents. In a third class there is no referent organization at all. However, before I describe the features and varieties of these other types, I must return to the question of environmental turbulence.

Confronted with the increasing organizational impact of the contextual environment and too little able to understand what was happening in projects with large-scale systems, Emery and I felt that an urgent social science necessity was to undertake at least a preliminary conceptualization of this unfamiliar field. We found a starting point in the idea of a field having a causal texture, a concept introduced into the study of perception by Tolman and Brunswick (1935). Developing this at the social level, we presented a first short joint paper to the International Psychology Congress in 1963 [Emery and Trist (1965)].

At that time the paper was not felt to be relevant. Most of our colleagues in organizational behavior had not yet been pushed, as we had been, into collaborative action research studies of systems larger than that of the single organization. They therefore felt no need for an additional concept. Since then, however, the word "turbulence" which we hit on seems to have become part of the popular language, suggesting that the phenomenon with which we were concerned has become generally recognized. Several scholars have now taken up the theme of the causal texture of organizational environments. I shortly expect the publication of papers which, with the aid of some of the new forms of structural mathematics such as catastrophe theory,[1] will attempt to formalize what has still remained a verbal model, even in the later expositions of Emery and Trist (1972) and Emery (1974).

In our joint endeavor we identified four ideal types of contextual environment, approaches to all of which are presumed to exist simultaneously in the real world, but whose mixture and weighting vary immensely between contemporary societies, and even more so historically. The first two types, the placid random and the placid clustered, imply no change or slow change in the environment. They will not be discussed in the present context, except to note that, historically, the placid clustered environment has been man's accustomed social habitat. In this world small is beautiful. This slogan of Schumacher's (1975), which headlines one of the new ideas which have recently come into good currency, suggests that there might be more of a future for this type of habitat than has commonly been supposed, though it would require linkage to an overall setting, non-existent before, and the support of some of the most sophisticated information and biological technologies.

Be this as it may, it is under the dominance of the third type, the disturbed-reactive environment, that most of the generations now on the human stage have grown up. This environment became salient as the industrial revolution proceeded. It has had the effect of making bureaucracies, in the sense intended by Weber (1947), the central form of organization in advanced industrial societies as distinct from patrimonial organizations, which, he said, were central to pre-industrial societies. These bureaucracies have become increasingly technocratic and increasingly large in both the private and public sectors. They survive by strategies of power and competitive challenge, absorbing or subjugating others whom they seek to acquire, or who stand in their way. Their efficiency has made them the engine of economic growth, and we owe to them in large measure the affluence we enjoy. Their religion is the Protestant Work Ethic which stimulates the drive to continous achievement. A cherished reward of those who thrive in them is the sweet smell of success when the high climb has been made.

The very success of the technocratic bureaucracy as an organizational modality, adaptive to disturbed-reaction environments, has led to dysfunctional effects. For these immense organizations go it alone without regard to what others are doing, while interdependencies in the contextual environment, social as well as economic, are increasing. Accepting the technological imperative, they accelerate a change-rate whose scope of diffusion has, with the aid of modern communication systems, become not only immensely broad but immensely rapid. This is leading to a situation in which response times for adaptation are becoming hazardously short. Concentrated largely on their own short-term specific objectives, they have given only marginal attention to the longer-term, more general effects of their actions on wider systems. These effects have not been supposed to be their business. As a result, unintended consequences pile up on the slag heaps of collective phenomena. Processes such as these are increasing the level of turbulence in the contemporary world and suggested to Emery and myself the idea of a turbulent field as the fourth type of contextual environment. As Don Schön (1971) has put it, we have lost the stable state.

For some time now there have been abundant signs that technocratic go-it-alone bureaucracies (our salient inherited organizational form) cannot adapt to conditions of persistent and pervasive environmental turbulence, however large they become and however massive the power they wield. Even with a bit of corporate planning, or for that matter with the planning efforts of specialized public agencies, they seem to increase instability rather than secure the stability they need by strategies which have become inappropriate. The endemic crises which they are increasingly experiencing—and endemic crisis is different from aberrations that can be expected to go away—cannot be met by the methods which have built their success.

The basic reason why bureaucratic organizations show diminishing adaptive capability in face of rising environmental turbulence is that, though they can cope with risk (which they can assess with all the arts of the calculable now available), they cannot cope with uncertainty, which throws them off the carefully programmed courses they have prepared. Furthermore, the greater the resources—human, material and financial—sunk in these programs, the more difficult it becomes for them to change direction.

In a turbulent field, uncertainty is raised to an altogether higher level than that existing under disturbed-reactive conditions. This is a direct consequence of the greater complexity of, and interdependence among, the immense number of activities making up the causal texture of the contextual field.

If to usher in this century Weber felt he could rightly unveil bureaucracy as a newly perfected organizational monument (ideally adapted to the then prevailing disturbed-reactive conditions), then our chances of reaching the year 2000 in reasonably good shape (now that turbulent conditions are increasing in salience) would appear to entail our identifying, and becoming skilled in practising, an alternative organizational principle. I believe this alternative will be found to lie in the characteristics of systems of organizational ecology.

These characteristics do not only reverse a number of key bureaucratic rules as regards the internal workings of single organizations. They tend for example to promote self-regulation of the parts rather than insist on their external regulation (from above). They accomplish a figure-ground reversal in transferring the focus of attention from the single organization to the larger system of which it is a part. This larger system I will call an organizational domain. The domain of an organization differs from its organization-set in that, while the latter references the field to the organization, the former references the organization to the field.

In his book *Beyond the Stable State,* Don Schön (1967) has referred to what I have called organizational domains as functional systems. In the industrial field he gives an amusing account of all the various activities and people contributing to a domain which he labels "keeping clothes clean." The point of this story is that the structure of the domain is chaotic because most of those in it do not correctly perceive the identity of the domain. He also gives a tragic account of another domain called "blindness in America." The point of this story is that the structure of the domain is obsolete because most of those in it have not yet appreciated that the dominant group in the composition of the blind has changed, from the young totally blind to the old partially blind, while the bulk of the available resources are still being deployed towards the former. Organizational domains, then, have structure, which might be too little or too much, appropriate or inappropriate. They also have boundaries, which might be too narrow, as when we think of hospitals instead of health care systems; or which might be too broad, as when we think rather nebulously of "industry." For now the picture of the domain has become too far abstracted from any concrete operational reality towards which effective courses of social action might be devised. In addition, organizational domains have direction. They might be moving in social space by moving towards closer relations with other domains or becoming more independent of them. Some time ago, for example, the British government put education and science together in a single ministry while separating off technology. In social time a domain might be increasing or decreasing in salience, or just newly emergent. It can be relatively large or relatively small, whatever its boundaries might be. Most important of all, it has an identity, and if this identity is mistaken, error creeps in to all the other dimensions.

The identities of organizational domains are discovered through what Sir Geoffrey Vickers (1965) has called acts of appreciation, which meld together judgments of fact with judgments of value. Appreciations guide the social perceptions in terms of which we construe the worlds of our domains; hence settle their identities, and thence take decisions concerning their structure, boundaries, direction, and magnitude. In a rapidly-changing, complex and highly interdependent environment, existing appreciations have to be checked and new appreciations have to be sought repeatedly.

New methodologies are needed to undertake the special type of inquiry involved in making such appreciations. One such methodology currently is being developed by Fred and Merelyn Emery and their associates at the Centre for Continuing Education of the Australian National University [Emery (1976b)]. The basis of the methodology, called a search conference, is to gather together for 2–5 days, in a residential setting, the various parties involved in an organizational domain to consider, in a constraint-free manner and in a futures time perspective, not only what they have been doing, but what they ought to be doing.

Organizational ecology is concerned with the level which is intermediate between the socially micro and the socially macro. Writers as different as Michel Crozier (1974) and Ronald Laing (1967) have noted that social science knowledge at this level is sparse compared with what is known about the individual, the family and the single organization on the one hand and processes in the overall society at the aggregate level on the other, whether in economics or sociology. Any strategy enabling us to make

headway at the middle level, such as the embryonic method of the search conference, is therefore welcome.

I noted earlier that the student of organizations had to make a figure-ground reversal in order to render the domain visible and I listed some of the dimensions of organizational domains. I described certain of their basic features such as network character and tendency towards a negotiated order. As to the sparseness of social science knowledge about them, let me make two suggestions: first, that organizational domains are not easy to see, even when the change of focus is made; second, that their special importance has not been appreciated until recently.

The difficulty of seeing organizational domains is not solely due to the absence of suitable techniques. To a very important extent it is due to the fact that in modern industrial societies the structuring of social fields at the middle level is weak. The clout and the high visibility belong to the singular organization: to the enterprise, not to the chamber of commerce or even the employers' confederation; to the individual union, not to the trades council; to the specific public departments more than city councils. Also, too few of the numerous voluntary organizations that haunt the middle level wield effective power. In our societies, control of the micro has been left in the hands of the macro. Our tradition has been to depend for control on organizations on the other side of the gap, such as national governments and their multitudinous outgrowths, and to a lesser extent state governments and their also formidable outgrowths in countries having a federal political structure. This tradition worked reasonably well so long as disturbed-reactive conditions prevailed and the outgrowths remained within limits. But with the increasing salience of turbulent conditions, systems of aggregate control are becoming increasingly insufficient and inefficient, no matter how large the outgrowths.

The outstanding triumph of industrial societies has been in production, delivered by the instrument of the individual free enterprise firm and mediated by a market mechanism which was largely auto-regulative. But production is no longer the central problem and the market mechanism is no longer as auto-regulative as it was during the nineteenth and earlier parts of the present century. Regulation has now become the central problem. With traditional aggregate economic and social controls proving insufficient and singular organizations, whether private or public, being unable to provide it because they were built for another purpose, what is to be done? How is the gap to be filled?

This leads me to the special importance of the middle level of societal organization, which has not been realized until recently, it having been left as a desert rather like the middle of Australia. The gap, I will argue, can be filled and the desert brought into cultivation, not by strengthening aggregate controls, but by strengthening societal organization at this very middle level, where it has remained so hazardously weak and ineffectual.

No good outcome, however, can be expected if the domains selected are wrongly appreciated or the subsequent modelling is developed in accordance with the bureaucratic principle. So far as this course is taken, it will make matters worse. For it will simply add to the already high level of turbulence that singular technocratic bureaucracies have generated.

If, however, the social architectural task should be approached according to a principle of organizational ecology, then there would be some reasonable hope that domains would be better appreciated and institutions would be built in more self-regulating ways.[2] This would not only absorb a good deal of turbulence adaptively, but eventually it would reduce it. A condition which would reestablish a more stable state might then be reached in the long run. Many messes would be cleared up and fewer subsequently made. This is the core of my argument in favor of a concept of organizational ecology and my reason for wishing to encourage the development of social practice in this direction.

A word, however, about what is likely to happen if the alternative path is taken of strengthening aggregate controls. This could only lead to a form of society in which a very high degree of totalitarianism was present. I do not wish to present my case against totalitarianism either on personal dislike of such societies or on whether they are founded on capitalist or socialist principles. For totalitarianism has appeared on both these backgrounds. My case rests rather on a theory that totalitarianism will not work in any society once this society has passed a certain point in its development. This is because totalitarianism is inherently bureaucratic and bureaucracies cannot cope with the complexities and interdependencies which further development would entail. The associated higher level of uncertainty would create a degree of turbulence which bureaucratic instruments could not control. The society would become locked in stagnation or begin to disorganize.

Totalitarianism apparently is working reasonably well in the Soviet Union, at least on the surface, though if Solzhenitsyn is correct it is at enormous cost. But the Soviet Union is still much less developed than Western societies, and the countries of the Third World which are trying out totalitarianism, in either capitalist or socialist forms, are far less developed still. Totalitarianism might provide one way of getting through the first and more simple stages of industrialism rather rapidly but there is no evidence to suggest that it can become a means through which post-industrialism, which seems to be inherently pluralistic, can be realized; and Western societies are already getting into, or approaching, a post-industrial stage.

Centralized bureaucratic control, however, is not the only way of industrializing rapidly, as the departure of China from the Soviet model would indicate. It is of the greatest interest from the point of view of this paper that this departure has entailed a thorough-going attempt to de-bureaucratize Chinese institutions, especially the communist party. I do not believe, however, that the Chinese model has direct application to Western societies. Our traditions are too different; and in any case, as Willett (1975) suggests, a degree of aggregate control—which would be unacceptable to us and unworkable in view of our greater complexity—would seem to persist in parallel with the decentralized communes, however much, from the outside, they look organizationally ecological. Though we might learn much from China, Western societies will have to build a new set of adaptive institutions capable of turbulence-reduction on the basis of their own traditions and experience.

Having established the relevance of a concept of organizational ecology, let me now return to the question of classes of organizational domain, and illustrate them by describing some projects currently under way by my colleagues and myself.

The first class is concerned with domains in which one of the constituent organizations becomes the referent organization, as in the Coventry case. In the second class of socio-ecological organization, no particular constituent organization becomes a central referent organization. The organizational population creates a new referent organization which none of them dominates, yet all control. In other instances there is no such referent organization at all. This latter can be considered a third class of organizational domain.

In the second class the fact that all the organizations belonging to the domain are represented in the referent organization gives the referent organization an aggregate character. This enables it to cohere the organizational field in a way which builds consensus among the members. It can thus maximize collaboration and minimize conflict, lower resistance to change, and thence undertake relevant and effective innovation. These are critical aspects of domain development.

One such organization, with which I have been working for the last three years, is the Labor-Management Committee of the City of Jamestown, a small manufacturing town in upper New York State. This Committee, having established a community-wide constituency, has proved to be innovative and effective to an unusual degree.

In the early 1970s, when the rest of America was booming, the largest plant in Jamestown closed down permanently and others moved south, so that unemployment rose to over 10 percent. Labor-management relations were notoriously bad and disputes were frequent. No new firms could be enticed to come in and still others were planning to depart. In the crisis thus created, a young charismatic mayor was elected with bi-partisan political support. As a result of this underlying consensus, his prestige was sufficient to enable him to call management and labor together in a way which had not previously been possible. He invited the general managers and local union presidents of all unionized plants in the area (and these were the large majority) to begin meeting regularly in order to transform the climate of industrial relations. With most of them responding, this goal was achieved after a year of sometimes exceedingly stormy meetings.

Since then the Committee, as a central referent organization, has facilitated a whole series of developments:

a shared skills development program has been initiated because the stock of in-house skills in the dominant industries was becoming seriously depleted;

in-plant labor-management committees, formed in most of the member plants, have developed extensive quality of work programs; these have increased both productivity and job satisfaction;

a major engineering company has been attracted to the town; it will employ 2000–3000 people;

several companies have expanded or have been salvaged when in difficulties;

better transport links are being considered and connections are being developed with neighboring areas with which there is a community of interests;

labor-management committees have begun to be established in one or two places in the public sector;

first steps have been taken to make Jamestown a "health city" and an energy conservation city as well as a labor-management city.

A sustained evolving process is under way which is linking various interests together in an active network. This is steering the city towards a more prosperous future which it will have chosen for itself.

I have described this project in some detail because it illustrates the processes, rather than the structures, that organizational ecology is concerned with. Processes of domain development are opened. They unfold through time in direct correlation with events in the environment in patterns and sequences which cannot be pre-programmed. Yet what has been happening in Jamestown is a process of continuous adaptive planning, in Ackoff's sense; it also is the establishment of a system of public learning, in Schön's sense. So far as the network of Jamestown-type communities materializes, they proactively will begin to choose futures for themselves different from and, hopefully, better than those that would await them if they passively allowed events to overtake them. One of the paradoxes in developing adaptive capability in turbulent environments is that the high level of uncertainty involves, more than ever before, making choices and taking the active role. As Etzioni (1968) has said, hope for the future lies in the creation of an active society.

In another variety, within the second class of organizational domain with new referent organizations, the organizational population is so large that it has to be represented by a sample of the constituents who then form some kind of panel. In a recent paper Emery (1976a) has suggested that this sampling be random. If each constituent organization were to nominate an individual, able and willing to serve, the sample required for the referent organization could be drawn by a procedure modelled on that of jury service. There would be a period of office, say two years. Special appointments would not be made, neither would there be voting. The panel members would not be representing their particular organizations but would be accountable as individuals to the domain. Emery has suggested such a procedure for selecting the members of the industrial councils recommended by the Jackson Committee (1975) in its report on policies for Australian manufacturing industry. The aim is to prevent the domination of such councils by the more powerful inhabitants of the domain and to minimize manipulation by specific interest groups. For these councils, Emery thought that 30 to 40 members would provide an adequate sample and that any one set, by and large, would be as good as any other. Of course, the members would be free to work in whatever task groups they wished to form.

The function of such bodies is regulation not production. Their work is appreciation not operation. It would involve making critical value judgments concerning the ways in which a domain might best develop. Though it requires multiple perspectives, such work is generalist, not specialist in orientation. Though technical staffs would be provided, the panels themselves would not be allowed to become technocratic. The proposed design reverses the bureaucratic model.

The various types of council suggested by the Jackson Committee (industrial, regional, state and federal) were intended to stand in non-hierarchical relation to each other. A system designed on these lines might be expected to strengthen and make more self-regulating the middle ground of society, absorbing some of the turbulence generated at the macro level and buffering the micro organizations.

Let me now pass to the third class of organizational domain: those organizations which have no referent organization initially or at any subsequent stage. They have no center and may be described as having a purely network character. Schön takes as an example of such a domain the youth movement which evolved during the 1960s and spread rapidly throughout most countries of the world. This movement, though revolutionary as regards the values and life styles it advocates, has never had any stated aims. There has been no political party, no specific program, no recognized leader, no kind of formal organization. The movement has remained fluid, with key individuals and groups passing in and out of focus, even when engaged in political protest. It has operated through a culture rather than a structure, the most salient patterns being rock music, drugs, a so-called underground, a penchant for Eastern forms of philosophy and religion, and communal forms of living which seek to recapture some of the support provided by the extended family systems of pre-industrial societies adapted to placid clustered environments.

How can a culture operate without a structure? Seemingly, through a technology: in this case the advanced information-based technologies of modern communication systems. Without records, tapes, cassettes, videos, radios, television, the telephone, air travel and automobiles the diffusion of the youth culture could never have taken place in the manner it did or with its rapidity. The modern youth culture is as much a socio-technical system as a factory, though a kind of counter-factory. In becoming this it carries a serious message concerning our need to un-program ourselves from bureaucracy.

The combination of culture and technology, working without formal structure as regards any referent organization and depending purely on social networks, would seem to be able to bring about the relatively rapid emergence of new values commonly shared over a wide field. Shared values, rather than formal structures, would seem to be necessary in order to cohere diverse social fields. They are what is needed above all for turbulence control. Of course, new values have to be relevant to the conditions emerging in the environment.

The role in the culture-technology combination of the new communications technology is that it enables new values to be diffused more widely and rapidly than has been possible by earlier methods. Scope and speed are critical attributes in the diffusion of relevant innovation in a rapidly changing world.

At the center of contemporary network movements is what I think of as the organizational revolution about which this paper has been concerned and which consists of a re-centering of organizational life, away from the principles of bureaucracy and towards the principles of organizational ecology. This re-centering involves a basic shift: from the primacy of the bounded single organization to the primacy of the unbounded networks through which the members of organizational domains become linked. This shift entails what I referred to as a figure-ground reversal.

As the capacity to build and manage organizational networks increases, it is as though a new medium were being created through which people in organizational life can become connected with and related to each other in more flexible and relevant ways. No longer are they bound in their fields of relations by their specific organizations and formal roles as much as they were in the heyday of bureaucracy under disturbed-reactive conditions. The individual is becoming more ready to break out of fixed organizational moulds, to challenge them, to use more of the role space around him and to cultivate the skills of the boundary spanner. He is in process of becoming a network man rather than an organization man. I believe that this process, which is arising, as it were, out of the social ground itself [Trist (1976)], is working in the direction of de-bureaucratizing organizations, that this is preparing the way for alternative forms to emerge, that these will be built on principles of organizational ecology and that they will prove adaptive under conditions of contextual turbulence.

The core relevant values involved are those associated with organizational democracy. It seems no accident to me that a movement towards organizational democracy has recently arisen, under various names, different forms and with varying emphasis, in all Western countries, twin aims being to improve the quality of life in the workplace and to share power [Trist (1974)]. Except in Norway and Sweden it is still in an infant state, faced with strong resistance from the bureaucratic heritage which it is endeavoring to replace. But the bureaucrats will fail to perceive that the change nevertheless is being accelerated quietly through innumerable supporting networks which are becoming naturally established by all kinds of persons, at all levels, across all kinds of boundaries in and between organizations of all types. More and more of these individuals are seeing for themselves the way they believe things should now go in organizational life. This kind of process has not been bargained for in the bureaucratic ethos. Perhaps bureaucracies will be in for a surprise. If they are, it might be possible to begin reducing contextual turbulence and to recover something of a stable state, sooner than the doomsayers maintain.

It has been my purpose in this paper to outline a concept of organizational ecology which can allow the study of inter-organizational relations to proceed more clearly at the level of what I have called organizational domains. Three classes of such domains were distinguished in terms of the role in each of what may be called the referent organization, which becomes progressively more cultural and less structural in character. Some of the characteristics of organizational domains were discussed, as were some of the processes of domain development. I have endeavored not only to trace the emergence of organizational ecology from earlier organization theory[3] and to illustrate this from empirical studies, but to argue in favor of its *relevance* to the task of institution-building in a world in which the environment has become exceedingly complex and more interdependent, with the consequence that organizations must face the future under conditions of a higher level of uncertainty than that to which they have hitherto been accustomed. In order to control the turbulence generated in such a world it is my submission that organizational forms in the middle level of society, between the macro and the micro, require strengthening. Further, I submit, that the function of organizations at this middle level is regulation and not production. And finally, I submit that it is critical for our well-being that they be fashioned on ecological and democratic rather than on bureaucratic and totalitarian lines. This choice seems to me to be central to the question of our becoming able to negotiate a reasonably safe passage from an industrial to a post-industrial order.

Notes

1. Peter Longdon, personal communication, Department of Commerce, University of Western Australia.

2. For the concept of social architecture, see Perlmutter (1965).
3. Since this address was given, there have been published: a book on alternatives to hierarchies by Herbst (1976) of the Institute of Work Psychology, Oslo; a much-expanded version of "Futures We Are In" [Emery (1977)]; and a newsletter entitled "Linkage," which has been started by J. Friend of the Institute for Operational Research at Tavistock, to create dialogue among researchers and practitioners, concerned with inter-organizational relations in providing community services. These works develop further the type of concept which will enable the field of organizational ecology to be established.

References

ACKOFF, R. L., 1975, Redesigning the Future (Wiley, N.Y.).

CHEVALIER, M., 1966, A Theory of Interest Group Planning (Ph.D. thesis, University of Pennsylvania, Philadelphia).

CROZIER, M., 1974, "The Relationship Between Micro and Macrosociology," *Human Relations,* 25, 239–252.

DILL, W. R., 1958, "Environment as an Influence on Managerial Autonomy," *Administrative Science Quarterly,* 2, 409–443.

DRUCKER, P. F., 1968, The Age of Discontinuity (Harper & Row, N.Y.).

EMERY, F. E.,1974, Futures We're In (Centre for Continuing Education, Australian National University, Canberra).

EMERY, F. E., 1976a, Adaptive Systems for our Future Governance (National Labour Institute Bulletin No. 4., New Delhi).

EMERY, F. E., 1976b, "Searching for New Directions," in: Emery, M., ed., New Ways for New Times (Centre for Continuing Education, Australian National University, Canberra).

EMERY, F. E., 1977, Futures We Are In (Martinus Nijhoff, Leiden).

EMERY, F. E., & E. L. TRIST, 1965, "The Causal Texture of Organizational Environments," *Human Relations, 18,* 21–31.

EMERY, F. E., & E. L. TRIST, 1972, Towards a Social Ecology (Plenum Press, London & N.Y.).

ETZIONI, A., 1968, The Active Society (Columbia University Press, N.Y.).

EVAN, W., 1966, "The Organization-Set," in: Thompson, J., ed., Approaches to Organizational Design (University of Pittsburgh Press, Pittsburgh).

FORRESTER, J. W., 1971, "The Counterintuitive Nature of Social Systems," *Technology Review, 73,* 52–68.

FRIEDMANN, J., 1973, Retracking America: A Theory of Transactive Planning (Doubleday-Anchor, N.Y.).

FRIEND, J., & N. JESSOP, 1969, Local Government and Strategic Choice (Tavistock Publications, London).

FRIEND, J., J. M. POWER, & C. J. YEWLETT, 1974, Public Planning: The Inter-Corporate Dimension (Tavistock Publications, London).

HERBST, P. G., 1976, Alternatives to Hierarchies (Martinus Nijhoff, Leiden).

HIGGIN, G. W., F. E. EMERY, & E. L. TRIST, 1966, Communications in the Farmers' Union (N.F.U. & Tavistock Institute, London).

JACKSON, R. G. (Chairman), 1975, Committee to Advise on Policies for Manufacturing Industry, Policies for Development of Manufacturing Industry (Australian Government Publishing Service, Canberra).

LAING, R. D., 1967, The Politics of Experience (Penguin, Harmondsworth).

LAWRENCE, P. R., & J. W. LORSCH, 1967, The Organization and the Environment (Research Division, Graduate School of Business Administration, Harvard University, Boston).

MANHEIM, K., 1936, Ideology and Utopia (Routledge and Kegan Paul, London).

MARCH, J. G., & H. A. SIMON, 1958, Organizations (Wiley, N.Y.).

METCALFE, J. L., 1974, "Systems Models, Economic Models, and the Causal Texture of Organizational Environments: An Approach to Macro-Organization Theory," *Human Relations, 27,* 639–664.

METCALFE, J. L., 1976, "Organizational Strategies and Interorganizational Networks," *Human Relations, 29,* 327–43.

PERLMUTTER, H., 1965, Towards a Theory and Practice of Social Architecture (Tavistock Publications, London).

SAMPSON, A., 1974, The Sovereign State of I.T.T. (Fawcett World Library, N.Y.).

SCHÖN, D., 1971, Beyond the Stable State (Penguin, Harmondsworth).

SCHUMACHER, E. F., 1975, Small is Beautiful (Harper & Row, N.Y.).

STRINGER, J., 1967, "Operational Research for 'Multi-organizations'," *Operational Research Quarterly, 18,* 105–20.

TOLMAN, E. C., & E. BRUNSWICK, 1935, "The Organism and the Causal Texture of the Environment," *Psychological Review, 42,* 43–77.

TRIST, E. L., 1974, Work Improvement and Industrial Democracy (European Economic Community, Brussels).

TRIST, E. L., 1976, "Action Research and Adaptive Planning," in: Clark, A. W., ed., Experimenting with Organizational Life (Plenum Press, London & N.Y.).

VICKERS, SIR G., 1965, The Art of Judgment (Chapman and Hall, London).

WARREN, R. L., 1967, "The Interorganizational Field as a Focus for Investigation," *Administrative Science Quarterly, 12,* 396–419.

WEBER, R. L., 1947, The Theory of Social and Economic Organization (The Oxford University Press, London & N.Y.).

WILLETT, J. F., 1975, "The Development of Administration in the People's Republic of China," *Current Scene, 13,* 1–18.

32

The Population Ecology of Organizations*

Michael T. Hannan and
John Freeman

I. Introduction

Analysis of the effects of environment on organizational structure has moved to a central place in organizations theory and research in recent years. This shift has opened a number of exciting possibilities. As yet nothing like the full promise of the shift has been realized. We believe that the lack of development is due in part to a failure to bring ecological models to bear on questions that are preeminently ecological. We argue for a reformulation of the problem in population ecology terms.

Although there is a wide variety of ecological perspectives, they all focus on selection. . . . The bulk of the literature on organizations subscribes to a different view, which we call the adaptation perspective.[1] According to the adaptation perspective, subunits of the organization, usually managers or dominant coalitions, scan the relevant environment for opportunities and threats, formulate strategic responses, and adjust organizational structure appropriately.

*This research was supported in part by grants from the National Science Foundation (GS-32065) and the Spencer Foundation. Helpful comments were provided by Amos Hawley, François Nielsen, John Meyer, Marshall Meyer, Jeffrey Pfeffer, and Howard Aldrich.

SOURCE: Michael T. Hannan and John Freeman, ''The Population Ecology of Organizations,'' *American Journal of Sociology*, 82:5, pp. 929–964.

The adaptation perspective is seen most clearly in the literature on management. Contributors to it usually assume a hierarchy of authority and control that locates decisions concerning the organization as a whole at the top. It follows, then, that organizations are affected by their environments according to the ways in which managers or leaders formulate strategies, make decisions, and implement them. Particularly successful managers are able either to buffer their organizations from environmental disturbances or to arrange smooth adjustments that require minimal disruption of organizational structure. . . .

Clearly, leaders of organizations do formulate strategies and organizations do adapt to environmental contingencies. As a result at least some of the relationship between structure and environment must reflect adaptive behavior or learning. But there is no reason to presume that the great structural variability among organizations reflects only or even primarily adaptation.

There are a number of obvious limitations on the ability of organizations to adapt. That is, there are a number of processes that generate structural inertia. The stronger the pressures, the lower the organizations' adaptive flexibility and the more likely that the logic of environmental selection is appropriate. As a consequence, the issue of structural inertia is central to the choice between adaptation and selection models. . . .

Inertial pressures arise from both internal structural arrangements and environmental constraints. A minimal list of the constraints arising from internal considerations follows.

1. An organization's investment in plant, equipment, and specialized personnel constitutes assets that are not easily transferable to other tasks or functions. . . .

2. Organizational decision makers also face constraints on the information they receive. Much of what we know about the flow of information through organizational structures tells us that leaders do not obtain anything close to

full information on activities within the organization and environmental contingencies facing the subunits.

3. Internal political constraints are even more important. When organizations alter structure, political equilibria are disturbed. As long as the pool of resources is fixed, structural change almost always involves redistribution of resources across subunits. Such redistribution upsets the prevailing system of exchange among subunits (or subunit leaders). So at least some subunits are likely to resist any proposed reorganization. Moreover, the benefits of structural reorganization are likely to be both generalized (designed to benefit the organization as a whole) and long-run. Any negative political response will tend to generate short-run costs that are high enough that organizational leaders will forego the planned reorganization. . . .

4. Finally, organizations face constraints generated by their own history. Once standards of procedure and the allocation of tasks and authority have become the subject of normative agreement, the costs of change are greatly increased. Normative agreements constrain adaptation in at least two ways. First, they provide a justification and an organizing principle for those elements that wish to resist reorganization (i.e., they can resist in terms of a shared principle). Second, normative agreements preclude the serious consideration of many alternative responses. For example, few research-oriented universities seriously consider adapting to declining enrollments by eliminating the teaching function. To entertain this option would be to challenge central organizational norms.[2]

The external pressures toward inertia seem to be at least as strong. They include at least the following factors.

1. Legal and fiscal barriers to entry and exit from markets (broadly defined) are numerous. Discussions of organizational behavior typically emphasize barriers to entry (state licensed monopoly positions, etc.). Barriers to exit are equally interesting. There are an increasing number of instances in which political decisions prevent firms from abandoning certain activities. All such constraints on entry and exit limit the breadth of adaptation possibilities.

2. Internal constraints upon the availability of information are paralleled by external constraints. The acquisition of information about relevant environments is costly particularly in turbulent situations where the information is most essential. In addition, the type of specialists employed by the organization constrains both the nature of the information it is likely to obtain (see Granovetter 1973) and the kind of specialized information it can process and utilize.

3. Legitimacy constraints also emanate from the environment. Any legitimacy an organization has been able to generate constitutes an asset in manipulating the environment. To the extent that adaptation (e.g., eliminating undergraduate instruction in public universities) violates the legitimacy claims, it incurs considerable costs. So external legitimacy considerations also tend to limit adaptation.

4. Finally, there is the collective rationality problem. One of the most difficult issues in contemporary economics concerns general equilibria. If one can find an optimal strategy for some individual buyer or seller in a competitive market, it does not necessarily follow that there is a general equilibrium once all players start trading. More generally, it is difficult to establish that a strategy that is rational for a single decision maker will be rational if adopted by a large number of decision makers. . . . We should not presume that a course of action that is adaptive for a single organization facing some changing environment will be adaptive for many competing organizations adopting a similar strategy.

A number of these inertial pressures can be accommodated within the adaptation framework. But to do so greatly limits the scope of one's investigation. We argue that in order to deal with the various inertial pressures the adaptation perspective must be supplemented with a selection orientation.

We consider first two broad issues that are preliminary to ecological modeling. The first concerns appropriate units of analysis. Typical analyses of the relation of organizations to environments take the point of view of a single organization facing an environment. We argue for an explicit focus on populations of organizations. The second broad issue concerns the applicability of population ecology models to the study of human social organization. Our substantive proposal begins with Hawley's (1950, 1968) classic statement on human ecology. We seek to extend Hawley's work in two ways: by using explicit competition models to specify the process producing isomorphism between organizational structure and environmental demands, and by using niche theory to extend the problem to dynamic environments. We argue that Hawley's perspective, modified and extended in these ways, serves as a useful starting point for population ecology theories of organizations.

II. Population Thinking in the Study of Organization-Environment Relations

. . . The comparison of unit choice facing the organizational analyst with that facing the bioecologist is instructive. To oversimplify somewhat, ecological analysis is conducted at three levels: individual, population, and community. Events at one level almost always have consequences at other levels. Despite this interdependence, population events cannot be reduced to individual events (since individuals do not reflect the full genetic variability of the population) and community events cannot be simply reduced to population events. Both the latter employ a population perspective which is not appropriate at the individual level.

The situation faced by the organizations analyst is more complex. Instead of three levels of analysis, he faces at least five: (1) members, (2) subunits, (3) individual organizations, (4) populations of organizations, and (5) communities of (populations of) organizations. Levels 3–5 can be seen as corresponding to the

three levels discussed for general ecology, with the individual organization taking the place of the individual organism. The added complexity arises because organizations are more nearly decomposable into constituent parts than are organisms. Individual members and subunits may move from organization to organization in a manner which has no parallel in nonhuman organization.

Instances of theory and research dealing with the effects of environments on organizations are found at all five levels. . . . But, the most common focus is on the organization and its environment. In fact, this choice is so widespread that there appears to be a tacit understanding that individual organizations are the appropriate units for the study of organization-environment relations.

We argue for a parallel development of theory and research at the population (and, ultimately, the community) level. . . . Unfortunately, identifying a population of organizations is no simple matter. The ecological approach suggests that one focus on common fate with respect to environmental variations. Since all organizations are distinctive, no two are affected identically by any given exogenous shock. Nevertheless, we can identify classes of organizations which are relatively homogenous in terms of environmental vulnerability. . . .

If we are to follow the lead of population biologists, we must identify an analogue to the biologist's notion of species. Various species are defined ultimately in terms of genetic structure. As Monod (1971) indicates, it is useful to think of genetic content of any species as a blueprint. The blueprint contains the rules for transforming energy into structure. Consequently all of the adaptive capacity of a species is summarized in the blueprint. If we are to identify a species analogue for organizations, we must search for such blueprints. These will consist of rules or procedures for obtaining and acting upon inputs in order to produce an organizational product or response.

The type of blueprint one identifies depends on substantive concerns. . . . For us, an organizational form is a blueprint for organizational action, for transforming inputs into outputs. The blueprint can usually be inferred, albeit in somewhat different ways, by examining any of the following: (1) the formal structure of the organization in the narrow sense—tables of organization, written rules of operation, etc.; (2) the patterns of activity within the organization—what actually gets done by whom; or (3) the normative order—the ways of organizing that are defined as right and proper by both members and relevant sectors of the environment.

To complete the species analogue, we must search for qualitative differences among forms. It seems most likely that we will find such differences in the first and third areas listed above, formal structure and normative order. The latter offers particularly intriguing possibilities. Whenever the history of an organization, its politics, and its social structure are encoded in a normative claim (e.g., professionalization and collegial authority), one can use these claims to identify forms and define populations for research. . . .

Just as the organizational analyst must choose a unit of analysis, so must he choose a system for study. Given a systems definition, a population of organizations consists of all the organizations within a particular boundary that have a common form. . . . We suggest that a population ecology of organizations must seek to understand the distributions of organizations across environmental conditions and the limitations on organizational structures in different environments, and more generally seek to answer the question, Why are there so many kinds of organizations?

III. Discontinuities in Ecological Analysis

Utilization of models from ecology in the study of organizations poses a number of analytic challenges involving differences between human and nonhuman organizations with regard to their essential ingredients. Consider, first, the nongenetic transmission of information. Biological analyses are greatly simplified by the fact that most useful information concerning adaptation to the environment (which information we call structure) is transmitted genetically. Genetic processes are so nearly invariant that extreme continuity in structure is the rule. . . . The extreme structural invariance of species greatly simplifies the problem of delimiting and identifying populations. . . . When a population with given properties increases its net reproduction rate following an environmental change, it follows that it is being selected for. . . .

Human social organization presumably reflects a greater degree of learning or adaptation. As a result it is more difficult to define fitness in a precise way. Under at least some conditions, organizations may undergo such extreme structural change that they shift from one form to another. As a result, extreme adaptation may give rise to observed changes that mimic selection. This is particularly problematic when the various organizational forms are similar on many dimensions. . . .

Many theorists have asserted that structural change attends growth; in other words, a single organization cannot grow indefinitely and still maintain its original form. For instance, a mouse could not possibly maintain the same proportion of body weight to skeletal structure while growing as big as a house. It would neither look like a mouse nor operate physiologically like a mouse. Boulding (1953) and Haire (1959) argue that the same is true for organizations. . . . If it is true that organizational form changes with size, selection mechanisms may indeed operate with regard to the size distribution. When big organizations prevail it may be useful to view this as a special case of selection, in which the movement from "small form" to "large form" is theoretically indistinguishable from dissolution ("death") of small organizations and their replacement by (the "birth" of) large organizations. . . .

IV. The Principle of Isomorphism

In the best developed statement of the principles of human ecology, Hawley (1968) answers the question of why there are so many kinds of organizations. According to Hawley, the diversity of organizational forms is isomorphic to the diversity of environments. In each distinguishable environmental configuration one finds, in equilibrium, only that organizational form optimally adapted to the demands of the environment. Each unit experiences constraints which force it to resemble other units with the same set of constraints. . . .

While the proposition seems completely sound from an ecological perspective, it does not address a number of interesting considerations. There are at least two respects in which the isomorphism formulation must be modified and extended if it is to provide satisfactory answers to the question posed. The first modification concerns the mechanism or mechanisms responsible for equilibrium. In this respect, the principle of isomorphism must be supplemented by a criterion of selection and a competition theory. The second modification deals with the fact that the principle of isomorphism neither speaks to issues of optimum adaptation to changing environments nor recognizes that populations of organizations often face multiple environments which impose somewhat inconsistent demands. . . .

V. Competition Theory

. . . Optimization raises two issues: Who is optimizing, and what is being optimized? It is quite commonly held, as in the theory of the firm, that organizational decision makers optimize profit over sets of organizational actions. From a population ecology perspective, it is the environment which optimizes.[3] Whether or not individual organizations are consciously adapting, the environment selects out optimal combinations of organizations. So if there is a rationality involved, it is the "rationality" of natural selection. Organizational rationality and environmental rationality may coincide in the instance of firms in competitive markets. In this case, the optimal behavior of each firm is to maximize profit and the rule used by the environment (market, in this case) is to select out profit maximizers. . . .

A focus on selection invites an emphasis on competition. Organizational forms presumably fail to flourish in certain environmental circumstances because other forms successfully compete with them for essential resources. As long as the resources which sustain organizations are finite and populations have unlimited capacity to expand, competition must ensue.

Hawley (1950, pp. 201–3) following Durkheim (1947) among others, places a heavy emphasis on competition as a determinant of patterns of social organization. . . . In Hawley's model, competition processes typically involve four stages: (1) demand for resources exceeds supply; (2) competitors become more similar as standard conditions of competition bring forth a uniform response; (3) selection eliminates the weakest competitors; and (4) deposed competitors differentiate either territorially or functionally, yielding a more complex division of labor. . . .

The first step in constructing an ecological model of competition is to state the nature of the population growth process. At a minimum we wish the model to incorporate the idea that resources available at any moment for each form of organization are finite and fixed. . . . We also wish to incorporate the view that the rate at which units are added to populations of organizations depends on how much of the fixed capacity has already been exhausted. The greater the unexhausted capacity in an environment, the faster should be the rate of growth of populations of organizations. But the rate at which populations of organizations can expand into unused capacity varies among forms of organization. So there are two distinctive ecological considerations: the capacity of the environment to support forms of organization and the rate at which the populations grow (or decline) when the environmental support changes. . . .

One can show that when growth in population is constrained only by resource availability, the number of distinct resources sets an upper bound on diversity in the system.[4] Even more generally, the upper bound on diversity is equal to the number of distinct resources plus the number of additional constraints on growth (Levin 1970). . . .

The increasingly important role of the state in regulating economic and social action provides numerous opportunities for analyzing the impact of changes in constraint structures on the diversity of organizational forms. Consider the impact of licensing laws, minimum wage, health, and safety legislation, affirmative action, and other regulations on organizational action. When such regulations are applied to the full range of organizations in broad areas of activity they undoubtedly alter the size distributions of organizations. Most often they select out the smallest organizations. But it is not difficult to imagine situations in which medium-sized organizations (more precisely, those with some minimum level of complexity) would be more adversely affected. Besides altering size distributions, such regulations undoubtedly affect the diversity of organizational arrangements in other ways. Here one could analyze the impact of state action on the diversity of accounting systems within industries, curricula within universities, departmental structures within hospitals, etc. In each case it would be essential to determine whether the newly imposed constraint replaced lower level constraints, in which case diversity should decline, or whether the constraint cumulated with the existing constraints in which case organizational diversity would be likely to increase. . . .

When large-sized organizations emerge they pose a competitive threat to medium-sized but hardly any threat to small organizations. In fact, the rise of large organizations may increase the survival chances of small ones in a manner not anticipated in the classical model. When the large organizations enter, those in the middle of the size distribution are trapped. Whatever strategy they adopt to fight off the challenge of the larger form makes them more vulnerable in competition with small organizations and vice versa. That is, at least in a stable environment the two ends of the size distribution ought to outcompete the middle. . . .

VI. Niche Theory

. . . Intuition suggests that isomorphism holds as a good approximation only in stable environments. Faced with unstable environments, organizations ought to develop a generalist structure that is not optimally adapted to any single environmental configuration but is optimal over an entire set of configurations. In other words, we ought to find specialized organizations in stable and certain environments and generalist organizations in unstable and uncertain environments. Whether or not this simple proposition holds for social organizations, only empirical research will tell. However, a variety of population ecology models suggests that it is too simplistic. . . .

The concept of "niche," initially borrowed by biologists from early social science, plays a central role in ecological theory. . . . The (realized) niche of a population is defined as that area in constraint space (the space whose dimensions are levels of resources, etc.) in which the population outcompetes all other local populations. The niche, then, consists of all those combinations of resource levels at which the population can survive and reproduce itself.

Each population occupies a distinct niche. For present purposes it suffices to consider cases where pairs of populations differ with respect to a single environmental dimension, E, and are alike with respect to all others. Then relative competitive positions can be simply summarized as in Figure 1. As we have drawn this figure, one population, A, occupies a very broad niche, whereas the other, B, has concentrated its fitness, denoted W, on a very narrow band of environmental variation. This distinction,

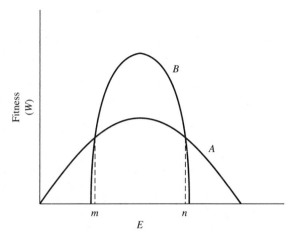

Figure 1
Fitness functions (niches) for specialists and generalists

which is usually referred to as generalism versus specialism, is crucial to biological ecology and to a population ecology of organizations.

In essence, the distinction between specialism and generalism refers to whether a population of organizations flourishes because it maximizes its exploitation of the environment and accepts the risk of having that environment change or because it accepts a lower level of exploitation in return for greater security. Whether or not the equilibrium distribution of organizational forms is dominated by the specialist depends, as we will see, on the shape of the fitness sets and on properties of the environment.

Part of the efficiency resulting from specialism is derived from the lower requirements for excess capacity. Given some uncertainty, most organizations maintain some excess capacity to insure the reliability of performance. In a rapidly changing environment, the definition of excess capacity is likely to change frequently. What is used today may become excess tomorrow, and what is excess today may be crucial tomorrow. . . .

The importance of excess capacity is not completely bound up with the issue of how much excess capacity will be maintained. It also involves the manner in which it is used.

Organizations may insure reliable performance by creating specialized units, as Thompson (1967) suggests, or they may allocate excess capacity to organizational roles, by employing personnel with skills and abilities which exceed the routine requirements of their jobs. . . .

Excess capacity may also be allocated to the development and maintenance of procedural systems. When the certainty of a given environmental state is high, organizational operations should be routine, and coordination can be accomplished by formalized rules and the investment of resources in training incumbents to follow those formalized procedures. . . . However, when certainty is low, organizational operations are less routine. Under these circumstances, a greater allocation of resources to develop and maintain procedural systems is counterproductive and optimal organizational forms will allocate resources to less formalized systems capable of more innovative responses (e.g., committees and teams). In this case, excess capacity is represented by the increased time it takes such structures to make decisions and by increased coordination costs.

The point here is that populations of organizational forms will be selected for or against depending upon the amount of excess capacity they maintain and how they allocate it. . . . Under a given set of environmental circumstances the fundamental ecological question is: which forms thrive and which forms disappear.

Generalism may be observed in a population of organizations, then, either in its reliance upon a wide variety of resources simultaneously or in its maintenance of excess capacity at any given time. This excess capacity allows such organizations to change in order to take advantage of resources which become more readily available. Corporations which maintain an unusually large proportion of their total assets in fluid form ("slack," in terms of theory of the firm; Penrose 1959; Cyert and March 1963) are generalizing. In either case, generalism is costly. Under stable environmental circumstances, generalists will be outcompeted by specialists. And at any given point in time, a static analysis will reveal excess capacity. An implication—shifting our focus to individual generalists—is that outside agents will often mistake excess capacity for waste. . . .

Variation is fine-grained when typical durations in states are short relative to the lifetime of organizations. Otherwise, the environment is said to be coarse-grained. Demand for products or services is often characterized by fine-grained variation whereas changes in legal structures are more typically coarse-grained.

The essential difference between two types of environmental variation is the cost of suboptimal strategies. The problem of ecological adaptation can be considered a game of chance in which the population chooses a strategy (specialism or generalism) and then the environment chooses an outcome (by, say, flipping a coin). If the environment "comes up" in a state favorable to the organizational form, it prospers; otherwise, it declines. However, if the variation is fine-grained (durations are short), each population of organizations experiences a great many trials and environment is experienced as an average. When variation is coarse-grained, however, the period of decline stemming from a wrong choice may exceed the organizational capacity to sustain itself under unfavorable conditions. . . .

Consider first the cases in which the environment is stable (i.e., $p = 1$). Not surprisingly, specialism is optimal. The results for unstable environments diverge. When the fitness set is convex (i.e., the demands of the different environmental states are similar and/or complementary), generalism is optimal. But when the environmental demands differ (and the fitness set is concave), specialism is optimal. This is not as strange a result as it first appears. When the environment changes rapidly among quite different states, the cost of generalism is high. Since the demands in different states are dissimilar, considerable structural management is required of generalists. But since the environment changes rapidly, these organizations will spend most of their time and energies adjusting structure. It is apparently better under such conditions to adopt a specialized structure and "ride out" the adverse environments.

The case of coarse-grained environments is somewhat more complex. Our intuitive understanding is that since the duration of an environmental state is long, maladaptation ought to be given greater weight. That is, the costs of maladaptation greatly outweigh any advantage incurred by the correct choice. . . .

The combination of coarse-grained environmental variation and concave fitness sets raises a further possibility. The optimal adaptation in the face of environmental uncertainty possesses fairly low levels of fitness in either state. It seems clear that there must be a better solution. . . .

Coarse-grained and uncertain variation favors a distinct form of generalism: polymorphism. We do not have to search very far to find an analogous outcome. Organizations may federate in such a way that supraorganizations consisting of heterogeneous collections of specialist organizations pool resources. When the environment is uncertain and coarse-grained and subunits difficult to set up and tear down, the costs of maintaining the unwieldy structure imposed by federation may be more than offset by the fact that at least a portion of the amalgamated organization will do well no matter what the state of the environment. In terms of the model suggested above there are no other situations in which such federated organizations have a competitive advantage. And even in this case, the only time during which they have such an advantage is when coarse-grained variation is uncertain. . . .

Much more can be said concerning applications of niche theory to organization-environment relations. We have focused on a simple version highlighting the interplay between competition and environmental variation in the determination of optimal adaptive structure in order to show that the principle of isomorphism needs considerable expansion to deal with multiple environmental outcomes and their associated uncertainty. The literature in ecology to which we have made reference is growing exponentially at the moment and new results and models are appearing monthly. The products of these developments provide students of organizations with a rich potential for the study of organization-environment relations. . . .

VII. Discussion

Our aim in this paper has been to move toward an application of modern population ecology theory to the study of organization-environment relations. For us, the central question is, why are there so many kinds of organizations? Phrasing the question in this way opens the possibility of applying a rich variety of formal models to the analysis of the effects of environmental variations on organizational structure.

We begin with Hawley's classic formulation of human ecology. However, we recognize that ecological theory has progressed enormously since sociologists last systematically applied ideas from bioecology to social organization. Nonetheless, Hawley's theoretical perspective remains a very useful point of departure. In particular we concentrate on the principle of isomorphism. This principle asserts that there is a one-to-one correspondence between structural elements of social organization and those units that mediate flows of essential resources into the system. It explains the variations in organizational forms in equilibrium. But any observed isomorphism can arise from purposeful adaptation of organizations to the common constraints they face or because nonisomorphic organizations are selected against. Surely both processes are a work in most social systems. We believe that the organizations literature has emphasized the former to the exclusion of the latter.

We suspect that careful empirical research will reveal that for wide classes of organizations there are very strong inertial pressures on structure arising both from internal arrangements (e.g., internal politics) and the environment (e.g., public legitimation of organizational activity). To claim otherwise is to ignore the most obvious feature of organizational life. Failing churches do not become retail stores; nor do firms transform themselves into churches. Even within broad areas of organizational action, such as higher education and labor union activity, there appear to be substantial obstacles to fundamental structural change. Research is needed on this issue. . . .

We suggest that the concrete implication of generalism for organizations is the accumulation and retention of varieties of excess capacity. To retain the flexibility of structure required for adaptation to different environmental outcomes requires that some capacities be held in reserve and not committed to action. Generalists will always be outperformed by specialists who, with the same levels of resources, happen to have hit upon their optimal environment. Consequently, in any cross-section the generalists will appear inefficient because excess capacity will often be judged waste. Nonetheless, organizational slack is a pervasive feature of many types of organizations. The question then arises: what types of environments favor generalists? Answering this question comprehensively takes one a long way toward understanding the dynamic of organization-environment relations. . . .

We have identified some of the leading conceptual and methodological obstacles to applying population ecology models to the study of organization-environment relations. We pointed to differences between human and nonhuman social organization in terms of mechanisms of structural invariance and structural change, associated problems of delimiting populations of organizations, and difficulties in defining fitness for populations of expandable units. In each case we have merely sketched the issues and proposed short-run simplifications which would facilitate the application of existing models. Clearly, each issue deserves careful scrutiny. . . .

We doubt that many readers will dispute the contention that failure rates are high for new and/or small organizations. However, much of the sociological literature and virtually all of the critical literature on large organizations tacitly accepts the view that such organizations are not subject to strong selection pressures. While we do not yet have the empirical data to judge this hypothesis, we can make several comments. First, we do not dispute that the largest organizations individually and collectively exercise strong dominance over most of the organizations that constitute their environments. But it does not follow from the observation that such organizations are strong in any one period that they will be strong in every period. Thus, it is interesting to know how firmly embedded are the largest and most powerful organizations. Consider the so-called Fortune 500, the largest publicly owned industrial firms in the United States. We contrasted the lists for 1955 and 1975 (adjusting for pure name changes). Of those on the list in 1955, only 268 (53.6%) were still listed in 1975. One hundred twenty-two had disappeared through merger, 109 had slipped off the "500," and one (a firm specializing in Cuban sugar!) had been liquidated. The number whose relative sales growth caused them to be dropped from the list is quite impressive in that the large number of mergers had opened many slots on the list. So we see that, whereas actual liquidation was rare for the largest industrial firms in the United States over a 20-year period, there was a good deal of volatility with regard to position in this pseudodominance structure because of both mergers and slipping sales.[5]

Second, the choice of time perspective is important. Even the largest and most powerful organizations fail to survive over long periods. For example, of the thousands of firms in business in the Unites States during the Revolution, only 13 survive as autonomous firms and seven as recognizable divisions of firms (*Nation's Business* 1976). Presumably one needs a longer time perspective to study the population ecology of the largest and most dominant organizations.

Third, studying small organizations is not such a bad idea. The sociological literature has concentrated on the largest organizations for obvious design reasons. But, if inertial pressures on certain aspects of structure are strong enough, intense selection among small organizations may greatly constrain the variety observable among large organizations. At least some elements of structure change with size (as we argued in Section III) and the pressure toward inertia should not be overemphasized. Nonetheless we see much value in studies of the organizational life cycle that would inform us as to which aspects of structure get locked in during which phases of the cycle. For example, we conjecture that a critical period is that during which the organization grows beyond the control of a single owner/manager. At this time the manner in which authority is delegated, if at all, seems likely to have a lasting impact on organizational structure. This is the period during which an organization becomes less an extension of one or a few dominant individuals and more an organization per se with a life of its own. If the selection pressures at this point are as intense as anecdotal evidence suggests they are, selection models will prove very useful in accounting for the varieties of forms among the whole range of organizations. . . .

Fourth, we must consider what one anonymous reader, caught up in the spirit of our paper, called the anti-eugenic actions of the state in saving firms such as Lockheed from failure. This is a dramatic instance of the way in which large dominant organizations can create linkages with other large and powerful ones so as to reduce selection pressures. If such moves are effective, they alter the pattern of selection. In our view the selection pressure is bumped up to a higher level. So instead of individual organizations failing, entire networks fail. The general consequence of a large number of linkages of this sort is an increase in the instability of the entire system (Simon 1962, 1973; May 1973), and therefore we should see boom and bust cycles of organizational outcomes. Selection models retain relevance, then, even when the systems of organizations are tightly coupled (see Hannan 1976).

Finally, some readers of earlier drafts have (some approvingly, some disapprovingly) treated our arguments as metaphoric. This is not what we intend. In a fundamental sense all theoretical activity involves metaphoric activity (although admittedly the term "analogue" comes closer than does "metaphor"). The use of metaphors or analogues enters into the formulation of "if . . . then" statements. For example, certain molecular genetic models draw an analogy between DNA surfaces and crystal structures. The latter have simple well-behaved geometric structures amenable to strong topological (mathematical) analysis. No one argues that DNA proteins are crystals; but to the extent that their surfaces have certain crystal-like properties, the mathematical model used to analyze crystals will shed light on the genetic structure. This is, as we understand it, the general strategy of model building. . . .

Instead of applying biological laws to human social organization, we advocate the application of population ecology theories. As we have indicated at a number of points, these theories are quite general and must be modified for any concrete application (sociological *or* biological). Our purpose has been twofold. First, we sketched some of the alterations in perspective required if population ecology theories are to be applied to the study of organizations. Second, we wished to stimulate a reopening of the lines of communication between sociology and ecology. It is ironic that Hawley's (1944, p. 399) diagnosis of some 30 years ago remains apt today: "Probably most of the difficulties which beset human ecology may be traced to the isolation of the subject from the mainstream of ecological thought."

Notes

1. There is a subtle relationship between selection and adaptation. Adaptive learning for individuals usually consists of selection among behavioral responses. Adaptation for a population involves selection among types of members. More generally, processes involving selection can usually be recast at a higher level of analysis as adaptation processes. However, once the unit of analysis is chosen there is no ambiguity in distinguishing selection from adaptation. Organizations often adapt to environmental conditions in concert and this suggests a systems effect. Though few theorists would deny the existence of such systems effects, most do not make them a subject of central concern. It is important to notice that, from the point of view embraced by sociologists whose interests focus on the broader social system, selection in favor of organizations with one set of properties to the disfavor of those with others is often an adaptive process. Societies and communities which consist in part of formal organizations adapt partly through processes that adjust the mixture of various kinds of organizations found within them. Whereas a complete theory of organization and environment would have to consider both adaptation and selection, recognizing that they are complementary processes, our purpose here is to show what can be learned from studying selection alone (see Aldrich and Pfeffer [1976] for a synthetic review of the literature focusing on these different perspectives).

2. Meyer's (1970) discussion of an organization's charter adds further support to the argument that normative agreements arrived at early in an organization's history constrain greatly the organization's range of adaptation to environmental constraints.

3. In biological applications, one assumes that power (in the physical sense) is optimized by natural selection in accordance with the so-called Darwin-Lotka law. For the case of human social organization, one might argue that selection optimizes the utilization of a specific set of resources including but not restricted to the power and the time of members.

4. A more precise statement of the theorem is that no stable equilibrium exists for a system of M competitors and $N < M$ resources (MacArthur and Levins 1964).

5. From at least some perspectives, mergers can be viewed as changes in form. This will almost certainly be the case when the organizations merged have very different structures. These data also indicate a strong selective advantage for a conglomerate form of industrial organization.

References

ALDRICH, HOWARD E., & JEFFREY PFEFFER. 1976. "Environments of Organizations." *Annual Review of Sociology* 2: 79-105.

ALDRICH, HOWARD E., & ALBERT J. REISS. 1976. "Continuities in the Study of Ecological Succession: Changes in the Race Composition of Neighborhoods and Their Businesses." *American Journal of Sociology* 81 (January): 846-866.

BLAU, PETER M. 1972. "Interdependence and Hierarchy in Organizations." *Social Science Research* 1 (April): 1-24.

BLAU, PETER M., & RICHARD A. SCHOENHERR. 1971. *The Structure of Organizations.* New York: Basic.

BLAU, PETER M., & W. RICHARD SCOTT. 1962. *Formal Organizations.* San Francisco: Chandler.

BOLTON, J. E. 1971. *Small Firms.* Report of the Committee of Inquiry on Small Firms. London: Her Majesty's Stationery Office.

BOULDING, KENNETH. 1953. "Toward a General Theory of Growth." *Canadian Journal of Economics and Political Science* 19: 326-340.

BURNS, TOM, & G. M. STALKER. 1961. *The Management of Innovation.* London: Tavistock.

CAPLOW, THEODORE. 1957. "Organizational Size." *Administrative Science Quarterly* 1 (March): 484-505.

CHURCHILL, BETTY C. 1955. "Age and Life Expectancy of Business Firms." *Survey of Current Business* 35 (December): 15-19.

CROZIER, MICHEL. 1964. *The Bureaucratic Phenomenon.* Chicago: University of Chicago Press.

CYERT, RICHARD M., & JAMES G. MARCH. 1963. *A Behavioral Theory of the Firm.* Englewood Cliffs, N.J.: Prentice-Hall.

DOWNS, ANTHONY. 1967. *Inside Bureaucracy.* Boston: Little, Brown.

DURKHEIM, É. 1947. *The Division of Labor in Society.* Translated by G. Simpson. Glencoe, Ill.: Free Press.

ELTON, C. 1927. *Animal Ecology.* London: Sidgwick & Jackson.

FREEMAN, JOHN. 1975. "The Unit Problem in Organizational Research." Presented at the annual meeting of the American Sociological Association, San Francisco.

FREEMAN, JOHN, & JACK BRITTAIN. 1977. "Union Merger Processes and Industrial Environments." *Industrial Relations,* in press.

FRIEDMAN, MILTON. 1953. *Essays on Positive Economics.* Chicago: University of Chicago Press.

GAUSE, G. F. 1934. *The Struggle for Existence.* Baltimore: Williams & Wilkins.

GRAICUNAS, V. A. 1933. "Relationship in Organizations." *Bulletin of the International Management Institute* (March), pp. 183-187.

GRANOVETTER, MARK S. 1973. "The Strength of Weak Ties." *American Journal of Sociology* 78 (May): 1360-1380.

HAIRE, MASON. 1959. "Biological Models and Empirical Histories of the Growth of Organizations." Pp. 272-306 in *Modern Organization Theory,* edited by Mason Haire. New York: Wiley.

HANNAN, MICHAEL T. 1975. "The Dynamics of Ethnic Boundaries." Unpublished.

———. 1976. "Modeling Stability and Complexity in Networks of Organizations." Presented at the annual meeting of the American Sociological Association, New York.

HANNAN, MICHAEL T. & JOHN FREEMAN. 1974. "Environment and the Structure of Organizations." Presented at the annual meeting of the American Sociological Association, Montreal.

HAWLEY, AMOS H. 1944. "Ecology and Human Ecology." *Social Forces* 22 (May): 398-405.

———. 1950. *Human Ecology: A Theory of Community Structure.* New York: Ronald.

———. 1968. "Human Ecology." Pp. 328-337 in *International Encylopedia of the Social Sciences,* edited by David L. Sills. New York: Macmillan.

HOLLANDER, EDWARD O., ed. 1967. *The Future of Small Business.* New York: Praeger.

HUMMON, NORMAN P., PATRICK DOREIAN, & KLAUS TEUTER. 1975. "A Structural Control Model of Organizational Change." *American Sociological Review* 40 (December): 812-824.

HUTCHINSON, G. EVELYN. 1957. "Concluding Remarks." *Cold Spring Harbor Symposium on Quantitative Biology* 22:415-427.

————. 1959. "Homage to Santa Rosalia, or Why Are There So Many Kinds of Animals?" *American Naturalist* 93: 145–159.

LEVIN, SIMON A. 1970. "Community Equilibrium and Stability: An Extension of the Competitive Exclusion Principle." *American Naturalist* 104 (September–October): 413–423.

LEVINE, SOL & PAUL E. WHITE. 1961. "Exchange as a Framework for the Study of Interorganizational Relationships." *Administrative Science Quarterly* 5 (March): 583–601.

LEVINS, RICHARD. 1962. "Theory of Fitness in a Heterogeneous Environment. I. The Fitness Set and Adaptive Function." *American Naturalist* 96 (November–December): 361–378.

————. 1968. *Evolution in Changing Environments.* Princeton, N.J.: Princeton University Press.

MacARTHUR, ROBERT H. 1972. *Geographical Ecology: Patterns in the Distribution of Species.* Princeton, N.J.: Princeton University Press.

MacARTHUR, ROBERT H., & RICHARD LEVINS. 1964. "Competition, Habitat Selection and Character Displacement in Patchy Environment." *Proceedings of the National Academy of Sciences* 51:1207–1210.

MARCH, JAMES G., & HERBERT SIMON. 1958. *Organizations.* New York: Wiley.

MARSCHAK, JACOB, & ROY RADNER. 1972. *Economic Theory of Teams.* New Haven, Conn.: Yale University Press.

MAY, ROBERT M. 1973. *Stability and Complexity in Model Ecosystems.* Princeton, N.J.: Princeton University Press.

MEYER, JOHN W. 1970. "The Charter: Conditions of Diffuse Socialization in Schools." Pp. 564–578 in *Social Processes and Social Structures,* edited by W. Richard Scott. New York: Holt, Rinehart & Winston.

MONOD, JACQUES. 1971. *Chance and Necessity.* New York: Vintage.

Nation's Business. 1976. "America's Oldest Companies." 64 (July): 36–37.

NIELSEN, FRANÇOIS, & MICHAEL T. HANNAN. 1977. "The Expansion of National Educational Systems: Tests of a Population Ecology Model." *American Sociological Review,* in press.

PARSONS, TALCOTT. 1956. "Suggestions for a Sociological Approach to the Theory of Organizations, I." *Administrative Science Quarterly* 1 (March): 63–85.

PENROSE, EDITH T. 1959. *The Theory of the Growth of the Firm.* New York: Wiley.

SELZNICK, PHILIP. 1957. *Leadership in Administration.* New York: Row, Peterson.

SIMON, HERBERT A. 1962. "The Architecture of Complexity." *Proceedings of the American Philosophical Society* 106 (December): 467–482.

————. 1973. "The Organization of Complex Systems." Pp. 1–28 in *Hierarchy Theory: The Challenge of Complex Systems,* edited by H. Patee. New York: Braziller.

SIMON, HERBERT A., & C. P. BONINI. 1958. "The Size Distribution of Business Firms." *American Economic Review* 48 (September): 607–617.

STINCHCOMBE, ARTHUR L. 1959. "Bureaucratic and Craft Administration of Production." *Administrative Science Quarterly* 4 (June): 168–187.

————. 1965. "Social Structure and Organizations." Pp. 153–193 in *Handbook of Organizations,* edited by James G. March. Chicago: Rand McNally.

TEMPLETON, ALAN R., & EDWARD A. ROTHMAN. 1974. "Evolution in Heterogenous Environments." *American Naturalist* 108 (July–August): 409–428.

THOMPSON, JAMES D. 1967. *Organizations in Action.* New York: McGraw-Hill.

TURK, HERMAN. 1970. "Interorganizational Networks in Urban Society: Initial Perspectives and Comparative Research." *American Sociological Review* 35 (February): 1–19.

WHITTAKER, ROBERT N., & SIMON LEVIN, eds. 1976. *Niche: Theory and Application.* Stroudsberg, Pa.: Dowden, Hutchinson & Ross.

WINTER, SIDNEY G., Jr. 1964. "Economic 'Natural Selection' and the Theory of the Firm." *Yale Economic Essays* 4:224–272.

ZALD, MAYER. 1970. "Political Economy: A Framework for Analysis." Pp. 221–261 in *Power in Organizations,* edited by M. N. Zald. Nashville, Tenn.: Vanderbilt University Press.

VI

Multiple Constituencies/Market Organization Theory

Multiple constituencies organization theory represents a major departure from the perspectives discussed in the previous two chapters. To communicate the magnitude of the change clearly, we will begin our introduction to the multiple constituencies perspective by comparing its basic assumptions with those of the "modern" structural and systems theories (Chapters IV and V).

The "modern" structural and systems perspectives are rational utilitarian theories, which assume that organizations are purposeful, goal-seeking entities that exist to accomplish utilitarian purposes: to make and sell products, deliver services, improve the well-being of citizens, return a profit to investors. Although this is an oversimplification, it is reasonably accurate to claim that the primary interest of these two rational perspectives is the identification of relationships between variables in the organization and its environment (independent variables) on the one hand, and the organization's ability to perform its utilitarian purposes (dependent variables) on the other. Bolman and Deal (1984) describe the first two assumptions of the structural-systems perspective:

1. Organizations are rational institutions whose primary purpose is to accomplish established objectives; rational organizational behavior is achieved best through systems of defined rules and formal authority. Organizational control and coordination are key for maintaining organizational rationality.
2. There is a "best" structure for any organization—or at least a most appropriate structure—in light of its given objectives, the environmental conditions surrounding it, the nature of its products and/or services, and the technology of the production processes.

Most empirical studies conducted from the "modern" structural and systems perspectives attempt to use objective, scientific, quasi-experimental designs and research approaches (Cook & Campbell, 1979, pp. 10–14) to discover the nature of the relationships among variables that affect the ability of organizations to accomplish their "given" purposes effectively and/or efficiently. Theories seek to combine, expand, and generalize the research findings and to point researchers in new, potentially fruitful directions. Systems and structurally oriented theorists and researchers *assume* the existence of cause-and-effect (logical-positivist) relationships among variables and seek to identify the nature and characteristics of these relationships. When the term *rational* is used relative to "modern" structural and systems theories, it means rational from a cause-and-effect, utilitarian, goals-oriented, organizational point of view. Structural and systems theorists assume that organizations are entities, and organizations (or populations of organizations) are the appropriate units of analysis for organization research and theorizing.

In contrast, the multiple constituencies/market perspective disputes the claim that organizations exist for the accomplishment of some shared utilitarian purposes. An organization is not a lifelike thing with an almost inherent right to exist because of its mission to accomplish utilitarian purposes; rather, an organization is simply a legal fiction, an "artificial construct under the law which allows certain organizations to be treated as individuals" (Jensen & Meckling, 1976, p. 310). From this perspective, an organization is only an extension of and a means for satisfying the interests of the individuals and groups that affect and are affected by it. The process by which individual rights or claims are allocated determines how resources are distributed among organizational stakeholders. Stakeholders include external constituencies (such as clients, customers, joint venturers, a state legislature or city council, government regulatory agencies, competitors, and suppliers), internal people and groups (for example, executives, direct production workers, staff specialists, and members of other subunits who may be collaborators or competitors), as well as quasi-insiders (including members of the board of directors, or executives in a parent holding company, in for-profit firms; elected executives, members of legislative oversight committees, or members of advisory boards, in public agencies; and clients who are also members of the board of directors in nonprofit organizations). These affected individuals and groups are variously referred to as *constituencies* (Connolly, Conlon, & Deutsch, 1980) and *stakeholders* (Mitroff, 1983) or, from a more limited viewpoint, *participants* or even *subunits* (Salancik & Pfeffer, 1977).

Each of the many constituencies shares some goals with others but also has its own distinctive (sometimes changing) goals, priorities, self-interests, and criteria of organizational effectiveness. Because each constituency brings its own interests and expectations to an organization, some priorities are always in competition with others for scarce organizational resources. Thus, organizations are webs of fluid interactions, constantly changing interests, and forever shifting balances of power among coalitions of constituencies. Given this perspective, it is easy to understand why conflict is inevitable even when all of the constituencies may agree upon the organization's broad purposes or mission (Wortman, 1983). Thus, the *negotiated order* theorists (Strauss, Schatzman, Bucher, Ehrlich, & Sabshin, 1963; Day & Day, 1977) visualize organizations as in constant states of change, with "contractual relations" providing a framework for the negotiation processes through which conflicting objectives are brought into equilibrium (Jensen & Meckling, 1976).

Jensen and Meckling articulate basic assumptions about the relationships among individuals and organizations that are typical of the perspective:

Viewing the firm as the nexus of a set of contracting relationships among individuals also serves to make it clear that the personalization of the firm implied by asking questions such as "what should be the objective function of the firm," or "does the firm have a social responsibility" is seriously misleading. *The firm is not an individual.* It is a legal fiction which serves as a focus for a complex process in which conflicting objectives of individuals (some of whom may "represent" other organizations) are brought into equilibrium within a framework of contractual relations. In this sense the "behavior" of the firm is like the behavior of a market; i.e., the outcome of a complex equilibrium process. We seldom fall into the trap of characterizing the wheat or stock market as an individual, but we often make this error by thinking about organizations as if they were persons with motivations and intentions (1976, p. 311).

Various multiple constituencies theories disagree about the nature of the relationships among constituencies and organizations, so they also differ widely in their assessments of implications for organizations and managers. For example, most multiple constituencies/market theories assume that individuals and groups are rational in defining their relationship with an organization. (Notice however, that this assumption does not imply *rational organizations,* as the systems and "modern" structural theories do.) "The distinctive character of market theories is attributable to their primary unit of analysis, namely, the self-interested individual seeking to maximize his or her utility through the exercise of rational choice" (Harmon & Mayer, 1986, p. 241).

Organizations do not have goals and objectives; rather, constituencies have goals and objectives that they wish to accomplish through involvement with an organization. Organizations remain as viable entities with their identities intact only as long as the diverse interests of their constituencies are satisfied. When their interests are not met (in fact or in perception), constituencies withdraw or change the nature of their association or their "psychological contracts" (Schein, 1980) with an organization. Thus, multiple constituencies theorists, such as Williamson (1975), Jensen & Meckling (1976), Day and Day (1977), Connolly, Conlon, and Deutsch (1980), and Keeley (1983, 1988), assume that individuals and groups consciously define the nature of their relationship— and the terms for continuing their relationship—with an organization in terms of their own rational goals or interests.

However, other organization theorists modify or completely reject the assumption that individuals are rational in their associations with organizations. For example, although Ian Mitroff (1983) views organizations from a multiple-stakeholders perspective, he recognizes that human rationality must be defined to include perceptions of reality, projections of self onto others, and imputed motivations.

[People] differ in their emotional make-up and psychological structure. They perceive the same "facts" differently, if not seeing entirely different facts to begin with. As a result, one *projects* an aspect of one's internal psyche onto one's external competition. . . . One's concept of one's competitors will be psychologically infected or contaminated. What is true of the single stakeholder "competitor" is true of all the stakeholders that constitute the complex social system in which the modern corporation is embedded (p. 7).

Other organization theorists who do not ascribe to the rational multiple constituencies perspective, including Weick (1979) and White and McSwain (1983), argue that individuals and groups do not act rationally. They do not know what their self-interests are until they learn about them through participation in organizational activities. Organizing is a sense-making task that follows after relatively unplanned activities. In other words, constituencies' self interests *emerge* from participation—they are not developed or pursued proactively or rationally.

In our opinion, the similarities in assumptions warrants identifying and grouping these theories as a separate, distinctive, emerging perspective of organization theory. The differences in approaches, focal interests, and the potentially exciting implications for organizations and constituencies clearly provide more than sufficient variety to justify including the perspective in this anthology. These differences have caused various theorists that we group together here to coin and use different labels for their theories. A few of the more widely known include *multiple constituencies, market, stakeholders, social contract, negotiated order* and, to a lesser extent, *strategic-contingency*.

The multiple constituencies/market perspective fits very neatly here between the systems/contingency/population ecology theories of organization (Chapter V) and the power and politics perspective (Chapter VII), by expanding upon and bridging aspects of both. For example, virtually all recent systems theories, contingency theories, and population ecology theories are open systems models that weave the environment into organizational systems. Multiple constituencies organization theory provides useful explanations about how the environment actually becomes and functions as a dynamic part of organizations through the bargaining and influencing activities of stakeholders— particularly with respect to decisions that involve allocations of resources among organizational activities and constituencies.

Multiple constituencies/market organization theory also sets the stage for the power and politics perspective that follows in Chapter VII. The power and politics perspective is a specific application (and an expansion) of multiple constituencies theory. It focuses on the tactics and strategies that constituencies or coalitions use to gain and maintain power in and around organizations. Thus, for example, Salancik and Pfeffer's strategic-contingency theory of power bridges the population ecology, multiple constituencies, and power perspectives. In a 1977 article in *Organizational Dynamics,* Salancik and Pfeffer see power as:

> something that accrues to organizational subunits (individuals, departments) that cope with critical organizational problems. . . . Because of the processes by which power develops and is used, *organizations become both more aligned and more misaligned with their environments* [1977, p. 4, emphasis added]
>
> To the extent that power is determined by the critical uncertainties and problems facing the organization and, in turn, influences decisions in the organization, the organization is aligned with the realities it faces. In short, *power facilitates the organization's adaptation to its environment—or its problems* [1977, p. 5, emphasis added]

The intellectual heritage of all multiple constituencies/market theories includes Richard Cyert and James March's seminal (1963) book *A Behavioral Theory of the Firm,* in which organizations are described as coalitions of self-interested participants. Organizational goals are series of constraints imposed on the organization through a bargaining process among potential coalition members and elaborated over time in response to short-term pressures. The goals of an organization are simply the dominant coalition's goals for an organization. Goals arise and change constantly through bargaining processes because an organization is a dynamic coalition of individuals and groups with different demands, changing foci of attention, and only limited ability to attend to all organizational problems simultaneously. Further, organizational goals change as new participants enter and old participants exit the coalition (Cyert & March, 1963, p. 115). Social contract theories, negotiated order theories, and multiple constituencies theories all trace their roots to John Locke's *Two Treatises of Government* (1967) and, to a lesser extent, Jean-Jacques Rousseau's *The Social Contract* (1947).

The first article reprinted here, "Organizational Effectiveness: A Multiple-Constituency Approach" (1980), introduces issues that are fundamental to multiple-constituencies theory even though its subject is the evaluation of organizational effectiveness. Connolly, Conlon, and Deutsch quickly reject the organizationally rational, goals-based and systems-based approaches to evaluating organizations, because "the multiple-constituency approach views organizations as intersections of multiple influence loops, each embracing a constituency biased toward the assessment of the organization's activities in terms of its own exchanges within the loop." Organizational effectiveness is many statements of goals and priorities, "each reflecting the evaluative criteria applied by the various constituencies involved to a greater or lesser degree with the focal organization." The article also assesses some implications of the multiple constituencies approach for the distribution of organizational resources, organizational purpose and location, and evaluation time frames.

In his 1983 *Academy of Managememt Review* article, "Values in Organizational Theory and Management Education," Michael Keeley attacks the prevailing aversion that proponents of rational, scientific research exhibit toward addressing values. "Many, if not most, researchers still feel there is something illegitimate about mixing value judgments with social science." Organizational theory and research cannot and should not be value free; the decision to use collective organizational goal attainment as *the* criterion for assessing organizational worth is itself a value decision. Keeley argues for consideration of a contract model as an alternative to the utilitarian, goals-based approach. "The key insight of a contractual view is that organizations normally exist by virtue of agreement on the activities alone, on joint *means* to separate [constituencies'] purposes (possibly profits for some persons, wages for others, goods or services for another group, etc.)." We have fallen into a counterproductive trap of equating organizational worth and organizational effectiveness. The multiple constituencies–contract approach requires us to redefine or expand our definition of organizational worth to include values such as voluntariness, justice, and the processes for distribution of rights—as well as utilitarian effectiveness.

As a rule, analysis of moral rights and obligations . . . has been regarded as "too normative." But it is no more normative, and far less objectionable, than attempts to derive the responsibilities of managers and other participants from imperatives of organizational goal attainment. . . . The primary responsibility of those who manage organizations is to promote voluntary cooperation—to facilitate agreements on institutional rights that respect the moral rights of *all* participants.

"External Influences on Managers," the third reading in this chapter, is from Ian Mitroff's 1983 book *Stakeholders of the Organizational Mind.* Mitroff explains how stakeholders—all of the "wide range of forces that influence any social system"— affect decision making about complex problems of organizational policy and design. This article describes ways to "generate and analyze stakeholders at the surface level of social systems." Mitroff emphasizes the interdependence among all members of social systems, thus articulating the multiple constituencies theory perspective of organizations as boundary-spanning networks or open systems. When thinking about stakeholders, it is important to think broadly and creatively. Mitroff calls nonobvious external stakeholders *snaildarters:*

> the endangered species of fish that held up a proposed hydroelectric project for years. In all their rational plans the designers of the dam had failed to take the snaildarter into account. As a result, one class of stakeholders, environmentalists, acted in behalf of another stakeholder, the snaildarter, that could not act in its own behalf. The lesson of the snaildarter is paramount. Just beneath the surface of the best laid and most rational plans swim forces of which people are entirely unaware and do not wish to consider.

The final reading in Chapter VI is from *Markets and Hierarchies: Analysis and Antitrust Implications* (1975), by the economist Oliver E. Williamson. For several reasons, we decided to deviate here from our pattern of presenting articles chronologically within chapters. "Understanding the Employment Relation" is written by an economist for economists, and it addresses a limited part of the subject area that is usually claimed by multiple constituencies theorists. Also, it is not easy to read. On the other hand, Williamson's article represents an important inclusion in this anthology because of the importance of the subject, the careful analytical methods employed, the depth of the analysis, and the high standing that Williamson and *Markets and Hierarchies* have in the field. Further, the discipline of economics has made very important contributions to the field of organization theory which we have not recognized adequately either in prior editions of *Classics of Organization Theory* or elsewhere in this edition.

"Understanding the Employment Relation" assesses organizational decisions to produce goods and services internally versus externally, by analyzing the applicability of various types of economic contract and market models to employment relations. Thus, Williamson limits his chapter to one small but very important aspect of the multiple constituencies arena—the relationship between organizations and employees. He conceives of the decision process leading to an employer–employee relationship as being analogous to a market transaction, and uses economic market analysis to assess the viability of alternative internal labor market and contract models. Then, "Understanding the Employment Relation'' turns to prior work by Herbert Simon (1957) to examine implications of the models for organizational authority and the ''transactional rationale for internal labor markets (in terms mainly of economizing on bounded rationality and attenuating opportunism).'' Williamson demonstrates how problems of labor organization involve the study of transactions and contracting, isolates and assesses the job features that characterize internal labor markets, explains why sequential spot contracting is unsuited to these types of job features, examines authority relations and the limitations associated with Simon's (1957) evaluation of alternative contracting modes, and develops the transactional rationale for internal labor markets mainly in terms of economizing on bounded rationality and attenuating opportunism.

References

BOLMAN, L. G., & DEAL, T. E. (1984). *Modern approaches to understanding and managing organizations.* San Francisco: Jossey-Bass.

CONNOLLY, T., CONLON, E. J., & DEUTSCH, S. J. (1980). Organizational effectiveness: A multiple-constituency approach. *Academy of Management Review, 5,* 211-217.

COOK, T. D., & CAMPBELL, D. T. (1979). *Quasi-experimentation: Design & analysis issues for field settings.* Boston: Houghton Mifflin.

CYERT, R. M., & MARCH, J. G. (1963). *A behavioral theory of the firm.* Englewood Cliffs, NJ: Prentice-Hall.

DAY, R., & DAY, J. V. (1977, Winter). A review of the current state of negotiated order theory: An appreciation and a critique. *The Sociological Quarterly, 18,* 126-142.

HARMON, M. M., & MAYER, R. T. (1986). *Organization theory for public administration.* Boston: Little, Brown.

HESSEN, R. (1979). A new concept of corporations: A contractual and private property model. *Hastings Law Journal, 13,* 1327-1350.

JENSEN, M. C., & MECKLING, W. H. (1976). Agency costs and the theory of the firm. *Journal of Financial Economics, 3,* 305-360.

KEELEY, M. (1980). Organizational analogy: A comparison of organismic and social contract models. *Administrative Science Quarterly, 25,* 337-362.

KEELEY, M. (1983). Values in organizational theory and management education. *Academy of Management Review, 8*(3), 376-386.

KEELEY, M. (1988). *A social-contract theory of organizations.* Notre Dame, IN: University of Notre Dame Press.

LOCKE, J. (1967). *Two treatises of government.* (Ed. by P. Laslett, 2d ed.). London: Cambridge University Press. (Original, 1690).

MITROFF, I. I. (1983). *Stakeholders of the organizational mind.* San Francisco: Jossey-Bass.

OTT, J. S. (1992, in press). Perspectives on organizational governance: Some effects on government-nonprofit relations. *Southeastern Political Review.*

ROUSSEAU, J. J. (1947). The social contract. In E. Barker, (Ed.). *Social contract* (pp. 167-307). London: Oxford University Press. (Original, 1762).

SALANCIK, G. R., & PFEFFER, J. (1977). Who gets power—and how they hold on to it: A strategic-contingency model of power. *Organizational Dynamics, 5,* 2-21.

SCHEIN, E. H. (1980). *Organizational psychology* (3d ed.). Englewood Cliffs, NJ: Prentice-Hall.

SIMON, H. A. (1957). *Models of man.* New York: Wiley.

STEERS, R. M. (1975, December). Problems in the measurement of organizational effectiveness. *Administrative Science Quarterly, 20,* 546-558.

STRAUSS, A. (1978). *Negotiations: Varieties, contexts, processes, and social order.* San Francisco: Jossey-Bass.

STRAUSS, A., SCHATZMAN, L., BUCHER, R., EHRLICH, D., & SABSHIN, M. (1963). The hospital and its negotiated order. In E. Freidson (Ed.), *The hospital in modern society* (pp. 147–169). New York: Free Press.

WEICK, K. E. (1979). *The social psychology of organizing* (2d ed.). Reading, MA: Addison-Wesley.

WHITE, O. F., JR., & McSWAIN, C. J. (1983). Transformational theory and organizational analysis. In G. Morgan (Ed.), *Beyond method: Strategies for social research.* Newbury Park, CA: Sage.

WILLIAMSON, O. E. (1975). *Markets and hierarchies: Analysis and antitrust implications: A study in the economics of internal organization.* New York: Free Press/Macmillan.

WORTMAN, M. (1983). Strategic planning in voluntary enterprises. In M. Moyer (Ed.), *Managing voluntary organizations. Proceedings of a conference held at York University. October 19–21, 1983* (pp. 147–167). Toronto, Ontario: York University.

33

Organizational Effectiveness: A Multiple-Constituency Approach

Terry Connolly, Edward J. Conlon, and Stuart Jay Deutsch

The field of organizational effectiveness research appears to be in conceptual disarray. Recent summaries of the literature reach uniformly negative conclusions: "There is only a rudimentary understanding of what is actually involved in or constitutes the concept [of organizational effectiveness]" [Steers, 1975]; "Measuring effectiveness is a critical but problematic issue" [Hrebiniak, 1978]; Organizational effectiveness . . . is an extremely untidy construct" [Campbell, et al., 1974]. Perspectives on effectiveness show little or no convergence [Molnar & Rogers, 1976] and quick improvement is unlikely [Kahn, 1977]. Some have even argued that the concept is not researchable, and should reside only as a conceptually rather than an empirically relevant construct [Hannan & Freeman, 1977]. We have no argument with such pessimism. We do, however, propose that hope not be entirely lost. This paper attempts to define a broad perspective on organizational effectiveness that encompasses rather than conflicts with existing perspectives. The proposed perspective will not attempt to

SOURCE: Terry Connolly, Edward J. Conlon, and Stuart Jay Deutsch, "Organizational Effectiveness: A Multiple-Constituency Approach," *Academy of Management Review* (1980), vol. 5, 211–217.

prescribe research directions or methodology. Rather, it will attempt to define areas of convergent theorizing and rich empirical domains.

Current Approaches to Organizational Effectiveness

Effectiveness statements are typically not descriptive; they are evaluative and often normative. That is, they are generally not attempts to answer the question "How is entity X performing?" Instead, they usually attempt to answer "How well is entity X performing?" and often "How much better should entity X perform?" The central differentiation among current effectiveness statements is in how they specify the evaluative criteria used to define "how well" the entity is performing or *could* perform.

Organizational Goals Approaches

To an "organizational goals" theorist, the problem of specifying criteria is exactly that of discovering goals. The use of "official" goal statements such as those found in articles of incorporation, organizational charter, or whatever, is seen as naive [Perrow, 1961; Porter, Lawler, & Hackman, 1976]. Instead, research effort is aimed at discovering the "operative" goals of those individuals most able to influence what the organization actually does—the "major decision makers" [Price, 1972], the "executive core" [Zald, 1963], or the "dominant coalition" [Pennings & Goodman, 1976]. This approach begs the empirical question of whether or not such a single dominant group actually exists in a given situation. Empirical studies such as those by Vroom [1960] and Lawrence and Lorsch [1967] suggest that strong goal consensus among senior managers of a single organization cannot be assumed. McCormick's [1973] suggestion that a broad survey of the organizational membership be used to identify goals allows for possible lack of consensus, but does not indicate what should be done if at least modest agreement is not found.

Systems Approaches

Theorists loosely grouped under the "systems" approach to organizational effectiveness offer a variety of ways to solve the criterion problem. At the most global level, functional analysis [Parsons, 1960; Lyden, 1975] argues that organizations may be evaluated by how well they solve the four essential problems: goal attainment, adaptation, integration, and pattern maintenance. More operationally, Evan [1976] draws on systems theory to suggest categories of measurable variables that might be related to effectiveness, but leaves the criterion problem essentially unresolved. An ingenious middle ground is proposed by Yuchtman and Seashore in what they call the "systems resource" approach. In essence, they argue that the three basic processes in an open-systems view of organizations—resource acquisition, transformation, and disposal—are tightly interconnected, so that overall effectiveness may be assessed at any point in the loop. They choose the input-acquisition process, and define effectiveness as "the ability of the organization . . . to exploit its environment in the acquisition of scarce and valued resources" [1967, p. 898].

The Crucial Assumption of Both Approaches

For all the considerable differences within and between these approaches, they share one crucial assumption: that it is possible, and desirable, to arrive at a *single* set of evaluative criteria, and thus a *single* statement of organizational effectiveness. We propose to relax this assumption. Specifically, we propose a view of organizational effectiveness in which several (or, potentially, many) different effectiveness statements can be made about the focal organization, reflecting the criterion sets of different individuals and groups we shall refer to as "constituencies." We should emphasize that this relaxation goes beyond the suggestion

[Steers, 1975] that effectiveness be treated multidimensionally, so that, for example, one could assess a given organization as highly effective in innovation, moderately effective in employee satisfaction, and so on. What we are proposing is a view of effectiveness that allows multiple evaluations from multiple constituencies, so that, for example, we might find the focal organization rated highly effective on various dimensions by its senior management, moderately effective by the employees' union, somewhat effective by its customers, and quite ineffective by a government regulatory agency. This multiplicity of ratings seems implicit in Hrebiniak's suggestion that "it may be useful to think in terms of effectiveness*es*" [1978, p. 326]. Some implications of this view are discussed in the following section.

A Multi-Constituency View of Effectiveness

We argue that an answer to the question "How well is entity X performing?" is inevitably contingent on whom one is asking. That is, the evaluative criteria required to transform a descriptive into an evaluative statement flow from the individuals or groups to whom we are referring as "constituencies," not from some abstract, value-free theory of organizations or systems. The point is, perhaps, rather obvious in the purposive, goal-seeking view of organizations: individuals become involved with an organization (as owners, managers, employees, customers, suppliers, regulators, etc.) for a variety of different reasons, and these reasons will be reflected in a variety of different evaluations. It appears somewhat arbitrary to label one of these perspectives a priori as the "correct" one. As an empirical matter, it may well be that a particular organization is so dominated by one individual or group that much of its behavior is explicable in terms of this single perspective; but this seems more appropriately a matter for empirical investigation than for assumption as the general case.

A parallel ambiguity as to purpose is implicit in a systems view of organizations—as, in fact, it is in all systems, even very simple ones. For example, the familiar furnace-thermostat system used in domestic heating appears, at first glance, to have an unambiguous purpose: the maintenance of internal temperature within preset limits. However, this purpose is not derivable from merely observing how the system operates. Such observational data are equally interpretable in terms of a "system purpose" such as "Maximize fuel consumption, subject to not exceeding an upper temperature limit," or "Minimize fuel consumption, subject to not falling below a lower temperature limit." Indeed, if the system were operated by a human thermostat and a human furnace operator, these two statements might well describe what each saw as the system purpose.

The example illustrates several important points. First, goals and constraints are, in general, interchangeable [Simon, 1961; Eilon, 1971]. Second, statements of purpose made by system members are likely to differ from one another, and do not provide an unambiguous statement of *the* system purpose. Third, such a single purpose is not derivable from observation of system behavior, no matter how detailed. Finally, the ambiguity is not the consequence of the complexity of organizations, but is found even in rather simple systems whose structural and dynamic properties are well understood.

In general, then, we treat effectiveness not as a single statement, but as a set of several (or perhaps many) statements, each reflecting the evaluative criteria applied by the various constituencies involved to a greater or lesser degree with the focal organization. In using the term "constituencies" rather than "participants," we mean to emphasize the possibility that individuals and groups not directly associated with the focal organization may form evaluations of its activities, and may be able to influence the activities of that organization to some extent. For example, an environmental group may form an assessment of the waste-disposal activities of the focal organization, and start legal proceedings aimed at enforcing a change in these practices. In doing so, the group becomes an active constituency of that organization, attempting to move the organization in a direction it sees, in terms of its own criteria, as "more effective."

Integration with Existing Views

The multiple-constituency view of organizational effectiveness may be seen as embracing as special cases several existing views of the effectiveness concept. For example, Pennings and Goodman's [1976] "dominant coalition" model presupposes the existence of a single group that has (by negotiation, side-payments, and so on) arrived at a workable shared set of evaluative criteria, and that has sufficient power to impose these criteria on the major activities of the organization. It may be the case that the objectives of all the relevant constituencies are reflected in the goals of this coalition. Whether, and in what circumstances, such dominant coalitions form is an empirical matter of considerable interest; but the multiple-constituency view has no trouble accommodating such situations as a special case of the more general phenomenon of multiple groups with more or less power to impose their evaluations on overall organizational functioning.

Systems approaches to effectiveness can be similarly accommodated as special cases. Parsonian functionalism [Parsons, 1960], for example, implies that ultimate weight be given to the evaluative criteria used by the larger society as a whole (though the mechanism by which these criteria are identified and applied is unclear). Yuchtman and Seashore's [1967] "systems resource" approach gives primary weight to the criteria applied by suppliers of scarce resources: an organization is defined as effective to the extent that it is able to maintain its supplies of such resources, presumably by satisfying the evaluative criteria of the suppliers. The evaluations of other constituencies are implicated indirectly. For example, the willingness of consumers to pay for final products generates the revenues that allow the manufacturing firm to purchase more "scarce resources" that allow further production. Thus, as with the "organizational goals" view, the "systems" approach to organizational effectiveness is embraced and, perhaps, extended by the multiple-constituency model.

The major difference between the "conceptual minimalist" perspective embraced herein and the more specific models discussed above resides in assumptions about how organizations deal with environmental (constituent) pressures. For example, the dominant coalition model presupposes that the demands of various constituencies are reflected in the goals generated by the dominant coalition. For example, if consumers demand reliable products, the goals of the dominant coalition should reflect quality control. Additionally, the potential influence of the various constituencies should also be reflected in the priority assigned to the goals of the dominant coalition. The systems resource perspective assumes that coalitions are influential to the extent that they can provide valued resources or influence resource acquisition. As suggested earlier, the general multiple-constituency approach avoids such assumptions and, by doing so, allows the case where no clear dominant constituency emerges or where influence does not directly operate through resources.

As an example of the integrative power of the multiple-constituency view, it is worth re-examining the only study of which we are aware [Molnar & Rogers, 1976] that attempted an empirical comparison of the "goals" and "systems" views of effectiveness. For 110 public agencies, these investigators obtained effectiveness ratings from agency administrators, from their peers, and from a variety of agency clients. The first two were interpreted in terms of agency goal attainment, the last in terms of systems resource effectiveness. The results showed a striking failure of convergence between the three ratings, a failure that Molnar and Rogers attribute to various conceptual and methodological problems. In a multiple-constituency view, of course, such divergence is to be expected: different constituencies rate a given organization in different ways. While Molnar and Rogers' results are thus an embarassment to both goal and systems-resource views of

effectiveness, they are perfectly consistent with multiple-constituency theory.

Some Implications of the Multiple-Constituency Approach

It is apparent that the proposed shift in the conceptual framework embracing the organizational effectiveness construct has profound implications for relevant empirical work. Without attempting a detailed research agenda, we would like to suggest three areas in which the conceptual shift might lead to a reorientation of empirical study addressing "effectiveness": the distribution of organizational satisfactions; issues of organizational location and change; and the time dimension as it relates to effectiveness.

Distributional Issues

The multiple-constituency view treats organizations as systems generating differential assessments of effectiveness by different constituencies. This view is close to that of such authors as Barnard [1938], Georgiou [1973], and Keeley [1978], who treat participant satisfaction, or inducement-contribution balance, as the central organizational issue. The present view is somewhat broader than that expressed by any of these authors. "Constituency" is intended as more inclusive than "direct participant"; and an "effectiveness statement" from any one of them is broader than their satisfaction with their own direct transaction with the focal organization. However, the conceptual similarity is strong, and it may be worth reviewing briefly the treatment of effectiveness by one of these authors, Keeley.

The first part of Keeley's argument is based directly on Barnard's participant-satisfaction model, in which the worth of an organization is assessed through "the ability of the system to maintain itself by returning human benefit in sufficient degree to induce participant cooperation" [Keeley, 1978, p. 277]. The second part of his argument proposes an overall optimality criterion for the resulting distribution of net satisfaction to participants, drawing on Rawls' [1971] criterion of "social justice." This criterion amounts to minimizing the regret of the least-advantaged participant, so that Keeley treats effectiveness in terms of this minimum point on the distribution of satisfactions across participants. It should be noted that, while the first part of this argument closely parallels the multiple-constituency view, the second part does not. We are uneasy at this point about the use of the "social justice" (or any other strongly normative) criterion to reduce multiple evaluations to a unitary effectiveness statement; and, by Keeley's argument, we would, for example, be forced to treat as highly *in*effective a prison in which the prisoners (the "most disadvantaged participants") were dissatisfied.

Despite these problems, we are impressed by the range of empirical questions that are opened up once "effectiveness" is so clearly seen as a distributional issue. For example:

How do participants (or, in our model, constituencies) become aware of their potential for shifting the distribution in their favor? What strategies are available to them to do so? How do other constituencies prevent such efforts? What coalitions are feasible and useful? Which actually form? Under what circumstances? Broadly, the concern here is with power issues, and with the ability of constituencies to recognize, develop, and exercise power so as to shift the distribution of satisfactions in their favor.

How do constituencies form? That is, how does an individual or group come to an awareness that the activities of the focal organization are both relevant to, and perhaps changeable by, appropriate action? For example, there appears to have been significant recent growth in the formation of "public-interest" (and private-interest) groups outside organizations that attempt, often successfully, to change corporate activities in areas such as environmental impact, minority and female hiring practices, and so on. The situational prerequisites and action strategies of such groups seem of considerable empirical interest, and are directly relevant to the "effectiveness" issue, as we conceive it.

Issues of Organizational Location

The multiple-constituency approach views organizations as intersections of multiple influence loops, each embracing a constituency biased toward the assessment of the organization's activities in terms of its own exchanges within the loop. In such a view, the organization's location is not merely geographic, but implies its existence as including some influence loops rather than (or more extensively than) others. In this sense, location may be a key strategic matter for currently powerful constituencies to manipulate. For example, a university may, over time, move from being primarily an undergraduate teaching school to a research and graduate-training operation. Such a change presumably implies a relative attenuation of the influence loops that connect the school to local employers, the community, the alumni, and so on, and a relative enhancement of such influence groups as federal funding agencies and the scholarly community. It is not clear how any of the current views of effectiveness would cope with such familiar organizational changes. They are, however, readily accommodated within the multiple-constituency view, which explicitly directs attention to the identification of constituencies, and thus to their possible succession over time, and to the organization's scope for the management of its constituency set.

The Temporal Dimension of Effectiveness

The issue of time frame for assessing effectiveness has generally confounded theoreticians and empiricists. The problem is that short-run organizational actions that appear ineffective (e.g., angering stockholders by withholding dividends and reinvesting) may actually be part of effective long-run strategies (e.g., growth through reinvestment rather than excessive debt). Hence an improved debt/equity ratio that attracts new investors might be highly effective in the long run. In a multiple-constituency perspective, the time issue becomes technically more complicated but conceptually clearer. Different constituencies may be dealt with by an organization in different time frames. This permits a focal organization to "time share" in terms of attention paid to the various constituencies. For example, a dean may choose to distribute raises to the faculty in a manner that appears inequitable to some portion of it (e.g., the stars) in the spring when it is too late for them to leave the organization, and then appease them with generous travel or teaching arrangements in the fall. This example illustrates several points. First, constituencies may not always be in a position to react immediately to the current distribution of satisfaction. Second, the time frames for feedback and the lag between organizational action and constituent response may permit the organization to "game" such that the bulk of satisfactions accrue to a constituency at key decision points (i.e., keep them happy when it matters most). Finally, it suggests that not *all* constituencies need managing *all* the time. The influence of time and the manner in which organizations use it is an intriguing issue with regard to effectiveness.

Conclusion

The primary intent of this essay has been to outline an alternative to the increasingly arid debate between the "organizational goals" theorists and the "systems" theorists as to which theory possesses the key to the effectiveness puzzle. In essence, we argue that neither theory does, and that the puzzle is primarily an artifact of a single, generally unstated assumption made by both: That a single statement about an organization's effectiveness is to be sought. No such assumption is, in our view, necessary or desirable.

With the obsession over a single statement removed, the door is opened to both conceptual clarification and empirical progress. In a multiple-constituency view, no surprise is engendered by the discovery that stockholders, senior managers, employee unions, and customers espouse divergent views of what the organization's goals should be. Nor is there any requirement that these groups and others should, in any particular setting, have reached a negotiated agreement or formed a dominant coalition generating operative goals. If they have done so, multiple-constituency research will reveal the fact; if not, the work is still not immobilized. Similarly, the multiple-constituency approach avoids such difficulties of systems views of effectiveness as identifying the organization's potential for acquiring scarce resources (whether or not it actually exploits this potential), or identifying the evaluative criteria applied to an organization by "society as a whole."

The multiple-constituency approach to effectiveness treats both goal and systems theories as valuable, though partial, insights into the linkages between the organization's activities and its constituencies. As we have tried to show, existing approaches, both goal-based and systems-based, can be treated as special cases of the general, multiple-constituency model. In general, the multiple-constituency approach asks: What constituencies exist in a particular setting? What effectiveness assessments does each now reach? What are the consequences of these assessments? From these questions flow a number of others: the distribution of satisfactions across constituencies, the opportunities for constituencies to affect the organization (and vice versa), the organization's location at the nexus of influence loops embracing its current and possible future constituencies, and others. In each case, the shift in conceptual base reorients empirical inquiry in directions we see as potentially fruitful.

On grounds both of conceptual clarity and empirical promise, then, the multiple-constituency approach appears to provide a more fruitful formulation of the effectiveness problem than do any of the current approaches. We specifically abandon the goal of answering questions such as "How effective is organization X?," where a single answer is expected. In our view, such questions are ill-formulated, and we feel no embarrassment that the approach we propose offers no answers to them.

We would argue that the question "Is General Motors more or less effective than HEW?" is of the same order as "Is an elephant more or less effective than a giraffe?" For both questions, we observe that both species exist, and can thus be assumed to be at least minimally adapted to their environments. Beyond that, we are more interested in the features of those environments, the adaptive mechanisms used by the organism (or organization), reactions to changes, and so on. We see no particular merit in an obsessional search for the single measure of merit on which organizations can be compared.

References

BARNARD, C. I. *The functions of the executive.* Cambridge, Mass.: Harvard University Press, 1938.

CAMPBELL, J. P.; et al. *The measurement of organizational effectiveness.* Unpublished paper, Personnel Decisions, Inc., Minneapolis, Minnesota, 1974.

EILON, S. Goals and constraints. *Journal of Management Studies,* 1971, *8*, 292–303.

EVAN, W. M. Organization theory and organizational effectiveness: An exploratory analysis. *Organizational and Administrative Science,* 1976, *7*, 15–28.

GEORGIOU, P. The goal paradigm and notes toward a counter paradigm. *Administrative Science Quarterly,* 1973, *18*, 291–310.

GOODMAN, P. S., & PENNINGS, J. M. (Eds.). *New perspectives on organizational effectiveness.* San Francisco: Jossey-Bass, 1977.

HANNAN, M. T., & FREEMAN, J. The population ecology of organizations. *American Journal of Sociology,* 1977, *82*, 929–964.

HREBINIAK, L. G. *Complex Organizations.* New York: West, 1978.

KAHN, R. L. Organizational effectiveness: An overview. In Goodman and Pennings, 1977, pp. 235–248.

KEELEY, Michael. A social-justice approach to organizational evaluation. *Administrative Science Quarterly,* 1978, *23*, 272–292.

LAWRENCE, P. R., & LORSCH, J. W. Differentiation and integration in complex organizations. *Administrative Science Quarterly,* 1967, *12*, 1–47.

LYDEN, F. J. Using Parson's functional analysis in the study of public organizations. *Administrative Science Quarterly,* 1975, *20*, 59–70.

McCORMICK, L. C. Comment on Price's "The study of organizational effectiveness." *Sociological Quarterly,* 1973, *14*, 271–273.

MOLNAR, J. J., & ROGERS, D. L. Organizational effectiveness: An empirical comparison of the goal and system resource approaches. *Sociological Quarterly,* 1976, *17*, 401–413.

PARSONS, T. *Structure and process in modern society.* Glencoe, Ill.: Free Press, 1960.

PENNINGS, J. M.; & GOODMAN, P. S. Toward a workable framework. In Goodman and Pennings, 1977, pp. 146–184.

PERROW, C. The analysis of goals in complex organizations. *American Sociological Review,* 1961, *26*, 854–866.

PORTER, L. W., LAWLER, E. E., & HACKMAN, J. R. *Behavior in organizations.* New York: McGraw-Hill, 1975.

PRICE, J. L. The study of organizational effectiveness. *Sociological Quarterly,* 1972, *13*, 3–15.

RAWLS, John. *A theory of justice.* Cambridge, Mass.: Harvard University Press, 1971.

SIMON, H. A. *Administrative behavior* (2nd ed.). New York: Macmillan, 1961.

STEERS, R. M. Problems in the measurement of organizational effectiveness. *Administrative Science Quarterly,* 1975, *20*, 546–558.

VROOM, V. H. The effects of attitudes on perceptions of organizational goals. *Human Relations,* 1960, *13*, 229–240.

YUCHTMAN, E., & SEASHORE, S. E. A system resource approach to organizational effectiveness. *American Sociological Review,* 1967, *32*, 891–903.

ZALD, M. M. Comparative analysis and measurement of organizational goals. *Sociological Quarterly,* 1963, *4*, 206–230.

34

Values in Organizational Theory and Management Education

Michael Keeley

Discussions of value issues involved in organizational theory and management education appear from time to time in the literature (Frost, 1980; Nord, 1978; Scott, 1979). But many, if not most, researchers still feel there is something illegitimate about mixing value judgments with social science. This is the case even in areas that appear most value-laden— for instance, in work on the evaluation of organizations (Steers, 1977) or their "social responsibilities" (Keim, 1978). Efforts to avoid normative judgments in the study of organizations may be misplaced. This paper proposes that values are implied in "descriptive" theories of organization and the manager's role therein; such values can be subjects of reasoned debate and relevant factors in theory assessment.

Fact and Value

Organizational and management theories impart both factual and normative information. This claim contradicts the widely held view that an administrative science can and should be

SOURCE: Michael Keeley, "Values in Organizational Theory and Management Education," *Academy of Management Review* (1983), vol. 8, no. 3, 376–386. Copyright © 1983 by the Academy of Management. Reprinted by permission.

value-free. Perhaps the most influential proponent of the value-free view in the discipline has been Herbert Simon, who states that "an administrative science, like any science, is concerned purely with factual statements. There is no place for ethical assertions in the body of a science" (1957, p. 253). Simon's ideal of nonnormative science might be maintained if researchers only collected factual statements in a haphazard fashion. But, of course, facts are sought in an organized manner. And it is the *organization* of facts that entails a normative orientation (Taylor, 1967). To illustrate, consider the sort of "value-free" research that guides modern management education.

A highly regarded attempt at empirically grounded, nonnormative description is Mintzberg's (1973) study, *The Nature of Managerial Work*. Mintzberg (relying on Simon) contends that values reflect "someone's arbitrary belief of what 'ought' to be. A statement of values can be neither correct nor incorrect" (1973, p. 72). Therefore, he prefers factual information, which "can be tested as to its validity." Mintzberg assumes that the prescriptive function of a science of management is limited to showing managers how they can do *what they already do* more efficiently. And the main point of his research is that a precise, factual description of the manager's job is necessary before one can prescribe even in this limited sense. Mintzberg's own description "is based exclusively on the evidence from empirical studies of managerial work. . . . Hence, this book was written without preconceptions of the manager's job. The results of empirical research do the talking" (1973, p. 4).

The basis of Mintzberg's report is "intensive" and "comprehensive" observation of five chief executives, which yields an "inductive" theory of what managers do. This theory consists of ten working roles, or categories of activity, and six basic purposes of the manager. These purposes are particularly interesting. A few are:

1. The prime purpose of the manager is to ensure that his organization serves *its* basic purpose—the efficient production of specific goods or services. . . . 2. The manager must design and maintain the stability of his organization's operations. . . . 3. The manager must take charge of his organization's strategy-making system, and therein adapt his organization in a controlled way to its changing environment. . . . 4. The manager must ensure that his organization serves the ends of those persons who control it. . . . (1973, p. 95).

Mintzberg concludes by suggesting how a science of management should help to further these purposes—for example, by "reprogramming" managerial activities (after Frederick Taylor) and reeducating managers to perform them more efficiently.

Mintzberg somehow draws much obviously normative information from his facts. One might ask how the results of empirical research can "do the talking" about what managers *must* do or what *should* be done to help them. The reason such normative things emerge is that this study is far from purely empirical. What Mintzberg recognizes but fails to solve is the problem of how to arrange facts—in this case, managerial activities—in a nonevaluative theoretical framework. He notes that descriptions must account for all managerial behavior:

There has been a tendency in the literature to exclude certain work that managers do as inherently nonmanagerial. . . . Omissions such as these are arbitrary—they suggest a preconceived notion of the job which may not be in accord with the facts. If a manager engages in an activity, we must begin with the assumption that this is part of his job and seek to understand why he does it in the broadest sense of his responsibilities (1973, pp. 57–58).

However, some preconception of the manager's responsibilities is necessary to set even broad limits on the job; not everything a manager

does can count as an *organizational* behavior. Mintzberg, in a methodological appendix, comments on his own problems in deciding whether to include "extra-organizational contacts":

Where was the line to be drawn in such cases as lunch with a competitor to discuss trade gossip, a board meeting of an organization in an unrelated industry, a board meeting of a golf club? The manager may or may not have received important information related to the running of his organization at each of these meetings. A specific case was Manager A's testimony as a private individual at congressional hearings. He emphasized that all his activities were related to his work and he explicitly included those associated with the hearings. The difficulty with this view is that it meant I would have to study every verbal and written contact, social or otherwise. But clearly this could not be done. . . . The rule I used was simply to include business-like work (for example, Chamber of Commerce board meeting) and exclude work that was ostensibly social in nature (golf club board meeting). I also decided, perhaps arbitrarily, to exclude the work associated with the hearings (1973, pp. 271–272).

Moreover, all contacts with the manager's secretary were excluded because "they were very numerous and different from the others" (1973, p. 271).

It is evident, now, that some prior idea of managerial responsibilities, some normative idea of "business-like work," is relied on in deciding that lunch with competitors is "extra-organizational gossip," that contacts with secretaries or congressional committees are unimportant (in the latter case, despite the apparent claims of the manager himself). Such an idea shows up in the normative purposes that Mintzberg attributes to his subjects: managers are responsible primarily for organizational goal attainment. This inference has an ethical dimension that cannot be derived solely from facts concerning what a manager does. Other observers, holding different values, might count different activities in the managerial job, find diverse individual (rather than organizational) purposes in the facts, or properly conclude that what managers actually do is not necessarily what they should or must do.

Of course, most management theorists have been trained to interpret things much as Mintzberg does. The value orientation implied in his study is not readily noticed because it has so long pervaded organizational and management theory (Georgiou, 1973). From classical through modern works, organizations continually have been defined as systems *for* the attainment of goals (Fayol, 1949; Hall, 1977; Scott, 1981). And organizational goal attainment continues to be a dominant value in administrative science—in the measurement of system success or effectiveness (Steers, 1977), in the selection of research questions and dependent variables (Meyer, 1977), and in explicit or implicit prescriptions for organziational design (Galbraith, 1977). The need for *some* value to direct organizational inquiry is apparent, even to a positivist like Simon, because researchers must extract from rich and complex social realities a manageable set of items for analysis. Though one may exclude from analysis "unscientific" value assertions and investigate only factual statements, the number of facts that can be gathered about organizations is virtually infinite. A choice must be made regarding which facts are interesting and which are not; and values affect the choice. Simon admits this in noting that certain "ethical premises" must be adopted in order to focus inquiry. But he simply assumes, as "given," that these premises can only be the objectives of the organization under study, that an administrative science *should* consist of facts about how organizations attain or fail to attain their goals.

There are, however, alternate values one might adopt in studying organizations. One can define organizations as systems *for* something besides collective goal attainment and seek facts that bear on other, possibly more interesting, problems. Alternative values deserve attention because it is less scientific—not more—simply to accept, as given, an ethical premise for inquiry. The empiricist's fear that values are potential sources of bias in organizational analysis is well-founded. But, like other sources of bias (e.g., measuring instruments), values are integral to the process of inquiry, and one does not become a purer scientist or educator by refusing to examine them (Hesse, 1978). Instead, knowledge is advanced by carefully weighing the choices. The empiricist's belief that values are arbitrary, beyond the scope of rational choice, is *not* well-founded. Some values arguably are better than others. Consider another study of managerial behavior.

Value Choice

Singer and Wooten (1976) describe the administrative methods of an individual who was years ahead of his time as a manager and organizational theorist. Through his career ended almost 40 years ago, he was "an exponent of some of the most advanced, participative, and 'humanistic' organization and management theories being endorsed today" (1976, p. 80). In response to the overly mechanistic management and resulting inefficiencies of a critical industry, he devised and implemented a theory he called "organized improvisation." This represented "an attempt to debureaucratize the . . . industry in order to make it 'results' oriented rather than authority oriented. The theory . . . consists essentially of four major components: collegial decision making, fluidity of organizational structures, temporary organizational structures, and industrial self-responsibility [for local managers]" (1976, p. 82). Each component was put into practice with impressive consequences. With respect to the fourth, for example, he found that when he delegated authority for accomplishing objectives and linked rewards to individual initiative in problem solving, "his managers exhibited an enthusiasm for their work that was heretofore not characteristic of the . . . work environment" (1976, p. 84). Thus, in line with current theory, "he recognized the importance of management principles that rest on the ability to reinforce positive commitment . . . to the goals of the organization." He anticipated other precepts of modern administrative science in developing strategies for enhancing organizational adaptiveness: he took steps to discourage "groupthink" among his subordinates, utilized project and matrix management structures, opened lines of communication, and built a climate supportive of contingency approaches to decision making. "The cumulative effect of all these strategies was to create a more flexible and 'results' oriented organization" (p. 85), and he thereby "molded one of the most productive and efficient industries known to man" (p. 88).

Yet, despite his considerable success in terms of organizational goal attainment, his efforts were admitted failures in more important respects. His goal-focused system caused untold suffering. He was Albert Speer, Hitler's Minister for Armaments and War Production, and his error was to fashion an organization that devalued individual human beings.

What made Speer's organizational achievement all the more remarkable and all the more deplorable was the fact that a large proportion of workers in his armaments industry were unwilling participants. In pursuing its objectives the Speer Ministry relied on millions of forced laborers from occupied countries, concentration camp inmates, and prisoners of war. For many of these, "life in the Reich was one long, continual nightmare of hard work, insufficient food, inadequate quarters, personal discrimination, and cruelty" (Homze, 1967, p. 297). Particularly severe treatment was experienced in Krupp armaments factories. Evidence produced at the Nuremberg trials illustrates the sort of "self-responsibility" exercised by Krupp management in order to achieve production goals, cut costs, and maintain discipline:

Records found in the Krupp files plainly indicate that the practice of beating and torturing prisoners of war and foreign workers was deliberately prescribed by Krupp officials. Steel switches which were used to beat the workers were distributed pursuant to the instructions of Kupke, head of the Krupp camp for foreign workers. . . .

The conditions under which the concentration camp workers existed at the Krupp camps and factories and the indignities and barbarities to which they were subjected are vividly described in affidavits by such workers. . . . In general, the affidavits disclose that these concentration camp laborers slept on bare floors of damp, windowless and lightless cellars; that they had no water for drinking or cleansing purposes; that they were compelled to do work far beyond their strength; that they were mercilessly beaten; that they were given one wretched meal a day, consisting of a dirty watery soup with a thin slice of black bread; and that many of them died from starvation, tuberculosis and overexertion (United States Chief of Counsel for Prosecution of Axis Criminality, 1946, 2, pp. 800–804).

For their participation in such activities, Albert Speer, Alfried Krupp, and others were imprisoned by the Allies (and Fritz Sauckel, who supplied them with forced labor, was hanged).

The point of the tale is not that Speer was an active advocate of cruelty, or that his form of organization ensured brutality. In fact, Speer seemed concerned about working conditions, because his system might have been even more efficient were captive labor better treated (Davidson, 1966; Speer, 1970). But Speer was not concerned *enough*. Both he and his system were ultimately indifferent to the abuse of some human beings for the sake of achieving greater "organizational" goals. It can be assumed that most people are not so indifferent, that virtually all are outraged at the kind of treatment described at Nuremberg. This suggests that organizational goals and their attainment are not, in the final analysis, the most important private concerns. If one believes, then, that there was something more basically problematic—wrong—about Speer's organization than whether or not its goals were accomplished, why should one accept system goals as primary values in a public science of organization, as "ethical givens" for focusing research? Why should their attainment be the main dependent variables in explanatory models, the main standards of worth in effectiveness models, and the main emphasis in management education? Why, in short, should system-goal-directed activities define "business-like work" for administrators and business-like problems for admininstrative science to solve?

One cannot reply that organizations just *are* goal-directed systems, whose behavior the models simply describe. Even if organizations do seek goals, it does not logically follow that such behavior is their most noteworthy feature or their reason for being, as goal models imply. The latter is a debatable value judgment, not an obvious fact. To defend this judgment against the suspicions raised by Speer's excesses, one might say that his organization is an historical anomaly, that societies, such as that in the United States, put pressure on organizations to avoid extreme "self-serving" policies and, hence, that most organizations do more good than harm in pursuing their goals. All this is plausible. But in supposing these things, it is presumed that fundamental problems of organizational control have already been solved (or are someone else's worry). Note that goal models rely heavily on extraneous, "environmental" factors (e.g., interest-group pressures, laws, customs, human recalcitrance) to set limits on the personal costs of producing organizational results. Furthermore, in goal-based theories such limiting factors appear chiefly as obstacles that organizations must "adapt to" or overcome, rather than things to be valued; it is taken for granted that these factors already are strong enough to prevent the sacrifice of individuals' interests for those of the organization. Yet, in Speer's case, they were not strong enough; and they may not be in all cases today, or tomorrow.

The real message of Speer's story is that it is possible to draw rather confident normative conclusions about the importance of organizational problems. Examination of the most troublesome social systems, discloses grounds for agreement on the most serious problems

social systems can present. Most would agree that the primary problem with Speer's organization was its lack of *voluntariness;* and it is here proposed that the preservation of voluntariness is a basic problem in any organization, more basic than, say, goal attainment, and too important to take for granted. The importance of voluntariness as a social concern and its priority over the value of collective goal attainment is affirmed in many everyday normative attitudes toward organizations—for instance, in researchers' personal regard for rights of tenure, in American labor and civil rights legislation, and in common law principles of tort liability. By conveying the opposite priority, goal-based theories of organization and management become questionable on both ethical and practical counts.

Theory Choice

It may be helpful here to summarize a few points of the argument. Social (and physical) theories are problem-specific. In other words,

Every *rational* theory, no matter whether scientific or philosophical, is rational in so far as it tries to *solve certain problems*. A theory is comprehensible and reasonable only in its relation to a given *problem-situation* (Popper, 1965, p. 199).

Kuhn (1970) advances a similar view. Scientific theories are problem-specific because everything about complex phenomena, like organizations, cannot be explained at once. Theorists must select *some aspects* of such realities for analysis, and choose what they wish to explain in the process. Thus, theories imply not only how a puzzling phenomenon *can* (in part) be explained—an empirical matter—but what *needs* to be explained—a normative matter. It is in giving priority to certain needs for explanation (problems) that a theoretical framework secretes its own notion of value and becomes subject to ethical, as well as empirical, criticism (Taylor, 1967).

The problem-specific nature of theoretical frameworks might not cause much ethical concern if one only set about solving "given" problems. One could, as Machlup (1967) suggests, simply select a theory to fit the problem at hand. But, of course, problems are not always given. In management education the problems to be solved, in addition to their solutions, are typically taught—all through ostensibly descriptive devices, such as general theories or models of organizations. It is common, for instance, to model organizations after biological systems. In most texts aimed at present or prospective managers, organizations are depicted as social "actors" that possess the distinguishing features of living beings: goals, needs, welfares of their own, and so on. Individual persons, in this model, are portrayed as functional "members," filling roles or serving as "human resources" to further the organization's ends. This sort of organismic model lends importance to particular problems by virtue of what it is able to explain; it is useful mainly for addressing questions of organizational well-being, that is, system survival and other forms of goal attainment. (Historically, organismic social models were devised—by Plato, Hegel, Comte, Fayol, and other designers—specifically to address perceived problems of collective disorientation.) However, problems that are not prominent in living things, such as the emergence of voluntary cooperation among self-interested members or the allocation of individual benefits and burdens of joint action, are not well explained or given great importance when organizations are described as personified, goal-seeking entities (Keeley, 1980; Scott, 1979). Organizations are not necessarily best described in this way.

Despite their long preeminence in organizational theory, models emphasizing shared goals and associated organismic properties have generated increasing criticism (Zey-Ferrell & Aiken, 1981). Some objections reveal empirical misgivings. It is difficult, for instance, to identify true *organizational* goals; goal models tend to confuse powerful individual's goals *for* an organization with goals *of* the organization as a whole (Silverman, 1970). In underestimating conflict over ends, these models present an overly unified, rational, and rigid picture of social systems (Georgiou, 1973). And they yield weakly supported propositions due to other operational difficulties (Freeman, 1978). Much of the objection to goal models, though, is normative in nature. Critics argue that such models idealize order, the functions of existing relations for system well-being, and, for the most part, the status quo (Krupp, 1961). They display a bias toward the interests of dominant participants, legitimating their purposes as goals of the organization (Albrow, 1973). They also divert attention from a number of interesting organizational questions, including questions of power and politics: who gets what, when, and how? (Allison, 1971; Pfeffer, 1981).

The latter kind of criticism may be the most telling. Even if a model has empirical content, it can be misleading in suggesting that facts about parochical problems are really of prime importance in describing organizations. Social models used as *general* descriptive frameworks are especially liable to normative criticism on grounds of a misplaced problem priority (one inconsistent with considered ethical judgments); and ethical standards are appropriate complements to empirical ones in choosing between such models. Certainly, general models or theories must have reasonable empirical content to be taken seriously at all; but alternatives may stress facts about different problems and thus be factually "incommensurable," in which case ethical considerations of problem priority are relevant. It is argued here that goal models of organization are questionable as general descriptive devices because they subordinate problems of voluntariness to problems of system goal attainment. Can an alternate model reverse this priority while providing an empirically sound description of organizations?

The Contract Model

A traditional alternative to modeling social systems after goal-seeking, biological entities is to model them after *contracts*. From a contractual perspective, organizations are seen to be sets of agreements for satisfying diverse, individual interests (Keeley, 1980). The model disputes popular claims that "[an] organization would not exist if it were not for some common purpose," which "is the basis for organizational activities" (Hall, 1977, p. 83). The key insight of a contractual view is that organizations normally exist by virtue of agreement on the activities alone, on joint *means* to separate purposes (possibly profits for some persons, wages for others, goods or services for another group, etc.).

Organizational theorists employing a more or less contractual framework include Cyert and March (1963), who propose that organizations are coalitions of self-interested participants. "Participant" is a broader term than "member," designating anyone who takes part in a system of behavior: for example, "managers, workers, stockholders, suppliers, customers" (Cyert & March, 1963, p. 27). The authors explain the behavior of large firms as the result of serial agreements among such participants to cooperate for incentives generated by their joint action. Similar explanations are offered by theorists who portray organizations as "markets," which ultimately consist of "sets of contracting relationships among individuals" (Jensen & Meckling, 1976, p. 311). See, also, Georgiou (1973) and Pfeffer and Salancik (1978). The negotiated order perspective of Strauss (1978) perhaps is the most specific in outlining how day-to-day working relations arise from processes of interpersonal bargaining. Strauss shows that many organizations that seem to be stable, functionally-ordered systems are, in fact, fragile products of continual negotiation over the rights and duties (claims) of the participants. He suggests that it is tentative agreement on these rights and duties—not shared goals or instrumental role-taking—that explains how social order is possible. Social order, of course, also may result from coercion and, therefore, what contractualists like Strauss primarily explain is how a *voluntary* social order is possible (Day & Day, 1977).

In emphasizing how voluntary cooperation can be achieved in organizations, a contractual model does not imply that most organizations have actually solved the problem of voluntariness (any more than organismic models imply that most organizations have actually solved problems of system goal attainment). The model simply stresses the common importance of the problem in contracts and organizations, and it draws attention to common features of these systems, agreements on individual rights, that might form the basis for solutions. This point requires clarification, because a related issue has been a source of confusion in contractual thought ever since John Locke's (1690/1967) famous theory of the social contract.

One cannot assert that organizations just *are* voluntary contracts, or one may misdescribe systems of enforced cooperation, as well as grant undeserved legitimacy to the social and economic inequalities they entail. Robert Hessen (1979a), for instance, does both in a book recently characterized in this journal as "brilliant, concise, timely, . . . [and perhaps] the most important book on corporations in the last 50 years" (Locke, 1979, p. 477). The merits of Hessen's analysis may be a bit overstated. His avowed aim is to defend modern corporations against their critics, and in so doing he claims that "at every stage throughout its growth, a corporation is a voluntary association based exclusively on contract" (Hessen, 1979a, p. 43). In other words, "the contract model holds that a corporation is simply and literally a voluntary association of individuals, united by a network of contracts" (Hessen, 1979b, p. 1330). The term "voluntary" is problematic in this context, however, creating empirical and normative difficulties. Hessen does not substantiate the voluntariness of all, or even many, corporate arrangements. In the manner of classical contractual theorists, he merely points out that *some* existing arrangements *could have* resulted from contract-like acts. He goes on to propose that the presumed voluntariness of these hypothetical acts ought to immunize corporations against most forms of governmental regulation (under the freedom of association and contract provisions of the U.S. Constitution). All this is very controversial (Hamilton, 1979).

Hessen's principal mistake, common in contractualist works (Hayek, 1976; Pilon, 1979), is to read freely given consent into agreements whose voluntariness is uncertain—for example, creditors' acceptance of the limited liability of shareholders for corporate debts. Hessen maintains:

> Limited liability actually derives from an implied contract between the corporate owners and their creditors. . . . Outsiders cannot be compelled to extend credit to a corporation on a limited liability basis. They can, and often do, insist that one or several of the shareholders become personal guarantors . . . for the debt. . . . Because creditors have a choice in the matter, limited liability cannot be viewed as a state-created privilege that benefits the corporation at the expense of the creditor (1979b, pp. 1332–1333).

Although certain creditors may have a choice, it is fair to question the voluntariness of some of these "implied contracts." Employees, because they lack either bargaining power or awareness of the risks they incur, may not be in a position to negotiate personal guarantees for unpaid wages. Several jurisdictions take account of this fact and impose liability on shareholders for such debts.

As Hessen admits, all kinds of organizational agreements are actually "contracts of adhesion," that is, agreements containing standardized terms set by dominant parties and only marginally negotiable, if understandable, by weaker parties to a transaction. (Classic examples are insurance policies, farm-leases, and product warranties: Kessler, 1943). In these contracts, terms often have been skillfully designed to minimize the legal liabilities of their authors; and, although the "adhering" party theoretically is free to shop around for a better deal, one finds similar terms offered by competing organizations. Such agreements have been considered troublesome by legal scholars for quite some time. Llewellyn, 50 years ago, stressed the importance as well as the problem of contract as an instrument of organizational control:

> Where bargaining power, and legal skill and experience as well are concentrated on one side of the type-transaction, . . . Law, under the drafting skill of counsel, now turns out a form of contract which resolves all questions in advance in favor of one party to the bargain. It is a form of contract which, in the measure of the importance of the particular deal in the other party's life, amounts to the exercise of unofficial government of some by others, via private law. . . . Factory employment, employment in a company town or on a sugar beet farm, or farm-lease in some share-cropping districts—these press to the point where contract may mean rather fierce control (1931, pp. 731–732).

No doubt, much has changed in the last half century to alter patterns of domination. Many contracts have been standardized by law with an eye toward equalizing the positions of the contracting parties; and the economic usefulness of standardized contracts, on the whole, is undeniable. But the voluntariness of adhesion contracts in organizations and their title to legal protection still are matters for debate with respect to consumer contracts (Mueller, 1969), "employment-at-will" contracts (Summers, 1976), and others. Thus, Llewellyn's point remains valid: " 'Agreement' does not even today carry any necessary connotation of real willingness. Acquiescence is the lesser evil is all that need be understood" and the problem of contract remains "essentially one of determining what types of pressure or other stimuli are sufficiently out of line with our general presuppositions of dealing to open the expression of agreement to attack" (1931, p. 728)—in short, the problem of voluntariness.

Empirical Implications

The following can reasonably be concluded. It does make sense to describe organizations as series of contract-like agreements on rules of conduct, which specify participants' rights and duties. These agreements, on the one hand, may be quite involuntary and quite unstable. On the other hand, they do signify a factual form of acquiescence. It probably is more accurate to describe even the most coercive systems (like Speer's) as sets of temporary understandings about rules of behavior, rather than as organic entities pursuing common goals. Whether systems under study are voluntary or not, an empirically valid picture of organizational life can be drawn from a contractual perspective. This picture is distinctive in bringing the concept of *rights* to the forefront of inquiry.

Other models focus attention on system "goals" or "roles," but these are derivative concepts in a contractual view. In the latter, rights are recognized as the fundamental currency of social interaction. This emphasis contrasts sharply with the neglect of rights in mainstream organizational theory; however, it is consistent with the importance placed on rights in daily affairs. Virtually all organizational participants *have* rights (if not always in equal measure) and *act* accordingly; and the general structure of an organization can be outlined entirely in terms of "who has what rights to which things." Empirically, rights can be defined as claims justified within a system of rules (Feinberg, 1973). Entailed in *organizational* rules and the agreements supporting them—articles of incorporation, employment contracts, grievance procedures, warranties, informal customs, and so on—are several kinds of rights. Four types are most easily identified: claim-rights, which entitle the holder to some benefit for performance by another; privileges, which grant freedom to act in particular ways; powers, which are capacities to alter the rights of others; and immunities, or protections against having one's rights so altered (Commons, 1924; Hohfeld, 1923). Rights specify relations *between* persons, and each type of right typically involves correlative obligations or expectations on the part of another: "duties" to honor others' claim-rights; "no rights" to expect waiver of others' privileges; "liabilities" to have one's rights altered by powerholders;

and "disabilities" to alter the rights of those with immunities.

For descriptive purposes, even such a simple classification is useful. It can help to clarify vague concepts (like "property" or "authority") and poorly understood processes (like organizational "governance" or "coupling") by breaking these down into the component rights held and exercised by various participants. It can expose interesting contradictions in the application of organizational rules, as it has in the case of legal rules (Perry, 1977). And, overall, it can add welcome detail to otherwise rough accounts of cooperative action. If analysts went to the trouble of identifying the claim-rights, privileges, powers, immunities, and their correlatives in relations between participants, studies of management might contain much richer descriptions of organizational behavior than those fashioned from gross *roles,* such as Mintzberg's, which usually reflect only some rights and duties relevant to system goal attainment (Storey, 1980). Descriptions can be enriched further by including those rights that organizational participants have by virtue of *extraorganizational* rules—say, legal or cultural rules. The addition of legal and cultural rights also introduces a definite dynamic into the framework.

If one catalogs the rights and correlatives of organizational participants under different rule systems, inconsistencies ordinarily will show up. Some organizational rights may not be legal or cultural rights: for example, claim-rights to the performance of contracts by certain unlicensed vendors. Some legal or cultural rights may not be recognized in organizations: for example, claim-rights to a minimum wage. A right may differ in type under cultural, legal, and organizational rules: for example, the legal claim-right of customers to prompt repair of warranted products may, in fact, be only an organizational privilege. And the same type of right may vary in strength under different rules: for example, under cultural rules, the rights of employers to fire workers at will may be a weak power (subject to many exceptions or immunities); under legal rules, a stronger power (subject to a few exceptions); and under organizational rules, a nearly absolute power (subject to almost no exceptions). Such inconsistencies represent tensions that, over time, prompt changes in organizational, legal, and cultural norms. Further research may be able to specify: the kinds of inconsistencies that lead to organizational, or legal, or social change; the kinds that cause violent change; the factors that facilitate or delay change, and so on.

There are other obvious empirical implications of a contractual perspective. The model urges more deliberate inquiry into how rights get created through cycles of bargaining and negotiation, how they are secured through systems of sanctions, and how conflicts among rights are resolved, as well as continuation of traditional research on how objects of rights are produced (goods, services, profits, wages, etc.).

Normative Implications

Above all, however, the contract view draws attention to a particular problem in organizations, the problem of voluntariness. Contracts, it is generally accepted, *should* be voluntary; Anglo-American common law, for instance, is designed to protect those that are and discourage those that are not. The contract model extends this same judgment to organizations. It ultimately directs inquiry into the sorts of rights and obligations that characterize truly voluntary systems. This has been the great contribution of the contract metaphor to political philosophy (Gough, 1957)—perhaps its greatest potential contribution to organizational theory, as well.

Rights are actually practical solutions to the problem of voluntariness. Organizational rights normally promise that the mutual expectations that cause people to enter a relationship voluntarily will be fulfilled. Legal and cultural rights normally set constraints on those expectations to inhibit coercive relationships. But, because conventional rights sometimes fail to guarantee voluntariness, another category of rights historically has followed from a contractual model.

These are "moral" or "human" rights, which can be thought of as those rights individuals would possess in *ideally* voluntary systems. Such rights often are abstract and subjects of heated debate. They are not exactly the "self-evident truths" proclaimed by the American colonists in 1776. Yet, they are not hopelessly indeterminate or inseparable from narrow political ideologies.

Many human rights are widely acknowledged in ideal, international agreements, like the United Nations Universal Declaration of Human Rights (accepted without dissent, if not always observed, as "a common standard of achievement for all peoples and all nations"). The least controversial of these rights include freedoms of religion, opinion, and expression and immunities from slavery, servitude, discrimination, and similar harms. Philosophers recently have made heavy use of the contract device to justify related rights (Phillips, 1979). More theoretical work is needed to derive reasonable human rights specific to participants in complex organizations; the key theoretical question to be answered is: "What concrete rights would self-interested participants agree to recognize *if* they were in a position to negotiate freely a set of rules for mutual benefit?" A number of employee rights, for example, might be derived from an ideal contract situation analogous to a collective-bargaining setting in which the principals each have effective veto power over the employment contract, such as the right to due process in termination decisions, to equal opportunity for promotions, or to a hazard-free working environment. [Note that reasoning from imaginary contracts is valid only insofar as conditions for an ideally voluntary agreement, such as an effective veto, are built into the theoretical setting for negotiation. Some contractual theorists are careful in setting up these conditions, especially Rawls, (1971); others overlook them, especially Hessen, (1979a, 1979b).]

As a rule, analysis of moral rights and obligations has not attracted much serious attention in organizational theory and management education. This type of analysis has been regarded as "too normative." But it is no more normative, and far less objectionable, than attempts to derive the responsibilities of managers and other participants from imperatives of organizational goal attainment. From a contractual perspective, the primary responsibility of those who manage organizations is to promote voluntary cooperation—to facilitate agreements on institutional rights that respect the moral rights of *all* participants. This clearly *is* a normative inference, as is the inference that Simon (1957) and Mintzberg (1973) draw from a goal-based perspective: that is, managers are responsible primarily for furthering organizational goals. Although neither inference can be directly checked against facts, the contractual claim is more credible when tested against common normative judgments. It is difficult to find fault with systems that display high degrees of voluntariness. The same cannot necessarily be said of systems that display high degrees of goal attainment, as illustrated in Albert Speer's case and in the routine findings of U. S. courts, the press, and other forums of public opinion.

In sum, organizational models have both normative implications for management and empirical implications for research. This suggests that scientific and ethical criteria can complement one another—not *substitute* for one another—in the evaluation of alternative views. Social science can indicate only whether a model yields good (factual) solutions to specific problems. Ethics, on the other hand, can indicate whether a model yields good (worthwhile) problems to begin with. Although neither scientific nor ethical tests are apt to be conclusive, only if both show reasonably acceptable results should much trust be placed in the *general* validity of a social model. The contract model is likely to prove trustworthy on both counts.

References

ALBROW, M. The study of organizations—objectivity or bias? In G. Salaman & K. Thompson (Eds.), *People and organizations*. London: Longmans, 1973, 396–413.

ALLISON, G. T. *Essence of decision.* Boston: Little, Brown, 1971.

COMMONS, J. R. *Legal foundations of capitalism.* New York: Macmillan, 1924.

CYERT, R. M., & MARCH, J. G. *A behavioral theory of the firm.* Englewood Cliffs, N.J.: Prentice-Hall, 1963.

DAVIDSON, E. *The trial of the Germans.* New York: Macmillan, 1966.

DAY, R., & DAY, J. V. A review of the current state of negotiated order theory: An appreciation and a critique. *Sociological Quarterly,* 1977, *18,* 126–142.

FAYOL, H. *General and industrial management.* London: Pitman, 1949.

FEINBERG, J. *Social philosophy.* Englewood Cliffs, N.J.: Prentice-Hall, 1973.

FREEMAN, J. H. The unit of analysis in organizational research. In M. W. Meyer (Ed.), *Environments and organizations*. San Francisco: Jossey-Bass, 1978, 335–351.

FROST, P. Toward a radical framework for practicing organizational science. *Academy of Management Review,* 1980, 5, 501–507.

GALBRAITH, J. R. *Organization design.* Reading, Mass.: Addison-Wesley, 1977.

GEORGIOU, P. The goal paradigm and notes towards a counter paradigm. *Administrative Science Quarterly,* 1973, 18, 291–310.

GOUGH, J. W. *The social contract.* 2d ed. London: Oxford, 1957.

HALL, R. H. *Organizations: Structure and process.* 2d ed. Englewood Cliffs, N.J.: Prentice-Hall, 1977.

HAMILTON, R. W. Response (to Hessen). *Hastings Law Journal,* 1979, *30,* 1351–1352.

HAYEK, F. A. *Law, legislation and liberty* (Vol. 2). Chicago: University of Chicago Press, 1976.

HESSE, M. Theory and value in the social sciences. In C. Hookway & P. Pettit (Eds.), *Action and interpretation*. London: Cambridge University, 1978, 1–16.

HESSEN, R. *In defense of the corporation.* Stanford, Cal.: Hoover Institution, 1979a.

HESSEN, R. A new concept of corporations: A contractual and private property model. *Hastings Law Journal,* 1979b, *30,* 1327–1350.

HOHFELD, W. N. *Fundamental legal conceptions.* New Haven, Conn.: Yale University Press, 1923.

HOMZE, E. L. *Foreign labor in Nazi Germany.* Princeton, N.J.: Princeton University Press, 1967.

JENSEN, M. C., & MECKLING, W. H. Theory of the firm: Managerial behavior, agency costs and ownership structure. *Journal of Financial Economics,* 1976, 3, 305–360.

KEELEY, M. Organizational analogy: A comparison of organismic and social contract models. *Administrative Science Quarterly,* 1980, 25, 337–362.

KEIM, G. D. Corporate social responsibility: An assessment of the enlightened self-interest model. *Academy of Management Review,* 1978, 3, 32–39.

KESSLER, F. Contracts of adhesion—Some thoughts about freedom of contract. *Columbia Law Review,* 1943, 43, 629–642.

KRUPP, S. *Pattern in organizational analysis.* Philadelphia: Chilton, 1961.

KUHN, T. S. *The structure of scientific revolutions.* 2d ed. Chicago: University of Chicago, 1970.

LLEWELLYN, K. N. What price contract?—An essay in perspective. *Yale Law Journal,* 1931, 40, 704–751.

LOCKE, E. A. Book review: *In defense of the corporation. Academy of Management Review,* 1979, 4, 475–477.

LOCKE, J. Second treatise of government. In P. Laslett (Ed.), *John Locke: Two treatises of government.* 2d ed. London: Cambridge, 1967, 283–446 (Originally published, 1690).

MACHLUP, F. Theories of the firm: Marginalist, behavioral, managerial. *American Economic Review,* 1967, 57, 1–33.

MEYER, M. W. *Theory of organizational structure.* Indianapolis, Ind.: Bobbs-Merrill, 1977.

MINTZBERG, H. *The nature of managerial work.* New York: Harper & Row, 1973.

MUELLER, A. Contracts of frustration. *Yale Law Journal,* 1969, 78, 576–597.

NORD, W. R. Dreams of humanization and the realities of power. *Academy of Management Review,* 1978, 3, 674–678.

PERRY, T. D. A paradigm of philosophy: Hohfeld on legal rights. *American Philosophical Quarterly,* 1977, 14, 41–50.

PFEFFER, J. *Power in organizations.* Marshfield, Mass.: Pitman, 1981.

PFEFFER, J., & SALANCIK, G. R. *The external control of organizations.* New York: Harper & Row, 1978.

PHILLIPS, D. L. *Equality, justice and rectification.* New York: Academic Press, 1979.

PILON, R. Corporations and rights: On treating corporate people justly. *Georgia Law Review,* 1979, 13, 1245–1370.

POPPER, K. R. *Conjectures and refutations.* 2d ed. London: Routledge & Kegan Paul, 1965.

RAWLS, J. *A theory of justice.* Cambridge, Mass.: Harvard, 1971.

SCOTT, W. G. Organicism: The moral anesthetic of management. *Academy of Management Review,* 1979, 4, 21–28.

SCOTT, W. R. *Organizations: Rational, natural, and open systems.* Englewood Cliffs, N.J.: Prentice-Hall, 1981.

SILVERMAN, D. *The theory of organisations.* London: Heinemann, 1970.

SIMON, H. A. *Administrative behavior.* 2d ed. New York: Free Press, 1957.

SINGER, E. A., & WOOTON, L. M. The triumph and failure of Albert Speer's administrative genius: Implications for current management theory and practice. *Journal of Applied Behavioral Science,* 1976, 12, 79–103.

SPEER, A. *Inside the Third Reich* (R. Winston & C. Winston, Trans.). New York: Macmillan, 1970.

STEERS, R. M. *Organizational effectiveness.* Glenview, Ill.: Scott, Foresman, 1977.

STOREY, J. *The challenge to management control.* London: Kogan Page, 1980.

STRAUSS, A. *Negotiations.* San Francisco: Jossey-Bass, 1978.

SUMMERS, C. W. Individual protection against unjust dismissal: Time for a statute. *Virginia Law Review,* 1976, 62, 481–532.

TAYLOR, C. Neutrality in political science. In P. Laslett & W. G. Runciman (Eds.), *Philosophy, politics and society.* 3d ser. Oxford: Blackwell, 1967, 25–57.

United States Chief of Counsel for Prosecution of Axis Criminality. *Nazi conspiracy and aggression.* Washington, D.C.: U.S. Government Printing Office, 1946.

ZEY-FERRELL, M., & AIKEN, M. (Eds.). *Complex organizations: Critical perspectives.* Glenview, Ill.: Scott, Foresman, 1981.

35

External Influences on Managers

Ian Mitroff

Stakeholders: The Constituent Elements of Purposeful Systems

One purpose of this chapter is to reveal a set of methods by which stakeholders can be generated at the institutional, organizational, political, and social levels of social system analysis. The other purpose is to show the kinds of properties associated with stakeholders and hence the kinds of assumptions that must be made about them.

The discussion in this and the preceding chapter follows from a rather complex view of social systems and a special philosophy of social science for understanding such systems. The best elaboration of this view can be found in the works of Ackoff and Emery (1974) and Churchman (1971, 1979). While it is difficult to capture the richness of their views, it is best attempted after we have examined some of the concrete properties of stakeholders. Before we do this, however, we shall discuss first several concrete methods for uncovering stakeholders.

Methods for Uncovering Stakeholders

There are no definite limits to the number of techniques that one could use to generate a

SOURCE: Ian I. Mitroff, *Stakeholders of the Organizational Mind*, pp. 32–47. Copyright © 1983 Jossey-Bass Inc., Publishers. Reprinted with permission.

set of stakeholders relevant to any given organizational problem. It must be kept in mind that we are dealing with complex, messy systems. As a result, we do not obtain the kind of closure and definitiveness that one does in simple, closed systems.

Seven methods have proved to be sufficient in stimulating the thinking of practitioners about the kinds of stakeholders inherent in the situations with which they must deal. The seven are imperative, positional, reputational, social participation, opinion-leadership, demographic, and organizational. Since each approach picks up stakeholders that the others miss, we (Mason and Mitroff, 1981) recommend that organizations use all of them in thinking about the forces in their environment.

The *imperative* approach identifies stakeholders who feel strongly enough about an organization's proposed policies or actions to act on their feelings. To use this method, one makes a list of as many as possible of the imperatives, slogans, and catch-words that have been uttered in the context of a policy issue. Also identified are any acts of defiance (for example, strikes, sit-ins, and lying in front of trucks) or other actions that suggest dissatisfaction with the policy system. The *sources* of the imperatives and acts are identified and each is considered as a potential stakeholder. The deficiency of this method is that it misses silent stakeholders who nevertheless may have a strong opinion on a policy issue.

Recent events painfully demonstrate the importance of using this method to think about one's organization. The placing of poisonous substances in the products of various drug companies reveals that the stakeholders that organizations must now deal with in their environment are no longer entirely benign. They include such evil characters as assassins, extorters, kidnappers, and saboteurs.

A fundamental point of this and the previous chapter is that while the pinpointing of such characters in one's particular organization can never be perfect or exact, it does not excuse organizations from thinking seriously about them and about what they can do to anticipate their vulnerable places. It does not follow that if one cannot have exact or perfect knowledge regarding every potential stakeholder, then one should not think about or anticipate them at all. This is precisely the attitude that must change if organizations are to survive in a more complex world. In today's world the systematic consideration of stakeholders might very well be a dire necessity and not a luxury.

The *positional* approach identifies those stakeholders that occupy formal positions in a policy-making structure, whether internal or external to the organization, for example, government. Organization charts and legal documents are a good source for this method. The deficiency of this approach is that it ignores important stakeholders that are not formally a part of the organization but have an impact on it nonetheless.

The *reputational* approach is a sociometric one. It entails asking various knowledgeable or important persons to nominate those whom they believe have a stake in the system. The deficiency here is that unorganized, nonelite, and disenfranchised groups may be ignored.

The *social-participation* approach identifies individuals or organizations as stakeholders to the extent that they participate in activities related to a policy issue. Membership in special organizations or committees, attendance at meetings, voting, and other instances or observable behavior are taken as evidence of having a potential stake in an issue. The obvious deficiency of this approach is that many latent, currently nonparticipatory stakeholders (for example, the silent majority, children, the aged, future generations) will be overlooked.

Since one of the reasons for identifying stakeholders is to assess their leverage and influence in a policy system, it is sometimes adequate to identify only those who tend to shape the opinions of other stakeholders. The *opinion-leadership* method does this. Examples would be the editors of important magazines, newspapers,

and journals. This approach has the advantage of identifying important stakeholders who are not part of the formal structure or do not have the same status as those selected by previous methods. Its disadvantage is that it is less precise and requires more judgment on the part of the analyst than do some of the other methods.

The *demographic* approach identifies stakeholders by such characteristics as age, sex, race, occupation, religion, place of birth, and level of education. For many policy, planning, and strategy issues, these distinctions are necessary, since it is to be expected that a policy will have a different impact on different demographic groups. The disadvantage of this approach is that it assumes homogeneity of interest within any particular group.

The last method selects a *focal organization . . .* in a policy system and seeks to identify the individuals and organizations who have important relationships with the focal organization. Typical relationships are those of (1) supplier, (2) employee, (3) customer or client, (4) ally, (5) competitor or adversary, (6) regulator or controller (for example, government), and (7) regulatee or controlee (for example, subdivisions of a parent organization, legally controlled entities). . . . The advantage of this approach is that it identifies potential parties or elements that other approaches can overlook. It has the disadvantage of not being comprehensive and of potentially missing some key stakeholders such as opinion leaders.

Stakeholder Assumptions

For ease of presentation, stakeholder properties may be subdivided into two categories: intrinsic and extrinsic. Intrinsic properties are those that may be defined independent of other stakeholders. Extrinsic properties are those that arise as a result of the interaction and relationships with other stakeholders. Extrinsic properties become especially important when one stakeholder attempts to change another. As we shall see, it is easier to state the difference between intrinsic and extrinsic properties than it is to keep them strictly apart.

My view of stakeholders and their associated properties may be summarized in a number of key propositions:

1. An organization or social system is an organized collection of internal and external stakeholders. This is not as trivial as it may appear. The word *organized* implies that at least one critical property of a stakeholder will be influenced by the property of at least one other stakeholder. Assumptions naturally come into play because parties will differ as to which stakeholder influences which other. . . .

2. Each stakeholder is a distinct and distinguishable entity that has resources, purposes, and a will of its own. Thus it is capable of volitional or purposeful behavior (Ackoff and Emery, 1974). The detailed kinds of properties that characterize a stakeholder's behavior may be subdivided as follows. Note that each stakeholder has at least one important property in at least one of the following categories:

   a. The purposes and motivations of a stakeholder.
   b. The beliefs that a stakeholder has or that can be ascribed to it.
   c. The resources a stakeholder commands; among these are
      (1) Material resources.
      (2) Symbolic resources (for example, those pertaining to political office).
      (3) Physical resources.
      (4) Positional resources (for example, privileged position in a social or informational network).
      (5) Informational resources (for example, access to special or privileged sources).
      (6) Skill.
   d. Special knowledge and opinions.
   e. Commitments, legal and otherwise.
   f. Relationships to other stakeholders in the system by virtue of

(1) Power.
(2) Authority.
(3) Responsibility.
(4) Accountability.

Disagreements among the proponents of different policies usually occur because they typically ascribe or impute very different properties to the same set of stakeholders. For instance, in the drug company case the proponents of the three policies disagreed across almost every one of the six categories listed earlier that characterize stakeholder properties. They ascribed different purposes and motivations to almost all of the stakeholders in their case; they imputed different beliefs to them; they perceived the resources of each stakeholder differently; and so forth.

3. There is a network of interdependent *relationships* among all stakeholders. Some relationships are *supporting* in that they provide movement toward the organization's purposes. Some relationships are *resisting* in that they serve as barriers or encourage movement away from the organization's purposes. (See the properties listed earlier under item 2f.) This is the minimal sense in which an organization or social system is an organized collection of stakeholders.

4. A new strategy, that is, a change in strategy for an organization, changes one or more of the relationships among the stakeholders. Hence, every action is dependent on stakeholder properties and vice versa.

5. Relationships with each stakeholder (that is, stakeholder properties) may be changed in one or more of the following ways. Note that whether a stakeholder is susceptible to a particular means of change is itself an additional property of a stakeholder:

   a. Convert (change) the stakeholder by means of:
      (1) Commanding him or her through the exercise of power and authority.
      (2) Persuading him or her by appealing to reason, values, and emotion.
      (3) Bargaining with him or her by means of economic exchange.

(4) Negotiating with him or her to reach "give and take" compromises.

(5) Problem solving with him or her by means of sharing, debating, and arriving at agreed upon mutual perceptions.

b. Fight the stakeholder and politic to overpower him or her by means of:

(1) Securing and marshalling the organization's resources.

(2) Forming coalitions with other stakeholders.

(3) Destroying the stakeholder.

c. Absorb aspects of a stakeholder's demands by incorporating them by means of co-optation.

d. Coalesce with the stakeholder by forming a coalition with joint decision-making powers.

e. Avoid or ignore the stakeholder.

f. Appease the stakeholder by giving in to some of his or her demands.

g. Surrender to the stakeholer.

h. Love the stakeholder by forming an intense emotional bond or special relationship with him or her.

i. Be or become the stakeholder by transforming the organization into the stakeholder through merger, imitation, idolatry, or role modeling.

Any strategy must be implemented through one or more of these ways of affecting change. Hence, all strategies presuppose power, that is, the ability to employ a relevant set of methods for bringing about change. Little wonder, having identified these different ways of changing stakeholders, that analysts of a social system and policy makers often advocate such different policies. All of the properties regarding stakeholders and their ability to change through a certain means are highly volatile, changing, and subject to debate. It is exceedingly easy to assume very different capabilities with regard to each stakeholder's ability to change.

6. The state of an organization at a certain point in time will be the result of the interaction of the behavior of all the organization's stakeholders from the beginning of its history up to a particular point in time. This extended history may be referred to as the "culture" of the organization or of the extended set of stakeholders.

7. A strategy undertaken at one point in time to achieve outcomes at a later point *must* be based on one or more *assumptions* about (a) the properties and behavior of the stakeholders, (b) the network of relationships that binds them to the organization, and (c) the organization's power to change relevant relationships. Assumptions must be made because (a), (b), and (c) taken by themselves, or even collectively, are too complex for any person (that is, stakeholder) to have complete, perfect, or certain knowledge about them.

A Further Word about Purposeful Systems

As mentioned earlier, everything in this chapter follows from a special view of social systems. This view is neither easy to state nor to summarize. One way to approach it is to discuss the functions necessary to the existence and maintenance of social systems. Philosophers of science such as Ackoff, Churchman, and Singer have proposed four such functions:

1. The ability to change purposes (ends) and to create new purposes. Ackoff, Churchman, and Singer call this the Aesthetic Dimension. By aesthetic they mean something more than the traditional concept of aesthetics—the pursuit and meaning of the Beautiful. As I construe it, this may be conceived of as the Creativity and Change Dimension. In this sense, aesthetics refers to the characteristic style of an organization. It also refers to the organization's sense of quality, that is, what it instinctively feels is worth pursuing.

2. The ability to acquire and mobilize adequate resources (means). This can be referred

to as the Political and Economic Dimension, for politics and economics in their broadest possible senses pertain to the effective acquisition and use of means.

3. The ability to discover and develop resources and to allocate the right resource in the right amounts to the right organizational component at the right time, that is, the ability to relate means to ends effectively. This dimension obviously relates to the proper use of knowledge and information. Thus, this is naturally referred to as the Information and Communication Dimension.

4. The ability to sustain cooperation and to eliminate conflict among all stakeholders so that basic purposes are achievable. This is referred to as the Ethical, Moral, Cooperative Dimension.

Each of these broad dimensions could be expanded indefinitely. Richard Mason and I have recently attempted to do this by showing some of the conditions that would have to be met to obtain each of the functions of Ackoff, Churchman, and Singer. Following each condition we have placed in parentheses some of the many key areas and concepts from the field of management and organizational sciences that would have to be considered in order to attain that condition. The concepts thus show the tremendous complexity and interdisciplinary nature of the task involved in attaining each condition. Note that the conditions have been deliberately worded in the ideal. As a result, they help to draw out even further the nature of the tremendous assumptions that must be made if an organization is to perform satisfactorily or even exist.

1. Change and Creativity.
   a. The leaders of the organization must have the inspiration and creativity necessary to reevaluate the organization's current missions, purposes, objectives, and goals and to conceptualize new purposes. (Leadership, Statesmanship, Goal-Setting, Missions, Management by Objectives.)
   b. The managers must have the capability for translating new concepts, ideas, and purposes into concrete, visualizable programs of action. (Innovation, Creativity, Management of Change, Organizational Change, Invention, Protection of Change through Patents and Copyrights, Flexibility, Changeability.)
   c. All stakeholders must have the spirit, dedication, and commitment necessary to secure new purposes. (Motivation, Incentives, Satisfaction, Promotions, Careers, Personal Values, Organizational and Individual Renewal, Burnout, Catharsis, Energy, Drive.)

2. Business—Political and Economic Functions.
   a. The total resources held by the collection of stakeholders must be adequate to accomplish their purposes. (Capital Availability, Recruitment, Capital Budgeting, Finance, Purchasing, Energy, Mergers, Acquisition, Plant Location, Working Capital, Cash Flow, Inventory, Dividend Policy.)
   b. The managers must reallocate the resources from stakeholder to stakeholder so that each stakeholder possesses the amount of resources necessary to carry out its tasks at the right time and place. (Budgeting, Decision Making, Resource Allocation.)
   c. The stakeholders must employ the resources they have effectively and efficiently when executing their tasks to ensure that maximally useful output is produced. (Productivity, Production, Job Assignment, Organization Structure, Materials Handling, Design of Jobs.)
   d. The managers must distribute the output effectively to all relevant stakeholders. (Marketing, Sales, Distribution, Sales Force, Sales Training, Advertising, Customer Relations.)

3. Information and Communication.
   a. The collection of stakeholders must have the capacity to acquire or produce basic knowledge—scientific, industrial, and operations—about the organization's

products, technology, operations, finances, markets, and customers. (R and D, Accounting, Management Information Systems, Market Research, Operations Research, Corporate Intelligence, Planning, Library.)

b. The managers must ensure that the right information is transmitted to the right stakeholder at the right time. (Communications, Organization, Reporting, Dissemination, Education, Training, Advertising, Public Affairs, Auditing, Storage and Retrieval, Telecommunications, Teleconferencing.)

c. Each stakeholder must have the capacity to use the knowledge and information he or she receives to make effective decisions. (Management Systems, Knowledge Utilization, Applied Research, Participation, Boards of Directors, Policy-Making Structure, Authority, Responsibility, Accountability, Cognitive Style, Intuitive Decision Making, Decision Processes.)

4. Ethical, Moral, Cooperative.

a. Stakeholders must have the necessary peace of mind within themselves to be effective in their organizational life and the other aspects of their life. (Mid-Life Crisis, Quality of Work Life, Human Potential Movement, Satisfaction, Health and Safety, Stability, Fringe Benefits, Stress, Psychic Energy.)

b. There must be a minimum of conflict between the internal stakeholders—individuals, groups, departments—that function within the organization. (Organization Development, Role Clarification, Conflict Resolution, Leadership, Dissention, Goldbricking.)

c. There must be a minimum of conflict between the organization and its external stakeholders such as governments, public interest groups, social activists, unions, and competitors. (Public Relations, Government Relations, Labor Relations, Ethics, Morality, Social Responsibility, Product Safety SEC, EPA, EEOC, OSHA, OPEC, Issues Management, Freedom of Information, Anti-Trust.)

Stakeholders and Rationality

Nothing that has been said in this chapter is meant to imply that the four functions that I have borrowed from Ackoff, Churchman, and Singer are necessarily unique to them. In a profound and undeservedly neglected book, *Reason in Society,* Diesing (1962) identifies four basic types of rationality or functions that he argues are fundamental to a complex society. These are economic, political, legal, and social rationality. While different on the surface, Diesing's four types of rationality or social system functions are, for all practical purposes, identical to the four discussed earlier. What is important is not the particular names of the functions but that Diesing gives independent support for the existence of the distinct kinds of functions necessary to the operation of complex social systems. Even more important, Diesing is able to show that none of the functions is really able to exist without some *minimal* existence of the others. For instance, consider what Diesing terms economic rationality. In the ideal, economic rationality is based on the notion of economic *order.* Economic order exists when there is a universally recognized system of measurement (for example, dollars) such that different things and commodities can be compared in terms of their value with regard to the accepted units of measurement. There must be some minimal social rationality or solidarity within the members of a social system for a *common* system of measurement to be recognized and accepted as universally valid. Thus, all of the functions are *interdependent* in some basic sense. None can exist or function without the others.

An important implication emerges from this insight. No single stakeholder has a complete or totally separate existence of its own. In a complex social system, each stakeholder is tied to or dependent upon *at least one other* important social system stakeholder for its existence and/or functioning. This implies that *the properties of each stakeholder are dependent upon or a function of the properties of at least one other stakeholder in the entire system of stakeholders.* Put somewhat differently, *the assumptions that are made about the behavior of each stakeholder are a function of the assumptions made about the behavior of at least one other stakeholder in the system. Thus, every intrinsic property of a stakeholder is influenced by an extrinsic property of at least one other stakeholder.* We are truly dealing with a network or a system of behavior.

The preceding point establishes one of the most important properties of stakeholders at the level of social system analysis. It does not, however, establish all of them. . . . One such principle holds that, since some assumptions are judged to be more important and certain than others, *stakeholders can be ranked hierarchically according to their importance and the confidence one has in determining their properties.*

The most important property of stakeholders at this level is the *presumption* of rationality. In its most basic sense, this means that stakeholders cannot possess contradictory properties. A stakeholder cannot be strong and weak, rich and poor, at the same time. This might seem to contradict the discussion in Chapter Two of the physician who was imputed to be both price-sensitive and price-insensitive. The key word, however, is *imputed.* The physician was *perceived by* different groups to be different things. Presumably, though, a given physician could not be both at the same time, nor could a *single* group perceive a given physician to be both price-sensitive and price-insensitive.

There presumably exists an objective way, or ways, of settling the dispute.

These beliefs make for a rational conception of stakeholders. Indeed, most of what currently passes for organization theory, social systems analyses, sociology, and political science adheres to the presumption of rationality. With few exceptions the overwhelming emphasis is on the disinterested, impersonal, supposedly rational analysis of stakeholders. This mode of thinking can take the following form: "*If* stakeholder X has properties p, q, and so on, *then* X can cause stakeholder Y to behave in such-and-such a way." The discovery of such if-then relationships or impersonal laws is the overriding aim of the vast bulk of what we know as contemporary social science. As such, its aim is to emulate the physical sciences.

What is wrong with this? Nothing—when it is taken in its proper perspective. . . . But when it extends outside its proper domain of meaning, it gives us an incomplete and distorted picture of the complexities of human behavior. It is vitally important to appreciate that the theory of stakeholders presented thus far holds only for *surface* social system stakeholders, that is, those stakeholders conceived of as rational, calculating devices. It does not hold for stakeholders endowed with highly complex, emotional makeups. To treat this emotionality— even to acknowledge it—necessitates that we penetrate beneath the surface of stakeholders rationally conceived and rationally endowed.

To illustrate my point, consider the fact that in all the times my colleagues and I have applied the method of assumptions analysis, we have never encountered a case wherein any in-depth, sophisticated attribution or treatment of stakeholder properties was achieved. This does not mean that the users of the method did not achieve important insights, for they did.

This surface level treatment of stakeholders is not particularly surprising. The participants have been, for the most part, lay social system analysts, not professional social scientists. Even the social scientists rarely penetrate beneath the surface of things to offer a "deep structure" theory of human motivations.

My colleagues and I have tried to aid and even to push participants into thinking more deeply about a wider class of stakeholders and a deeper set of properties. For instance, we have encouraged participants to think about nonobvious stakeholders. We call them *snaildarters* after the endangered species of fish that held up a proposed hydroelectric project for years. In all their rational plans the designers of the dam had failed to take the snaildarter into account. As a result, one class of stakeholders, environmentalists, acted in behalf of another stakeholder, the snaildarter, that could not act in its own behalf.

The lesson of the snaildarter is paramount. Just beneath the surface of the best laid and most rational plans swim forces of which people are entirely unaware and do not wish to consider. These seemingly tiny and insignificant forces, however, have a strange way of wrecking the most well-conceived plans and policies.

This chapter began by revealing some rather straightforward ways to generate and to analyze stakeholders at the surface level of social systems. Step by step we have been led to the need for digging deeper into the concept of stakeholders. Are there classes of stakeholders that lie beneath the surface of those stakeholders that are most visible? If so, what are they? How do these less visible stakeholders influence those that we can see? As we shall see, in the answers to these questions lies a deeper, more complex psychoanalytic theory for managing complex social systems. It is, however, . . . a psychoanalytic theory in a nontraditional sense. Although guided by the immense insights of such giants as Freud and Jung, it attempts to formulate them in ways more accessible and relevant to those charged with managing the ever-widening disarray of things.

Finally, I would be the first to acknowledge that there is a certain unsatisfying incompleteness to our discussion thus far, particularly in this chapter, which displays an all-too-common malaise in the social sciences: It is a laundry list of concerns and issues. I have despairingly referred to it as a "philosophy of lists."

Such lists are unfortunately due to the basic character of the phenomena we are dealing with. For one, the number of stakeholders one must deal with in complex systems is so large, so varied, and so quickly changing that it would be almost impossible to create with any confidence a single, unchanging, timeless theory for describing the behavior of all stakeholders and their impacts on one another for any extended period of time.

One can still have a general social science with special emphasis on the word *science*. But a different kind of social "science" is needed to deal with the changing, uncertain nature of stakeholders and their associated properties. The general features of this social science were outlined in the preceding chapter (see also Mason and Mitroff, 1981; and Mitroff and Kilmann, 1978). One of the basic purposes of such a social science is precisely to allow those with different perceptions to debate whether a certain stakeholder has a certain set of properties and whether a certain stakeholder influences other stakeholders. That is, it is more important to have a method whereby the members of an organization facing a particular problem can work the lists of stakeholders than to present a single list of stakeholders that holds for all organizations and their problems.

Even if we were to consider whether all of the properties of stakeholders in one category were in theory derivable from another, we would not really be out of a dilemma. For instance, suppose that one were a Marxist social scientist. As a result, suppose that one insisted that all of, say, what Diesing labels as legal, political, and social rationality were derived solely from economic conditions. Suppose, too, that one contended that legal, political, and social behavior were solely or primarily a function of the economic modes of production of a society. Now, there is nothing inherently wrong with this argument per se, except to say that it is an assumption. Not only is this assumption not accepted by all social analysts or stakeholders themselves but, more crucial still, it is an assumption that, although vitally important, is no more certain than many of the other assumptions that describe a complex social system.

The somewhat inevitable laundry-list character of our social science demonstrates the particular kinds of complexities that a social science of complex problems faces. The question that confronts us is whether this complexity will become even greater or paradoxically less as we discover the even greater complexity of stakeholders. That is, will recognizing the even greater complexity of stakeholders lead to a greater or less complex way of thinking about social systems? . . . Finally, if the elegance of social science is not necessarily to be found in its formal theories about the substance of social systems, can it thereby be found in the sophistication of its methods for investigating incredibly changing phenomena? If the essence of humanity is indeed truly invention, then let us invent a method that measures up to the phenomenon that is humanity.

References

ACKOFF, R. L. *Creating the Corporate Future: Plan or Be Planned For.* New York: Wiley, 1981.

ACKOFF, R. L., & EMERY, F. *On Purposeful Systems.* Chicago: Aldine-Atherton, 1974.

CHURCHMAN, C. W. *Prediction and Optimal Decision: Philosophical Issues of a Source of Values.* Englewood Cliffs, N.J.: Prentice-Hall, 1961.

CHURCHMAN, C. W. *The Design of Inquiring Systems.* New York: Basic Books, 1971.

CHURCHMAN, C. W. *The Systems Approach and Its Enemies.* New York: Basic Books, 1979.

DIESING, P. *Reason in Society, Five Types of Decisons and Their Social Conditions.* Champaign: University of Illinois, 1962.

MASON, R. & MITROFF, I. *Challenging Strategic Planning Assumptions.* New York: Wiley, 1981.

MITROFF, I., & KILMANN, R. *Methodological Approaches to Social Science: Integrating Divergent Concepts and Theories.* San Francisco: Jossey-Bass, 1978.

MITROFF, I., & MASON, R. "Structuring Ill-Structured Policy Issues: Further Explorations in a Methodology for Messy Problems." *Strategic Management Journal,* 1980, *1,* 331–342.

MITROFF, I., & MASON, R. *Creating a Dialectical Social Science.* Amsterdam: Reidel, 1981a.

MITROFF, I., & MASON, R. "Dialectical Pragmatism: A Progress Report on an Interdisciplinary Program of Research on the Dialectical Inquiry System." *Synthese,* 1981b.

SINGER, E. A. *Experience and Reflection.* Philadelphia: University of Pennsylvania Press, 1959.

36

Understanding the Employment Relation

Oliver E. Williamson

This chapter is concerned with the implications of an extreme form of nonhomogeneity—namely, job idiosyncrasy—for understanding the employment relation. Although it refers largely to production workers, the argument can be extended, with appropriate modifications, to cover nonproduction workers as well. The purpose is to better assess the employment relation in circumstances where workers *acquire,* during the course of their employment, significant job-specific skills and related task-specific knowledge. What Hayek referred to as knowledge of "particular circumstances of time and place" (1945, p. 521) and what was referred to as first-mover advantages . . . thus play a prominent role in the analysis. . . .

This is not to suggest, however that extra-economic considerations are thought to be unimportant. To the contrary, the proposition . . . that supplying a satisfying exchange relation is part of the economic problem, broadly construed, has special relevance where an employment relation is involved. Indeed, some of the ways in which internal labor markets bear on this proposition are developed in Section 3.3, below. But placing primary reliance on atmosphere to explain internal labor markets poses the following dilemma: Assuming that the same considerations of contractual satisfaction with

SOURCE: Reprinted with permission of The Free Press, a division of Macmillan, Inc. from *Markets and Hierarchies: Analysis and Antitrust Implications,* by Oliver E. Williamson. Copyright © 1975, 1983 by The Free Press.

respect to the nature of the exchange relationship applies to production jobs of all kinds, how is the coexistence of structured (internal) and structureless (recurrent spot) labor markets to be explained? By contrast, rationalizing the absence of structure, where jobs are fungible, and the conscious creation of structure, for idiosyncratic jobs, is relatively straightforward if an efficiency orientation is adopted. Accordingly, the argument runs throughout principally in efficiency terms.

Four alternative labor contracting modes are examined. Two of these, recurrent spot contracting and contingent claims contracting, rely entirely on market-mediated transactions. The other two modes involve a mixture of market-mediated exchange and hierarchy (internal organization). What is commonly referred to as the "authority relation" and the internal labor market mode are of this second kind. These several alternative contracting modes are assessed in cost-economizing terms, where costs include both production and transaction cost elements. Considering that the focus throughout is on contracting, transaction costs naturally receive primary attention.

My purposes, briefly, are as follows:

1. To demonstrate that the interesting problems of labor organization involve the study of transactions and contracting and, except in a rather special idiosyncratic sense, do not turn mainly on technology.
2. To isolate and assess the idiosyncratic job features which characterize internal labor markets with the help of the organizational failures framework.
3. To set out the transactional detail that would attend complex contingent claims contracting in idiosyncratic job circumstances, thereby to disclose why such contracts are prohibitively costly or infeasible.
4. To demonstrate that sequential spot contracting is unsuited to the idiosyncratic tasks in question, whence Alchian and Demsetz'

(1972) discussion of the employment relation requires qualification.

5. To examine the authority relation and indicate the limitations associated with Simon's (1957) evaluation of alternative contracting modes.

6. To develop the transactional rationale for internal labor markets (in terms mainly of economizing on bounded rationality and attenuating opportunism) where jobs are idiosyncratic in nontrivial degree. . . .

1. Technology: Conventional and Idiosyncratic Considerations

It is widely felt that technology has an important, if not fully determinative, influence on the employment relationship. I agree, but take exception with the usual view in several respects. First, for the reasons given in the preceding chapter, indivisibilities (of the usual kinds) are neither necessary nor sufficient for market contracting to be supplanted by internal organization. Second, I contend that nonseparabilities at most explain small-group organization. Third, and most important, I argue that the leading reason why an internal labor market supplants spot contracting is because of small-numbers exchange relations. This last turns on task idiosyncrasies as these appear in a moving equilibrium context.

1.1 Conventional Treatments

1.1.1 Indivisibilities

. . . It is entirely feasible, as a technological matter, for physical assets and informational services for which indivisibilities are significant to be monopoly owned and sold for hire. What impedes such ownership and exchange arrangements are the transactional difficulties which attend small-numbers trades. . . . I raise the issue at this time merely to restate my position that conventional arguments which rely on indivisibilities to explain the employment relation do not, without more, go through.

Recourse to transactional considerations is ultimately necessary.

1.1.2 Nonseparabilities

More relevant to our purposes here is the allegation that technological nonseparabilities constitute the principal reason for the employment relation, whence hierarchy, to appear (Alchian and Demsetz, 1972). But for such technological conditions, a "normal sales relationship" would purportedly govern the terms under which labor would be made available for hire.

. . . It is the joining of nonseparability with opportunism and a condition of information impactedness, rather than nonseparability by itself, that occasions the substitution of hierarchy for market exchange. Absent opportunism, free riding problems, of which shirking is one, would never appear. Absent information impactedness, opportunistic inclinations could be checked by paying the appropriate discriminating wage.

Regarded in transactional terms, technological nonseparability represents a case where information impactedness is particularly severe; but I emphasize that this is merely a matter of degree. Lesser degrees of information impactedness plainly exist that do not have these same technological origins but which can and often do occasion the supplanting of markets by hierarchies. (As urged in the preceding chapter, most tasks appear to be separable in a buffer inventory sense—often as between individual workers and almost invariably between small groups of workers—yet hierarchy commonly appears.) Our assessment of the technological nonseparability argument thus comes down to this: Such conditions are *merely symptomatic* of a set of underlying transactional factors which, both here and elsewhere, ultimately explain the organization of economic activity as between markets and hierarchies.

1.2 Small Numbers and Task Idiosyncrasies

It is generally agreed that small-numbers exchange conditions are attended by serious market exchange problems. . . . The frequency of and manner in which small-numbers labor exchange conditions develop, however, is less widely appreciated. It is the thesis of this chapter that task idiosyncrasies are common, that these give rise to small-numbers exchange conditions, and that market contracting is supplanted by an employment relation principally for this reason.

1.2.1 General

Doeringer and Piore describe idiosyncratic tasks in the following way (1971, pp. 15–16):

Almost every job involves some specific skills. Even the simplest custodial tasks are facilitated by familiarity with the physical environment specific to the workplace in which they are being performed. The apparently routine operation of standard machines can be importantly aided by familiarity with the particular piece of operating equipment. . . . In some cases workers are able to anticipate trouble and diagnose its source by subtle changes in the sound or smell of the equipment. Moreover, performance in some production or managerial jobs involves a team element, and a critical skill is the ability to operate effectively with the given members of the team. This ability is dependent upon the interaction skills of the personalities of the members, and the individual's work "skills" are specific in the sense that skills necessary to work on one team are never quite the same as those required on another.

More generally, task idiosyncrasies can arise in at least four ways: (1) equipment idiosyncrasies, due to incompletely standardized, albeit common, equipment, the unique characteristics of which become known through experience; (2) process idiosyncrasies, which are fashioned or "adopted" by the worker and his associates in specific operating contexts; (3) informal team accommodations, attributable to mutual adaptation; among parties engaged in recurrent contact but which are upset, to the possible detriment of group performance, when the membership is altered; and (4) communication idiosyncrasies with respect to information channels and codes

that are of value only within the firm. Because "technology is [partly] unwritten and that part of the specificity derives from improvements which the work force itself introduces, workers are in a position to perfect their monopoly over the knowledge of the technology should there be an incentive to do so" (Doeringer and Piore, 1971, p. 84).

Training for idiosyncratic jobs ordinarily takes place in an on-the-job context. Classroom training is unsuitable both because the unique attributes associated with particular operations, machines, the work group, and, more generally, the atmosphere of the workplace may be impossible to duplicate in the classroom, and because job incumbents, who are in possession of the requisite skills and knowledge with which the new recruit or candidate must become familiar, may be unable to describe, demonstrate, or otherwise impart this information except in an operational context (Doeringer and Piore, 1971, p. 20). Teaching-by-doing thus facilitates the learning-by-doing process. Where such uniqueness and teaching attributes are at all important, specific exposure in the workplace at some stage becomes essential. Outsiders who lack specific experience can thus achieve parity with insiders only by being hired and incurring the necessary startup costs.

The success of on-the-job training is plainly conditional on the information disclosure attitudes of incumbent employees. Both individually and as a group, incumbents are in possession of a valuable resource (knowledge) and can be expected to fully and candidly reveal it only in exchange for value. The way the employment relation is structured turns out to be important in this connection. The danger is that incumbent employees will hoard information to their personal advantage and engage in a series of bilateral monopolistic exchanges with the management—to the detriment of both the firm and other employees as well.

An additional feature of these tasks not described above but nevertheless important to an understanding of the contractual problems associated with the employment relation is that the activity in question is subject to periodic disturbance by environmental changes. Shifts in demand due to changes in the prices of complements or substitutes or to changes in consumer incomes or tastes occur; relative factor price changes appear; and technological changes of both product design and production technique types take place. Successive adaptations to changes of each of these kinds is typically needed if efficient production performance is to be realized. In addition, life cycle changes in the work force occur which occasion turnover, upgrading, and continuous training. The tasks in question are thus to be regarded in moving equilibrium terms. Put differently, they are not tasks for which a once-for-all adaptation by workers is sufficient, thereafter to remain unchanged.

1.2.2 Interpretation

The production tasks that are of transactional interest in this chapter are ones that are either themselves rather complex or are embedded in a complex set of technological and organizational circumstances. Furthermore, successive adaptations are required to realize efficiency in the face of changing internal and environmental events. A nontrivial degree of uncertainty/complexity may thus be said to characterize the tasks. Training for such tasks occurs in an on-the-job context because of the impossibility, or great cost, of disclosing job nuances, in a classroom situation. The relevant job details simply cannot be identified, accurately described, and effectively communicated in a classroom context on account of information processing limitations of both originators (teachers) and receivers (trainees). Sometimes, indeed, the requisite language will not even exist. The pairing of bounded rationality with an uncertainty/complexity condition thus gives rise to the job-specific training situation. *Teaching-by-doing and learning-by-doing both economize on bounded rationality in these idiosyncratic job circumstances.* [1]

Specialized skills and knowledge accrue to individuals and small groups as a result of their specific training and experience. But while such skills and information accrue naturally, they can be disclosed strategically—in an incomplete or distorted fashion—if the affected parties should choose to. Whether this will obtain depends on the structure of the bargaining relationship. Where job incumbents acquire nontrivial first-mover advantages over outsiders, and, in addition, are opportunistically inclined, what was once a large-numbers bidding situation, at the time original job assignments were made, is converted into a small-numbers bargaining situation if adaptations to unplanned (and perhaps unforeseeable) internal and market changes are subsequently proposed. The reasons for and consequences of this shift from a large-numbers bargaining relationship at the outset to bilateral bargaining subsequently are further developed below.

2. Individualistic Bargaining Models [2]

Four types of individualistic contracting modes can be distinguished: (1) contract now for the specific performance of x in the future: (2) contract now for the delivery of x_i contingent on event e_i obtaining in the future; (3) wait until the future materializes and contract for the appropriate (specific) x at the time; and (4) contract now for the right to select a specific x from within an admissible set X, the determination of the particular x to be deferred until the future. Simon's study of the employment relation (1957, pp. 183–195) treats contracts of the first type, which he characterizes as sales contracts, to be the main alternative to the so-called authority relation (type 4). This, however, is unfortunate because type 1 contracts, being rigid, are singularly unsuited to permit adaptation in response to changing internal and market circumstances. By contrast, contingent claims contracts (type 2) and sequential spot sales contracts (type 3) both permit adaptation. If complexity/uncertainty is held to be a central feature of the environment with which we are concerned, which it is, the deck is plainly stacked against contracts of type 1 from the outset. Accordingly, type 1 contracts will hereafter be disregarded.

2.1 Contingent Claims Contracts

Suppose that the efficient choice of x on each date depends on how the future unfolds. Suppose, furthermore, that the parties are instructed to negotiate a once-for-all labor contract in which the obligations of both employer and employee are fully stipulated at the outset. A complex contingent claims contract would then presumably result. The employer would agree to pay a particular wage now in return for which the employee agrees to deliver stipulated future services of a contingent kind, the particular services being dependent upon the circumstances which eventuate.

Contracting problems of several kinds can be anticipated. First, can the complex contract be written? Second, even if it can, is a meaningful agreement between the parties feasible? Third, can such agreements be implemented in a low cost fashion? The issues posed can all usefully be considered in the context of the framework sketched out above.

The feasibility of writing complex contingent claims contracts reduces fundamentally to a bounded rationality issue.

Recall in this connection the conclusion reached by Feldman and Kanter in their assessment of complex decision trees, to wit, "The comprehensive decision model is not feasible for most interesting decision problems" (1965, p. 615). Plainly, the complex labor agreements needed for comprehensive description of the idiosyncratic tasks in question are of this kind. Not only are changing market circumstances (product demand, rivalry, factor prices, technological conditions, and the like) impossibly complex to enumerate, but the appropriate adaptations thereto cannot be established with any degree of confidence *ex ante*. Changing life cycle conditions with respect to the internal labor force compound the complexities.

The enumeration problems referred to are acknowledged by Meade in his discussion of contingent claims contracts. "When environmental uncertainties are so numerous that they cannot all be considered . . . or, what comes perhaps to much the same thing, when any particular environmental risks are so hard to define and to distinguish from each other that it is impossible to base a firm betting or insurance contract upon the occurence or nonoccurrence of any of them, then for this reason alone it is impossible to have a system of contingency . . . markets" (1971, p. 183). Except for bounded rationality, Meade's concerns with excessive numbers, undefinable risks, and indistinguishable events would vanish.

But suppose, *arguendo,* that exhaustive complex contracts could be written at reasonable expense. Would such contracts be acceptable to the parties? I submit that a problem of incomprehensibility will frequently arise and impede reaching agreement. At least one of the parties, probably the worker, will be unable to meaningfully assess the implications of the complex agreement to which he is being asked to accede. Sequential contracting, in which experience permits the implications of various contingent commitments to be better understood, is thus apt to be favored instead.

Assume, however, that *ex ante* understanding poses no bar to contracting. *Ex post* enforcement issues then need to be addressed. First, there is the problem of declaring what state of the world has obtained. Meade's remarks that contingent claims contracts are feasible in circumstances where it is impossible, on the contract execution date, "to decide precisely enough for the purposes of a firm legal contract" what state of the world has eventuated (1971, p. 183) bear on this. While it is easy to agree with Meade's contentions, I think noteworthy to observe that, were it not for opportunism and information impactedness, the impediments to contracting which he refers to vanish. Absent these conditions, the responsibility for declaring what state of the world had obtained could simply be assigned to the best informed party. Once he has made the determination, the appropriate choice of x is found by consulting the contract. Execution then follows directly.

It is hazardous, however, to permit the best informed party unilaterally to make state of the world declarations where opportunism can be anticipated. If the worker is not indifferent between supplying services of type x_j rather than x_k, and if the declaration of the state of the world were to be left to him, he will be inclined, when circumstances permit, to represent the state of the world in terms most favorable to him. Similar problems are to be expected for those events for which the employer is thought to be the best informed party and unilaterally declares, from among a plausible set, which e_i has eventuated.[3] Moreover, mediation by a third party is no answer since, by assumption, an information impactedness condition prevails with respect to the observations in question.

Finally, even were it that state of the world issues could be settled conclusively at low cost, there is still the problem of execution. Did the worker really supply x_i instead in response to condition e_i, as he should, or did he (opportunistically) supply x_j instead? If the latter, how does the employer show this in a way that entitles him to a remedy? These are likewise information impactedness issues. Problems akin to moral hazard are posed.

Ordinarily, bounded rationality renders the description of once-for-all contingent claims employment contracts strictly infeasible. Occasions to examine the negotiability and enforcement properties of such contracts thus rarely develop. It is sufficient for our purposes here, however, merely to establish that problems of any of these kinds impair contingent claims contracting. In consideration of these difficulties, alternatives to the once-for-all supply relations ought presumably to be examined.

2.2 Sequential Spot Contracts

Alchian and Demsetz take the position that it is a delusion to characterize the relation between employer and employee by reference to fiat, authority, or the like. Rather, it is their contention that the relation between an employer and his employee is identical to that which exists between a shopper and his grocer in fiat and authority respects (1972, p. 777):

> The single consumer can assign his grocer to the task of obtaining whatever the customer can induce the grocer to provide at a price acceptable to both parties. That is precisely all that an employer can do to an employee. To speak of managing, directing, or assigning workers to various tasks is a deceptive way of noting that the employer continually is involved in renegotiation of contracts on terms that must be acceptable to both parties. . . . Long term contracts between employer and employee are not the essence of the organization we call a firm.

Implicit in their argument, I take it, is an assumption that the transition costs associated with employee turnover ar negligible. Employers, therefore, are able easily to adapt to changing market circumstances by filling jobs on a spot market basis. Although job incumbents may continue to hold jobs for a considerable period of time and may claim to be subject to an authority relationship, all that they are essentially doing is continuously meeting bids for their jobs in the spot market. This is option number three, among the contracting alternatives described at the beginning of this section, done repeatedly.

That adaptive, sequential decision-making can be effectively implemented in sequential spot labor markets which satisfy the low transition cost assumption (as some apparently do, for example, migrant farm labor)[4] without posing issues that differ in kind from the usual grocer-customer relationship seems uncontestable. I submit, however, that many jobs do not satisfy this assumption. In particular, the tasks of interest here are not of this primative variety. Where tasks are idiosyncratic, in nontrivial degree, the worker-employer relationship and the feasibility of sequential spot market contracting breaks down.

Whereas the problems of contingent claims contracts were attributed to bounded rationality and opportunism conditions, sequential spot contracts are principally impaired only by the latter. (Bounded rationality poses a less severe problem because no effort is made to describe the complex decision tree from the outset. Instead, adaptations to uncertainty are devised as events unfold.) Wherein does opportunism arise and how is sequential spot contracting impaired?

. . . Opportunism pose[s] a contractual problem only to the extent that it appears in a small-numbers bargaining context. Otherwise, large-numbers bidding effectively checks opportunistic inclinations and competitive outcomes result. The problem with the tasks in question is that while large-numbers bidding conditions obtain at the outset, before jobs are first assigned and the work begun, the idiosyncratic nature of the work experience effectively destroys parity at the contract renewal interval. Incumbents who enjoy nontrivial advantages over similarly qualified but inexperienced bidders are well-situated to demand some fraction of the cost savings which their idiosyncratic experience has generated.

One possible adaptation is for employers to avoid idiosyncratic technologies and techniques in favor of more well-standardized operations. Although least-cost production *technologies* are sacrificed in the process, pecuniary gains may nevertheless result since incumbents realize little strategic advantage over otherwise qualified but inexperienced outsiders. Structuring the initial bidding in such a way as to permit the least-cost technology and techniques to be employed without risking untoward contract renewal outcomes is, however, plainly to be preferred. Two possibilities warrant consideration: (1) extract a promise from each willing bidder at the outset that he will not use his idiosyncratic knowledge and experience in a monopolistic way at the contract renewal interval; or (2) require incumbents to capitalize the prospective monopoly gains that each will accrue and extract corresponding lump sum payments from winning bidders at the outset.

The first of these can be dismissed as utopian. It assumes that promises not to behave opportunistically are either self-enforcing or can be enforced in the courts. Self-enforcement is tantamount to denying that human agents are prone to be opportunists, and fails for want of reality testing. Enforcement of such promises by the courts is likewise unrealistic. Neither case by case litigation nor simple rule-making disposition of the issues is feasible. Litigation on the merits of each case is prohibitively costly, while rules to the effect that "all workers shall receive only competitive wages" fail because courts cannot, for information impactedness reasons, determine whether workers put their energies and inventiveness into the job in a way which permits task-specific cost savings to be fully realized—in which case disaffected workers can counter such rules by withholding effort.

The distinction between consummate and perfunctory cooperation is important in this connection. Consummate cooperation is an affirmative job attitude—to include the use of judgment, filling gaps, and taking initiative in an instrumental way.[5] Perfunctory cooperation, by contrast, involves job performance of a minimally acceptable sort—where minimally acceptable means that incumbents, who through experience have acquired task-specific skills, need merely to maintain a slight-margin over the best available inexperienced candidate (whose job attitude, of necessity, is an unknown quantity). The upshot is that workers, by shifting to a perfunctory performance mode, are in a position to "destroy" idiosyncratic efficiency gains. Reliance on pre-employment promises as a means by which to deny workers from participating in such gains is accordingly self-defeating.

Consider, therefore, the second alternative in which, though worker participation in realized cost savings is assumed to be normal, workers are required to submit lump sum bids for jobs at the outset. Assuming that large numbers of applicants are qualified to bid for these jobs at the outset, will such a scheme permit employers to fully appropriate the expected, discounted value of future cost savings by awarding the job to whichever worker offers to make the highest lump sum payment?

Such a contracting scheme amounts to long-term contracting in which many of the details of the agreement are left unspecified. As might be anticipated, numerous problems are posed. For one thing, it assumes that workers are capable of assessing complex future circumstances in a sophisticated way and making a determination of what the prospective gains are. Plainly, a serious bounded rationality issue is raised. Second, even if workers had the competence to complete such an exercise it is seriously to be doubted that they could raise the funds, if their personal assets were deficient, to make the implied full valuation bids. As Malmgren has observed, in a somewhat different but nevertheless related context: ". . . some [individuals] will see opportunities, but be unable to communicate their own information and expectations favorably to bankers, and thus be unable to acquire finance, or need to pay a higher charge for the capital borrowed" (1961, p. 416). The communication difficulties referred to are due to language limitations (attributable to bounded rationality) that the parties experience. That bankers are unwilling to accept the representations of loan-seekers at face value is because of the risks of opportunism.

Third, and crucially, the magnitude of the estimated future gains to be realized by workers often depends not merely on exogenous events and/or activities that each worker fully controls but also on the posture of coworkers and the posture of the employer. Problems with coworkers arise if, despite steady state task separability, the constant or active cooperation of workers who interface with the task in question must be secured each time an adaptation is proposed. This effectively means that related sets of workers must enter bids as teams, which complicates the bidding scheme greatly and offers opportunities for free riding. Problems also arise if gains cannot be realized independently of the decisions taken by management with respect, for example, to the organization of production, complementary new asset acquisitions, equipment repair policy, and so forth. Lump sum bidding is plainly hazardous where workers are entering bids on life cycle earnings streams that are repeatedly exposed to rebargaining.[6]

Finally, but surely of negligible importance in relation to the issues already raised, there is the question of efficient risk-bearing: which party is best situated to bear the risks of future uncertainties—the individual workers or the firm? That individual workers may be poorly suited to bear such risks and, as a group, can pool risks only with difficulty seems evident and further argues against the bidding scheme proposed.

Transactional difficulties thus beset both contingent claims and sequential spot market contracting for the idiosyncratic tasks of interest in this chapter. Consider, therefore, the so-called authority relation as the solution to the contracting problems in question.

2.3 The Authority Relation

Simon has made one of the few attempts to formally assess the employment relation. Letting B designate the employer (or boss), W be the employee (or worker), and x be an element in the set of possible behavior patterns of W, he defines an authority relation as follows (1957, p. 184):

> We will say that B exercises *authority* over W if W permits B to select x. That is, W accepts authority when his behavior is determined by B's decision. In general, W will accept authority only if x_o the x chosen by B, is restricted to some subset (W's "area of acceptance") of all the possible values.

An employment contract is then said to exist whenever W agrees to accept the authority of B in return for which B agrees to pay W a stated wage (1957, p. 184).

Simon then asks when will such an employment relationship be preferred to a sales contract, and offers the following two conjectures (1957, p. 185):

1. W will be willing to enter into an employment contract with B only if it does not matter to him "very much" which x (within the agreed upon area of acceptance) B will choose, or if W is compensated

in some way for the possibility that B will choose x that is not desired by W (i.e., that B will ask W to perform an unpleasant task).

2. It will be advantageous to B to offer W added compensation for entering into an employment contract if B is unable to predict with certainty, at the time the contract is made, which x will be the optimum one, from his standpoint. That is, B will pay for the privilege of postponing, until some time after the contract is made, the selection of x.

He then goes on to develop a formal model in which he demonstrates that the employment contract commonly has attractive properties, under conditions of uncertainty, *provided that the alternatives are* (1) the promise of a particular x in exchange for a given wage w (what he considers to be the sales contract option), or (2) a set of X from which a particular x will subsequently be chosen in exchange for a given wage w' (the employment contract option).

Put differently, the deterministic sales contract is shown to be inferior to an incompletely specified employment relation in which W and B do not agree on all terms *ex ante*, but "agree to agree later"—or better, "agree to tell and be told." But plainly the terms are rigged from the outset. As noted previously, the particular type of sales contract to which Simon refers in attempting to establish the rationale for an authority relations is the only one of the three types of sales contracts described at the beginning of this section that lacks adaptability in response to changing market circumstances. Since employment contracts of both the contingent and sequential spot marketing kinds are not similarly flawed, a better test of the authority relation would be to compare it with either of these instead.

Simon's modeling apparatus, unfortunately, does not lend itself to such purposes. It is simply silent with respect to the efficiency properties of alternative contracts in which adaptability is featured. Not only is it unable

to discriminate between the authority relation, contingent claims contract, and spot market contracting in adaptability respects, but Simon's model fails to raise transaction cost issues of the types described here.

This is not, however, to suggest that the authority relation has nothing to commend it. To the contrary, such a relation does not require that the complex decision tree be generated in advance, and thus does not pose the severe bounded rationality problems that the contingent claims contracting model is subject to. The authority relation also, presumably, reduces the frequency with which contracts must be negotiated in comparison with the sequential spot contracting mode. Adaptations in the small can be costlessly accomplished under an authority relation because such changes, to the worker, do not matter very much.

Assuming, however, that the parties are prospectively joined in a long-term association and the jobs in question are of the idiosyncratic kind, most of the problems of sequential spot contracting still need to be faced. Thus, how are wage and related terms of employment to be adjusted through time in response to either small, but cumulative, or large, discrete changes in the data? What happens when hitherto unforeseen and unforeseeable contingencies eventuate? How are differences between parties regarding state of the world determinations, the definition of the task, and job performance to be reconciled? Substantially all of the problems that are posed by idiosyncratic tasks in the sequential spot contracting mode appear, I submit, under the authority relation as well.

3. The Efficiency Implications of Internal Labor Market Structures

The upshot is that none of the above contracting schemes has acceptable properties for tasks of the idiosyncratic variety. Contingent claims contracting (Meade, 1971, Chap. 10) fails principally because of bounded rationality. Spot market contracting (Alchian and Demetz, 1972,

p. 777) is impaired by first-mover advantages and problems of opportunism. The authority relation (Simon, 1957, pp. 183–195) is excessively vague and, ultimately, is confronted with the same types of problems as is spot market contracting. Faced with this result, the question of alternative contracting schemes naturally arises. Can more effective schemes be designed? Do more efficient contracting modes exist?

The analysis here is restricted to the latter of these questions, which is answered in the affirmative. Although it cannot be said that internal labor market structures are optimally efficient with respect to idiosyncratic tasks, it is nevertheless significant that their properties have been little noted or understated by predominantly non-neoclassical interpretations of these markets in the past.

My assessment of the efficiency implications of internal labor market structures is in three parts. The occasion for and purposes of collective organization are sketched first. The salient structural attributes of internal labor markets are then described and the efficiency implications of each, expressed in terms of the language of the organizational failures framework, is indicated. Several caveats, including a brief discussion of atmosphere, follow.

3.1 Collective Organization

To observe that the pursuit of perceived individual interests can sometimes lead to defective collective outcomes is scarcely novel. Schelling has treated the issue extensively in the context of the "ecology of micromotives" (1971). The individual in each of his examples is both small in relation to the system—and thus his behavior, by itself, has no decisive influence on the system—and is unable to appropriate the collective gains that would obtain were he voluntarily to forego individual self-interest seeking. Schelling then observes that the remedy involves collective action. An enforceable social contract which imposes a cooperative solution on the system is needed (1971, p. 69).

Although it is common to think of collective action as action by the state, this is plainly too narrow. As Arrow (1969, p. 62) and Schelling (1971, p. 68) emphasize, both private collective action (of which the firm, with its hierarchical controls, is an example) and norms of socialization are also devices for realizing cooperative solutions. The internal labor market is usefully interpreted in this same spirit.

Although it is in the interest of each worker, bargaining individually or as a part of a small team, to acquire and exploit monopoly positions, it is plainly not in the interest of the *system* that employees should behave in this way. Opportunistic bargaining not only in itself absorbs real resources, but efficient adaptations are delayed and possibly foregone altogether. Accordingly, what this suggests is that the employment relation be transformed in such a way that systems concerns are made more fully to prevail and the following objectives are realized: (1) bargaining costs are much lower; (2) the internal wage structure is rationalized in terms of objective task characteristics; (3) consummate rather than perfunctory cooperation is encouraged; and (4) investments of idiosyncratic types, which constitute a potential source of monopoly, are undertaken without risk of exploitation. For the reasons and in the ways developed below, internal labor markets can have, and some do have, the requisite properties to satisfy this prescription.[7]

3.2 Structural Attributes and Their Efficiency Consequences

3.2.1 Wage Bargaining

A leading difficulty with individual contracting schemes where jobs are idiosyncratic is that workers are strategically situated to bargain opportunistically. The internal labor market achieves a fundamental transformation by shifting to a system where wage rates are attached mainly to jobs rather than to workers. Not only is individual wage bargaining thereby discouraged, but it may even be legally foreclosed (Summers, 1969, p. 531). Once wages are expressly removed from individual bargaining, there is really no occasion for the worker to haggle over the incremental gains that are realized when adaptations of degree are proposed by the management. The incentives to behave opportunistically, which infect individual bargaining schemes, are correspondingly attenuated.

Moreover, not only are affirmative incentives lacking, but there are disincentives, of group disciplinary and promotion ladder types, which augur against resistance to authority on matters that come within the range customarily covered by the authority relation.[8] Promotion ladder issues are taken up on conjunction with the discussion of ports of entry in section 3.2.4, below; consider, therefore, group disciplinary effects.

In this connection Barnard observes (1962, p. 169):

> Since the efficiency of organization is affected by the degree to which individuals assent to orders, denying the authority of an organization communication is a threat to the interests of all individuals who derive a net advantage from their connection with the organization, unless the orders are unacceptable to them also. Accordingly, at any given time there is among most of the contributors an active personal interest in the maintenance of the authority of all orders which to them are within the zone of indifference. The maintenance of this interest is largely a function of informal organization.

The application of group pressures thus combines with promotional incentives to facilitate adaptations in the small.[9] Even individuals who have exhausted their promotional prospects can thereby be induced to comply. System interests are made more fully to prevail. This concern with viability possibly explains the position taken in labor law that orders which are ambiguous with respect to, and perhaps even exceed, the scope of authority, are to

be fulfilled first and disputed later (Summers, 1969, pp. 538, 573).

3.2.2 Contractual Incompleteness/Arbitration

Internal labor market agreements are commonly reached through collective bargaining. Cox observes in this connection that the collective bargaining agreement should be understood as an instrument of government as well as an instrument of exchange. "The collective agreement governs complex, many-sided relations between large-numbers of people in a going concern for very substantial periods of time" (1958, p. 22). Provision for unforeseeable contingencies is made by writing the contract in general and flexible terms and supplying the parties with a special arbitration machinery. "One simply cannot spell out every detail of life in an industrial establishment, or even of that portion which both management and labor agree is a matter of mutual concern" (Cox, 1958, p. 23). Such contractual imcompleteness is an implicit concession to bounded rationality. Rather than attempt to anticipate all bridges that might conceivably be faced, which is impossibly ambitious and excessively costly, bridges are crossed as they appear.

However attractive, in bounded rationality respects, adaptive, sequential decision-making is, admitting gaps into the contract also poses hazards. Where parties are not indifferent with respect to the manner in which gaps are to be filled, fractious bargaining or litigation commonly result. It is for the purpose of forestalling the worst outcomes of this kind that the special arbitration apparatus is devised.

Important differences between commercial and labor arbitration are to be noted in this connection. For one thing, ". . . the commercial arbitrator finds facts—did the cloth meet the sample—while the labor arbitrator necessarily pours meaning into the general phrases and interstices of a document" (Cox, 1958, p. 23). In addition, the idiosyncratic practices of the firm and its employees also constitute "shop law" and, to the labor arbitrator, are essential background for purposes of understanding a collective agreement and interpreting its intent (Cox, 1958, p. 24).

In the language of the organizational failures framework, the creation of such a special arbitration apparatus serves to overcome information impactedness because the arbitrator is able to explore the facts in greater depth and with greater sensitivity to idiosyncratic attributes of the enterprise than could normal judicial proceedings. Furthermore, once it becomes recognized that the arbitrator is able to apprise himself of the facts in a discerning and low cost way, opportunistic misrepresentations of the data are discouraged as well.

3.2.3 Grievances

Also of interest in relation to the above is the matter of who is entitled to activate the arbitration machinery when an individual dispute arises. Cox takes the position that (1958, p. 24)[10]

> . . . giving the union control over all claims arising under the collective agreement comports so much better with the functional nature of a collective bargaining agreement. . . . Allowing an individual to carry a claim to arbitration whenever he is dissatisfied with the adjustment worked out by the company and the union . . . discourages the kind of day-to-day cooperation between company and union which is normally the mark of sound industrial relations—a relationship in which grievances are treated as problems to be solved and contracts are only guideposts in a dynamic human relationship. When . . . the individual's claim endangers group interests, the union's function is to resolve the competition by reaching an accommodation or striking a balance.

The practice described by Cox of giving the union control over arbitration claims plainly permits group interests, whence the concern for system viability, to supercede individual interests, thereby curbing small numbers opportunism.

3.2.4 Internal Promotion/Ports of Entry

Acceding to authority on matters that fall within the zone of acceptance[11] merely requires that employees respond in a minimally acceptable, even perfunctory way. This may be sufficient for tasks that are reasonably well-structured. In such circumstances, the zeal with which an instruction is discharged may have little effect on the outcome. As indicated, however, consummate cooperation is valued for the tasks of interest here. But how is cooperation of this more extensive sort to be realized?

A simple answer is to reward cooperative behavior by awarding incentive payments on a transaction-specific basis. The employment relation would then revert to a series of haggling encounters over the nature of the *quid pro quo*, however, and would hardly be distinguishable from a sequential spot contract. Moreover, such payments would plainly violate the nonindividualistic wage bargaining attributes of internal labor markets described in Section 3.2.1, above.

The internal promotion practices in internal labor markets are of special interest in this connection. Access to higher-level positions on internal promotion ladders are not open to all comers on an unrestricted basis. Rather, as part of the internal incentive system, higher-level positions (of the prescribed kinds)[12] are filled by promotion from within whenever this is feasible. This practice, particularly if it is followed by other enterprises to which the workers might otherwise turn for upgrading opportunities, ties the interests of the workers to the firm in a continuing way.[13] Given these ties, the worker looks to internal promotion as the principal means of improving his position.

The practice of restricting entry to lower-level jobs and promoting from within has interesting experience-rating implications. It permits firms to protect themselves against low productivity types, who might otherwise successfully represent themselves to be high productivity applicants, by bringing employees in at low level positions and then upgrading them as experience warrants. Furthermore, employees who may have been incorrectly upgraded but later have been "found out," and hence barred from additional internal promotions, are unable to move to a new organization without penalty.[14] Were unpenalized lateral moves possible, workers might, considering the problems of accurately transmitting productivity valuations between firms, be able to disguise their true productivity attributes from their new employers long enough to achieve some additional promotions. Restricting access to low level positions serves to protect the firm against exploitation by opportunistic types who would, if they could, change jobs strategically for the purpose of compounding evaluation errors between successive independent organizations.

Were it, however, that markets could perform equally well these experience-rating functions, the port of entry restrictions described would be unnecessary. The (comparative) limitations of markets in experience rating respects warrant elaboration. The principal impediment to effective interfirm experience-rating is one of communication.[15] By comparison with the firm, markets lack a rich and common rating language. The language problem is particularly severe where the judgments to be made are highly subjective. The advantages of hierarchy in these circumstances are especially great if those persons who are the most familiar with a worker's characteristics, usually his immediate supervisor, also do the experience-rating. The need to rationalize subjective assessments that are confidently held but, by reason of bounded rationality, difficult to articulate is reduced. Put differently, interfirm experience-rating is impeded in information impactedness respects.

Reliance on internal promotion has affirmative incentive properties because workers can anticipate that differential talent and degrees of cooperativeness will be rewarded. Consequently, although the attachment of wages to jobs rather than to individuals may result in an imperfect correspondence between wages and marginal productivity at ports of entry, productivity differentials will be recognized over a time and a more perfect correspondence can be expected for higher-level assignments in the internal labor market job hierarchy. . . .

4. Concluding Remarks

Organizational failure and systems considerations appear repeatedly in the foregoing assessment of the properties of alternative contracting modes in relation to idiosyncratic tasks. These highlights are briefly recapitulated here, after which some qualifications are offered.

4.1 Application of the Organizational Failures Framework

But for uncertainty, adaptive sequential decision-making problems would never be posed. Accordingly, the occasion to devise flexible contracts would never develop.

But for bounded rationality, complex contingent claims contracts could be written, and there would be no occasion to investigate other forms of contracting.

But for opportunism, individuals would honestly disclose all information pertinent to the bargain and would self-enforce promises to forego the monopoly powers which accrue to incumbents. Alternatively, were it not for task idiosyncracies, information impactedness conditions would never develop and outsiders would be on a parity with incumbents in bidding for jobs. In either event, the distortions associated with monopoly advantage would vanish and spot market contracting would suffice. In circumstances, however, where incumbents realize idiosyncratic knowledge and skill advantages over otherwise qualified outsiders, small-numbers conditions evolve. If, additionally, incumbents behave opportunistically, spot market contracting is hazardous.

4.2 The Collective Agreement as a Systems Solution

Frequently more important than the question of whether workers accept authority in the limited sense of "do this" or "do that," at the appointed time and place in some highly prescribed manner, is their attitude toward cooperation. We have accordingly distinguished between perfunctory and consummate cooperation and have argued that collective organization, in the form of an internal labor market, is well-suited to promote consummate cooperation.

In this respect and others, internal labor markets serve to promote efficiency. Job evaluation attaches wages to jobs, rather than to individuals, thereby foreclosing individual bargaining. The resulting wage structure reflects objective long-term job values rather than current bargaining exigencies. Internal promotion ladders encourage a positive worker attitude toward on-the-job training and enable the firm to reward cooperative behavior. A grievance procedure, with impartial arbitration as the usual final step, allows the firm and the workers to deal with continually changing conditions in a relatively nonlitigious manner. Contract revision and renewal take place in an atmosphere of mutual restraint in which the parties are committed to continuing accommodation. Unionization commonly facilitates the orderly achievement of these results, though it is not strictly necessary, especially in small organizations.

Notes

1. Doing-while-learning also contributes to the output of the firm. Classroom training is typically at a disadvantage in this respect.

2. Lest the ensuing discussion of autonomous bargaining modes be thought to be contrived and/or unnecessary, since "everyone knows" such bargaining modes are inapposite, I make the following observations: First, though it is widely recognized that complex contingent claims contracting is infeasible [for example, Radner notes that the Arrow-Debreu contracting model "requires that the economic agents possess capabilities of imagination and calculation that exceed reality by many orders of magnitude" (1970, p. 457)], the reasons for this are rarely fully spelled out—either in general or, even less, with respect to labor market contracting. I attempt to rectify this condition in Section 2.1. Second, as our discussion of Alchian and Demsetz in Section 2.2 reveals, it is plainly not the case that everyone appreciates that idiosyncratic tasks need to be distinguished from tasks in general and that sequential spot contracting is singularly unsuited for jobs of the idiosyncratic kind. Third, so as to correct the widely held belief that the authority relation represents a well-defined alternative to "normal" market contracting (as recently illustrated by Arrow's (1974, pp. 25, 63–65) reliance on Simon's treatment of the authority relation), I think it important that the ambiguities of the authority relation be exposed.

3. The issue here is somewhat more subtle, however. The employer, when he assumes the role of the best informed party, will not wish to declare a false state of the world *unless,* at the time he got the worker to agree to a wage w, he represented to the worker that services of type x_i would be called or when event e_i obtained when in fact x'_i services, which the worker dislikes, yield a greater e_i gain. The worker, being assured that he would be called on to perform x'_i services only when the unlikely event e'_i occurred, agreed to a lower wage than he would have if he realized that an x'_i response would be called or in both e_i and e'_i situations—because the employer will falsely declare e_i to be e'_i so as to get x'_i performed.

4. See Doeringer and Piore (1971, pp. 4–5); also Kerr (1954, p. 95).

5. Consummate cooperation involves working in a fully functional, undistorted mode. Efforts are not purposefully withheld; neither is behavior of a knowingly inapt kind undertaken. Blau and Scott are plainly concerned with the difference between perfunctory and consummate cooperation in the following passage (1962, p. 140):

> the contract obligates employees to perform only a set of duties in accordance with minimum standards and does not assure their striving to achieve optimum performance. . . . [L]egal authority does not and cannot command the employee's willingness to devote his ingenuity and energy to performing his tasks to the best of his ability. . . . It promotes compliance with directives and discipline, but does not encourage employees to exert

effort, to accept responsibilities, or to exercise initiative.

6. There is the related problem of comparing the bids of workers who have different age, health, and other characteristics. Possibly this could be handled by stipulating that winners have claims to jobs in perpetuity, so that a job can be put up for rebidding by the estate of a worker who dies or retires. Such rebidding, however, is hazardous if the new worker must secure anew the cooperation of his colleagues. Established workers are then in a position strategically to appropriate some of the gains. (This assumes that coalition asymmetries exist which favor old workers in relation to the new.)

7. Common's discussion with Sidney Hillman concerning the transformation of membership attitudes among the Amalgamated Clothing Workers illustrates some of the systems attributes of collective agreements (1970, p. 130):

> Ten years after World War I, I asked Sidney Hillman . . . why his members were less revolutionary than they had been when I knew them twenty-five years before in the sweatshop. . . . Hillman replies, "They know now that they are citizens of the industry. They know that they must make the corporation a success on account of their own jobs." They were citizens because they had an arbitration system which gave them security against arbitrary foremen. They had an unemployment system by agreement with the firm which gave them security of earnings. This is an illustration of the meaning of part-whole relations.

8. Authority relation is used here in the qualified short run sense suggested in our discussion of Simon in Section 2.3 above.

9. Of course, informal organization does not operate exclusively in the context of a collectivized wage bargain. Autonomous bargainers, however, are ordinarily expected to behave in autonomous ways. The extent to which group powers serve as a check on challenges to authority is accordingly much weaker where the individual bargaining mode prevails (March and Simon, 1958, pp. 59, 66). By contrast, the individual in the collectivized system who refuses to accede to orders on matters that fall within the customarily define zone of acceptance is apt to be regarded as cantankerous or malevolent, since there is no private pecuniary gain to be appropriated, and will be ostracized by his peers.

10. I am informed that his practice is changing and offer three comments in this regard. First, institutional change does not always promote efficiency outcomes; backward steps will sometimes occur—possibly because the efficiency implications are not understood. Second, relegating control to the union on whether a grievance is to be submitted to arbitration can sometimes lead to capricious results. Disfavored workers can be unfairly disadvantaged by those who control the union decision-making machinery. Some form of appeal may therefore be a necessary corrective. Third, that workers are given rights to bring grievances on their own motion does not imply that this will happen frequently. Grievances that fail to secure the support of peers are unlikely to be brought unless they represent egregious conditions on which the grievant feels confidently he will prevail. The bringing of trivial grievances not only elicits the resentment of peers but impairs the grievant's standing when more serious matters are posed.

11. The zone of acceptance is discussed in the quotation from Barnard in Section 3.2.1.

12. For a discussion, see Doeringer and Piore (1971, pp. 42–47).

13. Since access to idiosyncratic types of jobs is limited by requiring new employees to accept lower-level jobs at the bottom of promotion ladders, individuals can usually not shift laterally between firms without cost. "Employees in nonentry jobs in one enterprise often have access only to entry-level jobs in other enterprises. The latter will often pay less than those which the employees currently hold" (Doeringer and Piore, 1971, p. 78).

14. Agents seeking transfer may have gotten ahead in an organization by error. Experience-rating, after all, is a statistical inference process and is vulnerable to "Type II" error. When a mistake has been discovered and additional promotions are not forthcoming, the agent might seek transfer in the hope that he can successfully disguise his true characteristics in the new organization and thereby secure further promotions. Alternately, the agent may have been promoted correctly, but changed his work attitudes subsequently—in which case further promotion is denied. Again, he might seek transfer in the hope of securing additional promotion in an organization that, because of the difficulty of interfirm

communication about agent characteristics, is less able to ascertain his true characteristics initially.

15. Interfirm experience-rating may also suffer in veracity respects, since firms may choose deliberately to mislead rivals. The major impediment, however, is one of communication.

References

ALCHIAN, A. A., "Uncertainty, Evolution and Economic Theory," *Journal of Political Economy, 58:* 211-221, June 1950.

———, "Costs and Outputs," in M. Abramovitz et al., *The Allocation of Economic Resources: Essays in Honor of Bernard Francis Haley.* Stanford: Stanford University Press, 1959, pp. 23-40.

———, "Corporate Management and Property Rights," In H. G. Manne, ed., *Economic Policy and Regulation of Corporate Securities.* Washington: American Enterprise Institute for Public Policy Research, 1969, pp. 337-360.

——— and H. Demsetz, "Production, Information Costs, and Economic Organization," *American Economic Review, 62:* 777-795, December 1972.

ARROW, K. J., "Economic Welfare and the Allocation of Resources for Invention," in *The Rate and Direction of Inventive Activity.* Princeton: Princeton University Press, 1962, pp. 609-625.

———, "Comment," *The Rate and Direction of Inventive Activity.* Princeton: Princeton University Press, 1962, pp. 353-358.

———, *Aspects of the Theory of Risk Bearing.* Helsinki: Yrjo Jahnssonin Saatio, 1965.

———, "The Organization of Economic Activity," *The Analysis and Evaluation of Public Expenditure: The PPB System.* Joint Economic Committee, 91st Cong., 1st Sess., 1969, pp. 59-73.

———, *Essays in the Theory of Risk-Bearing.* Chicago: Markham, 1971.

———, "Gifts and Exchanges," *Philosophy and Public Affairs,* Summer 1972, 343-362.

———, *Limits of Organization.* New York: W. W. Norton & Company, Inc., 1974.

BARNARD, C. I., *The Functions of the Executive,* 2d ed., Cambridge: Harvard University Press, 1962.

———, "Functions and Pathology of Status Systems in Formal Organizations," in W. F. Whyte, ed., *Industry and Society.* New York: McGraw-Hill Book Company, Inc., 1946, pp. 46-83.

BLAU, P. M., & R. W. SCOTT, *Formal Organizations.* San Francisco: Chandler Publishing Company, 1962.

COMMONS, JOHN R., *Institutional Economics.* Madison: University of Wisconsin Press, 1934.

———, *The Economics of Collective Action.* Madison: University of Wisconsin Press, 1970.

COX, A., "The Legal Nature of Collective Bargaining Agreements," *Michigan Law Review, 57:* 1-36, November 1958.

DOERINGER, P., & M. PIORE, *Internal Labor Markets and Manpower Analysis.* Boston: D. C. Heath and Company, 1971.

FELDMAN, J., & H. KANTER, "Organizational Decision Making," in J. March, ed., *Handbook of Organizations.* Chicago: Rand McNally & Company, 1965, pp. 614-649.

HAYEK, F., "The Use of Knowledge in Society," *American Economic Review, 35:* 519-530, September 1945.

KERR, C., "The Balkanization of Labor Markets," in E. Wight Bakke et. al., *Labor Mobility and Economic Opportunity.* Cambridge and New York: The Technology Press of the Massachusetts Institute of Technology, and John Wiley & Sons, Inc., 1954, pp. 92-110.

MALMGREN, H., "Information, Expectations and the Theory of the Firm," *Quarterly Journal of Economics, 75:* 399-421, August 1961.

MARCH, J. G., & H. A. SIMON, *Organizations.* New York: John Wiley & Sons, Inc., 1958.

MEADE, J. E., *The Controlled Economy.* London: George Allen & Unwin, Ltd., 1971.

RADNER, R., "Competitive Equilibrium Under Uncertainty," *Econometrica, 36:* 31-58, January 1968.

———, "Problems in the Theory of Markets Under Uncertainty," *American Economic Review, 60:* 454-460, May 1970.

———, "Existence of Equilibrium of Plans, Prices, and Price Expectations in a Sequence of Markets," *Econometrica, 40:* 289-304, March 1972.

SCHELLING, T. C., *The Strategy of Conflict.* Cambridge: Harvard University Press, 1960.

———, "On the Ecology of Micromotives," *Public Interest, 25:* 61-98 Fall 1971.

SIMON, H. A., *Models of Man.* New York: John Wiley & Sons, Inc., 1957.

———, *Administrative Behavior*. 2d ed., New York: The Macmillan Company, 1961.

———, "The Architecture of Complexity," *Proceedings of the American Philosophical Society, 106:* 467–482, December 1962.

———, *The Sciences of the Artificial*. Cambridge: Massachusetts Institute of Technology Press, 1969.

———, "Theories of Bounded Rationality," in C. McGuire and R. Radner, eds., *Decision and Organization*. Amsterdam: North-Holland Publishing Company, 1972, pp. 161–176.

SUMMERS, C., "Collective Agreements and the Law of Contracts." *Yale Law Journal, 78:* 527–575, March 1969.

VII

Power and Politics
Organization Theory

The neatest thing about power is that we all understand it. We may have first discovered power as children when our mothers said, "Don't do that!" And we learn about power in organizations as soon as we go to school. Most of us have a pretty good intuitive grasp of the basic concepts of organizational power by the time we reach the third grade. So, the newest thing about power in organizations is not our understanding of it, but rather our intellectualizing about it.

Ordinary people—as well as scholars—have hesitated to talk about power. First, for many, power is not a subject for polite conversation. We have often equated power with force, brutality, unethical behavior, manipulation, connivance, and subjugation. Rosabeth Moss Kanter (1979) contends that "power is America's last dirty word. It is easier to talk about money—and much easier to talk about sex—than it is to talk about power." Second, many of the important writings from the power school are quite recent, and the theoretical grounding of the school is not as advanced as it is in the classical, "modern" structural, and systems schools. For both of the above reasons, fewer people have been exposed to analyses of organizational power. So, it will be useful to start our introduction to the power and politics school by contrasting some of its basic assumptions with those of its immediate predecessors, the "modern" structural and systems schools.

In both the "modern" structural and the systems schools of organization theory, organizations are assumed to be institutions whose primary purpose is to accomplish established goals. Those goals are set by people in positions of formal authority. In these two schools, the primary questions for organization theory involve how best to design and manage organizations to achieve their declared purposes effectively and efficiently. The personal preferences of organizational members are restrained by systems of formal rules, authority, and by norms of rational behavior (see Chapters IV and V for more complete discussions).

The power school rejects these assumptions about organizations as being naive, unrealistic, and therefore of minimal practical value. Instead, organizations are viewed as complex systems of individuals and coalitions, each having its own interests, beliefs, values, preferences, perspectives, and perceptions. The coalitions continuously compete with each other for scarce organizational resources. Conflict is inevitable. Influence—and the power and political activities through which influence is acquired and maintained—is the primary "weapon" for use in competition and conflicts. Thus, power, politics, and influence are critically important and permanent facts of organizational life.

Only rarely are organizational goals established by those in positions of formal authority. Goals result from ongoing maneuvering and bargaining among individuals and coalitions. Coalitions tend to be transitory: They shift with issues and often cross vertical and horizontal organizational boundaries. (For example, they may include people at several levels in the organizational hierarchy and from different product, functional, and/or geographical divisions or departments.) Thus, organizational goals change with shifts in the balance of power among coalitions. J. V. Baldridge (1971) found that organizations had many conflicting goals, and different sets of goals take priority as the balance of power changes among coalitions—as different coalitions gain and use enough power to control them. Why are organizational goals so important in the theory of organizational power and politics? Because they provide the "official" rationale and the legitimacy for resource allocation decisions.

Power relations are permanent features of organizations primarily because specialization and the division of labor result in the creation of many small, interdependent organization units with varying degrees of importance. The units compete with each other for scarce resources—as well as with the transitory coalitions. As James D. Thompson points out in *Organizations in Action* (1967), a lack of balance in the interdependence among units sets the stage for the use of power relations. Jeffery Pfeffer emphasizes this point in his Preface to *Power in Organizations* (1981): "Those persons and those units that have the responsibility for performing the more critical tasks in the organization have a natural advantage in developing and exercising power in the organization. . . . Power is first and foremost a structural phenomenon, and should be understood as such."

The "modern" structural school of organization theory places high importance on "legitimate authority" (authority that flows down through the organizational hierarchy) and formal rules (promulgated and enforced by those in authority) to ensure that organizational behavior is directed toward the attainment of established organizational goals. Structuralists tend to define power as synonymous with authority. In contrast, John Kotter (1985) argues that in today's organizational world, there is an increasing gap between the power one needs to get the job done and the power that automatically comes with the job (authority). The power and politics school views authority as only one of the many available sources of organizational power, and power is aimed in *all* directions—not just down through the hierarchy. For example, Robert W. Allen and Lyman W. Porter divide their 1983 book of readings on *Organizational Influence Processes* into three parts: downward influence (authority), lateral influence, and upward influence.

Other forms of power and influence often prevail over authority-based power. Several of this chapter's selections identify different sources of power in organizations, so we list only a few here as examples: control over scarce resources (for example, office space, discretionary funds, current and accurate information, and time and skill to work on projects), easy access to others who are perceived as having power (for example, important customers or clients, members of the board of directors, or someone else with formal authority or who controls scarce resources), a central place in a potent coalition, ability to ''work the organizational rules'' (knowing how to get things done or to prevent others from getting things done), and credibility (for example, that one's word can be trusted).

By now you should be wondering just what power, politics, and influence are. Many definitions have been proposed, and Jeffrey Pfeffer explores the advantages and limitations of some of the better ones in his chapter on ''Understanding the Role of Power in Decision Making'' from his 1981 book *Power in Organizations,* which is reprinted here. We like the following definition of power, which is a blending of definitions proposed by Gerald Salancik and Jeffrey Pfeffer (1977), and Robert Allen and Lyman Porter (1983): ''Power is the ability to get things done the way one wants them done; it is the latent ability to influence people.'' This definition offers several advantages for understanding organizations. First, it emphasizes the relativity of power. As Pfeffer points out, ''power is context or relationship specific. A person is not 'powerful' or 'powerless' in general, but only with respect to other social actors in a specific social relationship.''

Second, the phrase ''the way one wants them done'' is a potent reminder that conflict and the use of power often are over the choice of methods, means, approaches, and/or ''turf.'' They are not limited to battles about outcomes. This point is important because power is primarily a structural phenomenon—a consequence of the division of labor and specialization. For example, competing organizational coalitions often form around professions: hospital nurses versus paramedics, sociologists versus mathematicians in a college of liberal arts, business school–educated staff specialists versus generalists from the ''school of hard knocks'' in a production unit, or social workers versus educators in a center for incarcerated youth. Organizational conflicts among people representing different professions, educational backgrounds, sexes, and ages frequently do not involve goals. They center on questions about the ''right'' of a profession, academic discipline, or sex or age group to exercise its perception of its ''professional rights,'' to control the way things will be done, or to protect its ''turf'' and status. Why is this point important? Because it reemphasizes that organizational behavior and decisions frequently are not ''rational''—as the word is used by the ''modern'' structural school and the systems school, meaning ''directed toward the accomplishment of established organizational goals.'' Thus, this definition of power highlights a fundamental reason why the power and politics school rejects the basic assumptions of the ''modern'' structural school and the systems school as being naive and unrealistic, and considers those theories of organization to be of minimal value.

Jeffrey Pfeffer's chapter ''Understanding the Role of Power in Decision Making,'' provides an excellent synopsis of the power and politics perspective on organizations. We have placed it first among this chapter's selections in order to provide the reader with a macroperspective on the school. His basic theme is that power and politics are fundamental concepts for understanding behavior in organizations. He defines the concepts of power, authority, and organizational politics, and he identifies the ''place of power'' in the literature of organization theory.

David Mechanic's influential and pioneering 1962 *Administrative Science Quarterly* article ''Sources of Power of Lower Participants in Complex Organizations,'' which is reprinted here, examines sources of influence and power that can be aimed at targets who possess more formal authority than the potential "influencer" possesses. As John Kotter (1977) points out, power is related to dependence, and lower-level organizational members have an arsenal of weapons with which to make others dependent upon them. They include expertise, effort and interest, attractiveness (or charisma), location and position in the organization, coalitions, and rules. This is an intellectualization of something we all know instinctively—that some people are treated like prima donnas or "get away with murder" in organizations because they possess some special skill that gives them power in the context of their organization. The most ready examples are "Hawkeye" and "Trapper" from the *MASH* movie and television series. If they were not badly needed surgeons at the battlefront, they would have been court-martialled years before.

"Leadership in an Organized Anarchy" (reprinted here) is the concluding chapter from Michael Cohen and James March's 1974 general report prepared for The Carnegie Commission on Higher Education. It was published in book form as *Leadership and Ambiguity: The American College President.* The overall study was conducted in response to the almost continual crises, demonstrations, and fiscal deterioration of many colleges and universities in the United States in the late 1960s and early 1970s. During these turbulent years, university presidents lost much of their power; the role of university president that historically had been a blend of mediation and authoritative functions became predominantly mediative.

Through an extensive series of interviews conducted on and around campuses, Cohen and March found that universities have "uncertain goals, a familiar but unclear technology, and inadequate knowledge about who is attending to what." Thus, they introduced the phrase *organized anarchies* to communicate why American universities are distinctive organizational forms with unique leadership needs and problems: Most notably, the major characteristic of a presidency is ambiguity. Further, "presidents discover that they have less power than is believed, that their power to accomplish things depends heavily on what they want to accomplish, that the acceptance of authority is not automatic, that the necessary details of organizational life confuse power . . . , and that their colleagues seem to delight in complaining simultaneously about presidential weakness and presidential willfulness." *Ambiguity of power* is one of four important ambiguities of anarchy facing university presidents: The others are ambiguity of *purpose, experience,* and *success.* Cohen and March propose "elementary tactics of administrative action"—effective tactics for leading in an organized anarchy—that reflect the assumptions and strategies of power and politics organization theory. They also stress the importance of *sensible foolishness:* "The contribution of a college president may often be measured by his capability for sustaining that creative interaction of foolishness and rationality."

In her 1979 *Harvard Business Review* article "Power Failure in Management Circuits," which is reprinted here, Rosabeth Moss Kanter argues that executive and managerial power is a necessary ingredient for moving organizations toward their goals. "Power can mean efficacy and capacity" for organizations. The ability of managers to lead effectively cannot be predicted by studying their styles or traits; it requires knowledge of a leader's real power sources. Kanter identifies three groups of positions within organizations that are particularly susceptible to powerlessness: first-line supervisors, staff professionals, and top executives. However, she carefully distinguishes between "power" and "dominance, control, and oppression." Her primary concern is that at higher organizational levels, the power to "punish, to prevent, to sell off, to reduce, to fire, all without appropriate concern for consequences" grows, but the power needed for positive accomplishments does not. Managers who perceive themselves as being powerless and who think their subordinates are discounting them tend to use more dominating or punishing forms of influence. Thus, in large organizations, powerlessness (or perceived powerlessness) can be a more substantive problem than possession of power. By empowering others, leaders actually can acquire more "productive power"—the power needed to accomplish organizational goals. "Power Failure in Management Circuits" also contains an embedded subarticle on the particular problems that power poses for women managers.

"Organization Development: A Political Perspective" by Anthony T. Cobb and Newton Margulies (reprinted here), links the power perspective to the field of organizational behavior, or as it is also known, the human relations perspective of organization theory (Ott, 1989, Chapter VI).

> Organization development is a long-range effort to improve an organization's problem-solving and renewal processes, particularly through a more effective and collaborative management of organizational culture . . . with the assistance of a change agent, or catalyst, and the use of the theory and technology of applied behavioral science, including action research (French & Bell, 1984).

Typically, "the product or result of organization development (OD) activities is an ongoing set of processes for organizational renewal that are *in-and-of-themselves defined as criteria of organizational effectiveness*" (Ott, 1989, p. 513).

OD has often been characterized and criticized for lacking political sophistication and for not being sensitive to issues of power. In this article, Cobb and Margulies offer a refutation: OD has developed an unrecognized political orientation that aids OD change-agent consultants in the arena of organizational politics and supports their interventions in social *and* political subsystems. ("The political subsystem is composed of the sources, locations, and flow of power through the organization.") Those who advocate increased involvement by OD consultants in organizational politics "assume that not only are politics a fact of organizational life, but that some powerful and sophisticated members of the client system use politics to protect and extend their own selfish interests." Political activism is the best way to deal with them.

However, Cobb and Margulies warn of potentially serious utilitarian and values problems that may result from increased political activity by OD practitioners. "The political moderate position recognizes [the potential problems]. It seeks to work within the political subsystem to help establish the climate necessary to support such traditional change elements as honesty, openness, collaboration, and participation. There is no doubt that these elements are value laden," and they are not the values of the power/politics frame.

Henry Mintzberg describes his 1983 book *Power in and Around Organizations* as a discussion of a theory of organizational power. Organizational behavior is viewed as a power game. The "players" are "influencers" with varying personal needs, who attempt to control organizational decisions and actions. "Thus, to understand the behavior of the organization, it is necessary to understand which influencers are present, what needs each seeks to fulfill in the organization, and how each is able to exercise power to fulfill them." His chapter "The Power Game and the Players," which is reprinted here, focuses on the "influencers"—who they are and where their power comes from. Eleven groups of possible influencers are listed: five are in the "external coalition" and six in the "internal coalition." The external coalition consists of the owners, "associates" (suppliers, clients, trading partners, and competitors), employee associations (unions and professional associations), the organization's various publics (at large), and the corporate directors (which includes representatives from the other four groups in the external coalition and also some internal influencers). The internal coalition is comprised of six groups of influencers: the chief executive officer, operators (the organization's "producers"), line managers, analysts (staff specialists), and the support staff. The final "actor" in Mintzberg's internal coalition is the ideology of the organization—"the set of beliefs shared by its internal influencers that distinguishes it from other organizations." Factors like organizational ideology actually are more representative of our final school of organization theory, the organizational culture school, which is discussed in the next chapter.

References

ALLEN, R. W., & PORTER, L. W. (1983). *Organizational influence processes.* Glenview IL: Scott, Foresman.

BALDRIDGE, J. V. (1971). *Power and conflict in the university.* New York: Wiley.

COHEN, A. R., & BRADFORD, D. L. (1990). *Influence without authority.* New York: Wiley.

CUMMINGS, L. L., & STAW, B. M. (Eds.). (1981). *Research in organizational behavior* (Vol. 3). Greenwich, CT: JAI Press.

COBB, A. T., & MARGULIES, N. (1981). Organization development: A political perspective. *Academy of Management Review, 6*(1), 49–59.

COHEN, M. D., & MARCH, J. G. (1974). *Leadership and ambiguity: The American college president.* New York: McGraw-Hill.

CYERT, R. M., & MARCH, J. G. (1963). *A behavioral theory of the firm.* Englewood Cliffs, NJ: Prentice-Hall.

FRENCH, W. L., & BELL, C. H., Jr. (1984). *Organization development* (3d ed.). Englewood Cliffs, NJ: Prentice-Hall.

JAY, A. (1967). *Management and Machiavelli.* New York: Holt, Rinehart & Winston.

KANTER, R. M. (1977). *Men and women of the corporation.* New York: Basic Books.

KANTER, R. M. (July-August 1979). Power failure in management circuits. *Harvard Business Review, 57,* 65–75.

KAUFMAN, H. (March 1964). Organization theory and political theory. *American Political Science Review, 58,* 5–14.

KORDA, M. (1975). *Power! How to get it, how to use it.* New York: Random House.

KOTTER, J. P. (July-August 1977). Power, dependence, and effective management. *Harvard Business Review, 55,* 125–136.

KOTTER, J. P. (1985). *Power and influence: Beyond formal authority.* New York: Free Press.

MECHANIC, D. (December 1962). Sources of power of lower participants in complex organizations. *Administrative Science Quarterly, 7, 3,* 349–364.

MINTZBERG, H. (1983). *Power in and around organizations.* Englewood Cliffs, NJ: Prentice-Hall.

OTT, J. S. (Ed.), (1989). *Classic readings in organizational behavior.* Pacific Grove, CA: Brooks/Cole.

PFEFFER, J. (1981). *Power in organizations.* Boston: Pitman.

PORTER, L. W., ALLEN, R. W., & ANGLE, H. L. (1981). The politics of upward influence in organizations. In L. L. Cummings & B. M. Staw (Eds.), *Research in Organizational Behavior,* Vol. 3 (pp. 408–422). Greenwich, CT: JAI Press.

SALANCIK, G. R., & PFEFFER, J. (1977). Who gets power—and how they hold on to it: A strategic-contingency model of power. *Organizational Dynamics, 5,* 2–21.

SIU, R. G. H. (1979). *The craft of power.* New York: Wiley.

THOMPSON, J. D. (1967). *Organizations in action.* New York: McGraw-Hill.

TUSHMAN, M. L. (April 1977). A political approach to organizations: A review and rationale. *The Academy of Management Review, 2,* 206–216.

YATES, D., Jr. (1985). *The politics of management.* San Francisco: Jossey-Bass.

ZALEZNIK, A., & KETS DE VRIES, M. F. R. (1985). *Power and the corporate mind.* Chicago: Bonus Books.

37

Understanding the Role of Power in Decision Making

Jeffrey Pfeffer

More than 40 years ago Harold Lasswell (1936) defined politics as the study of who gets what, when, and how. Certainly, who gets what, when, and how, are issues of fundamental importance in understanding formal organizations. Nevertheless, organizational politics and organizational power are both topics which are made conspicuous by their absence in management and organization theory literature (Allen, et al., 1979). Why?

It is certainly not because the terms *power* and *politics* are concepts used infrequently in everyday conversation. Both are often used to explain events in the world around us. Richard Nixon's behavior while in the presidency has been ascribed to a need for power. Budget allocations among various federal programs are described as being the result of politics. Success in obtaining a promotion may be attributed to an individual's ability to play office politics. The fact that certain business functions (such as finance) or occupational specialties (such as law) are frequently important in organizations is taken to reflect the power of those functions or occupations. There are few events that are not ascribed to the effects of power and politics. As Dahl (1957: 201) noted, "The concept of power is as ancient and ubiquitous as any that social theory can boast." . . .

SOURCE: Jeffrey Pfeffer, *Power in Organizations* (Marshfield, Mass.: Pitman Publishing, 1981), 1–32.

Power has been neglected for several reasons. First, the concept of power is itself problematic in much of the social science literature. In the second place, while power is something it is not everything. There are other competing perspectives for understanding organizational decision making. These perspectives are frequently persuasive, if for no other reason than that they conform more closely to socially held values of rationality and effectiveness. And third, the concept of power is troublesome to the socialization of managers and the practice of management because of its implications and connotations.

Therefore, we begin at the beginning, with a discussion of these issues as they affect the study and analysis of power and politics in organizations. It is important to understand what power is and what it isn't; what alternative perspectives exist on organizational choice processes; and the place of power in the organization theory literature. With that as background, it will be possible then to proceed to the analysis of organizations using a political perspective.

The Concept of Power

The very pervasiveness of the concept of power, referred to in the earlier quote from Robert Dahl, is itself a cause for concern about the utility of the concept in assisting us to understand behavior in organizations. Bierstedt (1950: 730) noted that the more things a term could be applied to the less precise was its meaning. Dahl (1957: 201) wrote, ". . . a Thing to which people attach many labels with subtly or grossly different meanings in many different cultures and times is probably not a Thing at all but many Things." March (1966) has suggested that in being used to explain almost everything, the concept of power can become almost a tautology, used to explain that which cannot be explained by other ideas, and incapable of being disproved as an explanation for actions and outcomes.

Most definitions of power include an element indicating that power is the capability of one social actor to overcome resistance in achieving a desired objective or result. For instance, Dahl (1957: 202–203) defined power as a relation among social actors in which one social actor, A, can get another social actor B, to do something that B would not otherwise have done. Power becomes defined as force, and more specifically, force sufficient to change the probability of B's behavior from what it would have been in the absence of the application of the force. Emerson's (1962: 32) definition is quite similar: "The power of actor A over actor B is the amount of resistance on the part of B which can be potentially overcome by A." Bierstedt (1950: 738) also wrote of power as having incidence only in cases of social opposition. Power may be tricky to define, but it is not that difficult to recognize: "the ability of those who possess power to bring about the outcomes they desire" (Salancik and Pfeffer, 1977b: 3).

It is generally agreed that power characterized relationships among social actors. A given social actor, by which we mean an individual, subunit, or organization, has more power with respect to some social actors and less power with respect to others. Thus, power is context or relationship specific. A person is not "powerful" or "powerless" in general, but only with respect to other social actors in a specific social relationship. To say, for example, that the legal department in a specific firm is powerful, implies power with respect to other departments within that firm during a specific period of time. That same legal department may not be at all powerful with respect to its interactions with the firm's outside counsel, various federal and state regulatory agencies, and so forth. And, the power of the department can and probably will change over time.

Although power is relationship or context specific, it is not necessarily specifically related to a limited set of decision issues. Whether or not power is generalizable across decision issues

is an empirical question, not a matter of definition. Indeed, one of the interesting aspects in the study of power in organizations is the determination of under what circumstances power is general across decisions, and in what cases the power of a particular social actor is more issue-specific.

Most studies of power in organizations have focused on hierarchical power, the power of supervisors, or bosses over employees. The vertical, hierarchical dimension of power is important in understanding social life, but it is not the only dimension of power. As Perrow (1970: 59) wrote, "It is my impression that for all the discussion and research regarding power in organizations, the preoccupation with interpersonal power has led us to neglect one of the most obvious aspects of this subject: in complex organizations, tasks are divided up between a few major departments or subunits, and all of these subunits are likely to be equally powerful." Implicit in this statement is the recognition that power is, first of all, a structural phenomenon, created by the division of labor and departmentation that characterize the specific organization or set of organizations being investigated. It is this more structural approach to power that constitutes the focus of this book, although at times we will consider what individual characteristics affect the exercise of structurally determined power.

It should be evident why power is somewhat tricky to measure and operationalize. In order to assess power, one must be able to estimate (a) what would have happened in the absence of the exercise of power; (b) the intentions of the actor attempting to exercise power; and (c) the effect of actions taken by that actor on the probability that what was desired would in fact be likely to occur. Because the ability to diagnose power distributions is critical to understanding and acting effectively in organizations, we will consider the diagnosis of power in some detail in the next chapter. For now, it should be recognized that the definition and assessment of power are both controversial and problematic.

The Concept of Authority

It is important to distinguish between power and authority. In any social setting, there are certain beliefs and practices that come to be accepted within that setting. The acceptance of these practices and values, which can include the distribution of influence within the social setting, binds together those within the setting, through their common perspective. Activities which are accepted and expected within a context are then said to be legitimate within that context. The distribution of power within a social setting can also become legitimate over time, so that those within the setting expect and value a certain pattern of influence. When power is so legitimated, it is denoted as authority. Weber (1947) emphasized the critical role of legitimacy in the exercise of power. By transforming power into authority, the exercise of influence is transformed in a subtle but important way. In social situations, the exercise of power typically has costs. Enforcing one's way over others requires the expenditure of resources, the making of commitments, and a level of effort which can be undertaken only when the issues at hand are relatively important. On the other hand, the exercise of authority, power which has become legitimated, is expected and desired in the social context. Thus, the exercise of authority, far from diminishing through use, may actually serve to enhance the amount of authority subsequently possessed.

Dornbusch and Scott (1975), in their book on evaluation in organizations, made a similar point with respect to the evaluation process. They noted that in formal organizations, some people have the right to set criteria, to sample output, and to apply the criteria to the output that is sampled. Persons with such authority or evaluation rights are expected to engage in these authorized activities, and, instead of being punished for doing so, are punished when they fail to do so.

The transformation of power into authority is an important process, for it speaks to the issue of the institutionalization of social control. As such, we will return to this issue when political strategies are considered and when we take up the topic of institutionalized power. For the moment, it is sufficient to note that within formal organizations, norms and expectations develop that make the exercise of influence expected and accepted. Thus, social control of one's behavior by others becomes an expected part of organizational life. Rather than seeing the exercise of influence within organizations as a contest of strength or force, power, once it is transformed through legitimation into authority, is not resisted. At that point, it no longer depends on the resources or determinants that may have produced the power in the first place.

The transformation of power into authority can be seen most clearly in the relationship between supervisors and subordinates in work organizations. As Mechanic (1962) noted, lower level organizational members have, in reality, a great amount of power. If they refused to accept and accede to the instructions provided by higher level managers, those managers would have difficulty carrying out sanctions and operating the organization. Furthermore, the lower level participants have power that comes from specialized knowledge about the work process and access to information that higher level managers may not have. Thus, Mechanic (1962) argued, what is interesting is not that subordinates accept the instructions of managers because of the greater power possessed by the managers. Rather, it is interesting that in spite of the considerable degree of power possessed by lower level employees, these employees seldom attempt to exercise their power or to resist the instructions of their managers.

The point that is being made is important. Although it is true that the manager may have the power to fire employees, to control the amount of money they get paid, and to affect their promotion opportunities in the future, in most organizations such powers are severely limited and, in any event, are seldom exercised. Employees do not consciously compare their power (to withhold labor services, to quit, to withhold information, to do the work poorly) with the power that the manager has (to use and withhold rewards and sanctions), and then decide whether or not to comply depending on the relative power balance. Rather, most of the time in most work settings the authority of the manager to direct the work activities is so legitimated and taken for granted, that issues of relative power and sanctions seldom become consciously considered. Subordinates obey not because the supervisor has the power to compel them to, rather, they follow reasonable instructions related to the control of their work behavior because they expect that such directions will be given and followed. In this way, power becomes transformed into authority, and control can be exercised almost regardless of the balance of power possessed by the interacting groups.

When social understanding and social consensus develops to accept, ratify, and even prefer the distribution of power, then the power becomes legitimated and becomes authority. Authority is maintained not only by the resources or sanctions that produced the power, but also by the social pressures and social norms that sanction the power distribution and which define it as normal and acceptable. Such social acceptance and social approval adds stability to the situation and makes the exercise of power easier and more effective. Legitimation, of course, occurs in a specific social context, and what is legitimate in one setting may be illegitimate in another. The degree and kind of supervisor-subordinate control exercised in U.S. organizations, for instance, may be perceived as illegitimate in the organizations of countries where there is more worker self-management and industrial democracy. Legitimation of power is thus ultimately problematic and far from inevitable. The examination of the conditions under which power and social control become legitimated and transformed into authority is an important undertaking in trying to understand the governance and control of organizations.

Definition of Organizational Politics

The task of defining the term organizational politics is as difficult as that of defining power.

The problem is to distinguish between political activity and organizational or administrative activity in general. As in the case of power, if politics refers to all forms of administrative or managerial action, then the term becomes meaningless because it includes every behavior.

From Lasswell's (1936) definition of politics as who gets what, when, and how, and from Wildavsky's (1979) descriptions of the politics of the budgetary process, the inference is that politics involves how differing preferences are resolved in conflicts over the allocation of scarce resources. Thus, politics involves activities which attempt to influence decisions over critical issues that are not readily resolved through the introduction of new data and in which there are differing points of view. For our purposes, organizational politics will be defined as:

> Organizational politics involves those activities taken within organizations to acquire, develop, and use power and other resources to obtain one's preferred outcomes in a situation in which there is uncertainty or dissensus about choices.

If power is a force, a store of potential influence through which events can be affected, politics involves those activities or behaviors through which power is developed and used in organizational settings. Power is a property of the system at rest; politics is the study of power in action. An individual, subunit, or department may have power within an organizational context at some period of time; politics involves the exercise of power to get something accomplished, as well as those activities which are undertaken to expand the power already possessed or the scope over which it can be exercised. This definition is similar to that provided by Allen, et al. (1979: 77): "Organizational politics involve intentional acts of influence to enhance or protect the self-interest of individuals or groups."

From the definition of power, it is clear that political activity is activity which is undertaken to overcome some resistance or opposition. Without opposition or contest within the organization, there is neither the need nor the expectation that one would observe political activity. And, because political activity is focused around the acquisition and use of power, it can be distinguished from activity involved in making decisions which uses rational or bureaucratic procedures. In both rational and bureaucratic models of choice, there is no place for and no presumed effect of political activity. Decisions are made to best achieve the organization's goals, either by relying on the best information and options that have been uncovered, or by using rules and procedures which have evolved in the organization. Political activity, by contrast, implies the conscious effort to muster and use force to overcome opposition in a choice situation. . . .

It is clearly important to be able to distinguish between political activity and administrative action in general, and to distinguish between outcomes produced by social power and outcomes that occur by chance, because of precedent, or because of the application of rational decision procedures. At the same time, analysis should not be unnecessarily diverted by the interminable definitional and theoretical controversies that fill the literature surrounding these concepts. In a study of eighty-seven managerial personnel, Allen, et al. (1979: 77–78) reported:

> Respondents were asked to describe organizational political tactics and personal characteristics of effective political actors. . . . No definition of organizational politics was given to the respondents, nor did any of them ask what was meant by the term.

Similarly, in an interview study of twenty-nine department heads at the University of Illinois, during which each respondent was asked to rate the power of his and the other departments on the campus, only one department head found it necessary to ask for clarification of what was meant by the term *power*. It seems fair to state that *power* and *politics* are terms that have some shared meanings in the world of organizational actors. We shall see when we consider the assessment of power in organizations that such shared meanings guide and are anchored in consensually shared judgments concerning the distribution of power in organizational settings.

The Place of Power in Organization Theory Literature

If *power* and *politics* are terms which are used frequently in everyday conversation, understood at least at an intuitive level by practicing managers and administrators, and, as we shall demonstrate later, can help account for careers, budgets, structure, the relative size of personnel components, and their persistence over time, why then is power neglected in the literature of organization theory? One reason has already been suggested—the issues associated with the definition and measurement of these concepts. A second issue, that of competing perspectives for analyzing organizational choice processes, will be considered later in the chapter. For the moment, consider the place of power in the literature of organization theory and the role served by such literature.

Examination of the major textbooks now current in the field will indicate that the subject of power is either not mentioned at all in the subject index or, if it is, it receives short shrift in terms of the number of pages devoted to it. When the subject of power is found in the index, it is frequently associated with a discussion of the individual bases of power (e.g., French and Raven, 1968) or the need for power. Size, technology, and environment all receive much more time and attention, even in those books with a presumably more sociological perspective. And, in specialized books dealing with topics such as organization design or organization development, power typically receives no mention at all, even though it is a particularly critical variable for some of these more specialized concerns.

It is, of course, possible that this book and its treatment of organizations seriously overstates the importance of power and politics as phenomena of concern and explanations for behavior in organizations. This argument how-ever, not only flies in the face of a small but growing body of empirical research, but also the popular explanations for organizational phenomena which are found in sources such as *Fortune, Business Week,* or the *Wall Street Journal.* If power is unimportant, it is not only this author that has been fooled; I have plenty of company in the business press.

A more likely explanation for the neglect of power in the management and organizational behavior literature is found by considering the role of management writing in the management process, and the position of a topic such as power as implied by the various functions served by management writing. The argument to be developed is relatively straightforward: manage-ment writing serves a variety of functions; in virtually all of these functions there is a strong component of ideology and values; topics such as power and politics are basically incompatible with the values and ideology being developed; therefore, it is reasonable, if not theoretically useful, to ignore topics which detract from the functions being served by the writing, and this includes tending to ignore or to downplay the topics of power and politics.

To ask what functions are served by manage-ment writing, we can begin by asking who reads management books. The answer is that there are three important categories of persons who read management books, though the books they read are not necessarily the same: students in under-graduate and graduate programs in management and administration who read the books to acquire knowledge about the profession and practice of management; practicing managers and administrators in public and private sector organizations; and the general public, including those not involved with or in private business organizations. Consider next, what books or writings are needed in each case.

In the case of students, there is little doubt that one of the important functions of busi-ness education is socialization. This statement reflects both the more general importance of socialization in the educational process, and the specific prominence of socialization with respect to certain occupations and professions. It is not in just the fields of medicine and law that socialization plays an important part of the educational process. Although less frequently empirically examined, there are important con-siderations of socialization in the education of young, aspiring managers (e.g. Schein, 1968). Socialization involves the inculcation of norms and values that are central to the profession and that are, not incidentally, useful to the organiza-tions in which the professionals are going to work. There is no norm so central to the existing practice and ideology of management as the norm of rationality. . . . Rationality and rational choice models focus attention on the development of technologies to more effectively achieve a goal or set of goals, such as profit or efficiency. Concern is directed toward the development of alternatives, the development of sophisticated techniques for evaluating the alternatives, their possible consequences, and the assembling of information that facilitates the evaluation of performance along these specified dimensions. What is less salient and less cen-tral in this process of rational choice is the origin of these objectives or criteria and who benefits and who loses by having decisions made to optimize these particular decision criteria as opposed to others.

It is, we are suggesting, not by accident that in choosing among alternatives given certain specified preferences (March, 1978) the role of preferences has been neglected in theories of choice, relative to the role of technologies. It is around preferences, and the values and beliefs implicit in these preferences, that conflicts of interest emerge. And such conflicts may cause a diversion of effort from goal attainment which is not favored by those whose goals are being served well by the present arrangement. The point is that, by even raising the issue of prefer-ences or criteria as problematic, the institu-tionalized nature of goals such as profits or efficiency is challenged and is threatened by the mere fact of the challenge. It is in this sense that all normative theories of organization, whether within the domains of economics, organizational design, organizational development, or whatever, are inevitably political; it is also the case that most or perhaps all of the descriptive theories are equally political. These theories are political in the sense that each takes for granted certain assumptions abut the world and how it operates, thereby causing the indoctrination of these assumptions. The result is the unconscious, or at best semiconscious, acceptance of the implicit values by a widely varying set of participants. Some actors may benefit from the application of these values and some may lose. The same point has been nicely developed by Walter Nord (1974) in his critique of modern human resource management theory. It is equally and inevitably applicable to all organization theory.

In the socialization of professional managers, there are some components which are distinctly different from the socialization of other professionals. First, in contrast to doctors, lawyers, and to a lesser extent accountants, the professional manager will not practice in a relatively small organization with the legal structure of a partnership. Rather, he or she will work in a much larger organization which is legally structured as a corporation. The manager, then, can be expected to operate in a setting substantially more bureaucratized and in which there is a lesser likelihood of attaining such a great amount of ownership or control. Thus, the socialization must focus not so strongly on developing values that will serve the professional in solo or small group practice, but rather that will facilitate the manager's integration into large, formalized bureaucracies. Clearly, the acceptance of legitimate authority as implemented through a hierarchical structure is more important in the socialization of managers. Such authority will be more readily accepted to the extent that it *is perceived* to be legitimate. Given the social values stressing universalism and rationality, any organizational authority system and decision-making apparatus that operates according to these values will appear to be more legitimate and will encourage compliance on the part of the managers.

To socialize students into a view of business that emphasizes power and politics would not only make the compliance to organizational authority and the acceptance of decision outcomes and procedures problematic, but also it might cause recruitment problems into the profession. It is certainly much more noble to think of oneself as developing skills toward the more efficient allocation and use of resources—implicitly for the greater good of society as a whole—than to think of oneself as engaged with other organizational participants in a political struggle over values, preferences, and definitions of technology. Technical rationality, as a component of the managerial task, provides legitimation and meaning for one's career, fulfilling a function similar to healing the sick for doctors, or serving the nation's system of laws and justice for attorneys.

For the second group of practicing managers, as well as for the student, the ideology of rationality and efficiency provides an explanation for career progress, or lack thereof, that is much more likely to lead to the acceptance of one's position rather than an attempt at making a radical change. The theoretical foundations of economics, including human capital and labor market theories, emphasize the universalistic nature of the wage determination process. It is scarcely an exaggeration to note that the inclusion of socioeconomic background in multiple regressions explaining wages or change in wages is what distinguishes a sociological from an economic approach to the issues of stratification and inequality. The theory that efficiency considerations, bureaucratic rationality, or both, drive out power and politics, reassures those in or entering into the corporate world, that their success in rising through the ranks will be more a function of their marginal product than of their ability to diagnose power distributions and play politics. Inequality in outcomes becomes justified by the presumed decision-making processes which produce such outcomes; this process is deemed legitimate and accepted because of its association with valued social ideals. This acceptance of one's place and rewards in the organization clearly can discourage the unionization of the workforce, and can help to provide continuing motivation and purposefulness to work when career blockages or other career problems occur.

In this way, the ideology of efficiency and rationality provides comforting explanations for practicing managers who find the progress of their careers blocked or less than what they might like, or feel a general sense of malaise about their work and their future. The invisible hands of marginal productivity and human capital have put them where they deserve to be. If power is to be considered at all, it is in terms of individually-oriented political strategies (e.g. Korda, 1975), which provide the managers with the illusion that, with a few handy hints, they can improve their lot in the organization. Explanations which focus on structural variables, as most of the explanations for power and politics developed here do, are less popular, as they provide no easy palliatives and imply a need for much more fundamental change in terms of affecting decision outcomes.

For the third set of readers of the management literature, the general public, the emphasis on rationality and efficiency and the deemphasis on power and politics, assures them that the vast power and wealth controlled by organizations is, indeed, being effectively and legitimately employed. In this sense, organization theory and economic theory frequently find themselves fulfilling similar roles in explaining the status quo in terms which both justify and legitimate it. The theory of perfect competition or markets argues that when market processes are allowed to operate unimpeded by the intervention of politicians or monopolists, the best allocation results are obtained. Even those writers who have noted the existence of transaction costs and resulting problems (e.g. Williamson, 1975) have argued from a premise assuming efficiency interests on the part of the various economic actors involved.

In a similar fashion, the literature of organizational behavior has been dominated by a parallel form of functionalism. The strategic contingencies theories of organizational design (Lawrence and Lorsch, 1967; Galbraith, 1973; Woodward, 1965; Pennings, 1975) argued

that there existed some optimal organizational design, given the organization's technology, size or environmental uncertainty. The assumption was implicit in much of this work that if such contingencies could be uncovered, the implementation of the rational structures would be straightforward. The search for empirical regularities between context and structure presumes some functional imperative for organizations, as a collectivity, to be roughly in correspondence with the requirements of their technologies or environments. Discussion of the size of the administrative component (Pondy, 1969; Blau and Schoenherr, 1971), the degree of centralization and formalization present in organizations (Burns and Stalker, 1961; Thompson, 1967), and the degree of differentiation (Lawrence and Lorsch, 1967; Thompson, 1967), all proceeded from a premise of functional rationality, though only Thompson took pains to make this assumption explicit.

The ideology of functional rationality—decision making oriented toward the improvement of efficiency or performance—provides a legitimation of formal organizations, for the general public as well as for those working within specific organizations. Bureaucracies are, as Perrow (1972) argued, tremendous stores of resources and energy, both human and financial. Bureaucracies also represent concentrations of energy on a scale seldom seen in the history of the world. The legitimation and justification of these concentrations of power are clearly facilitated by theories arguing that efficiency, productivity, and effectiveness are the dominant dynamics underlying the operation of organizations.

To maintain that organizations are less than totally interested in efficiency, effectiveness or market performance is to suggest that it is legitimate to raise questions concerning the appropriateness of the concentration of power and energy they represent and makes it possible to introduce political concerns into the issues of corporate governance. The introduction of these concerns makes the present control arrangements less certain and permanent and would be resisted by all of those who benefit from the status quo.

The argument, then, is that the very literature of management and organizational behavior (as well, we might add, of much of economics, though that is a topic worthy of separate development) is itself political (Edelman, 1964), and causes support to be generated and opposition to be reduced as various conceptions of organizations are created and maintained in part through their very repetition. In this literature, efficiency-enhancing or profit-increasing behavior are not being taken as hypotheses about motivation and causes for action, but rather as accepted facts. Then, a theory is developed which is both consistent with these assumptions and finds excuses for why so much variation in actual decisions and behaviors is missed. Another way of seeing the very strong ideological basis and bias in organization theory is to contrast explanations of organizations developed in the U.S. with those found in the writings of European organizational scholars (e.g., Karpik, 1978; Crozier, 1964). The European treatment of organizations and of knowledge about organizations takes a much more context-specific, historical view. Organizations are much more clearly related to the broader social issues of power and politics in the society and it is assumed that conception of organizations themselves are products of a social construction of reality which also constitutes an ingredient of politics played out on a macro-social level. . . .

A study of the sociology of organizational science, although an interesting endeavor, is well beyond the scope of this book. Nevertheless, some casual observations about the political and ideological role of organizational behavior literature are in order. Consider a sampling of books randomly selected from the card catalogue of a major U.S. business school library with the terms power or politics in the title. Most of the books are by authors who are either European, political scientists, or sociologists. Few, if any, are in or from U.S. business schools. One could, in general, make the statement that the assumptions and topics covered by organization research are explainable by the political and social context in which researchers are working. This observation has already been made about social psychologists by Cartwright who noted:

> It is true, of course, that the substantive content of the knowledge attained in any field of science is ultimately determined by the intrinsic nature of the phenomena under investigation, since empirical research is essentially a process of discovery with an internal logic of its own. But it is equally true that the knowledge attained is the product of a social system and, as such, is basically influenced by the properties of that system and by its cultural, social and political environment (1979: 82).

A study of the politics of knowledge in the organizational behavior area, which traces changes in research issues, conclusions, and expressed values and ideologies, and relates these to changes in funding patterns, consultancy, social values, and political trends in the society in general, and to cultural differences, would be productive in terms of developing data and explanations for the phenomena discussed in this section.

Models of organizations which emphasize power and politics have their own political problems. It is important for those analyzing organizations to be able to figure out the kind of analytical framework that can be most usefully employed to diagnose the particular organization of interest. Kaplan's (1964) parable of the hammer is relevant. Because one has a hammer, one tends to use it on everything and for every task. Similarly, there is a tendency to take a noncontingent approach to the analysis of organizations, and to see them all as rational, bureaucratic, or political. Just as it is difficult to play football with baseball equipment, it is difficult to diagnose or effectively operate in an organization unless its dominant paradigm or mode of operation is understood. Furthermore, in order to evaluate the validity of a political approach to organizational analysis, there must be some alternatives with which to compare the model. For both of these reasons—to place the political model in a broader context of competing perspectives on organizational decision making and to raise issues relevant to diagnosing the form of system one is dealing with—we will describe the major contending models of organizational decision making.

Rational Choice Models

The model of rational choice is prominent in the social choice literature. It is not only prescribed as being the best way to make choices in organizations, but frequently claims to be descriptive of actual choice processes as well. The rational model presumes that events are "purposive choices of consistent actors" (Allison, 1971: 11). It is important to recognize, therefore, that the rational model presumes and assumes that "behavior reflects purpose or intention" (Allison, 1971: 13). Behavior is not accidental, random, or rationalized after the fact; rather, purpose is presumed to pre-exist and behavior is guided by that purpose. With respect to understanding organizations or other social collectivities, the rational model further presumes that there is a unified purpose or set of preferences characterizing the entity taking the action. As Allison (1971: 28–29) has noted:

> What rationality adds to the concept of purpose is *consistency*: consistency among goals and objectives relative to a particular action; consistency in the application of principles in order to select the optimal alternative (emphasis in original).

The rational choice model presumes that there are goals and objectives that characterize organizations. As Friedland (1974) has noted, rationality cannot be defined apart from the existence of a set of goals. Thus, all rational choice models start with the assumption of a goal or consistent goal set. In the case of subjective expected utility maximization models (Edwards, 1954), the goals are called utilities for various outcomes, associated with the pleasure or pain producing properties of the outcomes.

In the language of economics and management science, the goals are called the objectives or objective function to be maximized. Occasionally, goals are called preferences, referring to the states of the world the social actor prefers. Rational choice models require that these goals be consistent (March, 1976: 70).

Given a consistent set of goals, the next element in theories of rational choice is a set of decision-making alternatives to be chosen. Alternatives are presumed to be differentiable one from the other, so that each is uniquely identified. Such alternatives are produced by a search process. Until Simon (1957) introduced the concept of satisficing, it was generally assumed that search was costless and that large numbers of alternatives would be considered. Simon's contribution was to introduce the concept of bounded rationality, which held that persons had both limited capacities to process information and limited resources to devote to search activities. Thus a search for alternatives would be conducted only until a satisfactory alternative was uncovered. The concept of satisfaction was defined in terms of the social actor's level of aspiration (March and Simon, 1958).

Be they many or few, once a set of alternatives are uncovered, the next step in the rational decision-making process involves the assessment of the likely outcomes or consequences of the various possible courses of action. If there is risk or uncertainty involved, then estimates of the probability of the occurrence of various consequences would be used in making statements about the values of the consequences of different choices. At this stage in the decision process, it is assumed that consequences can be fully and completely anticipated, albeit with some degree of uncertainty. In other words, everything that can possibly occur as a result of the decision is presumably specified, though which of the various possibilities will actually occur may be subject to chance.

Then, a rational choice involves selecting that course of action or that alternative which maximizes the social actor's likelihood of attaining the highest value for achievement of the preferences or goals in the objective function.

In rational choice, decisions are related systematically to objectives (March, 1976: 70); that decision is made which shows the most promise of enabling the social actor to maximize the attainment of objectives. "Rationality refers to consistent, value-maximizing choice within specified constraints" (Allison, 1971: 30).

It is clear that in analyzing choice processes in organizations or other social collectives, the assumption of consistency and unity in the goals, information and decision processes is problematic. However, one of the advantages of the rational model is that it permits prediction of behavior with complete certainty and specificity if one knows (or assumes one knows) the goals of the other organization. Allison (1971: 13), in reviewing foreign policy analysis, has argued that this advantage is one important reason that "most contemporary analysts . . . proceed *predominantly* . . . in terms of this framework when trying to explain international events." The rational choice model facilitates the prediction of what the other social actor will do, assuming various goals; turning the model around, various goals can be inferred (though scarcely unambiguously) from the behavior of the other actor. It is inevitably the case that "an imaginative analyst can construct an account of value-maximizing choice for any action or set of actions performed" (Allison, 1971: 35).

Thus, to preserve the diagnostic and analytic properties of the rational model, goal consistency, and congruity are assumed. In economic theory, the goal of the firm is assumed to be profit maximization. In the theory of finance, the goal is assumed to be the maximization of shareholder wealth. In theories of public bureaucracies the goals are presumed to be those that are part of the agency's mission and which enable it to fulfill its assigned role in society. As Stava (1976: 209) has noted in discussing choice in larger political bodies, "legal-bureaucratic theories mostly argue that resources are allocated . . . according to some universalistic rules applied in a neutral way and in accord with the prima facie needs of the society." For society, one could as easily substitute the word organization. Stava continued by noting that

decisions were presumed to be both formally neutral and rational. "They are neutral in the sense that the necessary value premises for the decisions are given or treated as given. . . . The decisions should also be (formally) rational. This means that they are intended to realize goals" (Stava, 1976: 209). . . .

Bureaucratic Models of Decision Making

The rational model of choice implies the need for some substantial information processing requirements in organizational decision making. These may be unrealistic or unattainable in some cases, and organizations may operate using standard operating procedures and rules rather than engaging in rational decision making on a continuous basis. The bureaucratic model of organizations substitutes procedural rationality for substantive rationality (Simon, 1979); rather than having choices made to maximize values, choices are made according to rules and processes which have been adaptive and effective in the past.

The best explication of what is meant by bureaucratically-rational decision processes can be found in March and Simon (1958) and Cyert and March (1963). In this framework, goals are viewed as systems of constraints (Simon, 1964) which decisions must satisfy. Because of bounded rationality, search is limited and stops as soon as a satisfactory alternative is found. Uncertainty tends to be avoided in that, rather than making comprehensive assessments of risk and probabilities, decisions are made with relatively short time horizons. Conflict among different alternatives or points of view is never fully resolved, and priorities and objectives are attended to sequentially, first, for instance, worrying about profit, then about market share, then personnel problems, and so forth. Throughout this process, organizations learn and adapt, and their learning and knowledge takes the form of rules of action or standard operating procedures, repertoires of behavior which are activated in certain situations and which provide a program, a set of behaviors for organizational participants, that serve as a guide to action and choice.

Seen from this perspective, decisions are viewed "less as deliberate choices and more as *outputs* of large organizations functioning according to standard patterns of behavior" (Allison, 1971: 67). It is presumed that "most of the behavior is determined by previously established procedures" (Allison, 1971: 79). The model of organizations as bureaucratically rational presumes less conscious foresight and less clearly defined preferences and information. Both rely on habitual ways of doing things and the results of past actions, and constrain how the organization proceeds to operate in the future. Decisions are not made as much as they evolve from the policies, procedures, and rules which constitute the organization and its memory.

Perhaps one of the best examples to consider in understanding the difference between the rational choice model and the bureaucratic model is to examine the effect of precedence on budgeting decisions. The literature on governmental budgeting, for instance (Wildavsky, 1979; Davis, Dempster, and Wildavsky, 1966; Wildavsky and Hammond, 1965), indicates that the best predictor of this year's budget is last year's budget. Analysis of governmental budgeting indicates that precedence, coupled with some very simple rules for handling increased requests, can account for most of the variation in resource allocations. That this process is not perceived as completely rational is evidenced by the fact that great time and attention has been spent on developing alternative resource allocation schemes, such as Planning-Programming-Budgeting Systems (PPBS) and zero-based budgeting. The advocates of these systems argue that what was allocated last year may have little to do with rational, value maximizing goal attainment, and it is necessary to more systematically relate decisions to preferences and new information.

Of course, most of these new decision making processes have had tremendous problems in their implementation. Precedence and other similar simple rules may not be optimal, but they are at least computationally easy and require less heroic assumptions about information processing capacities. Furthermore, one could argue that except in circumstances of sudden and dramatic change in the contingencies confronting the organization, incremental budgeting is sufficient to maintain effective operations through the process of making small adjustments to the organization's operations. Thus, bureaucratic rationality, it is argued, can perhaps effectively substitute for substantive rationality.

Distinguishing Bureaucratic Organizations

It is relatively simple to distinguish between organizations which operate under the bureaucratic model and those which operate under the rational model. Bureaucratic organizations will typically have much less extensive information search and analysis activities, and rely more heavily on rules, precedent, and standard operating procedures. Less time and resources will be spent on decision making, and fewer alternatives will be considered before actions are taken. Indeed, it is the difference in the amount of analysis, search, and focused attention on goal attainment, that constitutes the difference between the bureaucratic and rational models.

Distinguishing between the bureaucratic and political models of organization may be somewhat more difficult. After all, if the distribution of power is stable in the organization, which is a reasonable assumption, particularly over relatively short time periods, and if power and politics determine organizational decisions, then organizational choices will be relatively stable over time. But, this stability is also characteristic of the use of precedent in decision making, which is one of the hallmarks of bureaucratic organizations. One way of distinguishing, then, would involve looking at the correlates of the incremental changes in decisions and allocations made within the organization. While both models might be consistent with the use of precedent for the bulk of the decisions, there are some implicit differences in how incremental resources will be allocated. In bureaucratic organizations, changes in resource allocation patterns should either follow a proportional basis, be based on some standard measure of operations and performance, or reflect an attempt to shift the resources to better achieve the goals and values of the organization. By contrast, political models of organizations would suggest that power would best predict changes and shifts in decisions and allocations.

Research which attempts to explore the use of rules and standard operating procedures in organizations has typically involved the use of computer programs which simulate the operation of such rules (e.g., Cyert and March, 1963; Crecine, 1967; Gerwin, 1969). Unfortunately, the validation of such models is complex because there may be many ways in which an observed outcome can be produced. This means that just because the application of a set of decision rules produces results that mirror what occurs in an organization, it is not necessarily true that these rules are actually guiding the organization's decision making.

Decision Process Models

Although they exist within much the same tradition as the bureaucratic model of organizations, decision process models differ in that they presume even less rationality and more randomness in organizational functioning. As power models depart from bureaucratic rationality by removing the assumption of consistent, overall organizational objectives and shared beliefs about technology, decision process models depart even further by removing the presumption of predefined, known preferences held by the various social actors. Decision process models posit that there are no overall organizational goals being maximized through choice, and no powerful actors with defined preferences

who possess resources through which they seek to obtain those preferences. Stava (1976: 209) described decision process models as follows:

> In *decision process theories* it is presumed that policy is the outcome of a choice made by one or several decision-makers. Which choice is made is determined by the situation in which the decision-maker finds himself. This situation is, in turn, largely caused by the processes preceding the choice. It is impossible, then, to predict policies without knowing the details of the preceding processes.

March (1966: 180) argued that in such decision process models, although one might posit that the various actors have preferences and varying amounts of power, the concept of power does not add much to the prediction of behavior and choice in such systems.

More recently, March (1978) and others (e.g., Weick, 1969) have questioned whether or not the concept of preferences makes sense at any level of analysis, individual or organizational. One of the arguments raised is that instead of preferences guiding choice, choice may determine preferences. In other words, one only knows what one likes after it has been experienced; or, as Weick has argued, one only knows what one has done after he or she has done it, since the meaning of action is retrospective and follows the action rather than preceeds it. In this framework, goals are seen as the products of sense making activities which are carried on after the action has occured to explain that action or rationalize it. The action itself is presumed to be the result of habit, custom, or the influence of other social actors in the environment.

One example of a decision process model of social choice is the garbage can model (Cohen, March, and Olsen, 1972). The basic idea of the model is that decision points are opportunities into which various problems and solutions are dumped by organizational participants. "In a garbage can situation, a decision is an outcome of an interpretation of several relatively independent 'streams' within an organization" (Cohen, March, and Olsen, 1976: 26). The streams consist of problems, solutions (which are somebody's product), participants, and choice opportunities. The decision process models developed by March and his colleagues emphasize the problematic nature of participation by various social actors in choices. They note that systems are frequently so overloaded with problems, solutions, and decision opportunities that any given social actor will attend to only certain decisions.

Cohen, March, and Olsen (1972) developed a simulation of the garbage can decision process. One of the important conclusions emerging from that simulation is:

. . . that although the processes within the garbage can are understandable and in some ways predictable, events are not dominated by intention. The processes and the outcomes are likely to appear to have no close relation with the explicit intention of actors. In situations in which load is heavy and the structure is relatively unsegmented, intention is lost in a context-dependent flow of problems, solutions, people, and choice opportunities (Cohen, March, and Olsen, 1976: 37).

March (1966) had earlier begun to explore the role of chance in organizational choice situations, and the garbage can simulation represents the formal incorporation of chance and randomness in a theory of choice.

The garbage can model emerged largely from a study of universities and university presidents (Cohen and March, 1974). Universities were characterized as organized anarchies, and garbage can decision process models were believed to be particularly appropriate in such contexts, although the assertion is also made that elements of these models are found in most organizations. Weiner (1976) has summarized some of the main features and assumptions of the organized anarchy model of organizations. First, "the existing theory of organized anarchies does not require that decisions be reached or problems solved by a specified time . . . the theory holds that such requirements are neither generated within the organization nor imposed by the organization's environment" (Weiner,

1976: 226). The garbage can model then, presumes and assumes no deadlines. Decisions are worked on until they are made. The theory also suggests that "the stream of problems entering or leaving an organization" is a "flow that is independent of the other streams of choices, solutions and energy. . . . The theory holds further that problems move autonomously among choice opportunities in search for a choice process in which the problem can be resolved" (Weiner, 1976: 243). Decision making is viewed as an activity which absorbs the energy of those available, works on problems, and comes up with solutions which are determined in large measure by a random stream of events.

Distinguishing Organized Anarchies

The key concept used in diagnosing whether or not the organization is an organized anarchy which can best be understood by using decision process organizational models is that of intention. Not only are there presumed to be no overarching organizational goals, but presumably intention is problematic even at the level of subunits and groups within the organization. Action occurs, but it is not primarily motivated by conscious choice and planning. Although not made explicit, there should be relatively little consistency or consensus over behavior in an organized anarchy. Events should unfold in ways predictable only by considering the process, and not through consideration of value maximization, precedent, power, or force.

If that seems like a difficult requirement to fulfill, those who advocate the decision process model of organizations argue that much of the consistency and intentionality observed in organizations is imputed by those doing the observing rather than being a characteristic of the organization being observed. Much as in Allison's (1971) treatment of foreign policy analysis, goals are imputed to organizations themselves. Similarly, rules and power may also be imputed rather than actually be properties of the system under study.

Although decision process models provide a language for describing the randomness that is sometimes observed, they do not provide a great amount of predictive power. Their theme is that such prediction is largely impossible, except for the use of complex programs of decision routines. Their de-emphasis of intention makes them unpopular with those who view the world in a more proactive, strategic fashion.

Political Models of Organizations

One criticism that has been leveled against rational choice models is that they fail to take into account the diversity of interests and goals within organizations. March (1962) described business firms as political coalitions. The coalitional view of organizations was developed by Cyert and March (1963) in their description of organizational decision making. In bureaucratic theories of organizations, the presumption is that through control devices such as rewards based on job performance or seniority, rules that ensure fair and standardized treatment for all, and careers within the organization, the operation of self-interest can be virtually eliminated as an influence on organizational decision making. Economic or incentive theories of organizations argue that through the payment of wage, particularly when compensation is made contingent on performance, individuals hired into the organization come to accept the organization's goals. Political models of organizations assume that these control devices, as well as others such as socialization, are not wholly effective in producing a coherent and unified set of goals or definitions of technology. Rather, as Baldridge (1971: 25) has argued, political models view organizations as pluralistic and divided into various interests, subunits, and subcultures. Conflict is viewed as normal or at least customary in political organizations. Action does not presuppose some overarching intention. Rather, action results "from games among players who perceive quite different

faces of an issue and who differ markedly in the actions they prefer" (Allison, 1971: 175). Because action results from bargaining and compromise, the resulting decision seldom perfectly reflects the preferences of any group or subunit within the organization.

Political models of choice further presume that when preferences conflict, the power of the various social actors determines the outcome of the decision process. Power models hypothesize that those interests, subunits, or individuals within the organization who possess the greatest power, will receive the greatest rewards from the interplay of organizational politics. In such models, power "is an intervening variable between an initial condition, defined largely in terms of the individual components of the system, and a terminal state, defined largely in terms of the system as a whole" (March, 1966: 168–169). Power is used to overcome the resistance of others and obtain one's way in the organization.

To understand organizational choices using a political model, it is necessary to understand who participates in decision making, what determines each player's stand on the issues, what determines each actor's relative power, and how the decision process arrives at a decision; in other words, how the various preferences become combined (majority rule; unanimity; ⅔ vote; etc.) (Allison, 1971: 164). A change in any one of these aspects—relative power, the rules of decision making, or preferences—can lead to a change in the predicted organizational decision.

Distinguishing Political Models of Organizations

March (1966) has argued that it is often difficult to distinguish chance models from power or force models in terms of the predictions that each would make. He argued that evidence for force models would include: whether or not power is stable over time, whether or not power is stable over subject matter, whether or not power is correlated with other attributes, and whether or not power could be experimentally manipulated. These are important criteria to keep in mind when thinking about the evidence for a political model of organizations to be presented in this book.

It is clear that a political or power model of choice need not assume that all issues are equally important and, therefore, equally worthy of effort. Incorporating ideas of activation in force or power models makes their testing even more difficult.

Power models can be distinguished from rational models if it can be demonstrated that either no overarching organizational goal exists or even if such a goal does exist, decisions are made which are inconsistent with maximizing the attainment of the goal. Power can be distinguished from chance or organized anarchy models by demonstrating that actors in organizations have preferences and intentions which are consistent across decision issues and which they attempt to have implemented. Further evidence for political models would come from finding that measures of power in social systems, rather than goals, precedent, or chance, bring about decision outcomes. Indeed, the ability to measure and operationalize power is critical both for diagnosing political systems and for testing political models of organizations.

Summary

One of the points of Allison's (1971) analysis of the Cuban missile crisis is that it is not necessary to choose between analytical frameworks. Each may be partly true in a particular situation, and one can obtain a better understanding of the organization by trying to use all of the models rather than by choosing among them. This point is different than saying that some organizations are characterized more by the political model and others by the rational model. Allison's argument is that insight can be gained from the application of all the frameworks in the same situation. This statement is

true, but only within limits. At some point, the various perspectives will begin to make different predictions about what will occur, and will generate different recommendations concerning the strategy and tactics to be followed. At that point, the participant will need to decide where to place his or her bets.

As we have already discussed, discovering which perspective best describes a particular organization is not easy, and the world will do little to make it easier. Some of the perspectives are more accepted and acceptable than others. This means that language will be used to make it seem that the organization is operating according to the more accepted paradigms. It also means that there will be various informational and other types of social influence imposed on the observer to make him construct a particular view of the organization.

In Figure 1, the four decision models described in this chapter are briefly summarized along eight relevant dimensions. The ability to perfectly distinguish between the models, using a single dimension in a particular situation, is likely to be limited. However, by considering the dimensions in combination and by using comparative frames of reference, it becomes feasible to assess the extent to which the organization in question is operating according to one or the other of the models.

It is evident from the title of this book what my view is concerning the relative applicability of the four models of organizational decision making. Circumstances of bureaucratically rational decision making occur only in certain conditions on an infrequent basis. As Thompson and Tuden (1959) have argued, consensus on both goals and technology, or the connections between actions and consequences, are necessary in order for computational forms of decision making to be employed. Where there is disagreement over goals, compromise is used; when there is disagreement over technology, judgment is employed; and when there is disagreement about both, Thompson and Tuden characterize the decision situation as one requiring inspiration. In the case of judgment, compromise, and inspiration, it is the relative power of the various

		Model		
Dimension	Rational	Bureaucratic	Decision Process/ Organized Anarchy	Political Power
Goals, preferences	Consistent within and across social actors	Reasonably consistent	Unclear, ambiguous, may be constructed ex post to rationalize action	Consistent within social actors; inconsistent, pluralistic within the organization
Power and control	Centralized	Less centralized with greater reliance on rules	Very decentralized, anarchic	Shifting coalitions and interest groups
Decision process	Orderly, substantively rational	Procedural rationality embodied in programs and standard operating procedures	Ad hoc	Disorderly, characterized by push and pull of interests
Rules and norms	Norm of optimization	Precedent, tradition	Segmented and episodic participation in decisions	Free play of market forces; conflict is legitimate and expected
Information and computational requirements	Extensive and systematic	Reduced by the use of rules and procedures	Haphazard collection and use of information	Information used and withheld strategically
Beliefs about action-consequence relationships	Known at least to a probability distribution	Consensually shared acceptance of routines	Unclear, ambiguous technology	Disagreements about technology
Decisions	Follow from value-maximizing choice	Follow from programs and routines	Not linked to intention; result of intersection of persons, solutions, problems	Result of bargaining and interplay among interests
Ideology	Efficiency and effectiveness	Stability, fairness, predictability	Playfulness, loose coupling, randomness	Struggle, conflict, winners and losers

Figure 1
Overview of four organizational decision-making models

social actors that provides both the sufficient and necessary way of resolving the decision.

Furthermore, if intention is not always a guiding force in the taking of action and if preferences are not always clear or consistent, then there are at least some participants in organizations who know what they want and have the social power to get it. The randomness implied by the decision process model of organizations is inconsistent with the observation that in organizational decision making, some actors seem to usually get the garbage, while others manage to get the can.

Standard operating procedures, rules, and behavior repertoires clearly exist and are important in organizations. Much organizational decision making involves issues that are neither important nor contested, and in such cases, standard operating procedures are sufficient to get the decisions made in an inexpensive fashion. However, it is necessary to be aware that these various rules, norms, and procedures have in themselves implications for the distribution of power and authority in organizations and for how contested decisions should be resolved. The rules and processes themselves become important focal points for the exercise of power. They are not always neutral and not always substantively rational. Sometimes they are part and parcel of the political contest that occurs within organizations.

One of the reasons why power and politics characterize so many organizations is because of what some of my students have dubbed the Law of Political Entropy: given the opportunity, an organization will tend to seek and maintain a political character. The argument is that once politics are introduced into a situation, it is very difficult to restore rationality. Once consensus is lost, once disagreements about preferences, technology, and management philosophy emerge, it is very hard to restore the kind of shared perspective and solidarity which is necessary to operate under the rational model. If rationality is indeed this fragile, and if the Law of Political Entropy is correct, then over time one would expect to see more and more organizations characterized by the political model.

References

ALLEN, R. W., MADISON, D. L., PORTER, L. W., RENWICK, P. A., & MAYES, B. T. (1979). Organizational politics: Tactics and characteristics of its actors. *California Management Review, 22,* 77–83.

ALLISON, G. T. (1971). *Essence of decision.* Boston: Little, Brown.

BALDRIDGE, J. V. (1971). *Power and conflict in the university.* New York: Wiley.

BARITZ, J. H. (1960). *The servants of power.* Middletown, CT: Wesleyan University Press.

BIERSTEDT, R. (1950). An analysis of social power. *American Sociological Review, 15,* 730–738.

BLAU, P. M. (1964). *Exchange and power in social life.* New York: Wiley.

———, and SCHOENHERR, R. A. (1971). *The structure of organizations.* New York: Basic Books.

BURNS, T., & STALKER, G. M. (1961). *The management of innovation.* London: Tavistock.

CAREY, A. (1967). The Hawthorne studies: A radical criticism. *American Sociological Review, 32,* 403–416.

CARTWRIGHT, D. (1979). Contemporary social psychology in historical perspective. *Social Psychology Quarterly, 42,* 82–93.

COHEN, M. D., & MARCH, J. G. (1974). *Leadership and ambiguity: The American college president.* New York: McGraw-Hill.

———, & OLSEN, J. P. (1972). A garbage can model of organizational choice. *Administrative Science Quarterly, 17:* 1–25.

———. (1976). People, problems, solutions, and the ambiguity of relevance. In J. G. March and J. P. Olsen, (Eds.), *Ambiguity and choice in organizations* (pp. 24–37). Bergen, Norway: Universitetsforlaget.

CRECINE, J. P. (1967). A computer simulation model of municipal budgeting. *Management Science, 13:* 786–815.

CROZIER, M. (1964). *The bureaucratic phenomenon.* Chicago: University of Chicago Press.

CYERT, R. M., & MARCH, J. G. (1963). *A behavioral theory of the firm.* Englewood Cliffs, NJ: Prentice-Hall.

DAHL, R. A. (1957). The concept of power. *Behavioral Science, 2,* 201–215.

DAVIS, O. A., DEMPSTER, M. A. H., & WILDAVSKY, A. (1966). A theory of the budgeting process. *American Political Science Review, 60:* 529–547.

DORNBUSCH, S. M., & SCOTT, W. R. (1975). *Evaluation and the exercise of authority: A theory of control applied to diverse organizations.* San Francisco, CA: Jossey-Bass.

EDELMAN, M. (1964). *The symbolic uses of politics.* Urbana, IL: University of Illinois Press.

EDWARDS, W. (1954). The theory of decision making. *Psychological Bulletin, 51:* 380–417.

EMERSON, R. M. (1962). Power-dependence relations. *American Sociological Review, 27,* 31–41.

FRENCH, J. R. P., Jr., & RAVEN, B. (1968). The bases of social power. In D. Cartwright & A. Zander (Eds.), *Group dynamics* (3rd ed.). (pp. 259–269). New York: Harper & Row.

GALBRAITH, J. R. (1973). *Designing complex organizations.* Reading, MA: Addison-Wesley.

GERWIN, D. (1969). A process model of budgeting in a public school system. *Management Science, 15:* 338–361.

KAPLAN, A. (1964). *The conduct of inquiry.* Scranton, PA: Chandler.

KARPIK, L. (1978). Organizations, institutions and history. In Lucien Karpik (Ed.), *Organization and environment: Theory, issues and reality* (pp. 15–68). Newbury Park, CA: Sage.

KORDA, M. (1975). *Power.* New York: Ballantine Books.

LASSWELL, H. D. (1936). *Politics: Who gets what, when, how.* New York: McGraw-Hill.

LAWRENCE, P. R., & LORSCH, J. W. (1967). *Organization and environment.* Boston: Graduate School of Business Administration, Harvard University.

MARCH, J. G. (1962). The business firm as a political coalition. *Journal of Politics, 24,* 662–678.

———. (1966). The power of power. In D. Easton (Ed.), *Varieties of political theory* (pp. 39–70). Englewood Cliffs, NJ: Prentice-Hall.

———. (1976). The technology of foolishness. In J. G. March and J. P. Olsen, (Eds.), *Ambiguity and choice in organizations* (pp. 69–81). Bergen, Norway: Universitetsforlaget.

———. (1978). Bounded rationality, ambiguity, and the engineering of choice. *Bell Journal of Economics, 9,* 587–608.

MARCH, J. G., & SIMON, H. A. (1958). *Organizations.* New York: John Wiley.

MAYES, B. T., & ALLEN, R. W. (1977). Toward a definition of organizational politics. *Academy of Management Review, 2,* 672–678.

MECHANIC, D. (1962). Sources of power of lower participants in complex organizations. *Administrative Science Quarterly, 7,* 349–364.

NEHRBASS, R. G. (1979). Ideology and the decline of management theory. *Academy of Management Review, 4,* 427–431.

NORD, W. R. (1974). The failure of current applied behavioral science: A Marxian perspective. *Journal of Applied Behavioral Science, 10,* 557–578.

PENNINGS, J. M. (1975). The relevance of the structural-contingency model for organizational effectiveness. *Administrative Science Quarterly, 20,* 393–410.

PERROW, C. (1961). The analysis of goals in complex organizations. *American Sociological Review, 26,* 859–866.

———. (1970). Departmental power and perspectives in industrial firms. In M. N. Zald (Ed.), *Power in organizations* (pp. 59–89). Nashville: Vanderbilt University Press.

———. (1972). *Complex organizations: A critical essay.* Glenview, IL: Scott, Foresman.

PFEFFER, J. (1978a). The micropolitics of organizations. In M. W. Meyer and Assoc., (Eds.), *Environments and organizations* (pp. 29–50). San Francisco: CA: Jossey-Bass.

PFEFFER, J., & SALANCIK, G. R. (1974). Organizational decision making as a political process: The case of a university budget. *Administrative Science Quarterly, 19,* 135–151.

———. (1978). *The external control of organizations: A resource dependence perspective.* New York: Harper & Row.

———, & LEBLEBICI, H. (1976). The effect of uncertainty on the use of social influence in organizational decision making. *Administrative Science Quarterly, 21,* 227–245.

PONDY, L. R. (1969). Effects of size, complexity, and ownership on administrative intensity. *Administrative Science Quarterly, 14,* 47–60.

PUGH, D. S. (1966). Modern organization theory. *Psychological Bulletin, 66,* 235–251.

SALANCIK, G. R., & PFEFFER, J. (1974). The bases and use of power in organizational decision making: The case of a university. *Administrative Science Quarterly, 19,* 453–473.

———. (1977b). Who gets power—and how they hold on to it: A strategic-contingency model of power. *Organizational Dynamics, 5,* 3–21.

SCHEIN, E. H. (1968). Organizational socialization and the profession of management. *Industrial Management Review, 9,* 1–16.

SIMON, H. A. (1957). *Models of man.* New York: Wiley.

———. (1964). On the concept of organizational goal. *Administrative Science Quarterly, 9:* 1–22.

———. (1979). Rational decision making in business organizations. *American Economic Review, 69:* 493–513.

STAVA, P. (1976). Constraints on the politics of public choice. In *Ambiguity and choice in organizations,* James G. March and Johan P. Olsen, pp. 206–224. Bergen, Norway: Universitetsforlaget.

THOMPSON, J. D. (1967). *Organizations in action.* New York: McGraw-Hill.

———, and TUDEN, A. (1959). Strategies, structures, and processes of organizational decision. In J. D. Thompson, P. B. Hammond, R. W. Hawkes, B. H. Junker, and A. Tuden, (Eds.), *Comparative studies in administration* (pp. 195–216). Pittsburgh: University of Pittsburgh Press.

WEBER, M. (1947). *The theory of social and economic organization.* New York: Free Press.

WEICK, K. E. (1969). *The social psychology of organizing.* Reading, MA: Addison-Wesley.

WEINER, S. S. (1976). Participation, deadlines, and choice. In J. G. March and J. P. Olsen, (Eds.), *Ambiguity and choice in organizations* (pp. 225–250). Bergen, Norway: Universitetsforlaget.

WILDAVSKY, A. (1979). *The politics of the budgeting process.* (3rd ed.). Boston: Little, Brown.

———, and HAMMOND, A. (1965). Comprehensive versus incremental budgeting in the department of agriculture. *Administrative Science Quarterly, 10:* 321–346.

WILLIAMSON, O. E. (1975). *Markets and hierarchies: Analysis and antitrust implications.* New York: Free Press.

WOODWARD, J. (1965). *Industrial organization: Theory and practice.* London: Oxford University Press.

ZALD, M. N. (1965). Who shall rule? A political analysis of succession in a large welfare organization. *Pacific Sociological Review, 8,* 52–60.

38

Sources of Power of Lower Participants in Complex Organizations

David Mechanic

It is not unusual for lower participants[1] in complex organizations to assume and wield considerable power and influence not associated with their formally defined positions within these organizations. In sociological terms they have considerable personal power but no authority. Such personal power is often attained, for example, by executive secretaries and accountants in business firms, by attendants in mental hospitals, and even by inmates in prisons. The personal power achieved by these lower participants does not necessarily result from unique personal characteristics, although these may be relevant, but results rather from particular aspects of their location within their organizations.

Informal versus Formal Power

Within organizations the distribution of authority (institutionalized power) is closely if not perfectly correlated with the prestige of positions.

Note: The editors acknowledge the sexist language of this article, but believe the importance of its contents warrants its inclusion in this collection.
SOURCE: David Mechanic, "Sources of Power of Lower Participants in Complex Organizations," in *Administrative Science Quarterly* 7 (December 1962): 349–364; reprinted by permission of *The Administrative Science Quarterly.* Copyright © 1962 *The Administrative Science Quarterly.*

Those who have argued for the independence of these variables[2] have taken their examples from diverse organizations and do not deal with situations where power is clearly comparable.[3] Thus when Bierstedt argues that Einstein had prestige but no power, and the policeman power but no prestige, it is apparent that he is comparing categories that are not comparable. Generally persons occupying high-ranking positions within organizations have more authority than those holding low-ranking positions.

One might ask what characterizes high-ranking positions within organizations. What is most evident, perhaps, is that lower participants recognize the right of higher-ranking participants to exercise power, and yield without difficulty to demands they regard as legitimate. Moreover, persons in high-ranking positions tend to have considerable access and control over information and persons both within and outside the organization, and to instrumentalities of resources. Although higher supervisory personnel may be isolated from the task activities of lower participants, they maintain access to them through formally established intermediary positions and exercise control through intermediary participants. There appears, therefore, to be a clear correlation between the prestige of positions within organizations and the extent to which they offer access to information, persons, and instrumentalities.

Since formal organizations tend to structure lines of access and communication, access should be a clue to institutional prestige. Yet access depends on variables other than those controlled by the formal structure of an organization, and this often makes the informal power structure that develops within organizations somewhat incongruent with the formally intended plan. It is these variables that allow work groups to limit production through norms that contravene the goals of the larger organization, that allow hospital attendants to thwart changes in the structure of a hospital, and that allow prison inmates to exercise some control, over prison guards. Organizations, in a sense are continuously at the mercy of their lower participants, and it is this fact that makes organizational power structure especially interesting to the sociologist and social psychologist. . . .

A Classic Example

Like many other aspects of organizational theory, one can find a classic statement of our problem in Weber's discussion of the political bureaucracy. Weber indicated the extent to which bureaucrats may have considerable power over political incumbents, as a result, in part, of their permanence within the political bureaucracy, as contrasted to public officials, who are replaced rather frequently.[4] Weber noted how the low-ranking bureaucrat becomes familiar with the organization—its rules and operations, the work flow, and so on, which gives him considerable power over the new political incumbent, who might have higher rank but is not as familiar with the organization. While Weber does not directly state the point, his analysis suggests that bureaucratic permanence has some relationship to increased access to persons, information, and instrumentalities. To state the hypothesis suggested somewhat more formally:

H1 Other factors remaining constant, organizational power is related to access to persons, information, and instrumentalities.

H2 Other factors remaining constant, as a participant's length of time in an organization increases, he has increased access to persons, information, and instrumentalities.

While these hypotheses are obvious, they do suggest that a careful scrutiny of the organizational literature, especially that dealing with the power or counter-power of lower participants, might lead to further formalized statements, some considerably less obvious than the ones stated. This kind of hypothesis formation is treated later in the paper, but at this point I would like to place the discussion of power within a larger theoretical context and discuss the relevance of role theory to the study of power processes.

Implications of Role Theory for the Study of Power

There are many points of departure for the study of power processes within organizations. An investigator might view influence in terms of its sources and strategies; he might undertake a study of the flow of influence; he might concentrate on the structure of organizations, seeing to what extent regularities in behavior might be explained through the study of norms, roles, and traditions; and, finally, more psychologically oriented investigators might concentrate on the recipients of influence and the factors affecting susceptibility to influence attempts. Each of these points of departure leads to different theoretical emphases. For our purposes the most important emphasis is that presented by role theorists.

Role theorists approach the question of influence and power in terms of the behavioral regularities which result from established identities within specific social contexts like families, hospitals, and business firms. The underlying premise of most role theorists is that a large proportion of all behavior is brought about through socialization within specific organizations, and much behavior is routine and established through learning the traditional modes of adaptation in dealing with specific tasks. Thus the positions persons occupy in an organization account for much of their behavior. Norms and roles serve as mediating forces in influence processes.

While role theorists have argued much about vocabulary, the basic premises underlying their thought have been rather consistent. The argument is essentially that knowledge of one's identity or social position is a powerful index of the expectations such a person is likely to face in various social situations. Since behavior tends to be highly correlated with expectations, prediction of behavior is therefore possible. The approach of role theorists to the study of behavior within organizations is of particular merit in that it provides a consistent set of concepts which is useful analytically in describing recruitment, socialization, interaction, and personality, as well as the formal structure of organizations. Thus the concept of role is one of the few concepts clearly linking social structure, social process, and social character. . . .

Role theory is useful in emphasizing the extent to which influence and power can be exercised without conflict. This occurs when power is integrated with a legitimate order, when sentiments are held in common, and when there are adequate mechanisms for introducing persons into the system and training them to recognize, accept, and value the legitimacy of control within the organization. By providing the conditions whereby participants within an organization may internalize the norms, these generalized rules, values, and sentiments serve as substitutes for interpersonal influence and make the workings of the organization more agreeable and pleasant for all.

It should be clear that lower participants will be more likely to circumvent higher authority, other factors remaining constant, when the mandates of those in power, if not the authority itself, are regarded as illegitimate. Thus as Etzioni points out, when lower participants become alienated from the organization, coercive power is likely to be required if its formal mandates are to be fulfilled.[5]

Moreover, all organizations must maintain control over lower participants. To the extent that lower participants fail to recognize the legitimacy of power, or believe that sanctions cannot or will not be exercised when violations occur, the organization loses, to some extent, its ability to control their behavior. Moreover, in-so-far as higher participants can create the impression that they can or will exert sanctions above their actual willingness to use such sanctions, control over lower participants will increase. It is usually to the advantage of an organization to externalize and impersonalize controls, however, and if possible to develop positive sentiments toward its rules.

In other words, an effective organization can control its participants in such a way as to make it hardly perceivable that it exercises the control that it does. It seeks commitment from lower participants, and when commitment is obtained, surveillance can be relaxed. On the other hand, when the power of lower participants in organizations is considered, it often appears to be clearly divorced from the traditions, norms, and goals and sentiments of the organization as a whole. Lower participants do not usually achieve control by using the role structure of the organization, but rather by circumventing, sabotaging, and manipulating it.

Sources of Power of Lower Participants

The most effective way for lower participants to achieve power is to obtain, maintain, and control access to persons, information, and instrumentalities. To the extent that this can be accomplished, lower participants make higher-ranking participants dependent upon them. Thus dependence together with the manipulation of the dependency relationship is the key to the power of lower participants.

A number of examples can be cited which illustrate the preceding point. Scheff, for example, reports on the failure of a state mental hospital to bring about intended reform because of the opposition of hospital attendants.[6] He noted that the power of hospital attendants was largely a result of the dependence of ward physicians on attendants. This dependence resulted from the physician's short tenure, his lack of interest in administration, and the large amount of administrative responsibility he had to assume. An implicit trading agreement developed between physicians and attendants, whereby attendants would take on some of the responsibilities and obligations of the ward physician in return for increased power in decision-making processes concerning patients. Failure of the ward physician to honor his part of the agreement resulted in information being withheld, disobedience, lack of cooperation, and unwillingness of the attendants to serve as a barrier between the physician and a ward full of patients demanding attention and recognition.

When the attendant withheld cooperation, the physician had difficulty in making a graceful entrance and departure from the ward, in handling necessary paperwork (officially his responsibility), and in obtaining information needed to deal adequately with daily treatment and behavior problems. When attendants opposed change, they could wield influence by refusing to assume responsibility officially assigned to the physician.

Similarly, Sykes describes the dependence of prison guards on inmates and the power obtained by inmates over guards.[7] He suggests that although guards could report inmates for disobedience, frequent reports would give prison officials the impression that the guard was unable to command obedience. The guard, therefore, had some stake in ensuring the good behavior of prisoners without use of formal sanctions against them. The result was a trading agreement whereby the guard allowed violations of certain rules in return for co-operative behavior. A similar situation is found in respect to officers in the Armed Services or foremen in industry. To the extent that they require formal sanction to bring about co-operation, they are usually perceived by their superiors as less valuable to the organization. For a good leader is expected to command obedience, at least, if not commitment.

Factors Affecting Power

Expertise

Increasing specialization and organizational growth has made the expert or staff person important. The expert maintains power because high-ranking persons in the organization are dependent upon him for his special skills and access to certain kinds of information. One possible reason for lawyers obtaining many high governmental offices is that they are likely to have access to rather specialized but highly important means to oganizational goals.[8]

We can state these ideas by hypotheses, as follows:

H3 Other factors remaining constant, to the extent that a low-ranking participant has important expert knowledge not available to high-ranking participants, he is likely to have power over them.

Power stemming from expertise, however, is likely to be limited unless it is difficult to replace the expert. This leads to two further hypotheses:

H4 Other factors remaining constant, a person difficult to replace will have greater power than a person easily replaceable.
H5 Other factors remaining constant, experts will be more difficult to replace than nonexperts.

While persons having expertise are likely to be fairly high-ranking participants in an organization, the same hypotheses that explain the power of lower participants are relevant in explaining the comparative power positions of intermediate- and high-ranking persons.

The application of our hypothesis about expertise is clearly relevant if we look at certain organizational issues. For example, the merits of medical versus lay hospital administrators are often debated. It should be clear, however, that all other factors remaining unchanged, the medical administrator has clear advantage over the lay administrator. Where lay administrators receive preference, there is an implicit assumption that the lay person is better at administrative duties. This may be empirically valid but is not necessarily so. The special expert knowledge of the medical administrator stems from his ability legitimately to oppose a physician who contests an administrative decision on the basis of medical necessity. Usually hospitals are viewed primarily as universalistic in orientation both by the general public and most of their participants. Thus medical necessity usually takes precedence over management policies, a factor contributing to the poor financial position of most hospitals. The lay administrator is not in a position to contest such claims independently, since he usually lacks the basis for evaluation of the medical problems involved and also lacks official recognition of his competence to make such decisions. If the lay administrator is to evaluate these claims adequately on the basis of professional necessity, he must have a group of medical consultants or a committee of medical men to serve as a buffer between medical staff and the lay administration.

As a result of growing specialization, expertise is increasingly important in organizations. As the complexity of organizational tasks increases, and as organizations grow in size, there is a limit to responsibility that can be efficiently exercised by one person. Delegation of responsibility occurs, experts and specialists are brought in to provide information and research, and the higher participants become dependent upon them. Experts have tremendous potentialities for power by withholding information, providing incorrect information, and so on, and to the extent that experts are dissatisfied, the probability of organizational sabotage increases.

Effort and Interest

The extent to which lower participants may exercise power depends in part on their willingness to exert effort in areas were higher-ranking participants are often reluctant to participate. Effort exerted is directly related to the degree of interest one has in an area.

H6   Other factors remaining constant, there is a direct relationship between the amount of effort a person is willing to exert in an area and the power he can command.

For example, secretarial staffs in universities often have power to make decisions about the purchase and allocation of supplies, the allocation of their services, the scheduling of classes, and, at times, the disposition of student complaints. Such control may in some instances lead to sanctions against a professor by polite reluctance to furnish supplies, ignoring his preferences for the scheduling of classes, and giving others preference in the allocation of services. While the power to make such decisions may easily be removed from the jurisdiction of the lower participant, it can only be accomplished at a cost—the willingness to allocate time and effort to the decisions dealing with these matters. To the extent that responsibilities are delegated to lower participants, a certain degree of power is likely to accompany the responsibility. Also, should the lower participants see his perceived rights in jeopardy, he may sabotage the system in various ways.

Let us visualize a hypothetical situation where a department concludes that secretarial services are being allocated on a prejudicial basis as a result of complaints by several of the younger faculty. Let us also assume that, when the complaint is investigated, it is found to be substantially correct; that is, some of the younger faculty have difficulty obtaining secretarial services because of preferences among the secretarial staff. If in attempting to eliminate discretion by the secretarial staff, the chairman establishes a rule ordering the allocation of services on the basis of the order in which work appears, the rule can easily be made ineffective by complete conformity to it. Deadlines for papers, examinations, and the like will occur, and flexibility in the allocation of services is required if these deadlines are to be met. Thus the need for flexibility can be made to conflict with the rule by a staff usually not untalented in such operations.

When an organization gives discretion to lower participants, it is usually trading the power of discretion for needed flexibility. The cost of constant surveillance is too high, and the effort required too great; it is very often much easier for all concerned to allow the secretary discretion in return for co-operation and not too great an abuse of power.

H7   Other factors remaining constant, the less effort and interest higher-ranking participants are willing to devote to a task, the more likely are lower participants to obtain power relevant to this task.

Attractiveness

Another personal attribute associated with the power of low-ranking persons in an organization is attractiveness or what some call "personality." People who are viewed as attractive are more likely to obtain access to persons, and, once such access is gained, they may be more likely to succeed in promoting a cause. But once again dependence is the key to the power of attractiveness, for whether a person is dependent upon another for a service he provides, or for approval or affection, what is most relevant is the relational bond which is highly valued.

H8   Other factors remaining constant, the more attractive a person, the more likely he is to obtain access to persons and control over these persons.

Location and Position

In any organization the person's location in physical space and position in social space are important factors influencing access to persons, information, and instrumentalities.[9] Propinquity affects the opportunities for interaction, as well as one's position within a communication network. Although these are somewhat separate factors, we shall refer to their combined effect as centrality[10] within the organization.

H9   Other factors remaining constant, the more central a person is in an organization, the greater is his access to persons, information, and instrumentalities.

Some low participants may have great centrality within an organization. An executive's or university president's secretary not only has access, but often controls access in making appointments and scheduling events. Although she may have no great formal authority, she may have considerable power.

Coalitions

It should be clear that the variables we are considering are at different levels of analysis; some of them define attributes of persons, while others define attributes of communication and organization. Power processes within organizations are particularly interesting in that there are many channels of power and ways of achieving it.

In complex organizations different occupational groups attend to different functions, each group often maintaining its own power structure within the organization. Thus hospitals have administrators, medical personnel, nursing personnel, attendants, maintenance personnel, laboratory personnel, and so on. Universities, similarly, have teaching personnel, research personnel, administrative personnel, maintenance personnel, and so on. Each of these functional tasks within organizations often becomes the sphere of a particular group that controls activities relating to the task. While these tasks usually are coordinated at the highest levels of the organization, they often are not co-ordinated at intermediate and lower levels. It is not unusual, however, for coalitions to form among lower participants in these multiple structures. A secretary may know the man who manages the supply of stores, or the person assigning parking stickers. Such acquaintances may give her the ability to handle informally certain needs that would be more time-consuming and difficult to handle formally. Her ability to provide services informally makes higher-ranking participants in some degree dependent upon her, thereby giving her power, which increases her ability to bargain on issues important to her.

Rules

In organizations with complex power structures lower participants can use their knowledge of the norms of the organization to thwart attempted change. In discussing the various functions of bureaucratic rules, Gouldner maintains that such rules serve as excellent substitutes for surveillance, since surveillance in addition to being expensive in time and effort arouses considerable hostility and antagonism.[11] Moreover, he argues, rules are a functional equivalent for direct, personally given orders, since they specify the obligations of workers to do things in specific ways. Standardized rules, in addition, allow simple screening of violations, facilitate remote control, and to some extent legitimize punishment when the rule is violated. The worker who violates a bureaucratic rule has little recourse to the excuse that he did not know what was expected, as he might claim for a direct order. Finally, Gouldner argues that rules are "the 'chips' to which the company staked the supervisors and which they could use to play the game";[12] that is, rules established a punishment which could be withheld, and this facilitated the supervisors' bargaining power with lower participants.

While Gouldner emphasizes the functional characteristics of rules within an organization, it should be clear that full compliance to all the rules at all times will probably be dysfunctional for the organization. Complete and apathetic compliance may do everything but facilitate achievement of organizational goals. Lower participants who are familiar with an organization and its rules can often find rules to support their contention that they not do what they have been asked to do, and rules are also often a rationalization for inaction on their part. The following of rules becomes especially complex when associations and unions become involved, for there are then two sets of rules to which the participant can appeal.

What is suggested is that rules may be chips for everyone concerned in the game. Rules become the "chips" through which the bargaining process is maintained. Scheff, as noted earlier, observed that attendants in mental hospitals often took on responsibilities assigned legally to the ward physician, and when attendants refused to share these responsibilities the physician's position became extremely difficult.[13]

The ward physician is legally responsible for the care and treatment of each ward patient. This responsibility requires attention to a host of details. Medicine, seclusion, sedation and transfer orders, for example, require the doctor's signature. Tranquilizers are particularly troublesome in this regard since they require frequent adjustment of dosage in order to get the desired effects. The physician's order is required to each change in dosage. With 150 patients under his care on tranquilizers, and several changes of dosages a week desirable, the physician could spend a major portion of his ward time in dealing with this single detail.

Given the time-consuming formal chores of the physician, and his many other duties, he usually worked out an arrangement with the ward personnel, particularly the charge (supervisory attendant), to handle these duties. On several wards, the charge called specific problems to the doctor's attention, and the two of them, in effect, would have a consultation. The charge actually made most of the decisions concerning dosage change in the back wards. Since the doctor delegated portions of his formal responsibilities to the charge, he was dependent on her good will toward him. If she withheld her cooperation, the physician had absolutely no recourse but to do all the work himself.[14]

In a sense such delegation of responsibility involves a consideration of reward and cost, whereby the decision to be made involves a question of what is more valuable—to retain control over an area, or to delegate one's work to lower participants.

There are occasions, of course, when rules are regarded as illegitimate by lower participants, and they may disregard them. Gouldner observed that, in the mine, men felt they could resist authority in a situation involving danger to themselves.[15] They did not feel that they could legitimately be ordered to do anything that would endanger their lives. It is probably significant that in extremely dangerous situations organizations are more likely to rely on commitment to work than on authority. Even within nonvoluntary groups dangerous tasks are regarded usually as requiring task commitment, and it is likely that commitment is a much more powerful organizational force than coercive authority.

Summary

The preceding remarks are general ones, and they are assumed to be in part true of all types of organizations. But power relationships in organizations are likely to be molded by the type of organization being considered, the nature of organizational goals, the ideology of organizational decision making, the kind of commitment participants have to the organization, the formal structure of the organization, and so on. In short, we have attempted to discuss power processes within organizations in a manner somewhat divorced from other major organizational processes. We have emphasized variables affecting control of access to persons, information, and facilities within organizations. Normative definitions, perception of legitimacy, exchange, and coalitions have all been viewed in relation to power processes. Moreover, we have dealt with some attributes of persons related to power: commitment, effort, interest, willingness to use power, skills, attractiveness, and so on. And we have discussed some other variables: time, centrality, complexity of power structure, and replaceability of persons. It appears that these variables help to account in part for power exercised by lower participants in organizations.

Notes

1. The term "lower participants" comes from Amitai Etzioni, *A Comparative Analysis of Complex Organizations* (New York, 1961) and is used by him to designate persons in positions of lower rank: employees, rank-and-file, members, clients, customers, and inmates. We shall use the term in this paper in a relative sense denoting position vis-à-vis a higher-ranking participant.

2. Robert Bierstedt, An Analysis of Social Power, *American Sociological Review,* 15 (1950), 730–738.

3. Robert A. Dahl, The Concept of Power, *Behavioral Science,* 2 (1957), 210–215.

4. Max Weber, "The Essentials of Bureaucratic Organization: An Ideal-Type Construction," in Robert Merton *et al., Reader in Bureaucracy* (Glencoe, Ill., 1952), pp. 18–27.

5. Etzioni, *op cit.*

6. Thomas J. Scheff, Control over Policy by Attendants in a Mental Hospital, *Journal of Health and Human Behavior,* 2 (1961), 93–105.

7. Gresham M. Sykes, "The Corruption of Authority and Rehabilitation," in A. Etzioni, ed., *Complex Organizations* (New York, 1961), pp. 191–197.

8. As an example, it appears that 6 members of the cabinet, 30 important subcabinet officials, 63 senators, and 230 congressmen are lawyers (*New Yorker,* April 14, 1962, p. 62). Although one can cite many reasons for lawyers holding political posts, an important one appears to be their legal expertise.

9. There is considerable data showing the powerful effect of propinquity on communication. For summary, see Thibaut and Kelley, *op. cit.,* pp. 39–42.

10. The concept of centrality is generally used in a more technical sense in the work of Bavelas, Shaw, Gilchrist, and others. For example, Bavelas defines the central region of a structure as the class of all cells with the smallest distance between one cell and any other cell in the structure, with distance measured in link units. Thus the most central position in a pattern is the position closest to all others. Cf. Harold Leavitt, "Some Effects of Certain Communication Patterns on Group Performance," in E. Maccoby, T. N. Newcomb, and E. L. Hartley, eds., *Readings in Social Psychology* (New York, 1958), p. 559.

11. Alvin W. Gouldner, *Patterns of Industrial Bureaucracy* (Glencoe, Ill., 1954).

12. *Ibid.,* p. 173.

13. Scheff, *op. cit.*

14. *Ibid.,* p. 97.

15. Gouldner, *op. cit.*

39

Leadership in an Organized Anarchy

Michael D. Cohen and
James G. March

The Ambiguities of Anarchy

The college president faces four fundamental ambiguities. The first is the ambiguity of *purpose*. In what terms can action be justified? What are the goals of the organization? The second is the ambiguity of *power*. How powerful is the president? What can he accomplish? The third is the ambiguity of *experience*. What is to be learned from the events of the presidency? The fourth is the ambiguity of *success*. When is a president successful? How does he assess his pleasures?

These ambiguities are fundamental to college presidents because they strike at the heart of the usual interpretations of leadership. When purpose is ambiguous, ordinary theories of decision making and intelligence become problematic. When power is ambiguous, ordinary theories of social order and control become problematic. When experience is ambiguous, ordinary theories of learning and adaptation become problematic. When success is ambiguous, ordinary theories of motivation and personal pleasure become problematic. . . .

Note: The editors acknowledge the sexist language of this article, but believe the importance of its contents warrants its inclusion in this collection.
SOURCE: Michael D. Cohen and James G. March, *Leadership and Ambiguity: The American College President*, pp. 195–229. Copyright 1974 Carnegie Foundation for the Advancement of Teaching. Reprinted by permission.

The Ambiguity of Purpose

Efforts to generate normative statements of the goals of a university tend to produce goals that are either meaningless or dubious. They fail one or more of the following reasonable tests. First, is the goal clear? Can one define some specific procedure for measuring the degree of goal achievement? Second, is it problematic? Is there some possibility that the organization will accomplish the goal? Is there some chance that it will fail? Third, is it accepted? Do most significant groups in the university agree on the goal statement? For the most part, the level of generality that facilitates acceptance destroys the problematic nature or clarity of the goal. The level of specificity that permits measurement destroys acceptance. . . .

Efforts to specify a set of consciously shared, consistent objectives within a university or to infer such a set of objectives from the activities or actions of the university have regularly revealed signs of inconsistency. To expose inconsistencies is not to resolve them, however. There are only modest signs that universities or other organized anarchies respond to a revelation of ambiguity of purpose by reducing the ambiguity. These are organizational systems without clear objectives; and the processes by which their objectives are established and legitimized are not extraordinarily sensitive to inconsistency. In fact, for many purposes the ambiguity of purpose is produced by our insistence on treating purpose as a necessary property of a good university. The strains arise from trying to impose a model of action as flowing from intent on organizations that act in another way.

College presidents live within a normative context that presumes purpose and within an organizational context that denies it. They serve on commissions to define and redefine the objectives of higher education. They organize convocations to examine the goals of the college. They write introductory statements to the college catalog. They accept the presumption that intelligent leadership presupposes the rational pursuit of goals. Simultaneously, they are aware that the process of choice in the college depends little on statements of shared direction. They recognize the flow of actions as an ecology of games (Long, 1958), each with its own rules. They accept the observation that the world is not like the model.

The Ambiguity of Power

Power is a simple idea, pervasive in its appeal to observers of social events. Like *intelligence* or *motivation* or *utility,* however, it tends to be misleadingly simple and prone to tautology. A person has power if he gets things done; if he has power, he can get things done. . . .

As a shorthand casual expression for variations in the potential of different positions in the organization, *power* has some utility. The college president has more potential for moving the college than most people, probably more potential than any one other person. Nevertheless, presidents discover that they have less power than is believed, that their power to accomplish things depends heavily on what they want to accomplish, that the use of formal authority is not automatic, that the necessary details of organizational life confuse power (which is somewhat different from diffusing it), and that their colleagues seem to delight in complaining simultaneously about presidential weakness and presidential willfulness.

The ambiguity of power, like the ambiguity of purpose, is focused on the president. Presidents share in and contribute to the confusion. They enjoy the perquisites and prestige of the office. They enjoy its excitement, at least when things go well. They announce important events. They appear at important symbolic functions. They report to people. They accept and thrive on their own importance. It would be remarkable if they did not. Presidents even occasionally recite that "the buck stops here" with a finality that suggests the cliché is an observation about power and authority rather than the proclamation of administrative style and ideology.

At the same time, presidents solicit an understanding of the limits to their control. They regret the tendency of students, legislators, and community leaders to assume that a president has the power to do whatever he chooses simply because he is president. They plead the countervailing power of other groups in the college or the notable complexities of causality in large organizations. . . .

The confusion disturbs the president, but it also serves him. Ambiguity of power leads to a parallel ambiguity of responsibility. The allocation of credit and blame for the events of organizational life becomes—as it often does in political and social systems—a matter for argument. The "facts" of responsibility are badly confounded by the confusions of anarchy; and the conventional myth of hierarchical executive responsibility is undermined by the countermyth of the nonhierarchical nature of colleges and universities. Presidents negotiate with their audiences on the interpretations of their power. As a result, during the recent years of campus troubles, many college presidents sought to emphasize the limitations of presidential control. During the more glorious days of conspicuous success, they solicited a recognition of their responsibility for events.

The process does not involve presidents alone, of course. The social validation of responsibility involves all the participants: faculty, trustees, students, parents, community leaders, government. Presidents seek to write their histories in the use of power as part of a chorus of history writers, each with his own reasons for preferring a somewhat different interpretation of "Who has the Power?"

The Ambiguity of Experience

College presidents attempt to learn from their experience. They observe the consequences of actions and infer the structure of the world from those observations. They use the resulting inferences in attempts to improve their future actions.

Consider the following very simple learning paradigm:

1. At a certain point in time a president is presented with a set of well-defined, discrete action alternatives.
2. At any point in time he has a certain probability of choosing any particular alternative (and a certainty of choosing one of them).
3. The president observes the outcome that apparently follows his choice and assesses the outcome in terms of his goals.
4. If the outcome is consistent with his goals, the president increases his probability of choosing that alternative in the future; if not, he decreases the probability.

Although actual presidential learning certainly involves more complicated inferences, such a paradigm captures much of the ordinary adaptation of an intelligent man to the information gained from experience.

The process produces considerable learning. The subjective experience is one of adapting from experience and improving behavior on the basis of feedback. If the world with which the president is dealing is relatively simple and relatively stable, and if his experience is relatively frequent, he can expect to improve over time (assuming he has some appropriate criterion for testing the consistency of outcomes with goals). As we have suggested earlier, however, the world in which the president lives has two conspicuous properties that make experience ambiguous even where goals are clear. First, the world is relatively complex. Outcomes depend heavily on factors other than the president's action. These factors are uncontrolled and, in large part, unobserved. Second, relative to the rate at which the president gathers experimental data, the world changes rapidly. These properties produce considerable potential for false learning. . . .

College presidents probably have greater confidence in their interpretations of college life, college administration, and their general environment than is warranted. The inferences they have made from experience are likely to be wrong. Their confidence in their learning is likely to have been reinforced by the social support they receive from the people around them and by social expectations about the presidential role. As a result, they tend to be unaware of the extent to which the ambiguities they feel with respect to purpose and power are matched by similar ambiguities with respect to the meaning of the ordinary events of presidential life.

The Ambiguity of Success

Administrative success is generally recognized in one of two ways. First, by promotion: An administrator knows that he has been successful by virtue of a promotion to a better job. He assesses his success on the current job by the opportunities he has or expects to have to leave it. Second, by widely accepted, operational measures of organizational output: a business executive values his own performance in terms of a profit-and-loss statement of his operations.

Problems with these indicators of success are generic to high-level administrative positions. Offers of promotion become less likely as the job improves and the administrator's age advances. The criteria by which success is judged become less precise in measurement, less stable over time, and less widely shared. The administrator discovers that a wide assortment of factors outside his control are capable of overwhelming the impact of any actions he may take.

In the case of the college president all three problems are accentuated. As we have seen earlier, few college presidents are promoted out of the presidency. There are job offers, and most presidents ultimately accept one; but the best opportunity the typical president can expect is an invitation to accept a decent version of administrative semiretirement. The criteria of success in academic administration are sometimes moderately clear (e.g., growth, quiet on campus, improvement in the quality of students and faculty), but the relatively precise measures of college health tend neither to be stable over time nor to be critically sensitive to presidential action. . . .

An argument can be made, of course, that the college president should be accustomed to the ambiguity of success. His new position is not, in this respect, so strikingly different from the positions he has held previously. His probable perspective is different, however. Success has not previously been subjectively ambiguous to him. He has been a success. He has been promoted relatively rapidly. He and his associates are inclined to attribute his past successes to a combination of administrative savoir-faire, interpersonal style, and political sagacity. He has experienced those successes as the lawful consequence of his actions. Honest modesty on the part of a president does not conceal a certain awareness of his own ability. A president comes to his office having learned that he is successful and that he enjoys success.

The momentum of promotion will not sustain him in the presidency. Although, as we have seen, a fair number of presidents anticipate moving from their present job to another, better presidency, the prospects are not nearly as good as the hopes. The ambiguities of purpose, power, and experience conspire to render success and failure equally obscure. The validation of success is unreliable. Not only can a president not assure himself that he will be able to lead the college in the directions in which others might believe, he also has no assurance that the same criteria will be applied tomorrow. What happens today will tend to be rationalized tomorrow as what was desired. What happens today will have some relation to what was desired yesterday. Outcomes do flow in part from goals. But goals flow from outcomes as well, and both goals and outcomes also move independently. . . .

One basic response to the ambiguities of success is to find pleasure in the process of presidential life. A reasonable man will seek reminders of his relevance and success. Where those reminders are hard to find in terms of socially validated outcomes unambiguously due to one's actions, they may be sought in the interactions of organizational life. George Reedy (1970) made a similar observation about a different presidency: "Those who seek to lighten the burdens of the presidency by easing the workload do no occupant of that office a favor. The 'workload'—especially the ceremonial work load—are the only events of a president's day which make life endurable."

Leader Response to Anarchy

The ambiguities that college presidents face describe the life of any formal leader of any organized anarchy. The metaphors of leadership and our traditions of personalizing history (even the minor histories of collegiate institutions) confuse the issues of leadership by ignoring the basic ambiguity of leadership life. We require a plausible basic perspective for the leader of a loosely coupled, ambiguous organization.

Such a perspective begins with humility. It is probably a mistake for a college president to imagine that what he does in office affects significantly either the long-run position of the institution or his reputation as a president. So long as he does not violate some rather obvious restrictions on his behavior, his reputation and his term of office are more likely to be affected by broad social events or by the unpredictable viscissitudes of official responsibility than by his actions. . . .

In this respect the president's life does not differ markedly from that of most of us. A leadership role, however, is distinguished by the numerous temptations to self-importance that it provides. Presidents easily come to believe that they can continue in office forever if they are only clever or perceptive or responsive enough. They easily come to exaggerate the significance of their daily actions for the college as well as for themselves. They easily come to see each day as an opportunity to build support in their constituencies for the next "election." . . .

The major consequence of a heroic conception of the consequences of action is a distrust of judgment. When college presidents imagine that their actions have great consequences for the world, they are inclined to fear an error. When they fear an error, they are inclined to seek social support for their judgment, to confuse voting with virtue and bureaucratic rules with equity. Such a conception of the importance of their every choice makes presidents vulnerable to the same deficiencies of performance that afflict the parents of first children and inexperienced teachers, lovers, or counselors.

A lesser, but important, result of a heroic conception of the consequences of action is the abandonment of pleasure. By acceding to his own importance, the college president is driven to sobriety of manner. For reasons we have detailed earlier, he has difficulty in establishing the correctness of his actions by exhibiting their consequences. He is left with the necessity of communicating moral intent through facial intensity. At the same time, he experiences the substantial gap between his aspirations and his possibilities. Both by the requirements of their public face and by their own intolerant expectations, college presidents often find the public enjoyment of their job denied to them.

The ambiguities of leadership in an organized anarchy require a leadership posture that is somewhat different from that implicit in most discussions of the college presidency. In particular, we believe that a college president is, on the whole, better advised to think of himself as trying to do good than as trying to satisfy a political or bureaucratic audience; better advised to define his role in terms of the modest part he can play in making the college slightly better in the long run than in terms of satisfying current residents or solving current problems. He requires an enthusiam for a Tolstoyan view of history and for the freedom of individual action that such a view entails. Since the world is absurd, the president's primary responsibility is to virtue.

Presidents occupy a minor part in the lives of a small number of people. They have some power, but little magic. They can act with a fair degree of confidence that if they make a mistake, it will not matter much. They can be allowed the heresy of believing that pleasure is consistent with virtue.

The Elementary Tactics of Administrative Action

The tactics of administrative action in an organized anarchy are somewhat different from the tactics of action in a situation characterized by clearer goals, better specified technology, and more persistent participation. Nevertheless, we can examine how a leader with a purpose can operate within an organization that is without one. . . .

As we will indicate later in this chapter, a conception of leadership that merely assumes that the college president should act to accomplish what he wants to accomplish is too narrow. A major part of his responsibility is to lead the organization to a changing and more complex view of itself by treating goals as only partly knowable. Nevertheless, the problems of inducing a college to do what one wants it to do are clearly worthy of attention. If presidents and others are to function effectively within the college, they need to recognize the ways in which the character of the college as a system for exercising problems, making decisions, and certifying status conditions their attempts to influence the outcome of any decision.

We can identify five major properties of decision making in organized anarchies that are of substantial importance to the tactics of accomplishing things in colleges and universities:

1. Most issues most of the time have *low salience* for most people. The decisions to be made within the organization secure only partial and erratic attention from participants in the organization. A major share of the attention devoted to a particular issue is tied less to the content of the issue than to its symbolic significance for individual and group esteem.

2. The total system has *high inertia*. Anything that requires a coordinated effort of the organization in order to start is unlikely to be started. Anything that requires a coordinated effort of the organization in order to be stopped is unlikely to be stopped.

3. Any decision can become a *garbage can* for almost any problem. The issues discussed in the context of any particular decision depend less on the decision or problems involved than on the timing of their joint arrivals and the existence of alternative arenas for exercising problems.

4. The processes of choice are easily subject to *overload*. When the load on the system builds up relative to its capacities for exercising and resolving problems, the decision outcomes in the organization tend to become increasingly separated from the formal process of decision.

5. The organization has a *weak information base*. Information about past events or past decisions is often not retained. When retained, it is often difficult to retrieve. Information about current activities is scant.

These properties are conspicuous and ubiquitous. They represent some important ways in which all organizations sometimes, and an organization like a university often, present opportunities for tactical action that in a modest way strengthen the hand of the participant who attends them. We suggest eight basic tactical rules for use by those who seek to influence the course of decisions in universities or colleges.

Rule 1: Spend time. The kinds of decision-making situations and organizations we have described suffer from a shortage of decision-making energy. Energy is a scarce resource. If one is in a position to devote time to the decision-making activities within the organization, he has a considerable claim on the system. Most organizations develop ways of absorbing the decision-making energy provided by sharply deviant participants; but within moderate boundaries, a person who is willing to spend time finds himself in a strong position for at least three significant reasons:

• By providing a scarce resource (energy), he lays the basis for a claim. If he is willing to spend time, he can expect more tolerant consideration of the problems he considers important. One of the most common organizational responses to a proposal from a participant is the request that he head a committee to do something about it. This behavior is an acknowledgement both of the energy-poor situation and of the price the organization pays for participation. That price is often that the organization must allow the participant some significant control over the definition of problems to be considered relevant.[1]

• By spending time on the homework for a decision, he becomes a major information source in an information-poor world. At the limit, the information provided need have no particular evidential validity. Consider, for example, the common assertions in college decision-making processes about what some constituency (e.g., board of trustees, legislature, student body, ethnic group) is "thinking." The assertions are rarely based on defensible evidence, but they tend to become organizational facts by virtue of the shortage of serious information. More generally, reality for a decision is specified by those willing to spend the time required to collect the small amounts of information available, to review the factual assertions of others, and to disseminate their findings.

• By investing more of his time in organizational concerns, he increases his chance of being present when something important to him is considered. A participant who wishes to pursue other matters (e.g., study, research, family, the problems of the outside world) reduces the number of occasions for decision making to which he can afford to attend. A participant who can spend time can be involved in more arenas. Since it is often difficult to anticipate when and where a particular issue will be involved (and thus to limit one's attention to key times and domains), the simple frequency of availability is relatively important.

Rule 2: Persist. It is a mistake to assume that if a particular proposal has been rejected by an organization today, it will be rejected tomorrow. Different sets of people and concerns will be reflected each time a problem is considered or a proposal discussed. We noted earlier the ways in which the flow of participants leads to a flow of organizational concerns.[2] The specific combination of sentiments and people that is associated with a specific choice opportunity is partly fortuitous, and Fortune may be more considerate another day.

For the same reason, it is a mistake to assume that today's victory will be implemented automatically tomorrow. The distinction between decision making and decision implementation is usually a false one. Decisions are not "made" once and for all. Rather they happen as a result of a series of episodes involving different people in different settings, and they may be unmade or modified by subsequent episodes. The participant who spends much time celebrating his victory ordinarily can expect to find the victory short-lived. The loser who spends his time weeping rather than reintroducing his ideas will persistently have something to weep about. The loser who persists in a variety of contexts is frequently rewarded.

Rule 3: Exchange status for substance. As we have indicated, the specific substantive issues in a college, or similar organization, typically have low salience for participants. A quite typical situation is one in which significant numbers of participants and groups of participants care less about the specific substantive outcome than they do about the implications of that outcome for their own sense of self-esteem and the social recognition of their importance. Such an ordering of things is neither surprising nor normatively unattractive. It would be a strange world indeed if the mostly minor issues of university governance, for example, became more important to most people than personal and group esteem.

A college president, too, is likely to become substantially concerned with the formal acknowledgment of office. Since it is awkward for him to establish definitively that he is substantively important, the president tends to join other participants in seeking symbolic confirmation of his significance.

The esteem trap is understandable but unfortunate. College presidents who can forgo at least some of the pleasures of self-importance in order to trade status for substance are in a strong position. Since leaders receive credit for many things over which they have little control and to which they contribute little, they should find it possible to accomplish some of the things they want by allowing others to savor the victories, enjoy the pleasures of involvement, and receive the profits of public importance.

Rule 4: Facilitate opposition participation. The high inertia of organizations and the heavy dependence of organizational events on processes outside of the control of the organization make organizational power ambiguous. Presidents sense their lack of control despite their position of authority, status, and concern. Most people who participate in university decision making sense a disappointment with the limited control their position provides.

Persons outside the formal ranks of authority tend to see authority as providing more control. Their aspirations for change tend to be substantially greater than the aspirations for change held by persons with formal authority. One obvious solution is to facilitate participation in decision making. Genuine authoritative participation will reduce the aspirations of oppositional leaders. In an organization characterized by high inertia and low salience it is unwise to allow beliefs about the feasibility of planned action to outrun reality. From this point of view, public accountability, participant observation, and other techniques for extending the range of legitimate participation in the decision-making processes of the organization are essential means of keeping the aspirations of occasional actors within bounds. Since most people most of the time do not participate much, their aspirations for what can be done have a tendency to drift away from reality. On the whole, the direct involvement of dissident groups in the decision-making process is a more effective depressant of exaggerated aspirations than is a lecture by the president.

Rule 5: Overload the system. As we have suggested, the style of decision making changes when the load exceeds the capabilities of the system. Since we are talking about energy-poor organizations, accomplishing overload is not hard. In practical terms, this means having a large repertoire of projects for organizational action; it means making substantial claims on resources for the analysis of problems, discussion of issues, and political negotiation.

Within an organized anarchy it is a mistake to become absolutely committed to any one project. There are innumerable ways in which the processes we have described will confound the cleverest behavior with respect to any single proposal, however imaginative or subjectively important. What such processes cannot do is cope with large numbers of projects. Someone with the habit of producing many proposals, without absolute commitment to any one, may lose any one of them (and it is hard to predict a priori which one), but cannot be stopped on everything. . . .

Rule 6: Provide garbage cans. One of the complications in accomplishing something in a garbage can decision-making process is the tendency for any particular project to become intertwined with a variety of other issues simply because those issues exist at the time the project is before the organization. A proposal for curricular reform becomes an arena for a concern for social justice. A proposal for construction of a building becomes an arena for concerns about environmental quality. A proposal for bicycle paths becomes an arena for discussion of sexual inequality.

It is pointless to try to react to such problems by attempting to enforce rules of relevance. Such rules are, in any event, highly arbitrary.

Even if they were not, it would still be difficult to persuade a person that his problem (however important) could not be discussed because it is not relevant to the current agenda. The appropriate tactical response is to provide garbage cans into which wide varieties of problems can be dumped. The more conspicuous the can, the more garbage it will attract away from other projects.

The prime procedure for making a garbage can attractive is to give it precedence and conspicuousness. On a grand scale, discussions of overall organizational objectives or overall organizational long-term plans are classic first-quality cans. They are general enough to accommodate anything. They are socially defined as being important. They attract enough different kinds of issues to reinforce their importance. An activist will push for discussions of grand plans (in part) in order to draw the garbage away from the concrete day-to-day arenas of his concrete objectives.

On a smaller scale, the first item on a meeting agenda is an obvious garbage can. It receives much of the status allocation concerns that are a part of meetings. It is possible that any item on an agenda will attract an assortment of things currently concerning individuals in the group; but the first item is more vulnerable than others. As a result, projects of serious substantive concern should normally be placed somewhat later, after the important matters of individual and group esteem have been settled, most of the individual performances have been completed, and most of the enthusiasm for abstract argument has waned.

The garbage can tactic has long-term effects that may be important. Although in the short run the major consequence is to remove problems from the arena of short-term concrete proposals, the separation of problem discussion from decision making means that general organizational attitudes develop outside the context of immediate decisions. The exercise of problems and the discussion of plans contribute to building of the climate within which the organization will operate in the future. . . .

Rule 7: Manage unobtrusively.   If you put a man in a boat and tell him to plot a course, he can take one of three views of his task. He can float with the currents and winds, letting them take him wherever they wish; he can select a destination and try to use full power to go directly to it regardless of the current or winds; or he can select a destination and use his rudder and sails to let the currents and wind eventually take him where *he* wants to go. On the whole, we think conscious university leadership is properly seen in third light. . . .

Unobtrusive management uses interventions of greater impact than visibilty. Such actions generally have two key attributes: (1) They affect many parts of the system slightly rather than a few parts in a major way. The effect on any one part of the system is small enough so that either no one really notices or no one finds it sensible to organize significantly against the intervention. (2) Once activated, they stay activated without further organizational attention. Their deactivation requires positive organizational action. . . .

Major bureaucratic interventions lie in the ordinary systems of accounting and managerial controls. Such devices are often condemned in academic circles as both dreary and inhibiting. Their beauty lies in the way in which they extend throughout the system and in the high degree of arbitrariness they exhibit. For example, students of business have observed that many important aspects of business life are driven by accounting rules. What are costs? What are profits? How are costs and profits allocated among activities and subunits? Answers to such questions are far from arbitrary. But they have enough elements of arbitrariness that no reasonable business manager would ignore the potential contribution of accounting rules to profitability. The flow of investments, the utilization of labor, and the structure of organization all respond to the organization of accounts.

The same thing is true in a college or university, although the process works in a somewhat different way because the convenient single index of business accounting, profit, is denied the university executive. Universities and colleges have official facts (accounting facts) with respect to student activities, faculty activities, and space utilization. In recent years such accounting facts have increased in importance as colleges and universities struggled first with the baby boom and now with fiscal adversity. These official facts enter into reports and filter into decisions made throughout the system. As a typical simple example, consider the impact of changing the accounting for faculty teaching load from number of courses to student credit hours taught. Or, consider the impact of separating in accounting reports the teaching of language (number of students, cost of faculty) from the teaching literature in that language at a typical American university. Or, consider the impact of making each major subunit in a university purchase services (e. g., duplication services, computer services, library services) at prices somewhat different from the current largely arbitrary prices. Or, consider the consequences of allowing transfer of funds from one major budget line to another within a subunit at various possible discount rates depending on the lines and the point in the budget year. Or, consider the effect of having students pay as part of their fees an amount determined by the department offering the instruction, with the amount thus paid returning to the department.

Rule 8: Interpret history.   In an organization in which most issues have low salience, and information about events in the system is poorly maintained, definitions of what is happening and what has happened become important tactical instruments. If people in the organization cared more about what happened (or is happening), the constraints on the tactic would be great. Histories would be challenged and carefully monitored. If people in the organization accepted more openly the idea that much of the decision-making process is a status-certifying rather than a choice-making system, there would be less dependence on historical interpretation. The actual situation, however, provides a tactically optimal situation. On the one hand, the genuine interest in keeping a good record of what happened (in substantive rather than status terms) is minimal. On the other hand, the belief in the relevance of history, or the legitimacy of history as a basis for current action, is fairly strong.

Minutes should be written long enough after the event as to legitimize the reality of forgetfulness. They should be written in such a way as to lay the basis for subsequent independent action—in the name of the collective action. In general, participants in the organization should be assisted in their desire to have unambiguous actions taken today derived from the ambiguous decisions of yesterday with a minimum of pain to their images of organizational rationality and a minimum of claims on their time. The model of consistency is maintained by a creative resolution of uncertainty about the past.

Presidents and Tactics

As we observed at the outset, practical tactics, if they are genuine, will inevitably be viewed as somewhat cynical. We will, however, record our own sentiments that the cynicism lies in the eye of the beholder. Our sympathies and enthusiasm are mostly for the invisible members of an organized anarchy who make such tactics possible. We refer, of course, to the majority of participants in colleges and universities who have the good sense to see that what can be achieved through tactical manipulation of the university is only occasionally worth their time and effort. The validity of the tactics is a tribute to their reluctance to clutter the important elements of life with organizational matters. The tactics are available for anyone who wants to use them. Most of us most of the time have more interesting things to do.

But presidents, as full-time actors generally occupying the best job of their lives, are less likely to have more interesting things to do. In addition, these tactics, with their low visibility and their emphasis on the trading of credit and recognition for accomplishment, will not serve the interests of a president out to glorify himself or increase his chances to be one of the very few who move up to a second and ''better'' presidency. Instead, they provide an opportunity chiefly for those who have some conception of what might make their institution better, more interesting, more complex, or more educational, and are satisfied to end their tenures believing that they helped to steer their institutions slightly closer to those remote destinations.

The Technology of Foolishness

The tactics for moving an organization when objectives are clear represent important parts of the repertoire of an organizational leader.[3] Standard prescriptions properly honor intention, choice, and action; and college presidents often have things they want to accomplish. Nevertheless, a college president may sometimes want to confront the realities of ambiguity more directly and reconsider the standard dicta of leadership. He may want to examine particularly the place of purpose in intelligent behavior and the role of foolishness in leadership.

Choice and Rationality

The concept of choice as a focus for interpreting and guiding human behavior has rarely had an easy time in the realm of ideas. It is beset by theological disputations over free will, by the dilemmas of absurdism, by the doubts of psychological behaviorism, and by the claims of historical, economic, social, and demographic determinism. Nevertheless, the idea that humans make choices has proved robust enough to become a matter of faith in important segments of contemporary Western civilization. It is a faith that is professed by virtually all theories of social policy making.

The major tenents of this faith run something like this:

Human beings make choices. Choices are properly made by evaluating alternatives in terms of goals and on the basis of information currently available. The alternative that is most attractive in terms of the goals is chosen. By using the technology of choice, we can improve the quality of the search for alternatives, the quality of information, and the quality of the analysis used to evaluate alternatives. Although actual choice may fall short of this ideal in various ways, it is an attractive model of how choices should be made by individuals, organizations, and social systems. . . .

Our cultural ideas of intelligence and our theories of choice display a substantial resemblance. In particular, they share three conspicuous interrelated ideas:

The first idea is the *preexistence of purpose.* We find it natural to base an interpretation of human-choice behavior on a presumption of human purpose. We have, in fact, invented one of the most elaborate terminologies in the professional literature: "values," "needs," "wants," "goods," "tastes," "preferences," "utility," "objectives," "goals," "aspirations," "drives." All of these reflect a strong tendency to believe that a useful interpretation of human behavior involves defining a set of objectives that (1) are prior attributes of the system, and (2) make the observed behavior in some sense intelligent vis-à-vis those objectives. . . .

The second idea is the *necessity of consistency.* We have come to recognize consistency both as an important property of human behavior and as a prerequisite for normative models of choice. Dissonance theory, balance theory, theories of congruency in attitudes, statuses, and performances have all served to remind us of the possibilities for interpreting human behavior in terms of the consistency requirements of a limited-capacity, information-processing system.

At the same time, consistency is a cultural and theoretical virtue. Action should be consistent with belief. Actions taken by different parts of an organization should be consistent with each other. Individual and organizational activities are seen as connected with each other in terms of their consequences for some consistent set of purposes. In an organization, the structural manifestion of consistency is the hierarchy with its obligations of coordination and control. In the individual, the structural

manifestation is a set of values that generates a consistent preference ordering.

The third idea is the *primacy of rationality.* By rationality we mean a procedure for deciding what is correct behavior by relating consequences systematically to objectives. By placing primary emphasis on rational techniques, we have implicitly rejected—or seriously impaired—two other procedures for choice: (1) the processes of intuition, through which people do things without fully understanding why; and (2) the processes of tradition and faith, through which people do things because that is the way they are done. . . .

These ideas are obviously deeply embedded in the culture. Their roots extend into ideas that have conditioned much of modern Western history and interpretations of that history. Their general acceptance is probably highly correlated with the permeation of rationalism and individualism into the style of thinking within the culture. The ideas are even more obviously embedded in modern theories of choice. It is fundamental to those theories that thinking should precede action; that action should serve a purpose; that purpose should be defined in terms of a consistent set of preexistent goals; and that choice should be based on a consistent theory of the relation between action and its consequences. . . .

The Problem of Goals

The tools of intelligence as they are fashioned in modern theories of choice are necessary to any reasonable behavior in contemporary society. It is inconceivable that we would fail to continue their development, refinement, and extension. As might be expected, however, a theory and ideology of choice built on the ideas outlined above is deficient in some obvious, elementary ways, most conspicuously in the treatment of human goals.

Goals are thrust upon the intelligent man. We ask that he act in the name of goals. We ask that he keep his goals consistent. We ask that his actions be oriented to his goals. We ask that a social system amalgamate individual goals into a collective goal. But we do not concern ourselves with the origin of goals. Theories of individual, organizational, and social choice assume actors with preexistent values. . . .

The conscious introduction of goal discovery for consideration in theories of human choice is not unknown to modern man. For example, we have two kinds of theories of choice behavior in human beings. One is a theory of children. The other is a theory of adults. In the theory of children, we emphasize choices as leading to experiences that develop the child's scope, his complexity, his awareness of the world. As parents, teachers, or psychologists, we try to lead the child to do things that are inconsistent with his present goals because we know (or believe) that he can develop into an interesting person only by coming to appreciate aspects of experience that he initially rejects.

In the theory of adults, we emphasize choices as a consequence of our intentions. As adults, educational decision makers, or economists, we try to take actions that (within the limits of scarce resources) come as close as possible to achieving our goals. We try to find improved ways of making decisions consistent with our perceptions of what is valuable in the world.

The asymmetry in these models is conspicuous. Adults have constructed a model world in which adults know what is good for themselves, but children do not. It is hard to react positively to the conceit. The asymmetry has, in fact, stimulated a large number of ideologies and reforms designed to allow children the same moral prerogative granted to adults— the right to imagine that they know what they want. The efforts have cut deeply into traditional childrearing, traditional educational policies, traditional politics, and traditional consumer economics.

In our judgment, the asymmetry between models of choice for adults and for children is awkward; but the solution we have adopted is precisely wrong-headed. Instead of trying to adapt the model of adults to children, we might better adapt the model of children to adults. For many purposes, our model of children is better. Of course, children know what they want. Everyone does. The critical question is whether they are encouraged to develop more interesting "wants." Values change. People become more interesting as those values and the interconnections made among them change. . . .

Introducing ambiguity and fluidity to the interpretation of individual, organizational, and societal goals obviously has implications for behavioral theories of decision making. . . . The main point here, however, is not to consider how we might describe the behavior of systems that are discovering goals as they act. Rather it is to examine how we might improve the quality of that behavior, how we might aid the development of interesting goals.

We know how to advise a society, an organization, or an individual if we are first given a consistent set of preferences. Under some conditions, we can suggest how to make decisions if the preferences are consistent only up to the point of specifying a series of independent constraints on the choice. But what about a normative theory of goal-finding behavior? What do we say when our client tells us that he is not sure his present set of values is the set of values in terms of which he wants to act? . . .

Within the context of normative theory of choice as it exists, the answer we give is: First determine the values, then act. The advice is frequently useful. Moreover, we have developed ways in which we can use conventional techniques for decision analysis to help discover value premises and to expose value inconsistencies. These techniques involve testing the decision implications of some successive approximations to a set of preferences. The object is to find a consistent set of preferences with implications that are acceptable to the person or organization making the decisions. Variations on such techniques are used routinely in operations research, as well as in personal counseling and analysis. . . .

Perhaps we should explore a somewhat different approach to the normative question of how we ought to behave when our value premises are not yet (and never will be) fully determined. Suppose we treat action as a way of creating interesting goals at the same time as we treat goals as a way of justifying action.

It is an intuitively plausible and simple idea, but one that is not immediately within the domain of standard normative theories of intelligent choice.

Interesting people and interesting organizations construct complicated theories of themselves. To do this, they need to supplement the technology of reason with a technology of foolishness. Individuals and organizations sometimes need ways of doing things for which they have no good reason. They need to act before they think.

Sensible Foolishness

To use intelligent choice as a planned occasion for discovering new goals, we require some idea of sensible foolishness. Which of the many foolish things that we might do now will lead to attractive value consequences? The question is almost inconceivable. Not only does it ask us to predict the value of consequences of action, it asks us to evaluate them. In what terms can we talk about "good" changes in goals? . . .

As we challenge the dogma of preexistent goals, we will be forced to reexamine some of our most precious prejudices: the strictures against imitation, coercion, and rationalization. Each of those honorable prohibitions depends on the view of man and human choice imposed on us by conventional theories of choice.

Imitation is not necessarily a sign of moral weakness. It is a prediction. It is a prediction that if we duplicate the behavior or attitudes of someone else, not only will we fare well in terms of current goals but the chances of our discovering attractive new goals for ourselves are relatively high. If imitation is to be normatively attractive, we need a better theory of who should be imitated. Such a theory seems to be eminently feasible. For example, what are the conditions for effectiveness of a rule that one should imitate another person whose values are close to one's own? How do the chances of discovering interesting goals through imitation change as the number of people exhibiting the behavior to be imitated increases? In the case of the college president we might ask what the goal discovery consequences are of imitating the choices of those at institutions more prestigious than one's own, and whether there are other more desirable patterns of imitation.

Coercion is not necessarily an assault on individual autonomy. It can be a device for stimulating individuality. We recognize this when we talk about education or about parents and children. What has been difficult with coercion is the possibility for perversion, not its obvious capability for stimulating change. We need a theory of the circumstances under which entry into a coercive relationship produces behavior that leads to the discovery of interesting goals. We are all familiar with the tactic. College presidents use it in imposing deadlines, entering contracts, making commitments. What are the conditions for its effective use? In particular, what are the conditions for goal-fostering coercion in social systems?

Rationalization is not necessarily a way of evading morality. It can be a test for the feasibility of a goal change. When deciding among alternative actions for which we have no good reason, it may be sensible to develop some definition of how "near" to intelligence alternative "unintelligent" actions lie. Effective rationalization permits this kind of incremental approach to changes in values. To use it effectively, however, we require a better idea of the metrics that might be possible in measuring value distances. At the same time, rationalization is the major procedure for integrating newly discovered goals into an existing structure of values. It provides the organization of complexity without which complexity itself becomes indistinguishable from randomness.

The dangers in imitation, coercion, and rationalization are too familiar to elaborate. We should, indeed, be able to develop better techniques. Whatever those techniques may be, however, they will almost certainly undermine the superstructure of biases erected on purpose, consistency, and rationality. They will involve some way of thinking about action now as occurring in terms of a set of future values different from those that the actor currently holds.

Play and Reason

A second requirement for a technology of foolishness is some strategy for suspending rational imperatives toward consistency. Even if we know which of several foolish things we want to do, we still need a mechanism for allowing us to do it. How do we escape the logic of our reason?

Here we are closer to understanding what we need. It is playfulness. Playfulness is the deliberate, temporary relaxation of rules in order to explore the possibilities of alternative rules. When we are playful, we challenge the necessity of consistency. In effect, we announce—in advance—our rejection of the usual objections to behavior that does not fit the standard model of intelligence.

Playfulness allows experimentation at the same time that it acknowledges reason. It accepts an obligation that at some point either the playful behavior will be stopped or it will be integrated into the structure of intelligence in some way that makes sense. The suspension of the rules is temporary. . . .

Playfulness is a natural outgrowth of our standard view of reason. A strict insistence on purpose, consistency, and rationality limits our ability to find new purposes. Play relaxes that insistence to allow us to act "unintelligently" or "irrationally" or "foolishly" to explore alternative ideas of purposes and alternative concepts of behavioral consistency. And it does this while maintaining our basic commitment to intelligence.

Although play and reason are in this way functional complements, they are often behavioral competitors. They are alternative styles and alternative orientations to the same situation. There is no guarantee that the styles will be equally well developed, that all individuals, organizations, or societies will be equally adept in both styles; or that all cultures will be sufficiently encouraging to both.

Our design problem is either to specify the best mix of styles or, failing that, to assure that most people and most organizations most of the time use an alternation of strategies rather than persevering in either one. It is a difficult problem. The optimization problem looks extremely complex on the face of it, and the learning situations that will produce alternation in behavior appear to be somewhat less common than those that produce perseverance.

Consider, for example, the difficulty of sustaining playfulness as a style within contemporary American society. Individuals who are good at consistent rationality are rewarded early and heavily. We define consistent rationality as intelligence, and the educational rewards of society are associated strongly with it. Social norms press in the same direction, particularly for men. "Changing one's mind" is viewed as feminine and undesirable. Politicians and other leaders will go to enormous lengths to avoid admitting an inconsistency. Many demands of modern organizational life reinforce the same rational abilities and preferences for a style of unchanging purposes.

The result is that many of the most influential and best-educated citizens have experienced a powerful overlearning with respect to rationality. They are exceptionally good at maintaining consistent pictures of themselves, of relating action to purposes. They are exceptionally poor at a playful attitude toward their own beliefs, toward the logic of consistency, or toward the way they see things as being connected in the world. The dictates of manliness, forcefulness, independence, and intelligence are intolerant of playful urges if they arise. The playful urges that arise are weak ones, scarcely discernible in the behavior of most businessmen, mayors, or college presidents.

The picture is probably overdrawn, but we believe that the implications are not. Reason and intelligence have had the unnecessary consequence of inhibiting the development of purpose into more complicated forms of consistency. To move away from that position, we need to find some ways of helping individuals and organizations to experiment with doing things for which they have no good reason, to be playful with their conceptions of themselves. We suggest five things as a small beginning:

First, we can treat *goals as hypotheses*. Conventional theories of decision making allow us to entertain doubts about almost everything except the thing about which we frequently have the greatest doubt—our objectives. Suppose we define the decision-making process as a time for the sequential testing of hypotheses about goals. If we can experiment with alternative goals, we stand some chance of discovering complicated and interesting combinations of good values that none of us previously imagined.

Second, we can treat *intuition as real*. We do not know what intuition is or even if it is any one thing. Perhaps it is simply an excuse for doing something we cannot justify in terms of present values or for refusing to follow the logic of our own beliefs. Perhaps it is an inexplicable way of consulting that part of our intelligence and knowledge of the world that is not organized in a way anticipated by standard theories of choice. In either case, intuition permits us to see some possible actions that are outside our present scheme for justifying behavior.

Third, we can treat *hypocrisy as a transition*. Hypocrisy is an inconsistency between expressed values and behavior. Negative attitudes about hypocrisy stem mainly from a general onus against inconsistency and from a sentiment against combining the pleasures of vice with the appearance of virtue. It seems to us that a bad man with good intentions may be a man experimenting with the possibility of becoming good. Somehow it seems more sensible to encourage the experimentation than to insult it.

Fourth, we can treat *memory as an enemy*. The rules of consistency and rationality require a technology of memory. For most purposes, good memories make good choices. But the ability to forget or overlook is also useful. If you do not know what you did yesterday or what other people in the organization are doing today, you can act within the system of reason and still do things that are foolish.

Fifth, we can treat *experience as a theory*. Learning can be viewed as a series of conclusions based on concepts of action and consequences that we have invented. Experience can be changed retrospectively. By changing our interpretive concepts now, we modify what we learned earlier. Thus we expose the possibility of experimenting with alternative histories. The usual strictures against "self-deception" in experience need occasionally to be tempered with an awareness of the extent to which all experience is an interpretation subject to conscious revision. Personal histories and national histories need to be rewritten continuously as a base for the retrospective learning of new self-conceptions.

If we knew more about the normative theory of acting before thinking, we could say more intelligent things about the functions of management and leadership when organizations or societies do not know what they are doing. Consider, for example, the following general implications.

First, we need to reexamine the functions of management decision making. One of the primary ways in which the goals of an organization are developed is by interpreting the decisions it makes, and one feature of good managerial decisions is that they lead to the development of more interesting value premises for the organization. As a result, decisions should not be seen as flowing directly or strictly from a preexistent set of objectives. College presidents who make decisions might well view that function somewhat less as a process of deduction or a process of political negotiation, and somewhat more as a process of gently upsetting preconceptions of what the organization is doing.

Second, we need a modified view of planning. Planning can often be more effective as an interpretation of past decisions than as a program for future ones. It can be used as a part of the efforts of the organization to develop a new consistent theory of itself that incorporates the mix of recent actions into a moderately comprehensive structure of goals. Procedures for interpreting the meaning of most past events are familiar to the memoirs of retired generals, prime ministers, business leaders, and movie stars. They suffer from the company they keep. In an organization that wants to continue to develop new objectives, a manager needs to be tolerant of the idea that he will discover the meaning of yesterday's action in the experiences and interpretations of today.

Third, we need to reconsider evaluation. As nearly as we can determine, there is nothing in a formal theory of evaluation that requires that criteria be specified in advance. In particular, the evaluation of social experiments need not be in terms of the degree to which they have fulfilled our prior expectations. Rather we can examine what they did in terms of what we now believe to be important. The prior specification of criteria and the prior specification of evaluational procedures that depend on such criteria are common presumptions that inhibit the serendipitous discovery of new criteria. Experience should be used explicitly as an occasion for evaluating our values as well as our actions.

Fourth, we need a reconsideration of social accountability. Individual preferences and social action need to be consistent in some way. But the process of pursuing consistency is one in which both the preferences and the actions change over time. Imagination in social policy formation involves systematically adapting to and influencing preference. It would be unfortunate if our theories of social action encouraged leaders to ignore their responsibilities for anticipating public preferences through action and for providing social experiences that modify individual expectations.

Fifth, we need to accept playfulness in social organizations. The design of organizations should attend to the problems of maintaining both playfulness and reason as aspects of intelligent choice. Since much of the literature on social design is concerned with strengthening the rationality of decision making, managers are likely to overlook the importance of play. This is partly a matter of making the individuals within an organization more playful by encouraging the attitudes and skills of inconsistency. It is also a matter of making organizational structure and organizational procedures more playful. Organizations can be playful even when the participants in them are not. The managerial devices for maintaining consistency can be varied. We encourage organizational play by insisting on some temporary relief from control, coordination, and communication.

Presidents and Foolishness

Contemporary theories of decision making and the technology of reason have considerably strengthened our capabilities for effective social action. The conversion of the simple ideas of choice into an extensive technology is a major achievement. It is, however, an achievement that has reinforced some biases in the underlying models of choice in individuals and groups. In particular, it has reinforced the uncritical acceptance of a static interpretation of human goals.

There is little magic in the world, and foolishness in people and organizations is one of the many things that fail to produce miracles. Under certain conditions, it is one of several ways in which some of the problems of our current theories of intelligence can be overcome. It may be a good way, for it preserves the virtues of consistency while stimulating change. If we had a good technology of foolishness, it might (in combination with the technology of reason) help in a small way to develop the unusual combinations of attitudes and behaviors that describe the interesting people, interesting organizations, and interesting societies of the world. The contribution of a college president may often be measured by his capacity for sustaining that creative interaction of foolishness and rationality.

Notes

1. For a discussion of this point in the context of public school decision making, see Stephen Weiner (1972).
2. For a discussion of the same phenomenon in a business setting, see R. M. Cyert and J. G. March (1963).
3. These ideas have been the basis for extended conversation with a number of friends. We want to acknowledge particularly the help of Lance Bennett, Patricia Nelson Bennett, Michael Butler, Søren Christensen, Michel Crozier, Claude Faucheux, James R. Glenn, Jr., Gudmund Hernes, Helga Hernes, Jean Carter Lave, Harold J. Leavitt, Henry M. Levin, Leslie Lincoln, André

Massart, John Miller, Johan Olsen, Richard C. Snyder, Alexander Szalai, Eugene J. Webb, and Gail Whitacre.

References

CYERT, RICHARD M., & JAMES G. MARCH: *A Behavioral Theory of the Firm,* Prentice-Hall, Inc., Englewood Cliffs, N.J., 1963.

LONG, NORTON A.: "The Local Community as an Ecology of Games," *American Journal of Sociology,* vol. 44, pp. 251–261, 1958.

REEDY, GEORGE E.: *The Twilight of the Presidency,* The World Publishing Company, New York, 1970.

WEINER, STEPHEN S.: "Educational Decisions in an Organized Anarchy," Ph.D. dissertation, Stanford University, Stanford, Calif., 1972.

40

Power Failure in Management Circuits

Rosabeth Moss Kanter

Power is America's last dirty word. It is easier to talk about money—and much easier to talk about sex—than it is to talk about power. People who have it deny it; people who want it do not want to appear to hunger for it; and people who engage in its machinations do so secretly.

Yet, because it turns out to be a critical element in effective managerial behavior, power should come out from undercover. Having searched for years for those styles or skills that would identify capable organization leaders, many analysts, like myself, are rejecting individual traits or situational appropriateness as key and finding the sources of a leader's real power.

Access to resources and information and the ability to act quickly make it possible to accomplish more and to pass on more resources and information to subordinates. For this reason, people tend to prefer bosses with "clout." When employees perceive their manager as influential upward and outward, their status is enhanced by association and they generally have high morale and feel less critical or resistent to their boss.[1] More powerful leaders are also more likely to delegate (they are too busy to do it all themselves), to reward talent, and to build a team that places subordinates in significant positions.

Powerlessness, in contrast, tends to breed bossiness rather than true leadership. In large

organizations, at least, it is powerlessness that often creates ineffective, desultory management and petty, dictatorial, rules-minded managerial styles. Accountability without power—responsibility for results without the resources to get them—creates frustration and failure. People who see themselves as weak and powerless and find their subordinates resisting or discounting them tend to use more punishing forms of influence. If organizational power can "ennoble," then, recent research shows, organizational powerlessness can (with apologies to Lord Acton) "corrupt."[2]

So perhaps power, in the organization at least, does not deserve such a bad reputation. Rather than connoting only dominance, control, and oppression, *power* can mean efficacy and capacity—something managers and executives need to move the organization toward its goals. Power in organizations is analogous in simple terms to physical power: it is the ability to mobilize resources (human and material) to get things done. The true sign of power, then, is accomplishment—not fear, terror, or tyranny. Where power is "on," the system can be productive; where the power is "off," the system bogs down.

But saying that people need power to be effective in organizations does not tell us where it comes from or why some people, in some jobs, systematically seem to have more of it than others. In this article I want to show that to discover the sources of productive power, we have to look not at the *person*—as conventional classifications of effective managers and employees do—but at the *position* the person occupies in the organization.

Where Does Power Come From?

The effectiveness that power brings evolves from two kinds of capacities: first, access to the resources, information, and support necessary to carry out a task; and, second, ability to get cooperation in doing what is necessary. (Figure 1 identifies some symbols of an individual manager's power.)

Both capacities derive not so much from a leader's style and skill as from his or her location in the formal and informal systems of the organization—in both job definition and connection to other important people in the company. Even the ability to get cooperation from subordinates is strongly defined by the manager's clout outward. People are more responsive to bosses who look as if they can get more for them from the organization.

We can regard the uniquely organizational sources of power as consisting of three "lines":

1. Lines of Supply. Influence outward, over the environment, means that managers have the capacity to bring in the things that their own organizational domain needs—materials, money, resources to distribute as rewards, and perhaps even prestige.

2. Lines of Information. To be effective, managers need to be "in the know" in both the formal and the informal sense.

3. Lines of Support. In a formal framework, a manager's job parameters need to allow for nonordinary action, for a show of discretion or exercise of judgment. Thus managers need to know that they can assume innovative, risk-taking activities without having to go through the stifling multi-layered approval process.

And, informally, managers need the backing of other important figures in the organization whose tacit approval becomes another resource they bring to their own work unit as well as a sign of the manager's being "in."

Note that productive power has to do with *connections* with other parts of a system. Such systemic aspects of power derive from two sources—job activities and political alliances:

1. Power is most easily accumulated when one has a job that is designed and located to allow *discretion* (nonroutinized action permitting flexible, adaptive, and creative contributions), *recognition* (visibility and notice), and *relevance* (being central to pressing organizational problems).

2. Power also comes when one has relatively close contact with *sponsors* (higher-level people who confer approval, prestige, or backing), *peer networks* (circles of acquaintanceship that provide reputation and information, the grapevine often being faster than formal communication channels), and *subordinates* (who can be developed to relieve managers of some of their burdens and to represent the manager's point of view).

When managers are in powerful situations, it is easier for them to accomplish more. Because the tools are there, they are likely to be highly motivated and, in turn, to be able to

---

To What Extent a Manager Can—

Intercede favorably on behalf of someone in trouble with the organization.
Get a desirable placement for a talented subordinate.
Get approval for expenditures beyond the budget.
Get above-average salary increases for subordinates.
Get items on the agenda at policy meetings.
Get fast access to top decision makers.
Get regular, frequent access to top decision makers.
Get early information about decisions and policy shifts.

Figure 1
Some common symbols of a manager's organizational power
(influence upward and outward)

motivate subordinates. Their activities are more likely to be on target and to net them successes. They can flexibly interpret or shape policy to meet the needs of particular areas, emergent situations, or sudden environmental shifts. They gain the respect and cooperation that attributed power brings. Subordinates' talents are resources rather than threats. And, because powerful managers have so many lines of connection and thus are oriented outward, they tend to let go of control downward, developing more independently functioning lieutenants.

The powerless live in a different world. Lacking the supplies, information, or support to make things happen easily, they may turn instead to the ultimate weapon of those who lack productive power—oppressive power: holding others back and punishing with whatever threats they can muster.

Figure 2 summarizes some of the major ways in which variables in the organization and in job design contribute to either power or powerlessness.

Positions of Powerlessness

Understanding what it takes to have power and recognizing the classic behavior of the powerless can immediately help managers make sense out of a number of familiar organizational problems that are usually attributed to inadequate people:

The ineffectiveness of first-line supervisors.
The petty interest protection and conservatism of staff professionals.
The crises of leadership at the top.

Instead of blaming the individuals involved in organizational problems, let us look at the positions people occupy. Of course, power or powerlessness in a position may not be all of the problem. Sometimes incapable people *are* at fault and need to be retrained or replaced. (See the ruled insert on pages 453–455 for a discussion of another special case, women.) But where patterns emerge, where the troubles associated with some units persist, organizational power

Factors	Generates Power When Factor Is	Generates Powerlessness When Factor Is
Rules inherent in the job	few	many
Predecessors in the job	few	many
Established routines	few	many
Task variety	high	low
Rewards for reliability/predictability	few	many
Rewards for unusual performance/innovation	many	few
Flexibility around use of people	high	low
Approvals needed for nonroutine decisions	few	many
Physical location	central	distant
Publicity about job activities	high	low
Relation of tasks to current problem areas	central	peripheral
Focus of tasks	outside work unit	inside work unit
Interpersonal contact in the job	high	low
Contact with senior officials	high	low
Participation in programs, conferences, meetings	high	low
Participation in problem-solving task forces	high	low
Advancement prospects of subordinates	high	low

Figure 2
Ways organizational factors contribute to power or powerlessness

failures could be the reason. Then, as Volvo President Pehr Gyllenhammar concludes, we should treat the powerless not as "villains" causing headaches for everyone else but as "victims."[3]

First-Line Supervisors

Because an employee's most important work relationship is with his or her supervisor, when many of them talk about "the company," they mean their immediate boss. Thus a supervisor's behavior is an important determinant of the average employee's relationship to work and is in itself a critical link in the production chain.

Yet I know of no U.S. corporate management entirely satisfied with the performance of its supervisors. Most see them as supervising too closely and not training their people. In one manufacturing company where direct laborers were asked on a survey how they learned their job, on a list of seven possibilities "from my supervisor" ranked next to last. (Only company training programs ranked worse.) Also, it is said that supervisors do not translate company policies into practice—for instance, that they do not carry out the right of every employee to frequent performance reviews or to career counseling.

In court cases charging race or sex discrimination, first-line supervisors are frequently cited as the "discriminating official."[4] And, in studies of innovative work redesign and quality of work life projects, they often appear as the implied villains; they are the ones who are said to undermine the program or interfere with its effectiveness. In short, they are often seen as "not sufficiently managerial."

The problem affects white-collar as well as blue-collar supervisors. In one large government agency, supervisors in field offices were seen as the source of problems concerning morale and the flow of information to and from headquarters. "Their attitudes are negative," said a senior official. "They turn people against the agency; they put down senior management. They build themselves up by always complaining about headquarters, but prevent their staff from getting any information directly. We can't

afford to have such attitudes communicated to field staff."

Is the problem that supervisors need more management training programs or that incompetent people are invariably attracted to the job? Neither explanation suffices. A large part of the problem lies in the position itself—one that almost universally creates powerlessness.

First-line supervisors are "people in the middle," and that has been seen as the source of many of their problems.[5] But by recognizing that first-line supervisors are caught between higher management and workers, we only begin to skim the surface of the problem. There is practically no other organizational category as subject to powerlessness.

First, these supervisors may be at a virtual dead end in their careers. Even in companies where the job used to be a stepping stone to higher-level management jobs, it is now common practice to bring in MBAs from the outside for those positions. Thus moving from the ranks of direct labor into supervision may mean, essentially, getting "stuck" rather than moving upward. Because employees do not perceive supervisors as eventually joining the leadership circles of the organization, they may see them as lacking the high-level contacts needed to have clout. Indeed, sometimes turnover among supervisors is so high that workers feel they can outwait—and outwit—any boss.

Second, although they lack clout, with little in the way of support from above, supervisors are forced to administer programs or explain policies that they have no hand in shaping. In one company, as part of a new personnel program supervisors were required to conduct counseling interviews with employees. But supervisors were not trained to do this and were given no incentives to get involved. Counseling was just another obligation. Then managers suddenly encouraged the workers to bypass their supervisors or to put pressure on them. The personnel staff brought them together and told them to demand such interviews as a basic right. If supervisors had not felt powerless before, they did after that squeeze from below, engineered from above.

The people they supervise can also make life hard for them in numerous ways. This often happens when a supervisor has himself or herself risen up from the ranks. Peers that have not made it are resentful or derisive of their former colleague, whom they now see as trying to lord it over them. Often it is easy for workers to break the rules and let a lot of things slip.

Yet first-line supervisors are frequently judged according to rules and regulations while being limited by other regulations in what disciplinary actions they can take. They often lack the resources to influence or reward people; after all, workers are guaranteed their pay and benefits by someone other than their supervisors. Supervisors cannot easily control events; rather, they must react to them.

In one factory, for instance, supervisors complained that performance of their job was out of their control: they could fill production quotas only if they had the supplies, but they had no way to influence the people controlling the supplies.

The lack of support for many first-line managers, particularly in large organizations, was made dramatically clear in another company. When asked if contact with executives higher in the organization who had the potential for offering support, information, and alliances diminished their own feelings of career vulnerability and the number of headaches they experienced on the job, supervisors in five out of seven work units responded positively. For them *contact* was indeed related to a greater feeling of acceptance at work and membership in the organization.

But in the two other work units where there was greater contact, people perceived more, not less, career vulnerability. Further investigation showed that supervisors in these business units got attention only when they were in trouble. Otherwise, no one bothered to talk to them. To these particular supervisors, hearing from a higher-level manager was a sign not of recognition or potential support but of danger.

It is not surprising, then, that supervisors frequently manifest symptoms of powerlessness: overly close supervision, rules-mindedness, and a tendency to do the job themselves rather than to train their people (since job skills may be one of the few remaining things they feel good about). Perhaps this is why they sometimes stand as roadblocks between their subordinates and the higher reaches of the company.

Women Managers Experience Special Power Failures

The traditional problems of women in management are illustrative of how formal and informal practices can combine to engender powerlessness. Historically, women in management have found their opportunities in more routine, low-profile jobs. In staff positions, where they serve in support capacities to line managers but have no line responsibilities of their own, or in supervisory jobs managing "stuck" subordinates, they are not in a position either to take the kinds of risks that build credibility or to develop their own team by pushing bright subordinates.

Such jobs, which have few favors to trade, tend to keep women out of the mainstream of the organization. This lack of clout, coupled with the greater difficulty anyone who is "different" has in getting into the information and support networks, has meant that merely by organizational situation women in management have been more likely than men to be rendered structurally powerless. This is one reason those women who have achieved power have often had family connections that put them in the mainstream of the organization's social circles.

A disproportionate number of women managers are found among first-line supervisors or staff professionals; and they, like men in those circumstances, are likely to be organizationally powerless. But the behavior of other managers can contribute to the powerlessness of women in management in a number of less obvious ways.

(continued)

One way other managers can make a woman powerless is by patronizingly overprotecting her: putting her in "a safe job," not giving her enough to do to prove herself, and not suggesting her for high-risk, visible assignments. This protectiveness is sometimes born of "good" intentions to give her every chance to succeed (why stack the deck against her?). Out of managerial concerns, out of awareness that a woman may be up against situations that men simply do not have to face, some very well-meaning managers protect their female managers ("It's a jungle, so why send her into it?").

Overprotectiveness can also mask a manager's fear of association with a woman should she fail. One senior bank official at a level below vice president told me about his concerns with respect to a high-performing, financially experienced woman reporting to him. Despite *his* overwhelmingly positive work experiences with her, he was still afraid to recommend her for other assignments because he felt it was a personal risk. "What if other managers are not as accepting of women as I am?" he asked. "I know I'd be sticking my neck out; they would take her more because of my endorsement than her qualifications. And what if she doesn't make it? My judgment will be on the line."

Overprotection is relatively benign compared with rendering a person powerless by providing obvious signs of lack of managerial support. For example, allowing someone supposedly in authority to be bypassed easily means that no one else has to take him or her seriously. If a woman's immediate supervisor or other managers listen willingly to criticism of her and show they are concerned every time a negative comment comes up and that they assume she must be at fault, then they are helping to undercut her. If managers let other people know that they have concerns about this person or that they are testing her to see how she does, then they are inviting other people to look for signs of inadequacy or failure.

Furthermore, people assume they can afford to bypass women because they "must be uninformed" or "don't know the ropes." Even though women may be respected for their competence or expertise, they are not necessarily seen as being informed beyond the technical requirements of the job. There may be a grain of historical truth in this. Many women come to senior management positions as "outsiders" rather than up through the usual channels.

Also, because until very recently men have not felt comfortable seeing women as businesspeople (business clubs have traditionally excluded women), they have tended to seek each other out for informal socializing. Anyone, male or female, seen as organizationally naive and lacking sources of "inside dope" will find his or her own lines of information limited.

Finally, even when women are able to achieve some power on their own, they have not necessarily been able to translate such personal credibility into an organizational power base. To create a network of supporters out of individual clout requires that a person pass on and share power, that subordinates and peers be empowered by virtue of their connection with that person. Traditionally, neither men nor women have seen women as capable of sponsoring others, even though they may be capable of achieving and succeeding on their own. Women have been viewed as the *recipients of sponsorship rather than as the sponsors themselves.*

(As more women prove themselves in organizations and think more self-consciously about bringing along young people, this situation may change. However, I still hear many more questions from women managers about how they can benefit from mentors, sponsors, or peer networks than about how they themselves can start to pass on favors and make use of their own resources to benefit others.)

(continued)

Viewing managers in terms of power and powerlessness helps explain two familiar stereotypes about women and leadership in organizations: that no one wants a woman boss (although studies show that anyone who has ever had a woman boss is likely to have had a positive experience), and that the reason no one wants a woman boss is that women are "too controlling, rules-minded, and petty."

The first stereotype simply makes clear that power is important to leadership. Underneath the preference for men is the assumption that, given the current distribution of people in organizational leadership positions, men are more likely than women to be in positions to achieve power and, therefore, to share their power with others. Similarly, the "bossy woman boss" stereotype is a perfect picture of powerlessness. All of those traits are just as characteristic of men who are powerless, but women are slightly more likely, because of circumstances I have mentioned, to find themselves powerless than are men. Women with power in the organization are just as effective—and preferred—as men.

Recent interviews conducted with about 600 bank managers show that, when a woman exhibits the petty traits of powerlessness, people assume that she does so "because she is a woman." A striking difference is that, when a man engages in the same behavior, people assume the behavior is a matter of his own individual style and characteristics and do not conclude that it reflects on the suitability of men for management.

Staff Professionals

Also working under conditions that can lead to organizational powerlessness are the staff specialists. As advisers behind the scenes, staff people must sell their programs and bargain for resources, but unless they get themselves entrenched in organizational power networks, they have little in the way of favors to exchange. They are seen as useful adjuncts to the primary tasks of the organization but inessential in a day-to-day operating sense. This disenfranchisement occurs particularly when staff jobs consist of easily routinized administrative functions which are out of the mainstream of the currently relevant areas and involve little innovative decision making.

Furthermore, in some organizations, unless they have had previous line experience, staff people tend to be limited in the number of jobs into which they can move. Specialists' ladders are often very short, and professionals are just as likely to get "stuck" in such jobs as people are in less prestigious clerical or factory positions.

Staff people, unlike those who are being groomed for important line positions, may be hired because of a special expertise or particular background. But management rarely pays any attention to developing them into more general organizational resources. Lacking growth prospects themselves and working alone or in very small teams, they are not in a position to develop others or pass on power to them. They miss out on an important way that power can be accumulated.

Sometimes staff specialists, such as house counsel or organization development people, find their work being farmed out to consultants. Management considers them fine for the routine work, but the minute the activities involve risk or something problematic, they bring in outside experts. This treatment says something about their expertise but also about the status of their function. Since the company can always hire talent on a temporary basis, it is unclear that the management really needs to have or considers important its own staff for these functions.

And, because staff professionals are often seen as adjuncts to primary tasks, their effectiveness and therefore their contribution to the organization are often hard to measure. This visibility and recognition, as well as risk taking and relevance, may be denied to people in staff jobs.

Staff people tend to act out their powerlessness by becoming turf-minded. They create islands within the organization. They set themselves up as the only ones who can control professional standards and judge their own work. They create sometimes false distinctions between themselves as experts (no one else could possibly do what they do) and lay people, and this continues to keep them out of the mainstream.

One form such distinctions take is a combination of disdain when line managers attempt to act in areas the professionals think are their preserve and of subtle refusal to support the managers' efforts. Or staff groups battle with each other for control of new "problem areas," with the result that no one really handles the issue at all. To cope with their essential powerlessness, staff groups may try to evaluate their own status and draw boundaries between themselves and others.

When staff jobs are treated as final resting places for people who have reached their level of competence in the organization—a good shelf on which to dump managers who are too old to go anywhere but too young to retire—then staff groups can also become pockets of conservatism, resistant to change. Their own exclusion from the risk-taking action may make them resist *anyone's* innovative proposals. In the past, personnel departments, for example, have sometimes been the last in their organization to know about innovations in human resource development or to be interested in applying them.

Top Executives

Despite the great resources and responsibilities concentrated at the top of an organization, leaders can be powerless for reasons that are not very different from those that affect staff and supervisors: lack of supplies, information, and support.

We have faith in leaders because of their ability to make things happen in the larger world, to create possibilities for everyone else, and to attract resources to the organization. These are their supplies. But influence outward—the source of much credibility downward—can diminish as environments change, setting terms and conditions out of the control of the leaders. Regardless of top management's grand plans for the organization, the environment presses. At the very least, things going on outside the organization can deflect a leader's attention and drain energy. And more detrimental, decisions made elsewhere can have severe consequences for the organization and affect top management's sense of power and thus its operating style inside.

In the go-go years of the mid-1960s, for example, nearly every corporation officer or university president could look—and therefore feel—successful. Visible success gave leaders a great deal of credibility inside the organization, which in turn gave them the power to put new things in motion.

In the past few years, the environment has been strikingly different and the capacity of many organization leaders to do anything about it has been severely limited. New "players" have flexed their power muscles: the Arab oil bloc, government regulators, and congressional investigating committees. And managing economic decline is quite different from managing growth. It is no accident that when top leaders personally feel out of control, the control function in corporations grows.

As powerlessness in lower levels of organizations can manifest itself in overly routinized jobs where performance measures are oriented to rules and absence of change, so it can at upper levels as well. Routine work often drives out nonroutine work. Accomplishment becomes a question of nailing down details. Short-term results provide immediate gratifications and satisfy stockholders or other constituencies with limited interests.

It takes a powerful leader to be willing to risk short-term deprivations in order to bring about desired long-term outcomes. Much as first-line supervisors are tempted to focus on daily adherence to rules, leaders are tempted to focus on short-term fluctuations and lose sight of long-term objectives. The dynamics of such a situation are self-reinforcing. The more the long-term goals go unattended, the more a leader feels powerless and the greater the scramble to prove that he or she is in control of daily events at least. The more he is involved in the organization as a short-term Mr. Fix-it, the more out of control of long-term objectives he is, and the more ultimately powerless he is likely to be.

Credibility for the top executives often comes from doing the extraordinary: exercising discretion, creating, inventing, planning, and acting in nonroutine ways. But since routine problems look easier and more manageable, require less change and consent on the part of anyone else, and lend themselves to instant solutions that can make any leader look good temporarily, leaders may avoid the risk by taking over what their subordinates should be doing. Ultimately, a leader may succeed in getting all the trivial problems dumped on his or her desk. This can establish expectations even for leaders attempting more challenging tasks. When Warren Bennis was president of the University of Cincinnati, a professor called him when the heat was down in a classroom. In writing about this incident, Bennis commented, "I suppose he expected me to grab a wrench and fix it."[6]

People at the top need to insulate themselves from the routine operations of the organization in order to develop and exercise power. But this very insulation can lead to another source of powerlessness—lack of information. In one multinational corporation, top executives who are sealed off in a large, distant office, flattered and virtually babied by aides, are frustrated by their distance from the real action.[7]

At the top, the concern for secrecy and privacy is mixed with real loneliness. In one bank, organization members were so accustomed to never seeing the top leaders that when a new senior vice president went to the branch offices to look around, they had suspicion, even fear, about his intentions.

Thus leaders who are cut out of an organization's information networks understand neither what is really going on at lower levels nor that their isolation may be having negative effects. All too often top executives design "beneficial" new employee programs or declare a new humanitarian policy (e.g., "Participatory management is now our style") only to find the policy ignored or mistrusted because it is perceived as coming from uncaring bosses.

The information gap has more serious consequences when executives are so insulated from the rest of the organization or from other decision makers that, as Nixon so dramatically did, they fail to see their own impending downfall. Such insulation is partly a matter of organizational position and, in some cases, of executive style.

For example, leaders may create closed inner circles consisting of "doppelgängers," people just like themselves, who are their principal sources of organizational information and tell them only what they want to know. The reasons for the distortions are varied: key aides want to relieve the leader of burdens, they think just like the leader, they want to protect their own positions of power, or the familiar "kill the messenger" syndrome makes people close to top executives reluctant to the bearers of bad news.

Finally, just as supervisors and lower-level managers need their supporters in order to be and feel powerful, so do top executives. But for them sponsorship may not be so much a matter of individual endorsement as an issue of support by larger sources of legitimacy in the society. For top executives the problem is not to fit in among peers; rather, the question is whether the public at large and other organization members perceive a common interest which they see the executives as promoting.

If, however, public sources of support are withdrawn and leaders are open to public attack or if inside constituencies fragment and employees see their interests better aligned with pressure groups than with organizational leadership, then powerlessness begins to set in.

When common purpose is lost, the system's own politics may reduce the capacity of those at the top to act. Just as managing decline seems to create a much more passive and reactive stance than managing growth, so does mediating among conflicting interests. When what is happening outside and inside their organizations is out of control, many people at the top turn into decline managers and dispute mediators. Neither is a particularly empowering role.

Thus when top executives lose their own lines of supply, lines of information, and lines of support, they too suffer from a kind of powerlessness. The temptation for them then is to pull in every shred of power they can and to decrease the power available to other people to act. Innovation loses out in favor of control. Limits rather than targets are set. Financial goals are met by reducing "overhead" (people) rather than by giving people the tools and discretion to increase their own productive capacity. Dictatorial statements come down from the top, spreading the mentality of powerlessness farther until the whole organization becomes sluggish and people concentrate on protecting what they can.

When everyone is playing "king of the mountain," guarding his or her turf jealously, then king of the mountain becomes the only game in town.

To Expand Power, Share It

In no case am I saying that people in the three hierarchical levels described are always powerless, but they are susceptible to common conditions that can contribute to powerlessness. Figure 3 summarizes the most common symptoms of powerlessness for each level and some typical sources of that behavior.

I am also distinguishing the tremendous concentration of economic and political power in large corporations themselves from the powerlessness that can beset individuals even in the highest positions in such organizations. What grows with organizational position in hierarchical levels is not necessarily the power to accomplish—productive power—but the power to punish, to prevent, to sell off, to reduce, to fire, all without appropriate concern for consequences. It is that kind of power—oppressive power—that we often say corrupts.

The absence of ways to prevent individual and social harm causes the polity to feel it must surround people in power with constraints, regulations, and laws that limit the arbitrary use

of their authority. But if oppressive power corrupts, then so does the absence of productive power. In large organizations, powerlessness can be a bigger problem than power.

David C. McClelland makes a similar distinction between oppressive and productive power:

The negative . . . face of power is characterized by the dominance-submission mode: if I win, you lose. . . . It leads to simple and direct means of feeling powerful [such as being aggressive]. It does not often lead to effective social leadership for the reason that such a person tends to treat other people as pawns. People who feel they are pawns tend to be passive and useless to the leader who gets his satisfaction from dominating them. Slaves are the most inefficient form of labor ever devised by man. If a leader wants to have far-reaching influence, he must make his followers feel powerful and able to accomplish things on their own. . . . Even the most dictatorial leader does not succeed if he has not instilled in at least some of his followers a sense of power and the strength to pursue the goals he has set.[8]

Organizational power can grow, in part, by being shared. We do not yet know enough about new organizational forms to say whether productive power is infinitely expandable or where we reach the point of diminishing returns. But we do know that sharing power is different from giving or throwing it away. Delegation does not mean abdication.

Some basic lessons could be translated from the field of economics to the realm of organizations and management. Capital investment in plants and equipment is not the only key to productivity. The productive capacity of nations, like organizations, grows if the skill base is upgraded. People with the tools, information, and support to make more informed decisions and act more quickly can often accomplish more. By empowering others, a leader does not decrease his power; instead he may increase it—especially if the whole organization performs better.

This analysis leads to some counterintuitive conclusions. In a certain tautological sense, the

Position	Symptoms	Sources
First-line supervisors	Close, rules-minded supervision	Routine, rules-minded jobs with little control over lines of supply
	Tendency to do things oneself, blocking of subordinates' development and information	Limited lines of information
	Resistant, underproducing subordinates	Limited advancement or involvement prospects for oneself/subordinates
Staff professionals	Turf protection, information control	Routine tasks seen as peripheral to "real tasks" of line organization
	Retreat into professionalism	Block careers
	Conservative resistance to change	Easy replacement by outside experts
Top executives	Focus on internal cutting, short-term results, "punishing"	Uncontrollable lines of supply because of environmental changes
	Dictatorial top-down communications	Limited or blocked lines of information about lower levels of organization
	Retreat to comfort of like-minded lieutenants	Diminished lines of support because of challenges to legitimacy (e.g., from the public or special interest groups)

Figure 3

Common symptoms and sources of powerlessness for three key organizational positions

principal problem of the powerless is that they lack power. Powerless people are usually the last ones to whom anyone wants to entrust more power, for fear of its dissipation or abuse. But those people are precisely the ones who might benefit most from an injection of power and whose behavior is likely to change as new options open up to them.

Also, if the powerless bosses could be encouraged to share some of the power they do have, their power would grow. Yet, of course, only those leaders who feel secure about their own power outward—their lines of supply, information, and support—can see empowering subordinates as a gain rather than as a loss. The two sides of power (getting it and giving it) are closely connected.

There are important lessons here for both subordinates and those who want to change organizations, whether executives or change agents. Instead of resisting or criticizing a powerless boss, which only increases the boss's feeling of powerlessness and need to control, subordinates instead might concentrate on helping the boss become more powerful. Managers might make pockets of ineffectiveness in the organization more productive not by training or replacing individuals but by structural solutions such as opening supply and support lines.

Similarly, organizational change agents who make a new program or policy to succeed should make sure that the change itself does not render any other level of the organization powerless. In making changes, it is wise to make sure that the key people in the level or two directly above and in neighboring functions are sufficiently involved, informed, and taken into account, so that the program can be used to build their own sense of power also. If such involvement is impossible, then it is better to move these people out of the territory altogether than to leave behind a group from whom some power has been removed and who might resist and undercut the program.

In part, of course, spreading power means educating people to this new definition of it. But words alone will not make the difference; managers will need the real experience of a new way of managing.

Here is how the associate director of a large corporate professional department phrased the lessons that he learned in the transition to a team-oriented, participatory, power-sharing management process:

"Get in the habit of involving your own managers in decision making and approvals. But don't abdicate! Tell them what you want and where you're coming from. Don't go for a one-boss grass roots 'democracy.' Make the management hierarchy work for you in participation. . . .

"Hang in there, baby, and don't give up. Try not to 'revert' just because everything seems to go sour on a particualar day. Open up—talk to people and tell them how you feel. They'll want to get you back on track and will do things to make that happen—because they don't really want to go back to the way it was. . . . Subordinates will push you to 'act more like a boss,' but their interest is usually more in seeing someone else brought to heel than in getting bossed themselves."

Naturally, people need to have power before thay can learn to share it. Exhorting managers to change their leadership styles is rarely useful by itself. In one large plant of a major electronics company, first-line production supervisors were the source of numerous complaints from managers who saw them as major roadblocks to overall plant productivity and as insufficiently skilled supervisors. So the plant personnel staff undertook two pilot programs to increase the supervisor's effectiveness. The first program was based on a traditional competency and training model aimed at teaching the specific skills of successful supervisors. The second program, in contrast, was designed to empower the supervisors by directly affecting their flexibility, access to resources, connections with higher-level officials, and control over working conditions.

After an initial gathering of data from supervisors and their subordinates, the personnel staff held meetings where all the supervisors were given tools for developing action plans for sharing the data with their people and collaborating on solutions to perceived problems. But then, in a departure from common practice in this organization, task forces of supervisors were formed to develop new systems for handling job and career issues common to them and their people. These task forces were given budgets, consultants, representation on a plant-wide project steering committee alongside managers at much higher levels, and wide latitude in defining the nature and scope of the changes they wished to make. In short, lines of supply, information, and support were opened to them.

As the task forces progressed in their activities, it became clear to the plant management that the hoped-for changes in supervisory effectiveness were taking place much more rapidly through conventional management training; so the conventional training was dropped. Not only did the pilot groups design useful new procedures for the plant, astonishing senior management in several cases with their knowledge and capabilities, but also, significantly, they learned to manage their own people better.

Several groups decided to involve shop-floor workers in their task fores; they could not see from their own experience the benefits of involving subordinates in solving job-related problems. Other supervisors began to experiment with ways to implement "participatory management" by giving subordinates more control and influence without relinquishing their own authority.

Soon the "problem supervisors" in the "most troubled plant in the company" were getting the highest possible performance ratings and were considered models for direct production management. The sharing of organizational power from the top made possible the productive use of power below.

One might wonder why more organizations do not adopt such empowering strategies. There are standard answers: that giving up control is threatening to people who have fought for every shred of it; that people do not want to share power with those they look down on; that managers fear losing their own place and special privileges in the system; that "predictability" often rates higher than "flexibility" as an organizational value; and so forth.

But I would also put skepticism about employee abilities high on the list. Many modern bureaucratic systems are designed to minimize dependence on individual intelligence by making routine as many decisions as possible. So it often comes as a genuine surprise to top executives that people doing the more routine jobs could, indeed, make sophisticated decisions or use resources entrusted to them in intelligent ways.

In the same electronics company just mentioned, at the end of a quarter the pilot supervisory task forces were asked to report results and plans to senior management in order to have their new budget requests approved. The task forces made sure they were well prepared, and the high-level executives were duly impressed. In fact, they were *so* impressed that they kept interrupting the presentations with compliments, remarking that the supervisors could easily be doing sophisticated personnel work.

At first the supervisors were flattered. Such praise from upper management could only be taken well. But when the first glow wore off, several of them became very angry. They saw the excessive praise as patronizing and insulting. "Didn't they think we could think? Didn't they imagine we were capable of doing this kind of work?" one asked. "They must have seen us as just a bunch of animals. No wonder they gave us such limited jobs.

As far as these supervisors were concerned, their abilities had always been there, in latent form perhaps, but still there. They as individuals had not changed—just their organizational power.

Notes

1. Donald C. Pelz, "Influence: A Key to Effective Leadership in the First-Line Supervisor," *Personnel*, November 1952, p. 209.
2. See my book, *Men and Women of the Corporation* (New York: Basic Books, 1977), pp. 164–205; and David Kipnis, *The Powerholders* (Chicago: University of Chicago Press, 1976).
3. Pehr G. Gyllenhammar, *People at Work* (Reading, Mass.: Addison-Wesley, 1977), p. 133.
4. William E. Fulmer, "Supervisory Selection: The Acid Test of Affirmative Action," *Personnel*, November-December 1976, p. 40.
5. See my chapter (coauthor, Barry A. Stein), "Life in the Middle: Getting In, Getting Up, and Getting Along," in *Life in Organizations*, eds. Rosabeth M. Kanter and Barry A. Stein (New York: Basic Books, 1979).
6. Warren Bennis, *The Unconscious Conspiracy: Why Leaders Can't Lead* (New York: AMACOM, 1976).
7. See my chapter, "How the Top is Different," in *Life in Organizations*.
8. David C. McClelland, *Power: The Inner Experience* (New York: Irvington Publishers, 1975), p. 263. Quoted by permission.

41

Organization Development: A Political Perspective

*Anthony T. Cobb and
Newton Margulies*

During the last several years the area of organizational politics (OP) has attracted the interest of social scientists and practitioners alike. In the field of organization development (OD), interest has focused on the use of OP in intervention programs. It is now generally recognized that such programs inevitably affect organizational politics and are affected by them [Bennis, 1969; Cobb, 1977; Pettigrew, 1975].

Despite this knowledge, the movement of OD into the study and use of OP had been cautious and conservative. At present, the interest OD displays in OP remains largely peripheral to what can be called its clinical or process orientation: one that relies on a relatively intimate client/consultant relationship to facilitate self-discovery, help, and renewal [Margulies & Raia, 1978, pp. 110–111]. There are a number of views regarding this level of OP interest. One extreme holds that any political orientations will necessarily divert attention from OD's clinical mission and inevitably subvert it. Another extreme view holds that OD consultants ought to assume a political activist role to ensure that program objectives are implemented. Both views maintain that OD has been devoid of any political orientation. The former maintains that

SOURCE: Anthony T. Cobb and Newton Margulies, "Organization Development: A Political Perspective," *Academy of Management Review* (1981), Vol. 6, No. 1, 49–59. Copyright © 1981 by the Academy of Management. Reprinted by permission.

this is how it should be, the latter that it must no longer remain so.

Our purposes in this article are two: First, we assert that, while OD is not politically sophisticated, neither is it devoid of a political orientation. OD has developed an unrecognized political orientation in many of its values and some aspects of its most frequently used technology. Although this political orientation is restricted in scope, it has proved useful in supporting OD's clinical objectives. We believe that the effectiveness of OD can be enhanced when professionals recognize, accept, and use this existing political orientation in the service of organizational change.

Our second purpose is to explore some of the ramifications of a greater level of political involvement in intervention programs. Although increased political involvement can aid the OD consultant and the host organization, so too can it do harm, particularly when it moves to the extreme of political activism.

To address these issues properly, a political perspective is developed first to view OD's past and its alternative political futures. This perspective provides focus for subsequent discussions.

A Political Perspective

A political perspective with sufficient range to deal with the issues here can be developed by briefly addressing two topics. First, a definition of the term "organizational politics" is provided and, second, what can be called the political subsystem is described.

The Meaning of Organizational Politics

The literature provides many definitions of OP developed from a variety of perspectives. Mayes and Allen [1977] provide an adequate survey of these. In terms relevant to OD, organizational politics can be defined as *the use of power to modify or protect an organization's exchange structure.* An exchange structure is composed of an organization's resource distribution system and those who have formal authority to decide to what purposes resources will be used. An exchange structure in equilibrium represents the status quo and is "legitimate." Efforts to change the status quo, then, involve political action both on the part of those who challenge and those who seek to maintain it.

As seen in this light, OP per se is neither good nor bad. Actually, OP can either help or hinder the organization, depending on the processes used and the objectives sought. Even though it is easy for the OD consultant to become involved in politics, it is entirely another matter to have the sophistication to manage the use of OP productively.

The Political Subsystem

For convenience, the notion of a social subsystem [Guest, Hersey, & Blanchard, 1977] is used here to denote the subsystem about which the OD consultant is expert and in which he or she operates. This subsystem co-exists with many others, one of which can be labeled the political subsystem.

The political subsystem is composed of the sources, locations, and flow of power through the organization. The basic criterion of effectiveness within the subsystem is the extent to which sufficient power can be accumulated and transferred to those locations (i.e., individuals) in the organization to maintain productive operations, solve problems, and implement solutions. A political subsystem is efficient to the extent that power can be accumulated and transferred quickly and with precision.

A tenet of general systems theory is that subsystems interact with one another. Therefore, changes in either the social or political subsystem will produce changes in the other. The interactive relationship poses at least two basic problems to OD consultants concerned with organizational politics. The first is determining how support can be generated within the social subsystem. The second is knowing what changes are necessary in the social subsystem to facilitate the development of an effective and efficient political subsystem.

Political Orientations in Organization Development

Because there is interaction between the social subsystem and the political subsystem, successful change in the former requires complementary and supportive changes in the latter. It is because OD is well aware of such subsystem interaction [Benne & Bernbaum, 1969; Leavitt, 1965] that there has been recent concern that OD consultants should become more politically sophisticated and active in order to increase intervention success [Burke, 1976; Pettigrew, 1975]. Yet, historically speaking, OD interventions on the whole have enjoyed a great deal of success. Given that OD consultants have traditionally displayed, at most, a minimal interest in OP, the issue must be raised of how they are able to survive at all, much less be successful. One reason may be just good fortune. Another may be that clients themselves come to see that political cooperation is necessary to protect their own self-interests. We will argue that there is still a third reason: OD has developed a largely unrecognized political orientation in addition to its clinical one and this political orientation complements the clinical one in producing successful interventions.

Where in OD does this political orientation lie? Even now, organization development does not appear to be an easily defined field or profession. For the purposes here, OD can be viewed as a profession built on a foundation composed of three basic interactive elements: its values, its technology, and its knowledge of the human side of organizations. If there is a political orientation in OD that helps guide the political behavior of consultants, then, it should reside in one or more of these elements.

The knowledge base of OD incorporates clinical concepts relevant to power, models of power, and even sources of power available to consultants for work in interventions [Huse, 1980, pp. 143–148]. Properly viewed, such concepts of power *can* form a foundation on which to build political theory and intervention strategy. Yet, even today the knowledge base of OD remains essentially lacking in political theory and models to help *guide* the consultant in terms of political intervention strategies [Beer, 1976; Bennis, 1969]. Therefore, if political assistance is given to the consultant, it must come from the value or technological base of the field. It is our view that it comes from both.

Political Support in the Value Base

For the purposes here, the value component of OD is viewed in structural terms. At its base lie fundamental philosophical or value orientations. These would include rationalism, pragmatism, existentialism [Friedlander, 1976], humanism, and democracy [Friedlander & Brown, 1974]. These basic orientations, then, provide the context for the development of more specific values: values concerning intervention concepts, means, and end-states. Valued clinical *aims,* or end-states of intervention, include individual growth and increased organizational effectiveness with the capability of self-renewal [French, Bell, & Zawacki, 1978]. Valued *means* for reaching this end-state include confrontation, honesty, open communications, the movement toward power equalization, and collaboration. Concepts that support these valued means include beliefs in the goodness of people, Theory Y assumptions, and the potential and desire for growth by organizational members. Such historically entrenched values of OD, then, provide the general context here for discussion.

The OD consultant is an expert in creating a social environment within which the client system can achieve full utilization of its own human resources to solve its problems [French et al., 1978]. Basic to the full utilization of human resources are such necessary processes as collaboration and participation. Collaboration, however, requires that power be exchanged, shared, and pooled. Participation in decision making requires a "franchise" that comes only with the power to make inputs. Thus, if the

consultant is to achieve collaboration and participation in the social subsystem, supportive changes must occur within the political subsystem to allow it. Some of these changes include the general reduction of power differentials between organizational members, the transfer of power to those who are to participate in decision making, and the removal of structural obstacles to the flow of power in the organization generally and between levels of authority in particular. The consultant is guided in these tasks by many of the values OD has developed.

The belief that power equalization should be used in interventions is a central concept in OD [Leavitt, 1965]. Strauss [1963, p. 41] stated, for example, that "the main thrust of the 'human relations movement' over the last 20 years has been toward . . . 'power equalization.' " In the nearly twenty years since Strauss's observation, this general orientation has become valued in its own right and is reflected in a number of other values that focus on more specific political problems. This can be demonstrated by examining specific values oriented to the individual, superior/subordinate relations, and organization structures paralleling the micro, intermediate, and macro perspectives of the organization.

The individual's political position. Participation raises the basic political issue of who should be given the right, and thus the power, to participate in decision making. On the level of the nation or state, for example, the extent of citizen participation is justified and supported by the assumptions made regarding the capabilities and traits of the polity (i.e., citizens).

The political position of organizational members is justified and supported as well by basic assumptions regarding workers. McGregor [1960] has articulated some of these assumptions. Theory X assumptions support a political structure in which power is centralized and participation removed from the rank and file. Theory Y assumptions support a political structure in which power is decentralized, justifying a wide base of participation. The clinical side of Theory Y assumptions focuses on the individual as a potential resource in problem solving. Theory Y also justifies the political necessity of transferring some measure of participatory power to the worker. Thus, although OD consultants may not recognize it, when they promote a clinical value orientation, coinciding with Theory Y, they are establishing as well some of the political subsystem changes needed to support their clinical aims.

Superior/subordinate relations. Historically, one of OD's principal concerns has been with leadership style. In its clinical context, OD has tied leadership style to interactions among subordinates, satisfaction, and productivity [Lewin, Lippitt, & White, 1939]. In terms of organizational change, OD has recognized that changes on one level require "complementary and reinforcing changes in organizational levels above and below that level" [Benne & Bernbaum, 1969, p. 331]. It is not surprising, therefore, to see that OD has developed a value orientation to leader/subordinate relations that supports the power exchange required for collaboration and interlevel adjustments between subordinates and superiors. Authoritarian leadership removes power from subordinates, thereby suppressing participation, collaboration, and the upward flow of influence, whereas democratic leadership facilitates them. The fact that OD values democratic leadership produces changes not only in the social subsystem, but complementary and reinforcing changes in the political subsystem as well.

The organization structure. In accordance with general systems theory, the structural subsystem [Guest et al., 1977] will affect the political subsystem. Although they did not address the political subsystem specifically, Burns and Stalker [1961] recognized this interactive effect. They noted that the rigid power structure of mechanistic organizations tends to hamper the power flow necessary for broad organizational problem solving. Organic organizations, on the other hand, facilitate problem solving by allowing an easier flow of power

through the political subsystem to wherever it is needed.

The behavioral administrative structures articulated by Likert [1961, 1967] are relevant to this discussion. System 1 tends to impede, but System 4 tends to facilitate the flow of power through the political subsystem. As a result, System 4 facilitates broad organizational collaboration, participation, and communication in the establishment of goals and resource distribution.

Organization development values an organic System 4 administrative structure for a number of clinical reasons. When such a structure is adopted by the client, however, it promotes changes within the political subsystem. These political changes, in turn, facilitate work within the social subsystem.

The practical and political utility of values. Fundamentally, OD values a democratic work place and the power equalization inherent in it. It was demonstrated above that this value orientation is manifest whether one takes a micro, intermediate, or macro perspective of the organization. Part of the reason OD may hold these values is that they are generally accepted in our society. Clinically speaking, they are valued because OD believes that they promote effective organizational performance and personal growth. One should not ignore, however, the political utility these values have in terms of the consultant's clinical objectives.

Consider the problems typically faced by the consultant and client system. They tend to be unstructured, complex, novel, and complicated. Evidence indicates that these types of problems are best solved by a broad-based participatory effort utilizing the resources of those best able to attend to them regardless of formal power position [Burns & Stalker, 1961; MacCrimmon & Taylor, 1976].

Such collaborative and participative efforts, however, require commensurate political subsystem support. Many OD values, some of which have been presented here, can be seen as helpful in promoting political support for clinical objectives.

Political Support in the Technological Base

The technological base of OD can be divided into two interdependent components. One includes the tools and techniques the consultant can use in intervention. The second includes the roles assumed by the consultant (e.g., facilitator, interviewer) and the operational know-how, expertise, or knowledge to use the tools, techniques, and roles available to the consultant. Political supports can be found in both components.

Tools and techniques. The value OD gives to power equalization finds expression in some of its techniques as well. Laboratory training, for example, promotes a commitment to open and honest communications regarding interpersonal relations, organizational life, and diagnosis. But such a commitment "does inevitably imply some democratization [that] . . . may indeed undermine formal authority to a considerable degree" [E. Schein, 1972, p 93]. Intervention techniques that include such components as these, then, serve to operationalize the political as well as clinical side of the democratic values held by OD consultants.

Other techniques appear to play a political part in integrating vested interests by facilitating actual change in the exchange structure. Techniques oriented toward roles provide a case in point. Organizational roles prescribe occupant behavior, areas of decision making, character of reporting relationships, legitimate power, and the like. In short, roles contain many components of the status quo exchange structure. Many role techniques, therefore, have a political side in that they intervene "directly in the relationship of power, authority, and influence" of role occupants and reciprocals [Harrison, 1978, p. 159]. When OD consultants facilitate change in such role components, then, they are working within both the social and political subsystems to accomplish their aims.

The political subsystem is also affected by a number of techniques oriented to "structural" or "work engineering." The negotiation of resource exchanges and integration of vested interests, for example, is a political subsystem change that occurs along with the institution of a management-by-objectives system. The clinical objectives of job enrichment include ownership of the task, increases in perceived task importance, and the like. To accomplish these objectives, however, "vertical loading" is required, whereby previous supervisory perogatives are given to the subordinate.

Consultant roles and operational knowledge. Consultants are called on to play a variety of roles when using their knowledge and techniques. The literature describes many of these roles; our focus here is on a distinctly political role that cuts across many others and is often ignored: the diplomatic role. The purpose of this role is to communicate the vested interests of one party to another in a language that can be fully understood. The diplomat then seeks to integrate these vested interests when possible and, when not, to reduce the friction caused by competition by negotiations, trade-offs, and the like.

In order to support the clinical objectives of intervention, the consultant often assumes one of at least two diplomatic roles. One might be called the "enfranchiser" role. The socio-organizational distance between higher- and lower- level participants is often large. So, too, is the power differential within the political subsystem. In order to communicate and facilitate the integration of vested interests, the consultant often becomes a "communications channel" between the parties. For low-level participants, consultants become surrogate participants in decision making; for higher-level decision makers they are representatives of the organizational citizenry.

The consultant often plays a diplomatic role horizontally in the organization as well. The consultant is frequently called on to mediate between organizational groups that are interdependent but have different vested interests, values, perceptions, and beliefs. Like Lawrence and Lorsch's integrator [1967], the consultant facilitates communication between parties by serving as a communications channel or by facilitating face-to-face interaction. By working with and between both groups, the consultant aids in the integration of their vested interests while focusing on their interaction process.

Whether moving vertically, horizontally, or obliquely in the organization, the OD consultant is in a unique position to carry the interests of one party to another. The parties can speak openly to the consultant, without fear of repercussions, and can be confident that the consultant is concerned about them as well as about the general welfare of the organization. This promotes the power generation and transfer necessary for effective political subsystem operation. Thus, the consultant plays the clinical role of communications channel and the political role of power channel at the same time for the same purpose: beneficial change in the social subsystem.

The Political Side of Organization Development

The more one explores OD, the more one can see its political side. It is true, however, that OD's clinical orientation remains paramount and that the political side plays a mostly unrecognized, supportive role. Evaluations made by Bennis [1969], Beer [1976], and Burke [1976] hold true today. Organization development has not come to fully appreciate the impact that OP has on change programs. Nor has OD developed the models, knowledge, and facts that represent a sophisticated political orientation.

Nevertheless, OD's brand of "political pacifism" should not be ignored. It needs to be further explored for at least three reasons. The first is to see if the direction it provides is appropriate for the various situations OD consultants encounter. Second, if OD is determined to become more politically active, a foundation for such growth may be found not only in the values and technology of OD but its knowledge base as well. Third, OD's present political orientation can serve as a reference point. As such, it is useful for exploring those issues involved in assuming a greater political role.

Political Involvement: Considerations for Organization Development

The OD profession has been urged to become more politically oriented and active [Bennis, 1969; Burke, 1976; Pettigrew, 1975]. In this regard at least two questions need to be raised. First, what would be the utility of increased political intervention? Second, what would be the consequences in terms of OD's ethical/value base? Before these questions can be answered, just what is meant by "increased political involvement" needs to be explored.

A Continuum of Political Involvement

It is possible to describe the extent and character of OP involvement along a continuum. At the extremes lie "political pacifism" and "political activism." The midrange is represented by the "political moderate" position.

Political pacifism. Political pacifism has been represented above. It includes a fundamental commitment to clinical rather than political intervention. While a political element does exist, it is minimal, generally unrecognized, and oriented to clinical support rather than being used as a means of change in its own right.

Political moderation. The political moderate advocates the development of knowledge, models, and strategies to overcome political blindspots [Bennis, 1969; Harrison, 1978; Pettigrew, 1975]. The use of these, however, remains subordinate to, and strictly supportive of, work within the social subsystem. The political role played by the consultant is at most one of a "political facilitator" who seeks to establish a political climate supportive of clinically oriented change. Honesty, truth, collaboration, participation, and the like are still pursued. Political facilitation works to overcome the political impediments to these components of change. The clients operating within this climate work toward the establishment of a new status quo, *one chosen by them.*

Political activism. Political activism advocates deep involvement in the political subsystem—at least as much as, if not more than, in the social subsystem. Here the consultant adopts the role of "political activist," of someone who has some vision of what the client system's condition ought to be. This vision is realized by politically overcoming resistance to it. In this sense, then, the political activist maintains that "the ends justify the means" and advocates such strategies as limiting and channeling communication for political purposes, the use of covert or hidden agendas, and the political use of intervention research [V. Schein, 1977]. Coercive politics may also be used. Damaging information gained in intervention, for example, might be used against those who stand in the way of the consultant [Pettigrew, 1975].

The Utility of Increased Political Involvement

It has been argued that increased political involvement will lead to greater chances of intervention success than that provided by the current approach of political pacifism. Because these arguments have been directly and indirectly stated in the literature [Bennis, 1969; Harrison, 1978; Pettigrew, 1975; V. Schein, 1977], they are only briefly reviewed here.

The moderate position takes due note of the evidence that supports the existence of OP and the political subsystem, and their effect on any change program [Bennis, 1969; Cyert & March, 1964; March, 1962; March & Simon, 1958; Thompson, 1967]. Ignoring this evidence creates a significant gap in the operational knowledge of OD and its approach to change. Furthermore, this knowledge gap makes it impossible to develop appropriate reactive and proactive strategies to support the clinical aims of the intervention program. Evidence can be cited demonstrating that once this gap is filled, political tools, techniques, and strategies can be developed to serve the clinical ends of the OD consultant [Harrison, 1978; Selznick, 1949]. Although individual studies are subject to criticism, the corpus of evidence represents a

systematic approach with generally positive results across applications. As a whole, then, the evidence lends support to the moderate position.

Political activism builds on the arguments provided by the moderate position. Activists assume that not only are politics a fact of organizational life but that some powerful and sophisticated members of the client system use politics to protect and extend their own selfish interests. These are formidable "opponents." Political activism, say the activists, is the best way to deal with them, and they cite evidence indicating that activist techniques (e.g., political manipulation of communication, research information) have successfully overcome such "opponents" [Pettigrew, 1975; V. Schein, 1977]. Unfortunately, most of this "evidence" is anecdotal and lacking in empirical validation. Much more empirical work needs to be done to support the activist position.

Some Caveats Regarding Increased Political Involvement

With all the arguments made for increased political involvement on the part of OD consultants, there is a surprising lack of attention given to some of the problems that may emerge. These potential problems deserve attention.

Political success requires political sophistication. Consultants in OD are probably more politically sophisticated than they realize or may be willing to admit. Nevertheless, OD consultants are clinicians, not politicians. Their training may have prepared them for political pacifism but not activism. To urge political pacifists to use techniques employed by activists can invite disaster. Recently, a broader base of political training and knowledge has been offered to OD consultants [Huse, 1980, pp. 143–148; NTL, 1980]. Though consultants now have the opportunity to develop greater political sophistication, the cautious and conservative progress of OD into OP may well be justified on utilitarian grounds. Little, if any, sophistication is required to enter the political arena, but a great deal is required to work productively within it.

Political reaction in the client system.
Largely ignored in arguments favoring political involvement are considerations of how the client system may react. Activists maintain, for example, that organizational "opponents" should be politically overcome. It must be remembered, however, that what is home ground to the opponent is foreign territory to the consultant. If opponents have any political sophistication, they will have identified and marshalled sources of power, formed long-standing alliances, and developed political strategies that have proven value in that particular system. One can expect such opponents to use their power and strategies when they perceive that their vested interests are attacked.

In addition, one needs to consider how the client system itself will react to political confrontation. It is one thing to be able to win a political confrontation; it is quite another to keep such confrontations from adversely affecting the political subsystem. Political pacifism seems to have evolved to minimize the danger of disruption. Political moderates, and activists in particular, need to carefully consider this aspect of political subsystem reactivity.

Reaction to the OD profession. Perhaps the biggest concern related to increased political activity, particularly political activism, is how clients will react to OD itself. Since its beginning, OD has developed an image of being close to what Charles Perrow [1977] called "the forces of light." This image derives from the emphasis on such fundamental values as honesty, openness, collaboration, and a steadfast concern for everyone in the client system. This image has utilitarian value. OD technology, for example, requires cooperation, trust, and client confidence in the consultant. The OD image supports these qualities, and the consultant depends on this image.

The success that political activists have enjoyed may be partly based on this image as well. Limiting and channeling communication for political purposes, the use of hidden or covert agendas, and the political manipulation of intervention research strategies may be successful partly because clients don't expect OD consultants to behave in this manner. Thus, using the element of surprise, the activist can catch opponents unprepared to effectively resist.

Images can change. As the reputation of the activist consultant grows, clients will no longer be caught by surprise. They can be expected, rather, to take the initiative and attack the consultant first. At the very least, the activist will no longer enjoy the trust and cooperation of clients who are preparing for political confrontation.

This would be a relatively minor concern for OD as a profession if clients could be counted on *not* to generalize their perceptions of activist consultants—an unrealistic hope. If the OD profession suffers an image change reflecting political activism, the chances of success even for political pacifists are reduced.

Consider the following example: A nationally known consultant company conducted management audits for a major governmental unit in the Pacific Southwest. Following the audits, high-ranking officials were fired, in light of evidence gained in some of the audits. Word quickly spread that these audits were political covers with the hidden agenda of marshalling evidence to do away with pre-selected officials. Whether or not this rumor was correct, from that point forward the audits created a great deal of political turmoil. Perhaps the activist is prepared for this type of reaction. The issue, however, is whether OD as a profession can accept this type of image change.

Facilitation vs activism. Political moderates remain committed to the traditional clinical orientation of organization development. They argue that political facilitation of social change is not only compatible with this orientation but will increase chances of intervention success as well. They conclude, therefore, that OD ought to promote such political involvement on the part of its practitioners. Although there is evidence to support this position, a number of caveats must be kept in mind. First, OD must take care to see that consultants are properly prepared to assume the role of a political facilitator. Second, political facilitation must be exercised with due caution lest the client system overreact. Third, OD must recognize that it is all too easy to slip from the facilitator role into the activist role. The boundaries between them are often difficult to define, particularly in the hour-to-hour day-to-day operation of an intervention program.

Political activists maintain that political facilitation is not enough to achieve intervention success in the face of determined political resistance. Greater rates of success can, however, be expected if the consultant uses whatever power politics are required to confront and remove such resistance. Political activism, however, carries with it not only the problems of client-system reaction, but also the problems of a negative image change for the OD profession as a whole.

On utilitarian grounds alone, OD is well advised to increase political involvement only with extreme caution and due deliberation. Beyond utilitarian considerations, OD consultants and the field as a whole should address as well the issue of how political involvement affects the value base of the profession.

Value Considerations

Political involvement, particularly as it approaches political activism, has consequences for the values of organization development. There has been a general lack of discussion regarding what these consequences may be, yet this is an important topic, because the distinctive character and practice of OD, as with any professional field, is based as much on its values as on its technology and knowledge [Margulies & Raia, 1978]. The value base plays an important role in the image of OD, the use of its technology, and in providing the context and objectives for intervention itself. The value base reflects the nature of the relationship between client and consultant and what constitutes acceptable consultant behavior. Clients depend on the value base of OD just as they do in any professional relationship. It has been argued above that consultants depend on it as well.

Political activism provides a good context for discussion. The sharp contrast between the values inherent in political activism and the traditional values of OD produces issues more easily discerned than when lesser levels of political involvement are addressed. At the same time, the issues raised by these contrasts provide some points of departure for addressing the more subtle issues of lesser forms of political involvement. The assertion that the ends justify the means, whether explicitly advocated [V. Schein, 1977] or implicitly assumed provides the focus for value considerations.

Can the means and ends be separated?
In theory, it may be possible to separate one's objectives and the means used to achieve them. In practice, and particularly in OD, the means used appear more often than not to affect the ends attained. From a value perspective, an OD intervention program is successful if the organizational health of a client system is improved and if it has achieved or expended its capacity for self-renewal [French et al., 1978]. These goals, in turn, are dependent on, and evolve from, the achievement of a host of other clinical objectives. Such objectives may well be displaced in an intervention program using the philosophy and techniques of political activism.

The displacement of clinical objectives can occur for a number of reasons. First, intense political activity often leads to the compromise of objectives for political expediency. One must consider the point at which such compromise becomes failure from a clinical perspective. Second, political activism, by its nature, fosters political activity in the client system of a similar character. Such activity can itself displace clinical goals. Moreover, the aftermath of political activism, with its tendency to produce win/lose conflict, can leave strains and tensions in the client system that drain energy from productive uses and future renewal. Finally, the capacity for self-renewal requires that the consultant teach those in the client system the concepts, methods, and values that will allow them to solve future as well as present problems

[French et al., 1978]. One must consider, then, whether political activism teaches the client methods of self-renewal, or suspicion, distrust, and the fine art of political warfare.

Presuming the ends that justify the means. Political activism is literally presumptuous: the activist presumes to know the good ends that justify the means used to achieve them. Traditionally, however, the OD consultant leaves the configuration of the ends (i.e., desired condition) to the decision making of the clients. In fact, the end traditionally pursued by OD consultants is to help establish the means by which the client can effectively and efficiently pursue a new status quo. Thus, within OD the means and ends are often the same.

The political moderate position recognizes this. It seeks to work within the political subsystem to help establish the climate necessary to support such traditional change elements as honesty, openness, collaboration, and participation. There is no doubt that these elements are value laden. To the extent that political activism replaces these traditional elements with a conscious restriction of openness and a limitation of both collaboration and participation, it is replacing the valued ends of OD for the means to reach some other set of objectives. Thus OD must consider, for example, if political resistance is a form of participation to be confronted and worked through or confronted and wiped out for some vision of what ought to be. In so considering, OD must consider as well whether it will still value the welfare of individuals, even those frightened enough to resist.

On the value of conserving OD values. If OD itself is to remain dynamic, the profession must constantly undergo changes to meet the challenges it faces. To the extent that OD values have promoted political naiveté within the profession, they may need to change to guide action in the political arena. It should be recognized, however, that the value base has served OD well in the past. If some values are to change, perhaps this would be best accomplished conservatively with the objective of *guiding* political involvement to reach *clinical ends.* Certainly traditional values should not be casually tossed aside to allow for politically expedient behaviors.

Concluding Remarks

We have focused on an important aspect of the growing field of organization development— its movement into the study and use of organizational politics. The present political orientations in the field, largely operationalized by OD consultants themselves, have been generally ignored and in some cases rejected. One purpose of the foregoing discussion has been to establish, as clearly as possible, the existence of these orientations. Broader recognition of OD's political orientations and the further development of political knowledge and skills can aid both the OD consultant and the field.

Political involvement is not, however, without its problems, and our second purpose has been to explore some of the utilitarian and value problems that can arise from increased political intervention. By exploring OD's present political orientation and its future political alternatives, we obtain a more complete understanding of the roles, skills, and strategies available to the OD consultant. This understanding, in turn, can only enhance the field.

References

BEER, M. On gaining influence and power for OD. *Journal of Applied Behavioral Sciences,* 1976, *12,* 45–51.

BENNE, K., & BIRNBAUM, M. Principles of changing. In W. G. Bennis, K. Benne, & R. Chin (Eds.), *The planning of change.* New York: Holt, Rinehart & Winston, 1969.

BENNIS, W. G. Unresolved problems facing organization development. *Business Quarterly,* 1969, *34*(4), 80–84.

BURKE, W. W. Organization development in transition. *Journal of Applied Behavioral Sciences,* 1976, *12,* 22–43.

BURNS, T., & STALKER, G. M. *The management of innovation.* London: Tavistock, 1961.

COBB, A. T. *Political planning and organizational innovation.* Paper presented at the annual meeting of the Academy of Management, Orlando, Florida, August 1977.

CYERT, R. M., & MARCH, J. G. *A behavioral theory of the firm.* Englewood Cliffs, N.J.: Prentice-Hall, 1964.

FRENCH, W., BELL, C., & ZAWACKI, R. Mapping the territory. In W. French, C. Bell, & R. Zawacki (Eds.), *Organization development: Theory, practice, and research.* Dallas: Business Publications, 1978, 5–12.

FRIEDLANDER, F. OD reaches adolescence: An exploration of its underlying values. *Journal of Applied Behavioral Science,* 1976, *12,* 7–22.

FRIEDLANDER, F., & BROWN, L. D. Organization development. In M. Rosenzweig & L. Porter (Eds.), *Annual review of psychology.* Palo Alto, Calif.: Annual Reviews, Inc., 1974, pp. 313–341.

GUEST, R., HERSEY, P., & BLANCHARD, D. *Organizational change through effective leadership.* Englewood Cliffs, N.J.: Prentice-Hall, 1977.

HARRISON, R. When power conflicts trigger team spirit. In W. French, C. Bell, & R. Zawacki (Eds.), 1978, pp. 158–164.

HUSE, E. F. *Organization development and change.* New York: West, 1980.

LAWRENCE, P., & LORSCH, J. *Organization and environment.* Boston: Harvard University Graduate School of Business Administration, 1967.

LEAVITT, H. J. Applied organizational change in industry: Structural, technological, and humanistic approaches. In J. G. March (Ed.), *Handbook of organizations.* Chicago: Rand-McNally, 1965, pp. 1144–1170.

LEWIN, K., LIPPITT, R., & WHITE, R. Patterns of aggressive behavior in experimentally created "social climates." *Journal of Social Psychology,* 1939, *10,* 271–299.

LIKERT, R. *New patterns of management.* New York: McGraw-Hill, 1961.

LIKERT, R. *The human organization: Its management and value.* New York: McGraw-Hill, 1967.

MacCRIMMON, K., & TAYLOR, R. N. Decision making and problem solving. In M. Dunnette (Ed.), *Handbook of industrial and organizational psychology.* Chicago: Rand-McNally, 1976, pp. 1397–1453.

MARCH, J. G. The business firm as a political coalition. *Journal of Politics,* 1962, *24,* 662–678.

MARCH, J. G., & SIMON, H. *Organizations.* New York: Wiley, 1958.

MARGULIES, N., & RAIA, A. P. *Conceptual foundations of organizational development.* New York: McGraw-Hill, 1978.

MAYES, B. T., & ALLEN, R. Toward a definition of organizational politics. *Academy of Management Review,* 1977, *2,* 672–678.

McGREGOR, D. *The human side of enterprise.* New York: McGraw-Hill, 1960.

NTL INSTITUTE. *1980 programs.* Arlington, Va.: NTL Institute, 1980.

PERROW, C. The short and glorious history of organizational theory. In H. Tosi & W. C. Hamner (Eds.), *Organizational behavior and management.* Chicago: St. Clair, 1977, pp. 8–19.

PETTIGREW, A. M. Toward a political theory of organizational intervention. *Human Relations,* 1975, *28,* 191–208.

SCHEIN, E. *Organizational psychology.* Englewood Cliffs, N.J.: Prentice-Hall, 1972.

SCHEIN, V. Political strategies for implementing changes. *Group & Organization Studies,* 1977, *2,* 42–48.

SELZNICK, P. *TVA and the grass roots.* Berkeley: University of California Press, 1949.

STRAUSS, G. Some notes on power-equalization. In H. J. Leavitt (Ed.), *The social science of organizations.* Englewood Cliffs, N.J.: Prentice-Hall, 1963.

THOMPSON, J. D. *Organizations in action.* New York: McGraw-Hill, 1967.

42

The Power Game and the Players

Henry Mintzberg

The core of this book is devoted to the discussion of a theory of organizational power. It is built on the premise that organizational behavior is a power game in which various players, called *influencers*, seek to control the organization's decisions and actions. The organization first comes into being when an initial group of influencers join together to pursue a common mission. Other influencers are subsequently attracted to the organization as a vehicle for satisfying some of their needs. Since the needs of influencers vary, each tries to use his or her own levers of power—*means* or *systems of influence*—to control decisions and actions. How they succeed determines what configuration of organizational power emerges. Thus, to understand the behavior of the organization, it is necessary to understand which influencers are present, what needs each seeks to fulfill in the organization, and how each is able to exercise power to fulfill them.

Of course, much more than power determines what an organization does. But our perspective in this book is that power is what matters, and that, if you like, everyone exhibits a lust for power (an assumption, by the way, that I do not personally favor, but that proves useful for the purposes of this book). When our conclusions here are coupled with those of the first book in this series, *The Structuring of*

SOURCE: Henry Mintzberg, *Power in and around Organizations,* © 1983, pp. 22–30. Reprinted by permission of Prentice-Hall, Englewood Cliffs, New Jersey.

Organizations (Mintzberg 1979a, which will subsequently be referred to as the *Structuring* book), a more complete picture of the behavior of organizations emerges.

The Exercise of Power

Hirschman (1970) notes in a small but provocative book entitled *Exit, Voice, and Loyalty,* that the participant in any system has three basic options:

To stay and contribute as expected, which Hirschman calls *loyalty* (in the vernacular, "Shut up and deal")

To leave, which Hirschman calls *exit* ("Take my marbles and go")

To stay and try to change the system, which Hirschman refers to as *voice* ("I'd rather fight than switch")

Should he or she choose voice, the participant becomes what we call an influencer.[1] Those who exit—such as the client who stops buying or the employee who seeks work elsewhere—cease to be influencers, while those who choose loyalty over voice—the client who buys without question at the going rate, the employees who do whatever they are told quietly—choose not to participate as active influencers (other than to support implicitly the existing power structure).

> To resort to voice, rather than exit, is for the customer or member to make an attempt at changing the practices, policies, and outputs of the firm from which one buys or of the organization to which one belongs. Voice is here defined as any attempt at all to change, rather than to escape from, an objectionable state of affairs . . . (Hirschman 1970, p. 30)[2]

For those who stay and fight, what gives power to their voice? Essentially the influencer requires (1) some source or basis of power, coupled with (2) the expenditure of energy in a (3) politically skillful way when necessary. These are the three basic conditions for the exercise of power. In Allison's concise words, "Power . . . is an elusive blend of . . . bargaining advantages, skill and will in using bargaining advantages . . ." (1971, p. 168).

The General Bases of Power

In the most basic sense, the power of the individual in or over the organization reflects some *dependency* that is has—some gap in its own power as a system, in Crozier's view, an "uncertainty" that the organization faces (Crozier 1964; also Crozier and Friedberg 1977). This is especially true of three of the five bases of power we describe here.[3] Three prime bases of power are control of (1) a resource, (2) a technical skill, or (3) a body of knowledge, any one critical to the organization. For example, a monopolist may control the raw material supply to an organization, while an expert may control the repair of important and highly complex machinery. To serve as a basis of power, a resource, skill or body of knowledge must first of all be *essential* to the functioning of the organization. Second, it must be *concentrated,* in short supply or else in the hands of one person or a small number of people who cooperate to some extent. And third it must be *nonsubstitutable,* in other words irreplaceable. These three characteristics create the dependency—the organization needs something, and it can get it only from the few people who have it.

A fourth general basis of power stems from legal prerogatives—exclusive rights or privileges to impose choices. Society, through its governments and judicial system, creates a whole set of legal prerogatives which grant power—*formal power*—to various influencers. In the first place governments reserve for themselves the power to authorize the creation of the organization and thereafter impose regulations of various sorts on it. They also vest owners and/or the directors of the organization with certain powers, usually including the right to hire and fire the top executives. And these executives, in turn, usually have the power to hire and perhaps fire the rest of the employees, and to issue orders to them, tempered by other legal prerogatives which grant power to employees and their associations.

The fifth general basis of power derives from access to those who can rely on the other four. That access may be personal. For example, the spouses and friends of government regulators and of chief executives have power by virtue of having the ear of those who exercise legal prerogatives. The control of an important constituency which itself has influence—the customers who buy or the accountants who control the costs—can also be an important basis for power. Likewise power flows to those who can sway other influencers through the mass media—newspaper editors, TV commentators, and the like.

Sometimes access stems from favors traded: Friends and partners grant each other influence over their respective activities. In this case, power stems not from dependency but from *reciprocity,* the gaining of power in one sphere by the giving up of power in another. As we shall see in many examples in this book, the organizational power game is characterized as much by reciprocal as by dependency—one-sided, or "asymmetrical"—relationships.[4]

Will and Skill

But having a basis for power is not enough. The individual must act in order to become an influencer, he or she must expend energy, use the basis for power. When the basis is formal, little effort would seem to be required to use it. But many a government has passed legislation that has never been respected, in many cases because it did not bother to establish an agency strong enough to enforce it. Likewise managers often find that their power to give orders means little when not backed up by the effort to ensure that these are in fact carried out. On the other hand, when the basis of power is informal, much effort would seem to be required to use it. If orders cannot be given, battles will have to be won. Yet here too, sometimes the reverse is true. In universities, for example, power often flows to those who take the trouble to serve on the committees. As two researchers noted in one study: "Since few people were involved and those who were involved wandered in and out, someone who was willing to spend time being present could often become influential" (March and Romelaer 1976, p. 272). In the game of power, it is often the squeaky wheel that gets the grease.

In effect, the requirement that energy be expected to achieve outcomes, and the fact that those with the important bases of power have only so much personal energy to expend, means that power gets distributed more widely than our discussions of the bases of power would suggest. Thus, one article shows how the attendants in a mental hospital, at the bottom of the formal hierarchy, could block policy initiatives from the top because collectively they were willing and able to exert far more effort than could the administrators and doctors (Scheff 1961), What this means is that influencers pick and choose their issues, concentrating their efforts on the ones most important to them, and, of course, those they think they can win. Thus Patchen (1974) finds that each influencer stakes out those areas that affect him or her most, deferring elsewhere to other influencers.

Finally, the influencer must not only have some basis for power and expend some energy, but often he or she must also do it in a clever manner, with political skill. Much informal and even formal power backed by great effort has come to naught because of political ineptness. Managers, by exploiting those over whom they have formal power, have often provoked resistance and even mutiny; experts regularly lose reasonable issues in meetings because they fail to marshall adequate support. Political skill means the ability to use the bases of power effectively—to convince those to whom one has access, to use one's resources, information, and technical skills to their fullest in bargaining, to exercise formal power with a sensitivity to the feelings of others, to know where to concentrate one's energies, to sense what is possible, to organize the necessary alliances.

Related to political skill is a set of intrinsic leadership characteristics—charm, physical strength, attractiveness, what Kipnis calls "personal resources" (1974, p. 88). *Charisma* is the label for that mystical quality that attracts followers to an individual. Some people become powerful simply because others support them; the followers pledge loyalty to a single voice.

Thus power derives from some basis for it is coupled with the efforts and the abilities to use the basis. We shall assume this in the rest of the book, and look more concretely at the channels through which power is exercised, what we call the *means* and *the systems of influence*—the specific instruments influencers are able to use to effect outcomes.

The Cast of Players in Order of Appearance

Who are these influencers to whom we have referred? We can first distinguish *internal* from *external* influencers. The internal influencers are the full-time employees who use voice, those people charged with making the decision and taking the actions on a permanent, regular basis; it is they who determine the outcomes, which express the goals pursued by the organization. The external influencers are nonemployees who use their bases of influence to try to affect the behavior of the employees.[5] The first two sections of our theory, on the elements of power, describe respectively the *External Coalition*, formed by the external influencers, and the *Internal Coalition*, formed by the internal influencers.

(As the word *coalition* was retained in this book only after a good deal of consideration, it is worth explaining here why it was chosen. In general, an attempt was made to avoid jargon whenever it was felt to be possible—for example, employing "chief executive officer" instead of "peak coordinator." "Coalition" proved to be a necessary exception. Because there are no common labels—popular or otherwise—to distinguish the power in from that around the organization, one had to be selected. But why *coalition?* Because it seems to fit best, even though it may be misleading to the reader at first. The word *coalition* is normally used for a group of people who band together to win some issue. As the Hickson research team at the University of Bradford notes, it has the connotation of "engineered agreements and alliances" (Astley et al. 1980, p. 21). Ostensibly, we are not using the word in this sense, at least not at first. We use it more in the sense that Cyert and March (1963) introduced it, as a set of people who bargain among themselves to determine a certain distribution of organizational power. But as we proceed in our discussion, the reader will find the two meanings growing increasingly similar. For one thing, in the External or Internal Coalition, the various influencers band together around or within the same organization to satisfy their needs. They do form some sort of "coalition." As Hickson et al. note in an earlier publication, "it is their coalition of interests that sustains (or destroys) [the] organization" (1976, p. 9).[6] More importantly, we shall see that the external and internal influencers each typically form rather stable systems of power, usually focussed in nature. These become semipermanent means to distribute benefits, and so resemble coalitions in the usual meaning of the term.)

Our power play includes ten groups of possible influencers, listed below in order of appearance. The first four are found in the External Coalition:

- First are the *owners,* who hold the legal title to the organization. Some of them perhaps conceived the idea of founding the organization in the first place and served as brokers to bring the initial influencers together.
- Second are the *associates,* the suppliers of the organization's input resources, the clients for its output products and services, as well as its trading partners and competitors. It should be noted that only those associates who resort to voice—for example, who engage in contacts of other than a purely economic nature—are counted as influencers in the External Coalition.

- Third are the *employee associations,* that is, unions and professional associations. Again these are included as influencers to the extent that they seek to influence the organization in other than purely economic ways, that is, to use voice to affect decisions and actions directly. Such employee associations see themselves as representatives of more than simple suppliers of labor resources. Note that employee associations are themselves considered *external* influencers, even though they represent people who can be internal influencers. Acting collectively, through their representatives, the employees choose to exert their influence on the organization from outside of its regular decision-making and action-taking channels, much as do owners and clients. (Singly, or even collectively but in different ways, the employees can of course bring their influence to bear directly on these processes, as internal influencers. Later we shall in fact see that it is typically their impotence in the Internal Coalition that causes them to act collectively in the External Coalition.)
- A fourth category comprises the organization's various *publics,* groups representing special or general interests of the public at large. We can divide these into three: (1) such general groups as families, opinion leaders, and the like; (2) special interest groups such as conservation movements or local community institutions; and (3) government in all of its forms—national, regional, local, departments and ministries, regulatory agencies, and so on.
- Another group of influencers, which is really made up of representatives from among the other four, as well as from the internal influencers, are the *directors* of the organization. These constitute a kind of "formal coalition." This group stands at the interface of the External and Internal Coalitions, but because it meets only intermittently, . . . it is treated as part of the External Coalition.

The Internal Coalition comprises six groups of influencers:

- First is the top or general management of the organization, Papandreou's peak coordinator.

We shall refer to this by the single individual at the top of the hierarchy of authority, in standard American terminology, the *chief executive officer,* or CEO.[7]

- Second are the *operators,* those workers who actually produce the products and services, or who provide the direct support to them, such as the machine operators in the manufacturing plant or the doctors and nurses in the hospital.

- Third are the managers who stand in the hierarchy of line authority from the CEO down to the first-line supervisors to whom the operators formally report. We shall refer to these simply as the *line managers.*

- Fourth are the *analysts of the techno-structure,* those staff specialists who concern themselves with the design and operation of the systems for planning and for formal control, people such as work study analysts, cost accountants, and long-range planners.

- Fifth is the *support staff,* comprising those staff specialists who provide indirect support to the operators and the rest of the organization, in a business firm, for example, the mailroom staff, the chef in the cafeteria, the researchers, the public relation officers, and the legal counsel.[8]

- Finally, there is an eleventh actor in the organizational power system, one that is technically inanimate but in fact shows every indication of having a life of its own, namely the *ideology* of the organization—the set of beliefs shared by its internal influencers that distinguishes it from other organizations.

Figure 1 shows the position of each of these eleven groups schematically. The Internal Coalition is shown in the center, with the Chief Executive Officer at the top, followed, according to the formal hierarchy of authority, by the line managers and then the operators. (In some parts of the discussion, we shall accept these notions of formal authority, in others, we shall not. For now, we retain them.) Shown at either side to represent their roles as staff members are the analysts and the support staff. Above the CEO is shown the board of directors to which the CEO formally reports. And emanating from the organization is a kind of aura to represent its ideology. Surrounding all this are the various groups of the External Coalition. The owners are shown closest to the top of the hierarchy, and to the board of directors, where they are often inclined to exert their influence. The associates are shown surrounding the operating core where the operators work, the suppliers on the left (input) side and the clients on the right (output) side, with the partners and competitors in between. The employee associations are shown closest to the operators, whom they represent, while the various publics are shown to form a ring around the entire power system, in effect influencing every part of it. Thus the organization of Figure 1 can be seen to exist in a complex field of influencer forces.

Each of these eleven groups of players in the organizational power game will be discussed in turn, together with the means of influence they have at their disposal. We assume in this discussion that each is driven by the needs inherent in the roles they play. For example, owners will be described as owners, not as fathers, or Episcopalians, or power-hungry devils. People are of course driven by a variety of needs—by intrinsic values such as the need for control or autonomy, or in Maslow's (1954) needs hierarchy theory, by physiological, safety, love, esteem, and self-actualization needs; by the values instilled in them as children or developed later through socialization and various identifications; by the need to exploit fully whatever skills and abilities they happen to have; by their desire to avoid repetition of painful experiences or to repeat successful ones; by opportunism, the drive to exploit whatever opportunities happen to present themselves. All of these needs contribute to the makeup of each influencer and lead to an infinite variety of behaviors. All are, therefore, important to understand. But they are beyond the scope of this book. Here we focus on those behaviors that are dictated strictly by role. We assume throughout that each group discussed above is driven to gain power in or over the organization—in other words, is an influencer; our discussion then focuses on what ends each seeks to attain, what means or systems of influence each has at its disposal, and how

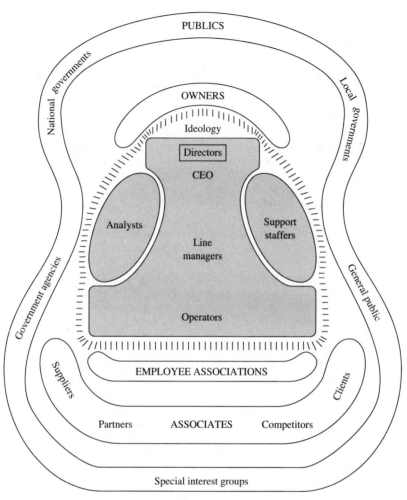

Figure 1
The cast of players

much power each tends to end up with by virtue of the role it plays in the power coalition to which it happens to belong. This is the point of departure for the discussion of our theory.

Notes

1. Some writers call the influencer a "stakeholder" since he or she maintains a stake in the organization the way a shareholder maintains shares. Other use the term "claimant," in that he or she has a claim on the organization's benefits. Both these terms, however, would include those who express loyalty as well as voice.

2. There are some interesting linkages among these three options, as Hirschman points out. Exit is sometimes a last resort for frustrated voice, or in the case of a strike (temporary exit), a means to supplement voice. The effect of exit can be "galvanizing" when voice is the norm, or vice versa, as in the case of Ralph Nader who showed

consumers how to use voice instead of exit against the automobile companies (p. 125). Of course, an inability to exit forces the disgruntled individual to turn to voice. Hirschman also makes the intriguing point that exit belongs to the study of economics, voice to that of political science. In economic theory, the customer or employee dissatisfied with one firm is supposed to shift to another: ". . . one either exits or one does not; it is impersonal" (p. 15). In contrast, voice is "a far more 'messy' concept because it can be graduated, all the way from faint grumbling to violent protest . . . voice is political action par excellence" (p. 16). But students of political science also have a "blind spot": ". . . exit has often been branded as *criminal,* for it has been labelled desertion, defection, and treason" (p. 17).

3. Related discussions of bases of power can be found in Allison (1971), Crozier and Friedberg (1977), Jacobs (1974), Kipnis (1974), Mechanic (1962), and Pfeffer and Salancik (1978).

4. French and Raven's (1959) five categories of power, as perhaps the most widely quoted typology of power, should be related to these five bases of power. Their "reward" and "coercive" power are used formally by those with legal prerogatives and may be used informally by those who control critical resources, skills, or knowledge (for example, to coerce by holding these back). Their "legitimate" power corresponds most closely to our legal prerogatives and their "expert" power to our critical skills and knowledge. Their fifth category, "referent" power, is discussed below in our section on political skill.

5. As we shall soon see, there are some circumstances in which external influencers can impose decisions directly on the organization, and others in which full-time employees acting in concert through their associations behave as external influencers by trying to affect the behavior of the senior managers. As Pfeffer and Salancik (1978, p. 30) point out, actors can be part of the organization as well as its environment. Nevertheless, the distinction between full-time employees— those individuals with an intensive and regular commitment to the organization—and others will prove to be a useful and important one in all that follows.

6. It might be noted that the Hickson group in the 1980 publication cited earlier (as Astley et al.) decided to replace the word *coalition* by *constellation.* That was tried in this book, but dropped as not having quite the right ring to it.

7. An alternate term which appears frequently in the more recent literature is *dominant coalition.* But we have no wish to prejudice the discussion of the power of one of our groups of influencers by the choice of its title.

8. For a more elaborate description of each of these five groups as well as clarification of the differences between technocratic and support staff and of line and staff in general, see Chapter 2 of the *Structuring* book.

References

ALLISON, G. T. (1971). *Essence of decision: Explaining the Cuban missile crisis.* Boston: Little, Brown. Copyright © 1971 by Graham T. Allison. Reprinted by permission of the publisher.

ASTLEY, W. G., AXELSSON, R., BUTLER, R. J., HICKSON, D. J., & WILSON, D. C. (1980). Decision making: Theory III. Working Paper, University of Bradford Management Centre. Used with permission.

CROZIER, M. (1964). *The bureaucratic phenomenon.* Chicago: University of Chicago Press. Used with permission.

———. (1974). Why is France blocked? In H. J. Leavitt, L. Pinfield, & E. J. Webb (Eds.). *Organizations of the future: Interaction with the external environment.* New York: Praeger. Used with permission.

———, & FRIEDBERG, E. (1977). *L'acteur et le système.* Paris: Editions du Seuil.

CYERT, R. M., & MARCH, J. G. (1963). *A behavioral theory of the firm.* Englewood Cliffs, NJ: Prentice-Hall.

FRENCH, J. R. P., Jr., & RAVEN, B. (1959). The bases of social power. In D. Cartwright (Ed.). *Studies in social power* (pp. 150–167). Ann Arbor: Institute for Social Research, University of Michigan.

HICKSON, D. J., BUTLER, R. J., AXELSSON, R., & WILSON, D. (1976). Decisive coalitions. Paper presented to International Conference on Coordination and Control of Group and Organizational Performance, Munich, West Germany.

HIRSCHMAN, A. O. (1970). *Exit, voice, and loyalty: Responses to decline in firms, organizations, and states.* Cambridge, MA: Harvard University Press.

JACOBS, D. (1974). Dependency and vulnerability: An exchange approach to the control of organizations. *Administrative Science Quarterly,* 45–59.

KIPNIS, D. (1974). The powerholder. In J. T. Tedeschi (Ed.), *Perspectives on social power* (pp. 82–122). Chicago: Aldine.

MARCH, J. G., & ROMELAER, P. J. (1976). Position and presence in the drift of decisions. In J. G. March & J. P. Olsen (Eds.), *Ambiguity and choice in organizations.* Bergen, Norway: Universitetsforlaget.

MASLOW, A. H. (1954). *Motivation and personality.* New York: Harper & Row.

MECHANIC, D. (1962). Sources of power of lower participants in complex organizations. *Administrative Science Quarterly,* 349–364.

MINTZBERG, H. (1979a). *The structuring of organizations: A synthesis of the research.* Englewood Cliffs, NJ: Prentice-Hall.

PATCHEN, M. (1974). The locus and basis of influence on organizational decisions. *Organizational Behavior and Human Performance,* 195–221.

PFEFFER, N., and SALANCIK, G. R. (1978). *The external control of organizations: A resource dependence perspective.* New York: Harper & Row.

SCHEFF, T. J. (1961). Control over policy by attendants in a mental hospital. *Journal of Health and Human Behavior,* 93–105.

VIII

Organizational Culture and Symbolic Management Organization Theory

The newest and most controversial perspective of organization theory is the organizational culture or symbolic management perspective. Its theories are based on assumptions about organizations and people that depart radically from those of the "mainline" schools of organization theory. In addition, the organizational culture perspective does not believe that quantitive, quasi-experimental, logical-positivist, research designs and methods are especially useful for studying organizations (Ott, 1989a, Chapter 5). In these respects, it shares similarities with the multiple constituencies and power theories.

What is organizational culture? First, it is the culture that exists in an organization, something akin to a societal culture. It is comprised of many intangible things such as values, beliefs, assumptions, perceptions, behavioral norms, artifacts, and patterns of behavior. It is the unseen and unobservable force that is always behind the organizational activities that *can* be seen and observed. According to Kilmann and others (1985), organizational culture is a social energy that moves people to act. "Culture is to the organization what personality is to the individual—a hidden, yet unifying theme that provides meaning, direction, and mobilization."

Secondly, organizational culture is an emerging set of organization theories with its own assumptions about organizational realities and relationships. It is yet another way of viewing, thinking about, studying, and trying to understand organizations. Like power and politics organization theory, the organizational culture perspective represents a counterculture within organization theory. Its assumptions, units of analysis, research methods, and approaches are very different from those of the dominant, rational, "modern" structural and systems theories. The organizational culture perspective challenges the basic views of the "modern" structural and systems perspectives about, for example, how organizations make decisions and how and why organizations—and people in organizations—act as they do.

In both the "modern" structural and the systems theories of organization, organizations are assumed to be utilitarian institutions whose primary purpose is to accomplish established goals. Those goals are set by people in positions of formal authority. The primary questions for organization theory thus involve how best to design and manage organizations to achieve their declared purposes effectively and efficiently. The personal preferences of organizational members are restrained by systems of formal rules, authority, and by norms of rational behavior. In a 1982 *Phi Delta Kappan* article, Karl Weick argues that four organizational conditions must exist in order for basic assumptions of the structuralists and systemists to be valid:

1. A self-correcting system of interdependent people
2. Consensus on objectives and methods
3. Coordination achieved through sharing information
4. Predictable organizational problems and solutions

But, unfortunately, Weick is forced to conclude that these conditons seldom—if ever—exist in modern organizations.

Consequently, the organizational culture perspective rejects the assumptions of the "modern" structural and systems theories. Instead, it assumes that many organizational behaviors and decisions are almost predetermined by the patterns of basic assumptions that are held by members of an organization. Those patterns of assumptions continue to exist and to influence behaviors because they repeatedly lead people to make decisions that "worked in the past" for the organization. With repeated use, the assumptions slowly drop out of peoples' consciousness but continue to influence organizational decisions and behaviors, even when the organization's environment changes. They become the underlying, unquestioned, but virtually forgotten reasons for "the way we do things here"—even when the ways are no longer appropriate. They are so basic, so pervasive, and so totally accepted as "the truth" that no one thinks about or remembers them.

Thus, a strong organizational culture literally controls organizational behavior: For example, an organizational culture can block an organization from making changes that are needed to adapt to a changing environment. From the organizational culture perspective, the personal preferences of organizational members are not restrained by systems of formal rules, authority, and by norms of rational behavior. Instead, they are controlled by cultural norms, values, beliefs and assumptions. In order to understand or predict how an organization will behave under varying circumstances, one must know and understand the organization's patterns of basic assumptions—its organizational culture.

Every organizational culture is different, for several reasons. First, what has "worked" repeatedly for one organization may not for another, so the basic assumptions differ. Second, an organization's culture is partially shaped by many factors including, for example, the societal culture in which it resides; its technologies, markets, and competition; and the personality of its founder(s) or dominant early leaders. Some organizational cultures are more distinctive than others; some organizations have strong, unified, pervasive cultures, whereas others have weaker cultures; some organizational cultures are quite pervasive, whereas others may have many *subcultures* existing in different functional or geographical areas (Ott, 1989a, Chapter 4).

Knowledge of an organization's structure, information systems, strategic planning processes, markets, technology, goals, and so forth, will give clues about an organization's culture, but not accurately or reliably. As a consequence, an organization's behavior can not be understood or predicted by studying its structural or systems elements; its organizational culture must be studied. And, the quantitative quasi-experimental research methods used by the "modern" structural and systems schools *cannot* identify or measure unconscious, virtually forgotten basic assumptions. Van Maanen, Dabbs, and Faulkner, in their 1982 book *Varieties of Qualitative Research,* describe a growing wave of disenchantment with the use of quantitative quasi-experimental research methods for studying organizations, mainly because these methods have produced very little useful knowledge about organizations over the last twenty years. Yet, quantitative research using quasi-experimental designs, control groups, computers, multivariate analyses, heuristic models, and the like are the essential "tools" of the systems and "modern" structural schools. More and more, the organizational culture school (and the power and politics school) are turning to qualitative research methods like ethnography and participant observation.

Earlier, we said that organizational culture represents a counterculture within the field of organization theory. The reasons should be becoming evident. The organizational culture perspective believes that the "modern" structural and systems schools of organization theory are using the wrong tools (or "lenses") to look at the wrong organizational elements in their attempts to understand and predict organizational behavior. In other words, they are wasting their time.

It takes courage to challenge the basic views of a mainstream school in any profession or academic discipline. Yet this is just what the organizational culture and the power and politics perspectives are doing when they advocate such radically different ways of looking at and working with organizations. For example, from the organizational culture perspective, AT&T's basic problems since deregulation and court-ordered splintering of the Bell System are not in its structure, information systems, or people. Rather, they rest in an organizational culture that no longer is appropriate for AT&T's deregulated world. The long-standing AT&T culture had been centered on assumptions about (1) the value of technical superiority, (2) AT&T's possession of technical superiority, and thus (3) AT&T's rightful dominance in the telephone and telecommunications market. Therefore, working to improve things like AT&T's goals, structure, differentiation and integration processes, strategic plans, and information systems will not solve AT&T's monumental problems. The solution requires changing an ingrained organizational culture: changing basic *unconscious* assumptions about what makes for success in a competitive telephone and communications market.

Lee Iacocca faced a similar problem (but different in its content) when he took over leadership of the Chrysler Corporation. Chrysler was a "loser"—in just about every way—in the eyes of employees, potential employees, investors, car dealers, financers, suppliers, and car buyers. It was simply *assumed* that Chrysler could not compete head-on. Iacocca had to change not only an organizational culture, but also *everybody's perception* of that culture. Chrysler needed and got in Iacocca what Warren Bennis (1984) and Tichy and Ulrich (1984) have called a "transformational leader," one who could totally transform an imbedded organizational culture by creating a new vision of and for the organization, and successfully selling that vision—by rallying commitment and loyalty to make the vision become a reality.

In Chapter VII, we said that much of the important writing from the power theories of organization is quite recent and its theoretical grounding is not as well developed as, for example, it is in the classical, "modern" structural, and systems theories. Most of the research and writing from the organizational culture perspective is even more recent. Thus, the organizational culture perspective suffers from the problems and limitations of youthfulness. Although phrases like *organizational culture* and *culture of a factory* can be found in a few books on management written as early as the 1950s (for example, Elliott Jaques' 1951 book *The Changing Culture of a Factory* and William H. Whyte, Jr.'s, 1956 book about conformity in business, *The Organization Man*), few students of management or organizations paid much attention to the nature and content of organizational culture until the late 1970s. (The few who did were mostly proponents of organization development [Ott, 1989b, Chapter VI].)

During the 1960s and early 1970s, several books on organizational and professional socialization processes received wide attention. As useful as these earlier works were, they *assumed* the presence of organizational or professional cultures and proceeded to examine issues involving the match between individuals and cultures. Some of the more widely read of these were the 1961 book *Boys in White* by Becker, Geer, Hughes, and Strauss, which chronicled the processes used to socialize medical students into the medical profession; Herbert Kaufman's 1960 study of how the United States Forest Service developed the "will and capacity to conform" among its remotely stationed rangers in *The Forest Ranger*; Ritti and Funkhouser's 1977 humorous-but-serious look at *The Ropes to Skip and the Ropes to Know*; John Van Maanen's articles on "Police Socialization" (1975) and "Breaking in: Socialization to Work" (1976). During this period, Edgar H. Schein contributed significantly to the knowledge about both organizational and professional socialization processes in numerous writings including, for example, "How to Break in the College Graduate" (1964), "Organizational Socialization and the Profession of Management" (1968), and *Career Dynamics: Matching Individual and Organizational Needs* (1978). Once again, however, these earlier writings did not address important questions such as how cultures are formed or changed, how cultures affect leadership, or the relationship between culture and strategic planning (establishing organizational directions); rather, they focused on the process of socializing employees into existing organizational cultures and the impacts of existing cultures on organizational members.

A different orientation to cultures in organizations started to appear in the organization theory literature during the late 1970's. This orientation is known as the symbolic frame, symbolic management, or organizational symbolism. Bolman and Deal (1984) identify the basic tenets of symbolic management as follows:

1. The meaning or the interpretation of what is happening in organizations is more important than what actually is happening.
2. Ambiguity and uncertainty, which are prevalent in most organizations, preclude rational problem solving and decision-making processes.
3. People use symbols to reduce ambiguity and to gain a sense of direction when they are faced with uncertainty.

Symbols are things like flags, logos, and creeds that carry a wider (or different) meaning than their intrinsic content. For example, the United States flag is a symbol because it embodies values, traditions, and emotions. Symbols also can be things such as words, phrases, organizational structures, management information systems, an office next to the president's, wood as opposed to steel office furniture, romanticized stories about organizational heroes, and ritualistic ceremonies—if they carry meanings that go beyond their intrinsic content. Thus, the focus of organizational symbolism is on the creation and management of the meaning of symbols.

The manipulation of symbols and the dramaturgy of symbolic acts are essential elements of managing people in organizations. While such manipulations may be conscious or unconscious on the part of management, they are invariably there. Frequently, symbolic acts are easily identifiable because of their obvious *beau geste* quality. They form an integral part of everyday manners and courtesies. When an organization's chief executive accidently meets a lower-echelon employee in a crowded elevator and says "How's your job coming along?" the executive is not using words to ask a question; the words are used simply to communicate sociability—a symbolic ritual. It would be quite out of place and both annoying and surprising to the executive if the employee actually answered the question instead of replying with a simple "Fine, thank you." In cases like these, language ceases to be an instrument of communication and becomes a symbol—a thing that carries a different meaning than its intrinsic content. Similar symbolic machinations are important devices for both control and motivation in any social system.

In their 1967 book, *The Social Construction of Reality*, Peter Berger and Thomas Luckmann define meanings as "socially contructed realities." In other words, things are not real in and of themselves; the perceptions of them are, in fact, reality. As W. I. Thomas said (1923), "If people believe things are real, they are real in their consequences." According to the organizational culture perspective, meanings (realities) are established by and among the people in organizations—by the organizational culture. Experimenters have shown that there is a strong relation between culturally determined values and the perception of symbols. People will distort their perceptions of symbols according to the need for what is symbolized (Davis, 1963). Thus, organizational symbolism is an integral part of the organizational culture perspective.

Symbolic management theory attracted only limited attention during the 1970s. The turning point for the organizational culture/symbolic management perspective did not arrive until 1981 or 1982. Then, almost overnight, organizational culture became a very hot topic in books, journals, and periodicals aimed at management practitioners and academicians, including Thomas Peters and Robert Waterman, Jr.'s, 1982 best-seller *In Search of Excellence* (and its sequels); Terrence Deal and Allan Kennedy's 1982 book *Corporate Cultures*; *Fortune* Magazine's 1983 story on "The Corporate Culture Vultures"; *Business Week*'s May 14, 1984 cover story "Changing a Corporate Culture." Also, both William Ouchi's 1981 best-seller *Theory Z* and Richard Pascale and Anthony Athos' *The Art of Japanese Management* (1981) certainly represent the organizational culture perspective.

The first definitive book on symbolic management was published in 1983, *Organizational Symbolism*, edited by Pondy, Frost, Morgan, and Dandridge. However, the first comprehensive, theoretically based, integrative writing on organizational culture did not appear until 1984 and 1985. Products of these two years include Thomas Sergiovanni and John Corbally's heady reader *Leadership and Organization Culture* (1984); Edgar Schein's pioneering *Organizational Culture and Leadership* (1985); Vijay Sathe's *Culture and Related Corporate Realitites* (1985); and the first of Ralph Kilmann's series of books built from interactive conference papers, *Gaining Control of the Corporate Culture.*

"Total Quality Management" (TQM) has thrust organizational culture onto the front pages of the management and organizational literature in the 1990s. Several professional management and behavioral sciences journals now carry articles regularly on a variety of issues that reflect the organizational culture and symbolic management perspective. And, books with important insights continue to roll off the publishers' presses: For example, *Developing Corporate Character* by Alan Wilkins (1989); *Organisational Cultures in Theory and Practice* by Pedersen and Sørensen (1989); *Organizational Climate and Culture* edited by Schneider (1990); *Corporate Culture and Organizational Effectiveness* by Dennison (1990); and *Cultural Knowledge in Organizations,* by Sackman (1991).

The first selection reprinted here is Edgar H. Schein's chapter from his 1985 book *Organizational Culture and Leadership* titled "Defining Organizational Culture." In it, Schein proposes a "formal definition" of organizational culture that has gained wide acceptance. His definition is a model of three levels of culture, which is particularly useful for sorting through myriad methodological and substantive problems associated with identifying an organizational culture.

In "The Making of an Organizational Saga," from his widely cited 1970 book *The Distinctive College: Antioch, Reed & Swarthmore,* Burton R. Clark examines how sagas and stories help to provide stability and continuity through symbolism, during and between the times of risks and tensions that inevitably accompany the stages in the development of "organizational distinctiveness." Clark's study represents an excellent example of the use of qualitative research methods to *explain* rather than simply to *understand* organizational phenomena.

Merle Reis Louis' 1983 article "Organizations as Culture-Bearing Milieux" provides a cogent overview of the cultural perspective. Louis conceives of meaning as "emergent"—as a socially constructed reality influenced by shared interpretations of symbols and social ideals that help organizational members interpret experiences and thus guide behavior. Louis explores culture from the psychological and sociological contexts and, like most proponents of organizational culture and symbolic management, argues that qualitative research methods hold the most promise for expanding useful knowledge of organizations.

As the title of the selection implies, "Organizations as Shared Meanings" (1983) by Linda Smircich (included here) examines how systems of commonly shared meaning develop and are sustained in organizations through symbolic communications processes. Smircich conducted a six-week study of an insurance company using ethnographic research methods in which data were collected mostly through observation and discussions with executives. Smircich identified a counterproductive "prevailing ethos"—a dominant shared interpretation—that inhibited management's ability to function effectively and that was disliked by almost all staff members: the belief that disagreements or problems that might prove difficult or uncomfortable to handle should not be discussed. "Problems get 'buried' instead of dealt with directly because 'it's easier to handle that way.'" Smircich explores several issues that are central to understanding the dynamics of the organizational culture/symbolic management perspective: why the staff sustained the dysfunctional ethos over an extended period (the functions served by maintaining it); how the staff made sense of its continuance and their willingness to abide by it (by sharing an interpreted meaning); the nature of its origins (an historical threat to the company's survival); how symbolic communications (rituals, slogans, and ceremonies) nurture and sustain it (for example, at Monday-morning staff meetings); and language clues an outsider observer or researcher might use to identify situations in which meaning is not being shared by members of a culture— and thus to alert an outsider to opportunities for gaining important understandings about the culture. Smircich reminds us that shared systems of meanings provide members of an organizational culture with "a sense of commonality, or taken for grantedness [that] is necessary for continuing organized activity so that interaction can take place without constant interpretation and reinterpretation of meanings. . . . The particular set of meanings that a group evolves provides it with its own ethos or distinctive character."

The organizational culture perspective is particularly important for understanding loosely structured organizations. Thus, our concluding reading, "Cultural and Competing Perspectives in Administrative Theory and Practice" by Thomas Sergiovanni, is written by a student of the most loosely structured form of organization: schools and universities. In our opinion, Sergiovanni (1984, pp. 2–8) articulates the fundamental underlying assumptions that define the essence of the organizational culture and symbolic management perspective:

- "The study of organizational behavior and administrative functioning might well be considered as 'artificial' sciences (Simon, 1969). . . . Reality is created by human conventions rather than by being inherent in the nature of the universe."
- "Actions have meaning in the sense that as preconditions change, meanings change regardless of the sameness of recorded behavior."
- "It is the scholar's perception of the dominant conventions that governs that nature of knowledge. . . . Knowledge is not a passive mirror of reality."
- "Efficiency principles persevere today [for our organizations because] . . . its strength is derived from the attractiveness of efficiency and technical rationality valued in Western thought."
- "Administrative activity is viewed as a cultural artifact."
- "What the leader stands for and communicates to others is considered important. The object of leadership is the stirring of human consciousness, the interpretation and enhancement of meanings, the articulation of key cultural strands, and the linking of organizational members to them."
- "Organizational and societal centers represent the locus of values, sentiments, and beliefs which provide the cultural cement for holding together human groups."

References

ALLEN, R. F., & KRAFT, C. (1982). *The organizational unconscious.* Englewood Cliffs, NJ: Prentice-Hall.
BECKER, H. S., GEER, B., HUGHES, E. C., & STRAUSS, A. L. (1961). *The boys in white: Student culture in medical school.* Chicago: University of Chicago Press.
BENNIS, W. G. (1984). Transformative power and leadership. In T. J. Sergiovanni & J. E. Corbally (Eds.), *Leadership and organizational culture* (pp. 64–71). Urbana, IL: University of Illinois Press.
BERGER, P. L., & LUCKMAN, T. (1967). *The social construction of reality.* Garden City, NY: Doubleday Anchor.
BOLMAN, L. G. & DEAL, T. D. (1991). *Reframing organizations: Artistry, choice, and leadership.* San Francisco: Jossey-Bass.
BUSINESS WEEK. (May 14, 1984). Changing a corporate culture: Can J&J move from bandaids to high tech?, pp. 130–138.
CLARK, B. R. (1970). *The distinctive college: Antioch, Reed & Swarthmore.* Chicago: Aldine.
DAVIS, J. C. (1963). *Human nature in politics: The dynamics of political behavior.* New York: Wiley.
DAVIS, S. M. (1984). *Managing corporate culture.* Cambridge, MA: Ballinger.
DEAL, T. E., & KENNEDY, A. A. (1982). *Corporate cultures.* Reading, MA: Addison-Wesley.
DENNISON, D. R. (1990). *Corporate culture and organizational effectiveness.* New York: Wiley.
FORTUNE. (October 17, 1983). The corporate culture vultures, pp. 66–71.
GRAVES, D. (1986). *Corporate culture: Diagnosis and change.* New York: St. Martin's Press.
HANDY, C. (1989). *The age of unreason.* Boston: Harvard Business School Press.
HELGESEN, S. (1990). *The female advantage: Women's ways of leadership.* New York: Doubleday/Currency.
HUNT, J. G., HOSKING, D. M., SCHRIESHEIM, C. A., & STEWART, R. (Eds.). *Leaders and managers.* New York: Pergamon.
JAQUES, E. (1951). *The changing culture of a factory.* London: Tavistock Institute.
JONES, M. O., MOORE, M. D., & SNYDER, R. C. (Eds.). (1988). *Inside organizations: Understanding the human dimension.* Newbury Park, CA: Sage.
KAUFMAN, H. (1960). *The forest ranger.* Baltimore, MD: The Johns Hopkins Press.
KILMANN, R. H., SAXTON, M. J., SERPA, R., & Associates (Eds.). (1985). *Gaining control of the corporate culture.* San Francisco: Jossey-Bass.
LOUIS, M. R. (1983). Organizations as culture-bearing milieux. In L. R. Pondy, P. J. Frost, G. Morgan, & T. C. Dandridge (Eds.). *Organizational symbolism* (pp. 39–54). Greenwich, CT: JAI Press.
OTT, J. S. (1989a). *The organizational culture perspective.* Pacific Grove, CA: Brooks/Cole.
OTT, J. S. (Ed.). (1989b). *Classic readings in organizational behavior.* Pacific Grove, CA: Brooks/Cole.
OUCHI, W. G. (1981). *Theory Z.* Reading, MA: Addison-Wesley.
PASCALE, R. T., & ATHOS, A. G. (1981). *The art of Japanese management.* New York: Simon & Schuster.
PEDERSEN, J. S., & SØRENSEN, J. S. (1989). *Organisational cultures in theory and practice.* Aldershot, UK: Gower.
PETERS, T. J. (Autumn 1978). Symbols, patterns, and settings: An optimistic case for getting things done. *Organizational Dynamics,* 3–23.
PETERS, T. J., & WATERMAN, R. H., Jr. (1982). *In search of excellence.* New York: Harper & Row.
PONDY, L. R., FROST, P. J., MORGAN, G., & DANDRIDGE, T. C. (Eds.). (1983). *Organizational symbolism.* Greenwich, CT: JAI Press.
QUINN, R. E., & CAMERON, K. S. (Eds.). (1988). *Paradox and transformation: Toward a theory of change in organization and management.* Cambridge, MA: Ballinger.
RITTI, R. R., & FUNKHOUSER, G. R. (1977). *The ropes to skip and the ropes to know.* New York: Wiley.
SACKMAN, S. A., (1991). *Cultural knowledge in organizations: Exploring the collective mind.* Newbury Park, CA: Sage.
SATHE, V. (1985). *Culture and related corporate realities.* Homewood, IL: Richard D. Irwin.
SCHEIN, E. H. (1964). How to break in the college graduate. *Harvard Business Review, 42,* 68–76.
SCHEIN, E. H. (1968). Organizational socialization and the profession of management. *Industrial Management Review, 9,* 1–15.

SCHEIN, E. H. (1978). *Career dynamics: Matching individual and organizational needs.* Reading, MA: Addison-Wesley.

SCHEIN, E. H. (1985). *Organizational culture and leadership.* San Francisco: Jossey-Bass.

SCHNEIDER, B. (Ed.). (1990). *Organizational climate and culture.* San Francisco: Jossey-Bass.

SERGIOVANNI, T. J. (1984). Cultural and competing perspectives in administrative theory and practice. In T. J. Sergiovanni & J. E. Corbally (Eds.), *Leadership and organizational culture: New perspectives on administrative theory and practice* (pp. 1–11). Urbana, IL: University of Illinois Press.

SERGIOVANNI, T. J., & CORBALLY, J. E. (Eds.). (1984). *Leadership and organizational culture.* Urbana, IL: University of Illinois Press.

SIEHL, C., & MARTIN, J. (1984). The role of symbolic management: How can managers effectively transmit organizational culture? In J. G. Hunt, D. M. Hosking, C. A. Schriesheim, & R. Stewart (Eds.), *Leaders and Managers* (pp. 227–239). New York: Pergamon.

SIMON, H. A. (1969). *The sciences of the artificial.* Cambridge, MA: MIT Press.

SMIRCICH, L. (1983). Organizations as shared meanings. In L. R. Pondy, P. J. Frost, G. Morgan, & T. C. Dandridge (Eds.), *Organizational symbolism* (pp. 55–65). Greenwich, CT: JAI Press.

THOMAS, W. I. (1923). *The unadjusted girl.* New York: Harper Torchbooks, 1967.

TICHY, N. M., & ULRICH, D. O. (Fall 1984). The leadership challenge—A call for the transformational leader. *Sloan Management Review, 26*(1), 59–68.

VAN MAANEN, J. (1975). Police socialization. *Administrative Science Quarterly, 20,* 207–228.

VAN MAANEN, J. (1976). Breaking in: Socialization to work. In R. Dubin (Ed.), *Handbook of work, organization and society* (pp. 67–130). Chicago: Rand McNally.

VAN MAANEN, J. (Ed.). (1979, 1983). *Qualitative methodology.* Newbury Park, CA: Sage.

VAN MAANEN, J., DABBS, J. M., Jr., & FAULKNER, R. R. (Eds.). (1982). *Varieties of qualitative research.* Newbury Park, CA: Sage.

WEICK, K. E. (June 1982). Administering education in loosely coupled schools. *Phi Delta Kappan,* 673–676.

WHYTE, W. H., Jr. (1956). *The organization man.* New York: Simon & Schuster.

WILKINS, A. L. (1989). *Developing corporate character: How to successfully change an organization without destroying it.* San Francisco: Jossey-Bass.

43

Defining Organizational Culture

Edgar H. Schein

Most of us—whether students, employees, managers, researchers, or consultants— live in organizations and have to deal with them. Yet we continue to find it amazingly difficult to understand and justify much of what we observe and experience in our organizational life. Too much seems to be "bureaucratic," or "political," or just plain "irrational." People in positions of authority, especially our immediate bosses, often frustrate us or act incomprehensibly, and those we consider the "leaders" of our organizations often disappoint us and fail to meet our aspirations. The fields of organizational psychology and sociology have developed a variety of useful concepts for understanding individual behavior in organizations and the ways in which organizations structure themselves. But the dynamic of why and how they grow, change, sometimes fail, and—perhaps most important of all—do things that don't seem to make any sense continues to elude us.

The concept of organizational culture holds promise for illuminating this difficult area. I will try to show that a deeper understanding of cultural issues in organizations is necessary not only to decipher what goes on in them but, even more important, to identify what may be the priority issues for leaders and leadership. Organizational cultures are created by leaders, and

SOURCE: Edgar H. Schein, *Organizational Culture and Leadership* (San Francisco, Calif.: Jossey-Bass, 1985), 1-22.

one of the most decisive functions of leadership may well be the creation, the management, and—if and when that may become necessary— the destruction of culture. Culture and leadership, when one examines them closely, are two sides of the same coin, and neither can really be understood by itself. In fact, there is a possibility—underemphasized in leadership research—that the *only thing of real importance that leaders do is to create and manage culture* and that the unique talent of leaders is their ability to work with culture. If the concept of leadership as distinguished from management and administration is to have any value, we must recognize the centrality of this culture management function in the leadership concept.

But before we examine closely the tie to leadership, we must full understand the concept of organizational culture. I would like to begin with two examples from my own consulting experience. In the first case (Company A), I was called in to help a management group improve its communication, interpersonal relationships, and decision making. After sitting in on a number of meetings, I observed, among other things, high levels of interrupting, confrontation, and debate; excessive emotionality about proposed courses of action; great frustration over the difficulty of getting a point of view across; and a sense that every member of the group wanted to win all the time. Over a period of several months, I made many suggestions about better listening, less interrupting, more orderly processing of the agenda, the potential negative effects of high emotionality and conflict, and the need to reduce the frustration level. The group members said that the suggestions were helpful, and they modified certain aspects of their procedure, such as lengthening some of their meetings. However, the basic pattern did not change, no matter what kind of intervention I attempted. I could not understand why my efforts to improve the group's problem-solving process were not more successful.

In the second case (Company B), I was asked, as part of a broader consultation project, to help create a climate for innovation in an organization that felt a need to become more flexible in order to respond to its increasingly dynamic business environment. The organization consisted of many different business units, functional groups, and geographical groups. As I got to know more about these units and their problems, I observed that some very innovative things were going on in many places in the company. I wrote several memos describing these innovations, added other ideas from my own experience, and gave the memos to my contact person in the company, hoping that he would distribute them to other managers who might benefit from the ideas. I also gave the memos to those managers with whom I had direct contact. After some months I discovered that whoever got my memo thought it was helpful and on target, but rarely, if ever, did the memo get past the person to whom I gave it. I suggested meetings of managers from different units to stimulate lateral communication, but found no support at all for such meetings. No matter what I did, I could not seem to get information flowing, especially laterally across divisional, functional, or geographical boundaries. Yet everyone agreed in principle that innovation would be stimulated by more lateral communication and encouraged me to keep on helping.

I did not really understand what happened in either of these cases until I began to examine my own assumptions about how things should work in these organizations and began to test whether my assumptions fitted those operating in my client systems. This step of examining the shared assumptions in the client system takes one into "cultural" analysis and will be the focus from here on. Such analysis is, of course, common when we think of ethnic or national cultures, but not sufficient attention has been paid to the possibility that groups and organizations within a society also develop cultures that affect in a major way how the members think, feel, and act. Unless we learn to analyze such organizational cultures accurately, we cannot really understand why organizations do some of the things they do and why leaders have some of the difficulties that they have. The concept of organizational culture is especially relevant to gaining an understanding of the mysterious and seemingly irrational things that go on in human systems. And culture *must* be understood if one is to get along at all, as tourists in foreign lands and new employees in organizations often discover to their dismay.

But a concept is not helpful if we misuse it or fail to understand it. My primary purpose in undertaking this book, therefore, is to explain the concept of organizational culture, show how it can best be applied, and relate it to leadership. To put it more precisely, I hope to accomplish the following things in this book:

1. Provide a clear, workable definition of organizational culture that takes into account the accumulated insights of anthropologists, sociologists, and psychologists. Much attention also will be given to what culture *is not,* because there has been a tendency in the last few years to link culture with virtually everything.

2. Develop a conceptual "model" of how culture works—that is, how it begins, what functions it serves, what problems it solves, why it survives, why and how it changes, and whether it can be managed and, if so, how. We need a dynamic evolutionary model of organizational culture, a model that tells us what culture *does,* not only what it is. In our rush to create more effective organizations in the last few years, we may well have latched on to culture as the new panacea, the cure for all our industrial ailments. How valid is this notion, and, if it is valid, how can we use culture constructively?

3. Show how culture, as a conceptual tool, can illuminate individual psychological behavior; what goes on in small groups and in geographically or occupationally based communities; how large organizations work; and how societal, multinational issues can be better understood through increased cultural insight. A dynamic model of culture will be especially useful in

improving our understanding of how human systems evolve over time.

4. Show how culture and leadership are really two sides of the same coin. One cannot understand one without the other.

Underlying these several purposes is a chronic fear I have that both students of culture and those consultants and managers who deal with culture in a more pragmatic way continue to misunderstand its real nature and significance. In both the popular and the academic literature, I continue to see simplistic, cavalier statements about culture, which not only confuse matters but positively mislead the reader and promise things that probably cannot be delivered. For example, all the recent writings about improving organizational effectiveness through creating "strong" and "appropriate" cultures continue to proliferate the possibly quite *incorrect* assumption that culture can be changed to suit our purposes. Suppose we find that culture can only "evolve" and that groups with "inappropriate" or "weak" cultures simply will not survive. The desire to change culture may become tantamount to destroying the group and creating a new one, which will build or evolve a new culture. Leaders do at times have to do this, but under what conditions is it possible or practical? Are we aware that we may be suggesting something very drastic when we say "Let's change the culture"?

So throughout this book I will be hammering away at the idea that culture is a *deep* phenomenon, that culture is *complex* and difficult to understand, but that the effort to understand it is worthwhile because much of the mysterious and the irrational in organizations suddenly becomes clear when we do understand it.

A Formal Definition of Organizational Culture

The word "culture" has many meanings and connotations. When we combine it with another commonly used word, "organization," we are almost certain to have conceptual and semantic confusion. In talking about organizational culture with colleagues and members of organizations, I often find that we agree "it" exists and is important in its effects but that we have completely different ideas of what the "it" is. I have also had colleagues tell me pointedly that they do *not* use the concept of culture in their work, but when I ask them what it is they do *not* use, they cannot define "it" clearly. Therefore, before launching into the reasons for studying "it," I must give a clear definition of what I will mean by "it."

Some common meanings are the following:

1. *Observed behavioral regularities* when people interact, such as the language used and the rituals around deference and demeanor (Goffman, 1959, 1967; Van Maanen, 1979b).

2. The *norms* that evolve in working groups, such as the particular norm of "a fair day's work for a fair day's pay" that evolved in the Bank Wiring Room in the Hawthorne studies (Homans, 1950).

3. The *dominant values espoused* by an organization, such as "product quality" or "price leadership" (Deal and Kennedy, 1982).

4. The *philosophy* that guides an organization's policy toward employees and/or customers (Ouchi, 1981; Pascale and Athos, 1981).

5. The *rules* of the game for getting along in the organization, "the ropes" that a newcomer must learn in order to become an accepted member (Schein, 1968, 1978; Van Maanen, 1976, 1979b; Ritti and Funkhouser, 1982).

6. The *feeling* or *climate* that is conveyed in an organization by the physical layout and the way in which members of the organization interact with customers or other outsiders (Tagiuri and Litwin, 1968).

All these meanings, and many others, do, in my view, *reflect* the organization's culture but none of them *is* the essence of culture. I will argue that the term "culture" should be reserved for the deeper level of *basic assumptions* and *beliefs* that are shared by members of an organization, that operate unconsciously, and that define in a basic "taken-for-granted" fashion an organization's view of itself and its environment. These assumptions and beliefs are *learned* responses to a group's problems of *survival* in its external environment and its problems of *internal integration.* They come to be taken for granted because they solve those problems repeatedly and reliably. This deeper level of assumptions is to be distinguished from the "artifacts" and "values" that are manifestations or surface levels of the culture but not the essence of the culture (Schein, 1981a, 1983, 1984; Dyer, 1982).

But this definition immediately brings us to a problem. What do we mean by the word "group" or "organization," which, by implication, is the locale of a given culture (Louis, 1983)? Organizations are not easy to define in time and space. They are themselves open systems in constant interaction with their many environments, and they consist of many subgroups, occupational units, hierarchical layers, and geographically dispersed segments. If we are to locate a given organization's culture, where do we look, and how general a concept are we looking for?

Culture should be viewed as a property of an independently defined stable social unit. That is, if one can demonstrate that a given set of people have shared a significant number of important experiences in the process of solving external and internal problems, one can assume that such common experiences have led them, over time, to a shared view of the world around them and their place in it. There has to have been enough shared experience to have led to a shared view, and this shared view has to have worked for long enough to have come to be taken for granted and to have dropped out of awareness. Culture, in this sense, is a *learned product of group experience* and is, therefore, to be found only where there is a definable group with a significant history.

Whether or not a given company has a single culture in addition to various subcultures then becomes an empirical question to be answered by locating stable groups within that company and determining what their shared experience has been, as well as determining the shared experiences of the members of the total organization.

One may well find that there are several cultures operating within the larger social unit called the company or the organization: a managerial culture, various occupationally based cultures in functional units, group cultures based on geographical proximity, worker cultures based on shared hierarchical experiences, and so on. The organization as a whole may be found to have an overall culture if that whole organization has a significant shared history, but we cannot assume the existence of such a culture ahead of time.

This concept of culture is rooted more in theories of group dynamics and group growth than in anthropological theories of how large cultures evolve. When we study organizations, we do not have to decipher a completely strange language or set of customs and mores. Rather, our problem is to distinguish—within a broader host culture—the unique features of a particular social unit in which we are interested. This social unit often will have a history that can be deciphered, and the key actors in the formation of that culture can often be studied, so that we are not limited, as the anthropologist is often limited, by the lack of historical data.

Because we are looking at evolving social units within a larger host culture, we also can take advantage of learning theories and develop a dynamic concept of organizational culture. Culture is learned, evolves with new experiences, and can be changed if one understands the dynamics of the learning process. If one is concerned about managing or changing culture, one must look to what we know about the learning and unlearning of complex beliefs and assumptions that underlie social behavior.

The word "culture" can be applied to any size of social unit that has had the opportunity to learn and stabilize its view of itself and the environment around it—its basic assumptions. At the broadest level, we have *civilizations* and refer to Western or Eastern cultures; at the next level down, we have *countries* with sufficient ethnic commonality that we speak of American culture or Mexican culture. But we recognize immediately that within a country we also have various *ethnic groups* to which we attribute different cultures. Even more specific is the level of *occupation, profession,* or *occupational community.* If such groups can be defined as stable units with a shared history of experience, they will have developed their own cultures. Finally, we get to the level of analysis that is the focus of this book—*organizations.* Within organizations we will find subunits that can be referred to as groups, and such groups may develop group cultures.

To summarize, at any of these structural levels, I will mean by "culture": *a pattern of basic assumptions—invented, discovered, or developed by a given group as it learns to cope with its problems of external adaptation and internal integration—that has worked well enough to be considered valid and, therefore, to be taught to new members as the correct way to perceive, think, and feel in relation to those problems.*

Because such assumptions have worked repeatedly, they are likely to be taken for granted and to have dropped out of awareness. Note that the definition does not include overt behavior patterns. I believe that overt behavior is always determined both by the cultural predisposition (the assumptions, perceptions, thoughts, and feelings that are patterned) and by the situational contingencies that arise from the external environment. Behavioral regularities could thus be as much a reflection of the environment as of the culture and should, therefore, not be a prime basis for *defining* the culture. Or, to put it another way, when we observe behavior regularities, we do not know whether we are dealing with a cultural artifact or not. Only after we have discovered the deeper layers that I am defining as the culture can we specify what is and what is not an artifact that reflects the culture.

Two Case Examples

To illustrate the problem of definition, I will briefly review the two company examples mentioned earlier. In Company A, hereafter referred to as Action Company, one encounters at the visible level an organization with open office landscape architecture; extreme informality of dress and manners; an absence of status symbols (so that it is hard to decipher who has what status in the organization); a very dynamic environment in the sense of rapid pace, enthusiasm, intensity, energy, and impatience; and, finally, a high level of interpersonal confrontation, argumentativeness, and conflict. One also discovers that people are constantly busy going to meetings of various sorts and expressing considerable ambivalence about committees and meetings. Committees are considered frustrating but necessary, and the level of debate and argument within meetings is intense.

If one goes beyond these surface phenomena and talks to people about what they do and why, one discovers some of their *values:* high regard for individual creativity, an absolute belief in individual accountability, but, at the same time, a strong commitment to obtaining consensus on important matters before moving ahead to a decision. Individuals at all levels in the organization are expected to think for themselves and take what they consider to be the correct course of action, even if it means going against a previous decision. Insubordination is positively valued if the action leads to a better outcome. The language one hears in the company reflects these values in that it glorifies "arguing back," "doing the right thing," and so on.

Inquiries about what the "boss" wants are typically considered irrelevant, giving one the impression that authority is not much respected in the organization. In fact, there are frequent complaints that decisions made at higher levels do not get implemented, that people at lower levels feel they can reverse a decision if their insight tells them to do something different, and that insubordination is rarely if ever punished. When people in higher authority positions are asked why they are not more decisive, why they let groups work things out, they state that they are "not smart enough" to make the decision by themselves. Consequently, they stimulate group debate and argument and create the kind of group atmosphere that I described above.

To understand this behavior, one must seek the *underlying assumptions* and premises on which this organization is based. The founding group comes from an engineering background, is intensely practical and pragmatic in its orientation, has built a strong and loyal "family" spirit that makes it possible to confront and have conflict without risk of loss of membership, and clearly believes that "truth" lies not in revealed wisdom or authority but in "what works," both technologically and in the marketplace. The assumption that the individual is the source of ideas but that no one individual is smart enough to evaluate his or her own ideas is at the root of the organization's problem-solving/decision-making model. Thus, creativity is always strongly encouraged, but new ideas have to be sold to all potentially affected parties before they will be blessed by higher authority.

Without understanding these assumptions, one cannot decipher most of the behavior observed, particularly the seeming incongruity between intense individualism and intense commitment to group work and consensus. Similarly, one cannot understand why there is simultaneously intense conflict with authority figures and intense loyalty to the organization without also understanding the assumption "We are one family who will take care of each other." Finally, without these assumptions one cannot decipher why a group would want a consultant to help it become more effective, yet ignore most of the suggestions on how to be more effective.

I now realize that what the group members meant by "effective" was, within their cultural assumptions, to be better at sorting out the truth. The group was merely a means to an end; the real process going on in the group was a basic, deep search for solutions that one could have confidence in because they stood up. Once I shifted my focus to improving the *decision* process instead of the *group* process, my interventions were more quickly acted on. For example, I began to help more with agenda setting, time management, clarifying some of the debate, summarizing, consensus testing once debate was running dry, and in other ways

focusing on the "task process" rather than the "interpersonal process." But the basic confrontive, interruptive style continued because the culture of the group legitimized operating that way, based on the assumption that truth is determined through confrontive debate.

Company B, hereafter referred to as the Multi Company, offers a sharp contrast. Multi is headquartered in Europe, and most of its managers are European. At the level of what is visible, it is more formal—the formality symbolized by large buildings and offices with closed doors; a hushed atmosphere in the corridors; obvious deference rituals among people who meet each other in the hall; many status symbols, such as private dining rooms for senior managers (in contrast to Action's open cafeteria); the frequent use of academic and other titles, such as Dr. so-and-so; a slower, more deliberate pace; and much more emphasis on planning, schedules, punctuality, and formal preparation of documents for meetings.

Multi managers come across as much more serious, more thoughtful, less impulsive, more formal, and more concerned about protocol. Whereas Action ties rank and salary fairly strictly to the actual job being performed by the individual, Multi has a system of managerial ranks based on length of service, overall performance, and the personal background of the individual rather than on the actual job being performed at a given time.

In meetings I observed much less direct confrontation and much more respect for individual opinion. Recommendations made by managers in their specific area of accountability are generally respected and implemented. Insubordination tends *not* to be tolerated. Rank and status thus clearly have a higher value in Multi than in Action, whereas personal negotiating skill and the ability to get things done in an ambiguous social environment have a higher value in Action than in Multi.

I could not understand the culture of Multi, however, until I attempted to circulate memos to the various branches of the Multi organization. Although I was supposed to "stimulate innovation," the ideas never got to certain managers unless I presented them personally. When I asked one of my colleagues in the organization *why* the information did not circulate freely, he indicated that unsolicited ideas might not be well received. Only if information was asked for was it acceptable to offer ideas, unless they came down the hierarchy as an official position. To provide unsolicited information or ideas could be seen as a challenge to the information base the manager was using, and that might be regarded as an insult, implying that the person challenged had not thought deeply enough about his own problem or was not really on top of his job.

To understand this and related behavior, it was necessary to consider the underlying assumptions that this company had evolved. It has grown and achieved much of its success through fundamental discoveries made by a number of basic researchers in the company's central research laboratories. Whereas in Action truth is discovered through conflict and debate, in Multi truth has come more from the wisdom of the scientist/researcher. Both companies believe in the individual, but the differing assumptions about the nature of truth led to completely different attitudes toward authority and the role of conflict.

In Multi authority is much more respected, and conflict tends to be avoided. The individual is given areas of freedom by the boss and then is totally respected in those areas. If the role occupant is not well enough educated or skilled enough to make decisions, he is expected to train himself. If he performs poorly in the meantime, that will be tolerated. In both companies there is a "tenure" assumption that once someone has been accepted he is likely to remain unless he fails in a major way.

In Action conflict is valued, and the individual is expected to take initiative and fight for ideas in every arena. In Multi conflict is suppressed once a decision has been made. In Action it is assumed that, if a job is not challenging or is not a good match between what the organization needs and what the individual can give, the individual should be moved to a new assignment or would quit anyway. In Multi

the person would be expected to be a good soldier and do the job. Both companies are successful, yet in certain respects their cultures are almost totally different.

Recognition of these assumptions has led me to change my role as a consultant at Multi. I found that if I gave information directly, even if it was unsolicited, it was accepted because I was an "expert." If I wanted information to circulate, I sent it out to the relevant parties on my own initiative. But I have not yet found reliable mechanisms for stimulating lateral communication as a means of achieving the basic goal of increasing innovativeness.

Levels of Culture

Throughout the previous discussion, I have referred to various cultural "elements," such as the physical layout of an organization's offices, rules of interaction that are taught to newcomers, basic values that come to be seen as the organization's ideology or philosophy, and the underlying conceptual categories and assumptions that enable people to communicate and to interpret everyday occurrences. As Figure 1 shows, I distinguish among these elements by treating basic assumptions as the essence—what culture really is—and by treating values and behaviors as observed manifestations of the cultural essence. In a sense these are "levels" of the culture, and they need to be carefully distinguished to avoid conceptual confusion.

Level 1: Artifacts. The most visible level of the culture is its artifacts and creations—its constructed physical and social environment. At this level one can look at physical space, the technological output of the group, its written and spoken language, artistic productions, and the overt behavior of its members. Since the insiders of the culture are not necessarily aware of their own artifacts, one cannot always ask about them, but one can always observe them for oneself.

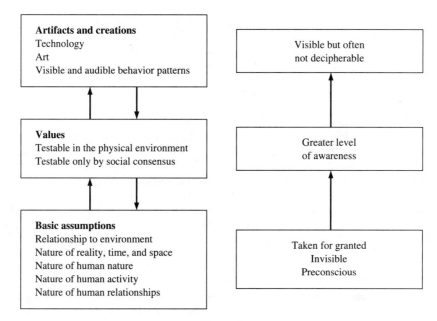

Figure 1
Levels of culture and their interaction
Source: Adapted from Schein, 1980, p. 4.

Every facet of a group's life produces artifacts, creating the problem of classification. In reading cultural descriptions, one often notes that different observers choose to report on different sorts of artifacts, leading to noncomparable descriptions. Anthropologists have developed classification systems, but these tend to be so vast and detailed that cultural essence becomes difficult to discern.

Moreover, whereas it is easy to observe artifacts—even subtle ones, such as the way in which status is demonstrated by members—the difficult part is figuring out what the artifacts mean, how they interrelate, what deeper patterns, if any, they reflect. What has been called the "semiotic" approach to cultural analysis (Spradley, 1979; Frake, 1964; Barley, 1983; Manning, 1979; Van Maanen, 1977) deals with this problem by collecting enough data on how people communicate to enable one to understand, from the point of view of the insider, what meanings are to be attached to the visible

behavior. If the anthropologist lives in the cultural environment long enough, the meanings gradually become clear.

If one wants to achieve this level of understanding more quickly, one can attempt to analyze the central values that provide the day-to-day operating principles by which the members of the culture guide their behavior.

Level 2: Values. In a sense all cultural learning ultimately reflects someone's original values, their sense of what "ought" to be, as distinct from what is. When a group faces a new task, issue, or problem, the first solution proposed to deal with it can only have the status of a value because there is not as yet a shared basis for determining what is factual and real. Someone in the group, usually the founder, has convictions about the nature of reality and how to deal with it, and will propose a solution based on those convictions. That individual may regard the proposed solution as a belief or principle based on facts, but the group cannot feel that same degree of conviction until it has collectively shared in successful problem solution. For example, in a young business if sales begin to decline, the leader may say "We must increase advertising" because of his* *belief* that "advertising always increases sales." The group, never having experienced this situation before, will hear that assertion as a statement of the leader's *values*: "He thinks that one should always advertise more when one is in trouble." What the leader initially proposes, therefore, cannot have any status other than a value to be questioned, debated, and challenged.

If the solution works, and the group has a shared perception of that success, the value gradually starts a process of *cognitive transformation* into a belief and, ultimately, an assumption. If this transformation process occurs—and it will occur only if the proposed solution continues to work, thus implying that it is in some larger sense "correct" and must reflect an accurate picture of reality—group members will tend to forget that the values were therefore debated and confronted. As the values begin to be taken for granted, they gradually become beliefs and assumptions and drop out of consciousness, just as habits become unconscious and automatic. Thus, if increased advertising consistently results in increased sales, the group begins to believe that the leader is "right" and has an understanding of how the world really works.

Not all values undergo such transformation. First of all, the solution based on a given value may not work reliably. Only those values that are susceptible of physical or social validation, and that continue to work reliably in solving the group's problems, will become transformed into assumptions. Second, certain value domains, those dealing with the less controllable elements of the environment or with aesthetic matters, may not be testable at all. In such cases consensus through social validation is still possible,

*The author uses *his* and *he* for reasons of convenience and acknowledges the inequity of the traditional use of masculine pronouns.

but it is not automatic. By social validation I mean that values about how people should relate to each other, exercise power, define what is beautiful, and so on, can be validated by the experience that they reduce uncertainty and anxiety. A group can learn that the holding of certain beliefs and assumptions is necessary as a basis for maintaining the group.

Many values remain conscious and are explicitly articulated because they serve the normative or moral function of guiding members of the group in how to deal with certain key situations. For example, if a company states explicitly in its charter and other public documents that it strongly values people, it may be doing so because it wants everyone to operate by that value, even without any historical experience that such a value actually improves its performance in its environment. A set of values that become embodied in an ideology or organizational philosophy thus can serve as a guide and as a way of dealing with the uncertainty of intrinsically uncontrollable or difficult events. Such values will predict much of the behavior that can be observed at the artifactual level. But if those values are not based on prior cultural learning, they may also come to be seen only as what Argyris and Schön (1978) have called "espoused values," which predict well enough what people will *say* in a variety of situations but which may be out of line with what they will actually *do* in situations where those values should be operating. Thus, the company may *say* that it values people, but its record in that regard may contradict what it says.

If the espoused values are reasonably congruent with the underlying assumptions, then the articulation of those values into a philosophy of operating can be helpful in bringing the group together, serving as a source of identity and core mission (Ouchi, 1981; Pascale and Athos, 1981; Peters and Waterman, 1982). But in analyzing values one must discriminate carefully between those that are congruent with underlying assumptions and those that are, in effect, either rationalizations or aspirations for the future.

If we can spell out the major espoused values of an organization, have we then described and understood its culture? And how do we know whether we have *really* understood it? The answer often lies in our own feelings as observers and analysts. Even after we have listed and articulated the major values of an organization, we still may feel that we are dealing only with a list that does not quite hang together. Often such lists of values are not patterned, sometimes they are even mutually contradictory, sometimes they are incongruent with observed behavior. Large areas of behavior are often left unexplained, leaving us with a feeling that we understood a piece of the culture but still do not have the culture as such in hand. To get at that deeper level of understanding, to decipher the pattern, to predict future behavior correctly, we have to understand more fully the category of "basic assumptions."

Level 3: Basic underlying assumptions. When a solution to a problem works repeatedly, it comes to be taken for granted. What was once a hypothesis, supported by only a hunch or a value, comes gradually to be treated as a reality. We come to believe that nature really works this way. Basic assumptions, in this sense, are different from what some anthropologists call "dominant value orientations" (Kluckhohn and Strodtbeck, 1961) in that such dominant orientations reflect the *preferred* solutions among several basic alternatives, but all the alternatives are still visible in the culture, and any given member of the culture could, from time to time, behave according to variant as well as dominant orientations. Basic assumptions, in the sense in which I want to define that concept, have become so taken for granted that one finds little variation within a cultural unit. In fact, if a basic assumption is strongly held in a group, members would find behavior based on any other premise inconceivable. For example, in a group whose basic assumption is that the individual's rights supercede those of the group, members would find it inconceivable that they should commit suicide or in some other way sacrifice themselves to the group even if they had dishonored the group. In a company in a capitalist country, it is inconceivable that one might sell products at a financial loss or that it does not matter whether a product works.

What I am calling basic assumptions are congruent with what Argyris has identified as "theories-in-use," the implicit assumptions that actually guide behavior, that tell group members how to perceive, think about, and feel about things (Argyris, 1976; Argyris and Schön, 1974). Basic assumptions, like theories-in-use, tend to be nonconfrontable and nondebatable. To relearn in the area of "theories-in-use," to resurrect, reexamine, and possibly change basic assumptions—a process that Argyris and others have called "double-loop learning"—is intrinsically difficult because assumptions are, by definition, not confrontable or debatable.

Clearly, such unconscious assumptions can distort data. If we assume, on the basis of past experience or education, that other people will take advantage of us whenever they have an opportunity (essentially what McGregor, 1960, meant by his "Theory X"), we expect to be taken advantage of and then interpret the behavior of others in a way that coincides with those expectations. We observe people sitting idly at their desk and perceive them as loafing rather than thinking out an important problem; we perceive absence from work as shirking rather than doing work at home. In contrast, if we assume—as the previously mentioned Action Company does—that everyone is highly motivated and competent (McGregor's "Theory Y"), we will act in accordance with that assumption. Thus, if someone at Action Company is absent or seems to be idle, the managers ask themselves what has happened to their job assignment process, not what is wrong with the individual. The person is still seen as motivated, but the environment is perceived as somehow turning him or her off. Managerial energy then goes into redesigning the work or the environment to enable the person to become productive once again.

Unconscious assumptions sometimes lead to "Catch 22" situations, as illustrated by a common problem experienced by American supervisors in some other cultures. A manager who comes from an American pragmatic tradition assumes and takes it for granted that solving a problem always has the highest priority. When that manager encounters a subordinate who comes from a different cultural tradition, in which good relationships and protecting the superior's "face" are assumed to have top priority, the following scenario can easily result.

The manager proposes a solution to a given problem. The subordinate knows that the solution will not work, but his unconscious assumption requires that he remain silent because to tell the boss that the proposed solution is wrong is a threat to the boss's face. It would not even occur to the subordinate to do anything other than remain silent or even reassure the boss that they should go ahead and take the action.

The action is taken, the results are negative, and the boss, somewhat surprised and puzzled, asks the subordinate what he would have done. When the subordinate reports that he would have done something different, the boss quite legitimately asks why the subordinate did not speak up sooner. This question puts the subordinate into an impossible bind because the answer itself is a threat to the boss's face. He cannot possibly explain his behavior without committing the very sin he is trying to avoid in the first place—namely, embarrassing the boss. He might even lie at this point and argue that what the boss did was right and only bad luck or uncontrollable circumstances prevented it from succeeding.

From the point of view of the subordinate, the boss's behavior is incomprehensible because it shows lack of self-pride, possibly causing the subordinate to lose respect for that boss. To the boss the subordinate's behavior is equally incomprehensible. He cannot develop any sensible explanation of his subordinate's behavior that is not cynically colored by the assumption that the subordinate at some level just does not care about effective performance and therefore must be gotten rid of. It never occurs to the boss that another assumption—such as "One never embarrasses a superior"—is operating and that, to the subordinate, that assumption is even more powerful than "One gets the job done."

In this instance probably only a third party or some cross-cultural education could help to find common ground whereby both parties could bring their implicit assumptions to the surface. And even after they have surfaced, such assumptions would still operate, forcing the boss and the subordinate to invent a new communication mechanism that would permit each to remain congruent with his culture— for example, agreeing that, before any decision is made and before the boss has stuck his neck out, the subordinate will be asked for suggestions and for factual data that would not be face threatening.

I have dwelled on this long example to illustrate the potency of implicit, unconscious assumptions and to show that such assumptions often deal with fundamental aspects of the culture. But such assumptions are hard to locate. If we examine carefully an organization's artifacts and values, we can try to infer the underlying assumptions that tie things together. Such assumptions can usually be brought to the surface in interviews if both the interviewer and the interviewee are committed to trying to piece together the cultural pattern. But this requires detective work and commitment, not because people are reluctant to surface their assumptions but because they are so taken for granted. Yet when we do surface them, the cultural pattern suddenly clarifies and we begin to feel we really understand what is going on and why.

Ethnographic versus Clinical Perspective

In reviewing my own "data base," the sources of my own knowledge about organizational culture, I have found it necessary to distinguish the perspective of the *ethnographer* from that of the *clinician*. The ethnographer obtains concrete data in order to understand the culture he is interested in, presumably for intellectual and scientific reasons. Though the ethnographer must be faithful to the observed and experienced data, he brings to the situation a set of concepts or models that motivated the research in the first place. The group members studied are often willing to participate but usually have no particular stake in the intellectual issues that may have motivated the study.

In contrast, a "clinical perspective" is one where the group members are clients who have their own interests as the prime motivator for the involvement of the "outsider," often labeled "consultant" or "therapist" in this context. In the typical ethnographic situation, the researcher must obtain the cooperation of the subjects; in the clinical situation, the client must get the cooperation of the helper/consultant. The psychological contract between client and helper is completely different from that between researcher and subject, leading to a different kind of relationship between them, the revelation of different kinds of data, and the use of different criteria for when enough has been "understood" to terminate the inquiry.

Clients call in helpers when they are frustrated, anxious, unhappy, threatened, or thwarted; when their rational, logical approaches to things do not work. Inevitably, then, the clinical view brings one to the topic of the "irrational" in organizations. I have found and hope to show in this book that one of the simplest ways of understanding the seemingly irrational is to relate such phenomena to culture, because culture often explains things that otherwise seem mysterious, silly, or "irrational."

Consultants also bring with them their models and concepts for obtaining and analyzing information, but the function of those models is to provide insight into how the client can be *helped*. In order to provide help, the consultant must "understand" at some level. Some theories, in fact, argue that only by attempting to change a system (that is, giving help) does one demonstrate any real level of understanding (Lewin, 1952; Schein, 1980). For me this criterion has always been the relevant one for "validating" my understanding, even though that understanding often is incomplete, since the

clinical relationship does not automatically license the helper to inquire into areas the client may not wish to pursue or considers irrelevant. On the other hand, the level of understanding is likely to be deeper and more dynamic.

The point of spelling all of this out now is to let the reader know that my data base is a clinical one, not an ethnographic one. I have not been a participant-observer in organizations other than the ones I had membership in, but in being a consultant I have spent long periods of time in client organizations. I believe that this clinical perspective provides a useful counterpoint to the pure ethnographic perspective, because the clinician learns things that are different from what an ethnographer learns. Clients are motivated to reveal certain things when they are paying for help that may not come out if they are only "willing" to be studied.

So this kind of inquiry leads, I believe, to a "deeper" analysis of culture as a phenomenon— deeper in the sense of its impact on individual members of the organization. This perspective also leads inevitably to a more dynamic view of how things work, how culture begins, evolves, changes, and sometimes disintegrates. And, as we will see, this perspective throws into high relief what leaders and other change agents can or cannot do to change culture deliberately.

References

ARGYRIS, C. (1976). *Increasing leadership effectiveness.* New York: Wiley-Interscience.

ARGYRIS, C., & SCHÖN, D. A. (1974). *Theory in practice: Increasing professional effectiveness.* San Francisco: Jossey-Bass.

ARGYRIS, C., & SCHÖN, D. A. (1978). *Organizational learning.* Reading, MA: Addison-Wesley Publishing.

BARLEY, S. R. (1983). Semiotics and the study of occupational and organizational cultures. *Administrative Science Quarterly, 28,* 393–413.

DEAL, T. E., & KENNEDY, A. A. (1982). *Corporate cultures.* Reading, MA: Addison-Wesley Publishing.

DYER, W. G., Jr. (1982). Culture in organizations. A case study and analysis. Unpublished paper, Sloan School of Management, MIT.

FRAKE, C. O. (1964). Notes on queries in ethnography. *American Anthropologist, 66,* 132–145.

GOFFMAN, E. (1959). *The presentation of self in everyday life.* New York: Doubleday.

GOFFMAN, E. (1967). *Interaction ritual.* Hawthorne, NY: Aldine.

HOMANS, G. (1950). *The human group.* New York: Harcourt Brace Jovanovich.

KLUCKHOHN, F. R., & STRODTBECK, F. L. (1961). *Variations in value orientations.* New York: Harper & Row.

LEWIN, K. (1952). Group decision and social change. In G. E. Swanson, T. N. Newcomb, & E. L. Hartley (Eds.), *Readings in Social Psychology* (rev. ed.). New York: Holt, Rinehart & Winston.

LOUIS, M. R. (1983). Organizations as culture bearing milieux. In L. R. Pondy & others (Eds.), *Organizational symbolism.* Greenwich, CT: JAI Press.

McGREGOR, D. M. (1960). *The human side of enterprise.* New York: McGraw-Hill.

MANNING, P. (1979). Metaphors of the field: Varieties of organizational discourse. *Administrative Science Quarterly, 24,* 660–671.

OUCHI, W. G. (1981). *Theory Z.* Reading, MA: Addison-Wesley.

PASCALE, R. T., & ATHOS, A. G. (1981). *The art of Japanese management.* New York: Simon & Schuster.

PETERS, T. J., & WATERMAN, R. H., Jr. (1982). *In search of excellence.* New York: Harper & Row.

RITTI, R. R., & FUNKHOUSER, G. R. (1982). *The ropes to skip and the ropes to know.* Columbus, OH: Grid.

SCHEIN, E. H. (1968). Organizational socialization and the profession of management. *Industrial Management Review, 9,* 1–15.

SCHEIN, E. H. (1978). *Career dynamics: Matching individual and organizational needs.* Reading, MA: Addison-Wesley.

SCHEIN, E. H. (1980). *Organizational psychology* (3rd ed.). Englewood Cliffs, NJ: Prentice-Hall. (First published 1965, 2nd ed. 1970.)

SCHEIN, E. H. (1981a). Does Japanese management style have a message for American managers? *Sloan Management Review, 23,* 55–68.

SCHEIN, E. H. (Summer 1983). The role of the founder in creating organizational culture. *Organizational Dynamics,* pp. 13–28.

SCHEIN, E. H. (1984). Coming to a new awareness of organizational culture. *Sloan Management Review, 25,* 3–16.

SPRADLEY, J. P. (1979). *The ethnographic interview.* New York: Holt, Rinehart & Winston.

TAGIURI, R., & LITWIN, G. H. (Eds.). (1968). *Organizational climate: Exploration of a concept.* Boston: Division of Research, Harvard Graduate School of Business.

VAN MAANEN, J. (1976). Breaking in: Socialization to work. In R. Dubin (Ed.), *Handbook of work, organization and society.* Chicago: Rand McNally.

VAN MAANEN, J. (1977). Experiencing organizations. In J. Van Maanen (Ed.), *Organizational careers: Some new perspectives.* New York: Wiley.

VAN MAANEN, J. (1979b). The self, the situation, and the rules of interpersonal relations. In W. Bennis & others, *Essays in interpersonal dynamics.* Pacific Grove, CA: Brooks/Cole.

44

The Making of an Organizational Saga

Burton R. Clark

The Leader, the Group, and the Community

The three case studies and the foregoing discussion suggest how distinctiveness is achieved in an American college. It is initiated by a single individual, or a small band, in a setting conducive in normative and structural openness. It is sustained by a much larger number of people, on and off campus, through many interlocking components of durable organization.

When we look for how distinctive emphasis gets under way, we find typically a single individual, usually the president, or a very small group. The innovator formulates a new idea, a mission; he has, with varying degrees of deliberateness, found his way to a particular college that is in a particular stage of development and that is structurally open, and he starts to design appropriate means of embodying his idea in the organization and to enhance the conduciveness of the setting. Although this is the function of a strong president, it can likely be performed also by a unified junta.

When we look for the way distinctive emphasis is maintained in a college, we find it typically firmly expressed in interlocking stable structures. The key structure is usually a tenured faculty armed with power. The senior faculty members are personally committed to the emphasis, are collectively the center of power or are

SOURCE: Burton R. Clark, *The Distinctive College: Antioch, Reed and Swarthmore* (Chicago: Aldine Publishing, 1970), 255–262.

so powerful that they can veto attempts at change, and are replaced over time in such a way as to continue the embodiment of the historic purpose in faculty values.

The question of who is most important in the making of a distinctive college, one raised often in educational circles, becomes then not a useful question. It leads toward simple answers and polarized arguments that obscure more than they reveal. For example, if we ask: "Is not Antioch the lengthened shadow of Morgan, a creature of his ideals and introduced practices?" the answer "yes" is a partial truth that overlooks the essential work of full development and institutionalization that took place under Henderson in the thirties; the essential, permanent commitment of the senior faculty; and the essential expression of an Antioch legend in student subculture, public image, and social base. If we answer the same question with a flat "no," we underestimate the great impact of one man in designing a change and getting it under way. The question requires an answer informed by an awareness of the stages of development in a college; the differing roles of the leader and the group in initiating and sustaining a distinctive style; and the complicated, ongoing interaction of purpose, leadership, environment, and the means of organization. The question of how distinctiveness is achieved must at least be broken into the two parts of how it was initiated and how it is sustained. That the question can be further specified and fruitfully posed in other ways has been demonstrated in earlier discussion.

We may note particularly that distinctiveness in a college involves and encourages those characteristics of group life commonly referred to as community. It offers an educationally relevant definition of the difference of the group from all others. And salient elements in the distinctiveness become foci of personal awareness and of a sense of things held in common with others currently on the scene, those who have been there before, and those yet to arrive. Distinctiveness captures loyalty, inducing men to enlist and to stay against the lures of career-ism. And it arrests the most transient members, the students, extending their devotion for years to come.

In turn, the conditions most favorable to the existence of a community assist in the development and maintenance of distinctive character. One such condition in a formal organization is singularity of purpose. Group integration is promoted when all are headed in the same direction. A second condition is smallness of size, which allows informal as well as formal links across the specializations and internal divisions inherent in formal organization. An aggregate of strangers brought together to pursue a common purpose within a small organization is more likely to develop a community than is an aggregation set to multiple purposes in a large enterprise. These conditions favor frequent and intense interaction across the system and encourage convergent rather than divergent personal experiences leading toward a sense of oneness. They then obviously can be put to the service of distinctiveness.

However, other conditions can sometimes compensate. Multipurpose universities of the size of ten thousand can still have a relatively strong sense of community and a distinctive character, e.g., Harvard and Yale. Here, long tradition, slow growth, high status, and units promoting intensive interaction combine to combat the structural and subjective fragmentation inherent in largeness and multiplicity of purpose. Tradition contributes an aura. Slow growth helps preserve a sense of unity, by granting time for the assimilation of newcomers into established staff and of new thought into traditional conceptions. High status encourages close identification with the institution: Harvard professor and Yale man are terms usually seized rather than resisted by those entitled to them. Structures promoting interaction—the Harvard residential houses, the Yale residential colleges—help students cope psychologically and socially with the potential stress of individual detachment among thousands of strangers. But these conditions are in short supply in American colleges and universities. The common situation is one of little tradition, rapid growth, modest status, and weak structures for promoting interaction. With these conditions, large size and multiple purpose sharply diminish the possibilities for a sense of community and for distinctive character in the whole.

We may also reflect on the achievement of distinctiveness by asking about its failure to occur. The explanatory scheme here suggests three main sources of nonoccurrence. One is lack of will, or essentially no man with a mission. The second is the absence of structurally conducive conditions for the introduction and early working-out of the mission. The third is weakness or breakdown in the structures of institutionalization, the major components of the organization highlighted earlier, whose embodiment of the mission to an important degree turns it into a saga. Thus we have the denial of distinctiveness when the mission-oriented leader cannot be found or induced to come to the organization; or having arrived, cannot loosen the organization from its web of traditional expectations and commitments; or having broken tradition and established the mission, the mission does not endure because one or more major structural supports develop weakly or give way. The latter problems include weakness in the social base, as nonbelievers stiffen their resistance and withhold support; attenuation of belief in the faculty, as nonselective recruitment introduces nonbelievers; fragmentation of the student subculture, as a growing student body becomes more heterogeneous and draws from the youth of a new age; and loss of unity and distinctiveness in curricular practices, as adaptations are made to placate external and internal interests. Above all, as emphasized, vulnerability lies in weak power of the believing group, for then agents of change can divert the organization to a new course.

The Risks and Tensions of Distinctiveness

Distinctive colleges, because they attempt to be special and not all things to all men, are likely to have one or more distinctive strains, exhibiting in higher degree tensions found elsewhere. In emphasizing one value, they underplay, oppose, or ignore others. In securing the loyalty of one segment of society, they may secure the hostility of others. In committing the organization strongly to one path of action, they find it difficult at a later time to take another route or otherwise to adapt as new demands are made upon them.

Among the three colleges of this study, we have seen a number of tensions and risks: the strain between adult responsibility and the freedom of students; the struggle between specialization and general education; the split between teaching and research; the risk of being a cult in a hostile countryside; the danger of getting cut off from ordinary funding sources. At Antioch, as we have seen, the freedom of students was a persisting source of institutional strain, presenting problems with which only a true believer would willingly live. The salient commitment to general education also produced a severe problem when the more specialized interests of modern academic men demanded to be served. And for decades the general liberality, nonconformity, and political action have produced local disdain and hostility, complicating severely the task of raising necessary funds. To become distinctive the college lived through two decades of being heavily in debt. After the retirement of the debt, the college continued to find its fund-raising efforts heavily mortgaged by its reputation. Antioch has had only a few quiet years since 1920, and it has had very few financially easy years.

Reed has shared with Antioch a deep institutional strain over student freedom. The internal anxiety and the external antipathy have been an enduring part of institutional affairs. One president after another has found student behavior his cross to bear, and trustees could hardly help resting uneasy, no matter how strong their pride in accomplishments. The college proved better oriented than Antioch for an age of specialization in that its posture was not rooted in an equally broad version of general education; but its dogged commitment to teaching meant

stubborn resistance to the interest in research growing everywhere in the academic world. And no other college of similar national standing has had such a problem of fund-raising. In its business affairs, it was a shoestring operation, with all that that entails in administrative anxiety, lack of physical plant, and underpayment of faculty. The strain and the risk have been high, again only tolerable to determined men who are sure they are right.

Of the three colleges, Swarthmore has been least subject to strain because of distinctiveness. To effect a major change it did not undergo the uncertainties of new organization or the difficulties of crisis. The change was more evolutionary and considerably better funded than was the case in the other two colleges. But Swarthmore could have lived an easier life if it had stayed more in the normal mold. The many changes of the twenties and thirties had to be fought out; alumni resistance made the whole effort a precarious one for several years and a matter of some stress for a longer period. Although the college was well oriented (for its size) for the growing interests in specialization and research, it, too, had to struggle to attract and hold an appropriate faculty against the lures of the universities. Even more than Antioch and Reed, the college could not make do with faculty members whose job alternatives were in average small colleges. Student brightness alone would make this foolhardy, and the self-concept and national leadership role of the college make it highly inappropriate. As a result, the college pitted itself against Ivy League universities in recruitment, not a soft road for any small college to travel. And then, too, the college found student freedom and nonconformity a steady source of strain within its membership and especially with the surrounding community.

The ultimate risk of distinctive character is that of success in one era breeding rigidity and stagnation in a later one. Commitments are precise rather than diffuse, sharply made rather than dully connected, articulated rather than unspoken; in short, they constitute a formula for later trouble. But in such matters, involving stages of organizational development and degrees of openness to later change, we know little about compelling restraints and open options. Surely the organization that turns a mission into a saga, a good idea into a fruitful legend, moves, in the full flush of success, toward the possibility of its distinctiveness becoming an antiquated mode, one from which it cannot unhook itself until torn by trouble. But surely, just as ordinary routinized colleges can vary in degree of openness to change, distinctively fixed colleges can also vary. Among the three colleges, for example, one can speculate that Reed is the least open to change. The Reed capacity, one may say the Reed necessity, to endure through sheer stubbornness gives it a sharp problem of adaptability. Swarthmore appears in a middle ground, conservative in habit but with possible flexibility within its open Quaker ethos and its general institutional health. Antioch appears the most open to change, even to diffusion of hard-won character. Its central educational values leave the curriculum exposed: To believe that the young learn from work in jobs off campus and from campus experiences outside the classroom is to unbutton things, for then why not this and why not that, why not course credit for making pottery or for living and working three month with a farm family in France? The ideals of social reform, strongest at Antioch, also spill over into a sense that one's own campus can stand improvement. The values institutionalized at Antioch have, in general, left the college somewhat experimental-minded, with a passion for self-study and for leadership in experimental-college circles.

In the face of the common institutional danger that distinctiveness may lead in time to rigidity and stagnation, we may note several features that are favorable to change and that are likely to be present in all distinctively excellent colleges. One feature is the challenge of bright students. To have a bright student body is to have a steady infiltration of critical minds. The faculty and administration then come under heavy pressure to remain alert, first in the performance of traditional practice, and second to the possibilities of altering practices to meet the changing needs and demands of the students.

In the best colleges, the students tend to become brighter than the faculty. Many faculty members must then struggle to maintain their credibility as teachers, reading widely and critically, staying abreast of the latest perspectives and findings of the discipline so that they at least know more than the students even if their mental gears do not go around so fast. On affairs that engage the whole campus, the bright students offer rational arguments that are qualitatively different from those students at average small colleges. At an Antioch or Reed or Swarthmore, time and again one can observe students getting the best of an administrator in an argument, driving him back against the wall as he tries to give a rational explanation for traditional controls over student behavior. In such settings, effective administrators not only must be intelligent and quick but also must be capable of adapting to the changing nature of sophisticated youth.

A second feature favorable to change is the expression of new views that occurs when the authority structure is relatively democratic and when discussion is relatively open. The students, faculty, and administrators who flow in from the outside, not as well socialized to what the college has been, as are the old-timers, are often the source of new thought. In time, on the average, they become socialized or they go away. The chance for them to express themselves in influential ways while they are young in the organization becomes an important factor in change. Forms of organization at Antioch, for example, have allowed young faculty members to have influence. The young ones do not sit in hushed silence, in awe or fear of their elders, as young men do in many small colleges. With the faculty meeting allowing a reasonable chance for men to be equal, Young Turks cannot be ignored. Community government, in addition, has allowed the voices of students to be heard. As a result, the oligarchs are not completely in control. There is always a group with a new plan that must be considered and in some cases adopted. Other leading colleges, in somewhat lesser degree, usually possess this source of adaptation.

Finally, sources of openness to change are found in the tensions and risks, described earlier in the section, that inhere in distinctive character. The tensions force small crises in organizational viability; the risks generate anticipation that present character may not be able to cope with future pressures. The small crises and worries about the future are commonly generated by problems of finance and retention of faculty. The frequent annual deficit shocks everyone when, in the current year, it jumps to a new high. The normal loss of faculty members to other places becomes abnormal and threatening when four associate professors leave in a single year. Such events can be taken as signs of a gathering storm, for if repeated because the college has become out of joint with the times, then the institution, beloved character and all, will decline in health and quality.

The Rewards of a Saga

When we hold educational ideals in mind, the making of a college is much more than raising money, erecting buildings, recruiting professors, organizing courses, and enrolling students. Past minimal competence lies the problem of whether the operations of the college will reflect to a significant degree certain educational and social values. To build effectively is to incorporate purpose effectively, and not any purpose but purpose congruent with the general ideals of a class of organizations and of a large social institution; e.g., the ideals of the liberated arts college and the ideals of excellence in higher learning. The reflected purpose can be a specific imitation of what the leading colleges of a given period are doing; and that is hard to do, requiring as it does supportive settings that are in short supply and organizational means that must be obtained in a competitive market. Even more difficult is to find the specific formula that allows the college to reflect general values in a new, highly productive, and esteemed form. The vision that drives the best educational leaders is to approach a general ideal of man by developing new organizational devices and practices.

Antioch, Reed, and Swarthmore are among the handful of colleges that, through ingenuity and persistence in the four decades of 1920 to 1960, came to reflect most fully distinctive excellence in liberal education on the American scene. Their stories tell us how they did it and suggest what is essential and what may be accidental to doing as well in other efforts. Optimistically, we see elements of organizational development that could be widely replicated. The common elements discussed here can at least inform the images of the future held by college administrators and faculties. Pessimistically, however, we see conditions, men, and events that have rarely conspired. No one should suggest that it is easy to get purpose and men together under conditions that permit effective expression of cherished educational ideals.

Either way, we find at root in these successful cases a willingness to risk much, personally and organizationally, to try a different route. The personal commitment required of many actors in the situation can be set in motion by the charisma of a single man. It can be fully invested and steadily carried over the years, however, only by a fusing of an idea and the organization. Careerist motives are not enough; an embodied idea is the institutional chariot to which individual motive becomes chained. When the idea is in command, men are indifferent to personal cost. They often are not even aware of how much they have risked and how much they sometimes have sacrificed. As ideologues, as believers, they do not care. They are proud of what they have been through, what they have done, and what they stand for. They feel highly involved in a worthwhile collective effort and wish to remain with it. For the organization the richly embellished institutional definition that we call a saga can then be invaluable in maintaining viability in a competitive market. It is also invaluable as a foundation for trust within the institutional group, easing communication and cooperation.

The individual and group returns are thus considerable. In offering so much thrill and pleasure, a saga maximizes for the individual the esthetic rewards of administration and group membership. The organizational means become beautiful ends in themselves. In turn, in binding and motivating the individual, even in fusing personal and organizational identities, the legend becomes a precious resource for those who fashion the enterprise, a resource created out of the social components of organization. In such efforts, the task—and the reward—of the institutional leader is to create and initiate an activating mission. The task—and the reward—of the institutional group is to have purpose and organization become a saga.

45

Organizations as Culture-Bearing Milieux

Meryl Reis Louis

Any social group, to the extent that it is a distinctive unit, will have to some degree a culture differing from that of other groups, a somewhat different set of common understandings around which action is organized, and these differences will find expression in a language whose nuances are peculiar to that group. Members of churches speak differently from members of tavern groups; more importantly, members of any particular church or tavern group have cultures, and languages in which they are expressed, which differ somewhat from those of other groups of the same general type (Becker & Geer, 1970, p. 134).

My aim in this paper is to present a view of organizations as culture-bearing milieux, that is, as distinctive social units possessed of a set of common understandings for organizing action (e.g., what we're doing together in this particular group, appropriate ways of doing in and among members of the group) and languages and other symbolic vehicles for expressing common understandings. The timeliness of such a view is indicated in several trends in the organizational sciences. First, there has been a growing dissatisfaction with traditional research efforts, especially those grounded in essentially positivistic views of organizations. Many have

SOURCE: L. R. Pondy and others, eds., *Organizational Symbolism*, 39–54. Copyright 1983 JAI Press. Reprinted with permission.

become disillusioned with fundamental inadequacies in traditional methods and the meager grasp and leverage on organizational phenomena they have provided (Silverman, 1970; Burrell & Morgan, 1979; Pondy & Mitroff, 1979; Van Maanen, 1979b; Evered & Louis, 1981).

Simultaneously, there has been a groundswell of interest in things cultural in organizations. Organizational researchers have undertaken studies of symbols, myths, legends and metaphors, of language systems and other artifacts of organizational cultures (Clarke, 1970; Mitroff & Kilmann, 1976; Wilkins & Martin, 1979; Dandridge, Mitroff & Joyce, 1980; Evered, 1983). Additionally, there has been an increasing concern with cognitive processes of individuals in organizations, with issues of how individuals make meaningful their interactions and encounters in daily organization life (Van Maanen, 1979a; Weick, 1979; Louis, 1980b).

A final impetus for developing a cultural view of organizations stems from a practical problem faced by increasing numbers of organizational participants. With the rising rate of voluntary turnover at all organizational levels has come a greater appreciation for cultural aspects of organizations by participants. Specifically, recognition of the need to become acculturated, to "learn the ropes," when entering an unfamiliar organizational setting suggests that some cultural stratum is present in any organization, and that its mastery is critical for the well-functioning of new organizational members (Schutz, 1964; Van Maanen, 1977; Louis, 1980a, 1980b).

The concept of culture is not new. It has long been used by anthropologists, among others, in studying ethnic and/or national groups through ethnographic and cross-cultural research. For example, Beres & Portwood (1979, p. 141) have proposed a comprehensive model of the influence of ethnic/national culture in the development of an individual's frame of reference and, in particular, orientations to work. They define culture as a "cognitive frame of reference and a pattern of behavior transmitted to members of a group from previous generations of the group," emphasize the role of socialization in the transmission of culture, suggest the need to consider psychological, social and historical dimensions, review deficiencies in cross-cultural research, and provide results of a test of one segment of the model. Although organizational (versus ethnic) culture is not considered per se, their paper offers a recent perspective on cross-cultural research and a conceptualization of cultural influence processes (or, more appropriately, factors in the process) directly relevant to work on organizational culture.

What is new and what is my particular aim here is to map dimensions of culture relevant in organizations and to suggest that researchers incorporate a cultural view of organizations into the repertoire of perspectives on organizations. The discussion: What constitutes a cultural perspective? What are psychological and sociological processes and contexts of cultural phenomena in organizations? And in what ways are organizations culture-bearing milieux? While this effort is necessarily exploratory (we are just beginning to map the territory and this will be a brief essay), the purpose is to broadly consider what a cultural view of organizations might entail.[1]

A Cultural Perspective

The idea of culture rests on the premise that the full meaning of things is not given a priori in the things themselves. Instead, meaning results from interpretation. Consider, for instance, a hiker encountering a fallen tree. The significance to the hiker of a tree laying across the trail depends on whether he is idly strolling through the morning woods, scouting ahead for hazards for other hikers on a pack train, making a getaway from a minimum security prison, or surveying drought damage in the forest. Whether the hiker views the fallen tree as the result of drought or of prison guards and, more basically, whether causes of the tree falling are relevant, depend on the larger historical and situational contexts of the hiker. The meaning as the significance of some event, utterance, etc. may derive from any of several aspects of the situation in which meaning is to be assigned. Meaning may involve definition, consequence, antecedents, and/or intention (Black, 1962, p. 193), as the example of the hiker demonstrates.

In a cultural view, meaning is produced through an *in situ* interpretive process. The process encompasses universal, cultural and individual levels of interpretation. The universal level refers to the broad set of objective or physically feasible meanings or relevances of each thing. For instance, universally speaking, dogs can be eaten, worshipped, or befriended, but not flown. These basic physical constraints are what Weick (1979) referred to as "grains of truth."

The cultural level refers to the set of potential meanings or relevances indigenous to the local social group. In one sense, this local code is a subset of the universal set of feasible relevances. In another sense, the local code is an elaboration of the universal set. Each of the objective or physically feasible meanings may be exploded into a whole range of meanings. For instance, consider the myriad social meanings of dog in our society—companion, family member, guide dog for the blind, shepherd, guard dog, drug detective. This array of meanings derives less from objective features or universal meanings of the creature dog and more from the creative differentiation from universal meanings into contextually relevant cultural meanings. The cultural code describes the repertoire of meanings that may appropriately be assigned to a thing by members of the particular social system. That, strictly speaking, dogs are befriended, but not eaten or worshipped in 1980 America reflects the code of relevances for dog in our Western culture.

The final level in interpretation is the individual one. Here the person's idiosyncratic adaptation of cultural codes leads to a set of personal codes of relevance. In turn, personal codes are applied in the moment of encountering a thing and meaning is produced. Whether you greet or run from the dog in front of you at this moment depends on your history with dogs and your recognition of this one as your neighbor's friendly puppy.

So, from the universe of feasible relevances of any thing, a cultural set of possible meanings appropriate through time and space for the social group is carved out, and based on this cultural code, social system members derive their own codes of relevance. As I have indicated in Figure 1, the universal can be thought of as an objective realm. Only at the universal level is meaning given a priori. The cultural stratum can be thought of as an intersubjective realm, studied through clinical means.

With few exceptions researchers in the organizational sciences have proceeded as if study of the universal stratum *alone* were sufficient to produce understandings of organizational behavior; organizational phenomena have been studied implicitly as universal matters devoid of any cultural component.[2] It is time to begin studying cultural phenomena as distinct aspects of organizational life. It is increasingly clear that much of what matters in organizational life takes place at the cultural level. From the "informal organization" first recognized in the Hawthorne studies to the "organizational politics" currently in vogue among researchers, cultural phenomena pervade organizational life. Yet, by and large, cultural phenomena seem to elude, be overlooked by, and/or remain on the fringe of mainstream organizational science. I suspect this is due in part to the lack of a coherent integral image conveyed in symbols and language sufficient to distinguish it from other images (e.g., culture versus machine). And so, in the following pages, I will begin to flesh out and give language to such an image. (The paradox is that traditional images, ideals and language of organizational science [i.e., our culture] tend to blind us to supplementary images of organization phenomena.)

The next two sections will consider aspects of culture relevant to a view of organizations as culture-bearing milieux. For purposes of discussion, a distinction is made between what goes on inside any one individual vis-à-vis cultural processes and what goes on outside the person; that is, between persons or, more generally, within the social system. The former is termed the psychological context and the latter the sociological context of culture.

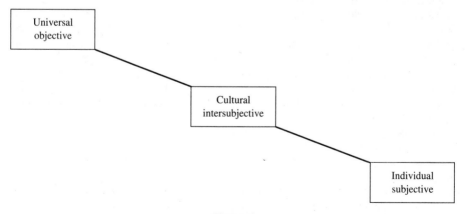

Figure 1
Levels of interpretation in producing meaning

Culture in Organizations: The Sociological Context

In a brief but classic statement, Kroeber and Parsons (1958) define culture as the ". . . transmitted and created content and patterns of values, ideas, and other symbolic-meaningful systems as factors in the shaping of human behavior . . ." as distinct from social system, or ". . . the specifically relational system of interaction among individuals and collectivities" (pp. 86–87). As discussed above, the codes of meaning or relevance indigenous to a social system serve as behavior-shaping social ideals (i.e., "thou shalt," "thou shalt not"). Social ideals constitute a system of values and relevances by which individuals and institutions set goals and aspirations, sanction behavior, and judge performances. A set of social ideals is represented in a kind of hierarchy or prioritization of meanings, a coherent meaning system. A cultural view then encompasses the system of social ideals and the set of symbolic devices (i.e., myths, rituals, signs, metaphors, special languages) that embody and are used to convey the ideals. While these symbolic devices are used to convey the local culture, they are simultaneously the artifacts of that culture.

Culture provides for social system continuity, control, identity and integration of members. The stability (through time) of shared ideals across generations of social system members provides continuity and serves a homeostatic function.[3] The stability (through space) of the standards or goals conveyed in the commonly-held set of ideals serves the control function of deviance detection and reduction.[4] Ouchi's (1979) work on control by clan illustrates this function. Further, ideals shared among members into the social group, a kind of individual-to-institution linking. Etzioni's (1961) work on moral involvement of organization members illustrates the integrating function of culture.[5]

More diffusely, culture embodies the identity of the social group. What we, as members, stand for and how we deal with one another and with outsiders is carried in and through our culture. Discussions of corporate personality are concerned at least implicitly, with the identity aspect of organizational culture (O'Toole, 1979).

Culture in Organizations: The Psychological Context

At the individual level, ". . . human beings act toward things on the basis of the meanings that things have for them . . ." (Blumer, 1969, p. 2). And those meanings, or significances, are the products of an in situ interpretive process. Meaning is essentially and endlessly negotiated by social system members. In one sense of negotiated, meaning production represents navigation of an experiential landscape by which one controls one's course or position. In the other sense of negotiated, it represents bargaining among alternative meanings differentially preferred by the various parties to an interaction.

At the micro-interactional level, the navigational aspect of cultural processes produces the individual's definitions of the situation.[6] Features as landmarks are identified and interpreted in light of present sociological position and destination. In an interaction, the person's individualized version of the local set of social ideals (i.e., personal code of meanings or frame of reference) guides perception, interpretation, and action. Through a series of steps, it allows the individual to assess whether, for instance, a particular performance constitutes a job well done. First, one's culturally derived meaning system facilitates the identification of a performance from a continuous stream of experience, or parsing as Weick (1969) refers to it. What is noticed is, to a great extent, given in our cultural set. Second, it directs attention to certain features of the performance considered worth assessing. Third, it provides the yardstick for assessing those features of the performance. Fourth, assessment or interpretation guides action; or, as W. I. Thomas (1951, p. 584) has phrased it, "If men define situations as real, they are real in their consequences." Responses are made in terms of features assessed and assessments of those features.

The psychological context of cultural processes has been discussed at length by Schutz (1964, 1970b) who has shown how the individual's interpretive scheme or meaning system is embedded and operational in a particular culture. As a result of this communal embeddedness of members' meaning systems, meaning produced in situ is extensively intersubjective. Discussions of specific subprocesses in which individuals make meaning in social interaction based on an intersubjective perspective are found in McHugh (1968) and Louis (1980b).

Figure 2 reviews the aspects of a cultural perspective outlined so far.

Culture in Organizational Settings

Ways in which organizations can be viewed as culture-bearing milieux and critical issues encountered in doing so are explored in this section. In addition, we will consider defining characteristics of cultural participation (e.g., physical versus psychological connection, self-perception, competence) and issues of boundary and perspective in studying culture in organizations.

Organizations provide regularly convening settings in which cultures may develop; thus, an organizational setting is analogous to a petri dish. Whether or not, or, more precisely, the extent to which, a particular organizational setting fosters the development of a local culture depends on a great many factors, only a few of which seem apparent at this stage of study. Some organizational settings may "bear" (in the sense of supporting the development of) elaborate cultures, while, in others, no appreciable culture may develop. In the latter case, the settings may be characterized by more purely instrumental involvement of members and individually oriented behaviors. This is analogous at the organizational level to what Hall (1976) has referred to at the societal level as a "low-context" setting. Further, multiple nested and/or overlapping cultures may be borne by any given organization in correspondence to the potential multitude of physical/sociological/cognitive settings convened within the bounds of organizational activities. For example, somewhat distinct local cultures may form in each of several departments within a division of an organization, and at the level of the division as an organizational setting. In this view, then, the organization provides the setting

Sociological Context		Psychological Context
Shared Ideals	*Symbolic Devices*	*Interpretive Scheme*
Cultural system of relevances Through the functions of culture, social systems achieve: Continuity—transtemporal stability Control—contemporaneous stability Integration of individual members Identity of social group		Personal system of relevances Within a culture: Meaning is emergent and intersubjective Individuals negotiate meaning Negotiation as: Navigation Bargaining The *in situ* interpretive process: Perception → Negotiation → Meaning ⇒ Definition of situation → Behavior

Figure 2
Aspects of cultural perspective

or milieu in and through which cultures may develop; thus, the phrase, "organizations as culture-bearing milieux."

Several features of organizational settings are hypothesized to contribute to the development of local cultures, regardless of the organizational level at which culture is investigated (e.g., whether we consider organization-wide culture or the work-group culture). For instance, more extensive cultures are expected to be associated with: stability of membership; the extent to which key members "consistently point to (a set of) general ideas or frameworks (Wilkins, in this volume, pp. 81–92); "members' perceptions of the relative youth and smallness of the organization; identification of human qualities of key people (i.e., idiosyncrasies, personal values, interpersonal style); impermeability of organizational boundaries (e.g., for purposes of product secrecy in an R&D lab or societal privacy in a nudist colony); membership restrictions (essential acquired or innate attributes, e.g., education or experience, sex, or race). There are undoubtedly other features of organizational settings that contribute to the development of local cultures which remain to be identified through further study.

I believe we will discover in future studies that patterns of features, the relative importance of some over others, will differ depending on the organizational level (e.g., organization-wide versus work-group) at which we are investigating cultures in organizations. Additionally, I believe we will discover different cultural processes and culture-shaping processes in operation depending on the developmental stage of the organizational unit qua setting under study. For instance, in entrepreneurships (organizations in early stages of development), culture-creating processes are expected to be in evidence. Stories and the values they convey are being shaped from the actions of key people. In contrast, cultural revitalization in mature or stagnating organizations (mid and late stages) may be fostered through the development and dissemination of new images and accompanying rationales for breaking with the past. The literal bringing in of "young blood" in the form of new leadership is often used to symbolically represent a new "life for the organization."

Changes in organizational settings can alternatively disrupt or support local cultures. For instance, the imposition of new technology may disrupt the local culture. Witness the example documented by Trist and Bamforth (1951) in their coal-mining studies. Previous to the change, task planning, coordination and control, interpersonal bonds and interfamily relationships were facilitated and mediated by the work group culture. The new technology imposed a different set of interpersonal relationships and externalized planning and control. The basic features of the work-group setting were altered; the structural arrangements in and of the work-group were dismantled and reassembled. Like a spider's web between garden tools resting against the walls of a shed, the web of the work-group culture was torn when the tools were rearranged.

Changes in organizational settings can also foster new cultural developments. For instance, establishing an identified task team creates a setting in and through which a local culture may develop. Creation of project teams, new geographically distinct divisions, and even matrix structures all represent the convening of potentially culture-bearing milieux. Each "new" unit created in an organizational change effort (e.g., adding project teams) may be new "in name only;" that is, it may be made up of people who have been members of the organization doing tasks done before in buildings and at desks long familiar. But, what matters is the "name." Organizational settings refer essentially to sociologically and cognitively identifiable spaces, not merely or even necessarily to physical aspects of setting; identifiability is facilitated by shared namings of space and/or by physical bounding of space. So, in a number of ways, organizational settings represent milieux which may foster, enhance, hinder, and/or disrupt the development of local cultures, depending on specific features of the setting.

In terms of membership in a particular organizational culture, an individual may be a member of a social system and its culture by virtue of regular ongoing physical presence and participation in face-to-face interactions with other members. One may also be a member of a culture by virtue of affiliation without necessarily being physically present in a face-to-face interaction system. For instance, being a member of the Academy of Management constitutes membership in a social system which convenes in the strict physical sense only once a year. Yet the culture of the Academy of Management seems clearly distinguishable from the culture of the Association for Humanistic Psychology or other professional groups. Further, membership by affiliation may be purely informal, as in the case of "regulars" at the culture-rich Monterey Jazz Festival, which convenes 3 days per year and has done so for more than 25 years. Thus, in two distinct ways, as opportunities for affiliation and as physically convening social systems, organizations can be seen as culture-bearing milieux.

An individual may be a member of a social system and participate superficially or deeply in the local culture. What determines the level of cultural membership is the individual's self-perception. This is particularly true when we consider cultures in work organizations as opposed to national and ethnic group cultures. In contrast to participation in a culture of birth, participation in an organizational culture is more temporary or transitory and more a matter of voluntary choice (though not necessarily the product of a conscious rational decision process). Ultimately, one is a participant in a particular culture to the extent that one considers him or herself to be a member.

In addition to self-perception as a factor in cultural participation, the competence of the participation must be considered. Competence is more at issue in organizational culture than societal culture in part because of the relative frequency with which individuals change organizations and therefore have an opportunity and an attendant need to master a new culture. Has the person sufficiently internalized core ideals and values, and appreciated key symbols? Adequate grasp of the local intersubjective or social reality is necessary in order for the individual to function within the culture.

In an organizational setting, the definition of a situation by an individual may be guided by several nested and/or overlapping cultural systems. These may be differentially dominant depending on the individual, his or her tenure in the social system, the congruence among cultural systems, the situation to be defined, etc. For instance, incongruence between overlapping cultures may result for individuals who have both professional and organizational affiliations (e.g., an attorney or CPA working at GM corporate headquarters). Similarly, nested cultures can exert incompatible pulls on individuals. This is illustrated in the case of the division manager torn between loyalty to his division and loyalty to the company, particularly when performance is assessed at divisional profit centers. Such situations have been studied in terms of role conflict and organizational commitment without adequate attention to relevant cultural elements.

The prevalence of nested and overlapping cultures (by affiliation and/or physical colocation) and the self-perceptual nature of cultural membership indicate the need to clarify issues of boundary and perspective in conducting organizational research. In studying culture, especially when organizations are studied at a distance, from the outside (Evered & Louis, 1981), one can't tell whether a particular boundary—e.g., the IBM culture as a whole—is a meaningful level of analysis, a substantially rich culture in comparison with other nested or overlapping cultures—e.g., the culture of IBM systems engineers in which individuals are simultaneously members. As well, different members of IBM may consider different boundaries relevant; they may consider their dominant affiliation at the organization-wide, or subunit or functional speciality level. The challenge, then, is to identify which culture(s) is being studied and from whose point of view.

In addition to the organizational phenomena previously identified (e.g., control systems, nature of involvement, role conflict, organizational/professional commitment), a number of other phenomena (e.g., organizational climate, goal setting/performance feedback) imply that cultural processes are present in organizations and suggest vehicles for studying culture in organizations. Organizational climate has dealt at least conceptually almost directly with culture in organizations. Goal setting and performance feedback, which serve to guide and assess actions of organizational members, can be seen through a cultural view as the formalization and individualization of shared social ideals.

Conclusion

In this essay I have proposed that organizations be viewed as culture-bearing milieux. Essential ingredients of a cultural perspective were outlined and a number of organizational phenomena implicated in a cultural perspective were identified. A key premise of a cultural view is that meaning is emergent and intersubjectively negotiated. It was proposed that shared social ideals, frames of reference and symbols for conveying them are indigenous to social systems in organizations, as elsewhere; and that these aid members in interpreting experience and that they facilitate expression and guide behavior.

Conceptual development is needed to flesh out a cultural perspective. For instance, it may be useful to develop what seem to be natural categories of cultural facets. Prescriptive, descriptive, and expressive facets correspond on first glance to the cultural manifestations of, respectively, shared ideals, present images of local life, and symbol sets. And, by viewing culture as the context of individual action, the temporal/real-time, self-referencing, context-embedded, and actionable qualities of culture could be studied in much the same way that discourse is studied distinctly from language (Ricoeur, 1971).

Traditional analytic, etic-oriented research strategies (e.g., survey research) must be supplemented with more synthetic emic-oriented strategies in order to tap contextual aspects of phenomena and the perspectives of system members. Ethnography, participant observation, and

intensive case study techniques may be appropriate. Certain types of interaction analysis may also be appropriate (e.g., sociolinguistics), native knowledge (especially as in Frake's work [1964] on elicitation frames), and information management schemes (e.g., Mehan, 1978) constituting the underlying structures by which people organize each other and build environments for one another. (See McDermott & Roth [1978] for a review of interactional approaches and Cicourel [1978] for a comparative illustration of three models of discourse analysis.) Whatever specific methods are used, appropriate study of cultural phenomena requires that researchers avoid objectifying intersubjective phenomena and consider critical issues of boundary and perspective.

Culture in organizations needs to be studied both as a primary focus (i.e., cultural processes in organizations) and as an additional level of analysis (i.e., cultural aspects of organizational phenomena). There are abundant opportunities to study culture as a primary focus. For instance, at the sociological level, evolution of culture could be examined by studying the initial convening and early history of a social system, its shared ideals, metaphors, and symbol systems. Pettigrew's (1979) work in tracing the development of a newly established organization illustrates this type of study. The start of a project team, the commissioning and initial staffing of a new ship in the Navy, and the beginning of classes each semester are all situations in which the evolution of culture in organizations can be studied. And what happens during a corporate takeover, the shifts in priorities, images, and even languages reflect sometimes massive and sudden alterations of culture.

I close this essay by suggesting a final rationale for adding a view of organizations as culture-bearing milieux to our repertoire of perspectives on organizations. Historically, organizational scientists have adopted a reductionistic approach in studying organizational phenomena. Parts and pieces have been studied; 2 to 5 variable causal models have predominated (e.g., in studies of leadership, technology, structure). Results and conclusions about organizational functioning drawn from such research have been weak and necessarily tentative. Perhaps progress in the organizational sciences has suffered due to a pattern of pursuing the whole by exclusively examining the parts, without a balanced recognition that the whole, especially in the case of organizations, is greater than the sum of the parts. In contrast to the traditional reductionistic approach, considerations of culture require, support, and themselves imply a more holistic and integrative approach to studying organizational phenomena. The themes and images characterizing particular cultures are lost when examined piecemeal. When considered as a whole, the character of a culture is rather readily detected, for instance, through its imprint on social system members. In sum then, a cultural perspective might help us to move from a fairly exclusive reliance on a reductionistic approach to more diverse and, in particular, more holistic approaches to organizational inquiry.

Notes

1. This paper was completed in 1980. Since then, organizational scientists have written much on this subject; my thinking has evolved; I have become concerned that our pursuit of culture may not prove fruitful (Louis, 1983). My notions of culture in organizational settings have been influenced by writings in cultural anthropology, sociology, linguistics, and philosophy. The works of Schutz (1964, 1970a, 1970b), Berger and Luckmann (1966), Geertz (1973), Thomas (1951) and Ball (1972) have been particularly influential. Basic material on anthropological approaches to meaning and culture, can be found in Hammel and Simmons (1970), Spradley (1972), Gamst and Norbeck (1976). Nida (1964) provides a helpful and detailed discussion of linguistic, referential and emotive meanings.
2. A detailed critique of deficiencies arising from the exclusive use of universalistic approaches in organizational research is found in Louis (1981). Discussions in Ritzer (1975), Burrell and Morgan (1979), and Pondy and Mitroff (1979) provide other characterizations of limitations of traditional perspectives on organizations.

3. See Buckley (1967, p. 206) for a discussion of systematic orgins of this function.
4. McHugh's (1968) temporal and spatial themes are analogous at the individual psychological level to what is suggested here at the social systems level.
5. This emphasis on stabilizing functions of culture is not meant to suggest that cultural systems are static. On the contrary, they are more appropriately viewed as in-process, evolving and emergent. For example, the changing attitudes toward career/family trade-offs that are being reflected in changes in work cultures in America illustrate the evolving character of culture.
6. "The definition of the situation" is used here to refer to the meanings given by the individual to particular experiences in an immediate sense, that is, in the moment of experience; the interpretive scheme refers to the meaning set that the setting and social system typically has for the individual, across particular situations.

References

BALL, D. W. (1972). The definition of situation: Some theoretical and methodological consequences of taking W. I. Thomas seriously. *Journal for the Theory of Social Behavior, 2,* 61–82.

BECKER, H. S., & GEER, B. (1970). Participant observation and interviewing: A comparison. In W. J. Filstead (Ed.), *Qualitative methodology.* Chicago: Rand McNally.

BEER, M. (1980). *Organization change and development: A systems view.* Santa Monica, CA: Goodyear.

BERES, M. E., & PORTWOOD, J. D. (1979). Explaining cultural differences in the perceived role of work: An intranational cross-cultural study. In G. N. England, A. Negandhi, & B. Wilpert (Eds.), *Organizational functioning in a cross-cultural perspective.* Kent, OH: Kent State University Press.

BERGER, P., & LUCKMANN, T. (1966). *The social construction of reality: A treatise in the sociology of knowledge.* New York: Anchor Books.

BLACK, M. (1962). Meaning. In D. D. Runes (Ed.), *Dictionary of philosophy.* Patterson, NJ: Littlefield, Adams & Co.

BLUMER, H. (1969). *Symbolic interactionism: Perspective and method.* Englewood Cliffs, NJ: Prentice-Hall.

BUCKLEY, W. (1967). *Sociology and modern systems theory.* Englewood Cliffs, NJ: Prentice-Hall.

BURRELL, G., & MORGAN, G. (1979). *Sociological paradigms and organisational analysis.* London: Heinemann.

CICOUREL, A. V. (1978). *Three models of discourse analysis: The role of social structure.* Unpublished paper, Department of Sociology, University of California, San Diego.

CLARKE, B. (1970). *The distinctive college: Antioch, Reed and Swarthmore.* Chicago: Aldine Publishing.

DANDRIDGE, T. C., MITROFF, I. I., & JOYCE, W. F. (1980). Organizational symbolism: A topic to expand organizational analysis. *Academy of Management Review, 5,* 77–82.

ETZIONI, A. (1961). *A comparative analysis of complex organizations.* New York: Free Press.

EVERED, R., & LOUIS, M. R. (1981). Alternative perspectives in the organizational sciences: 'Inquiry from the inside' and 'Inquiry from the outside.' Under review with the *Academy of Management Review, 6,* 385–395.

FRAKE, C. O. (1964). Notes on queries in ethnography. *American Anthropologist, 66,* Part 2, No. 3, 127–132.

GAMST, F. C., & NORBECK, E. (1976). *Ideas of culture: Sources and uses.* New York: Holt, Rinehart & Winston.

GEERTZ, C. (1973). *The interpretation of cultures.* New York: Basic Books.

HALL, E. T. (1976). *Beyond culture.* New York: Anchor Press.

HAMMEL, E. A., & SIMMONS, W. S. (1970). *Man makes sense: A reader in modern cultural anthropology.* Boston: Little, Brown.

HARRISON, R. (1972). Understanding your organization's character. *Harvard Business Review, 5*(3), 119–128.

KROEBER, A. L., & PARSONS, T. (1958). The concepts of culture and of social systems. *American Sociological Review, 23,* 582–583.

LOUIS, M. R. (1980a). Career transitions: Varieties and commonalities. *Academy of Management Review, 5,* 329–340.

LOUIS, M. R. (1980b). Surprise and sense making: What newcomers experience in entering unfamiliar organizational settings. *Administrative Science Quarterly, 25,* 226–251.

LOUIS, M. R. (1981). Culture in organizations: The need for and consequences of viewing organizations as culture-bearing milieux. *Human Systems Management, 2,* 246–258.

LOUIS, M. R. Prerequisites for fruitful research on organizational culture. Unpublished paper.

McDERMOTT, R. P., & ROTH, D. R. (1978). The social organization of behavior: Interactional approaches. *Annual Review of Anthropology, 7,* 321–345.

McHUGH, P. (1968). *Defining the situation: The organization of meaning in social interaction.* New York: Bobbs-Merrill.

MEHAN, H. (1978). Structuring school structure. *Harvard Educational Review, 48,* 32–64.

MITROFF, I. I., & KILMANN, R. (1976). On organizational stories: An approach to the design and analysis of organizations through myths and stories. In R. H. Kilmann, L. R. Pondy & D. P. Slevin (Eds.), *The management of organization design: Strategies and implementation.* New York: Elsevier.

NIDA, E. A. (1964). *Toward a science of translating.* Leiden: E. J. Brill.

O'TOOLE, J. J. (1979). Corporate and managerial cultures. In C. L. Cooper (Ed.), *Behavioral problems in organizations.* Englewood Cliffs, NJ: Prentice-Hall.

OUCHI, W. G. (1979). A conceptual framework for the design of organizational control mechanisms. *Management Science, 25,* 833–848.

PETTIGREW, A. M. (1979). On studying organizational cultures. *Administrative Science Quarterly, 24,* 570–581.

PIKE, K. L. (1954). *Language in relation to a unified theory of the structure of human behavior.* Glendale, CA: Summer Institute of Linguistics.

PONDY, L. R., & MITROFF, I. I. (1979). Beyond open system models of organization. In B. M. Staw (Ed.), *Research in organizational behavior* (Vol. 1). Greenwich CT: JAI Press.

RICOEUR, P. (1979). The model of the text: Meaningful action considered as a text. In P. Rabinow & W. M. Sullivan (Eds.), *Interpretive social science: A reader.* Berkeley: University of California Press. (Reprinted from *Social Research,* 1971, *38.*)

RITZER, G. (1975). *Sociology: A multiple paradigm science.* Boston: Allyn & Bacon.

SCHUTZ, A. (1964). *Collected papers II: Studies in social theory.* (Arvid Brodersen, Ed.) The Hague: Martinus Nijhoff.

SCHUTZ, A. (1970a). *On phenomenology and social relations.* (Helmut R. Wagner, Ed.) Chicago: The University of Chicago Press.

SCHUTZ, A. (1970b). *Reflections on the problem of relevance.* (Richard M. Zaner, Ed.) New Haven, CT: Yale University Press.

SILVERMAN, D. (1970). *The theory of organizations.* New York: Basic Books.

SPRADLEY, J. P. (1972). *Culture and cognition: Rules, maps, and plans.* San Francisco: Chandler.

THOMAS, W. I. (1951). *Social behavior and personality: Contribution of W. I. Thomas to theory and social research.* (Edmund H. Volkart, Ed.) New York: Social Science Research Council.

TRIST, E. L., & BAMFORTH, K. W. (1951). Some social and psychological consequences of the Longwall method of coal-getting. *Human Relations, 4,* 1–38.

VAN MAANEN, J. (1977). Experiencing organization: Notes on the meaning of careers and socialization. In J. Van Maanen (Ed.), *Organizational careers: Some new perspectives.* New York: John Wiley & Sons.

VAN MAANEN, J. (1979a). On the understanding of interpersonal relations. In W. Bennis, J. Van Maanen, E. H. Schein, & F. I. Steele (Eds.), *Essays in interpersonal dynamics.* Pacific Grove, CA: Brooks/Cole.

VAN MAANEN, J. (1979b). Reclaiming qualitative methods for organizational research: A preface. *Administrative Science Quarterly, 24,* 520–526.

WEICK, K. E. (1969). *The social psychology of organizing.* Reading, MA: Addison-Wesley.

WEICK, K. E. (1979). Cognitive processes in organizations. In B. M. Staw (Ed.), *Research in organizational behavior* (Vol. 1) Greenwich, CT: JAI Press.

WILKINS, A., & MARTIN, J. (1979). *Organizational legends.* Unpublished paper, Stanford University.

46

Organizations As Shared Meanings

Linda Smircich

The overall purpose of this paper is to illustrate how organizations exist as systems of shared meanings and to highlight the ways in which shared meanings develop and are sustained through symbolic processes. The paper is derived from an ethnographic study of the executive staff of an Insurance Company. It describes the system of meaning the group members used to make sense of their experience and traces its emergence from their interaction and its influence on their further interaction. The paper shows how such symbolic processes as organizational rituals, organizational slogans, vocabulary, and presidential style contribute to, and are part of, the development of shared meanings which give form and coherence to the experience of organization members.

The stability, or organization, of any group activity depends upon the existence of common modes of interpretation and shared understanding of experience. These shared understandings allow day to day activities to become routinized and taken for granted. Through the development of shared meanings for events, objects, words and people, organization members achieve a sense of commonality of experience that facilitates their coordinated action.

In a particular situation the set of meanings that evolves gives a group its own ethos, or distinctive character, which is expressed in patterns of belief (ideology), activity (norms and

SOURCE: L. R. Pondy and others, eds., *Organizational Symbolism*, 55–65. Copyright 1983 JAI Press. Reprinted with permission.

rituals), language and other symbolic forms through which organization members both create and sustain their view of the world and image of themselves in the world. The development of a world view with its shared understanding of the group identity, purpose and direction are products of the unique history, personal interactions and environmental circumstances of the group. Yet the particular world view may continue to shape organizational existence long after the key actors have departed from the scene and environmental conditions have changed. Acknowledgement of this provides the impetus for the study of the symbolic processes which facilitate the continued existence of particular organizational realities.

Background

The Insurance Company[1] studied is one division of a Corporation that has 10,000 employees in 12 northeastern states. The Corporation was formed in 1964 as a result of a merger of three well-established regional farmer's cooperatives with the formal objective of building and maintaining a strong, diversified, cooperative business organization to improve the economic well-being of its members. Before the merger each of the three cooperatives had developed their own insurance programs to protect the lives and property of their farmer members and to provide them with lower group rates. In 1968, the Insurance division was developed out of these programs and was eventually expanded into insurance services for the general public as well as the membership. The Insurance Company employs 250 people and is housed in a modern two story building two blocks from the corporate headquarters located in a medium size northeastern city.

An agreement was reached whereby the researcher was invited to spend six weeks in the Insurance Company as an observer of the top management group. The researcher's role was negotiated as that of an observer, to learn about the organization not to serve as a consultant. There was to be no presentation of "results" to the company. The fact that the President agreed to have an observer in the organization, but did not want feedback on the experience, is itself a piece of data, and one which is consistent with much of what is said here about the ways of life in this group.

The specific techniques used in this setting were similar to those of many anthropologists and sociologists doing field work (Bogdan & Taylor, 1975; Schatzman & Strauss, 1973). The researcher maintained the work hours of the organization and was provided with office space. Early on she met individually with each of the staff members and explained the project. The researcher's activity consisted of observing the management staff in a variety of situations: staff meetings, planning sessions, interactions with their subordinates, on coffee breaks and in casual conversation. The work proceeded in a way which allowed the themes present in the setting to emerge and to be explored in cycles of data collection and analysis (Glaser & Strauss, 1968; Diesing, 1971). Towards the end of the stay in the organization tape recorded conversations/interviews were held with each of the 10 staff members including the president. The conversation was oriented around several topics or themes which appeared to be relevant to the people in the organization. The raw data from this study consist of: daily field notes, documents from the organization, tapes of conversation, and the researcher's experience.

The Ethos

The dominant interpretation that the executive staff used to account for their way of life was the belief that, in their group, differences or problems which may be difficult or painful to handle were submerged. There was widespread agreement that "if you've got anything that is controversial, you just don't bring it up."

They saw their mode of behavior as a direct result of the style and preferences of the company president. The staff claimed that the president "likes to keep it cool," "doesn't like to see any friction or animosity," and "doesn't like to hear if things are bad." Consequently, there was a belief that in the company "people say what they know everyone else wants to hear." Problems get "buried" instead of dealt with directly because "it's easier to handle that way." Staff members perceived the president as having the philosophy that "you shouldn't air problems or disagreements." They feared that if they were to surface a disagreement they would be labelled a "troublemaker" or accused of "pointing a finger." The atmosphere in the organization was described as "a fiction, not reality." The corporate secretary believed that the president was aware that the staff members did not say what they really thought but that he allowed it to continue because "he'd like to finish out his time with the company having everything quiet, without any uproar."

Thus the staff made sense of their experience in similar ways ("we maintain a smooth surface of agreement") and they shared a rationale for why the situation was as it was ("we behave this way because of the president"). It is these areas of shared meaning which give the executive group a sense of commonality and unity to their experience. These beliefs contributed to coordinated, albeit restrained, interaction and an aura of passivity among the staff members. To the outside observer the beliefs appeared to function in rule-like fashion and lent the staff member's activity a programmed character.

In private almost all the staff members complained to the researcher about their mode of behavior and the president's style. Some expressed a preference for dealing with differences directly but they felt blocked from doing so. In public they tried scrupulously to maintain a facade of agreement and politeness. They shared the perception that they were behaving according to the president's preferences and to do otherwise would invite disaster.

With the executive staff we see at least two meaning systems, the public and the private, in operation. What is striking is the high degree of overlap across executives in both public and private systems of meaning. It is also striking that even though some staff members had an awareness of the dynamics of their situation, they felt dominated by their perception of a third meaning system, that of the president, and felt powerless to change it. Through the action of the president, the participation of the staff members, and the enactment of particular symbolic forms cultivated by the president, the ethos of apparent harmony was sustained and elaborated and came to dominate the ways in which the organization members interpreted their situation.

In addition to understanding the nature of the shared meaning systems of a group it is also important to understand the ways in which they come to be shared and by what mechanisms they are perpetuated. The remainder of the paper addresses these issues.

The Emergence of the Ethos

The emergence of this dominant system of meaning can be understood as a consequence of the historical development of the company, the struggles for leadership within it, and the personal ideology of the current president.

The formative period (1968–1978) of the Insurance Company, described as "traumatic" and "chaotic" was marked by several specific events: the demotion of the first head of the company, the firing of the second, the hiring of an executive vice president, and the hiring of a cadre of insurance professionals to strengthen the staff. These events surfaced struggle and conflict in the developing company between those staff members originally employed by one of the original farmers' cooperatives and those brought in from the insurance industry.

The distinction between the outside people and the inside people was heightened by the fact that most of the new personnel came directly from the same company as the executive vice president or had worked for that company at some time in the past. Discussions would frequently involve statements such as "This was how we did it at the other company." which would further alienate the outside group from

the inside group. It was perhaps awareness of the potential harmful effects of such a division which led to the creation of a ritual, a form of initiation rite, for each new member of management.

Rituals are behavior patterns which are stylized or formalized and which are repeated in that form. While it is common to associate rituals with events of religious significance there are also rituals carried out in everyday organizational life which are imbued with significance and which hold various meanings for the participants.

At special management meetings the staff became an Indian tribe; each new addition was given a headband with a feather and was christened with an Indian name. For example, one staff member was dubbed "Chief Running Water" because of his habitual lateness. As part of this ritual, the executive vice president instituted a 50¢ fine, levied any time anyone mentioned the name of the other firm.

Although the Indian tribe and the 50¢ fine were intended as symbols of the starting of new allegiances to a new company, the split between the people who had been associated with the corporation and those from the competitive firm was real and difficult to overcome. That the memory of the distinction between the inside and outside people was still quite vivid many years later is obvious from the talk of one executive who was with the company before the executive vice president was hired. He described the presence of a "division here in the company between that other company and the rest of us" because "if somebody wanted something and the guy was from the other company, he got it. If you weren't from there, you didn't get it." Those who came from the competitive firm to the Insurance Company seemed to remain aloof and not mingle with the others. It appeared to the veteran employees that the "executive vice-president's boys" were shown favoritism which contributed to a clandestine and political atmosphere. During this time period the executive vice president was responsible for the daily operations of the company while the president's efforts were devoted to external relationships. This arrangement came to an end in November of 1977 when the executive vice president entered the hospital with cancer. His death in January of 1978 marked the end of an era at the Insurance Company. When the executive vice president died a decision was made not to replace him; instead the vice presidents and directors began to report directly to the president.

The president was the central figure in the emergence and shaping of an ethos of apparent harmony which stood in contrast to these earlier conditions. He saw his task as the blending of the traditions and orientations of the people from inside the parent corporation with those brought in from the outside because of their knowledge of the insurance business. The desire to blend the inside and the outside was the basis upon which the symbols of the Insurance Company, connoting harmony and integration, were developed. We turn now to an examination of the symbolic processes associated with the president and the shared meanings which evolved around them.

An Organizational Ritual: The Monday Morning Staff Meeting

With the death of the executive vice president, weekly staff meetings were instituted to bring the president up to date on operations. The meanings that the executive staff members associated with these meetings were tied up with the historical context in which they began and their feelings about the president's style of management. At the time of the field work the staff members shared an interpretation of these meetings. To them they appeared to represent the way their president wanted business to be conducted: calmly, coolly, politely, harmoniously with no conflict, controversy or upset, but also with an air of unreality.

The Monday morning staff meetings had very much of a ritualistic quality. "We sit in the same seats, like cows always go to the same stall" said one executive. The tone of the meetings was low key, polite, calm, restrained and seemed to reflect the president's personal style of interaction which was also calm, reserved,

and restrained. There was very little discussion among staff members in the meetings, instead comments were directed to the president in one-to-one fashion. This one-to-one mode of interaction also reflected the president's favored style of management. The meetings appeared to resemble "show and tell" sessions more than anything else. They began promptly at 8:15. One member was habitually late and this was a source of humor and irritation. But although his lateness bothered some of the staff members, and was the target of covert derision, neither they nor the president said anything when he made his late entrances, instead, his entry was ignored.

The president's role at the staff meetings appeared to be that of a newscaster, funnelling information from the external environment into the system. He usually spoke about ten minutes. When he was finished each member in turn would report about the activities in his or her area. While this was being done the other staff members usually kept their eyes downcast. Only one staff member consistently took notes. There was rarely any interchange between staff members that was of a susbstantive nature, although there were upon occasion quick questions or minor barbs.

There was a shared belief among the staff members that these meetings were empty formality; they consisted of "superficial" communication. Discussion was kept at a surface level. People reported how many policies were handled; but they did not "delve as deep" into what they really felt about certain things which may be going on in their own departments or the departments of others. "You'll never see the nitty-gritty in the staff meeting," one executive told the researcher. "But I think I know why (the president) does it—to keep us together." One executive said their meetings were "just like coming home and the wife says 'How was your day at the office today?' " They believed the president did not ask the staff members hard questions because "it's not his policy to say or do anything that would offend anyone or hurt anyone's feelings" which led to the opinion that "It's a real waste of time. It's a situation where you can say just about anything and no one will refute it.'' One member observed that people ''are very hesitant to speak up, afraid to say too much.'' (They think) ''If I say this, will this happen?'' or ''(the president) likes to keep it cool. He doesn't like to see any friction or any animosity.'' Thus, the staff members see their behavior in these meetings as superficial where they say ''what everyone else wants to hear.'' They considered ''maybe (the president) doesn't want to know.'' Another staff member felt sure that the president was aware of the superficiality of their behavior but that he preferred it that way.

On the other hand, the president expressed the belief to the researcher that the staff meetings were ''a forum where we exchange information and keep up to date, on external and internal (issues) and on major decisions. They provide a forum for a little bit of important debate and discussion.''

The staff members did not see the meetings in those terms. Instead they were seen as a ritual for bringing them together but from which nothing of any substance emerged.

An Organizational Slogan: "Wheeling Together"

Shortly after the death of the executive vice president there was a deliberate effort to create an image or symbol for the Insurance Company. It took the form of a slogan ''Wheeling Together'' and was represented by an actual wagon wheel mounted on a flat base. The various spokes on the wheel represented the different parts of the Insurance Company; at the center was the customer. The wheel, about 4 feet high, was kept at the top of a file cabinet and was moved around from department to department. Lucite paper weights were produced embedded with the wheel image. There were even ''Wheeling Together'' rubber stamps for use on outgoing mail.

This image was originally created as a theme for a sales contest to convey the relationship between the agents in the field and the people in the home office, but was adopted by the president of the Company and incorporated into his annual ''kick off'' speech. Most of the staff members believed that the president meant his symbolic message to be applied to the executive staff members because of the divisiveness and conflicts between staff members which surfaced after the executive vice president's death. One staff member recalled ''There was a lot of dissension around the staff, a lot of disagreements, fights, an inordinate amount of finger-pointing . . . ''Wheeling Together'' is a theme that developed in order to promote teamwork.

The symbol of the wheel and the slogan ''Wheeling Together'' were intended to communicate a spirit of interdependence and teamwork. But at the time of the study the symbol and its accompanying slogan were clearly not alive as a positive image for the staff. In fact, the symbol became a shared image but in a negative way; it gave the staff members a common way to understand and talk about how poorly they worked together. ''Wheeling Together'' was the counterpoint or antithesis of their experience and they used it derisively to mock and ridicule their own behavior. One staff member talking about a series of incidents which demonstrated the hostile behavior between two departments summed up his description with a sarcastic ''now that's wheeling together.'' For the most part the executives were sympathetic to the ideal the symbol represented but questioned its applicability to their group. ''The philosophy was that each of the departments was a spoke of this wheel and if all the spokes were there and functioning you had a smooth-riding trip. But some of the departments are a little splintered and as a result the thing isn't really working together.'' Another staff member joked ''Actually we've got four wheel drive, but every wheel is going in its own direction.''

The image of the wheel served to highlight to the staff members that which was absent in their organization: a sense of cooperativeness with all parts of the company going in the same direction. Although the symbol and the slogan were ineffective in creating a feeling of harmony, they did capture the staff's attention, and provided a common way of understanding their experience. They mentioned for example the belief that one department was a "weak spoke" and therefore "the whole wheel can break," and that the "executive staff does not wheel together."

The image was part of the president's language. In talking about his role to the researcher he said he tried to encourage people to see their interdependence, "You really don't go very far unless everybody's got their shoulder to the wheel." But he also voiced some reservations. "You can't overdo this to the point where you threaten to suppress some spirited debate . . . You could have people not speaking their minds just because they feel they might undermine the teamwork." He believed "that would be wrong," there should be "some confrontation between people as long as it doesn't get personal." He said he stressed to his staff that "you just can't get personal about these things" because "then you've injected a little poison into the outfit." He felt that "debate should be encouraged if you're going to make the best decisions." He added, "the main thing is just to keep the personalities out."

It is obvious from the behavior and talk of the staff members that they have clearly received the message about keeping personalities out. This message is so important to the president and his concern about keeping things impersonal is so strong, the staff feel that there really is no room for any confrontation or debate. Although the president says it would be "wrong to suppress debate," it appears that that is exactly what has occurred here. The president paid lip service to the belief that "debate should be encouraged if you're going to make the best decisions" but through his actions and the enactment of these symbolic forms, the ethos which places value on the appearance of harmony is sustained and remains dominant.

Organizational Vocabulary: The Meaning of "Challenge"

The executive group sustained an appearance of smoothness and nonconfrontation not only in their activities but in their choice of vocabulary as well. This was most obvious in their use of the word "challenge" as a cover up word to mask what were really problems. The inability or unwillingness to call a situation a problem was consistent with the whole interaction pattern of keeping things hidden.

The staff members privately shared the view that challenge means "a problem." Some members put it more forcefully. "It means a very god-damn severe problem—my god what a mess." Another said, "It's an excuse word, it's a soft way of putting things. We don't want to hurt each other." Even the president said to the researcher, "I think the word challenge is sometimes overused. When people have problems or when an organization has problems, it's often considered a challenge, at least that's the way everybody uses it, to put it in a better light, I guess."

In this instance the way a particular word is used is congruent with and supportive of the larger pattern of behavior. Shared meanings for other words, events, objects, can provide a sense of commonality to experience and allow for coordinated responses without a great deal of re-negotiation of meaning at each encounter. In this group the members had a shared but unspoken agreement about using the word challenge, instead of problem, to spare a person who had a "challenge" from the harsher implications of a problem.

Conclusion

Organizations exist as systems of meanings which are shared to varying degrees. A sense of commonality, or taken for grantedness is necessary for continuing organized activity so that interaction can take place without constant interpretation and re-interpretation of meanings. Much of this commonality is developed through and perpetuated by such symbolic processes as the rituals, slogans and specialized vocabularies considered in this paper. The particular set of meanings that a group evolves provides it with its own ethos or distinctive character. The ethos may reflect historical circumstances, critical events, and unique attributes and preferences of key people. It emerges from social processes and shapes their course as part of the ongoing reality of the group.

The methods which ultimately emerged in the executive group of the organization here were a product of the difficulties of the search for leadership for the new division and the need to mesh a diverse group of people into a new organization, coupled with the calm, reserved, polite style of the president. The experiences of the formative period, characterized by interpersonal conflict, worked their way into the fabric of meanings shared by the executive group, including the president. They were not mere memories or artifacts but were kept alive as part of the ongoing reality of the organization in that the prevailing ethos was designed to encourage a completely opposite form of experience. The ethos of maintaining a smooth surface of agreement and avoiding confrontation seemed to serve as both a rationale and a guide for behavior. It was sustained through the rituals of the staff meeting and the president's one-on-one style of management; it was reflected and elaborated in the "Wheeling Together" slogan and the wheel symbol, and was firmly embedded in the patterns of speech.

The case study illustrates the way organization members forge common grounds for action, although in the situation presented here, it was more often inaction. These common grounds for action stem from mutual beliefs and the enactment of patterns of meaningful activities. Some of these may be purposely designed by those with influence as in the case of the "Wheeling Together" slogan, whereas many others take their significance as a consequence of the particular context and circumstances of action. Such processes are central to the existence of organized activity, which though so often taken for granted as routing and real, rests upon a complex system of shared meaning.

Note

1. Additional analyses of the dynamics of the executive staff of this organization can be found in Smircich, L., & Morgan, G. Leadership: The Management of meaning. *Journal of Applied Behavioral Science,* 1982, *18*(3), 257–273.

References

BOGDAN, R., & TAYLOR, S. J. *Introduction to qualitative research methods.* New York: Wiley, 1975.

DIESING, P. *Patterns of discovery in the social sciences.* Chicago: Aldine, 1971.

GLASER, B. G., & STRAUSS, A. L. *The discovery of grounded theory.* Chicago: Aldine, 1967.

SCHATZMAN, I., & STRAUSS, A. L. *Fieldwork.* Englewood Cliffs, N.J.: Prentice-Hall, 1973.

TURNER, G. A. *Exploring the industrial subculture.* London: Macmillan, 1971.

47

Cultural and Competing Perspectives in Administrative Theory and Practice

Thomas J. Sergiovanni

A number of perspectives in administration and organizational behavior compete for the attention of professionals involved in the leading and managing of educational organizations. The most well known reflect a high concern for efficiency, the person, and politics. The newest and most controversial are cultural perspectives. Controversy stems in part from cultural perspectives adopting assumptions that depart from other views, from the suspicion in which they hold norms of traditional science, and from their emphasis on understanding as well as explanation. Each of these four perspectives provides administrators with a framework for actions and decisions. Since determined reality and sensible events in organizational life differ depending upon the view adopted, actions and decisions differ accordingly. Perspectives, be they explicit or implicit, are the means by which actions and decisions are rationalized as legitimate and sensible.

In this introductory chapter the four perspectives are described with greater attention given to the cultural view. The cultural perspective provides the theme thread for subsequent chapters. A basic assumption of the book is that

SOURCE: T. J. Sergiovanni and J. E. Corbally (Eds.), *Leadership and Organizational Culture*, 1–11. Copyright 1984 University of Illinois Press. Reprinted with permission.

administrative and organizational analysis in schools and universities, and in other public organizations, should best be viewed as a multiple-perspective activity. Theories of administration, therefore, should not be viewed as competing, with the thought that one best view might emerge. Instead, the alternate and overlapping lenses metaphor is offered. When viewed in this way, each theory of administration is better able to illuminate and explain certain aspects of the problems administrators face but not others. Increased understanding depends upon the use of several theories, preferably in an integrated fashion.

Heretofore, cultural perspectives have been neglected and the other perspectives have typically been used singularly as separate truths in competition with an array of assumed falsehoods. The singular use of a particular perspective or brand of theory stems in part from viewing administration as an applied science. When this occurs, principles of action are determined by the direct—either implicit or explicit—application of laws presumed to be established by social science. Neglected is the extent to which this applied knowledge fits the particular characteristics of the problem and its context. When several theoretical perspectives are brought together to bear on a problem, the administration of educational organizations is viewed as an art where principles of action result from the judgments of administrators at work. The role of the various social sciences and related administrative theories in this case is not that of surrogate to the administrator's intuition, but serves instead to inform this intuition. Intuition allows the artful application of knowledge in a setting where particulars of the situation are taken into account.

Explicit and Background Assumptions

Theoretical perspectives in administration are comprised of at least two distinguishable components. One component is the explicitly formulated and stated assumptions which give a particular perspective structure, form, and definition. The other component is the background assumptions which are tacit (Gouldner 1970). Background assumptions define how events ought to be interpreted and what events are to be accepted as fact and real.

Explicitly formulated and stated assumptions central to any theoretical perspective are influenced as much by the prevailing background assumptions as by the properties of events and situations under study. In administrative practice, for example, how problems are defined, what factors are to be considered, how events are to be evaluated, which decision-making strategies are to be used, and what the standards are by which truth is to be determined can all be traced to the prevailing background assumptions of the administrator and the group in question. As the assumptions change so do the characteristics of practice. In this sense there is no separate reality in organizational behavior and administrative functioning. Objectivity and truth are evasive and no order exists beyond that which is created in the minds of persons and that which is imposed upon the organization by persons. It is in this sense, as well, that the study of organizational behavior and administrative functioning might well be considered as "artificial" sciences (Simon 1969).

In the artificial sciences, reality is created by human conventions rather than by being inherent in the nature of the universe. Chemical elements and genetic characteristics, for example, respond according to natural laws. Traditional science aims to discover these laws and to test them by predicting natural behavior. The human sciences, by contrast, are unique. Except for instinctive and other low-level functioning, humans do not behave; they *act*. Actions differ from behavior in that they are born of preconceptions, assumptions, and motives. Actions have meaning in the sense that as preconditions change, meanings change regardless of the sameness of recorded behavior.

To bring order to this apparent confusion, conventions are invented to help determine what is true, to guide appropriate action, and to establish standards by which action might be evaluated. It is the scholar's perception of the dominant conventions that governs the nature of knowledge production and the professional's perception of dominant perspectives that governs professional practice. Among Kant's many contributions was his idea that knowledge is not a passive mirror of reality; its nature and substance is determined by the ways in which people comprehend (Bleicher 1980).

The efficiency perspective is reflected in the commonly accepted principles of "good" management which characterize the organization and operation of schools and universities. A division of labor exists whereby instructional and coordinative tasks are allocated to specific roles. Roles are defined by job descriptions which are clearly linked to some overall conception of what the organization is to accomplish. Certain guides, such as span of control and student/faculty ratio, have been accepted to help decide the number of faculty needed and how they should be assigned. Tasks are subdivided and specialists are hired for various functions. Roles are ordered according to rank, with some enjoying more authority and privilege than others. Day-by-day decisions are routinized and controlled by establishing and monitoring a system of policies and rules. These in turn ensure more reliable behavior on behalf of organizational goals. Proper communication channels are established and objective mechanisms are developed for handling disputes, allocating resources, monitoring quality, and evaluating personnel. Good management, defined in this sense, is directed at the efficient achievement of certain ends. But efficiency cannot be accidental; it requires deliberate and calculated planning. The ends must be clearly defined and the means carefully determined and stipulated. If means are implemented precisely according to plan, ends are likely to be accomplished efficiently.

Much of what is taken for granted as good management can be traced to an era of development in administration referred to as scientific management (Taylor 1911). Scientific management did not offer a theory of administration and organization as such, but a set of principles and injunctions for administrators to follow. Efficiency was to be maximized by defining objectives clearly, by specializing task through division of labor, and, once the *best way* was identified, by introducing a system of controls to ensure uniformity, reliability, and standardization of product.

Efficiency principles persevere today as strong considerations in curriculum development, selecting educational materials, developing instructional systems, and in other aspects of educational administration. This continued interest in scientific management can be attributed to a period of economic instability and to demands for accountability felt by all public organizations. But its strength is derived from the attractiveness of efficiency and technical rationality valued in Western thought.

Historically scientific management principles were applied directly. Traditional control mechanisms such as face-to-face supervision, however, have now been replaced by more impersonal, technical, or rational control mechanisms. It is assumed that if visible standards of performance, objectives, or competencies can be identified and measured, then the work of teachers and that of students can be better controlled by holding them accountable to these standards thus ensuring greater reliability, effectiveness, and efficiency in performance. These standards are reflected in the attention university administrators give to such "quality" indicators as grades distributed by curricula, admissions scores by program major, number of students taught by faculty FTE (Full Time Equivalent), and number of books and papers published.

Karl Weick (1982) suggests that efficiency management principles assume the existence of a self-correcting rational system among closely linked and interdependent people, consensus on goals and means, coordination by dissemination of information, and predictability of problems and problem responses. Schools and universities, by contrast, are loosely structured with ambiguous goals and large spans of control. Weick notes that when the efficiency principles are applied to schools and universities and other loosely structured organizations "effectiveness declines, people become confused, and work doesn't get done." With respect to schools he concludes that "they are managed with the wrong model in mind" (Weick 1982, 673).

When viewing administrative theory and practice from a single perspective, certain aspects of organizations and administration are emphasized and better understood but other aspects are neglected or given secondary status. The efficiency perspective did not give adequate attention to the human side of life in educational organizations. Such issues as individual personality and human needs and such conditions as job satisfaction, motivation, and morale seemed to be clearly secondary.

By 1930 an effective counterforce on behalf of the human side of enterprise was to emerge. This force was later to evolve into a distinct pattern of thought about administration with a strong emphasis on the person. The metaphor "organic" is often used to describe the person perspective. The analogy is to that of a biological organism capable of feeling and growing but also capable of ill health if not properly nurtured. The building blocks to organizational health are individuals and their needs as groups of individuals. According to this view, an ideal school department or unit is one characterized by highly motivated individuals who are committed to objectives from which they derive satisfaction. These individuals are linked together into highly effective work groups. The work groups are characterized by commitment to common objectives, group loyalty, and mutual support. Efficiency views emphasized specialization by tasks; personal views emphasized specialization by people. Specialization by people permits individuals to function as experts who enjoy discretionary prerogatives and who are influenced more by client needs and their own expert abilities than by carefully delineated duties and tasks. The concepts of collegiality in universities and shared decision-making in schools are allied with this view.

The person perspective is reflected in human relations and human resources management theories. The bench mark most frequently mentioned as the beginning of the human relations movement in administration is the work of the research team which functioned from 1924 to 1933 at the Hawthorn plant of the Western Electric Company in Cicero, Illinois (Roethlisberger and Dickson 1939). Elton Mayo (1945), a prominent pioneer in this movement, offered a set of assumptions to characterize people which was quite different from that of efficiency management. He suggested that persons are primarily motivated by social needs and obtain their basic satisfactions from relationships with others. He maintained that management had robbed work of meaning, and therefore meaning must be provided in the social relationships of the job. Mayo also concluded that persons were more responsive to the social forces of their peer groups than to extrinsic incentives and management controls. Finally, a person's identity and loyalty to management and organization depended upon the extent to which interaction and acceptance needs were provided for at work.

Human resources theory represented a maturation of earlier human relations principles (Miles 1965). Both human relations and human resources lamented the loss of meaning in work. But in human resources this loss was not attributed to neglect of a person's social needs as much as to inability to use talents fully. A person's presumed capacity for growth received the greatest attention by human resources theorists. They urged that shared decision-making, joint planning, common goals, increased responsibility, and positive provision for more autonomy were the sorts of strategies to be developed by administrators. Motivation was to be intrinsic because jobs were to become interesting and challenging. Human resources theorists reflected not only an interest in people at work but a new regard for their potential. A great deal of emphasis was placed on autonomy, inner direction, and the desire for maximum self-development at work (McGregor 1960; Likert 1967; Argyris 1964).

The political perspective represents a recent and important development in the literature of educational administration. Four critical emphases distinguish the political perspective from those which emphasized efficiency or the person.

Each of the other views is primarily concerned with forces, events, and activities internal to the organization. The political perspective is concerned with the dynamic interplay of the organization with forces in its external environment. Schools and universities, for example, are viewed as open rather than closed systems, as integral parts of a larger environment not as bounded entities isolated from their environment. They receive inputs, process them, and return outputs to the environment. Inputs are presumed to be diverse and output demands often conflicting. As a result there is constant interplay between school and environment. The university is expected to meet its commitments to teaching but at the same time to win enough research contracts to help maintain financial solvency. The high school is expected to maintain tight control over students but at the same time to teach them self-responsibility and initiative. The nature of this interplay is political. As issues are resolved, bargains are struck and agreements reached. Internally, school and universities are comprised of interdependent subunits and groups with self-interests which compete with each other.

The emphasis in other views is on the administration of policy decisions. In the political perspective the emphasis is on policy development. Political views do not consider goals as givens to be administered. Goals are considered to be highly unstable and constantly changing. Therefore, understanding the process of bargaining in the development of consensus and understanding that sensitivity of such agreements to external forces are considered important.

The other views seek to suppress, program, gloss-over, or resolve conflict. In the political perspective conflict is considered as both natural and necessary. Conflict resolution is an important concern to administrators who work from the person perspective for they view conflict as unnatural and pathological. Since finding and using the "one best way" are characteristics of the efficiency perspective, conflict is regarded as a deviation to be corrected. The emphasis in the political perspective is on policy formulation. This emphasis requires debates over appropriate goals, values, and strategies and is naturally accompanied by conflict.

Each of the other views assumes norms of rationality in decision-making. The political perspective is not based on similar interpretations of rationality. For example, since it is assumed that goals are not givens but negotiated, and since the interplay within the organization and between the organization and its environment is viewed as bargaining, then the rational pattern of establishing clear goals and subsequently programming individual and organizational behavior to maximize these goals is suspect. Instead, a "satisficing" image of person and organization is offered as a substitute for more traditional rational images. Administrators do not seek optimal solutions to the problems they face but seek solutions that will satisfy a variety of demands. The "best" research program is not adopted but the one that is easier to implement and which costs less is chosen. In the schools the "best" reading program is not selected for children but the one which teachers will accept and implement with the minimum amount of difficulty is chosen.

The political perspective began to receive attention by administrators in the late fifties as scholars from political science and the decision sciences systematically began to study the problems of organization and administration. Herbert A. Simon's now classic work *Administrative Behavior: A Study of Decision-Making Processes in Administrative Organization* (1945) is considered by many as the forerunner of this movement. In recent years James G. March and his colleagues have turned their attention to the analysis of educational organizations (Cohen and March 1974), coining the label "organized anarchies" to characterize the way these organizations function (March and Olsen 1976).

The Cultural Perspective

Within the cultural perspective organizations are viewed as artificial entities subject to the whims of human predispositions and conventions, and within organizations administrative activity is viewed as a cultural artifact. The emphasis in analysis and practice is more on understanding than explaining and on making sense of events and activities than on describing.

The cultural perspective is the most recent view of theory and practice among the four and the view likely to receive more attention in the near future. This view looks to phenomenology, symbolic-interactionism, anthropology, ecology, hermeneutics, and critical theory as relevant scholarly traditions. More particularistic in focus and with a higher regard for the practical and the practitioner's way of knowing than the other three views, the cultural is concerned with the unique aspects of issues and situations and with grass-roots approaches to studying educational organizations and environments. Individuals, for example, are studied in context where both context and individual are assumed to be relatively equal. According to this view individuals are not masters of context but integral parts. Thus the study of human behavior separate from the unique characteristics of the specific organizational context is viewed with suspicion.

Underlying the cultural perspective is the concept of community and the importance of shared meanings and shared values. Within the university there exist several subcultures each seeking to promote and maintain its values. To understand the university is to understand the nature of multicultural societies, and to administer the university requires that one deal with the web of conflict and tension which exists as several subcultures try to protect their way of life. The administrator accepts the fact that differences among subgroups are greater than values shared in common; that often administrative practices represent the intrusion of one culture on another; that how people interpret events is very important; and that normative and persistent qualities of each subculture are sacro-sanct. The need exists, nonetheless, to identify and articulate those cultural strands which can evoke enough common human consciousness among groups to enable concerted action.

Leadership within the cultural perspective takes on a more qualitative image; of less concern is the leader's behavioral style, and leadership effectiveness is not viewed merely as the instrumental summation of the link between behavior and objectives. Instead, what the leader stands for and communicates to others is considered important. The object of leadership is the stirring of human consciousness, the interpretation and enhancement of meanings, the articulation of key cultural strands, and the linking of organizational members to them. As Pondy suggests,"What kind of insights can we get if we say that the effectiveness of a leader lies in his ability to make activity meaningful for those in his role set—not to change behaviors but to give others a sense of understanding about what they are doing, and especially to articulate it so they can communicate about the meanings of their behavior" (1978, 94). He characterizes the difference between behavior and meaning as the difference between "playing notes" and "making music." Within the cultural perspective concern is greater for the music-making aspects of leadership than note-playing aspects.

The concept of "center" is important to the cultural perspective. Organizational and societal centers represent the locus of values, sentiments and beliefs which provide the cultural cement for holding together human groups. As Edward A. Shils states:

Society has a center. There is a central zone in the structure of society. This central zone impinges in various ways on those who live within the ecological domain in which the society exists. Membership in the society, in more than the ecological sense of being located in a bounded territory and of adapting to an environment affected or made up by other persons located in the same territory, is constituted by a relationship to this zone.

The center, or the central zone, is a phenomenon of the realm of values and beliefs. It is the center of the order of symbols, of values and beliefs, which govern the society. It is the center because it is the ultimate and irreducible, and it is felt to be such by many who cannot give explicit articulation to its irreducibility. The central zone partakes of the nature of the sacred. In this sense, every society has an official "religion" even when that society or its exponents and interpreters conceive of it, more or less correctly, as a secular, pluralistic, and tolerant society. . . . The center is also a phenomenon of the realm of action. It is a structure of activities, of roles and persons, within the network of institutions. It is in these roles that the values and beliefs which are central are embodied and propounded [1961, 119].

As repositories of values, organizational and group centers are sources of identity for individuals and groups from which their organizational lives become meaningful. Developing and nurturing center value patterns and accepting center norms which dictate what one should believe and how one should behave represent a response to felt needs of individuals and groups for stability and order and for a mechanism whereby the new and varied can be absorbed in a meaningful fashion. Centers provide a sense of purpose to seemingly ordinary events and bring worth and dignity to human activity within organizations. Centers, therefore, are cultural imperatives—normal and necessary for establishing social order and providing meaning.

Since the development of centers within organizations occurs naturally in response to human needs, left unattended several "wild" centers may develop with only accidental congruence with official organizational purposes and ideals. Further, "wild" centers developed by various subgroups within an organization may not only contradict administrative and organizational aspirations but may conflict as well among themselves. Thus the "domestication" of centers becomes an important leadership responsibility of administrators who work within the cultural perspective. To this effort, leaders consciously work to build unity, order, and meaning within the organization as a whole by giving attention to organizational purposes, the philosophical and historical traditions of the organization, and the ideals and norms which define the way of life in the organization for purposes of socialization and of obtaining compliance.

Summary

Perspectives are images of reality and not truths in themselves. Since educational administration and organizational behavior are linked to human conventions, perspectives of practice are not truth seeking in the traditional sense but rather serve to enhance one's understanding and to illuminate one's view of the world.

Though it is natural to debate the relative usefulness of various perspectives, some scholars continue to emulate the more exact sciences by seeking the replacement of one perspective with another. An assumption basic to this book is that multiple-perspective and integrative views are more appropriate in fields such as public and educational administration. A multiple-perspective view requires that technical and practical matters, explanation and understanding, be brought together. In analyzing Habermas's (1970) views on the nature of knowledge and its integration, McCarty notes "the real problem . . . is not technical reasons as such but universalization, the forfeiture of a more comprehensive concept of reason in favor of the exclusive validity of scientific and technological thought, the reduction of *praxis* to *techne* and the extension of purposive-rational action to all spheres of life. The proper response, then, lies not in a radical break with technical reason but in properly locating it within a comprehensive theory of rationality" (1978, 22).

It should be clear, then, that our argument is not with other views of administrative theory and practice, only with their universalization.

A multiple-perspective view cannot be realized, however, in the absence of parity for the cultural perspective, a problem we seek to remedy with this book.

References

ARGYRIS, CHRIS (1964). *Integrating the Individual and the Organization.* New York: Wiley.

BLEICHER, JOSEF (1980). *Contemporary Hermeneutics: Hermeneutics as Method, Philosophy and Critique.* London: Routledge & Kegan Paul.

COHEN, MICHAEL D., & JAMES G. MARCH (1974). *Leadership and Ambiguity: The American College President.* New York: McGraw-Hill.

GOULDNER, ALVIN (1970). *The Coming Crisis of Western Sociology.* New York: Avon Press.

HABERMAS, JURGEN (1970). "Technology and Science as Ideology." *Toward a Rational Society.* Translated by Jeremy J. Shapiro. Boston: Beacon Press.

LIKERT, RENSIS (1967). *The Human Organization: Its Management and Value.* New York: McGraw-Hill.

McCARTHY, THOMAS (1978). *The Critical Theory of Jurgen Habermas.* Cambridge, Mass.: MIT Press.

McGREGOR, DOUGLAS (1960). *The Human Side of Enterprise.* New York: McGraw-Hill.

MARCH, JAMES G., and JOHAN P. OLSEN (1976). *Ambiguity and Choice in Organizations.* Bergen: Universitetsforlaget.

MAYO, ELTON (1945). *The Social Problems of an Industrial Civilization.* Boston: Harvard Graduate School of Business.

MILES, RAYMOND E. (1965). "Human Relations or Human Resources?" *Harvard Business Review* 43(4), 148–156.

PONDY, LOUIS R. (1978). "Leadership as a Language Game." In Morgan W. McCall, Jr., and Michael M. Lombardo, eds. *Leadership: Where Else Can We Go?* Durham: Duke University Press.

ROETHLISBERGER, FREDERICK, & WILLIAM DICKSON (1939). *Management and the Worker.* Cambridge, Mass.: Harvard University Press.

SHILS, EDWARD A. (1961). "Centre and Periphery." In *The Logic of Personal Knowledge: Essays Presented to Michael Polanyi.* London: Routledge & Kegan Paul, pp. 117–131.

SIMON, HERBERT A. (1945). *Administrative Behavior: A Study of the Decision Making Processes in Administrative Organization.* New York: Macmillan Co.

——— (1969). *The Sciences of the Artificial.* Cambridge, Mass.: MIT Press.

TAYLOR, FREDERICK (1911). *The Principles of Scientific Management.* New York: Harper & Row.

WEICK, KARL E. (1982). "Administering Education in Loosely Coupled Schools." *Phi Delta Kappan* (June), 673–676.